C0-AOF-810

Also in the Variorum Collected Studies Series:

NELSON H. MINNICH
The Fifth Lateran Council (1512–1517)

LOUIS-JACQUES BATAILLON
La prédication au XIIIe siècle en France et Italie

JOHN W. O'MALLEY
Religious Culture in the Sixteenth Century

PETER A. LINEHAN
Past and Present in Medieval Spain

JEAN RICHARD
Croisades et Etats latins d'Orient

JEAN-PIERRE DEVROEY
Etudes sur le grand domaine carolingien

ALFRED SOMAN
Sorcellerie et justice criminelle: Le Parlement de Paris (16e–18e siècles)

PAUL GRENDLER
Culture and Censorship in Late Renaissance Italy and France

C.R. CHENEY
The English Church and Its Laws, 12th–14th Centuries

C.R. CHENEY
The Papacy and England, 12th–14th Centuries

ANTOINE DONDAINE
Les hérésies et l'Inquisition, XIIe–XIIIe siècles

ROBERT SOMERVILLE
Papacy, Councils and Canon Law in the 11th–12th Centuries

JEAN BECQUET
Vie canoniale en France aux Xe–XIIe siècles

E. WILLIAM MONTER
Enforcing Morality in Early Modern Europe

HENRY KAMEN
Crisis and Change in Early Modern Spain

The Catholic Reformation:
Council, Churchmen, Controversies

Professor Nelson H. Minnich

Nelson H. Minnich

The Catholic Reformation:
Council, Churchmen, Controversies

VARIORUM

This edition copyright © 1993 by Nelson H. Minnich

Published by VARIORUM
        Ashgate Publishing Limited
        Gower House, Croft Road,
        Aldershot, Hampshire GU11 3HR
        Great Britain

        Ashgate Publishing Company
        Old Post Road,
        Brookfield, Vermont 05036
        USA

Bx
830
1512
,M55
1993

ISBN 0-86078-350-2

A CIP catalogue record for this book is available
from the British Library.

The paper used in this publication meets the minimum requirements of
    American National Standard for Information Sciences
— Permanence of Paper for Printed Library Materials, ANSI Z39.48-1984.

Printed by   Galliard (Printers) Ltd
              Great Yarmouth, Norfolk
              Great Britain

COLLECTED STUDIES SERIES CS403

CONTENTS

This volume contains x + 313 pages

PREFACE

The title of this collection of studies, *The Catholic Reformation*, may at first glance seem misleading since all of its essays do not relate directly to the question of reform. From the healing of the Great Western Schism to the opening of the greater divisions by the Protestant Reformation, the Latin Church had three principal concerns: reform, unity, and faith, as evidenced by the tasks assigned to conciliar deputations from Pisa (1409) to Lateran V (1512-17). Because the issue of reform came to overshadow all other considerations and because scholars have devoted appreciably more energy to tracing the various reform efforts, this whole period (ca. 1409-ca. 1545) has come to be called the Catholic Reformation. Given that the studies in this volume fall within this time frame, the title *The Catholic Reformation* seems appropriate.

The Council here treated is the Fifth Lateran (1512-17). It, too, was concerned with the issues of reform, unity, and faith. The two studies that most directly treat the reform proposals brought before this Council are to be found in my companion volume, *The Fifth Lateran Council (1512-17)*. The two studies that trace the efforts to implement its reform measures in Rome (IV) and explain why the poor reception of its decrees elsewhere raised questions about the validity of its legislation (X) are included here. The Council's relations with Eastern Christians are examined while trying to identify the orator of the patriarch of Jerusalem (II) and while reconstructing the career of the Council's most prominent Greek member (VI). Lateran V's concern for doctrinal issues can be viewed from the perspective of how it used Sacred Scripture when formulating its decrees (III). For a recent study of the Council's work in an area that combined doctrinal and disciplinary questions, please see my "Prophecy and the Fifth Lateran Council (1512-17)," in *Prophetic Rome in the High Renaissance Period*, edited by Marjorie E. Reeves [=Oxford-Warburg Studies] (Oxford, 1992), 63-87. Study I offers a overview both of the history of this Council and of the significance of the diary of the papal master of ceremonies, Paride de Grassi, for understanding its ceremonies, organization, dynamics, and factions. An analysis of the life and thought of a conciliarist writing in Rome at the time of the Lateran Council can be found in my "Girolamo Massaino: Another Conciliarist at the Papal Court, Julius II to Adrian VI," in *Studies in Church History in Honor of John Tracy Ellis*, edited by Nelson H. Minnich, Robert B. Eno, S.S., and Robert F. Trisco (Wilmington, Del., 1985), 520-65.

The careers of some notable churchmen from this period are also examined. With the help of a previously little known autobiography, the fascinating life of the Florentine Antonio degli Agli can be traced from a childhood in rags to an adolescence spent working by day and studying at night. He then became a cleric to escape debtors' prison and was subsequently a tutor to the future Paul II and dedicated humanist-bishop who promoted a synthesis of Christian and classical learning and virtuous conduct by his numerous writings and personal example (V). A collaborative study (IX) with the psychiatrist William W. Meissner, S.J., offers a psychoanalytic interpretation of the character of the prince of humanists and Augustinian canon,

Desiderius Erasmus of Rotterdam. It suggests that Erasmus in his anger at having been abandoned by his priest-father lashed out at a host of father substitutes, especially his teachers and many of the clerics of his day. His ambivalent longing for parental acceptance, yet desire to take revenge, may help to explain his conflicted relations with the Church. For a differing view of his character offered by John C. Olin and our response, please see the *American Historical Review* 84 (1979) 906-09. The career of the Greek emigré Alexios Celadenus who ultimately failed to achieve his life's goal of promotion to the cardinalate and raising a crusade to liberate his homeland is here reconstructed. The reprinted version of this article (VI) is furnished with a reproduction of the miniature frontispiece that is missing from the original printing and depicts Celadenus presenting a Greek lectionary to Julius II. For details on Alexios' relations with his dioceses of Gallipoli (1480-1508) and Molfetta (1508-17), please see Luigi Michele de Palma, *Vescovi Molfettesi del '500 al servizio della sede apostolica* [=Corona Lateranensis, 37] (Rome, 1987), 21-57. In the context of analyzing his diary of Lateran V, the life of Paride de Grassi is also reviewed (I).

An examination of three controversies involving clergy and laity are included in this collection. With the help of a previously unknown letter of April, 1512 of the recently professed Camaldolese hermit Pietro (Vincenzo) Querini to his old friends the Venetian patricians Gasparo Contarini and Niccolò Tiepolò, Professor Elisabeth G. Gleason and I in Study VII have been able to document further the emergence of a new spirituality that allows for a life of holiness in the world. This letter also testifies to Querini's concern for the welfare of his other friends following the Battle of Ravenna and to his unwavering support for the cause of Julius II in his struggle with the Pisan Council. The outbreak of the Protestant Reformation led to numerous controversalist writings. The Italian prince-diplomat and humanist, Alberto Pio of Carpi, accused Erasmus of supporting the Protestants and of espousing positions similar to theirs. In Study XI their debate over the use of sacred images is traced. On the urgings of the laymen and clerics, Johannes Eck composed his famous *Enchiridion locorum communium*. Study VIII examines three previously ignored documents to determine the context in which work on the *Enchiridion* was begun, how the earlier manuscript versions were compiled, and how they differed from the first printed edition dedicated to Henry VIII.

Many debts of gratitude are owed to those scholars who helped to make this volume possible and I am happy to acknowledge these: to Paul F. Grendler who suggested that I publish this collection, to my co-authors Elisabeth G. Gleason and William W. Meissner who agreed to the inclusion of our articles in it, to A. Lynn Martin who called my attention to the Chigi codex with its stray treasures, to those scholars who personally invited me to write various pieces for conferences and/or publication (Marc Dykmans, S.J., for Study I, Walter Brandmüller for III and XI, and Herbert Immenkötter for VIII), to John Smedley who provided editorial assistance, and to Joseph C. Linck who helped with the index. The American Philosophical Society, the American Council of Learned Societies, and the Societas Internationalis Historiae Conciliorum Investigandae provided funding for research on some of these topics and for the presentation of my findings at conferences in Jerusalem, Istanbul, Rotterdam, and Ingolstadt.

This volume is dedicated to my parents Hubert M. Minnich and the recently deceased Alberta (Berdie) Pfadt Minnich. My mother, who always encouraged my education, passed on to me her love of the past. She faithfully read my various publications, but would ask what relevance they have for further reforming the Church following Vatican II. My father has taken a certain paternal pride in his son's publications, but often wonders aloud why I spend so much time and energy writing articles for which I am not paid. Although I have never been able to explain my scholarly publications in a way that satisfied their concerns, I offer them this collection as a filial token of my deepest appreciation for their loving and loyal support over the years.

NELSON H. MINNICH

The Catholic University of America
Washington, D.C.
4 July 1992

ACKNOWLEDGEMENTS

Grateful acknowledgement is made to the following publishers, journals and editors, for kindly permitting the reproduction in this volume of articles originally published by them: Ferdinand Schöningh, Paderborn (for studies I, III, XI); the editors of *Orientalia Christiana Periodica*, Rome (II); The Catholic University of America Press, Washington, D.C. (IV, VII); Giunti Barbèra, Florence (V); the editors of *Historical Reflections/Réflexions Historiques*, Alfred, N.Y. (VI); Aschendorff Verlag, Münster (VIII); the editors of the *American Historical Review*, Washington, D.C. (IX); E.J. Brill, Leiden (X).

PUBLISHER'S NOTE

The articles in this volume, as in all others in the Collected Studies Series, have not been given a new, continuous pagination. In order to avoid confusion, and to facilitate their use where these same studies have been referred to elsewhere, the original pagination has been maintained wherever possible.

Each article has been given a Roman number in order of appearance, as listed in the Contents. This number is repeated on each page and quoted in the index entries..

I

Paride de Grassi's Diary of the Fifth Lateran Council

Introduction*

The publication of a reliable edition of those sections of the Diary of Paride de Grassi (1470—1528) which deal directly with the preparations for and events of the Fifth Lateran Council (1512—17) is a major contribution to the study of this church assembly which met on the very eve of the Reformation. Unlike the extensive scholarly publication of sources for the councils immediately preceding and following it[1], the records of this Lateran Council still await a critical edition. Guglia has shown how deficient are the official acts of this Council issued under a mandate from Leo X by their compiler cardinal Antonio del Monte in 1521 and republished in subsequent conciliar collections[2]. A few of

* Support for some of the research on which this study is based was provided by the National Endowment for the Humanities through Villa I Tatti in Florence and the American Academy in Rome. I should like to thank Professors Paul F. Grendler and John F. D'Amico for their helpful suggestions toward improving the text.

[1] Critical editions of relevant documents for these councils exist in such modern collections as, e. g.: for Konstanz (1414—18) Acta Concilii Constanciensis, ed. Heinrich FINKE, Johann HOLLNSTEINER, and H. HEIMPEL, 4 vols. (Münster, 1896—1928); for Basel (1431—49) Concilium Basiliense, Studien und Quellen zur Geschichte des Concils von Basel, ed. Johann HALLER for vols. 1—4 and with the assistance of the Historische und Antiquarische Gesellschaft von Basel for vols. 5—8 (Basel, 1896—1936); for Ferrara—Firenze—Roma (1438—45) Concilium Florentinum. Documenta et Scriptores, ed. by the Pontifical Institute of Oriental Studies, II vols. (Roma, 1940—77) — an overview of this project by Joseph GILL appeared in Orientalia Periodica Christiana 43 (1977) 5—17, and the other collections of G. HOFMANN published by the same Institute and by the Gregorian University; and for Trent (1545—63) the modern collection Concilium Tridentinum diariorum, actorum, epistularum, tractatuum nova collectio ed. by the Görres-Gesellschaft (Freiburg im Breisgau, 1901—).

[2] Although a collection of Lateran decrees was published by Etienne GUILLERY in Rome during the same year the Council ended and reissued by Alessandro MINUZIANO in Milan the following year, the official acts of the Council were edited by Antonio DEL MONTE, published in Rome in 1521, and subsequently reprinted in the collections of QUENTEL-CRABBE (1551), and in those of BINIUS, LABBE-COSSART, HARDOUIN, and MANSI — for a partial survey of these editions and their merits, see: François SALMON, Traité d'étude des conciles et de leur collections, Paris 1724, 197—201; Henri QUENTIN, Jean-Dominique Mansi et les grandes collections conciliares: Étude d'histoire litteraire, Paris 1900, 12—16; Eugen GUGLIA, Studien zur Geschichte des V. Laterancconcils, (1512—1517), in: Sitzungsberichte der philosophisch-historischen Classe der kaiserlichen Akademie der Wissenschaften — Wien 140 (1899), X. Abhandlung, 1—34, esp. 1—13; Hubert ELIE, Un Lunevillois imprimeur à Rome au début du XVIème

I

371   *Paride de Grassi's Diary of the Fifth Lateran Council*

the extant working papers of the Council were published in 1887 by cardinal Joseph Hergenroether as appendices to the eighth volume of his continuation of Carl von Hefele's *Conciliengeschichte*[3]. While some minor documents have been published by subsequent scholars[4], the most important source for the Council

siècle: Etienne Guillery, in: Gutenberg-Jahrbuch (1939) 185—96, (1944—49) 128—37, esp. 129—30, 137, and Nelson H. MINNICH, The Participants at the Fifth Lateran Council, in: AHP 12 (1974) 157—206, esp. 168—70.

I have not as yet been able to locate a copy of this Guillery collection. Elie cites a colophon which is almost identical (*furunt* vs. *fuerunt*) with that at the end of the pamphlet *Bulla absolutionis concilii Lateranensis cum decreto expeditionis in Turchos generalis ac impositionis Decimarum per Triennium Lecta in Duodecima et Ultima Sessione per R. D. Patriarcham Aquilegien.*, namely, *Impresse fuerunt Rome hae Bulle Sacri concilii Lateranensis. Per Magistrum Stephanum Guillireti de Lunarivilla Tullen. Dioc. Anno a Nativitate Dni. M. D. XVII. Die vero Vigesima Octava Mensis Julii Pont. S.D.N. Dni. Leonis Pape. X: Anno eiusQuinto. FINIS.* — included in a copy of Sigismondo Tizio's Historiarum Senensium Tomus VIII. *Hoc est voluminis* 5[ti] *pars* 2[a] *ab anno 1515 ad annum 1520* . . ., for year MDXVI, see BAV, Chigiana, G II 38. Whether this pamphlet was published by itself or is part of a collection of bulls is not clear.

The edition of Antonio del Monte is entitled Sacrum Lateranense concilium novissimum sub Julio. II. et Leone. X. celebratum, Romae: per Jacobum Mazochium, 1521.

My citations will be to the reprint of this edition in the widely available collection Sacrorum conciliorum nova et amplissima collectio, ed. Giovanni Domenico MANSI and a Florentine and Venetian editor (Paris 1902 reprint), vol. 32, cols. 649D—999C, hereafter cited as MANSI.

[3] Carl Joseph von HEFELE, Conciliengeschichte nach den Quellen bearbeitet, vol. 8, fortgesetzt von Joseph HERGENROETHER, Freiburg im Breisgau 1887, 810—31, 845—55.

[4] The memorials of the Spanish bishops, a record of the ceremony of adhesion, and the royal instructions to the ambassador to the Council are printed in José M. DOUSSINAGUE, Fernando el Católico y el Cisma de Pisa, Madrid 1946, II 504—12, 520—25, 528—43; they are studied by J. GOÑI GAZTAMBIDE, España y el Concilio V de Letrán, in: AHC 6 (1974) 154—222; much of the correspondence between Fernando and his ambassador to the Council, Jeronimo Vich, has been published by the Baron de TERRATEIG (Jesús de Manglano y Cucaló de Montull), Politica en Italia de Rey Católico 1507—1516: Correspondencia inedita con el embajador Vich, vol. 2: Documentos e indice general which is número XII, vol. 2 of Estudios published by the Biblioteca "Reyes Catolicos", Madrid 1963.

In the supplement to his collection of conciliar documents, Giovanni Domenico Mansi has published the correspondence of Angelo Fondi defending the Lateran Council, a brief of Leo to universities requesting help on a reform of the calendar and thirteen propositions of the conciliar deputies for such a reform discussed at the Council, and two edicts and a *monitorio* requiring the observance of the Council's reform decrees at Rome — see MANSI 35, 1565A—88B. The papal and imperial correspondence related to the calendar reform has been printed in Demitrio MARZI, La questione della riforma del calendario nel quinto concilio lateranese (1512—1517) (= Pubblicazioni del Reale Istituto di studi superiori pratici e di perfezionamento in Firenze. Sezione di filosofia e filologia 27) Firenze 1896, 78—79, 89, 167—68, 185—86.

The sections from the conciliar speeches of Julius II and Tommaso de Vio missing in the edition of del Monte and in all subsequent acts, together with the consistorial and deputation speeches of Raffaele Riario have been published as appendices to Nelson H. MINNICH, Concepts of Reform Proposed at the Fifth Lateran Council, in: AHP 7 (1969) 163—252, esp. 237—52.

The speech of the imperial ambassador defending the reputation of Maximilian I is printed as an appendix to his study, The *Protestatio* of Alberto Pio (1513), in: Società, politica e cultura a Carpi ai tempi di Alberto III Pio (= Medioevo e Umanesimo 46) Padova 1981, 261—89, esp. 285—89.

A working paper of the reform deputation on curial offices and fees is printed in Walther von HOFMANN, Forschungen zur Geschichte der kurialen Behörden vom Schisma bis zur Reformation (= Bibliothek des kgl. preuß. historischen Instituts in Rom 12, 13) Roma 1914, II 242—48.

Among the published reform proposals for the consideration of the pope and Council, the most significant was probably that by Paolo (Tommaso) Giustiniani and Pietro (Vincenzo) Quirini, two Camaldolese hermits, entitled Libellus ad Leonem X. Pontificem Maximum, in: Annales Camaldulenses Ordinis Sancti Benedicti, ed. Giovanni Benedetto MITTARELLI and Anselmo COSTADONI, IX Venezia 1773, 612—719.

after its acts and working papers is the Diary of the principal master of ceremonies at the Council. This document provides, among other things, detailed accounts of the preparations for and ceremonies of this Council, revealing glimpses at its leading figures, factions, and alliances, explanations of the conflicts which caused it to be prorogued and almost boycotted or cancelled, and judgment on its ultimate failure.

Historians of this Council have long recognized the significance of this Diary. In his continuation of Cesare Baronio's *Annales Ecclesiastici*, Odorico Rainaldi in 1663 quoted extensively from this document when treating the Council[5]. Recognizing its importance for understanding the Church of Rome on the eve of the Reformation, Johann Joseph Ignaz von Döllinger published in 1882 a large section of the Diary supplementing Rainaldi's treatment of the later years of the pontificate of Julius, notably the conciliar period, and Pio Delicati and Mariano Armellini in 1884 edited excerpts from the pontificate of Leo X[6]. While Döllinger used a reasonably good manuscript for his transcription, Delicati and

---

An edition of the Libellus by Giuseppe ALBERIGO, apparently still in preparation, was announced by Paolo PRODI in his Riforma cattolica e controriforma, in: Nuove Questioni di Storia Moderna, ed. Luigi BULFERETTI, I Milano 1964, 357—418, esp. 366—68, 409. The Libellus has been studied in some detail by many scholars, the most notable of whom is Silvio TRAMONTIN in his two studies: Un programma di riforma della chiesa per il Concilio Lateranense V: Il Libellus ad Leonem dei veneziani Paolo Giustiniani e Pietro Quirino, in: Venezia e i concilii, ed. Antonio NIERO et alii (= Quaderni del Laurentianum I) Venezia 1962, 67—93 and Il problema delle chiese separate nel Libellus ad Leonem dei veneziani Paolo Giustiniani e Pietro Quirini, in: Studia patavina 11 (1964) 275—82.

Much of the correspondence and many of the reports of the Venetian ambassadors have been published in Marino Sanudo, I Diarii 1496—1535, ed. Federico STEFANI, Guglielmo BERCHET, Nicolò BAROZZI, 58 vols. Venezia 1879—1903, vols. 14—24.

For the scarce printed correspondence of the French ambassadors, see Alberto CAVIGLIA, Claudio di Seyssel (1450—1520): La vita nella storia de' suoi tempi (= Miscellanea di storia italiana 23 ser. III) Torino 1928. Royal correspondence can be found in Lettres du Roy Louis XII avec plusieurs autres lettres, memoires et instructions écrites depuis 1504 jusques et compris 1514, ed. Jean GODEFROY, 4 vols. Brussels 1712.

For the published English correspondence, see the appendices in Richard FIDDES, The Life of Cardinal Wolsey, London ²1726 and David Sanderson CHAMBERS, Cardinal Bainbridge in the Court of Rome 1509 to 1514, Oxford 1965.

[5] Cesare BARONIO, Annales Ecclesiastici, vols. 20—34 are the work of Odorico RAINALDI, rev. and ed. Giovanni Domenico MANSI and Augustin THEINER, 37 vols., Paris 1864—83, vols. 30 and 31, Paris 1877—80 reprint Rainaldi's 1663 account of the Council. For Mansi's analysis of Rainaldi's life and work, see vol. 20, Barri/Ducis 1870, iii—xi.

[6] Paride de GRASSI, Das Pontificat des Papstes Julius II. nach dem Tagebuch des Großceremoniars Paris de Grassis, in: Beiträge zur politischen kirchlichen und Cultur-Geschichte der sechs letzten Jahrhunderte, ed. Johann Joseph Ignaz von DÖLLINGER, III Wien 1882, 363—433, esp. 413—33; and the Il Diario di Leone X, ed. Pio DELICATI and Mariano ARMELLINI, Roma 1884. Other scholars have also published excerpts from this Diary, but for the conciliar material Rainaldi, Döllinger, and Delicati/Armellini are the principal editors to be considered until now. For a listing of manuscript copies of the Diary kept at the Vatican Library, see Pierre SALMON, Ordines Romani Pontificaux Rituels Cérémoniaux, Città del Vaticano 1970 (= Les manuscripts liturgiques latins de la Bibliothèque Vaticane 3) (= Studi e Testi 260) 355—56, 359—61, 382, 399, 404, 406, 419, 431—32, 467—69, 478, 499—500, pp. 107—09, 114, 119—20, 124, 126—27, 135, 137, 141—42.

I

Armellini were either dependent on a very defective copy or else exercised great liberty in their editorial practices. Scholars of the Council have thus been left with printed editions of the Diary which provide excerpts of conciliar material of varying degrees of reliability. The edition by Marc Dykmans, based on nearly contemporaneous and autograph copies of this Diary, at last remedies this situation.

The Fifth Lateran Council

The origins and course of the Council which de Grassi so carefully described have already been studied in detail by scholars[7] and need only to be reviewed in their broader outlines here.

The origins of the Lateran Council can be traced to a combination of secular and religious factors. The attempt by Julius II (1503—13) to recover sections of the Papal States which had been seized by Venice resulted in the formation of the League of Cambrai. With the help principally of his French, Imperial, and Spanish allies, Julius not only restored the territorial integrity of the Lands of the Church, but brought Venice to its knees. Fearful lest the demise of the Republic as a major force on the peninsula would open the way to foreign domination of all Italy and of the papacy itself, Julius betrayed his former allies and formed a new league. With the help of his new ally, Venice, and of Spain, he hoped to expel the French whose control of Genoa and Milan he suspected would be followed by an attempt to regain Naples. When the papal vassal, Alfonso I d'Este, duke of Ferrara (1505—34), refused to turn his arms against his former ally France, Julius excommunicated him and his supporters[8].

---

[7] Some of the more important modern treatments of this Council can be found in: Vincenzo Tizzani, I concilii Lateranensi, Roma 1878; Mandell Creighton, A History of the Papacy from the Great Schism to the Close of Rome, vols. 4—5 New York 1897; Charles-Joseph Hefele, Histoire des conciles d'après les documents originaux, continued by Joseph Hergenroether, French translation augmented with critical notes and bibliography by Henri Leclercq, VIII — I Paris 1917, 239—565; Ludwig von Pastor, The History of the Popes from the Close of the Middle Ages, London ⁴1923; F. Vernet, Latran (Vᵉ Concile, occuménique du), in: Dictionnaire de théologie catholique VIII — II, Paris 1925, 2667—86; Roger Aubenas and Robert Ricard, L'Eglise et le Renaissance (1449—1517) (= Histoire de l'Eglise depuis les origines jusqu'à nos jours 15) Paris 1951, 163—89; Olivier de la Brosse, Latran V in: Latran V et Trente, I (= Histoire des conciles oecuméniques 10) Paris 1975, 11—114, with bibliography on 469 bis 473; Petro B. T. Bilaniuk, The Fifth Lateran Council (1512—1517) and the Eastern Churches (Toronto 1975); Richard J. Schoeck, The Fifth Lateran Council: Its Partial Successes and Its Larger Failures, in: Reform and Authority in the Medieval and Reformation Church, ed. Guy Fitch Lytle, Washington, D.C. 1981, 99—126; and Nelson H. Minnich, Episcopal Reform at the Fifth Lateran Council (1512—1517), doctoral dissertation, Harvard University, 1977.

In the following review of the history of this Council, references will not be made to all the literature available, but only to the two most important general surveys, Rainaldi and Hergenroether/Leclercq, and to a few of the other more specialized studies which introduce one to further research on the topic.

[8] Rainaldi, 1504, nr. 1—13, 1505, nr. 1, 1506, nr. 19—33, 1507, nr. 1—3, 1508, nr. 1—8, 21—23, 1509, nr. 1—21, 1510, nr. 1—16; Hergenroether/Leclercq 255—75; for a survey of the intricate

Angered by the pope's ingratitude and treachery, Louis XII, king of France (1498—1515), resolved to oppose Julius with all means available. Having helped Julius regain numerous cities in Romagna, the French king now supported a restoration of the rebellious Bentivogli to power in Bologna. And if Julius could use such spiritual weapons as excommunication and interdict against political enemies, so too could his opponents. With the support of his clergy, Louis cut off the flow of revenues from French lands to the Roman Curia and threatened to call a general council, ostensibly for the reform of the Church, extirpation of heresy, and raising of a crusade, but in reality to discipline the pontiff for his treachery. Not only the Emperor-elect Maximilian I, but also a group of rebellious cardinals eventually joined him in the call for such a council[9].

These cardinals had a variety of reasons for supporting this council and their action was not without a legal basis. The decree *Frequens* (1417) of the Council of Konstanz had mandated the regular holding of general councils. Although this legislation was never formally abrogated, papal observance of it was initially half-hearted. As the power of the papal monarchy grew, the popes labored to repeal it in practice by prohibiting appeals to councils, by punishing Andreas Zamometič who attempted to convene one at Basel in 1481, and by the nullifying effect of many years of continuous non-observance. Despite such efforts to destroy *Frequens*, this decree was still considered by many as binding on the popes and appeals to it as valid[10].

The cardinals' case was also based on the election capitularies Julius had sworn. Both before and after his elevation in 1503, the new pope had promised to convoke within two years a general council for restoring peace among Christians, reforming the Church, reducing taxes, and organizing a crusade. This council was to be held in a free and safe place to be determined by the pontiff with the consent of two thirds of the cardinals. The agreement of the same proportion of cardinals was necessary for the pope to postpone the council or for them to convoke it on their own authority in case of papal neglect. In the subsequent years Julius had ignored this pledge with the tacit approval of the cardinals[11].

---

political history of this period by a contemporary, see Books 6—9 of Francesco GUICCIARDINI, Storia d'Italia, ed. Costantino PANIGADA, Bari 1929, vols. 2—3.

[9] RAINALDI, 1510, nr. 18—20, 22—23; HERGENROETHER/LECLERCQ 275—80; L. SANDRET, Le Concile de Pise (1511), in: Revue des questions historiques 34 (1883) 425—56, esp. 426—30.

[10] RAINALDI, 1510, nr. 18—20; HERGENROETHER/LECLERCQ 280—81; Walter ULLMANN, Julius II and the Schismatic Cardinals, in: Schism, Heresy, and Religious Protest, ed. Derek BAKER (= Studies in Church History[9]) Cambridge 1972, 177—93, esp. 178—80; CREIGHTON, History of Papacy IV 106—09; DOUSSINAGUE, Cisma de Pisa II 539.

[11] ULLMANN 177—78, 184; RAINALDI, 1503, nr. 8; Acta primi concilii Pisani celebrati ad tollendum schisma anno Domini MCCCCIX et concilii Senensis MCCCCXXIII ex codice manuscripto; item constitutiones sanctae in diversis sessionibus sacri generalis concilii Pisani ex bibliotheca regia, Paris 1612, 15—20.

By 1511 Julius had lost some of his support in the Sacred College. His autocratic manner and imprisonment of cardinals he suspected of opposing him raised fears for their personal safety, especially among the non-Italian members of the College. In August of 1510 a group of five cardinals (Carvajal, Briçonnet, de Prie, Sanseverino, and Borja) managed to escape from his control and fled to the protection of the French king. Whether for reasons of personal animosity toward Julius and hopes of eventual reward for backing Louis and Maximilian in their opposition to this pope, or for their publicly stated desire to reform and defend the Church, three cardinals (Carvajal, Briçonnet and de Prie) supported the convocation of a council by the procurators of the French and German rulers on 16 May 1511; and on their own authority three days later these prelates also then convoked a council to meet later that year. The three convokers of the council named six other cardinals whom they claimed, unjustifiably in the case of four as later events proved, supported them in this action. Due to their fear of the pontiff, still other cardinals were said to back this council secretly, but feared to express their views openly. The edict of convocation cited as justification the decree *Frequens*, Julius' election capitularies, and the pressing needs of the Church[12].

If the legal arguments for the convocation of the Pisan Council were such as to win the support of such eminent canonists as Filippo Decio and Giasone del Maino, the juridical basis for this council was soon undercut by Julius II[13]. On the advice of both Tommaso de Vio, O. P., and Antonio del Monte and with the support of the majority of the cardinals, the pope convoked by the bull *Sacrosanctae Romanae ecclesiae* dated 18 July 1511 a rival council of his own to meet at the Lateran in Rome in the spring of the following year. From the papal perspective, the Pisan cardinals by insisting on their own council were guilty of schism and deserving of the penalties of excommunication and deprivation of honors and benefices. His official warning of 25 July 1511 having gone unheeded, Julius on October 24th formally penalized four of the Pisan cardinals[14].

Undeterred at first by such measures, the rebellious cardinals assembled their council at Pisa on 1 November 1511. A continuous and vigorous papal campaign using the diplomatic skills of nuncios and the writings and preachings of the friars succeeded in turning public opinion against the Pisans and forced this council to spend its energies in a struggle for survival. Local opposition com-

---

[12] Ullmann 178—83; Rainaldi, 1510, nr. 18—19, 1511, nr. 1—8, 20—21; Acta primi 20—37; Sandret 432—33; Hergenroether/Leclercq 280—84, 297; Terrateig, II 144—45.

[13] Ullmann 180—81, 185—87; Hergenroether/Leclercq 314—17; Rainaldi, 1511, nr. 19; Myron P. Gilmore, Humanists and Jurists: Six Studies in the Renaissance, Cambridge, Mass. 1963, 72—79. On the literary battle among theologians over the Pisan Council, see: Olivier de La Brosse, Le Pape et le Concile, la comparaison de leur pouvoirs à la veille de la Réforme, Paris 1965; Hergenroether/ Leclercq 317—23; and Rainaldi, 1511, nr. 30—31, 37—41.

[14] Rainaldi, 1511, nr. 9—15, 24—29, 32—36; Hergenroether/Leclercq 297—302; Aluigi Cossio, Il cardinale Gaetano e la Riforma, Cividale 1902, I (and only) 144, 146—47; Mansi 652 C.

bined with the military reversals suffered by the French led the conciliar fathers to seek security by relocating successively in Milan, Asti, and Lyon where the tenth and final session was held on 6 July 1512. Such fierce papal opposition did not precipitate the fathers into quickly adopting rash measures. Until the Lateran Council actually opened in May of 1512, the Pisans could claim that the Julian bull of convocation was merely a ploy to undermine Pisa and would never be implemented. Instead of proceeding immediately to an attack on Julius, the Pisans repeatedly sought to negotiate a compromise whereby their council would be transferred to a place mutually acceptable to themselves and the pope, who would then adhere to it and send his own supporters to attend. Only after Julius had harshly rejected these conciliatory efforts did the Pisan Council finally suspended him from the exercise of his temporal and spiritual powers[15]. Given their canonical arguments for convoking the council and their moderation, it is not surprising that Carvajal and Sanseverino were eager to defend themselves on juridical grounds and not to beg for mercy when attempting a reconciliation with Julius' successor, Leo X.

The goals set for the rival Lateran Council by Julius II and reiterated by Leo X in their bulls of convocation and proroguement and in their speeches to the assembly came under three major headings. The primary goal was a restoration of church unity by an ending of the Pisan Schism, abrogation of the Pragmatic Sanction of Bourges (1438), and extirpation of heresies — probably a reference to the doctrinal errors of the Hussites and to some of the philosophical stances of the Averroists. The second area of concern was political: restoring peace among Christian princes and organizing a crusade to meet the Moslem threat. The final goal of the Council was a reform of the offices and fees of the Roman Curia and of the morals of clergy and laity alike[16].

The Council opened with much pomp on 3 May 1512 and was followed by twelve sessions, the final one sitting on 16 March 1517.

Under Julius five formal sessions were held from 10 May 1512 to 16 February 1513. In these sessions, the Council tried to defeat the Pisan Schism by decrees condemning the Pisan Council and its supporters, by attacks on the Pragmatic Sanction which helped sustain these schismatics, and by successful efforts to win

---

[15] RAINALDI, 1511, nr. 16—18, 20—23; HERGENROETHER/LECLERCQ 304—05, 323—35, 357—60; Acta primi, for the Pisan cardinals' response to the emissary of the Sacred College (11. IX. 1511) 67—74, for Pisan delegates to Rome 75, for a report of the Pisan Council's rebuffed efforts to find a solution (4. I. 1512) 109—15, for the accusation of contumacy against Julius for refusing to send a representative (24. III. 1512) 152, for warnings to the pope (24. III. 1512) 172—82, for a declaration of his guilt (19. IV. 1512) 185—86; and for the official suspension of Julius from the administration of his temporal and spiritual powers (21. IV. 1512) 193—206; ULLMANN 188—89; for Florentine diplomatic reports concerning this council, see Augustin RENAUDET, Le concile gallican de Pise-Milan: Documents florentins (1510 — 1512), Paris 1922.

[16] MANSI 657E, 667D, 687BC, 688D, 692B, 695B, 783AB, 788DE; RAINALDI, 1513, nr. 24; MINNICH, Concepts of Reform 167, 238.

the adherence of most of Europe to this Council sitting in Rome. It passed two reform measures: a reaffirmation of a bull against simony in papal elections issued eight years earlier, and a decree ordering observance of the curial reforms hastily published on the eve of the Council in the hope of eliminating some of the more flagrant abuses before the fathers assembled[17]. The Julian phase of the Council was characterized by very tight papal control of the agenda and by a strategy of going through the motions of a council with great care for legal forms and ritual, but of producing nothing new or of substance in the areas of a suppression of heresy, establishment of peace, organization of a crusade, or reform of the Church. Julius probably felt that the defeat of the Pisan Council was his highest priority and that the preparation of decrees aimed at accomplishing the other conciliar goals could preceed at a slower pace[18].

The key to understanding what did or did not happen during the Julian phase is to be found in the pope's ultimate goals and personal fears. Julius had dedicated himself to restoring the territorial integrity and political independence of the Papal States and to reasserting papal power in the areas of ecclesiastical appointments, jurisdiction, and finance. Until the papacy was thus strengthened, all other major programs were to be postponed or implemented only insofar as they advanced the primary goals. At this juncture in his pontificate, the chief obstacles to realizing these aims were the French military might in Italy endangering his territorial base and the Pisan Council threatening to undermine his spiritual authority.[19]

While Julius employed with ease the tactic of a counter military league, he feared the power of his Lateran Council which could be used against its papal convoker. He confessed to de Grassi an almost childlike fear of its ability to discipline him, and for a time he hesitated to make church appointments in the belief that the Council limited his powers in this important area. Lest the con-

---

[17] MANSI 714A—15D (affirming three earlier measures against the Pisan Council), 733D—35A (condemning all the acts of the Pisan Council and confirming a former interdict on France and transfer of the fair from Lyon to Geneva), 750D—52D (issuing a *monitorium* against the Pragmatic Sanction), 753A—54E (confirming the earlier reform of curial offices, asking for a report on the abrogation of the Pragmatic Sanction from the conciliar congregation for the next session, and demanding that those who have received benefices from the Pisan Council resign them), 768A—72B (reissuing the earlier condemnation against simony in papal elections), and 772D—73E (ordering French prelates to come to discuss an abrogation of the Pragmatic Sanction).

[18] GUGLIA, Studien zur Geschichte 26—28, 32—34; de Grassi's Diary also confirms this characterization — see in DYKMANS' text, section 840: parts 6—7, 845 : 3, 921 : 2, 985 : 2 — hereafter references to Dykmans' edition will be cited as DE GRASSI, section number: part number.

[19] The character and policies of Julius II are examined in greater depth in such studies as: M. A. J. DUMESNIL, Histoire de Jules II: Sa vie et son pontificat, Paris 1873; M. BROSCH, Papst Julius II. und die Gründung des Kirchenstaates, Gotha 1878; CREIGHTON III 68—202; PASTOR VI 212—607; Emmanuel RODOCANACHI, Histoire de Rome: Le Pontificat de Jules II, Paris 1928; Loren PARTRIDGE and Randolph STARN, A Renaissance Likeness: Art and Culture in Raphael's 'Julius II', Berkeley 1980; and Felix GILBERT, The Pope, His Banker and Venice, Cambridge, Mass. 1980.

ciliar fathers play any other role than that of merely approving what he and the cardinals decided, Julius made from the start no provision for a system of congregations and deputations. An initial fear of the Council seems also to have produced some surprising changes in his behavior. He repeatedly left late from his bedroom for the sessions and with unusual patience sat through the long conciliar ceremonies which were new to him[20].

Eventually some of his anxieties diminished. De Grassi's careful orchestration of the Council's ceremonies and Julius' own demonstrable ability to control its agenda insulated him from any possible conciliar censures. He was also relieved to learn that his position at the Lateran Council differed from that of disputed popes at Konstanz and hence his powers of appointment were not limited by the Council. His fear of a free council was eventually overcome by his even greater fear lest his Council be rejected as illegitimate for not having followed the organizational structure of such previous councils as Konstanz and Basel, especially when the fathers at the Lateran complained of not having been consulted on the agenda. While avoiding an organization based on congregations divided along national lines, he provided for a system of controlled consultation. At first the bishops were divided into groups under the chairmanship of one of nine trusted cardinals, but then Julius replaced this system with a committee of cardinals and twenty-four prelates of his own choosing who formally functioned as a conciliar congregation and did his bidding. With increased confidence in his ability to manage the Council, his behavior began to change. Reports of tardiness ceased. Instead of freezing with fright or resorting to a halting and repetitive delivery when called upon to speak, Julius was now composed enough to give a short address to the assembly on his reasons for having called this Council. So confident did Julius become in his power over the Council that he insisted over de Grassi's protest on having the fathers recast their votes, this time individually and in a loud voice. Julius, nonetheless, still regarded the Council as a potentially dangerous weapon that could backfire on him instead of striking down the French. To protect the authority and independence of the papal office and to prevent any possible French influence in the selection of his successor, Julius on his deathbed ordered the cardinals not to allow the Council a role in that election[21]. He died never having relinquished his tight control on the Lateran Council.

---

[20] DE GRASSI 844 : 37 (his fear of being disciplined), 883 : 4 (questioning of his ability to make appointments), 844 : 4 and 847 : 3 (tardiness), 844 : 26 (patience).

[21] DE GRASSI 844 : 2 and 38 (Julius praises de Grassi's organization), 848 : 7 (Julius controls agenda), 848 : 4, q. 6 and 968 : 2 (congregations), 846 : 1 und 847 : 20 (Julius speaks), 901 : 29 (recast vote), 924 : 4 (deathbed); DE GRASSI, Diarium Leonis, Vat. Lat. 12275, vols. 40r, 52r–v (Julius' fear of public speaking), Ferdinand Adolf GREGOROVIUS, History of the City of Rome in the Middle Ages, 8, 1, London 1902, 189, n. 1 (for his poor delivery style).

Under his successor Leo X (1513—21), seven sessions of the Council were held, three in his first year, and one in each of the subsequent years. The Leonine phase can be divided into two periods.

The first period, extending from the sixth to eighth sessions, that is from April 27th to December 19th of 1513, was typified by an apparent greater participation of the council fathers in the formulation of the conciliar program and by a renewed energy and progress toward accomplishing the goals set for the Council. With the agreement of pope and cardinals, three deputations (peace, faith and reform) were established. The Council fathers elected twenty-four prelates who were subsequently divided among these three deputations. What brought the membership on each deputation to twenty was the addition by the pope of eight cardinals and four other prelates, often curialists or religious[22]. The specific contributions these working groups made in the formulation of the conciliar decrees is difficult to determine given the paucity of surviving documents. Whatever their role may have been, the Council was by year's end on its way toward achieving its stated goals.

The clearest achievement registered at the Council was the healing of the Pisan Schism. At the seventh session the Council's secretary read a document signed by the penitent Carvajal and Sanseverino who admitted their error in having supported the Pisan Council and acknowledged the legitimacy of the Lateran to which they now adhered; at the eighth the mandate and letter of the King of France were read denouncing the Pisan Schism, promising to move against its supporters, and committing France to the Lateran Council and its forthcoming delegation to negotiate there the question of the Pragmatic Sanction[23]. The Pisan Schism was thus in effect ended.

Bulls approved at the seventh and eighth sessions of the Council commissioned legates and nuncios to visit the various Christian princes in hopes of negotiating a universal peace in Christendom, preparatory to the organization of a crusade against the Turks[24].

An extirpation of heresy was provided for in two decrees of the eighth session. The first stated that Tamás Bakócz, the cardinal primate of Hungary, was empowered to negotiate with the Hussites in hopes of reuniting them to the Church.

---

[22] The decision to establish three deputations was taken at the consistory of 2 May 1513 — see DE GRASSI, Diarium Leonis, Vat. Lat. 12275, fol. 40ᵛ. On the election of twenty-four prelates and their division into deputations, see DE GRASSI 968: 1—2; MANSI 794B—97E; MINNICH, Episcopal Reform 357—65.

[23] MANSI 814D—15B, 832A—36B. A detailed analysis of how Leo healed this schism is currently in preparation.

[24] MANSI 815C—18A, 843E—45D. For studies of Leo's efforts to organize such a crusade, see: Eugen GUGLIA, Die Türkenfrage auf dem V. Lateranconcil, in: MIÖG 21 (1900) 679—91, and Kenneth M. SETTON, Pope Leo X and the Turkish Peril, in: Proceedings of the American Philosophical Society 113 (1969) 367—424.

Another bull condemned as heretical those philosophic views challenging Christian teachings on the immortality of the individual human soul, on the creation of the world, and on the unity of truth; it ordered professors of philosophy to defend the Christian position[25].

In the area of reform the Council enacted two measures. At the seventh session it reaffirmed the curial reform issued by Julius II and at the eighth it approved a list of penalties for those failing to observe the bull *Pastoralis officii*. Issued six days earlier, this bull had retreated from some of the sterner Julian reforms and sought to regularize curial practices and fees[26].

Had the Council ended with its eighth session, Leo could have claimed with some justification that under his presidency it had enacted measures furthering the achievement of all its announced goals. But two major factors led to its continuance.

Leo was eager that the Council under his leadership register a victory which had eluded his predecessors. Given the pledge of Louis XII to send a French delegation, Leo hoped to overturn with the cooperation of the French bishops themselves those decrees of Basel incorporated in the Pragmatic Sanction of Bourges. The Lateran Council would thus formally abrogate the charter of the Gallican Liberties[27].

The second factor leading to a continuation of the Council was a solemn oath Leo had sworn in his election capitularies. He had not only pledged himself to see that the Council achieved its stated ends, but had promised not to transfer or conclude it without the consent of a majority of the conciliar fathers. These bishops were not satisfied with the Council's accomplishments to date and at

---

[25] MANSI 842A—43C, 845AB; on Bakócz, see Vilmos FRAKNÓI, Erdödi Bakócz Tamás Élete, Budapest 1889, 130—142 and Petro B. T. BILANIUK, The Fifth Lateran Council (1512—1517) and the Eastern Churches, Toronto 1975, 135—37; on the decree against philosophical errors, see A. DENEFFE, Die Absicht des V. Laterankonzils, in: Scholastik 8 (1933) 358—79, Siro OFFELLI, Il pensiero del concilio Lateranese V sulla dimonstrabilità razionale dell'immortalità dell'anima umana, in: Studi Patavina 2 (1955) 3—17; Etienne GILSON, Autour de Pomponazzi: Problématique de l'immortalité de l'âme en Italie au debut du XVIe siècle, in: Archives d'histoire doctrinale et littéraire du Moyen Age 28 (1962) 163—277; Giovanni di NAPOLI, L'immortalità dell'anima nel Rinascimento, Torino 1963; Felix GILBERT, Cristianesimo, umanesimo, e la bolla 'Apostolici Regiminis' del 1513, in: RSIt 79 (1967) 976—90.

[26] MANSI 816C—17A, 845D—46E; the bull Pastoralis officii is registered in ASV, Reg. Vat. 1200, fols. 425r—47v and 1211, fols. 134r—76r and printed in Bullarum diplomatum et privilegiorum sanctorum pontificum Taurinensis editio, ed. Francesco GAUDE, vol. 5 Ab Eugenio IV (1431) ad Leonem X (1521) Torino 1860, 571—601 — hereafter this volume is cited as Bullarum Tauriensis editio.

[27] MANSI 835DE, 864BC; that this was Leo's primary goal during the second period is implicit in his continuance of the Council, despite troubles, proroguement of it in hopes of securing French attendance, special efforts to get the French to come by obtaining for them safe-conducts and by issuing threats, and closing of the Council soon after he had the Pragmatic Sanction abrogated. Cajetan recognized this as Leo's great achievement in his preface to the pope written some months after the Council's close — see Secunda secundae partis summae sacrosanctae theologiae sancti Thomae Aquinatis doctoris angelici Reverendissimi Domini Thomae a Vio Caietani tituli sancti Xisti presbyteri cardinalis commentarius illustra, Lyon 1558, a2r.

the eighth session a significant number of them demanded that the reformation of the Church be more comprehensive than the weak measures incorporated in *Pastoralis officii*. In response to their demand, Leo reportedly almost smiled and promised to treat again at the next session the question of reform[28].

The second period so aggravated the pontiff that he rued the Council's continuance and threatened to prorogue it indefinitely. The initiative passed from the pope and cardinals to the disgruntled bishops. In some respects the eighth session marked the completion of the papally sponsored agenda, the notable exception being an abrogation of the Pragmatic Sanction. Until the arrival of the French delegation, the Council was in need of an agenda. On 15 January 1514, less than a month after the eighth session, Leo requested all prelates, masters, doctors, and other religious men wishing to propose material for the consideration of the Council to bring it to the attention of the senior cardinals on the appropriate conciliar deputation. What was specifically proposed in response to this request is not clear, but by the eve of the ninth session the bishops were formulating their own program of reform and were ready to insist on its enactment[29].

The crisis which occurred in the Spring of 1514 resulted only in part from the assertion of episcopal power. De Grassi attributed Leo's reluctance to continue a council he now felt burdensome to the conflict between the pope's obligations to the cardinals and the opposing demands of the bishops. But more was involved here. Leo became convinced that the leading princes of Christendom were in a conspiratorial league to strip him of his power through the agency of their national delegations at the Council[30]. Like Julius before him, Leo came to perceive the Lateran Council as a potentially dangerous tool that could sabotage rather than serve the ends of papal power. But unlike his predecessor, Leo had lost an absolute control over it.

The way out of his difficulties was along the path of negotiated compromises and skillful diplomacy. In order to obtain the bishops' approval of an abrogation of the Pragmatic Sanction and agreement to close the Council, the pope would have to meet some of their demands. These were focused primarily on a restoration of their prestige and jurisdictional authority and on the establishment of an agency in Rome to safeguard their interests once the Council ended. The pope's fears of domination by the princes acting through the Council were al-

---

[28] For the text of Leo's promise, see: ASV, Miscel. Arm. II, nr. 43, fol. 16ᵛ and A.A. Arm. I—XVIII, nr. 5037, n. 23, fol. 16ʳ; SANUTO XVI 109; the Florentine ambassadors reported to the Dieci di Balia on 24 April 1513 that Leo had been dispensed by the cardinals from many of his election promises, but it is not clear if these were those of a financial nature or included those affecting the Council — see: BAV, Vat. Lat. 6232, fol. 112ᵛ; on Leo's promise at the eighth session, see DE GRASSI 1039: 14.

[29] MANSI 847C—E, 848D—50D, DE GRASSI 1081: 1—3.

[30] DE GRASSI 1081: 2; Hubert JEDIN, Vincenzo Quirini und Pietro Bembo, in: Kirche des Glaubens, Kirche der Geschichte, Freiburg 1966, I 153—66, esp. 157—59; PASTOR VII 161.

layed by the failure of any significant foreign delegation to arrive and by the success of his diplomatic measures which helped create and preserve a balance of powers and openings to his political opponents[31].

The history of the final four sessions of the Council was in large part that of a struggle between the bishops on one side and on the other the cardinals and those enjoying exemption from local episcopal jurisdiction, notably the mendicant friars. While Leo cast himself in the role of mediator, his loyalties were with the college of cardinals and his sympathies with those enjoying papal exemptions, despite any initial promise he may have made to the bishops[32].

On the eve of the ninth session the resentment of the bishops toward the cardinals broke out into the open. A series of meetings were held and deputies elected in the hope of resolving an impasse created by the bishops' threat that if they received no relief from the burdens imposed on them by cardinals, they would either boycott the Council or vote down any measures submitted for their approval. The bishops became more tractable when they were assured that measures in the up-coming Great Reform Bull which they found offensive would be eliminated, that nothing would be enacted which did not apply equally to both them and the cardinals, and that a special session of the Council would meet to hear their complaints[33].

In return for these pledges Leo obtained episcopal approval of the decrees submitted at the ninth session on 5 May 1514. These included the Great Reform Bull by which Leo redeemed his earlier promise of a more comprehensive reform of the Church. Another bull exhorted Christian princes to make peace, prescribed prayers for a crusade, and repeated the commands of his predecessor that all prelates, especially those under the obligation of *ad limina* visitation, attend the Lateran Council and that all rulers grant them permission and safe-conduct. Pleading their inability to obtain safe-passage from the rulers of either Genoa or Milan, the bishops in the French delegation presented their excuse in a letter to Leo which he had read at this session. While the pope accepted their excuse this time, he later secured from the doge of Genoa a pledge of safe-conduct for these prelates[34].

Instead of the hoped for arrival of the French delegation and abrogation of the Pragmatic Sanction at the following session, Leo was forced to deal once again with the complaints of the bishops already in Rome. In addition to their continued attack on the power cardinals had over bishops, the latter insisted on a termination of the privileges of exempt religious. The friars used various ploys

---

[31] MINNICH, Participants 176—78; Letter of Francesco Vettori to the Deici di Balia, Rome, 18 April 1514, in Archivio di Stato, Firenze, Dieci di Balia, Carteggio-Responsive nr. 118, fols. 568ʳ⁻ᵛ; Francesco NITTI, Leone X e la sua politica: secondo documenti e carteggi inediti, Firenze 1892, 11—13.

[32] DE GRASSI 1081: 2, 1116: 3, 1185: 1—6.

[33] MANSI 848A—50D, DE GRASSI 1081: 2—3.

[34] MANSI 864B—85D, 899A—900C.

to protect their traditional exemptions, but the bishops rejected any measures short of a conciliar rescission, and backed their demand with a renewed threat of boycott[35]. Leo once again secured the agreement of the bishops to approve the conciliar legislation at the tenth session on 4 May 1515 by promising a special session to deal with their demands. Two of the four bulls whose approval Leo thereby secured treated questions of orthodoxy. The first sided with the Franciscans in defending the *montes pietatis* against the attacks of the Dominicans and Augustinians who claimed that these pawn shops were usurious institutions. The second mandated a censorship of all printed books. As a partial answer to the bishops' demands for a curtailment of exemptions, another bull restored episcopal jurisdiction over many clerics and curial officials residing in their dioceses. What Leo obtained from this session was a bull ordering any French prelate or noble who alleged the legitimacy of the Pragmatic Sanction to appear in person at the next session of the Council or else be declared guilty of contumacy[36].

Both the pope's and bishops' respective legislative programs for this second period of the Leonine phase of the Council culminated in the bulls presented at the eleventh session. In the year and a half since the previous session, major developments had transpired. When the new king of France, Francis I, trounced Leo's allies in the battle of Marignano (13—14 September 1515), the pope quickly reached in a series of face-to-face negotiations with the king at Bologna in December of 1515 an agreement which resolved the major outstanding political and ecclesiastical questions between them. This Concordat of Bologna replaced the Pragmatic Sanction of Bourges which was to be formally abrogated in France[37]. Leo was eager that both the concordat and the abrogation be confirmed by conciliar authority. The bishops were willing to cooperate for a price. They had waited years now for the oft promised session that would give a favorable hearing to their demands. Should they approve Leo's new arrangements for the French Church without obtaining at the same time the reforms they so passionately desired, they would have surrendered their strongest bar-

---

[35] De Grassi 1116: 2—3; Hergenroether—Leclercq 451—52.

[36] Mansi 905C—07B, 907D—12A, 912C—13D, 913E—14D; a good survey on the question of the *montes pietatis* is to be found in Michele Monaco, La questione dei Monti di Pietà al Quinto Concilio Lateranense, in: Rivista di Studi Salernitani 7(1971) 85—136; on the preventive censorship of the press, see: Joseph Hilgers, Der Index der verbotenen Bücher in seiner neuen Fassung dargelegt und rechtlich-historisch gewürdigt, Freiburg i. Br. 1904/07, esp. 6, 133—36, 206, 395—96, 408, and C. J. Pinto de Oliveira, Le premier document pontifical sur la presse. La constitution 'Inter Multiplices' d'Innocent VIII (17 novembre 1487), in: RSPhTh 50 (1966) 628—43; Rudolf Hirsch, Bulla Super Impressione Librorum, 1515, in: Gutenberg-Jahrbuch (1975) 248—51.

[37] Jules Thomas, Le concordat de 1516: Ses origines, son histoire au XVIᵉ siècle, 3 vols. Paris 1910; Louis Madelin, France et Rome, Paris 1913, esp. 103—196; Terrence Mulkerin, The Fifth Council of the Lateran (1512—1517): A Chapter in the Struggle against Gallicanism, in: St. Meinrad Essays 12 (1961) 42—53; R. J. Knecht, The Concordat of 1516: A Reassessment (1963), reprinted in Government in Reformation Europe, 1520—1560, ed. Henry J. Cohn, New York 1971, 91—112.

gaining chip. Should they then agree to the Council's close, they would have lost the opportunity of a lifetime to reverse the centuries-long process of declining episcopal power. Now was the time to insist on their program: an end to the exemptions of religious and the establishment of an episcopal "confraternity."

Having obtained little relief after a fierce struggle with the powerful cardinals, the bishops had hopes of greater success in their conflict with the religious who could easily be overwhelmed in any vote at the Council. The bishops were determined to bring these religious under their jurisdiction. At least two petitions, one containing some eighty points and the other fifteen, were drawn up detailing the bishops' complaints. The latter document has survived. So too have an anonymous item by item refutation of it, a speech apparently written by Egidio Antonini of the Augustinians and addressed to the three cardinals commissioned to hear this case, and a letter of his commenting on this struggle.[38] The intent of the bishops was to eliminate the exemptions of the mendicant friars contained in the bull known as *Mare magnum* and to reduce to common law their many privileges which the bishops considered pretexts for abuses and violations of their jurisdiction. Among the defenses used by the friars were appeals to the wisdom of papal authority which the bishops were implicitly attacking, recitals of the numerous benefits conferred on the Church and papacy by the labors of the mendicants, and claims that the friars were for the most part innocent of the charges brought against them and that present law was adequate to punish anyone shown to be guilty[39].

Only with difficulty could the bishops pressure the pope and cardinals into agreeing to a conciliar rescission of the mendicants' exemptions. The friars enlisted supporters from the highest ranks of ecclesiastical and civil society and

---

[38] For a general survey of this conflict in the early sixteenth century, see Alaphridus de BONHOME, Jurisdiction des évêques et exemption des réguliers selon le projet de bulle de Paul III 'Superni dispositione consilii' (Décembre 1540 — Janvier 1542), in: RDC 15 (1965) 97—138, 214—39, 331—49, 16 (1966) 3—21.

Mention of the eighty articles against the friars is to be found in the letter of Egidio Antonini to the Augustinian house in Paris (s. l., s. d.) printed in Veterum scriptorum et monumentorum historicorum, dogmaticorum, moralium, amplissima collectio, ed. Edmond MARTÈNE and Ursin DURAND, 9 vols. Paris 1724—33, III, Ep. 23, 1262—64, esp. 1263, his letter from Rome of 15 January 1517 to the whole order is printed as Ep. 24, 1264—67; the bishops' fifteen-point petition is printed as appendix C in HERGENROETHER, Conciliengeschichte, VIII 813—14, the anonymous response in the name of all religious as App. D, 814—18, the speech as App. E, 818—31. That Antonini was the author of App. E is suggested not only by its elegant Ciceronic style, but also by references in it to the quarter tax he opposed and to the scheme of history he adopted which dated the end of the apostolic era with pope Sylvester who allowed the Church to grow wealthy — see HERGENROETHER/LECLERCQ 827; MARTÈNE/DURAND 1265B; MANSI 670A; John W. O'MALLEY, Giles of Viterbo on Church and Reform: A Study in Renaissance Thought, Leiden 1968, 139—42.

This conflict between the bishops and friars at Lateran V is studied in detail in MINNICH, Episcopal Reform 407—34.

[39] HERGENROETHER/LECLERCQ 813—14; 817, 820—23, 825, 829.

sought to undercut the bishops' criticisms by a rapid and thorough self-reform. The bishops would be satisfied, however, with nothing less than a conciliarly mandated reform which could not be easily set aside. Realizing that the Council would be forced to enact some kind of reform, Leo sought a compromise which would placate the bishops but protect the financial resources and internal autonomy of the religious. The draft of a bull presented to the bishops for their approval four days prior to the eleventh session was openly criticized by all. A second draft presented the following day met such strong opposition that it was finally revised in accordance with many of the bishops' wishes[40]. They were able to obtain Leo's consent to such a decree only by dropping their other major demand, the establishment of an episcopal confraternity.

This sodality or confraternity was the most interesting and potentially revolutionary proposal made by the bishops. This guild-like organization with its own set of officers and officials would be composed of episcopal delegates from the nations of Christendom. These representatives would reside in Rome in order to protect at the Curia the interests of their colleagues. Such an organization could easily have become a rival to the Sacred College and eventually have freed the bishops from the domination of the cardinals. It would also have given bishops continued leverage in the Roman Curia once the Council ended[41].

When Leo submitted this proposal to the College of Cardinals for their consideration, he found them so adamantly opposed to it that he imposed a perpetual silence on this plan. Because the cardinals in trying to justify their opposition had alleged that episcopal interests were already represented at court by the papal assistants, the bishops who still overwhelmingly backed their proposal revised it so that these court prelates would now become their official representatives. The pope and cardinals, however, wanted nothing to do with so dangerous a proposal in any guise. They not only totally rejected it, but Leo threatened to prorogue the Council indefinitely and allow the privileges of the mendicants to stand intact should the bishops persist in demanding such a confraternity[42]. Having been forced to drop this proposal for the sake of a victory over the mendicants, the bishops were determined to curtail the friars' privileges as much as possible.

---

[40] MARTÈNE/DURAND 1263—67; Margarete HAUSNER, Die Visitation des Aegidius von Viterbo im Kloster der Augustinereremitinnen zu Memmingen 1516, in: Memminger Geschichtsblätter 1972, 5—92; on Leo's role as protector of the friars, see also the preface of CAJETAN to Secunda secundae partis summae ... theologiae ... Aquinatis, a₂ʳ; DE GRASSI 1116: 2—3; MANSI 935E—39A.

[41] The contents of this first and no longer extant proposal can be partially reconstructed from the memorial attacking it — see HERGENROETHER, Conciliengeschichte, App. J, 847—53.

[42] Ibid., 852—53 and App. H, 845—46; DE GRASSI, 1185: 1—7; for a detailed study of these proposals, see MINNICH, Episcopal Reform, 380—404 and Francis OAKLEY, Conciliarism at the Fifth Lateran Council? in: Church History 41 (1972) 452—63.

The eleventh session, four times prorogued, finally met on 19 December 1516. After a reading of the mandate of the Maronite patriarch, four major documents were proposed for the bishops' approval. The first, which gave bishops control over the pulpits in their dioceses, was easily passed by the fathers. Rather than then submitting a short bull rescinding a number of the friars' exemptions, Leo took no chances and had a very lengthy document and its briefer companion piece read. After delineating the many abuses said to exist in the French Church due to the Pragmatic Sanction, this extended document reiterated the provisions of the Concordat of Bologna which were said to remedy this situation. The shorter bull formally abrogated the Pragmatic Sanction of Bourges and declared that the pope alone has the power to convoke, transfer, and dissolve a council. But for a few minor objections raised against various provisions in these two documents, the bishops overwhelmingly approved them. Leo at last obtained what he most wanted from the Council. The bull on the friars was now read and submitted to a vote. So numerous were the bishops' protests to various provisions in it that the debate dragged on and only after a careful counting of the votes was the bull finally approved. For all their years of bitter struggle, the bishops had not succeeded in restoring to any appreciable degree the dignity and power of their office. Leo, however, took great satisfaction in the results of the eleventh session, declaring that the abrogation of the Pragmatic Sanction pleased him greatly and the limited curtailment of the friars' privileges had his absolute approval. Despite the objections of the Spanish master of ceremonies, Leo joyfully intoned the *Te Deum* which ended the session[43].

Having secured what he wanted from the Council, Leo now worked to end it quickly. Such items as a reform of the calendar still under study were set aside. Instead of accepting a delay in order to work out a compromise on a conciliar confirmation and extension of Paul II's decree against alienation of church property, the cardinals decided to drop the matter when it met some opposition in the general congregation preceeding this session[44]. The agenda for this session was thus limited to approving two documents: a decree forbidding the plundering of cardinals' residences during conclaves and a bull imposing a crusade tax and closing the Council.

The twelfth session on 16 March 1517 witnessed a last ditch effort by the bishops to assert their power. While they approved the decree protecting the cardinals' residences, they vigorously attacked the other measure claiming that now that the princes were at peace, it was time for opening a council rather than terminating one, and voicing doubts that a crusade against the Turks would ever be launched. So close was the vote on this bull, that it was approved by a

---

[43] MANSI 947E—64E, 965E—74E, DE GRASSI 1206: 11, 14—16, 1207: 1.

[44] MANSI 979B—E; HERGENROETHER, Conciliengeschichte, App. K, 853—55; the *Paulina* decree is probably *Ambitiosae cupiditati* (1468) = C. un., III, 4, Extr. comm. = FRIEDBERG II 1269.

mere two or three vote margin[45]. Nonetheless, Leo had kept his election pledge and had dissolved the Council with the consent of a majority of its members. And regarding the declared goals of the Council, he had seen that a variety of decrees were issued which at least on paper seemed to further their accomplishment.

The History of the Office of Master of Ceremonies and of His Diary

The literary form and content of the Diary of Paride de Grassi, an important primary source for the history of this Council, can best be understood in the context of the office of its author and of the tradition of liturgical writings established by his predecessors.

The origins of the office of master of ceremonies are difficult to establish. The earlier *ordines Romani* suggest that the pope himself by such gestures as a nod of the head directed at times the ceremonies of his chapel. A special official entrusted with the supervision of these rites does not seem to have existed in the Middle Ages, despite Gaetano Moroni's claim that Lotario dei Segni prior to his promotion to the cardinalate in 1190 had held the office of papal master of ceremonies. The existence of such an official is not confirmed by any mention of him in the lists of those clerics and officers participating in the papal coronation and procession of 1316. During the fourteenth century a variety of papal officials, such as camerlengo, sacristan, and chaplain wrote about ceremonies and may have also functioned as ceremonialists. Recent scholarship suggests that the office of cleric of ceremonies evolved out of that of the clerics of the chapel. Pierre Salteti of Mende, named a cleric of the inner chapel in 1369, is known to have functioned as a ceremonialist. The first mention of the office of cleric of the ceremonies of the papal chapel seems to have occurred on 13 November 1415 when Giovannello de Alderisio, known as Bramerico, was officially named to this post[46]. The office was thus less than a century old when de Grassi was appointed to it in 1504.

---

[45] Mansi 986D—93B; de Grassi 1231: 8.

[46] An early study of this office which concentrates on its later developments is found in Gaetano Moroni, Maestro delle ceremonie pontificie, in: Dizionario di erudizione storico-ecclesiastico, 41 (Venice 1846) 163—181, esp. 163, 168—70, 177; for the pope signaling the choir to stop the music so that the liturgy could progress and for a brief over-view of the evolution of liturgical writings up to the time of de Grassi, see: Aimé Georges Martimort, The Church at Prayer, 2: The Eucharist, ed. A. G. Martimort, Noële Maurice Denis Boulet, Roger Béraudy, Austin Flannery, and Vincent Ryan, Shannon, Eire 1973, 6—48, for the pope's role in *Ordo I*, 39—40, 42, and also useful is Le cérémoniale apostolique avant Innocent VIII: Texte du manuscrit Urbinate Latin 469 de la Bibliothèque Vaticane, éstabli par Dom Filippo Tamburini, Introduction par Msgr. Joaquim Nabuco (= Bibliotheca "Ephemerides Liturgicae": Sectio Historica 30) Roma 1966, 11*—38*; the basis for Moroni's assertion that de Grassi claimed that Innocent III prior to becoming cardinal had been a master of ceremonies (Dizionario XLI 177) seems to be the state-

In the course of the fifteenth century the office of the clerics of the ceremonies of the papal chapel developed an organization of its own. Until Guido de Busco's appointment by the year 1405 as his colleague, Bramerico had discharged by himself the functions of that office. For the remainder of that century at least two clerics jointly held the post, by the death of Eugenius IV there is mention of five. On the basis of stipendary rights they were apparently divided into two groups. Those known as *ordinarii et participantes* were usually two in number, but the appointment of Humbert Rolet brought their number to at least three. He who held the office longest was known as the senior ordinary and enjoyed special claims on revenues. They were called *participantes* because they shared the income of the office. Those without direct rights to these revenues were known as *non-participantes*, *socii*, and *supernumerarii*. Such a ceremonialist was employed only occasionally in the middle in that century but by its end it was common practice to name two. They were often clerics of the papal chapel such as deacons, subdeacons, and acolytes, and would substitute for an absent *ordinarius*, but did not automatically succeed to his office when vacant. The reform bull *Pastoralis officii* approved by the Lateran Council in 1513 institutionalized this division of the college of masters of ceremonies into two ordinary masters and two substitutes selected from among the clerics of the papal chapel. These substitutes should neither share in the revenues of the ordinary masters nor receive a special stipend from the curia, but should be content with their income from the papal chapel. Apparently they acted as substitutes in papal ceremonies and served papal legates on their journeys.

In order to continue to utilize the expertise of an experienced master even after his promotion to the episcopacy which required the resignation of all curial posts, a special honorific office of president was created. Agostino Patrizi (d. 1494) seems to have been the first to occupy it (ca. 1485). De Grassi on his nomination to the bishopric of Pesaro (1513) was also allowed to stay on as *praesidens* of the college of ceremonialists, but had to delegate his functions to another, his nephew Ippolyto Morbioli. But as even a casual reading of his Diary will show, de Grassi continued in fact to function as master. Later that year, his activities were regularized when *Pastoralis officii* decreed that with the

---

ment Innocentius Pontifex Max. eius nominis Tertius, in nostra professione doctor illustris . . . in DE GRASSI, De caeremoniis cardinalium et episcoporum in eorum dioecesibus libri duo, Venice 1582, fol. 3ʳ; the descriptions of the papal ceremonies of 1316 are in Marc DYKMANS, Le cérémonial papal de la fin du moyen âge à la renaissance, II: De Rome en Avignon ou le cérémonial de Jacques Stefaneschi, (= Bibliothèque de l'Institut Historique Belge de Rome 25) Bruxelles/Rome 1981, 318—21; a brief survey of early writings on ceremonies is given by Pierre SALMON, Les manuscripts liturgiques latins de la Bibliothèque Vaticane, III: Ordines Romani, Pontificaux, Rituels, Ceremoniaux, (= Studi e testi 260) Città del Vaticano 1970, ix-x; studies on the beginnings of the office of ceremonialist are provided by Gustave CONSTANT, Les maîtres de cérémonies du XVIᵉ siècle: leur Diaires, in: Mélanges d'archéologie et d'histoire de l'École Française de Rome 23 (1903) 161—229, 319—43, esp. 161—62 and by Franz WASNER, Guido de Busco: ein Beitrag zur Frühgeschichte des päpstlichen Zeremonienamtes, in: AHP 4 (1966) 79—104, esp. 81 n. 4, 97—100.

consent of the pope and of the other masters of ceremonies a newly appointed bishop could remain in this ceremonial office[47].

The international character of this college of ceremonialists fluctuated over its first century to be fixed with the approval of the Lateran Council in 1513. Of the eighteen known ordinary clerics of ceremonies from Bramerico to de Grassi, seven were Italians, probably four from the Empire, four French, two Spanish, and one of unidentified origin. While the French were more numerous in the first half of the fifteenth century (two were from the diocese of Rouen and one from Toulon), the Italians came to dominate the later period (three from Siena, and one each from the Marches(?), Naples, Bologna, and Viterbo). The ceremonialists from the Empire continued to hold office at various times throughout the century and came from the region west of the Rhine (Tournai, Verdun, Toul, Lüttich(?), and Strassburg). A balance between the cis- and ultra-montane groups was a concern of the Lateran Council which agreed to the provision in *Pastoralis officii* that the two ordinary masterships be divided between these two groups. Because at the time of the Council both masters were Italians (de Grassi of Bologna and B. Nicolai of Viterbo), the Spaniard Bernardino Guttierez, who had in 1504 resigned his post in favor of de Grassi, was in December of 1513 temporarily reappointed as master, but he seems to have been only a *supernumerarius*[48].

---

[47] WASNER 81, 98—104; and his Tor der Geschichte: Beiträge zum päpstlichen Zeremonienwesen im 15. Jahrhundert, in: AHP 6 (1968) 113—162, esp. 121—22; CONSTANT 163—67; Marc DYKMANS, Le cérémonial de Nicholas V, in: RHE 63 (1968) 365—78, 785—825, esp. 792—93 n. 1; Agostino PATRIZI, Rituum Ecclesiasticarum sive sacrarum cerimoniarum sacrosanctae Romanae Ecclesiae libri tres, ed. Cristoforo MARCELLO, Venice 1516 / reprint Ridgewood, N.J. 1965, fol. 124ᵛ; LEO X, Pastoralis Officii, in: Bullarum Taurinensis editio V 572—73; HOFMANN II 186—190; Rino AVESANI, Per la biblioteca di Agostino Patrizi Piccolomini vescovo di Pienza, in: Mélanges Eugène Tisserant, VI: Bibliothèque Vaticane, Première partie, (= Studi e Testi 236) Città del Vaticano 1964, 1—87, esp. 17—18; L. THUSANE, Notice Biographique in: Johannes Burchardi Diarium sive rerum urbanarum commentarii (1483—1506), 3 vols. Paris 1883—85, III, i—lxviii, esp. xii—xiii, n. 4.

[48] The ceremonialists can be divided into the following national groups: Italians (Guido de Busco of the Marches[?], Giovannello de Alderisio known as Bramerico of Naples, Enea Silvio Piccolomini of Siena, Agostino Patrizi of Siena, Aldello Piccolomini of Siena, Paride de Grassi of Bologna, and Baldassare Nicolai of Viterbo); French (Hambert Roleti of Rouen, Michel Brunout of Rouen, Matthieu Petri of Quimper, and Antoine Rébiol of Toulon); Empire (Michael Goie of Tournai[?] — while Tournai and the Tournaisis were still French, much of the diocese lay within the Empire), Randulphus Dandrenas of Lüttich[?], Nicholas Gilquin of Verdun, and Johann Burckard of Strassburg); Spanish (Pedro Gonzalez de Villaverde of Burgos and Bernardino Guttierez of Salamanca); unknown (Vincentius) — see WASNER, Guido de Busco 99—102 and Tor der Geschichte 115—32; HOFMANN II 183; and THUSANE II 356—57 n. 2. That Guido de Busco came from a French speaking area (does the Angevin court of Naples qualify?) is asserted by Bernhard SCHIMMELPFENNIG, Zum Zeremoniell auf den Konzilien von Konstanz und Basel, in: QFIAB 49 (1969) 273—92, esp. 275. This gradual Italianization of the office was furthered by de Grassi who personally urged Leo X to ignore the Lateran decree and replace the deceased Nicolai with another Italian instead of either the Spaniard Guttierez or German Michael Sander (a former supernumerarius) as proposed. With Leo's appointment of Biagio Martinelli of Cesena in 1518 this provision of the Lateran Council became a dead letter — see: CONSTANT 226—27; THUSANE III, xliii n. 4; LEO X, Pastoralis officii, in: Bullarum Taurinensis editio V 572. This process of excluding "foreigners" occurred throughout the Roman curia — see HOFMANN I 238—42.

Appointment to the office of ceremonialist was by the pope. He could on his own initiative name someone a cleric of the ceremonies of the papal chapel as did Eugenius IV in 1445 when he appointed Pedro Gonzalez. The more common practice, however, seems to have been to appoint someone in response to the petition of an influential patron or relative. Guido de Busco secured his post through the efforts of his uncle Guglielmo Dalla Vigna, the papal sacristan. Varieties of nepotism were not uncommon. Agostino Patrizi who was adopted into the Piccolomini family resigned his office to Aldello Piccolomini. Onofrio Nicolai, a *supernumerarius*, was followed by Baldassare Nicolai as an *ordinarius*. On his promotion to the episcopacy de Grassi succeeded in having his sister Lodovica Morbioli's son Ippolyto appointed as his substitute while retaining for himself the right of regress. In his own case, de Grassi was named *ordinarius* in 1504 with the backing of cardinals Raffaelle Riario and Petrus Isvalies. Whether his curialist brother Achille had secured for him this support from the cardinals is not clear. That it probably cost him a good deal of money is suggested by the report that Burckard paid Patrizi about 450 golden ducats for the expenses of investiture[49].

The revenues attached to this office amply compensated its holder for such an initial investment. From the appointment of de Busco, ca. 1404 onwards, the two *ordinarii* shared these revenues, while the *supernumerarii*, added later in that century, apparently received a portion of them only at the consent of the *ordinarii* in return for specific services rendered. When in 1469 Patrizi complained to Paul II that his income of six golden ducats for the past three years as a *supernumerarius* was inadequate for the expense of maintaining a fitting household with himself, two retainers, and a horse to feed and with himself to clothe, the pope supplemented his income with a parochial benefice and promoted him to *ordinarius*. A summary by de Busco in the 1430's of the revenues earned by the *ordinarii* indicates a monthly income of ten ducats plus numerous service fees and *spolia*. While Eugenius IV drastically reduced this monthly stipend, the other revenues of the office grew over the years. In 1470 Paul II fixed the fees and which shares went to whom. But under Sixtus IV and his successors these fees and *spolia* increased once again. The list of *spolia* due to the masters ranged from handkerchiefs, wax candles, and torches to pillows, covers, clothing, and utensils. So intently did officials assert their rights to these fringe benefits that in 1508 de Grassi came to blows with two Augustinian friars at Santa Maria del Popolo, ripping the scapular and tunic of one, and grabbing the other by his hair and ears. And what did they fight over? A waxen taper! As part of his reforms related to the Lateran Council, Julius lowered the fees

---

[49] WASNER, Guido de Busco 81; and his Tor der Geschichte 123; AVESANI 18—19 n. 89; HOFMANN II 183; CONSTANT 227; Pompeo LITTA, Famiglie celebri italiane, Milano 1820—56, VII, Grassi di Bologna, tavola II; THUSANE I 3, II 350, III, xliii n. 4, 357 n. 2.

and *spolia* due to the ceremonialists. De Grassi tried to reconcile himself to these conciliar reforms. Under Leo X the bull *Pastoralis officii* detailed the limits on such emoluments. Once again de Grassi was unhappy. These reductions of his income probably help to explain his later contempt for the Council's accomplishments[50].

Among the principal emoluments of the office in the early sixteenth century were three benefices and a residence attached to a Roman church. Prior to the time of the Grassi the masters of ceremonies apparently had no special place of residence. For a time Patrizi may have resided in the household of cardinal Francesco Todeschini-Piccolomini. Burckard accumulated enough money to have built his own palace and thereby give the name of his adopted city of Strassburg *(Argentina)* to his palace and to the city square abutting it, the Largo Argentina of today. De Grassi was able to obtain from Julius II a Roman benefice with residence attached, the archpresbyterate of Saints Celso and Giuliano near the Ponte Sant'Angelo which was conveniently close to the Vatican. This benefice included a spacious residence with a large hall, two studies, a storeroom, and garden. The efforts of the collegiate clergy of this church to block his appointment were of no avail. By the bull *Pastoralis officii* of 1513 the archpresbyterate, a canonry, and a prebend of this church were permanently attached to the office of the masters of ceremonies to help provide them a fitting income[51].

What probably made the office of master of ceremonies so highly desirable was neither its revenues nor residence, but rather the opportunities it afforded for winning the support of high churchmen in the pursuit of benefices, pensions, curial posts, and prelacies. Many of the masters were very successful in accumulating a variety of benefices and pensions, often in their native lands but also in Rome. Like other ceremonialists, de Grassi also constantly sought benefices and pensions[52]. As part of the papal court, the masters could participate actively in

---

[50] WASNER, Guido de Busco 85, 90—98; HOFMANN II 28—29; AVESANI 11—12; DYKMANS, Le cérémonial 792—93 n. 1; CONSTANT 195—222; THUSANE II 354 n. 1; DE GRASSI, Diarium Julii, Vat. Lat. 12414, fol. 206ᵛ and Diarium Leonis, Vat. Lat. 12275, fol. 179ʳ—80ʳ, 197ʳ; LEO X, Pastoralis officii, in: Bullarum Taurinensis editio V 572—73; DE GRASSI 1231: 10.

[51] AVESANI 9—10; Roma e Dintorni, Milano ⁵1950, 35—36; for de Grassi's residence, see his account of first obtaining it in 1509 from Julius in DÖLLINGER III 389—90 and the confirmation in Joseph HERGENROETHER, Regesta Leonis, Freiburg i. Br. 1884, I 17, nr. 268 (19 March 1513); and for the detail of the 1474 map of Alessandro Strozzi showing the church's form and location, see Richard KRAUTHEIMER, Rome: Profile of a City, 312—1308, Princeton, N.J. 1980, 270, 272; the reference to this church in Pastoralis officii is in Bullarum Taurinensis editio V 573.

[52] Noteworthy for their pluralism were: Radulphus Dandrenas who held important benefices in Arras, Rouen, Autun, Metz, Konstanz, Châlons, and Lüttich (see WASNER, Guido de Busco 101 n. 14, 16), Humbert Roleti in Lausanne and Bourges (Ibid 101—02 n. 19, 20, 22—24, 26—27), Pedro Gonzalez in Toledo, Valencia, Seville and Leon (WASNER, Tor der Geschichte 124 n. 38), and especially Antoine Rébiol with numerous benefices in France (Ibid 130—32, n. 58—60, 62—63, 65). Johann Burckard's skills at obtaining benefices in Strassburg, Metz, and Basel were amply demonstrated before his promotion to the mastership and his appetite was not satisfied by this appointment — see: J. LESELLIER, Les méfaits du cérémoniaire Jean Burckard, in: Mélanges d'archéologie et d'histoire de l'Ecole Française de Rome 44

the competition for curial posts; many obtained positions as solicitors, readers, writers, and abbreviators of various papal documents, but only a few reached the more important posts of protonotary, prelate of the palace, and *referendarius* of letters of favor attained by Burckard. By the end of the century masters were often rewarded for their various services with promotion to the episcopacy: E. S. Piccolomini to Trieste and Siena, Patrizi to Pienza, A. Piccolomini to Soana, Burckard to Orte, and de Grassi to Pesaro. The custom also developed that these episcopal masters were named papal assistants. Given the papal practice of often choosing cardinals from among their assistants, it is not surprising that an ambitious prelate such as Burckard may have held such hopes — at least de Grassi claimed that Julius II had joked that Burckard was bringing up the end of a line of new cardinals in hopes of being promoted along with them[53].

De Grassi considered the office of master of ceremonies to be both demanding and difficult. To corroborate his opinion he cited the words of one of his predecessors who had gone on to become pope, Enea Silvio Piccolomini (Pius II). According to this Sienese humanist, a ceremonialist needs strength of body, alertness of mind, and great knowledge of his duties so that he can consider each factor and in every respect serve and satisfy all. His actions and teachings are to be so guided by rules that they may be regarded as models of what is to be done; for the learning process is dependent upon a teacher, example, practice, and experience[54].

In response to Innocent VIII's concern that splendor and order characterize divine services and that they be conducted with gravity and dignity, with smoothness and tranquility, and without disturbance, Agostino Patrizi prepared with help from the writings of his predecessors and from his own colleague Johann Burckard an account of the ceremonies of the papal court. In describing the duties of the masters, he echoed the pope's concerns. The masters are thus to perform their functions decorously, deftly, quietly, modestly, and seriously, interspersing their actions with fitting pauses so as to inspire greater reverence and devotion. That such qualities did not always characterize their actions is suggested by the provisions in the never enacted reform bull of Pius II which

---

1927) 11—34, esp. 14—16, 19—20. For some of de Grassi's benefices and pensions, see: ASV, Reg. Vat. 942, fol. 238; 951, fol. 87; 958, fols. 83, 169.

[53] On curial posts, see WASNER, Guido de Busco 99—102 and his Tor der Geschichte 122, 124, 130, 132; THUSANE III, v, xli, xliii; Konrad EUBEL, Hierarchia catholica medii et recentioris aevi, II Münster 1914, 216, 243, III Münster 1923, 211, 274; DE GRASSI, Diarium Julii, Vat. Lat. 12414, fol. 193v, and his Diarium Leonis, Vat. Lat. 12275, fol. 151r; on two differing interpretations of Burckard's actions see THUSANE III, xliii and 427 n.

[54] Paride DE GRASSI, De caeremoniis cardinalium et episcoporum in eorum dioecesibus libri duo, Venice 1582, fol. 4v—5r — after much personal searching of Piccolomini's writings for this text and after correspondence with leading experts on Pius II, Franz WASNER was unable to locate the original source for de Grassi's quote — see his Tor der Geschichte 120 n. 21. De Grassi's description of the diocesan master of ceremonies (fol. 4r—v) is apparently modeled on Pius II's statement.

urged the masters to fulfil their functions with the greatest diligence and modesty, and which forbad them to speak loudly, nod awkwardly, or gesture unbecomingly. In his efforts to assure proper order in the papal chapel, Patrizi described in detail the responsibilities of each ceremonialist[55].

In general the senior of the two ordinary masters was to concern himself with the pope. Stationing himself near the altar or at the credence table, he was to fix his attention on the pontiff, being ever ready to carry out his commands. Only if personally called on, or for an urgent reason, should he approach the pope and then only with gravity and reverence, and with care to make the customary gesture of respect to the cardinals[56].

The junior of the two ordinary masters was responsible primarily for the liturgy at the altar, its celebrant and his ministers. The actual assistance given to the celebrant must have been on occasion found wanting, for the reform bull *Pastoralis officii* of 1513 ordered the masters to help with dutiful respect and charity the cardinals and prelates who celebrated the liturgy. Without seeking a special financial compensation for their services, the masters were sincerely to admonish the celebrants at an opportune moment as to what was fitting and necessary. Should the rituals necessitate the services of a third ceremonialist, he was to be employed in accordance to what the ordinary masters deemed fitting[57].

Orderly ceremonies also depended on good relations and agreement among the masters. Patrizi urged the senior master to treat his junior and less-experienced partner as a good colleague and brother. The junior was to defer to his senior and assist him in carrying out his numerous responsibilities. Both were encouraged to cooperate. Before a ceremony took place, the masters were to forsee what needed to be done, make a plan, and divide up the tasks among themselves. If they could not agree and the junior refused to yield to the senior, it was deemed advisable that only one master direct all the ceremonies. That discords did occur was recognized by Pius II who, however, blamed them on variants in the ceremonial books used and ordered that one version be established as normative — a project on which both Patrizi and Burckard labored, but whose completion was not achieved by the time of de Grassi who found himself in conflict with Guttierez, both at times appealing to differing ceremonial texts, precedents, and authorities[58].

---

[55] Patrizi, Caeremoniale Romanum, Appendix, fol. Eeee, and fol. 124ᵛ; Pius II, Pastor Aeternus n. 137 printed in Rudolf Haubst, Der Reformentwurf Pius' des Zweiten, in: RQ 49 (1954) 188—242, esp. 227.

[56] Patrizi fol. 121ᵛ—22ʳ, 124ᵛ.

[57] Ibid., Leo X, Pastoralis officii, in: Bullarum Taurinensis editio V 572.

[58] Patrizi 124ᵛ; Haubst 227; the Caeremoniale Romanum is one of the major projects on which Patrizi and Burckard collaborated — see the conclusion to the 1488 dedicatory letter printed as an appendix in the Gregg Press reprint. This letter also acknowledges that quarrels among the masters of ceremonies have occurred when ceremonies were not written down and where the oral traditions differed.

The masters were also to safeguard the dignity and good order of the ceremonies by quieting any disturbances in the chapel. Patrizi wanted them to see that those present at the services stayed in their places and did not move about without reason. Pius ordered his ceremonialists to keep a careful watch on everyone who spoke or laughed in the chapel. The masters were to admonish them modestly to maintain silence. But should the noise continue, they were to refer the case to the pope who would have the papal sacristan punish the culprits for their excesses[59].

De Grassi's own understanding of the office of master of ceremonies and of what norms should regulate its activities, together with an analysis of his relations with his fellow masters and of how he carried out that office, will be treated later in detail. But first some consideration should be given to another of the master's responsibilities and to how his predecessors shaped the way in which he fulfilled it.

By the time of de Grassi the long tradition of writing about liturgical services in general and the more recent practice of recording noteworthy historical instances of these ceremonies had become an obligation of the master's office to maintain a journal. Descriptions of the ceremonies used at various liturgical functions from the eighth to the fifteenth centuries, known to scholars as the fifteen *ordines Romani* which Mabillon published in 1689, were preserved at the Vatican in numerous manuscript copies placed at the disposition of the masters. Ordo XIV, recently analyzed and edited by Marc Dykmans in his on-going study of the evolution of papal ceremonials in the later Middle Ages and Renaissance is attributed to Giacomo Stefaneschi (c. 1261—1341) and contains descriptions of a number of ceremonies which can be related to specific historical events such as the coronation of king Robert d'Anjou of Sicily in 1309 and of pope John XXII in 1316. The ceremonial (Ordo XV) of the papal sacristans, Pierre Ameilh of Brénac (d. 1401) and his nephew Pierre Assalbit (d. 1441) was chronological in format[60]. From such writings seems to have developed the practice of keeping a journal.

---

[59] PATRIZI fol. 124v; HAUBST 227; for a humorous example of de Grassi's attempts to restore order in the chapel when a lengthy and rambling sermon of a friar provoked laughter from the cardinals present, see John W. O'MALLEY, Praise and Blame in Renaissance Rome: Rhetoric, Doctrine, and Reform in the Sacred Orators of the Papal Court c. 1450—1521 (= Duke Monographs in Medieval and Renaissance Studies 3) Durham, N.C. 1979, 20—21.

[60] For a general study of medieval liturgical writings, see C. VOGEL, Introduction aux sources de l'histoire du culte chrétien au moyen âge (= Biblioteca degli "Studi Medievali" of the Centro Italiano di Studi sull'Alto Medioevo 1) Spoleto 1966, esp. 101—181. For the first scholarly publication of these Ordines Romani (mostly collections of rubrical prescriptions) see: Jean MABILLON and Michel GERMAIN, Museum Italicum seu collectio veterum scriptorum ex bibliothecis italicis, 2 vol. Paris 1687—89, vol. 2 contains the Ordines; some of these have been carefully studied by recent scholars, e. g.: Michel ANDRIEU, Les Ordines Romani du haut moyen âge, Part I, Les manuscrits, II, Les textes, 5 vols. (= Spicilegium sacrum Lovaniense 11, 23—24, 28—29 Louvain 1931—61 and for his study of the pontificals used in

The diary tradition originated in the fifteenth century. Pierre Salteti, who was named a cleric of the papal chapel in 1369, kept a diary-like account of the activities of the chapel of the Avignonese pope Benedict XIII for the years 1404—09 and is thus credited with being the founder of the tradition of maintaining a journal. François de Conzié (d. 1432) who authored the *Avisamenta* of 1409 on this pope's household also kept a diary of papal ceremonies. During the reign of Eugenius IV (1431—47) three ceremonialists seem to have kept accounts. The Frenchman Matthieu Petri apparently recorded the ceremonies of the papal court; while the Sienese Piccolomini, who served both the Council of Basel and the anti-pope Felix V in the capacity of ceremonialist, wrote a history of what transpired at this council and in the entourage of the Savoyard claimant. Piccolomini's attention, however, was focused less on the ceremonies than on the issues, personalities, and events of this period. Yet another diary which described the ceremonies of the papal court from the time of Eugenius IV to Pius II was actually used by de Grassi. Its author was probably Pedro Gonzales who functioned in the papal chapel at least from the time of his appointment as master by Eugenius IV in 1445 until replaced by Agostino Patrizi in 1469. An extant excerpt from this diary for the pontificate of Nicholas V reveals a primary concern for the details of the ceremonies surrounding such events as the funeral of a curial official, the marriage and coronation of Friedrich III, and the visit of the Greek patriarch. The author's attention to wider issues of interest to historians is not of the scope of a Piccolomini but foreshadows the mixture of liturgical and other considerations which characterize the writings of Burckard and de Grassi. The diaries of Antoine Rébiol (master from 1450 to 1484) and of Agostino Patrizi were apparently known to both Burckard and de Grassi, but do not seem to have survived[61]. Because the writings of Patrizi and Burckard were so influential on de Grassi, special attention will be here given to their careers and liturgical works.

---

combination with these ceremonials Le Pontifical Romain au moyen âge: I, Le Pontifical Romain du XIIe siècle, II, Le Pontifical de la Curie Romaine au XIIIe siècle, III, Le Pontifical de Guillaume Durand, IV, Tables alphabétiques, 4 vols., (= Studi e testi 86—88, 99) Città del Vaticano 1938—41; these studies have been continued by Marc Dykmans, Le Cérémonial papal de la fin du moyen âge à la Renaissance: I, Le Cérémonial papal du XIIIe siècle, II, De Rome en Avignon ou Le Cérémonial de Jacques Stefaneschi 24—25 (= Bibliothèque de l'Institut Historique Belge de Rome 24, 25) Bruxelles 1977—81 and his Mabillon et les interpolations de son Ordo Romanus XIV, in: Gregorianum 47 (1966) 316—42; for a study of the Vatican collection of liturgical manuscripts, see Pierre Salmon, Les manuscrits liturgiques latins de la Bibliothèque Vaticane (= Studie e testi 251, 253, 260, 267, 270) Città del Vaticano 1968—72, esp. vol. 3: Ordines Romani Pontificaux Rituels Ceremoniaux, v—xii; for these coronations described in Ordo XIV and the chronological character of Ordo XV, see Dykmans, Cérémonial de Stefaneschi 153, 290—305, 448—57 and his Mabillon 341; on Pierre Assalbit, see also Schimmelpfennig 275—76.

[61] The evidence of early diaries is studied in Dykmans, Mabillon 341, and Wasner, Guido de Busco 98—99, and his Tor der Geschichte 117—19, 123—29, 134—36; Piccolomini's contemporary account of the Council of Basel and its aftermath has been published as De gestis concilii Basiliensis commentariorum, ed. and trans. Denys Hay and W. K. Smith, Oxford 1967; for a study and critical edition of diary excerpts attributed to Gonzalez, see: Marc Dykmans, Le cérémonial de Nicholas V, in: RHE 63 (1968) 365—78, 785—825, esp. 371 (on de Conzié), 374—75, 389, 790, 795—815, 820—21.

Agostino Patrizi was a humanist, curialist, and bishop, whose lasting fame rests principally on his liturgical writings. These were highly esteemed by his contemporaries, especially pope Innocent VIII, and enjoyed a lasting influence. De Grassi consulted them as reliable authorities and regarded their compiler as the most eminent reformer of papal ceremonies. The form into which Patrizi reduced the often conflicting written and oral traditions of his office as master of ceremonies has determined these rites ever since[62].

Patrizi did not begin his career as a ceremonialist. Born in Siena in the 1430s or '40s and educated there, notably by the famed canonist Fabiano Benci of Montepulciano, this son of Aloysius Patrizi, a notary, at an early age came under the influence of two humanist prelates. His relative Francesco Patrizi, a governor of Foligno and bishop of Gaeta (ca. 1460—d. 1494) encouraged his interests in classical literature. The bishop of Siena, Enea Silvio Piccolomini, took Agostino under his protection and provided for his physical needs. When Piccolomini was elected pope in 1460, Patrizi went to Rome where he was quickly employed as the pope's private amanuensis, taking dictation (part of Pius II's *Commentaries* are in Agostino's hand) and proof-reading the writings of the pope and his copyists. He accompanied Pius to Ancona and when the pontiff died there, he entered the service of the pope's nephew cardinal Francesco Todeschini-Piccolomini (the future Pius III) whose friendship he retained throughout his life. From this cardinal he received the right of adding the Piccolomini family name to his own[63].

To support himself, Patrizi accumulated a number of ecclesiastical posts. Already a priest by 1461, he was appointed by Pius II as a papal chaplain, familiar, and abbreviator, and as pastor of the parish of S. Angelo in the diocese of Fermo. Although Paul II abolished the college of abbreviators, he eventually retained Patrizi as a papal familiar. By 1466 or '67 this former amanuensis of Pius II, who had early on in his career been named a conciliar and papal master of ceremonies, was himself functioning in that capacity. When Patrizi complained to Paul II that the office of substitute ceremonialist was poorly compensated, this pope, who had earlier granted him the parish church of S. Maurizio in Siena, now gave him in addition that of S. Vito in Vesuri in the diocese of Fermo and toward the end of 1469 appointed him an ordinary ceremonialist, succeeding Pedro Gonzalez in that office. Probably in his capacity as a master of cere-

---

[62] AVESANI 17—20; DE GRASSI 841: 1; NABUCO 9*—13*.
    Until the publication of the learned study of Patrizi's life and writings which will introduce Dykmans' forthcoming critical edition of his ceremonial in the series Studi e testi, scholars must depend upon the two standard works on this topic: the biography of Apostolo Zeno reprinted in his Dissertazione vossiane di Apostolo Zeno, cioè, giunte e osservazioni intorno agli storici italiani che hanno scritto latinamente, 2 tomes Venice 1752/53, II, 96—102 and the more recent study by AVESANI 1—31.
[63] ZENO II 96, 100—01; AVESANI 3—9; DYKMANS, Mabillon 316—17 n. 2; Caeremoniale Romanum, fol. 51ᵛ.

monies, Patrizi accompanied both his patron cardinal Francesco Todeschini-Piccolomini on his 1471 legation to Regensburg in behalf of a crusade, and cardinal Giovanni Battista Zeno in the summer of 1477 on his legation to northern Italy. Patrizi is also reported to have held a canonry in Siena. In 1479 Sixtus IV reappointed him an apostolic abbreviator, a post he resigned in 1483 to Agostino Piccolomini. This resignation and that of his mastership in 1484 to Johann Burckard were necessitated by his promotion to the bishopric of Pienza and Montalcino, where he already held a cathedral canonry. Despite this appointment, he seems to have remained in Rome and on the resignation of Antoine Rébiol in 1485, to have assumed a position as prefect of the office of master of ceremonies. In 1489 he resigned his mastership again, this time to Aldello Piccolomini. His final years seem to have been spent in Pienza and he probably died there in 1494[64]. If Patrizi's quest for ecclesiastical posts did not distinguish him from previous masters, his success in being named bishop and his reputation as a humanist brought him closest to the most famous of his predecessors and patrons, Enea Silvio Piccolomini.

Apart from his liturgical works, Patrizi gained a reputation as a biographer and chronicler. Thus, he wrote a life of his former teacher Benci and accounts of the visit of Friedrich III to Italy and of the legation of cardinal Todeschini-Piccolomini to the Diet at Regensburg. His 1488 epistle to this cardinal, defending his uncle Pius II against the attacks of Giovanni Simonetta, was never published due to the intervention of the secretary of the duke of Milan. He may also have written a treatise on learned men and inventors. His efforts at writing history were not distinguished. His two works treating the history of Siena from its origins to 1404 were based on fables and apocryphal stories, and plagiarized a popular chronicle. His account of Monte Cassino in the form of an epitome is a continuation of an earlier chronicle. The summary of the history of the Council of Basel which he wrote is taken from Domenico Capranica's *Collectaneae* and Juan de Segovia's *Historia*[65]. This same interest in recording contemporary and historical events and this ability at compiling a coherent account from the writings of others are also evident in his liturgical writings.

Patrizi seems to have authored at least four ceremonials writings. A treatise on *Caeremoniae legati de latere*, probably based in part on his experiences as a member of the legations of Todeschini-Piccolomini and Zeno and already composed by 1483, has recently been identified as his and published. The diary he

---

[64] Zeno II 101—02; Avesani 9—19, 27—28; Hofmann II 183, 186, 190, 258; Eubel II 216; Thusane I 2—3 n. 2, III, xii, xiv; Nabuco 22*—24* n. 41.

[65] Zeno II 102—05 — he also mentions a treatise De annatis; Avesani 12, 21—27 — he suggests on p. 6 that Agostino may have helped his relative Francesco compose the De institutione rei publicae and cites numerous letters written by Agostino to Francesco and other humanists, especially associates of Pomponio Leto's Roman Academy, whose dangerous views on religion he censured — see p. 13—15.

kept was known to Burckard and de Grassi, but does not seem to have survived[66]. Thus, his fame over the centuries rests principally on his *Pontificale* and *Caeremoniale*.

His *Liber Pontificalis* was commissioned by Innocent VIII who was concerned with regularizing Church ceremonies as part of his program of reform. Patrizi's skills at synthesizing and organizing others' materials were put to the test. With the assistance of Johann Burckard he examined carefully the conflicting texts and sought to produce a pontifical that would replace that compiled by Guillaume Durand (1230—96). He borrowed heavily from this thirteenth-century liturgist and canonist not only specific rituals and prayers, but also the arrangement given them. Patrizi's pontifical, however, was intended strictly for bishops and he eliminated from the texts he used whatever was intended for priests. This material he hoped to arrange in a second book intended for priests. The thus revised pontifical was published in Rome by Stephen Planck on 20 December 1485. Twelve years later, soon after the death of Patrizi, it was reprinted and the name of Giacomo Luzzi was added to Burckard's as a fellow collaborator on this project. Apparently Luzzi's contribution was to have listed the printing errors in the 1485 edition on an appended folio. So appreciative was Innocent VIII of this pontifical of 1485 that he ordered Patrizi to compose another collection — this time of the rites and ceremonies used by the Church at Rome[67].

This work, entitled *Rituum ecclesiasticorum sive sacrarum cerimoniarum sacrosanctae Romanae Ecclesiae libri tres*, taxed Patrizi's abilities. He felt unequal to the command given him by a pontiff who was deeply concerned for the tranquil order and grave dignity of papal ceremonies. The liturgical writings preserved at the Vatican, eight of which are known to have been by orders of Innocent VIII handed over to Patrizi and Burckard in 1487 to "facilitate" their work, were often more a source of headaches than of help because they frequently contradicted each other. Their variations Patrizi ascribed to the accretions of time, to the fallibility of human memory, to the confused opinions of scribes, to the influence of local customs on a peregrinating papal curia, and to disagreements among masters of ceremonies. His intent was not only to establish the correct ritual, but also to eliminate what was superfluous and antiquated. The actual revisions which were made have, however, been faulted for having replaced the simple grandeur of a pastoral liturgy with a papal Mass that was so lengthy, complicated, and pompous that it was celebrated but thrice annually[68].

---

[66] Franz WASNER, Fifteenth-century Texts on the Ceremonial of the Papal 'Legatus a Latere', in: Traditio 14 (1958) 295—358, esp. 304-05, 307, 310—16, 322, 327, 329—35 (prints PATRIZI's Cerimonie), 354, and his 'Legatus a latere': Addenda Varia, in: Ibid. 16 (1960) 405—16, esp. 413—14, and his Guido de Busco 134—36; AVESANI 19.

[67] MABILLON/GERMAIN II 584; ZENO II 106—08; AVESANI 17—19; SALMON 102; THUSANE III, xii n. 2, xx n. 2; Nabuco 23*—24* n. 42—43.

[68] MABILLON/GERMAIN II 584—85; a printed edition of this work published in 1516 has been reprinted

Patrizi did not discharge his commission without assistance. He assumed responsibility for describing such procedures as those used to elect and crown a new pontiff, to canonize a saint or celebrate a council, to invest papal officials, to raise someone to the office of cardinal, bishop, or abbot, to receive civil dignitaries, and to show reverence toward high ecclesiastics. He also described the garb and functions of the various papal officials and how the Eucharistic liturgy was to be celebrated. But when it came to detailing the ceremonies proper to specific feast days and anniversary commemorations, Patrizi depended upon his comaster of ceremonies, Johann Burckard, for an accurate report.[69]

The results of their labors were submitted to the careful scrutiny of a commission of cardinals. Patrizi's apologies for using the current technical liturgical vocabulary instead of finding the most appropriate classical term did not prevent the cardinals from approving his work[70]. It was not, however, until the time of the Lateran Council that this collection was printed under the editorship of the Venetian Cristoforo Marcello. The then master of ceremonies, Paride de Grassi, became so enraged because the rites of the papal chapel had thus been divulged that he sought to have all copies of this work together with their editor burnt. He failed on both accounts. Neither the commission of cardinals entrusted with examining the matter, one of whose three members was his own brother and protector of the ceremonialists' office, Achille de Grassi, nor the pope, Leo X, agreed with the master and the *Caeremoniale* went through many subsequent editions[71].

Because de Grassi felt this *Caeremoniale* revealed material pertinent to the papal ritual of his day, that section of the work devoted to conciliar ceremonies most likely served in good part as de Grassi's guide in planing the Lateran Council.

Section XIV of Patrizi's Book One of the *Caeremoniale* devotes five chapters to conciliar matters. Although never personally present at a general council (the Congress of Mantova was not a true council), Patrizi describes in some detail its location and seating arrangements, its officials and voting members, its agenda and prayers, and its division into general congregations and public sessions. The explicit attention he gives to the Councils of Konstanz and Basel,

---

as Caeremoniale Romanum — see footnote 47 above; manuscript copies of this work at the Vatican are identified in SALMON 101, 103, 118, 123—24, 127—28, 140; in his journal entry for 4 March 1487, Burckard records having been given on orders of Innocent VIII eight ancient ceremonial books to assist him and Patrizi in their efforts at compiling a new ceremonial — see Johannis Burckardi Liber notarum ab anno MCCCCLXXXIII usque ad annum MDVI, ed. Enrico CELANI, Tome 32 (= Rerum italicarum scriptores: Raccolta degli storici italiani del cinquecento al millecinquecento 1, 2) Città di Castello 1906—42, I 184; for the criticism of their revisions and the suggestion that they utilized in their work the Ordo of Stefaneschi and a Liber caeremoniarum of Pedro Gonzalez, see NABUCO 22*, 28*—33*, 5—210 (prints Gonzalez's Liber which has no section devoted to councils).

[69] MABILLON/GERMAIN II 586; NABUCO 30*—31*.
[70] MABILLON/GERMAIN II 586.
[71] Ibid. II 586—92; AVESANI 19—20.

echoed in the Diary of de Grassi, suggests that their ceremonies provided the model for his conciliar prescriptions. His information on these rites probably came not only from standard liturgical works and the acts of these councils, but also from such narrative accounts as those he had used earlier in writing his own history of the Council of Basel. For that portion of chapter five dedicated to these two councils which treats the order and prayers of a public session, one of his sources has been identified — the *Nota de sessione* whose author(s) remains anonymous. Patrizi borrowed from this text the formulae for the prayers to be recited at a public session. The changes he made in these prayers were in general minor, but on occasion significant when his intention was to eliminate any suggestion of conciliaristic theology[72].

That de Grassi read this conciliar section of Patrizi's *Caeremoniale* carefully in planning the Lateran Council is apparent from a comparison of Patrizi's description of the seating arrangements and of the ceremonies at the opening session with de Grassi's account of how he constructed the conciliar chamber and arranged the ceremonies of that session. While differences do exist, the parallels are too striking to explain otherwise. A detailed analysis of a woodcut representing the eighth session of that council suggests to what extent the prescriptions of Patrizi and de Grassi were actually implemented[73]. Where Patrizi's regulations were vague, found inappropriate, or disagreed with other authors consulted, de Grassi had recourse to the cardinals or pope for an official resolution of the difficulty[74]. Otherwise, Patrizi's *Caeremoniale* seems to have been considered for the most part normative.

The man who most influenced the literary form in which de Grassi recorded the ceremonies and events of the Lateran Council was Patrizi's initial replacement as master and eventual collaborator in writing his major liturgical works,

---

[72] Caeremoniale Romanum, fol. 58ᵛ—62ʳ, SCHIMMELPFENNIG 276—77, 288—92.
For some examples of the changes made by PATRIZI (= P) in the text edited by SCHIMMELPFENNIG (= S): *Esto solus subgestor et effector* (S, 289) — *Esto salus et effector:* (P, 61ᵛ); *nomen possides gloriosum, qui* (S. 289) — *nomen possides gloriosum: non patiaris perturbatores esse iusticiae, qui* (P, 61ᵛ); *in nullo deviemus* (S, 289) — *in nullo aberremus* (P, 61ᵛ); the anti-conciliaristic intent of Patrizi's alterations is more evident in a comparsion of the following two texts: the *praesidens* prays, *Oremus. Mentibus nostris, quesumus domine, spiritum sanctum benignus infunde quatenus in nomine tuo collecti, sic in cunctis teneamus cum moderamine pietatis iusticiam, ut hic a te in nullo dissencia voluntas nostra, sed semper racionabilia meditantes, que tibi sunt placita, exequamur in factis. Per dominum nostrum Ihesum Christum etc.* (S, 290) becomes the pope's prayer *Mentes nostras, quaesumus Domine, Paracletus, qui a te procedit, illuminet et in omnem: sicut tuus promisit filius: inducat veritatem. Qui tecum uiuit et regnat in unitate eiusdem.* (P, 61ᵛ). On this prayer, de Grassi followed Patrizi's version — see 843: 26.
[73] Caeremoniale Romanum, fol. 59ʳ—60ᵛ; DE GRASSI 840: 12—18, 843: 14—31, 847: 5—14; Nelson H. MINNICH and Heinrich W. PFEIFFER "Two Woodcuts of Lateran V," in: AHP 8 (1970) 179—241, esp. 184, 190—99 and their De Grassi's Conciliabulum at Lateran V: The De Gargiis Woodcut of Lateran V Re-examined, in: Ibid, 19 (1981) 147—72.
[74] DE GRASSI 840: 7, 841: 1—2.

Johann Burckard. For the first two years (1504—06) of de Grassi's tenure in the office of master, Burckard was his senior colleague. Although he disliked Burckard intensely, de Grassi acknowledged this German's mastery of the office and tried to understudy him[75].

Burckard's rise to power and fame was inspite of the disadvantages of his youth, some of his own making. Born (ca. 1450) of humble parents in the village of Nieder-Haslach, some thirty kilometers west of Strassburg, Johann received his early education there probably as a choirboy in the collegiate church of Sankt Florenz. His later interest in ceremonies may have stemmed in part from this experience. Lacking funds to continue his education, he entered the service of Johann Wegeraufft, a canon of the church of St. Thomas in Strassburg and vicar general for spiritual affairs of the prince-bishop Ruprecht von Simmern. Burckard labored as one of the numerous scribes employed to copy official documents. His handwriting at this point was clearly legible and not the later scourge of his contemporaries and more recent editors. Perhaps in an effort to overcome his poverty, he resorted to forgery and thievery. He produced a number of dispensations from the obligation of publishing the banns of matrimony, leaving blank a space to insert the names. He also stole a broad two-edged sword and a florin coin. When these were discovered in his bedroom at Wegeraufft's house, Johann was expelled and found all prospects of honest advancement closed to him in Strassburg. Hoping to make his career elsewhere, he arrived in Rome in November of 1467[76].

Within a few years Burckard's future looked brighter. By the summer of 1471 Paul II had granted him an expectative on an altar chaplaincy in Strassburg. This pope's nephew, Marco Barbò, was appointed cardinal-legate to the German emperor on 22 December 1471 and ten days later the name of the youthful Burckard in the capacity of a minor valet appeared the second from the bottom on a list of some eighty members of Barbò's household. From Sixtus IV he received two other expectatives, one on a canonry in his hometown of Haslach in the church were he had sung as a boy and the other in Strassburg also on a canonry at the church where his former employer Wegeraufft functioned as canon. In order to protect his right to these canonries, Burckard went through

---

[75] THUSANE III 426—27 n. 2.

[76] The most recent account of Burckard's life is that of Ingeborg WALTER, Burckard, Johannes, in: Dizionario biografico degli Italiani, 15 (Rome 1972) 405—08, for his youth see 405. That by E. VANSTEEN-BERGHE, Burckard (Jean), in: Dictionnaire d'histoire et de géographie ecclesiastique 10 (Paris 1938) 1249—51 incorporated the revisionary materials on his youth reported in J. LESELLIER, Les méfaits du cérémoniaire Jean Burckard, in: Mélanges d'archéologie et d'histoire de l'École Française de Rome 44 (1927) 11—34. Until Lesellier's findings, the standard study was that by L. THUSANE, Notice biographique, i—lxviii at the beginning of the third volume of his edition of Burckard's diary. De Grassi's criticism of his senior colleague's handwriting was wholeheartedly seconded by the editor of his autograph diary Enrico Celani — see Liber notarum, xv—xvi.

the humiliating process of obtaining a papal pardon for the crimes of his youth which would otherwise have disqualified him — in 1473 for his forgery and in 1475 for his theft. That he was still given to deceit and pilferage in his old age was asserted by his colleague de Grassi[77].

With the elimination of these canonical impediments, Burckard went on to accumulate a significant number of benefices and curial posts. His benefices were located in the Empire. During 1478 he received two chaplaincies and two canonries in Strassburg, Metz, and Basel, at the conclave of 1484 the office of praepositus of Teurstatt outside Bamberg, in 1485 the same post at St. Florenz in Haslach, and in 1488 the deanry of the chapter of St. Thomas in Strassburg from whose collegiate community he had been expelled as a youth[78].

Considering his humble origins, the impressive list of curial posts he acquired should probably be attributed to his driving ambition and the backing of patrons. That he increased his qualifications for some of these posts by pursuing a course of study at Rome in theology and canon law, even acquiring the doctorate in canon law, is a matter of some dispute among scholars. The cardinal whose household he joined in 1473, Giovanni Arcimboldi, obtained for him the title of papal familiar and continual commensal. By entering the service two years later of the papal treasurer, Tommaso Vincenzi, Burckard gained access to the papal palace. Within three years he was appointed papal acolyte and chaplain and abbreviator of apostolic letters — both of these posts would have soon brought him into contact with Patrizi, if their acquaintance had not already begun years earlier through their mutual patron cardinal Barbò. In 1481 Sixtus IV appointed Burckard apostolic protonotary and in November of 1483 ordinary master of ceremonies, replacing Patrizi who had been promoted to the episcopacy. On the payment of fees totaling 450 golden ducats to Patrizi and the curia for the bull of investiture, Burckard was formally presented for the post as *numerarius et participans* on December 21st and began functioning on 26 January 1484. With the resignation of the senior co-master Antoine Rébiol on Christmas Eve of 1485, Burckard gained the position of seniority which he never relinquished. His quest for curial posts and prelacies did not end with this mastership. In 1488 he was also named master of the register of supplications. Pius III appointed him bishop of Orte and Città Castellana, a provision confirmed by Julius II who also named him in 1503 a prelate of the palace and papal assistant and in 1504 referendarius of letters of favor. Two weeks prior to his death on 6 May 1506, he obtained his final curial post as one of the sixty

[77] WALTER 405—06; LESELLIER 14—16, 32—34; EUBEL II 15, 37, nr. 311; THUSANE III, xliii, xlvii, 424 n, 427 n.
[78] WALTER 405—06; VANSTEENBERGHE 1249; THUSANE III, xi; LESELLIER, 13, 16; CELANI, Liber notarum I 52—53.

abbreviators of the *parco minore*[79]. While in some respects Burckard's accumulation of ecclesiastical offices was in keeping with the practice of his predecessors, his success at it was remarkable even by their standards.

Unlike his predecessor Patrizi, Burckard seems to have written exclusively on liturgical topics. In addition to his collaboration on Patrizi's *Liber Pontificalis* and *Caeremoniale Romanum*, Burckard composed his own *Opus de caeremoniis curiae Romanae*, wrote instructions for the ceremonies of a papal legate, collected liturgical data from the writings of his predecessors, and compiled a number of *ordines* specially written for the ceremonies conferring all the major orders on the invalid, newly elected Pius III in 1503, for the priestly ordinations of cardinals Galeotto della Rovere and Raffaelle Riario, and for his own episcopal consecration in 1504. He published in 1498 a small manual for priests entitled *Ordo Missae secundum consuetudinem sanctae Romanae ecclesiae* which enjoyed a wide diffusion and was often reprinted. But the work on which his fame justly rests, and which probably provided materials for some of his other liturgical writings, was his *Liber notarum* or journal covering the years 1483 to 1506. While historians over the centuries have published excerpts from it, not until this century was a reliable edition of the complete diary published. De Grassi, who had access to the original autograph, corrected, annotated, and even cancelled out whole sections of the diary, made repeated references in his own writings to its entries, and seems at least in part to have used it as a model for his own Diary[80].

Burckard's diary evolved, not only beyond the form used by his predecessors, but also away from his own initial brief jottings to a fuller narrative account. The extant excerpts from the journal of his predecessor Gonzalez gave minimal attention to the sequence of the rites, and the apparel worn during them. Gonzalez's historical perspective was mostly limited to such issues as how this rite differed from what was done on another occasion or the place of origins of a particular missal. The historical significance of the event was not seriously discussed. The style was that of a narrative chronicle and did not incorporate documents[81].

---

[79] WALTER 405—06; VANSTEENBERGHE 1249; LESELLIER 17; HOFMANN II 85—86, 167—68, 172; THUSANE III, vi, xl—xliii; NABUCO 26* n. 51 (summarizes the evidence for Burckard's doctorate); EUBEL II 211.

[80] WALTER 406—07; VANSTEENBERGHE 1249—50; SALMON, Ordinis Romani, 9, 102, 105—06, 108, 114, 120, 124, 126, 140; WASNER, Ceremonial of Legate 305—06, 311, 314, 316, 318—23, 343—52 (prints his instruction for the cardinal legate de Lunate), and his Addenda Varia 410—411; CONSTANT, Les maîtres 327—29; THUSANE III, i—ii, liii; CELANI xi—xii, xxii—xxviii. For a study of the manuscripts used by Thusane and Celani and of the relative merits of their respective editions, see Giovanni SORANZO, Studî intorno a papa Alessandro VI (Borgia) (= Nuova serie of Pubblicazioni dell'Università Cattolica del Sacro Cuore 34) Milano 1950, 51—56.

[81] WASNER, Tor der Geschichte 124—29, 145—62; a critical edition of Gonzalez's texts is provided in DYKMANS, Le Cérémonial de Nicholaus V, 790—820 — on 790 he notes that Gonzalez was concerned merely with ceremonial questions, while Burckhard's account resembles a newspaper with its abundance of information on a variety of topics.

While the first nine months of Burckard's diary, from Christmas Eve of 1483 until 12 August 1484 (the death of Sixtus IV) recorded but bare sketches of the ceremonies on festivals and special occasions (dates, places, celebrants, etc.), the new master soon came to recognize the benefit of giving fuller descriptions. His accounts accordingly grew in length and detail, providing an almost day-by-day record, not only of what pertained to the ceremonies but also of many other things such as the activities of popes and cardinals and reports of international intrigues and battles[82].

What had begun as a freely-willed continuation of a tradition and as a matter of convenience became by the end of Burckard's tenure an obligation of the office of master of ceremonies. Burckard was concerned that his journal be as reasonably complete as possible. When he was away serving on a legation or visiting his German homeland on vacation or business, one of the other masters would take notes on what happened at the papal court. On his return he transcribed this information into his diary. The lacunae which still remain in the diary are attributed to the summertime inactivity of the papal chapel, to his own illness (he suffered from gout), to the pressure of other official and personal affairs or even to occasional indolence which might prevent him from attempting to record the events until after his memory of them had faded. Just when this concern for maintaining a complete and detailed journal became an obligation of the masters is unclear. But by the time de Grassi began his tenure as master in 1504 one of the two masters was required to keep the written record of what transpired each day in that office[83].

For the most part Burckard's diary was a personal record of the ceremonies of the papal chapel. Due to its simple style and references to "today" or "yesterday", it was probably usually written on a day-by-day basis. The information contained in it came for the most part from his direct observations or else involved things with which he was directly associated. When he was dependent on others for his information and suspected that this source might not be reliable, Burckard would condition his statements by mentioning that it was thus and thus rumored or reported. He made his account especially useful to historians by including copies of a variety of documents: from papal election capitularies and lists of conclavists and curial officials to papal bulls and letters and pasquinades. In general he let the events and documents speak for themselves; but he did on occasion pass oblique moral judgments on persons, notably the Borgias and their associates, and he felt pity even for those justly punished for their crimes. Toward the leaders in the Church he showed the outward marks of deference and spoke with respect of religious rites. Political

---

[82] CELANI I, xxiii, 3—13 (for initial jottings), 6 (cites the usefulness of giving a fuller account).

[83] CELANI I, xxi—xxiv, 207—09, II, 454; THUSANE I 1 n. 2, III, xv—ixx, xxxviii, 353—54 n. 1, 360 n. 1; CONSTANT 333; SORZANO 44—48.

I

issues were not followed with great interest or deep loyalties. His attention, rather, focused primarily on the details of the ceremonies and here he showed himself an expert, diligent, and self-critical functionary. His opinions on ceremonies were often sought and followed by the highest ecclesiastical and civil authorities, although he was known to resist their wishes. His frank and intrepid manner was also balanced by tact and prudence[84].

Burckard was not without his critics, the most hostile of whom was probably his junior co-master, Paride de Grassi. From the beginning their relationship was strained. As his junior co-master Burckard had the Spaniard Bernardino Guttierez and as his substitute the German Michael Sander. On learning that de Grassi aspired to the office of co-master, Burckard wished to be assured that Guttierez had actually resigned his office. Only then would Burckard accept the Italian as his colleague. De Grassi interpreted this delay as an attempt to block and reject his appointment[85].

Burckard's failure to teach him personally the duties of his office only deepened de Grassi's suspicions and antagonism. When the seasoned ceremonialist showed himself reluctant to share immediately with his novice colleague the detailed workings of an office which he had mastered by twenty years of painstaking note taking, de Grassi was bitter. Guttierez, instead, became his instructor. To de Grassi's displeasure, Burckard does not seem to have brought him into the planning process for the ceremonies. His journal, however, was available. On finding his personal record of papal ceremonies initially very difficult to read, the Italian exclaimed in frustration that no one except Satan, Burckard's protector and scribe, or the Sybil herself could decipher his script. Having once mastered it, he proceeded to mark up this journal with "corrections" and marginal notes, and even cancelled out whole passages he disliked. He resented having to learn his office by such difficult study and quiet observation. As his expertise grew he became more critical of his senior and accused him of making mistakes, of varying the ritual according to his personal vanities, and of concocting on the spur of the moment ridiculous improvisations. Because Burckard did not intervene to prevent Julius from dining with women at the banquet celebrating the marriage of his nephew with the illegitimate daughter of Alexander VI, de Grassi denounced him as a corrupter of papal ceremonies[86].

His attacks were not limited to matters of ceremonies but extended to slurs on Burckard's character. He claimed that he was "always and everywhere con-

---

[84] THUSANE III, i—ii, xvi, xxvii; CELANI, Liber notarum, e.g., I, 26—28 (conclavists), 30—45 (capitularies), 428—38 (curial officials), 491—503 (bulls and oaths of investiture), etc.; SORZANO 37—41, 44—51.

[85] CELANI II 451, 512; THUSANE III, xliii, 356—57 n. 2.

[86] THUSANE I 186 n. 1, 189 n. 1, 194 n. 1, 195 n. 1—2, II, 16 n. 1, III, 389 n. 2, 407n. 1 , 419 n. 1, 426 n. 2; CELANI I xv, xxii—xxiii; DYKMANS, "Le Cérémonial de Nicolas V," 787 n. 2.

trary, dissatisfied, and unfriendly," "the most inhuman, insidious, and bestial of all beasts," someone given to deceit and thievery. De Grassi could not acknowledge even after the death of Burckard that his colleague had advanced liturgical learning without also referring to him sarcastically as "that great thrice-over magisterial and genial master of our ceremonies."[87]

As much and as unfairly at times as de Grassi railed against his predecessor, he, nonetheless, seems to have taken Burckard as a model for his own mastership and diary.

Paride de Grassi

Career

De Grassi's career can be traced only in part. He was born about 1450 in Bologna, the son of Baldassare and his wife Orsina d'Amerigo Bucchi. The ancient and noble family of the de Grassis seems to have given many of its members to the Church. His uncle Antonio was a curialist bishop of Tivoli (1485—91) and his brother Achille also made a career at Rome becoming an auditor of the Rota and the bishop of Città di Castello in 1506 and soon after his promotion to the cardinalate in 1511, of his native city of Bologna. Like others in his family Paride was early on destined for a clerical career and given a legal training, eventually earning the doctorate in both civil and canon laws. He accumulated numerous benefices in and around Bologna, eventually becoming canon of the cathedral[88].

When he left Bologna to pursue a career elsewhere is not known. The obligations attached to his major benefices there may have detained him for awhile or have required repeated visits home. By 1476 he held a canonry in the large church of St. Petronio which he exchanged in 1484 for one in the cathedral. He continued to share in the revenues of the cathedral *mensa* until 1494, the year he was made a governor of Orvieto under the protection of Cesare Borgia. He seems to have first visited Rome in 1473 or '74. For the next thirty years, according to his claim of 1504, he served in the Roman Curia a variety of popes and cardinals. In just what capacities he did this is not clear. Among the names of the officials of the November 1503 conclave which elected Julius II, de Grassi's appears immediately after those of the two ordinary masters of ceremonies and before that of the secretary of the college. But his function at the

---

[87] THUSANE III 410 n. 1, 424 n. 1, 426 n. 2, 427 n. 1; a nationalistic bias is suggested by HOFMANN I 242 n. 2; SORZANO 36—37.

[88] The standard study of the de Grassi family is that by Pompeo LITTA, Famiglie celebri italiane, Milan 1820—56, vol. 7, Grassi di Bologna, for Paride's immediate family see tavola II. Litta's account of Paride's life has been superseded by that of Luigi FRATI as an introduction to his Le due spedizione militari di Giulio II tratte dal Diario di Paride de Grassi bolognese (= Documenti e studi pubblicati per cura della Reale Deputazione di storia patria per le provincie di Romagna 1) Bologna 1886, iii—xxxiv, esp. iii—xxi; HOFMANN II 28, 134, 190; EUBEL II 251; III 12, 136, 168.

conclave is not described. In December of 1503 Julius rejected his petition to be appointed a *supernumerarius* cleric of the camera. A few months later, in May of 1504, with the assistance of cardinals Riario and Isvalies, he was presented for the office of ordinary master of ceremonies. When apparently his brother, Achille, succeeded in getting Guttierez to resign, he was formally installed in that post, being invested personally by the pope with the surplice of office[89].

De Grassi's tenure as master differed little from that of his predecessors. He too was not content with the mastership and its revenues, but continued to collect offices, benefices, and pensions. Not until he was appointed bishop (of Pesaro in 1513) and papal assistant (in December of 1515) did de Grassi feel in some respects equal to his predecessors Patrizi, Piccolomini, and Burckard[90].

Like them, he also added to the literature on the liturgy. In addition to his most important work, the Diary covering the years 1504—21, de Grassi composed a number of ceremonial works. In 1507/08 he compiled a *Brevis ordo Romanus* which was postumously published in the eighteenth century. Ceremonials also came from his pen: one written in 1506, a volume of additions to the second book of Patrizi's *Caeremoniale Romanum* which had been compiled by Burckard, and the *De caeremoniis capellae papalis* from the time of Leo X. Two of his smaller treatises dealt with particular papal ceremonies: *De equitatione papae per urbem in solemnitate non pontificali* and *Modus servatur in infirmitate papae et eius morte*. Another treatise was more general in nature: *Tractatus de funeribus et exequiis in Romanae curiae peragendis*. A piece he prepared for the ceremonies at Bologna in 1507 entitled *De ceremoniis ad cardinales episcopos spectantibus* was published in Rome, 1564, as *De caeremoniis cardinalium et episcoporum in eorum dioecesibus libri duo*. A treatise *De consecratione episcoporum* is also attributed to him. In his *Tractatus de oratoribus Romanae curiae* and *De oratorum praecedentia* he described who were considered true ambassadors and how they were ranked.

---

[89] FRATI, Due spedizioni, vi—vii claims de Grassi basically retained his residency at Bologna until 1494, making numerous trips back and forth from Rome. Paride's presence in Rome for the early months of 1485 is attested by him in his annotation on Burckard's diary account of the obeisance ceremonies of the Knights of Rhodes and in his own diary comments on the canonization ceremonies for Bl. Leopold — see THUSANE I 135 n. 3, 136—37 n. 1; Thusane seems to err on II 287, in listing a "P. de Grassi" among the sollicitors of apostolic letters in 1496. CELANI I 612 (entry for 1 June 1496) lists the sollicitor as "L. de Grassi," perhaps the same "L. de Grossi" of the 4 June 1493 list (see I, 431). Paride's permanent residency in Rome by 1499 is suggested by his appointment that year as a canon of S. Lorenzo in Damaso — see FRATI vi; on his rejection for the post of cleric of the Camera, see: CELANI II 426, on his presence at the conclave and appointment as master, see Ibid. II 451; THUSANE III 299, 356—57 n. 2, and FRATI viii—ix.

[90] For examples of de Grassi's continued accumulation of offices and revenues, see: BAV, Reg. Vat. 942, fol. 238 (pension), 951, fol. 87 (pension in Cuenca), 958, fols. 83, 169 (parochial benefice in Modena); EUBEL III 274, Pisaurien, n. 5 lists the monastery of S. Maria de Babali in the diocese of Pesaro, a prebend, canonry, and parish church in Fano, and the right of access to a portion of the hospital and canonry revenues of an Augustinian church in Pamplona; and Fondo Santini, nr. 23, fol. 126[r] records his autograph matriculation as a notary with his signature and personal emblem of the letter "P" in a monstrance-like device. On his appointment as a papal assistant, see Diarium Leonis, Vat. Lat. 12275, fol. 151[r], and on the masters as bishops, EUBEL II 216, 243; III, 274, 305.

Perhaps also to be numbered among his liturgical writings are the annotations, corrections, and cancellations he made in the writings of his predecessors such as Gonzalez and Burckard[91].

Given de Grassi's concern for following the example set by his predecessors, especially Patrizi and Burckard, both of whom published liturgical works during their lifetimes, it is surprising that not one of de Grassi's many writings was published before his death at Rome in 1528. He claimed his bitter opposition to Marcello's printing of Patrizi's *Caeremoniale* was in part based on his concern lest the mysteries of the papal chapel be divulged to the public[92]. But beneath his rage at Marcello and his failure to publish a single one of his own works is to be suspected another factor — his reluctance to share with his contemporaries the expertise of his profession which he had acquired after years of labor. By his almost exclusive control over this information, he was able to dominate papal ceremonies, win plaudits and preferments, and protect himself from criticism for his own departures from the script. Some of the very traits he so disliked as a junior master in his senior colleague Burckard seem to have marked on his own later years.

To what extent de Grassi followed the prescriptions in the *Caeremoniale Romanum* regulating relations between the masters is open to question. As the junior master, he did defer to Burckard, but not without grumbling and resentment at the authority this veteran ceremonialist commanded. The death of Burckard in 1506 made Paride the senior master. The man appointed as his junior colleague was the apostolic notary, Baldassare Nicolai of Viterbo, who had formally been a substitute for the papal sacristan. Baldassare does not seem to have challenged Paride's position. His illnesses, however, especially during the busy time of the Lateran Council necessitated that some provision be made. Paride's nephew and substitute master, Ippolito Morbioli, does not seem to have been much help and de Grassi complained that he often bore alone the burdens of being master. The appointment of Guttierez as Nicolai's temporary

---

[91] On de Grassi's writings, see: FRATI xxi; DYKMANS, Mabillon 342; SALMON, Ordines Romani: De caeremoniis nr. 342, 430, 491, 499, 504, pp. 104, 126, 140—41, 143; De equitatione, nr. 430, p. 126; Modus servatur, nr. 436, p. 128; De funeribus, nr. 436, 518, pp. 128, 145; De consecratione, nr. 335, p. 102; De oratoribus, nr. 347, 467, 499, pp. 106, 135, 141; for a copy of de Grassi's treatise on the precedence of ambassadors, see BAV, Ottoboniani latini 2366; de Grassi's annotations on Gonzalez's diary are noted in WASNER, Tor der Geschichte 145, 149—53, 158—59, 161, de Grassi's marginalia, corrections and cancellations in Burckhard's diary are noted by SORZANO 55; CELANI I, xxii—xxiii; and THUSANE, e. g. I 186 n. 1, 189 n. 1, 192 n. 1, 194 n. 1, 195 n. 1—2, 196 n. 1—3, etc.; a portion of de Grassi's Supplementum et additiones to Patrizi's Caeremoniale Romanum (1488), completed by the spring of 1505, has recently been published in John W. O'MALLEY, The Feast of Thomas Aquinas in Renaissance Rome: A Neglected Document and Its Import, in: RSCI 35 (1981) 1—27, esp. 26—27.

[92] For de Grassi as the champion of preserving the secrecy of the Roman ceremonies, see NABUCO 34* and suggestions in DE GRASSI, De caeremoniis cardinalium et episcoporum in eorum dioecesibus libri duo, Venice 1582, fol. 1ʳ—3ʳ.

replacement seems to have created more problems for de Grassi than to have lightened his burdens[93].

De Grassi's relations with Bernardino Guttierez were strained. By the time de Grassi replaced him in 1504, this Spaniard had already functioned in the office of ordinary master for over nine years. His resignation of this post in de Grassi's favor did not terminate his services as a ceremonialist. Up to the time of Burckard's death, he continued to function as a colleague of the ordinary masters, perhaps like Michael Sander, as a substitute. When Burckard failed to give de Grassi the personal instructions he desired in the duties of his new office, Guttierez became his teacher. A close rapport between them does not seem to have developed. The new master is known to have disagreed with his teacher and Guttierez did not always share important information with him. With the appointment of Nicolai, Guttierez seems to have devoted his energies to his various curial posts as a writer, abbreviator, and solicitor[94].

When Leo X in December of 1513 reappointed Guttierez as master of ceremonies, the stage was set for conflict. Whether his formal title was that of *supernumerarius* or of principal ceremonialist, he was a veteran in the office and de Grassi's former teacher. When he questioned Paride's handling of certain ceremonies, de Grassi felt challenged. He accused Bernardino of disparaging his abilities and of acting as if he knew more about conciliar ceremonies, even though he had never attended either a council or the many meetings of the Lateran's preparatory commission. To safeguard his own position as the leading ceremonialist at the papal court, de Grassi failed to bring Guttierez into the planning process — something for which years earlier he had faulted his senior co-master Burckard. To block any alterations in the ceremonies proposed by this Spaniard, de Grassi had recourse to Leo who backed his fellow Italian[95]. If de Grassi ignored the *Caeremoniale's* prescriptions to yield to one's senior in the office and to consult with one another in order to reach agreement, he did follow its ruling that where disagreements exist it is better that only one master direct the ceremonies. De Grassi saw to it that that one master was himself.

In his treatise *De caeremoniis cardinalium et episcoporum*, de Grassi gave prescriptions for a master of ceremonies' relations with his fellow ministers. Because his subject was the diocesan master of ceremonies, who apparently functioned without a colleague, de Grassi never treated relations between co-mas-

---

[93] On de Grassi's *relationes* with Burckard, see: CELANI II 462 and THUSANE III 410 n. 1, 419 n. 1, 423 n. 1; on Baldassare de Nicolai, see: THUSANE III xliii n. 4, 429; MANSI 697B; DE GRASSI, 847: 24; and CELANI I 583 n. 2; on Morbioli, see: DE GRASSI, Diarium Leonis, Vat. Lat. 12275, fol. 167r and THUSANE III xliii n. 4.

[94] CELANI I 583 n. 2; THUSANE III 369, 379, 392 n. 3, 393 n. 1, 410 n. 1, 423, n. 1; HOFMANN II 183.

[95] Scholars differ on the title of Guttierez's position: HOFMANN II 183 holds it was as *supernumerarius*, while CELANI I 583 n. 2 claims it was as principal ceremonialist. For examples of conflict between the two masters at the Council, see DE GRASSI 1039: 5, 1081: 4—5, 1206: 16, 1231: 3.

ters. He did, however, urge the master to deal courteously with his fellow ministers and to show himself affable and kind, rather than severe and domineering, unless, of course, such conduct was truly called for. The master was to see to it that each minister at the liturgy knew and had practiced his own role. De Grassi admonished the ceremonialist to so master his profession that no one could find fault in his actions and that he could ever remain the master who corrected others and yet was himself not subject to criticism. Guttierez's questioning of his handling of certain ceremonies implied that de Grassi had not mastered his profession and thus seems to have created the situation in which a severe and imperious response was deemed necessary[96].

Diary

De Grassi's statements on the office, norms and duties of the master of ceremonies as found in this treatise on diocesan ceremonies will be compared to his teachings and practices recorded in his Diary, but first a closer look at his reasons for keeping this journal and its particular style and sources.

Purpose

De Grassi's reasons for keeping a diary were multiple. His initial decision to write on a daily basis, or whenever it seemed necessary, a record of what was done regarding papal ceremonies was not in order to fulfill the obligation of the master's office to maintain such a journal. Burckard's diary was apparently the official one and de Grassi's over-lapped it for two years. His principal reason for recording the papal ceremonies was the same as that of Burckard before him — a convenient way of learning the responsibilities and procedures of the office of master. By keeping a record for study and future consultation of what he had seen, by reading the treatises and journals of his predecessors, and by participating repeatedly in these papal ceremonies, de Grassi hoped to gain the experience and knowledge proper for a master[97]. He seems to have been concerned, too, that his own successors would come to have a high regard for his expertise and find in his writings guidance and help. With Burckard's death the responsibility for keeping the official journal became his. Given the relative infrequency of a council and the scarcity of prescriptions in the writings of his predecessors on how to celebrate one, it is not surprising that he would devote special attention to recording his own handling of conciliar ceremonies.

De Grassi's stated intention in keeping that section of his Diary related to the Council was not to write a secret history of the papal court for the entertainment or edification of the curious, but to record information on the struc-

---

[96] DE GRASSI, De caeremoniis cardinalium et episcoporum in eorum dioecesibus libri duo, Venice 1582, fol. 4r–v; DE GRASSI, 1081; 4 shows de Grassi interpreting Guttierez's comment as an attack on his professional competency.

[97] THUSANE III 357 n.

I

ture, decorations, and ceremonies of the Lateran Council and on how various controversies related to them were resolved. He hoped that such a record would be of service to those well-disposed and studious successors in the office of ceremonialist who were also burdened with the task of organizing a council. He noted that the writings of Patrizi were of much assistance to him, but ultimately proved inadequate, for their author had never seen a real council, but discoursed on it like one seeking to cross a body of water dry-shod. He hoped that those who read his own writings would not consider him rash, conceited, and inept, but should feel free to correct and emend them. Had he not made a record of things, they might slip forever into oblivion[98].

While his primary intent was to write a history of the ceremonial aspects of the Lateran Council, de Grassi did not neglect opportunities to portray himself to posterity as a master with great expertise and importance at the papal court. When questioned about precedents, he would produce texts from diaries and treatises on ceremonies and even from codices in the Camera and Chancellery which supported his opinions. He identified deficiencies in the ceremonial of his great predecessor Patrizi and recommended remedies which were approved by pope and cardinals. As noted earlier, when Guttierez challenged his handling of the ceremonies, de Grassi almost invariably received the backing of Leo[99].

According to de Grassi, popes valued his opinions and rewarded his services. He was consulted on many matters, some outside his immediate competency, and Leo found in him a reliable spokesman for the concerns of his fellow bishops. Even when his advice had not been solicited, de Grassi would volunteer it to the pope at the opportune or crucial moment. On the particularly delicate matter of honoring papal relatives at the conciliar ceremonies, Leo seems to have deferred to de Grassi's good judgment. Julius, who was most anxious that the Council be properly celebrated and tightly controlled, was lavish in his praise of de Grassi's management of it and promised him a rich monastery as a reward. Leo, neither so nervous nor profuse in his praise, awarded him a bishopric of greater fiscal value and dignity and granted him and his co-master a one-sixth share in the materiel of the conciliar chamber which had cost a thousand ducats to construct and decorate. In addition to such financial remunerations, both Julius and Leo rewarded their master with the honor of being taken into their confidence. De Grassi eagerly recorded such incidents since they confirmed his own sense of self-importance[100].

---

[98] DE GRASSI 840: 7—8; 841: 1; 847: 28.

[99] On his use of ceremonial writings, see, for example, DE GRASSI 842: 8 and 1116: 14, on the deficiencies of Patrizi and his own recommendations which were approved: 840: 7; 841: 1—2; 842: 4, 8, 10, 12—13, 15; on his controversy with Guttierez: 1039: 5; 1081: 4—6; 1206: 16.

[100] On de Grassi as a papal advisor, see: DE GRASSI 883: 5—6, 1039: 14, 1081: 2; on his handling of papal relatives, see 1116: 9, 1206: 5, 1230: 1; on papal rewards, see 840: 6—7, 843: 33, 844: 2, 34, 37—38,

Style

The style of de Grassi's Diary is similar to that of Burckard's. Both recorded on an almost day-by-day basis the ceremonies of the papal court. They embellished their accounts with occasional digressions into the historical background of an institution or issue, with a narrative of the events leading up to or accompanying a ceremony, and with copies of relevant documents. De Grassi, however, gave a full historical account less often, spoke in terms of groups rather than individual persons, protected the pope's reputation, and concerned himself more with the details of the ceremonies[101]. Burckard's journal, nonetheless, was the model for his own Diary.

Although the daily chronicle format characterizes much of de Grassi's narrative, his Diary underwent later revisions. His style initially suggests that each entry was the evening's recollection of the more notable happenings of that day. There is even the interjection of a fervent hope that Julius will not forget the monastic benefice promised him that day. But this diary-like format is not always maintained: background information on an issue which developed over many months and years is summarized with no day-by-day record of its development given, copies of documents thought important and occasionally updated are inserted into the narrative, information about future events is at times used to correct or revise statements which would otherwise have proven untrue, and cross-references to earlier and later accounts are provided at various places in the narrative. These revisions not only eliminated errors but also assisted the reader in finding related materials elsewhere in the text. Such revisions rarely referred to materials in a later year and thus suggest that they were carried out toward the close of the year under consideration. That de Grassi himself thought of the calendar year as the organizing principle of his Diary is implied in his reference to an account *in libro ephemeridum mearum sive annualium* which cited the year and folio number[102].

Sources

The information recorded in his Diary seems to have been drawn for the most part from direct personal experience and observation. The freshness of eye-witness reporting, accompanied by occasional accounts of personal participation in and judgments on these events, characterize many of the entries. In

---

1231: 10; on being taken into the pope's confidence, see 848: 8, 28, 964: 11, 989: 5—6, 1039: 14—15, 1081: 2, 1206: 13.

[101] THUSANE III, i; CONSTANT 327—332.

[102] On the hoped for monastery, see DE GRASSI 844: 38; for examples of background summaries, 1081: 2—3, 1116: 2—3, 1185: 1—4; of documents, 842—43, 846: 2, 848: 4, 990—91, 1185: 5—7, 1207; of revisions, 842: super 14 (see 848: 4, q. 3 where the issue was really decided later), 846: 2, q. 5, 846: 17, 848: 4, 848: 4, q. 2, 1039: 11, 1206: 15; of cross-references, 848: 4, q. 2, 10, 1039: 3, 1206: 1; on his referring the reader to a particular year and folio number, see 844: 38.

general de Grassi avoided hearsay, unless of course he was recording what he personally heard the pope report or something commonly known. At times he presented the popes' words or those to or about them as direct quotations, but more often he paraphrased them. He does not seem, however, to have realized the importance of providing his accounts with the proper names of all the major participants, not to mention supplying lists of officials' names so common in Burckard's journal. For the Council the only two lists he provided were of the cardinals attending the opening session and of the Council's officials, one of whom was himself. Pleading an inability to recall their names, he did not record the twenty-four prelates elected by their colleagues, and he also left blank the name of the French ambassador at the eighth session who was Louis Forbin. Such omissions may in part be explained by his tendency to describe events in terms of groups and factions, rather than of individuals and their leaders[103].

That he was actually present at the event he records can often be borne out from the conciliar rolls. Although his name does not appear in the list of participants for the eighth and twelfth sessions, his presence at the former can be established from his recorded comments during a vote. The evidence for his participation or not in the final session is mixed. Not only is his name missing from that roll and from the record of individual votes accompanied by an explanation or qualification, but he gave an unusually imprecise figure for the number of prelates attending this session and mentioned that he was absent when Leo improperly blessed M. Bruno Corvino. That he may have meant by that statement that he was merely not in the immediate vicinity to prevent this, but was at the Council itself, is suggested by his noting that Carvajal read only one instead of the customary three prayers and that Leo bestowed the benediction at the time he had suggested. De Grassi's attendance at the congregation preparatory to the twelfth session three days earlier is recorded in the Council's acts and thus establishes his presence in Rome just prior to that session. It must be remembered, though, that his predecessor Burckard would record in his journal descriptions of events he had never attended personally, relying on his co-masters to supply him with the necessary information. A similar procedure here cannot be automatically ruled out. Other events he reported which he may not have attended are the meeting of the cardinals and architects in the Lateran Basilica to plan the Council and many of the meetings and negotiations of his fellow bishops to defend their interests. But even in these cases, a subsequent statement or indications of strong support for and possibly deeper involvement in the struggle of his fellow bishops suggest a personal presence at the events

---

[103] For examples: of a papal comment made to him (1206: 13), of something commonly known (883: 4), of direct quotations (845: 3, 848: 28, 925: 4, 1039: 14), and of paraphrases of them (844: 38, 924: 4, 1039: 14); for examples of lists of names, see 844: 30 and 847: 24; for his failure to include names, see 968: 2 and 1039: 9.

he reported. He was not, however, elected by his fellow bishops to any of the deputations or commissions entrusted with representing their interests and he was not even privy to the decisions of the congregation held on the eve of the eighth session[104]. Because his Diary does not attempt to describe the proceedings of these committees, even though such reports would have enhanced his accounts, the impression is strengthened that de Grassi in general narrated only what he personally witnessed.

Documents Incorporated into the Diary

In addition to these reports, de Grassi's Diary also contains copies of a number of important documents. The choices he made of conciliar materials to incorporate into his Diary are somewhat peculiar. None of the sermons, secular mandates, or bulls read at the Council itself received anything but the briefest description. Perhaps he felt that these would be recorded in its official acts and were also often available as separate publications[105]. The documents he did record in some detail were the mandates of the Scandinavian king and Maronite patriarch, the formulae used in the reconciliation of the Pisan cardinals, the questions he submitted regarding conciliar ceremonies, and the formal proposal for making the papal assistants into a representative body of the whole episcopate.

A paraphrasing of the 10 April 1512 mandate of the Danish king Hans von Oldenburg (d. 1513) may have been included for fear that no record would be kept elsewhere. The official acts of the Council, indeed, made no mention of this adhesion of the Scandinavian kingdoms, neither at the subsequent third session nor at the fourth session where this mandate was apparently read, nor at the final session in which cardinal Lorenzo Pucci represented the new king Christiern II, the Wicked[106]. Since de Grassi could only have suspected such

---

[104] On his presence at the eighth session and at the congregation prior to the twelfth, see MANSI 849E and 978E; for his estimate that the prelates present were 90 or 100 and that he was absent *(me absente)*, see DE GRASSI 1231: 1, 4; for his reports on meetings and negotiations he probably never attended, see Ibid. 840: 4—5, 1081: 2—3, 1116: 2—3, 1185: 1—4; for indications of his deeper involvement in these issues, see Ibid. 840: 6, 1081: 2 and MANSI 849E; and for his non-participation in the working deputations, see MANSI 794E—95B, 796B—97D, 850D and DE GRASSI 1039: 14.

[105] For a listing of many of these separately published conciliar documents, see: Fernanda ASCARELLI, Le Cinquecentine Romane: Censimento delle edizione romane del XVI secolo posseduto dalle biblioteche di Roma, Milano 1972, 145—46, 153—56.

[106] For a paraphrasing of the Danish king's mandate, see DE GRASSI 877: 3, also printed in Rainaldi 1512 nr. 83; for the absence of any notice of this mandate in the official acts, see MANSI 716C, 733C, 986D; for the reports of the Venetian ambassadors that the Danish mandates were presented, see SANUDO XV 390 and XXIV 105 — the mandate read at the twelfth session was from king Christiern and dated 26 February 1515, see ASV, Arch. Vicecancell. 2, fol. 22ᵛ; for the mandate of 10 April 1512, see Arild HUITFELD, Kong Hansis krønicke som vaar Danmarckis Suerigis Norgis Vendis oc Gotthis konge hertrug vdi Slesuig Holsten Stormarn oc Dytmersken greffue vdi Oldenborg oc Delmenhorst som regaerede i 32 aar fra anno 1481 oc til anno 1513 (= General Krønnicke 6) Kiøbenhaffn 1599, 294—95 and Acta Pontifi-

I

omissions at the time, a more likely reason was the importance of this mandate. Julius was desperately trying to win to his side those favoring the Pisan Council, among whom were the Emperor and the rulers of Scotland, Navarre, and the Scandanavian union of Kolmar. This adhesion to the papal Council by the Danish king Hans whose ambassador Johan Wulf reported to the pope in August of 1512 that the king's nephew, James IV of Scotland, was advised by his uncle to send his own orators to Julius and that Hans would urge the schismatic duke of Muscovy to do the same must have appeared to de Grassi a major victory for the papal side well worth recording.

Given such conciliar goals as unity among Christians and a combined crusade against the Moslems, the mandate of the Maronite patriarch deserved note. De Grassi was apparently fascinated by these Maronites and provided a brief description of them in his Diary. In addition to the mandate of the patriarch, he also recorded, but at the end of his *Ceremoniale*, the mandate of the civil ruler, the mouqaddam of Mt. Lebanon, read at a secret consistory on 17 December 1516, two days before the eleventh session[107].

De Grassi's transcription of the patriarch's mandate is an important document. The original letter in Arabic and its Latin translation read at the Council do not seem to have survived. Three apparently contemporary copies of this mandate are available to historians: that contained in de Grassi's Diary, the version printed in del Monte's official acts of the Council, and the one published as an appendix by Philippe Labbe who obtained his version, thanks to Domenico Magri, from the Library of Latino Latini at the Cathedral of Viterbo. Besides variants in spelling, choice of conjunctions, inverted word order, and stylistic alterations with synonyms, these versions also differ through the omission of whole phrases[108]. Since none of the three can stand alone as the authentic complete version, textual critics will be grateful to de Grassi as an important witness.

---

cum Danica: Pavelige Aktstykker Vedrørende Danmark 1316—1536, ed. L. MOLTESEN et alii, 7 vols. København 1904—43, V (1492—1513), ed. A. KRARUP and J. LINDBAEK, p. 579, nr. 4272.

[107] For his account of the Maronites, see DE GRASSI 1206: 11, for his transcription of the patriarch's mandate, Ibid. 1207; for his transcription of the moquaddam's letter, see DE GRASSI, Ceremoniale, BAV, Vat. Lat. 12270, fol. 154r—57r, also printed in MANSI 1014B—16A.

[108] The more significant variants occur in the acts at MANSI 942E 8 where after *susciptamus* de Grassi inserts *quamvis, absit iactanie verbo, ter in anno, videlibet, in pascate Domini nostri Iesu Christi et sanctorum Petri et Pauli natali hoc consueverimus adimplere*, while Latino has *Quamvis absit jactantia, ter in anno, videlicet in paschate, in natali domini nostri Jesu Christi, et festo SS. apostolorum Petri et Pauli hoc consuevimus adimplere* MANSI 1013B 2—6). The Latino version, however, drops a clause by replacing the fuller text: *et propterea apprime in domino exultavimus et animi nostri immodicam spiritualem conceperunt laetitiam, Deoque . . .* (MANSI 943A 9—12) with *Propterea exultavimus in domino, Deoque . . .* (MANSI 1013C 2—3). The Rainaldi version is closer to the Del Monte edition, but is more confused on the question of receiving the Eucharist.

Del Monte's version is reprinted in MANSI 942B—43D and with slight variation in RAINALDI, 1516 nr. 7—8. Latino's version is in MANSI 1012D—14A. This patriarchal mandate dated 14 February 1515 was not published with the collection of papal bulls and briefs issued later in 1515 and sent to the Maronite patriarch — see Bulle et brevia apostolica plumbata: que S.D.N.D. Leo divina providentia papa X. ad

Historians are also indebted to de Grassi for his detailed account of the reconciliation of the penitent Pisan cardinals. He alone has preserved for posterity the speeches of these cardinals and of Leo X, the penitents' confession of guilt and promise of emendment, and the pope's formula reuniting them to the Church and restoring them to their former honors and benefices. The confession was to have been entered into the public acts of the Camera and recorded in the acts of the domestic secretaries of the pope and Lateran Council. Some seven years later Antonio del Monte, hoping to include this confession in his published edition of the official acts of the Council, searched for it in vain among the papers of the former papal and conciliar secretary, Tommaso (Phedra) Ingirhami who had died in 1516. The reports sent back to rulers from their representatives in Rome described the public events surrounding the reconciliation, but gave mere summaries and isolated phrases from the formulas used. The pope's letters to Christian princes announcing this event were similarly devoid of copies of the actual texts used in the ceremonies. The only surviving source for these documents has been the Diary of de Grassi. Historians ever since have followed the example of Rainaldi who borrowed copiously from the Diary in reporting the reconciliation[109].

De Grassi's reasons for having gone into such detail on this reconciliation ceremony are open to speculation. The event itself was very significant and the ceremonies surrounding it probably had to be devised by de Grassi. He himself played a major role in them as intermediary, choreographer, and attendant. Having devoted so much effort to these ceremonies, he, no doubt, wanted posterity to have a record of them. Insofar as they set a precedent, de Grassi was apparently not happy, for he felt Leo had dealt too leniently with these former schismatics[110].

The one conciliar document clearly of his own authorship which de Grassi included in his Diary was the set of questions he had submitted to the college of cardinals for resolution prior to the opening of the Council. Because the cardinals requested personal copies so that they could reflect on the issues in-

---

Petrum Patriarcham Maronitarum in monte Libano partium Syrie per certos sue Sanctitatis Nuncios misit Rome: M. Silber 1515, in B.A.V., Racc. I, IV, 1734, int. 8 — see Ascarelli 156.

On Labbe's role as publisher of the Viterbo copy, see Guglia, Studien zur Geschichte 5.

[109] The documents of the reconciliation ceremony are recorded in de Grassi 990—991; on their deposition, see Ibid. 989: 6 and Mansi 814D—15A; for diplomatic reports and the papal letters, see Sanudo XVI 429—32, 479—81, Pastor VII App. 4—5, pp. 448—50, Regesta Leonis I 198 nr. 3373—77 (27. VI. 1513) for letters to the kings of France, Scotland, Portugal, and England and to the Regent of the Netherlands and I 200 nr. 3410 (28. VI. 1513) for the letter to Emperor Maximilian I, and Rainaldi, 1513, nr. 50; for Rainaldi's account of the reconciliation, see Ibid. 1513, nr. 44—49.

[110] For his caustic comment that the cardinals returned to their homes as if victors, see de Grassi 989: 12. The restoration of the cardinals with a banquet and joyful celebrations reminds one of the return of the Prodigal Son in Luke 15: 22—24.

volved before giving their responses, de Grassi had copies made. The thirty-one questions he recorded in his Diary, however, are not an exact transcription of a list of twenty questions which still survives in the Vatican Secret Archive[111].

---

[111] On the cardinals' request, see DE GRASSI 841: 8; for the wording of the thirty-one questions, Ibid. 842: 1—31; the copy of twenty questions, preserved in ASV, Con. Trid. nr. 6, fol. 428ʳ—29ʳ, but with most of the references provided by DYKMANS' notes on 842: 1—19, is here transcribed:

1 *Quando placeat quod publicetur dies prima concilii: an in die pascatis in pulpito alto super plateam ex loco bene-dictionis per diaconum cardinalem qui etiam publicat indulgentias?*

2 *Qui habeant vocem decisivam in concilio et qui consultivam tantum? Et utrum abbates omnes habeant decisivam, non obstante opinione domini cardinalis scribentis in capitulo Sane* [c. 1. X, I. 43 = FRIEDBERG II 230] *et in capitulo Grave, De prebendis* [c. 29, X, III, 5 = FRIEDBERG II 478]?

3 *Utrum admittendi sint barones et laici ac etiam ecclesiastici non prelati, ut sunt theologi et canoniste? Et utrum sem-per etiam in decisionibus admittantur isti theologi et canoniste? Et an ac quando et qualiter?*

4 *In quo habitu pontifex non celebrans Missam sedebit in concilio quia in cerimoniali reformato hec disciplina est confuse descripta, idest, cum pluviali et mitra ac sandaliis et cum lectione psalmorum? In aliis autem antiquis libris et in ipso ritu tunc observato aliter dicitur, videlicet, quod esse debet prout fuit Innocentius iiii et Gregorius x, perinde ac si celebrat cum fanone et planeta et pallio paratus. Et tunc cardinales et prelati, parati sicut pontifice celebrante, prestabunt obedientiam eidem ut sit communiter hodie.*

5 *Si autem papa non celebrat, quomodo et in quo habitu prestabunt predicti obedientiam? Et an predicti omnes de concilio et in omni consilio prestare debent obedientiam?*

6 *Si papa non est presens sed aliquis cardinalis presideat concilio, in quo loco sedebit, attento modulo concilii, ubi altare est inter solia pape et imperatoris superius et sedilia cardinalium inferius?*

7 *Et quia presidens non semper solet celebrare, queritur in quo habitu esse debeat quando non celebrat, an in planeta aut in pluviali, et in qua mitra simplici an pretiosa?*

8 *An placeat forma precum que est in moderno cerimoniali reformato, an prout in antiquis libris in quibus expresse jubetur ut concilium incoetur per prefationem hymni Veni Creator Spiritus sicut dogmatizat Dominicus de Sancto Geminiano in tractatu de Conciliis et Petrus de Monte confirmat sic fuisse factum in Basiliensi ubi ipse fuit presens?*

9 *An placeat antiqua forma versuum videlicet Orate et erigite vos, an moderna Flectamus genua, levate?*

10 *An placeat quod finita una quaque sessione detur solemnis benedictio per pontificem, etiam si fuerit prius post Missam data? In nostro cerimoniali nihil dicitur, sed in aliquibus antiquis expresse precipitur.*

11 *An casu quo sit danda per papam, etiam eodem absente detur benedictio huiusmodi per presidentem?*

12 *An placeat quod, conclusa aliqua materia magne importantie, cantetur Te Deum laudamus sicut in duobus antiquis conciliis factum fuit, licet in nostro cerimoniali nihil dicatur de hoc?*

13 *In quo colore paramentorum erunt tam pontifex quam cardinales et prelati sedentes in sessionibus que fient inter Pasca et Pentecostem, attento quod in nostro cerimoniali expresse cavetur quod in rubeo quia Missa erit de Spiritu Sancto, sed in conciliis duobus quibus Innocentius iiii et Gregorius x Lugduni interfuerunt expresse legitur quod erant vestiti paramentis albis propter tempus Resurrectionis tunc instantis, licet Missa et officium esset de Spiritu Sancto?*

14 *An placeat quod diaconus cardinalis omnia legat que erunt legenda, ut in Constantiensi? An vero principium sce-dularum, quas postea notarius prosequatur in pulpito, vel qualiter?*

15 *Declarentur que sint evangelia convenientia materiis diversis, quia nihil difinitum reperitur et dentur ex nunc ut possuit scribi in libro concilii huiusmodi.*

16 *An prelati sessuri debeant sedere prius vel posterius iuxta tempora promotionis singulorum, vel quomodo? An forte pontifex in prima sessione decernet nulli preiuditium fieri propter huiusmodi confusas sessiones, sicut in aliis factum legitur?*

17 *Declaretur de patriarchis presertim Antiocheno presente, ubi sedebit? Et quid de aliis 4or videlicet Aquilegensi, Bituricensi, Gradensi, et Pisano? An stetur consuetudini vel iuris dispositioni secundum quod distinguit Dominicus de Sancto Geminiano in predicto tractatu?*

18 *Quid de abbatibus Urbis, an sint privilegiati in huiusmodi conciliis, sicut in processionibus quibus pontifex vadit ad Lateranum coronatus?*

19 *An omnes milites Hierosolimitani habendi sint pro custodia aditus ad concilium, quia sic in antiquo Constantiensi et Pisano legitur factum?*

20 *Quid de conservatoribus Urbis, ubi stabunt aut ubi sedebunt? Habeatur liber de Conciliis qui erat in Camera apo-stolica et datus fuit domino secretario nuper defuncto.*

The differences between the Diary's questions and the Archive's list provide clues as to how this section of the Diary was composed. Dykmans records a marginal note in the Diary stating that the wording of the questions was not exact. A comparison with the Archive's list confirms this statement. Although the substance of the first nineteen questions is the same, not one of these has the identical wording throughout as its counterpart in the Diary. In general the same question appears in the Diary with fuller explanations, more specific details, stylistic embellishments, and altered syntax. The only reverse tendencies in the Diary are to drop specific citations of the *Corpus Juris Canonici* and references to the number of codices used. The one major addition to the first nineteen questions was in the Diary's question 3 where the protonotaries and penitentiaries were treated, but no corresponding answer was provided in the response section. Question 20 in the Archive's copy is not raised in questions 20—31 of the Diary, but an answer to it is given in the Diary's response to question 19. The concluding request in the final question of the Archive's list that the book on councils be recovered, which was in the Apostolic Camera and had been given to the pope's secretary who died recently (Sigismondo de' Conti died in March of 1512)[112], not only helps to date this document but seems to be a likely conclusion to such a list of questions. It suggests that the Archive's copy is, indeed, one of those given to the cardinals and that the Diary's additions to question 3 and questions 20—31 were written later.

Supporting evidence for this suspicion can be found in questions 3[bis] and 14 of the Diary. The wording of 3[bis] is very close to that of the first question de Grassi submitted to a congregation of cardinals prior to the second session. That the issue of the seating place of the protonotaries was first formally raised on this occasion and not prior to the Council's opening is suggested by de Grassi's comments on the first session. Noting that the protonotaries had taken a position he felt belonged properly to the papal assistants, de Grassi claimed they were given it due to a ruling in the *Ordinario*. He makes no mention of a decision of the pope or cardinals — the first mention of such a decision comes in answer to his question posed prior to the second session[113]. His proposal in question 14 of the Diary, which is not repeated in the corresponding question in the Archive's copy, that prelates might read conciliar documents from a wooden pulpit may also be later interpolation. While mention of a similar procedure appeared in question 8 discussed prior to the first session on May 5th, it took the complaint of the bishops, that cardinal Farnese reading from the papal dais could not be heard in the rear of the chamber, before the conciliar commission of cardinals on May 16th decided where to locate such a pulpit and to appoint prelates as lectors[114].

---

112 HOFMANN II 124.

113 DE GRASSI 842: 3 bis, 847: 8, 848: 4, 10.

114 DE GRASSI 842: 14 suggests as lectors prelates reading from a wooden pulpit, the response 842:

That questions 20—31 were later additions is suggested by de Grassi's confused treatment of whether and when Julius was to address the Council. Question 24 and its response established that the pope was not to address the opening session but could, should he so wish, speak as much as he wanted at the first
formal session. In the scenario of the ceremonies for the opening session which
de Grassi drew up and submitted for the approval of the pope and cardinals no
provision was made for a papal discourse. At that opening session on May 3rd,
however, de Grassi seems to have been surprised that Julius did not speak and
reported that the pope excused himself on the grounds that he had not foreseen
that it was expected of him and hence had not come prepared. On the following
day de Grassi found Julius determined to address the next session, even trying
out his speech on a critical master of ceremonies. Given the pope's announced
intention, de Grassi reportedly asked the next day in question 6 submitted to
the commission of cardinals whether a prelate should also give a sermon at that
session. As things worked out both Julius and Bernardo Zane, the archbishop
of Spljet, gave sermons at the first session. In both question 24 submitted prior
to the opening session and question 6 following that session de Grassi pointed
to the papal practice at Konstanz which Lateran sought to follow. De Grassi's
narration of the sequence of events does not make much sense. If the commission had decided that Julius was not to speak at the opening session, why was
de Grassi surprised and Julius apologetic when he had no speech to deliver?
The question may have first arisen at the session itself or from a closer reading
of the prescriptions in Patrizi's *Caeremoniale Romanum*, and de Grassi, failing to
have made proper provision, covered over his negligence by claiming the cardinals had decided against it based on the precedent established at Konstanz.
Question 24 was thus inserted to suggest that de Grassi had foreseen the need
for such a sermon but its absence was the responsibility of the cardinals[115].

Toward the end of his account of Lateran V, de Grassi provided an overview
and key document which help to explain the dynamics and mounting power
struggle which determined the second period of the Leonine phase of the Coun-

---

super 14 agrees to this procedure, 843: 10 mentions a pulpit for the orators to the left of the pope and
outside the chancel, 846: 2, q. 8 asks whether a prelate should read conciliar documents from the wooden
pulpit, and 848: 4 q. 3 orders the wooden pulpit placed behind the cardinal deacons' bench and that lectors
reading from it be prelates — prior to this decision of 16 May 1512, the acts of the Council record no prelate
reading a conciliar document, but instead the weak-voiced Farnese read all the documents, e. g., MANSI
654AB, 667B, 680E, 695A, 697B,E.

[115] For question 24 and its response, see DE GRASSI 842: 24 and super 24; for the scenario of the ceremonies of the opening session, see 843: 1—33; for Julius' excuse that he had not foreseen that such a speech
was expected of him, see 844: 28; del Monte claimed that Julius had not given a speech because he was
indisposed, see MANSI 653C; on Julius' intention to speak at the first session and his draft speech which
de Grassi criticized, see DE GRASSI, 846: 1; for question 6 and its response, see 846: 2, q. 6; for the speeches
at the first session, 847: 17, 20 and MANSI 653D, 680D; for Patrizi's ruling that the pope should address
the opening session of a council, see his Caeremoniale Romanum, fol. 62ʳ: *Pontifex patres hortatur verbis
convenientibus ad facienda decreta assignans rationes cur ita sit facienda.*

cil. So contrary was the conflict over an episcopal confraternity to the image of concord and cooperation, which del Monte wanted to convey in his edition of the Council's acts, that this cardinal avoided any mention of it[116]. Even though de Grassi's own account is often sketchy and vague, historians remain in his debt.

De Grassi's interest in and support for the bishops' causes seem to have deepened insofar as they affected him directly. His open espousal of their concerns followed closely on his own promotion to the episcopal rank. Within a year he added his voice to the chorus of those protesting the power cardinals had to appoint to benefices in another's diocese. He also joined his fellow bishops in their opposition to the privileges of the mendicants and noted with interest his colleagues' initial proposal for an episcopal confraternity to represent their interests in Rome. But on none of these three occasions did he provide specific details, names of leading exponents, or copies of proposals. Historians must look elsewhere for this information. The only time he became interested enough to record in his Diary one of the bishops' formal petitions was in June of 1516. By then they had recast their initial proposal for a confraternity to meet the objections of the cardinals and had assigned its functions to an enlarged college of papal assistants. His reason for including a copy of this reworked petition cannot be attributed to any of the ceremonies at a particular conciliar session, since Leo and the cardinals adamantly opposed any formal vote on this proposal, threatening to prorogue the Council indefinitely if necessary to block such a measure. Rather, the reason seems to lie in the fact that Paride de Grassi, like many of the masters of ceremonies before him who were bishops, was also a papal assistant, having recently been appointed such in December of 1515. Had the proposal been accepted by pope and cardinals, de Grassi would have found himself in a potentially powerful position in the Roman curia. Such an opportunity for greatness lost to him and his successors deserved some notice in his Diary. That de Grassi himself shared in the formulation and advancement of this proposal is doubtful. His naive disclaimer to any knowledge of why the cardinals found the proposal abhorrent suggests that he was not a part of the leadership behind the proposal[117].

While the initial proposal for an episcopal confraternity has not survived and can be reconstructed only in part from a detailed rebuttal of it, the revised proposal centering on the papal assistants is extant in two versions. What seems to have been the formal copy presented to the pope and amended by another hand to explain in greater detail a specific proposal, to point out that certain proposed agencies and officials of the college were not necessary, and to make the petition appear more acceptable to the pope, has been preserved in the

---

[116] GUGLIA, Studien zur Geschichte (1899) 12.
[117] DE GRASSI 1081: 2, 1116: 3, 1185: 1—7; MANSI 849E.

Vatican Secret Archive and was published by Hergenroether in 1887. The version which appears in de Grassi's Diary was published by Rainaldi in 1663, but it is based on a text inferior to Dykmans' autograph. In addition, the copy in the Diary is not identical to that preserved in the Archive. While the variants do not alter the general sense of the document, but touch such minor points as added or deleted words, choice of pronouns, and case endings, they do indicate that no one version is clearly superior, but that each deserves to be considered carefully by a future editor of this document[118].

As Ceremonialist

De Grassi's role at the Council was first and foremost that of ceremonialist. Except for the cause of restoring episcopal rights and dignity, his interests were focused on the ceremonial aspects of the Council and he had to exert himself initially to have his expertise in these matters acknowledged by all. Preparations for the Council were entrusted to a commission of ten cardinals. When they failed to solicit his advice, de Grassi felt personally slighted and was quick to criticize the proposals submitted by the architects and engineers consulted by these cardinals. He scoffed at the various plans advanced, deriding their vanity, shallowness, and ignorance of conciliar ceremonies. De Grassi felt that his expertise in managing papal ceremonies qualified him to direct those of a council. In an effort to establish his credentials and stave off any possible challenges to his directing the ceremonies of the upcoming Lateran Council, he circumvented the commission of cardinals and submitted for the approval of Julius II a wooden model he had made of how the conciliar chamber should be constructed, arranged, and decorated. He was delighted when the pope vindicated his professional reputation by praising his model before the cardinals and entrusting to him sole responsibility for its realization. De Grassi promptly took control not only of preparing the conciliar chamber but also of organizing the Council's ceremonies. Where the writings of his predecessors provided inadequate guidance, de Grassi had recourse to the commission of cardinals or to the pope and sacred consistory for a decision. It is interesting to note that while the names of de Grassi and his colleague Nicolai appear in the list of conciliar officials appointed at the first session, their function was that of assigning places to the conciliar fathers. Unlike Enea Silvio Piccolomini at the previous Council of Basel or Pompeo de' Spiriti later at Trent, de Grassi does not seem to have held a special office of conciliar master of ceremonies, for it is mentioned neither in the acts nor in his Diary. Instead, he functioned in his capacity as papal ceremonialist[119].

---

[118] DE GRASSI 1185: 7; HERGENROETHER, Conciliengeschichte VIII App. H, 845—46; RAINALDI, 1516, nr. 3.

[119] DE GRASSI 840: 4—7, 847: 24; MANSI 697B, E; Hubert JEDIN, A History of the Council of Trent,

Guided by Principles

In de Grassi's opinion the master of ceremonies was a professional guided by his own discipline. The rules de Grassi set out in his earlier work on diocesan ceremonies were repeated or echoed in these sections from his Diary. The master is described as being in some sense an overseer *(suis ceremoniis quasi antistitem)*, leader, and director of those engaged in divine worship. His rulings were not to be arbitrarily devised, but to conform to divine law, the teachings of the fathers, current usage, and personal experience. Certain theological principles were to govern his prescriptions — thus an altar representing Christ should be more honored than the pope, His vicar. An expert knowledge of tradition and precedent was important and this could be obtained from studying: the ceremonial writings of one's predecessors and those belonging to the Camera and Chancellery; treatises on councils; literary, architectural, and pictorial evidence; one's own and others' diaries; and from personal experience. What was learned from such sources was to be applied in a rational and learned manner and adapted according to time and place[120].

Concern for Reverence and Splendor

De Grassi shared with Innocent VIII and Patrizi before him concern that ceremonies be characterized by reverence, adornment, and order. To promote an attitude of prayerful reverence a fast was imposed at the beginning of the Council on all who would attend, especially on those with the right to vote. The litany and other prayers were ordered to petition divine guidance. And to enhance this sense of reverence during the services, de Grassi sought to maintain a hush in the Basilica. When noise distracted from the dignity of the ceremonies, the conservator of Rome was called upon to enforce a fitting silence. To add splendor to the ceremonies de Grassi decorated the conciliar chamber with costly fabrics as backdrops and as coverings for the altar, seats, and floor. In memory of this Council, Julius donated to the Lateran Basilica a *pallium dossale* made of gold cloth, a Greek cross, two beautifully worked candelabra, plus a set of golden outer vestments, linen under garb, and silken cords. Once these were blessed, cardinal Domenico Grimani and his assistants vested in them to celebrate the Mass for the first session. In addition to his own ornate vestments, the pope wore his tiara on his way to the chamber and a lavishly adorned mitre

---

II New York 1961, 18; that DE GRASSI was skillful enough to construct a wooden model of the conciliar chamber two cubits long is in keeping with his own prescriptions that a ceremonialist should be able to make with his own hands whatever is needed to carry out his office — see his De caeremoniis libri duo, fol. 4ᵛ.

[120] Ibid. fols. 2ᵛ, 3ᵛ—4ʳ; DE GRASSI, 883: 6 (profession with a discipline), 840: 23 (theological principle), 840: 5 (knowledge of tradition), 840: 7, 841: 1, 842: 4, 10, 1116: 14 (ceremonial writings), 842: 8, 844: 20 (treatises on councils), 840: 7 (artistic remains), 848: 4, q. 10, 1116: 14 (diaries), 841: 1, 1081: 4 (personal experience), 840: 23 (theological consideration overrules tradition).

during much of the ritual there. On the altar were placed candelabra, a cross, and a number of relics, and the heads of Sts. Peter and Paul were exhibited to public view. A choir sang at various points in the liturgy and when an important matter was decreed at a session, it was closed with a *Te Deum*[121].

Concern for Order

Of great concern to de Grassi was the proper ordering of the ceremonies. Both earlier in describing the responsibilities of the master and at the time of the Council when he sought to carry out these duties, his concern was that the ceremonies be performed *rite recteque* and at a council also *legaliter* and *regulariter*. This care was shared by Julius II who was eager that no deficiency in the organization or rituals of the Lateran Council be found which could serve as a pretext for refusing attendance at it. An important element in the perceived correctness of the Council's ceremonies was their conformity to the practices of former councils, especially those of the previous century, and in particular of Konstanz and Basel. Of these previous assemblies the most normative for de Grassi seems to have been Konstanz. Its procedures were cited by him on numerous occasions. This may in part have been due to the attention Patrizi had devoted to this council in his *Caeremoniale Romanum*. Precedent was a major factor in determining what was to be done at the Lateran Council. A legally and ritually perfect council was seen by Julius II as his best weapon against the rival Pisan assembly which was desperately struggling for an acknowledgement of its legitimacy. In the opinion of de Grassi, Julius was interested not in matters of substance, but only in the appearances of a council and these rituals were to be done with the greatest reverence and majesty[122].

If de Grassi and the popes shared the same general concern for the correctness of the conciliar ceremonies, they did not always agree on particulars. Although Julius often yielded to de Grassi's judgment as to what was proper, at the fourth session the pope overruled with an angry glare his discretely protesting master of ceremonies and insisted that each conciliar father clearly and individually restate his approval of the bull interdicting France, despite a just completed unanimous voice vote. When the mild mannered Leo X came to the papal throne, the master became more bold in his asserting a contrary opinion. So convinced was de Grassi of the correctness of his understanding of diplomatic

---

[121] DE GRASSI, De caeremoniarum libri duo, fols. 3ʳ, 5ʳ and see supra nn. 55 and 59; DE GRASSI 842: super 21 (fast), 843: 24, 26 (prayers), 1039: 13 (silence), 840: 23—27 and 846: 2 q. 19 (fabrics and items on altar), 843: 23 (tiara), 842: super 7 (ornate mitre), 27 (altar), 28 (heads of Apostles), 842: super 8 and 12 (choir), 848: 18, 29, 1039: 15 *(Te Deum)*, and 847: 4 (Julius' gifts to Basilica).

[122] DE GRASSI, De caeremoniarum libri duo, fol. 4ʳ; DE GRASSI 840: 7 (rite recteque ac legaliter), 923: 13 (regulariter), 845: 3 (pretext), 840: 7, 841: 1, 842: 8 (former councils as norms), 842: 14, 19, 24 super 12, super 16, 845: 1, 846: 2, qq. 7, 8, 848: 5, 921: 5 (Konstanz), 985: 2 (appearances), 921: 2 (majesty).

protocol that at the seventh session he defied the decision of the recently elected pope favoring the orator, Laurentius Miedzyleski, of the fraternal dukes of
Mazowsze, Stanisław and Janusz Piastri, and denied him a seat in the section
reserved for the ambassadors of civil rulers[123].

That was not the only occasion when de Grassi asserted himself in his official capacity as the assigner of seats in the Council. At the fifth session when
Julius was confined to his deathbed and the moderator of the Council, Raffaelle
Riario, did not intervene to restrain him, de Grassi was ready to make a public
scene in order to secure others' compliance with his sense of propriety. He
ordered the moderator's brother, Cesare Riario, to assume his proper seat as a
patriarch and removed an archbishop from his place for failing to wear the
correct attire[124]. Granted the need for someone to maintain order, de Grassi
seems at times to have devoted excessive attention to minor details and to have
brooked no opposition to his orders. Ordering about leaders of Church and
state must have confirmed his own sense of self-importance.

Maintenance of Order Among the Lay Participants and Knights

De Grassi's Diary provides ample evidence that his office as assigner of
places at conciliar ceremonies consumed a good deal of his attention. In an era
of warring rulers and of ambitious dignitaries sensitive to the least slighting of
their honors and privileges, and in the absence of published rules settling questions of protocol but with conflicting claims often based on ambiguous precedents, inevitably a number of officials and ambassadors at the Lateran Council
quarreled over the positions assigned them.

Under Julius controversies were contained or at least temporarily resolved
by decisions made by the pope or the cardinals. One of the principles which
seems to have underlain the Julian ordinances was the desire to win over potential Roman rebels and enlist them instead as papal guards. Thus positions
of honor on the papal dais were granted to the Roman barons, senator, and
conservators. Proximity to the pontiff in the processions to the Council was
also granted by Julius to the conservators who assisted the City's governor in
protecting the pope while on his way to the Council, and when once there they
either sat in positions of honor opposite the ambassadors or served as guards at the
entrance to the conciliar chamber. These officials seem to have felt that this
special honor was due them as representatives of Rome, the seat of the Empire.
Julius' absence from the fifth session allowed a heated controversy to flare up
over the privileges of the heir to Mantova[125].

---

[123] De Grassi 905: 3 (Julius accepts de Grassi's suggestion), 1116: 9 (Leo defers to him), 901: 29
(de Grassi overruled), 985: 11 (de Grassi defies papal decision).

[124] De Grassi 923: 13—14.

[125] De Grassi 843: 19, 844: 7—8, 1116: 14 (honoring potential rebels), 844: 33, 847: 25, 901: 8,
1039: 13, 1081: 4, 1116: 10 (conservators of Rome), 923: 15—17 (Pio versus Gonzaga).

I

The election of a new pope provided the opportunity for pressing claims to precedence. Despite Leo X's reaffirmation of Julius' decision that the Knights of Jerusalem and Rhodes, rather than the papal mazzieri (mace-bearers), were to ride closer to him in his first procession to the Lateran Council, these minor papal officials did not want to yield to the Knights. They insisted that as members of the pope's court, their dignity was greater than that of the Knights. The reasons which had swayed Julius were also convincing to Leo: mazzieri were inferior to Knights who were chosen by the pope as his personal bodyguards, a function they seem also to have performed at the councils of Pisa and Konstanz a century earlier, and the way in which the mazzieri would protect the pope, marching directly before him like an armed phalanx going into battle, was deemed less appropriate than that afforded by the Knights with their ceremonial weapons. To obtain compliance with his decision favoring the Knights, Leo instructed the Master of the House and governor of the City to see that all mazzieri preceded the Knights in the procession to the tenth session and that any who disobeyed were punished. As a concession to the bruised honor of the mazzieri and of Bernardino Guttierez who had supported them against the Julian ruling so ably defended by de Grassi, Leo ordered that the Knights should not accompany him too closely[126].

A similar controversy involving the conservators of the City and the diplomatic corps came to Leo's attention. Julius had determined that the conservators flank the governor who in a procession went immediately before the Captain of the Church who preceded the subdeacons carrying the papal cross. The conservators interpreted their close proximity to the pontiff as an indication that they were higher in dignity than the ambassadors who were further away. At first they claimed superiority only to those ambassadors who represented a ruler less than a king. But by the end of the Council they claimed precedence over all ambassadors, even imperial. Instead of directly refuting these pretensions, Leo sought to eliminate the problem. Since the conservators accompanied the governor, the pope called upon him to perform his customary function of riding ahead to insure the pope's safe passage and upon the conservators to assist him. Instead of complying with the pope's wishes, the conservators absented themselves from the procession to the tenth session. Two years later, when they attempted to resume their place of honor in the papal entourage, de Grassi and Guttierez together rejected them and Leo told them to go to the heads of the streets over which he would pass. Thereafter they came no more to advance their claims[127].

---

[126] DE GRASSI 847: 2, 28, 964: 2 (claims of the mazzieri), 842: 19 and super 19, 844: 1, 1039: 5 (Knights' case), 1116: 11 (Knights to keep a distance).

[127] DE GRASSI 1116: 10 (Julian ruling), 1081: 4 (proximity as superiority), 1230: 1 (superior to all ambassadors), 1081: 4, 1116: 10, 1230: 1 (Leonine rulings and non-attendance of the conservators).

Whereas Julius was less hesitant to make rulings regarding his own papal officials, did not easily tolerate challenges to them, and forestalled possible disputes involving Roman officials by placating them with flattery due to his delicate political situation, Leo's authority over these groups was but slowly established and his decisions made only after due consideration of rival claims. His key consultant would appear to have been de Grassi, the depository of information on how and why cases were previously resolved.

As an expert on how disputes over precedence among ambassadors had been previously resolved, de Grassi's advice was highly valued. The most interesting case to occur during the Council was probably that at the tenth session involving Savoy. While desirous of honoring the ambassadors of duke Charles III of Savoy, the brother-in-law of Leo's brother Giuliano, the Medici pope feared alienating the dukes of Milan and Venice, neither of whose ambassadors at Rome were willing to yield the place of honor to Savoy. In hope of finding a solution to his difficulties by an appeal to precedent, the pope asked the master of ceremonies how in accordance with papal law and practice Savoy ranked in relation to Venice and Milan. De Grassi responded that according to what is found in the books of the Camera and Chancellery and in his own books on ceremonies the juridical order was Savoy, Milan, and Venice. To overcome the pontiff's surprise and disbelief, de Grassi showed him the texts on which this ranking was based. He added that in practice Milan customarily yielded its place to Venice, but that neither was willing to accept the precedence of Savoy. Both Alexander VI and Julius II had dealt with the controversy by having the contending ambassadors alternate with Savoy the times when they would attend official functions. Leo was at first attracted to this solution, but then decided that the representatives of all three dukes should attend that session and that controversy could be avoided if the ambassadors of Savoy accompanied Giuliano de' Medici who as Captain of the Church held a position of high honor in the procession and if they did not sit in the benches reserved for lay orators, but sat instead on the opposite side in the row between those of the cardinal deacons and that of Roman officials[128]. Leo thus sought to side-step controversy by eliminating its occasions rather than by making a clear decision on precedence which could alienate a present or potential ally. De Grassi was

---

[128] In February of 1515, Giuliano de' Medici married Filiberta of Savoy, the sister of Duke Charles and aunt of Francis I of France — see CREIGHTON V 236; on 27 February 1485 the representatives of Savoy and Milan who had earlier alternated attending services in the papal chapel were both forbidden by Innocent VIII to come due to their squabbling, on 2 June 1493 the ambassador of Savoy was allowed to attend a service but those of Venice and Milan were told by Alexander VI to stay away lest a scandalous controversy ensue — see CELANI I 110, 427; on 25 November 1512 Julius II temporarily resolved the controversy between Savoy and Venice by ordering that they alternate between them the place of honor — see BAV, DE GRASSI, Diarium Julii, Vat. Lat. 12269, fol. 593ᵛ; the Leonine phase of this controversy is in DE GRASSI 1116: 14.

there to assist him by pointing out similar solutions adopted by Leo's predecessors.

When, in de Grassi's eyes, an ambassador lacked legal or precedential grounds for claiming a position of honor, he was prepared to defend traditional procedures, even if this meant going against the wishes of the pope. When the Knights of Rhodes had won over Leo to according them the honors of sovereign lords, de Grassi protested that they were properly members of a religious order and refused to seat them with the diplomatic corps, but directed them instead to the benches reserved for religious. And as noted earlier, de Grassi also contravened Leo's orders by refusing admission to the ambassadors' section to the representatives of the dukes of Maszowze on the grounds that they were not independent rulers but vassals of the King of Poland[129].

Maintenance of Order Among the Ecclesiastical Participants

De Grassi's insistence on established order was perhaps most adamant in the area of ecclesiastical rankings. The supremacy of the pope was clearly evident in his organization of processions and conciliar ceremonies. The arrangement of the papal and imperial thrones left no doubt that the pope claimed superiority over temporal rulers. De Grassi saw him as the head of all Christendom and was concerned that he be an exemplar of faith. On the pope's relation to a council, de Grassi distinguished between two scenarios. When the pope has not submitted himself to a council but presides over it, he is in no way limited by it. When, however, he is subject to it, he can do nothing and must defer all things to its authority. Such was not the case regarding Julius and the Lateran Council. De Grassi's suggestion that the pope must willingly submit himself to a council before it can exercise supremacy over him seems to have been a reconciliation of traditional papal teachings with the decrees of Konstanz and Basel, an interpretation known to one who acknowledged his lack of expertise in theology and canon law and readily accepted by a pope who doubted his own authority. The attack on papal authority mounted by the rebellious Pisan cardinals under French and Imperial auspices was for de Grassi a heinous crime. He found it difficult to support the concessions of leniency granted by Leo to the penitent cardinals, stressing in his account the harsher aspects of the punishments and, like the obedient brother in the story of the Prodigal Son, criticizing the festivities which accompanied the reconciliation[130]. While his respect for the papal office was high, the master of ceremonies was not blind to the personal failings of those who held it.

---

[129] On 31 October 1504, Julius had already granted the Knights seats in the section reserved for the representatives of princes — see Thusane III 369; for de Grassi's rejection of their claim at the time of the Council, see Diarium Leonis, Vat. Lat. 12275, fols. 103r—05r; de Grassi 985: 11 (Maszowze).

[130] De Grassi 840: 12, 24 (superiority of papal to imperial throne), 924: 2 (pope as exemplar of faith), 883: 4—6 (when a pope is subject to a council), 989: 12 (criticism of the festivities).

De Grassi's attitude toward the cardinals was ambivalent. They were the prelates of his every day professional experience and among their number was his own brother, Achille. That they were the only group attending the Council for whom de Grassi gave a detailed listing by name at the opening session and a separate counting at most subsequent ones is probably less due to any special theological significance he attached to their office than to an initial desire to show that the majority of the cardinals backed the Lateran rather than the Pisan Council. The conciliar functions performed by the cardinals were those assigned them by the popes and tradition. Julius entrusted to a select number of them the tasks of supervising the preparations for the Council, deciding controverted points in the ceremonies, and directing the conciliar commissions charged with bringing materials to the floor of the assembly for a vote. At first the cardinals exercised a monopoly too as principal ministers at the Eucharistic celebrations and as lectors of the drafts of bulls put to a vote, but complaints about Farnese's weak voice and difficulty in finding willing celebrants led to an ever increasing role for bishops in the Council's liturgy. The cardinals retained, however, their key role as advisers to the pope on all important matters having to do with the Council. At times the pope would overrule the advice of his cardinals but in general they were in agreement. Leo in particular seems to have felt himself bound by their wishes and even had to go back on a promise to the bishops when the cardinals opposed it. So deferential was he that after the very lengthy eleventh session he even refused a return ride to the Vatican in the comfort of a litter out of respect for the senior cardinals who apparently lacked such a mode of transport[131].

De Grassi both acknowledged that the cardinals were in some way sharers in the papal dignity yet in many respects no more eminent than bishops. Their position in the first quadrangle of the conciliar chamber implied that they were participants in the papal honor and higher in dignity than the patriarchs who were considered leaders of the archbishops and of all prelates. The cardinals' functions as councillors and ministers of the pope were considered more important in determining their location in the conciliar chamber than the fact that among their number were patriarchs, primates, archbishops, and bishops. Nonetheless, their dignity derived from their prelacies apart from their function as papal advisers was also highly esteemed by the master of ceremonies. The cardinals' role as council fathers he compared to judges rendering their decision and therefore it was fitting that they be seated and wear appropriate attire, notably the mitre. He thus protested at what seemed obsequious behavior when some cardinals stood bare-headed and announced their vote in response to

---

[131] De Grassis 844: 30—31, 848: 1, 905: 13, 964: 1 (cardinals at Council), 1039: 5, 1206: 6, 1116: 5 (archbishops as celebrants), 846: 2 qq. 7—9, 848: 4 qq. 4—5 (Farnese replaced as regular lector), 846: 2 q. 5, 846: 17, 905: 3, 1116: 5 (popes overruling cardinals), 1081: 2, 1185: 1—4 (Leo bound to cardinals), 1206: 17 (Leo's deference to senior cardinals).

Julius' order that they clearly and individually voice their approval or rejection of a proposed conciliar decree. While thus protective of the cardinals' dignity as prelates, de Grassi was also strongly opposed to many of their claims to superiority over bishops. By seeing that both cardinals and bishops had elevated seats and footbenches, wore mitres, voted in a similar manner, and paid their individual obesiance to the pope, de Grassi emphasized their equality. He seems to have personally resented the cardinals' lording it over the bishops and their privileges which trampled on the rights and jurisdiction of local episcopal ordinaries. Their opposition to reform measures sponsored by the bishops was attributed by the Grassi to their addiction to license and abuse[132].

Preservation of the dignity befitting the patriarchs was of some concern to the master of ceremonies. In his design for the conciliar chamber, he positioned special seats for them in a prominent place within the first quadrangle, forming the side directly opposite the pope's throne and beginning as it were the episcopal section. Because two of the privileged Latin patriarchs (Bakócz of Constantinople and Carvajal of Jerusalem) were cardinals, C. Riario of Alexandria and Carafa of Antioch were not seated alone on the section originally reserved for them, but joined the papal assistants on the papal dais. At the fifth session when there were no papal assistants due to Julius' absence and Carafa celebrated the Mass, Riario chose to sit in the section reserved for bishops. Having recognized this irregularity, de Grassi admonished the patriarch to occupy his proper place, but Riario protested that such honors did not interest him. The master of ceremonies insisted that for reasons of personal humility he could not degrade the patriarchal dignity and had either to leave the ceremonies or take his proper place. Some cardinals who had been auditors of the Rota joined in persuading Riario to relocate himself at the head of the archiepiscopal seats[133].

What to do about the four non-privileged patriarchs (Aquileja, Bourges, Pisa, and Venice) became a problem when Andrew Forman of Bourges and Marino Grimani of Aquileja pressed claims to preferential treatment and ignored the ruling of the preparatory commission of cardinals that they sit in the section reserved for primates and archbishops and be ranked according to the seniority of their promotions. De Grassi in the winter of 1516/17 claimed that the Scot had at a conciliar session earlier that year (the eleventh?) attempted to take a place of preeminence above all ambassadors and bishops, but that he had been ejected from the Council by de Grassi with the backing of the pope and cardinals. When the Venetian also insisted on a place of honor greater than that of the ambassadors, a solution was found in having him sit with the papal assist-

---

[132] DE GRASSI 840: 14, 16, 26 (cardinals' seats in first quadrangle), 905: 9 (cardinals to be mitred and seated when voting), 840: 17, 842: super 14, 846: 2 q. 5, 848: 4 q. 3, 905: 9, 1081: 6 (similar treatment of cardinals and bishops), 1081: 3, 1185: 1 (de Grassi's criticism of the cardinals).

[133] DE GRASSI 840: 15 (location of patriarchal seats), 842: 32 super 17 (seated with papal assistants), 923: 13 (incident at fifth session).

ants on the papal dais. Guttierez warned the Spanish ambassador, Pedro Urrea, the bishop of Siracusa, of Grimani's effort to outrank him; and at the congregation before the twelfth session where there were no seats for papal assistants due to Leo's absence, an altercation between Grimani and Urrea broke out over precedence. When de Grassi intervened on Grimani's side, Urrea was indignant and pointed out that he was not only a bishop but an ambassador of Spain. To this de Grassi responded that he was the master of the pope, cardinals, and other masters of ceremonies. The controversy at this congregation was temporarily resolved when the presiding cardinals waivered a seating arrangement based on rank and allowed each prelate to sit where he wished. Later on Leo backed the ruling of his master of ceremonies, dismissing the complaints of the Spanish ambassador[134].

The prerogatives of the group which de Grassi came to care the most to protect were those of the bishops. Even in the planning stages of the Council de Grassi had been careful to respect the rights of bishops. He lobbied vigorously to preserve episcopal honor against the protonotaries' pretensions of superiority by getting Julius to reaffirm a ruling of Pius II. But his efforts went for naught when the papal assistants (a select group of patriarchs, archbishops, bishops, and occasional curial officials from whose ranks Julius often selected his cardinals) yielded without protest their positions of honor on the papal dais to these aggressive curialists. With his own promotion to the bishopric of Pesaro, de Grassi came to identify more closely with episcopal causes. At the eighth session he joined with his fellow bishops in attacking the Curia-sponsored reform measures for not being broad enough and failing to include a reform of its authors. In the struggles from the ninth to eleventh sessions which pitted the bishops against the cardinals and friars, his espousal of the episcopal cause led him at times to attribute base motives and deceitful tactics to this opposition. He was not only out to protect the splendor, power, and jurisdictional authority of the episcopate in general, but his own interests in Pesaro as well. De Grassi's accounts of the bishops' motivations, strategies, dilemmas, and protests, even to the point of threatening to vote down any measures proposed in the Council and attempting to postpone or refuse the traditional act of obesiance to the pontiff, provide the historian with information not easily found elsewhere[135].

---

[134] On the Forman controversy, see DE GRASSI Diarium Leonis, Vat. Lat. 12275, fols. 128v—29r and 193v—95r — that Forman was ejected from the Council is questionable, rather the place was more likely the papal chapel and the occasion a papal ceremony held there to commemorate either the feast of St. Cornelius, pope and martyr, or the vigil of Sts. Cosmas and Damian, the patrons of the Medici family, on 26 September 1514, or the vigil of All Saints on 31 October 1514; for the ruling of the preparatory commission, see DE GRASSI 842: super 17; on the Grimani controversy, see DE GRASSI, Diarium Leonis, Vat. Lat. 12275, fol. 194r—95r and MANSI 977AB.

[135] DE GRASSI 842: 3 bis, 847: 8, 848: 4, 10, 901: 6 (bishops versus protonotaries), 1116: 3, 1185: 2 (hostility to cardinals and friars), 1081: 2, 1116: 2, 1185: 1 (defense of episcopal interests), 1081: 2, 1185: 4, 1206: 6 (bishops' struggles); MANSI, 846E—47A (de Grassi's espousal of curial reform).

I

Principles of Order

The order which de Grassi, therefore, sought to safeguard and make manifest in his ceremonies was one sanctioned by tradition and by feudal and canonico-theological principles. Precedents and vassalage were important in determining ranks among princes and diplomats. Respect for the ecclesiastical hierarchy with the papacy at its summit governed his ordering of clerics. An extension of the papal prerogatives not only to the cardinals but also to a wide variety of curial officials, from protonotaries to mazzieri, and even to mendicants as exempt religious, could and often did raise numerous concerns for a defender of the traditional feudal and episcopal order such as de Grassi. This loyal servant of the popes recognized such grants of papal privilege as disruptive of the hierarchial order of the Church and destructive of episcopal authority. His thinking on the episcopacy seems to have extended beyond questions of jurisdiction as evidenced in his struggle with the protonotaries, but it is not clear that he espoused a theological position such as that enunciated by Vicenzo Fanzi on the eve of the eleventh session. Fanzi held that bishops are not merely papal appointees, like any curial official, but are raised to the episcopal dignity by Christ Himself. De Grassi's own deep sense of the splendor and power of the episcopacy and any diminution of these as abuses seems to suggest that this ceremonialist also saw these attributes as inherent in the episcopal office. In his earlier treatise on diocesan ceremonies, however, he referred to cardinals and bishops as successors of the apostles and disciples, men summoned to share in the pastoral office and to assist Christ's vicar who enjoys the fulness of power[136]. De Grassi's own elevation to the episcopacy may have led him to a deeper understanding and appreciation of the office of bishop.

In addition to the evidence it gives of de Grassi's understanding of his office and of his concerns, the Diary also provides valuable information about the Council itself. In general this confirms and supplements what is known from other sources, but on occasion it corrects the official acts of del Monte.

The Council of de Grassi's Diary

Goals

De Grassi's Diary provides some clues as to which, if any, of the announced goals of the Council merited more of the pope's attention. In his bull of convocation, address read for him at the inaugural ceremonies, and discourse delivered at the first session Julius spoke in generalities. His favorite imagery seems to have been the field of the Lord which needed to be weeded and restored to productive cultivation. This metaphor is used both in his inaugural address and in the one

---

[136] For Fanzi's position, see Mansi 938E—39A; for de Grassi's earlier statement on the episcopacy, see his De caeremoniis libri duo, fol. 3ʳ⁻ᵛ; on episcopal splendor and power, see DE GRASSI 1116: 2.

Gospel text he personally selected for the conciliar liturgy. In his speech the tares are corrupted morals. Given the agenda of the fourth session, which was to be reflected in the scriptural passage chosen (Julius selected the parable of the seed falling on various soils from Matthew 13), the weeds and thorns are apparently the evils of the Pragmatic Sanction of Bourges. Except for defeating the Pisan cardinals "on account of whom the Council was called," the Julian goals may at first seem so vague as to suggest a ritualistic reiteration of traditional conciliar aims. The inadequacy of such a harsh judgment on this pope's conciliar aims is apparent when one recalls that Julius established a commission of twenty-four prelates, plus some cardinals, to deliberate on how he could best enact a reform of morals, restoration of peace, and end to the schism. De Grassi, nonetheless, accused Julius of being concerned with the mere appearances of a council and not with its substantial achievements[137].

Of the several goals officially assigned to the Council Leo singled out two in his first address to the fathers. He urged a reform of the City and world and a restoration of peace and quiet to the Christian republic. That Leo was not alone in attaching great importance to the goal of reform is evident in de Grassi's earlier statement that it is for the sake of reform that prelates assemble and form a council. At Lateran the scope of this reformation was determined from the start not to extend into the interior of one's soul, cases of conscience, but to be limited to external matters. On various occasions under Leo this reform was specified as involving "morals and things," all the officials of Rome and their offices, and even the reformers themselves and the pope[138]. Reform efforts during the second period of the Leonine phase aimed at a restoration of episcopal dignity and jurisdictional rights were not part of the conciliar programs envisioned by either Julius or Leo.

For the Medici pope the second principal purpose of the Council was the establishment of peace and quiet in the Christian republic. Given his subsequent

---

[137] For the official statements of purpose, see MANSI 667B—D, 680D, 687BC, 688D; for the full text of Julius' inaugural address, see MINNICH, Concepts of Reform 237—38. While some of the Gospel texts to be chanted during the conciliar liturgy were already prescribed by the *Pontificale* (DE GRASSI, 842: 15), others varied according to the topics to be treated at that session (PATRIZI, Caeremoniale Romanum, fol. 62ʳ). At first Julius allowed the commission of cardinals which in turn delegated one of its members, Marco Vigerio, to make these selections (DE GRASSI 842: 15 and super 15). However, for the fourth session Julius determined that the Gospel reading should be from Matthew 13 (DE GRASSI 905: 2; MANSI 747C). Del Monte clearly states that the text was the parable of the sower who went out to sow his seed (Mt 13: 3—23), de Grassi's description of it as "containing the matter of the weeds" suggests Mt 13: 24—30, 36—43. For the Pisan cardinals as the reason for calling the council, see DE GRASSI 844: 18; for Julius' establishment of a commission of prelates and cardinals, 968: 2, and for de Grassi's accusation that this pope's concern was for appearances and not substance, 985: 2.

[138] DE GRASSI 840: 2 (council meets to reform), 968: 2 (here de Grassi uses the term *reformanda* to include morals, peace, and schism), 842: 3ᵗᵉʳ (penitentiaries may not attend in their official capacity but as university graduates, because the Council's reform does not treat a reform of souls), 964: 9 (Leo's goals), 968: 2 (morals and things), 985: 13 (reform of officials), 1039: 14 (*quod omnium reformatio fiat, tam sui quam reformatorum*).

conciliar bull urging peace among Christian princes and mandating the dispatch of nuncios to promote this goal, the pope's intention would seem to have been the restoration of peace in civil society. He did not, however, neglect efforts aimed at eliminating discord in the Church; for when he set about organizing the work of the Council, he assigned to the deputation charged with finding ways to establish peace among Christian princes, the additional task of extirpating schism[139].

The third deputation at the Lateran Council was charged with preparing materials related to doctrine, especially ecclesiological questions. Julius does not seem to have been worried about abstract philosophical and theological errors, but directed the attention of his conciliar commission to the practical problem of ending the Pisan schism. The question of heresy during the Julian phase of the Council was focused on the Pisan cardinals and their supporters who were denounced as heretics and schismatics. This sentiment was even echoed in the Venetian mandate read at the fourth session. From the perspective of Rome the greatest danger to the Church was a denial of the doctrine of papal supremacy. Leo was in agreement with this assessment. He, however, assigned to the deputation on peace the task of ending the Pisan schism and gave a more speculative scope to the third deputation, committing to it the problem of the Pragmatic Sanction which had been used to justify the Pisan schism. Probably in imitation of the deputations at Konstanz and Basel, he enlarged its mandate to deal with other questions of the faith. This eventually led to the condemnation of such speculative errors as those of the Averroists which denied the multiplicity and immortality of the human soul[140].

Location

De Grassi's Diary also provides detailed information on the everyday functioning of the Council and allows one to determine with some precision the location of its formal sessions. In his bull of convocation Julius stated that the council would be held *apud Lateranum*, where many councils had been previously celebrated. Precisely where in this Lateran complex is not specified. According to the *Caeremoniale Romanum* of Patrizi a council could be celebrated either in a cathedral church or in another place suitable for the purpose. Despite the existence of an *aula concilii* in the Lateran palace, Julius seems early on to have favored the Council's location in the Basilica. He ordered the preparatory com-

---

[139] DE GRASSI 964: 9; MANSI 788E (goal of peace), 796B (conciliar deputation on peace), 817BC and 843E—45A (conciliar bulls providing measures for peace). Julius' concern for peace was registered at the Council was evidenced from the beginning by the inclusion of collects for peace in the conciliar Eucharistic liturgy; but even in this case, the use of this collect may have been more in imitation of a practice followed at Konstanz, than as a signal of his deep concern — see DE GRASSI 846: 2 q. 4, 847: 16, 901: 4, 923: 3. This practice seems to have continued under Leo, e. g., 964: 5. A more significant indication of his concern was the establishment of a commission of cardinals and prelates to deliberate on the question of peace and quiet in Christendom — see, 968: 2.

[140] DE GRASSI 968: 2 (Julian and Leonine deputations), 844: 18, 848: 22, 901: 26, 905: 4 (Pisan cardinals as heretics); MANSI 796B, 797B (tasks of two deputations); PATRIZI, *Caeremoniale Romanum*, fol. 60ᵛ (deputation for matters touching the "Catholic faith" at Konstanz and Basel).

mission of cardinals and the architects with their skilled workmen to meet in the church for determining the actual site and structures to be used. When they had difficulty making their decision, de Grassi came forward with his own model. His Diary explains in elaborate detail the location, measurements, internal organization of seats, furnishing, and decorations of a conciliar chamber, which he called a *conciliabulum*. This walled enclosure, based on information he had gathered from Patrizi and the surviving pictorial and literary evidence of the councils of the fifteenth century, was constructed in the nave of the Basilica and used at the Council's opening on 3 May 1512[141].

The *conciliabulum* was not the only place readied for conciliar functions. At the banquet following the inaugural ceremonies, Julius learned that at Konstanz special quarters had been put at the private disposition of the civil rulers, pope, and cardinals so they could consult in secret on the agenda of the council. Lest the absence of such a place be used as a pretext by the emperor or kings for not attending the Lateran Council, Julius ordered de Grassi to ready a similar room. The site chosen for this *secreta mansio* was none other than the *aula concilii*. De Grassi borrowed for it the design of his *conciliabulum*. Benches for bishops could apparently be added or removed depending on the function. Within a mere two days time de Grassi claims to have prepared this hall for conciliar ceremonies[142].

The conciliar commission of cardinals now had to choose between two possible locations for the public sessions. When asked where the first session was to be held, the cardinals opted for the Basilica. The *conciliabulum* was not without its problems. Although the church was to be cleared of all unauthorized persons during the deliberative portion of a session, a great downpour drove people back into the Basilica at the eighth session. Lest noise from the crowd continue to disrupt the conciliar proceedings, one of the conservators of Rome was sent out to impose silence and quiet. Noise was not the only problem brought on by the rain. The roof leaked in a number of places. The efforts of the bishops to escape a bath created such a commotion that the obeisance ceremony was almost postponed. Rain fell during or threatened three other sessions. Despite the drawbacks of the *conciliabulum*, the cardinals did not relocate the session. De Grassi's suggestion that with the pope absent the fifth session

---

[141] MANSI 687D (bull of convocation); PATRIZI, *Caeremoniale Romanum*, fol. 59 *(in Ecclesia cathedrali, sive alio capaci loco)*; De GRASSI 840: 5 (commission studies sites in Basilica), 840: 6—28 (de Grassi's plans), 844: 22—23 *(conciliabulum* used at opening ceremonies); for a detailed study of the conciliar chamber, see MINNICH and PFEIFFER, De Grassi's Conciliabulum at Lateran V, in: AHP 19 (1981) 148—68.

[142] DE GRASSI 845: 1—4 (decision to prepare the mansio and description of it); at one point de Grassi claims the hall lacked benches for bishops (845: 2) and there was only one row behind the cardinals for princes and ambassadors (845: 4); two days later in the second question submitted to the cardinals he announced that the hall was already prepared for receiving all the conciliar fathers (846: 2, q. 2). Given the remarkable speed with which he readied this hall, one wonders if work had not been already underway on preparing the hall for conciliar use. Julius II is reported to have had windows constructed in the hall to provide natural lighting for the Council — see, G. Rohault de FLEURY, Le Latran au Moyen Age, Paris 1877, 258.

be held in the *aula concilii* was not accepted by the cardinals. His labors in preparing that hall for conciliar functions were not totally in vain, for an important general congregation was held there after the sixth session[143].

The Eucharistic liturgy at each formal session was celebrated on the portable altar constructed inside the *conciliabulum*. The high altar of the Basilica was used only for the Mass at the beginning of the inaugural ceremonies and as the altar before which the popes subsequently prayed while making their way to the conciliar chamber[144].

Scheduling

Details regarding the scheduling of the formal sessions of the Council can be found scattered throughout these sections of the Diary. Due primarily to the battle of Ravenna and its aftermath, Julius twice postponed the opening of the Council. But once the Council began, all of the five sessions of the Julian phase, except for one, met on the days initially assigned them. Only the third session had to be postponed. De Grassi gave two possible explanations for this prorogation: either Julius' desire to name cardinals which he felt he could not do while a council was sitting or the pope's fear that Matthew Lang, the emperor's representative, would attend the session and propose something at variance with the pontiff's wishes[145].

Under Leo not one of the sessions met on the day set for it at the conclusion of the previous session. Explanations for some these prorogations are offered by de Grassi. Thus, the ninth session was postponed for almost two months due to the bishops' threatened boycott and resolution to vote down any measures unless their grievances against the cardinals were resolved. This same issue, together with the demand for a rescission of the exemptions of religious from episcopal jurisdiction, delayed twice the tenth session. Leo's meeting at Bologna with Francis I, the hoped for arrival of a delegation of French bishops, the continuing insistence of the conciliar bishops that the privileges of religious be curtailed, and the struggle over an episcopal college resulted in repeated postponements of the eleventh session[146]. Leo's inability to hold a single session on the day first appointed is thus at least in part directly attributable to the a-

---

[143] DE GRASSI 846: 2 (decision of 5 May 1512), 1039: 13 (rain at eighth session), 848: 19 (leaks at second session), 901: 2, 31, 1206: 4—5 (rain at third and eleventh sessions), 964: 3 (fear of rain at fourth); 922: 1 (proposal to relocate session for fifth), 968: 1 (congregation of 13 May 1513 in the *aula concilii*).

[144] DE GRASSI 844: 6 (opening Mass on high altar), 847: 3 (subsequent Masses in *conciliabulum*), 847:3 and 964: 5 (Julius and Leo pray before high altar).

[145] DE GRASSI 840: 3 (postponement of opening session), 844: 27 and 847: 1 (first session), 848: 1 (second session), 848: 23 and 883: 4 (postponement of third session), 901: 26 and 905: 1 (fourth session), 905: 8 and 923: 1 (fifth session).

[146] DE GRASSI 923: 11 and 964: 1 (postponement of sixth session), 964: 2 and 985: 1 (postponement of seventh), 985: 14 and 1039: 1 (postponement of eighth), 1081: 1—2 (postponement of ninth), MANSI 885E, 898B—E, DE GRASSI 1081: 12 and 1116: 1 (postponement of tenth), 1116: 13, 21 and 1206: 1 (postponement of eleventh), 1206: 15 and 1231: 1 (postponement of twelfth).

wakened sense of episcopal power and the threat of the bishops to use it. The difficulty of preparing controversial material and of working out compromises helped to make this Lateran assembly the third longest general council in the history of the Church.

The Diary also provides information on the more practical aspects of scheduling. Under Julius, the opening and first two sessions met on Mondays, the third and fourth on Fridays, and the fifth on Wednesday. Except for the opening ceremonies and tenth session which fell on the feast of the Finding of the Holy Cross, no effort seems to have been made to schedule sessions to coincide with significant feasts. Under Leo the sixth session was held on a Wednesday, the eighth and twelfth on Mondays, and the rest on Fridays. Thus, half of all the sessions were held on this traditional day of penance and prayer. The three days of the week on which sessions were celebrated were also the traditional days for holding a consistory[147].

The sessions began in the morning. Julius, who at times had some difficulty in rising early, seems to have favored a later hour. For only two of the Julian sessions did de Grassi specify the hour at which the ceremonies began and in both cases it was 10 o'clock in the morning. After the sessions Julius usually dined at the Lateran palace or at one of the church complexes along the return route to the Vatican. The starting time under Leo seems to have been 6 o'clock in the morning or sunrise. The sixth and seventh sessions lasted until 11 o'clock, the ninth till 1 in the afternoon and the tenth until 1:30 p.m. The eleventh session was very long and the pope did not return to the vicinity of the Vatican until almost sunset. The times for the eighth session are difficult to determine given the fact that many of the fathers dined just before attending. The length of a session depended on its agenda. The shortest session whose hours de Grassi noted lasted three hours, the longest seven and a half. The eleventh must have consumed almost the whole day[148].

Attendance

De Grassi often recorded in his Diary the number of those attending various sessions. Those whom he consistently singled out for a counting were mitred prelates who enjoyed a deliberative vote. His summary numbers of all mitres seem to have included cardinals, patriarchs, archbishops, and bishops, but not mitred abbots, even though the congregation of cardinals ruled that abbots ap-

---

[147] For the days of the week, see DE GRASSI 844: 1, 847: 1, 848: 1, 901: 1, 905: 1, 923: 1, 964: 1, 985: 1, 1039: 1, 1081: 1, 1116: 4, 16, 1206: 5, 1231: 1; on the days for consistories and on the importance of the feast of the Finding of the Holy Cross, see PATRIZI, Caeremoniale Romanum, fol. 142ᵛ—43ʳ.

[148] For indications of when the session were held, see DE GRASSI 844: 4, 847: 3, 27, 848: 8, 30, 901: 2—4, 31, 905: 1, 11, 923: 18, 964: 13, 985: 16, 1039: 16, 1081: 7, 12, 1116: 16, 21, 1206: 5, 17, 1231: 1; de Grassi began counting the hours of the day from sunset of the previous day, hence to derive the modern equivalent, six hours must be subtracted — see John Rigby HALE, Renaissance Europe: Individual and Society, 1480—1520, London 1971, 13.

pointed for life and exercising jurisdiction over people, such as the abbot of San Gregorio de Urbe, enjoyed a deliberative voice in the Council. Whether such abbots did in fact vote is not clear — the acts make no mention of one casting a vote. While the cardinals ruled that the four generals of mendicant orders were not to be excluded from the deliberative proceedings, their voting rights are not specified. The description in the acts of de Vio's interventions at the eighth and twelfth sessions would seem to indicate that the generals enjoyed a vote that was deliberative and not merely consultative. Procurators, at least those who were mitred prelates in their own right, could apparently cast a vote in the name of the prelates who empowered them. There is no record, however, of other procurators or of abbots with a three-year term of office having voted at the sessions. Apparently neither procurators nor religious superiors were counted as mitred fathers by de Grassi. Usually he divided those with mitres into cardinals and other prelates and gave separate figures for each. The highest number of cardinals at any one session seems to have been twenty-five at the tenth, and the total number of all mitres never exceeded one hundred and fifty, the eighth session being the best attended. According to de Grassi's numbers average attendance was about one hundred and sixteen mitres[149].

A comparison between the attendance figures given by de Grassi and the lists of names recorded by del Monte shows more discrepancies than agreements. Their numbers agree only for the second, third, and eleventh sessions, but in the latter the name of an additional prelate appears in the acts of that session, thus disqualifying even the eleventh session. De Grassi's figures are generally higher than the numbers derived from counting the names furnished by del Monte. The most notable discrepancies are for the fifth session where de Grassi gives 135 while del Monte only 100 names in his list, plus an additional one in the acts, and for the eighth session where the master of ceremonies counted 146 but the editor provided only 116 names. The disparity in their numbers is not resolved by counting abbots and generals. The only times when the master's numbers were lower than the editor's were the count for cardinals at the twelfth session and the number of prelates at the congregation prior to the

---

[149] DE GRASSI 842: 32 super 2—3 (ruling in voting rights), 905: 13 (cardinals counted as mitres), 848: 27, 901: 12 (cardinals included in count of all mitres); for the number of prelates present: 842: 30—31 (16 cardinals and 83 mitres at opening ceremonies), 847 (no numbers given for first session), 848: 1, 27 (16 cardinals and 86 mitres for a total of 102 at the second session), 901: 12 (111 total mitres at the third), 905: 13 (19 cardinals and 104 other mitres at the fourth), 923: 19 (135 mitres at the fifth), 964: 1 (22 cardinals and 90 mitres at the sixth), 985: 8 (111 mitres at the seventh), 1039: 9 (24 cardinals and 122 mitres at the eighth), 1081: 10 (140 mitres in all at the ninth), 1116: 9, 17 (25 cardinals and 93 mitres at the tenth), 1206: 5 (80 mitres in all which includes 16 cardinals at the eleventh), 1231: 1 (16 cardinals and 90 or 100 mitred prelates at the twelfth). To arrive at an average attendance figure of 116.5 mitres, the opening ceremonies are counted, the first session is not since de Grassi provides no figures, the numbers 90 or 100 for the twelfth are treated as 95 and the pope who attended all sessions except the fifth is included in the counts. For the vote of de Vio, see MANSI 843D and 993A, of a procurator, 975BC, D.

eleventh session. Given the already noted flaws in the del Monte lists, de Grassi's figures are probably to be preferred[150].

Care was exercised to see that only authorized persons were present during the deliberative portion of a session. After the opening ceremonies for the Council which included a solemn Mass on the high altar of the Basilica and an outdoor procession to the *conciliabulum* attended by an estimated 50,000 people, the number of those present at the subsequent sessions was drastically reduced because all these ceremonies were held in the restricted space of the conciliar chamber. The first part of a session was open to the public. This usually included the ritual for the pope's arrival, the celebration of the Mass, the sermon, the benediction and publication of an indulgence, the obeisance by cardinals and prelates, the prayers and litanies, the chanting of the Gospel, the reading of mandates from civil rulers, and the presentation by procurators and acceptance by the pope of credential letters excusing prelates who were legitimately impeded from attending. Significant variants in this ritual were two. At the fourth session on urgings from de Grassi Julius allowed the people to remain to hear both the reading of a letter of Louis XI to Pius II abrogating the Pragmatic Sanction and the diatribe of Melchiorre Baldassini, the Council's promotor, denouncing the Pragmatic Sanction and its supporters. At the eleventh session, no sermon was delivered due to the actual or feigned illness of the orator and the benediction and indulgences were inserted after the prayers following obeisance. The public portion of a session usually ended with the citation for contumacy of all those who lacked a legitimate excuse for not coming. Lest unauthorized persons be present at any of the deliberations which followed, they were at this point ordered to leave[151].

A number of officials were given responsibility for seeing that the Council chamber was cleared of everyone except for the council fathers, their deputies, and the necessary officials. The order to leave the chamber was announced by the master of ceremonies. The confirming nod of Julius was needed before his order was taken seriously at the fourth session. The officials charged with removing people were the mazzieri and apostolic cursores, who were to be as-

---

[150] For del Monte's list of prelates, see MANSI 676E—79E (15 cardinals and 79 prelates at I), 707B—10B (16 + 86 at II), 727D—30E (17 + 94 at III), 743B—46C (19 + 96 at IV), 762E—65E (19 + 80 + 1 who comes from distinguishing Andreas Literen. and Philippus Adriacensis from the conflated Andreas Adriacensis of 765C + Laurentius Montisregalis of 774D at V), 785A—88A (22 + 89 at VI), 805E—08E (22 + 86 at VII), 827C—30D (23 + 93 at VIII), 858B—62B (25 + 112 at IX), 901A—04C (23 + 90 + Fernandus Scalensis of 916C at X), 936A—37E (5 + 60 at congregation prior to XI), 939B—41D (16 + 64 + Johannes Algarensis of 975B—D of XI), 980A—83B (18 + 90 at XII). Not included in these figures as prelates are abbots and generals. For a study of the flaws in del Monte's lists, see MINNICH, Participants 165—74.

[151] For examples of this order with some minor variations, see DE GRASSI 901: 9—24, 964: 5—11, 1039: 5—13, 1206: 6—10, 1231: 2—6, for the exception at fourth session 905: 3—7, for the absence of a sermon and relocation of the benediction and indulgences at the eleventh 1206: 7, 9. De Grassi basically followed the order prescribed by PATRIZI, Caeremoniale Romanum, fol. 61r—62r.

sisted if necessary by the palatine stipendiaries. At least at the eighth session one of the conservators of Rome also assisted in this removal. Their efforts were hindered not only by the reluctance of many to leave, but also by the narrowness of the place. Most were jammed into the aisle behind the last row for prelates (where religious superiors and some protonotaries were to sit) and the walls of the chamber. This space was assigned to theologians and canonists, but they seem to have been crowded out by curious courtiers, curialists, and clerics. Those who were successfully removed seem to have awaited the end of the session in the cloister, Constantinian halls, or porticos of the Basilica. Minor officials such as cantors needed for the concluding ceremonies withdrew to the *cellulas* of the Council, that is, to the latrine area located behind panels on either side of the papal dais[152].

The list of those allowed to stay gradually grew as the Council progressed. The commission of cardinals decided from the start that the voting members of the Council included all mitred prelates and abbots with jurisdiction over people. Major religious superiors were also allowed to stay; abbots elected for a three-year term, however, normally had only a consultative voice and needed the pope's permission to speak. Similarly, civil rulers and their representatives also remained, enjoyed a consultative voice, and yet had to clear their comments first with the pope. They had the additional function of serving as formal witnesses to the acts of the Council. Procurators of absent cardinals, impeded prelates, and ecclesiastical chapters and colleges could propose nothing for the Council's consideration without prior clearance of the pope or of those deputized to examine their mandates. These ecclesiastical procurators were denied admission to the deliberative portion of the session. Allowed to stay were the specifically designated officials of the Council and of the papal chapel. Julius also permitted by special favor a number of other persons to remain, such as his own secretary, two medical doctors, assisting chamberlains, cantors, and the trainbearers of the cardinals. Arguing from the presence of the latter, the papal chamberlains under Leo also secured papal permission to remain[153].

Officials

De Grassi's Diary in conjunction with del Monte's acts identifies the various officials of the Council and describes their functions. The most important of-

---

[152] DE GRASSI 901: 25, 905: 8 (categories of those allowed to remain), 905: 7 (Julius backs de Grassi's order), 846: 2 q. 18 and 1039: 13 (officials charged with removing people), 847: 14 (difficulty of removal), 847: 14, 848: 4 q. 2, and 848: 10 (occupants of last row), 840: 18 and 842: 32 super 3 (location of theologians and canonists who were to be excluded), 847: 13, 848: 11 and 901: 9 (others who occupied their space), 846: 2 q. 15 (waiting places), 840: 13, 20 and 848: 18 (cantors were to wait in the cells, but since the only cells mentioned in the chamber were latrines, they must have retired there).

[153] DE GRASSI 842: 32 super 2, 3 and 846, 2 q. 12 (those with deliberative and consultative voices), 847: 5—13 (location of officials), 846: 2 qq. 12, 13 (rights of civil and ecclesiastical procurators), 843: 31 (ambassadors as witnesses), 848: 1 (officials), 846: 2 q. 5, 848: 18, and 1116: 15, 17 (special papal permits to remain eventually given).

ficial was the president. Both Julius and Leo held this office at the Lateran Council. At the fifth session when Julius was absent due to illness, he was represented by the Dean of the Sacred College of Cardinals, his cousin, Raffaelle Riario, who is referred to in the documents as the president of the Council. The majesty and power of the papal office were so fully transferred to the presidency when held by a pope that the Council was initially overshadowed by this office. The large dais with throne for a papal president placed against the rear wall of the chamber dominated visually the whole chamber. At the beginning of each session, every prelate was obliged to pay his individual obeisance to the pope — a ceremony on which the popes insisted despite the delays it caused in an already lengthy ritual, despite the confusion occasioned by the leaky roof at the third session, and despite the protests of the rebellious bishops at the eleventh session. The only time this ceremony was eliminated was when Riario occupied the presidency. In his office as president, the pope controlled every significant action at a session. He alone set the agenda. Appointments of conciliar officials were subject to his approval. Whether by himself or after consultation in consistory, he approved or altered the ceremonies proposed by the master of ceremonies and preparatory commission of cardinals. He could also have a major influence on the content of a conciliar decree. While Julius seems to have delegated to others the choice of celebrants and homilists, he determined at least initially who would read the *cedula*, once cardinal Farnese's voice proved too weak to be heard by all. Before any non-cardinal could read aloud a document, he had to come before the pope to obtain his permission. Major mandates were usually first submitted to the pope prior to their recitation. When it came to deliberating, no one with a consultative voice could speak without papal clearance. The pope cast the first vote, could stop further action by refusing to respond, could determine the method of voting and even demand that a vote be retaken[154]. Without question, the papal president was the most important official at the Lateran Council.

[154] DE GRASSI 842: 32 super 6, 7, 11 and 846: 2 q. 1 (presidency and pope's intention always to exercise it), 922: 2, 3 (position and garb of Riario at fifth session), 923: 5—7, 10 (Riario referred to as praesidens), MANSI 762CD, 766DE, 793E, (Riario as praesidens seated in front of altar as prescribed in PATRIZI, Caeremoniale Romanum, fol. 59ᵛ), 842: 32 super 5, 843: 25, 846: 2 q. 5, 847: 18, 848: 19, 964: 7, 1039: 9, 1206: 8 (when, how, and insistence on the paying of obeisance), 847: 19 versus 848: 19 (contradictory statements on obeisance at the first session), 923: 3—11 (no mention of obeisance to the non-papal president at the fifth session), 848: 7 (Julius alone sets the agenda of the Council), 842: 32 super 25 (appointment of officials subject to his approval), 841—843, 922: 9 (ceremonies approved by pope), 844: 3, 883: 1—3 (after consultation in consistory), 846: 2 q. 5, 921: 4 (cardinals yield to pope's wishes), 1039: 14 (Leo resolves on new reform decree), 842: 32 super 30, 846: 2 q. 3, 921: 5 (pope delegates to cardinals and master the choice of celebrant), 846: 2 q. 9 (cardinals choose Zane), 1116: 4, 7 (Teglatius appointed homilist by Leo probably after consultation in a consistory), 848: 4 q. 3 (Julius to choose recplacements for Farnese), 1116: 13 (Leo chooses lectors), 848: 13, 22 (Julius blesses lectors before they read), 901: 16 (papal blessing indicates permission to ascend pulpit and read), 905: 8 (Julius allows bishop to read a *cedula*), 848: 16, 985: 9—10, and 1039: 10 (major mandates handed to popes), 842:32 super 2, 3 and 846: 2 q. 12, 13 (papal permission needed to exercise consultative voice), 905: 6 (official of Council needs papal

I

Second in importance to the president was the c o n c i l i a r c o m m i s s i o n appointed by Julius in 1512. Although initially composed of ten cardinals, only eight of their names appear on a reform decree issued at the end of March in preparation for the Council. By May de Grassi was referring to this commission as the congregation of nine cardinals *(novemviratus congregatione, patribus novemviris)*. By the time of Leo this congregation had apparently been replaced by other structures. Under Julius these cardinals frequently made the practical decisions regarding the Council, often as responses to questions put to them by de Grassi. In general Julius went along with their decisions, but not always[155].

Deeply involved in the smooth running of the Council was the m a s t e r o f c e r e m o n i e s. He probably ranked technically, however, only as an official of the papal chapel. His role in the design and construction of the chamber, in determining and directing the conciliar ceremonies, and in assigning places and resolving controversies over precedence has already been noted. In addition, at the sessions themselves, he ordered at the proper moment the citation for contumacy of those absent and the exclusion of unauthorized persons. During the deliberative portion of the session, he handed to the pope to give to the lectors the *cedulas* to be voted on. The master's vote was cast immediately after the pope's and cardinals' and on occasion he instructed the fathers on the method of voting, reported to the pope the results of the election, and told the cantors to begin the *Te Deum* ending the session[156].

Apart from the master of ceremonies, the most prominent of the middle level conciliar officials was probably the p r o m o t e r of the Council. This title was given to one of the c o n c i l i a r p r o c u r a t o r s, often the fiscal procurator. Mariano de Cuccini held this post until his death early in 1513 and Leo appointed as his successor on March 30th Mario de Peruschi. When a procurator acted as a promoter is not always clear; at times functions performed by a promoter are ascribed to an official identified only as a procurator. According to Patrizi, the conciliar promoter was like a public manager who saw to it that items of business were taken up and brought to conclusion. Unlike the lectors and homilists he was not to address the assembly from the pulpit, but seems to have positioned himself within the first quadrangle[157].

---

permission to speak), 848: 25, 964: 13, 1039: 14 (pope votes first), 901: 23, 905: 7, 964: 11 (popes prevent further action by their refusal to respond), 901: 28—29 (Julius determines method of voting), 905: 9 (Julius orders fathers to repeat their vote louder).

[155] De Grassi 839, 840: 4—5 (Julius appoints ten cardinals who reform officials and attempt to determine the Council's site in the Basilica), 848: 4 q. 6 and 848: 5 (congregation is of nine cardinals), 846: 2 and 848: 3—5 (questions submitted to deputized cardinals), 846: 2 q. 5 and 905: 3 (Julius goes against the wishes of some of the cardinals).

[156] De Grassi 847: 23, 964: 10 (directs officials), 901: 28 (instructs fathers and reports voting results), 901: 21, 25 (orders citations and exclusion), 901: 30 and 964: 13 (orders singing of *Te Deum*).

[157] Hofmann II 95 (the fiscal procurators of the Camera), de Grassi 843: 31 and 901: 19 (promotor as fiscal procurator), 901: 19 and Mansi 773E (Mariano de Cuccini under Julius), Mansi 657E and 993A (Mario Peruschi under Leo), Patrizi, Caeremoniale Romanum, fol. 60ᵛ.

At the Lateran Council these procurators made sure that legal documents were drawn up recording important acts. At the opening ceremonies the promoter, de Cuccini, called upon the protonotaries as *stipulatores* and the ambassadors as witnesses to consign to writing and memory the important *cedula* just read which officially began the Council and set the date for its first session. At that meeting, Thomas Regis called upon the protonotaries and notaries to draw up the public documents recording its acts. When Matthew Lang, the personal representative of the Emperor, read at the third session a *cedula* by which Maximilian renounced the Pisan Council and adhered to the Lateran, the promoter, Mariano de Cuccini, quickly ordered the notaries to make a verbatim record of this document. At the fourth session, de Cuccini, described as procurator of the fisc and of the sacred Council, participated in the proceedings against the Pragmatic Sanction. After the conciliar advocate, Melchiorre Baldassini, had eloquently urged its abrogation, de Cuccini asked if the measures against its supporters proposed by Baldassini should be put into execution. When the conciliar fathers approved a *monitorium* against the Sanction and its adherents and determined the date for the next session, de Cuccini ordered the notaries and others to draw up instruments documenting this approval. At the sixth session under Leo, de Peruschi tried unsuccessfully to have an edict issued against the king of France to force him to lift the Pragmatic Sanction[158].

The promoter of the Council had a role in the citation of absent prelates. The responsibility for issuing this summons seems to have belonged to the fiscal procurator. At the fifth session, the promoter and fiscal procurator were one and the same official, de Cuccini. His citation resulted in a number of procurators coming forward with the mandates of absent bishops. A description of the ritual of citation as carried out at the third session is provided by de Grassi and del Monte. De Cuccini, the fiscal procurator, accompanied by Petrus Mengivar, an apostolic cursor, and by two prelates processed down the central passageway of the *conciliabulum*, stopping at the center of the chamber, at the entrance apparently to the second quadrangle, and at the gates of the *conciliabulum*, where each time in a loud voice all prelates and others accustomed to attending a council were cited to come and warned that their failure to comply brought the accusation of contumacy and made them liable to the legal penalties and censures contained in the bull *Coena Domini*. After Mengivar reported back to the pope on their citations, de Cuccini on bended knee confirmed this report, accused those absent of being contumaciously negligent, and asked that legal

---

According to Jedin, Ercole Severoli, as promotor at the Council of Trent, "was the assembly's legal assistant and defender of its rights." This able jurist advised on the legal form given to decrees, supervised the notaries' authentication of the acts, and began proceedings against those absent prelates declared contumacious. See JEDIN II 511.

[158] DE GRASSI 843: 31 and 844: 29 (opening session), 847: 26 (first session), 901: 19 and MANSI 733C (third session), 905: 6—7, 12 (fourth session), 964: 11 (sixth session), for de Peruschi ordering similar instruments, see, e. g. MANSI 930D, 943E, 993A.

proceedings be initiated against them. Julius promised to give his response at the next session. At this fourth session, de Cuccini accompanied by two cursores Mengivar and Joannes Bernardi, repeated this ritual and this time Julius declared that those absent fell under the penalties prescribed. Riario, as president at the fifth, reiterated this sentence. At the sixth session, the new fiscal procurator de Peruschi was accompanied by the promoter, unidentified, and to their request for judgment that the absent were subject to penalties Leo said nothing. This pope admitted the excuses of the French prelates at the ninth, but at the tenth declared them liable to the penalties if they did not attend the next session[159].

Other prominent officials of the Council were its secretaries. At the first session Julius appointed to this office Bartolomeo Saliceto of Bologna and Tommaso (Phedra) Inghirami of Volterra, who was succeeded on his death in 1516 by Andreas Piperarius. Among their functions as secretaries was the public and open production of a record of the proceedings of the Council, a task for which their known industry commended them. They were also called upon to act as witnesses and to summon the newly appointed conciliar officials to come forward to swear their oath of office. One of the secretaries was commissioned to notify Zane of his appointment as lector at the first session. Inghirami was often charged with reading aloud to the assembly the mandates of civil rulers, and on occasion the letter of a king or a *cedula* at a congregation. His successor Piperarius was also a frequent lector. Saliceto does not figure prominently. Important conciliar documents may also have been entrusted to the care of Inghirami[160].

The appointment of the humanist and papal librarian Inghirami and of the former apostolic secretary Saliceto did not sit well with the current college of apostolic secretaries which petitioned that four of its members be appointed as secretaries of the Council. Given the divisions already in the Church due to the Pisan Council, the commission of nine cardinals sought to placate them by appointing two of their number, Marino Caracciolo of Naples and Angelo Colucci of Jesi. Because Julius later rejected the appointment of a married man

---

[159] DE GRASSI 923: 9 and MANSI 773A—74B (promoter summons procurators of absent bishops), DE GRASSI 1206: 16 (fiscal procurator issues citations), 901: 21 and MANSI 733CD (ritual at third session), DE GRASSI 905: 12 and MANSI 755A (fourth session: de Grassi has Julius issuing his sentence, while del Monte claims he said nothing), MANSI 773E—74A (Riario agrees to imposition of penalties), DE GRASSI 964: 10—11 (sixth session), MANSI 864B—69B (ninth session), 915E (Leo's conditional judgment at the tenth session is reported without the condition in DE GRASSI 1116: 19), 697B (Bernardus Mocharus and Thomas Regis appointed as procurators and Mariano de Cuccini as fiscal procurator).

[160] DE GRASSI 847: 24 (appointment of Saliceto and Inghirami), 1206: 11 (Piperarius succeeds Inghirami), 848: 5 (task of writing the proceedings), 847: 23 (secretaries summon officials to take oaths), 846: 2 q. 9 (secretary is to notify Zane that he is lector), 848: 16, 901: 16, 905: 4, 923: 10, 964: 10 (Inghirami reads mandates), 905: 5 and 968: 1 (he reads letter and *cedula*), 1206: 11 and 1231: 6 and MANSI 983E (Piperarius reads mandate of Maronite patriarch and letter of emperor), MANSI 814D, 815A (documents entrusted to the secretaries), 935C (secretaries as witnesses).

That the office of conciliar secretary at Trent was "obviously created on the model of the papal secretaries at the fifth Lateran council" is asserted in JEDIN II 497.

to this conciliar office as inappropriate, Colucci was replaced by Juan Carroz of Valencia. As honorific appointees and mere deputies they were warned by de Grassi not to presume to rush about the Council nor to record in public its proceedings. While they could attend the Council, they were to do any of their writing at home. To their displeasure, de Grassi's admonitions prevailed with the backing of the cardinals[161].

The production of the official acts of the Council was entrusted to specially deputized scribes and notaries. The actual writing down of the minutes of the sessions was apparently done by four scribes, each from a different nation: Benôit Troilet from France, Bernhard Schulz from the Empire, Bernardino Contreras from Spain, and Francesco Attavanti from Italy. Schulz and Contreras were twice called upon by cardinal del Monte acting on orders from Leo to provide legal documents in the case of the absent French prelates. In April of 1515 they saw to it that the letter of safe-conduct for the French prelates granted by the doge of Genoa was authenticated and delivered to the French ambassadors in Rome. And in July of that year they furnished Forbin with an authentic instrument of his protest at the tenth session excusing the absent French prelates. The scribes also functioned as subalternate notaries[162].

Supervising and subscribing the work of the scribes were the notaries. Julius appointed four: the Spaniard Alfonso de Lerma and the Italians Paolo de Cesi, Francesco Spinola, and Nicolò Lippomani. At least the first two were already participating protonotaries and when Lippomani was made bishop of Bergamo, Lorenzo de Laureliis of Amelia was apparently appointed in his place. The principal responsibility of the conciliar notaries was to review the conciliar documents, seeing that they were in a fitting order and agreement. Notaries were also to sign everything ordained in the Council. In conjunction with the clerics of the Camera they were to investigate public documents and examine the faculties of nuncios and legates. Both these protonotaries and the clerics of the Camera enjoyed at the Council positions of honor on the papal dais. The presence of the protonotaries at the beginning of the ceremonies was necessitated by their function as official witnesses. When many mandates of absent bishops were produced at the time of citation, the protonotaries relieved the pope of the task of receiving these minor mandates by collecting them themselves[163].

The protonotaries and scribes cooperated with the scrutators in collecting the votes. The scrutators appointed at the first session were the Greek Manilius Rhallis, an acolyte of the papal chapel, and the Italians Jacopo Simonetta,

---

[161] HOFMANN II 119, 183; DE GRASSI 848: 5.

[162] DE GRASSI, 847: 24 (names and nationalities of scribes), MANSI 899A—900C (letter of safe-conduct), 914D—15D, 934C—35E (instrument of protest), 696E (scribes as subalternate notaries).

[163] DE GRASSI 847: 24 (names of notaries), 989: 6 (Laureliis), MANSI 697C (de Lerma and de Cesi as protonotaries), 935C (Laureliis as conciliar notary), 729D (Lippomani as bishop), 696E (duties of notaries), DE GRASSI 848: 6—7 (notaries examine documents), 848: 4 q. 2 (position on dais), 901: 6 (protonotaries to be present at beginning), 985: 10 (protonotaries receive episcopal mandates).

auditor of causes of the apostolic palace, Alvaroto degli Alvaroti, abbreviator of apostolic letters de parco majore, and Girolamo Chinucci, auditor of the apostolic Camera and soon to be named bishop of Ascoli-Piceno. Chinucci's successor was probably the apostolic *rescribendarius*, Cristoforo Barozzi, deputized as a scrutator earlier on the petition of the apostolic writers who had appealed to the practice of Konstanz where one of their number had held that office. The four scrutators were so divided that half collected the votes on one side of the conciliar chamber, while the other two did the same on the opposite side. In the gathering of the returns, each scrutator was always to be accompanied by a notary and a scribe of the Council. The method of voting was to be determined at each session, but a written ballot was apparently never used, Julius not only preferring an individual voiced vote, but insisting that it be spoken very loudly. Leo seems to have continued the practice of voting by voice. The prelates were to signify their approval or not of the measure proposed by using the words *Placet* or *Non placet*. The pope was to use the plural form. While de Grassi encouraged the fathers at the second session to express their opinions as the Holy Spirit so inspired them, by the fifth session he was trying to prevent additional comments from being added to the votes and by the tenth session he had harsh words for those who regularly appended clauses to their votes. It was probably the duty of the scribes to record the votes and comments. When the voting was completed, the results were reported back to the pope by various persons — thus at the third session by de Grassi, at the fourth by the scrutators, and at the sixth by a protonotary. At the eighth, Leo questioned the protonotary about the size of the opposition[164].

The last group of officials described in some detail in the Diary and acts were the guards. They were divided into three groups. The protection of the Council was entrusted to Costantino Comneno Arianiti who enjoyed the titles of duke of Macedonia, prince of Achaia, sole and general guardian of the Council, and captain of its guard. His function was to secure the outside of the Basilica with the assistance of his troops, a strong militia composed of armed infantry[165].

The protection of the single entrance way into the *conciliabulum* was committed to the three conservators of Rome assisted by the tribunes of the people. At the opening ceremonies, these conservators had been given by the pope a special position of honor with the ambassadors in hopes of securing thereby their

---

[164] DE GRASSI 847: 24 (names of only three scrutators, Chinucci's missing), MANSI 697A (names of four scrutators), 729DE (Chinucci as bishop), DE GRASSI 848: 5 (Barozzi), MANSI 697A (teams), DE GRASSI 846: 2 q. 10 (method of voiting), 901: 28—29 and 905: 9 (loud voiced votes), 846: 2 q. 10, 848: 26 and 905: 9 *(Placet)*, 848: 25 and 901: 27 (pope to respond in the plural person), 848: 26 (free to add comments), 923: 11 (effort to prevent comments), 1116: 17 (attack on those who always add comments), 901: 28 (de Grassi reports results), 905: 10 (scrutators report), 964: 13 (protonotary reports), 1039: 14 (Leo questions). For a more detailed examination of the voting procedure, see GUGLIA, Studien zur Geschichte (1899) 23—25.

[165] MANSI 696D (titles of Arianiti), DE GRASSI 842: 32 super 19 (sole guardian assisted by troops outside the Basilica), 847: 25 (captain of armed troops).

loyalty. At the first session they were seated with the barons of Rome opposite the ambassadors, a position not originally assigned them in de Grassi's model of the *conciliabulum*, but allotted them for this session by Julius, for it was during these ceremonies that they swore on the Gospels before the pope the oath of their office. In response to a petition that at least one of the three be admitted to the sessions, the pope ruled that they should all be stationed as guards outside the entrance to the conciliar chamber. Although they apparently succeeded at the second session in reoccupying their former seats in the first quadrangle, by the third session they were standing guard outside the chamber. Apparently sometime before the fifth session which Julius never attended, the decision was made to admit to the ceremonies one of the three conservators. Under Leo the number of those present increased at least to two from the sixth to tenth sessions. In addition to their function of guarding the entrance to the chamber, the conservators were charged with preventing anything unbecoming or violent or noisy from occurring there. Their duties also included quieting the people inside the Basilica so that the conciliar services would not be disturbed. As noted earlier, the conservators were responsible, too, for removing unauthorized persons from the *conciliabulum*[166].

The third group of guards were the Knights of St. John of Jerusalem and Rhodes. Based on the precedent of the councils of Pisa and Konstanz a century earlier, these knights should have guarded the entrance to the Council. That task, however, was assigned to the conservators. Julius chose the knights, instead, as his personal bodyguard, a function exercised normally by the mazzieri. These minor papal officials tried under both Julius and Leo to assert their claim to being the pope's primary protectors during the formal processions to the Lateran Basilica. The knights, nonetheless, were positioned closer to the pope in the procession and once at the Lateran, they guarded the interior of the Basilica. Of the fifty or so knights there, three were chosen by Julius as his personal bodyguards within the *conciliabulum* and were assigned places of honor with the barons of Rome. The knights so honored were: Fabrizio de Caretto, Admiral of the Order, its representative at the papal court, and brother of cardinal

---

[166] MANSI 697D (names and function of conservators), DE GRASSI 844: 16, 847: 25 and 1039: 9 (conservators to guard entrance, together with the *tribunis populi, capurionibus* or heads of the 13 Roman rioni, and four mazzieri — apparently they sat during the lengthy sessions), 840: 16 (no mention of seats for conservators in de Grassi's model), 844: 7 (pope honors conservators at opening ceremonies), 846: 2 q. 17 (Julius rejects request that at least one of them be admitted to the session), 847: 11 (conservators seated at first session), 847: 25 (they take oath), MANSI 710E (conservators at second session), DE GRASSI 901: 8 (conservators outside chamber at third session), MANSI 766C (one of conservators present at fifth session), DE GRASSI 1039: 9 (*pristina institutio* prescribed that but one of the three be admitted, while the other two stood guard, but at this eighth session two conservators were seated), 1116: 14 (conservators seated at tenth session), MANSI 788C (two at sixth), 809C (*Conservatores* — Benzon *cum sociis* at the seventh session), 863A (two at ninth), 904E—05A (two at tenth); see supra nn. 125 and 127 for dispute; DE GRASSI 844: 33 and 1039: 19 (conservators silence people), 901: 8 (conservators to prevent disturbances); for removing people, see supra n. 152.

Carlo Domenico; Pietro Grimani, prior of Hungary and brother of cardinal Domenico; and Sisto della Rovere, prior of Rome, future bishop of Saluzzo, and relative of the pope. On Caretto's departure for Rhodes and election as Grand Master, he was replaced by Filippo Provana, commendatore of Chieri, and by Francesco de Guidono. At the ninth session, Antonio de Zúñiga, who was in litigation over the priorship of Castile, was also present. When Julius was prevented by illness from attending the fifth session, the knights gave their protection to the college of cardinals. After the Mass at which all the armed knights had been present, only three remained in the chamber for the deliberative portion of that session[167].

To round out this brief survey of the officials of the Council, two other groups of functionaries should be mentioned. The **assigners of places** in the Council, Paride de Grassi, Baldassare de Nicolai, and probably the latter's replacement Bernardino Guttierez, have already been treated and some of the controversies over precedence studied. Also named as officials at the first session were the **advocates** of the Council: Giustino de Carosi appointed fiscal advocate and the other advocates Paolo de Planca from Rome, Angelo de Cesi from Narni, Giovanni Batista Ricci (?) of Siena, and Melchiorre Baldassini of Naples whose denunciation of the Pragmatic Sanction at the fourth session has already been noted. These advocates do not figure prominently either in de Grassi's Diary or in del Monte's acts. The **officials of the papal chapel** such as acolytes and cantors who functioned during the liturgical ceremonies at the beginning or end of each session are described in passing in the Diary but will not be considered here[168].

---

[167] For the knights' dispute with the mazzieri, see supra n. 126; Mansi 696D, 697D (names and functions of the knights); DE GRASSI, 842: 32 super 19 and 844: 15 (knights as guardians of the pope and present inside the Basilica but outside the *cancelli* or *conciliabulum*), 846: 2 q. 17 and 847: 11 (of fifty knights, admit the procurator and the priors or Rome and Hungary); the Grand Prior of England, Thomas Docwra or Docrey (d. 1527), was appointed a member of the English delegation to the Council but seems never to have attended — see A. MIFSUD, The Knights Hospitallers of the Venerable Tongue of England in Malta, Valletta, Malta 1914, 42—43, 121—22, 187, and The Letters and Papers, Foreign and Domestic, of the Reign of Henry VIII, ed. J. S. BREWER, I London 1862, no. 2085 (4. II. 1512) p. 320 — in the commission of 11 April 1512 Sir Robert Wyngfeld replaced Docwra — see no. 3109, p. 342; on the contested priorship of Castile, see Luis SERRANO, Primeras negociaciones de Carlos V, Rey de España, con la Santa Sede (1516—1518), in: Escuela Española de Arqueología é Historia en Roma, Cuadernos de Trabajos; II Madrid 1914, 21—96, esp. 35—37, 72; for the efforts of Julius to obtain many knights to guard the Council, the reluctance of the knights on Rhodes to strip their defenses for this purpose, their order to the Italian and other Mediterranean provinces to send knights to Rome, and the replacement of Caretto with Provana, see Iacomo BOSIO, Dell'Istoria della Sacra Religione et Illustrissima Militia di San Giovanni Gierosolimitano, Pars Prima, Roma 1594, 501—06; for the dispensation from coming to Rome to defend the Council granted by Leo X on 5 June 1513 to the Commendatore of Brindisi who was also under orders both from the Admiral of the Knights to come to Rhodes to defend it and from his civil ruler Fernando of Aragon to go to Otranto for its defense, see ASV, Arm. XXXIX, vol. 30, fol. 30ʳ—31ʳ; for Provana as Caretto's representative, see MANSI 850E; DE GRASSI 921: 3, 21 (knights at fifth session).

[168] For a treatment of de Grassi, de Nicolai, and Guttierez and of the controversies over precedence, see supra nn. 48, 93—95, 123—29, 133—34; on the masters of ceremonies as the ordinary assigners of seats, see PATRIZI, Caeremoniale Romanum, fol. 60ʳ; DE GRASSI 847: 24 (naming of officials), MANSI

According to the Diary, de Grassi made an attempt about the time of the second session to have yet other officials appointed for the Council. He called to the attention of the commission of nine cardinals a passage in Patrizi's *Caeremoniale* which ordered that magistrates and ministers be nominated who would suggest material for the consideration of the council and would examine the faculties and public documents of those sent to it. In response the cardinals noted that the pope himself determined the agenda of the Lateran Council and that the four conciliar protonotaries had already been charged with examining the faculties of those sent to the Council — hence, neither group of new officials was needed. When de Grassi observed that the examination of faculties required legal learning and experience such as is had by auditors of the Rota and clerics of the Camera but not usually by protonotaries, the cardinals compromised by agreeing to have deputized at the third session clerics of the Camera who would assist the conciliar notaries in this task[169]. That such assistants were so deputized is not clear either in the Diary or in the official acts.

Consultative Structures

Although the organizational structure of the Lateran Council has already been studied elsewhere in some detail, the sources used were inadequate[170]. Dykmans' edition of de Grassi's Diary now allows for a fuller understanding of the development of consultative structures and of the seats of real power.

Julian Phase

Only gradually were bishops brought into the planning of the Council. Despite the papal exhortation read by cardinal Alessandro Farnese at the first session urging each and every member who had something useful and opportune to propose to the Council to bring it to the pope's attention, the agenda of the Council was most likely determined initially by Julius, the preparatory commission of cardinals, and the whole college of cardinals meeting in consistory. The frustration of the bishops at having been assigned a minor consultative role in the planning process was accentuated when at the first session they were also called upon to approve documents whose public recitation some could not even hear. The voice of cardinal Farnese, who was standing on the papal dais, was too weak to be understood by the prelates seated at the other end of the chamber. The bishops complained not only about the inaudibility of the lector, but also

---

697A—C (appointment of officials), 905: 6 (Baldassini's intervention at the fourth session); for a description of the position and functions of some of the officials of the papal chapel, see, for example, DE GRASSI 843: 2—29 and 847: 5—27.

[169] DE GRASSI 846: 2 q. 13 (officials appointed to examine faculties), 848: 6—7 (proposal for new officials and cardinals' responses), and PATRIZI, Caeremoniale Romanum, fol. 60ʳ (description of official suggesters and examiners).

[170] GUGLIA, Studien zur Geschichte (1899), 26—34; MINNICH, Episcopal Reform 352—65; for the notable lacunae in DOELLINGER, see his edition of the Diarium, 418—19.

about being required to vote on issues they had not previously considered. In response to their complaints, the pope and cardinals agreed that the reading of a *cedula* prior to a vote on its approval would be entrusted to a specially deputized prelate who was to stand in a wooden pulpit placed behind the benches of the cardinal deacons. To inform the prelates beforehand of the contents of a decree under consideration, a system of consultations was instituted[171].

The procedure used was not modeled on Konstanz and Basel, nor on the organizational structure of the rival Council of Pisa-Milan. A division of the fathers into four thematic groups organized according to the four conciliar nations was rejected by the commission of cardinals for fear that national rulers would thereby come to influence and dominate the Council. Instead, the nine cardinals of the commission decided that the conciliar fathers should be divided into nine groups by lot and not along national lines. Each of the cardinals would then take responsibility for the prelates in one of the groups, calling them to himself to inform them fully that at the next session, which was the second, the schismatic Council of Pisa would be declared null. The opinions of each prelate were to be ascertained by these cardinals. If most or all of the prelates agreed to this sentence against the Pisan Council, it would be freely proposed for enactment at the next session. If this was not agreeable to the prelates, some other provision would be made. But at least for the second session, this method of consultation would be employed. As regards subsequent sessions, another system would be devised[172].

That the cardinals did consult with the prelates prior to the second session is suggested by the actions of a bishop at that session. Only one of the one-hundred and two prelates did not fully approve the decree nullifying the Pisan Council and confirming three earlier papal measures against that council and its adherents. While these former condemnations had declared the supporters of Pisa to be heretics and schismatics, the Lateran decree did not specifically repeat this particular denunciation. The reason the Greek bishop, Alexius Celadoni, gave for his qualified vote was his desire that the Pisan fathers not be condemned unless first given the opportunity to be heard, should they so wish. To explain his position to the pope at greater length, Celadoni openly beckoned de Grassi to come to him. The Greek then handed the master a *cedula* elaborating on the reasons for his vote. He begged him to give it to Julius when the pope was at repose in his room. De Grassi honored his request. Celadoni's actions would suggest that he had been informed beforehand of the specific provision in the

---

[171] MANSI 695A—96A (exhortation to offer proposals), DE GRASSI, 848: 4 qq. 3 and 6 (complaints of prelates).

[172] DE GRASSI 848: 4 q. 6; Acta primi concilii Pisani, 159; on the voting procedures at Basel, see HEFE-LE-LECLERCQ VII—II 757—58, CREIGHTON II 72, and Joseph GILL, The Council of Florence, Cambridge 1959, 50—51, n. 4.

decree indirectly condemning the Pisan fathers and that he had time enough to formulate his objection and write it up in a document which could be presented to the pope. Prior consultation by a cardinal fits well into this scenario[173].

What provision, if any, was made for consultation of the prelates prior to the third and fourth sessions celebrated seven months later is not known. In the bull *Saluti gregis* of the fourth session, however, Julius declared his intention to appoint a commission of prelates from the various nations represented at the Lateran Council. They were to prepare reform measures for approval at subsequent sessions. The recommendations for dealing with the Pragmatic Sanction which were to come out of the meetings in the upper hall of the Lateran *(aula concilii?)* of the congregations of cardinals and other prelates were also to be presented at later sessions. Thus by the end of the first year, Julius was setting in place consultative structures. As is evident in his decree *Inter alia* of the fifth session, these commissions had yet to draw up specific measures by February of the following year. De Grassi relates in passing that Julius chose twenty-four prelates together with some cardinals to deliberate on how the Council could properly and juridically achieve its goals. The phrase *rite et iuridice* suggests that their concern may have been more with the legal form of the conciliar bulls than with their content, which Julius probably intended to decide[174].

Leonine Phase

On assuming the presidency of the Council, Leo like Julius before him urged the conciliar fathers at the sixth session to consider what should be done for the good of Christendom. Five days later, on 2 May 1513, a proposal was made in the sacred consistory to establish three conciliar commissions. At the command of Leo, a general congregation of all the prelates in Rome who are accustomed to vote in a council gathered on the afternoon of Friday the 13th of May in the *aula concilii* of the Lateran Palace. There the deans of the three orders of cardinals, Raffaelle Riario, Tamás Bakócz, and Alessandro Farnese, presided over a group of eighty-seven patriarchs, archbishops, and bishops. Riario informed them of Leo's wish to facilitate the business of the Council in three areas which demanded action: the reformation of morals and other things at Rome and elsewhere, the peace and quiet of the Christian republic, and the removal of schism. This tripartite division was later rearranged and expanded and the names by which these three deputations were known signified their principal tasks: peace, faith, and reform. Riario justified the establishment of

---

[173] DE GRASSI 848: 22, 27—28 (condemnation and Celadoni's reaction), MANSI 714A—15D (Lateran bull condemning the Pisan Council).

[174] MANSI 753B, D (Julius appoints working congregations), 772E—73A, C (they fail as yet to produce any measures); DE GRASSI 968: 2 (Julius appoints 24 prelates and charges them).

deputations to work on each of these topics on the grounds of the difficulty of assembling all the prelates for each item of business and by an appeal to the procedures used by other councils[175].

Unlike Julius who chose the prelates who were to collaborate with the cardinals in planning the Council's agenda, Leo requested through Riario that these assembled fathers themselves choose twenty-four grave and learned prelates to serve with the cardinals in the pope's presence regarding what is to be proposed to the Council. The fathers agreed to this proposal. A dispute over election procedures was resolved by resorting to white and black beans and declaring as winners those who received the least negative votes[176].

The twenty-four prelates thus selected shared a number of things in common. Most had some experience of working in the Roman curia where they could have become known to the bishops who chose them, many of whom were also curialists. Three out of four were members of the secular clergy, the religious bishops being four Franciscans, two Dominicans, and one Knight of St. John. Prominent Italian families were well represented. When it came to assigning these twenty-four prelates to particular deputations, Leo tended to appoint prelates from noble families to the deputation on peace, religious with training in philosophy and theology to the deputation on faith, and curialists to that on reform. Not all of those elected were in fact assigned. Leo apparently replaced two of these elected prelates, G. Contugi and G. Magnani, with G. P. Carafa and F. Piccolomini. While no reason for these changes was given, it may be suspected that the pope wanted men more experienced in diplomacy. Contugi seems to have been unhappy with his exclusion from the deputations and became, thereafter, a vocal opponent of many of the measures put to a vote before the Council[177].

In addition to the eight elected prelates who sat on each of the three deputations of peace, faith, and reform, Leo assigned to each working group eight cardinals, two bishops, and two heads of religious orders. These papal appointees who thus outnumbered by far the elected members could determine the direction and decisions of a deputation. Leo also seems to have presided over many of their meetings[178].

Little is known of what happened at the meetings of these deputations. De Grassi who was neither elected nor appointed to membership gave scant

---

[175] Mansi 788D (Leo urges fathers to consider Council's agenda), 794C—D (congregation of 13 May 1513 — the date of the 14th here given is incorrect since Friday that year fell on the 13th), de Grassi 964: 9 (Leo's exhortation at sixth session), 968: 1—2 (election of deputation members).

[176] De Grassi 968: 2 and Mansi 794DE.

[177] Mansi 794E—95B (names of elected members), 796A—97D (division of prelate into deputations); Minnich, Participants 181—96; Eugen Guglia, Craynensis - Tranensis ?, in: MIÖG 21 (1900) 536—39; and Minnich, Episcopal Reform 358—60.

[178] Mansi 796A—97D (Leo's appointees), Minnich, Concepts of Reform 244—46, 248—51, esp. 250 (Leo present at meetings).

attention to their workings. In a bull of the twelfth session Leo claimed that these three deputations had continued to function until then. That they were active until the time of the eighth session is evident from comments in the Council's official acts and from the few surviving working papers of Riario and the reform deputation. Provided the deputation on faith was entrusted with the task of reforming the calendar, its activities can be traced in part up to the eve of the last session. Scarcely anything is known about the discussions or decisions of the peace deputation after the eighth session. Up until that crucial session of 19 December 1513, the preparation of conciliar materials was initially done in these deputations. Two days prior to that session they met in the newly decorated Sistine Chapel for a formal reading of their *cedulae*. This important step toward finalizing the text of the conciliar bulls was itself preceded by a meeting of the Sacred Consistory which lasted for eight continuous hours, one of the lengthiest that men could then recall. The topic of this marathon meeting was the agenda of the eighth session. Immediately following this meeting, that session was postponed for three days so that the deputations could put their material in a fitting format. This sequence of events suggests that under Leo, too, the prelates were to be restricted to a consultative role and were to formalize decisions ultimately made in the Sacred Consistory[179].

The decision to continue the Council resulted in a number of important changes which de Grassi's Diary documents. The dissatisfaction of the bishops with the nature and scope of the conciliar reform registered at the eighth session soon grew into almost open rebellion. Leo's efforts to funnel all proposals through his carefully controlled deputations failed, for the bishops violently opposed what was being submitted for their approval. They began to meet on their own, even inviting the pope to attend and hear their complaints. Instead of conciliar materials being worked out in the deputations, new structures emerged. Leo, who claimed to have sympathy with the bishops, admitted that he was ultimately bound to the wishes of the cardinals and urged the bishops

---

[179] DE GRASSI 1039: 14 (de Grassi complains of not having been invited to congregation of the deputations); MANSI 989DE, 990B (Leo claims deputations continued to function to the end; HEFELE-HERGENROETHER VIII 810—13 (working papers of reform deputation), MINNICH, Concepts of Reform 244—51 (Riario's comments); HOFMANN II 242—48 (reform draft); for the propositions of the conciliar deputies on the reform of the calendar, see supra n. 4 and HEFELE-HERGENROETHER VIII 855; MANSI 819 A, C (peace deputation prior to eighth session); 819C (meeting in the cappela superiori palatii aposto-lici which is identified by ASV, Arch. Consist., Acta Vicecancell. 2, fol. 21 in combination with MANSI 664D and 977A as the Sistine Chapel — *superiori* because it was above the original library); for a report on the meeting of the Sacred Consistory, see the letter of Alberto Pio to Maximilian, Rome, 3 January 1514 in the Haus-, Hof- und Staatsarchiv (Wien), Maximiliana, box 31, folder I, fol. 10ᵛ: *Tribus aut quattuor interpositis diebus* (after Lang's official entry into Rome on 9 December 1513) *Summus consistorium habuit quo forte numquam nec ipse Julius et raro pontifices priores longius habuerunt, octo horis continuis in consistorio fuerunt patres ante prandium . . . in eo enim consistorio agendum erat de his quae in proxima sessione conciliari decernenda erant, quapropter plura et magna erant disserenda et rogandae sententiae patrum . . .* MANSI 819A (postponement of eighth session for three days *quia tamen resolutiones per eos factae in debitam schedulam adhuc reduci non potuerunt.*)

to deal directly with them. To handle these negotiations the bishops elected their own representatives. Before any document was submitted for approval at a formal session, it usually had first to be approved at a general congregation of all the cardinals and bishops meeting just prior to that session. And before this document was brought to the attention of a general congregation, it was probably cleared by the pope and cardinals[180].

Composition of Documents

The preparation of the documents to be approved by the Council was entrusted over the years to a variety of persons. The commission of ten cardinals appointed by Julius apparently drew up the decrees reforming curial and urban officials which were issued prior to the Council and reaffirmed at its fourth session. The bulls and other conciliar documents read at the opening ceremonies and first session by cardinal Farnese were written by him or else were either verbatim reiterations of previous papal decrees or adaptations made by him of the decrees of Konstanz. The role of the supervisory commission of nine cardinals was limited to deciding that the various items to be enacted at the first session were not to be divided up into separate bulls but collected into one. De Grassi and others seem to have reviewed a draft composed by Farnese to see that it conformed to its purpose and was well conceived. The master's criticism of the draft, however, did not alter, the cardinal's recitation. Whether Farnese continued to author the conciliar decrees is not known. At the congregation of cardinals prior to the fifth session, it was decided to reaffirm the earlier bull against simony in papal elections. The format given this decree was, however, criticized by the cardinals. The identity of its author was not given by de Grassi. Up until this time the cardinals and prelates specially deputized by Julius to draft conciliar materials had failed as yet to produce a single decree[181].

The evidence for establishing how conciliar documents were composed during the presidency of Leo is fragmentary. The initial drafting of the bulls approved at the eighth session was apparently entrusted to the three conciliar

---

[180] DE GRASSI 1039: 14 (bishops protest reform measures), MANSI 847C (Leo urges all to submit their propopals to the three senior cardinals from the congregation of the three deputations); DE GRASSI 1081: 2, 1116: 2—3, 1185: 1—6 (bishops go into almost open rebellion), 1081: 2 and 1185: 6 (Leo bound to cardinals), 1185: 2 (Leo sympathetic to bishops), MANSI 850CD and DE GRASSI 1185: 2 (bishops elect their own deputies to negotiate for them with cardinals), MANSI 848D—50D, 900 DE, 935E—39A, 977A—79E (general congregations meeting prior to the ninth through twelfth sessions), HEFELE-HERGENROETHER VIII 853-55 (report on the congregation prior to the last session).

[181] HOFMANN I 309 (pre-conciliar reforms), MANSI 753AB (reforms reaffirmed by Council), DE GRASSI 842: 14 and 32 super 14 (Farnese to read), 842: 23 and 32 super 23 (Farnese entrusted with the composition and form of the documents), 846: 2 qq. 7—8 (Farnese to write a composite bull and adapt the decree of Konstanz), 842: 23 and 844: 27 (de Grassi checks Farnese's draft), 922: 1 (criticism of format of decree), MANSI 773C (deputies' measures not yet readied). The important role played by Farnese at the Council (he was also a member both of the preparatory commission and of the deputation for peace) was acknowledged by Raffaele Lippo Brandolini in his Dialogus Leo nuncupatus, ed. Francesco FOGLIAZZI, Venezia 1753, where Farnese is portrayed as a leader at the Lateran Council.

deputations. One of these deputations, also referred to as a particular congregation, had a role in shaping the text presented for the approval of a general congregation on 29 April 1514 prior to the ninth session. The contents of the final version, however, were worked out two days later by a commission of cardinals and bishops. The material for the tenth session was discussed by the cardinals and congregations of prelates and finally approved at a general congregation. As a result of the numerous objections of the bishops, two general congregations had to be held prior to the eleventh session to work out the wording of both the narrative and prescriptive sections of the bull curtailing the exemptions of religious. Because of the disagreements among bishops consulted at a general congregation prior to the twelfth session, the *cedula* confirming and extending the legislation of Paul II against alienation of ecclesiastical property was dropped from the agenda of that session on the advice of three cardinals. Given such protests at the last minute, it is questionable whether the bishops had a significant role in preparing the drafts of conciliar documents[182].

It is much more probable that the contents of these decrees were determined in the tight inner circle of Tuscan curialist cardinals who were expert in canon law and functioned as Leo's intimate advisers. Although Leo's cousin, Giulio, was his most intimate adviser, he probably seldom involved himself directly in the preparation of documents. Instead, the person who most influenced their composition was probably Antonio del Monte. He had urged Julius to call the Council, was a member of its preparatory commission and reform deputation, and was the only cardinal to be a member of all four cardinalitial commissions charged with major conciliar affairs: negotiating the French adherence, resolving the dispute between bishops and friars, and presiding over the general congregations prior to the last two sessions. Leo's choice of him as editor of the official acts of the Council would also suggest that he was the man principally responsible for the formulation of its decrees. The two other cardinals who sat with him on three of the four special commissions, but not on that involving the religious, were Lorenzo Pucci and Pietro Accolti, also eminent canonists. Farnese helped with the French negotiations and was one of the presiding cardinals at the congregation prior to the eleventh session. Grimani was also at that congregation, probably due to his theological expertise and the pending decree on preaching. Vigerio, a Franciscan, assisted del Monte in hearing the

---

[182] MANSI 816BC (conciliar materials discussed in particular deputations prior to presentation at session), 819A (deputations draft *cedulas*), 797E and 819C (numerous discussions of material prior to its submission to Council), 849BC (texts shaped in deputation), DE GRASSI 1081: 2 (bishops insist on revisions in sections of a decree proposed), MANSI 850CD (text negotiated by cardinals and bishops), 898B—E (drafts discussed by cardinals and congregations of prelates), 900DE (general congregation prior to tenth session), 935E—39A (congregations prior to eleventh session), 977A—79E and HEFELE-HERGENROETHER VIII 853—55 (congregation prior to the twelfth session).

case of the bishops against the friars[183]. Thus, the most influential cardinals in determining the specifics of the decrees were probably del Monte, Pucci, and Accolti.

Given Leo's concern that official church documents be written in elegant, Ciceronian Latin, it is not surprising that he entrusted to his two domestic secretaries the final drafting of most of these decrees. Jacopo Sadoleto seems to have authored many of the decrees from the seventh to the tenth sessions, and Pietro Bembo those for the eleventh. Paolo Francesco Biondi, an apostolic secretary, apparently drafted the documents of the final session[184]. The role of the conciliar secretaries (Ingirhami, Saliceto, and Piperarius) did not, therefore, under Leo extend to the actual composition of the decrees.

The opening few words of the decrees indicated by whose authority they were being promulgated. Unlike those bulls at Konstanz, Basel, and the rival Pisan Council which were issued in the name of the council due to the prevailing conciliarist sentiment and the absence of a pope, both Julius and Leo followed for the most part the instructions in Patrizi's *Caeremoniale* and promulgated the Lateran decrees in their own names with the Council approving. This formula was also used for the decrees of the fifth session which Julius never attended, despite Patrizi's prescription that when the pope is not present, the decrees were to be issued in the name of the council[185].

---

[183] MANSI 834E—35A (commission handling negotiations with France), 936AB and 977BC (presiding cardinals at congregations); HEFELE-HERGENROETHER VIII 830 (del Monte and Vigero as judges of dispute between bishops and friars), 853—55 (report of Pucci probably to Giulio dei Medici on the final congregation); MANSI 652 BC (Leo commissions del Monte, who persuaded Julius to call the Council, to edit its acts); how it would have happened that both del Monte and Accolti, who presided over the congregation reviewing the material for the twelfth session, did not remove earlier from a *cedula* put to a vote at that session material they both disliked but waited for the session itself to complain is somewhat puzzling — see MANSI 977B and 986DE.

[184] For the official copies of Lateran decrees copied into the Vatican Registers, see for example: ASV, Reg. Vat. 1198, fols. 12ʳ—15ᵛ (*Meditatio cordis nostri* — Sadoleto), 1198, fols. 37ʳ—38ᵛ (*Apostolici regiminis solicitudo* —?, but checked by Bembo), 1198, fols. 38ᵛ—40ʳ (*Ad omnipotentis* —?, but checked by Bembo), 1198, fols. 36ʳ—37ʳ (*In apostolici culminis* —?, but checked by Bembo), 1195, fols. 95ʳ—99ʳ (*Posteaquam ad universalis*—Sadoleto), 1195, fols.85ʳ—94ʳ (*Supernae dispositionis arbitrio*—Sadoleto), 1195, fols. 168ʳ—70ʳ (*Inter multiplices* — Sadoleto), 1195, fols. 161ʳ—65ʳ (*Regiminis universalis ecclesiae* — Sadoleto), 1195, fols. 166ᵛ—67ᵛ (*Inter solicitudines* — Sadoleto), 1195, fols. 165ᵛ—66ʳ (*Cum inter alia* — Sadoleto), 1193, fols. 131ʳ—41ʳ (*Divina disponente clementia* — Bembo), 1197, fols. 46ʳ—55ʳ and 1204, fols 50ᵛ—61ᵛ (*Primitiva illa ecclesia* — Bembo), 1196, fols. 205ʳ—10ʳ (*Pastor aeternus* — Bembo), 1207, fols. 220ʳ—22ʳ (*Dum intra mentis* — P. Blondus), 1196, fols. 223ʳ—25ᵛ (*Constituti juxta verbum* — ?, a triplicated copy, this same document in the form of bulls signed by Bembo is still extant in two copies — see A. A. Arm. I—XVIII, nrs. 1905 and 1906; on the prominent role of Sadoleto and Bembo in Leo's Secretariat, see Richard M. DOUGLAS, Jacopo Sadoleto 1477—1547: Humanist and Reformer, Cambridge, Mass. 1959, 14—28; on Blondus, see HOFMANN II 119; on the Secretariat under Leo, see John A. F. THOMSON, Popes and Princes 1417—1517: Politics and Polity in the Late Medieval Church, London 1980, 101—02.

[185] PATRIZI, Caeremoniale Romanum, fol. 62ʳ; MANSI 768A and 772E (decrees of the fifth session issued in the name of the absent Julius); the suggestion of a surviving conciliarist mentality is to be found in Lang's cedula read at the third session which referred to the Lateran Council as representing the universal Church — see MANSI 733B.

The legal form of the documents read to the Council was on one occasion of concern to de Grassi. The procedure prescribed by Patrizi and apparently followed under Julius was that the *cedula* or draft of the decree (usually written on a scroll) was first read to the fathers assembled in a formal session, approved by a vote, marked by the protonotaries and scribes, put into the form of a public document, and only then furnished with the embossed apostolic seal of a bull. At the eighth session Leo handed to the lectors for reading not *cedulae* but bulls. De Grassi protested to the pope, noting that only after a *cedula* was approved should the bull be drawn up. Leo overruled his master, ordered the bulls read, and promised to revise them should they be found wanting[186].

To what extent documents were revised as the result of complaints registered during the voting at a formal session is an interesting problem. None of the *cedulae* read at a session are extant for study. Despite the literary format of del Monte's acts which supposedly record what the lectors read, the documents therein published are in fact not the draft *cedulae* subject to revisions but the final bulls which were promulgated. How the two versions may have differed is difficult to determine. Despite Leo's promise to emend the decrees at the eighth session if they did not please, a comparison of the prelates' complaints with the text published indicates that no alterations were made. At the ninth session, Leo explicitly promised to revise the wording of the Great Reform Bull in the light of the criticisms of the bishops, but once again there is no evidence of this having been done. When the cardinals complained at the twelfth session about specific points in the decree protecting their households from plunder during conclaves, the acts record that the *cedula* was revised according to their wishes. The petition of some bishops to have similar protection extended to their households was ignored. Even when a majority of the bishops openly opposed a decree, and singled out particular phrases for emendation, Leo overruled their requests and with the support of the cardinals achieved the electoral majority to have the law enacted intact[187]. This brief review suggests that once a *cedula* was approved at a general congregation, it was rarely revised as the result of adverse

---

[186] Patrizi, Caeremoniale Romanum, fol. 62ʳ; DE GRASSI 985: 13 (documents written on scrolls), 844: 29 (notaries called upon to draw up public instruments of an approved decree), 1039: 14 (de Grassi protests reading documents already sealed).

[187] That the supposed cedulae in del Monte are in fact the final texts can be established by comparing the del Monte versions with the bulls copied into the Vatican Registers cited above in n. 184; for examples of where complaints at the eighth session produced no revisions, compare Mansi 842D with 843C, 842E with 843D, and 846BC with 846E—47A. For the ninth session, see DE GRASSI, 1081: 10 and compare for example MANSI 886C (Trivulzio) with 878A, 886BC (complaints against the non-observance of common law by allowing cardinals and others to hold incompatible benefices, commendas, pensions, etc.) with 876A—77C, 886C (Aegidian constitutions) with 883A, 886C (blasphemers), with 881D—82D; for the twelfth session, see MANSI 986D—88B. DE GRASSI 1206: 3 (effectiveness of episcopal protests at a general congregation), 1206: 15 and 1231: 8 (futility of bishops' protests at a formal session), and MANSI 975A—B compared with 974A for specific complaints which were overruled.

votes cast at the formal session, unless, of course, the complaints came from powerful cardinals.

Use of Sacred Scripture

The prominence given at the Lateran Council to the Sacred Scriptures varied. While the sermons were generally replete with scriptural references, most of the decrees made only passing references or allusions to biblical texts. This was probably due to the literary style of the canonists and humanists who formulated them. The three decrees dealing with the soul's immortality, the *montes pietatis*, and preaching did quote Scripture more freely[188]. This is attributable most likely both to the need to furnish proof texts and to a mode of writing more common among theologians who were well represented on the faith deputation.

The degree of reverence accorded to books containing the Sacred Scriptures differed at various points in the conciliar ceremonies. A Gospel text was not only read as part of the Mass, but a passage specially selected for its relevance to the particular agenda of that session was chanted by a cardinal deacon. The texts were chosen from those used at the Sunday liturgies during the year and contained in a book of Gospels. This lectionary was paid great respect: it was accompanied by candles, incensed, and kissed by the pope. Although the lectionary was taken from atop the altar before the chanting ritual, it is not clear that it was replaced there afterwards[189].

No provisions were made for enthroning the Gospels at the Council. Patrizi ordered that, in addition to the high altar already in the church, another altar be erected before which the pope could pray on his arrival and face while saying the prayers of the conciliar liturgy. On this altar were to be placed a cross, the Blessed Sacrament, and some relics. Because of Julius' weakness which made genuflections before the Blessed Sacrament excessively difficult for him, de Grassi placed only a cross, some relics, and two candelabra on the altar of the *conciliabulum*. He makes no mention of the Gospel Book being put there. Instead, the pope and the college of cardinals ruled that the Bible was not to be displayed openly, but placed *under* the altar! Also kept there for reference were the book of canon law, ceremonial, and pontifical. At the ceremony for the swearing in of the conciliar officials the Scriptures were used. A missal opened to the page where the Crucifixion was depicted was placed at the feet of Julius.

---

[188] MANSI 842A—43C, 905C—07B, 944A—47D.

[189] DE GRASSI 847: 16 and 985: 6 (Gospel at Mass), 843: 29, 847: 20, 848: 21 (Gospel chanted after the litanies and prayers at the session); PATRIZI, Caeremoniale Romanum, fol. 62ʳ (reverence shown Gospel Book and regulation that the passage read should fit the agenda); DE GRASSI 843: 29 (lectionary taken from atop the altar), 848: 4 q. 5 (the cardinal deacons could share the task of chanting the Gospels), 842: 15, 848: 21, 1116: 6 (appropriate passages selected from Sunday liturgies).

Each official was brought to the pope and took his oath while touching "the most holy Scriptures"[190].

The great attention paid in the arrangement of the conciliar chamber and in the ordering of the ceremonies to highlight the preeminence of the pope indicates that symbolism was esteemed at the Council. The failure to pay throughout the conciliar ceremonies the symbolic honors to be accorded the Sacred Scriptures such as was done in the ritual of the Eastern Church and would soon be done in the Protestant liturgies, is one of the problematic aspects of the Roman Church on the eve of the Reformation[191].

Comments on Specific Participants

De Grassi's Diary is valuable for the information it provides not only about the ceremonies, organization, factions, and functioning of the Council, but also about some of its leading personalities. His comments about what these prelates said or did are often revealing. Julius is portrayed as so weak that he cannot, or but barely, genuflect during the services. He sits patiently through the ceremonies of a Council whose authority he fears. De Grassi's overall estimate of this pope is put in the mouth of others who praise Julius at the time of his death. His successor, Leo X, is described as a man of personal piety, who climbs the Holy Stairs and exorcizes a possessed woman. His promise to enact a conciliar reform of himself was not kept. Rather, he was tempermentally easy-going, able to smile and joke, eager to please every one, but ultimately allied with the college of cardinals and deferential to its senior members. His diplomatic handling of the French is evidenced in his private remarks to de Grassi. At the sixth session he said nothing in response to the request for a declaration of contumacy against the absent French prelates because, as he told de Grassi, he was unwilling to do anything contrary to the French king. At the eleventh session he confided that the absent French ambassadors, Denys and Guillaume Briçonnet, had secretly agreed to the abrogation of the Pragmatic Sanction but did not want to do so publicly at the Council lest they offend their fellow French prelates and country[192].

---

[190] Patrizi, Caeremoniale Romanum, 59r-v; De Grassi 840: 27 (items put atop the altar), 842: 29 and 32 super 29 (items put under the altar), 847: 23, 25 and Mansi 697C (swearing in ceremony).
[191] Romeo de Maio, The Book of the Gospels at the Oecumenical Councils, Città del Vaticano 1963, 14—15, 25, 33 — perhaps the lectionary used at the Lateran Council is the famous Codex Urbinas Latinus 10 written by Matteo di Ser Ercolano de' Contugi of Volterra.
[192] De Grassi 843: 26, 844: 17, 25 (Julius' weakness), 844: 26 (Julius' patience), 844: 37 and 883: 4—6 (Julius fears Council), 925: 4 (judgment on Julius' pontificate), 1039: 2 (Leo's personal piety), 985: 16 (Leo exorcizes possessed woman), 1039: 14 (promises to reform himself at next session), 989: 6 and 1039: 14 (Leo smiles and jokes), 1039: 14 and 1116: 15 (Leo tries to satisfy everyone), 1206: 16 (Leo deferential to senior cardinals), 964: 11 (not offend French king), 1206: 13 (Leo has the private consent of French ambassadors); Sanuto, I Diarii XXIV 105.

De Grassi also commented on some of the cardinals. His sympathies were not with the penitent Pisan cardinals whose humiliations at the reconciliation ceremonies he recorded in detail and whose further embarrassment he secured by having the Spaniard Carvajal sing the Mass at the final session. He was also critical of other foreign cardinals, accusing Lang and Bakócz of pomp and arrogance. What seems to have particularly irritated de Grassi was their failure to wear Roman style clerical garb. He made some interesting comments about three Italian cardinals. Vigerio is hailed as an expert in selecting scriptural texts for the liturgy. Despite complaints about his weak voice, Farnese continued to have a prominent role in the conciliar ceremonies and even volunteered to sing the Gospel at the tenth session. When Dovizi chanted the Gospel at the last session, it was for the first time in his life. Except for Celadoni and Cesare Riario, the homilists, and the lectors, individual bishops at the sessions did not generally merit comment[193].

Concluding Observations

This tendency to describe the activities of only a select group of prelates at the Council points to one of the weaknesses of the Diary. As mentioned earlier, de Grassi viewed the events at the Council either from the perspective of a ceremonialist or of a bishop interested in protecting the prestige and powers of his office. Not having membership on a conciliar deputation nor elected a delegate by his colleagues, de Grassi was not privy to the inner workings of the Council. Instead, he described them in general terms of the bishops and their opponents, the cardinals and friars. Individual prelates appear in these selections from his Diary only in so far as they had a role in the ceremonies or disrupted its smooth functioning. The Diary was never intended to be a full history of the Council, but rather a record of its ceremonies with some occasional digressions.

The information provided by the Diary is, nonetheless, invaluable, for it adds to, confirms, and corrects what is found elsewhere. Of particular merit are both the numerous details it provides on the actual functioning of the ceremonies and its surveys of the bishops' struggles with their opponents. The relationship between the Diary and the official acts of del Monte has already been studied by Guglia and the discrepancies between these two principal sources are noted by Dykmans. For supplementary accounts of individual sessions, the researcher should consult the reports sent by the ambassadors at the Council to their respective rulers[194]. Now that de Grassi's Diary is here

---

[193] DE GRASSI 989: 1—7, 10 (humiliations of Pisan cardinals), 990: 1 (their confession of guilt), 1231: 2 (Carvajal to sing final Mass), 848: 8 (Bakócz), 901: 10 (Lang), 842: 31 super 15 (Vigerio), 848: 4, qq. 3—4 (Farnese's weak voice, yet to continue reading), 1116: 6 (he volunteers to sing), 1231: 5 (Dovizi), 848: 27—28 (Celadoni), 923: 13 (Riario).

[194] Eugen GUGLIA, Studien zur Geschichte (1899) 1—21 (for the relationship between del Monte's acts and de Grassi's Diary, and for a survey of the extant ambassadors' reports).

published in a most useful edition by Dykmans, let us hope that future scholars of this Council will direct their attention to collecting and editing these ambassadors' reports.

II

The Orator of Jerusalem at Lateran V

The Problem

The official acts of the Fifth Lateran Council (1512-17) published at Rome by papal mandate four years later under the editorship of Cardinal Antonio del Monte list among the *oratores, senator,
illustres domini temporales* present at the ninth session on 5 May
1514 a certain *orator patriarchae Hierosolymitani* (¹). This entry
appears but once in the fourteen different rolls of council participants. No Christian name is given for either the orator or his
patriarch. Their identity poses many problems, thus far ignored
by historians of the Council (²).

Patriarchs of Jerusalem

The patriarchal seats of Jerusalem were probably not represented by an orator at Lateran V. The Latin patriarch from

(¹) *Sacrum Lateranense Concilium novissimum sub Iulio .II. et
Leone .X. celebratum.* ed. Antonius de MONTE, Romae 1521, reprinted in
Sacrorum conciliorum nova et amplissima collectio, ed. J. D. MANSI et al.,
Vol. 32 (1438-1459), Paris 1902 reprint, cols. 649-999 plus appendices;
the reference to the orator of the patriarch of Jerusalem is at col. 863a.
Hereafter references to this volume of MANSI are cited as "M" followed
by the column number and alphabetic subdivision.

(²) E.g., HEFELE-LECLERCQ, *Histoire des Conciles d'après les documents originaux* VIII-I, Paris 1917, 429; L. von PASTOR, *Storia dei papi
dalla fine del medio evo*, Vol. IV-I: *Storia dei papi nel periodo del Rinascimento: Leone X*, versione italiana di A. MERCATI, Roma 1960, 534-36;
O. RAYNALDUS, *Annales Ecclesiastici*, ed. A. THEINER, Paris 1877, ad
annum 1514, #3-36, hereafter cited as "RAYNALDUS" followed by the
year and numeric subdivision. For my recent study of the council's
rolls, see: *The Participants at the Fifth Lateran Council, Archivum Historiae
Pontificiae* 12 (1974).

1503/04 until shortly before his death in 1523 was the Spanish cardinal Bernardino López de Carvajal. Following his humiliating absolution in June of 1513 for having presided over the rival Council of Pisa, this high prelate was faithful in frequenting the Fifth Lateran. Since he attended the ninth session, there was no reason or right for him to have an orator also present (¹). The Greek patriarch Dorotheos II (1505-43) was apparently unsympathetic toward Rome given his discrimination against Latins a couple years later when Selim placed the major Christian shrines of Jerusalem under his jurisdiction. It is unlikely that he sent a representative to the council in Rome. The Armenian patriarch(s) Petros (1501-   ) or/and Sarguis III (1507-23) who had recently reestablished residence in the church-convent of St. James the Apostle in Jerusalem probably never sought relations with Rome — or, if this *patrik* did, available sources fail to report it (²).

(¹) G. van GULIK and C. EUBEL, *Hierarchia catholica media et recentioris aevi*, rev. L. SCHMITZ-KALLENBERG, reprinted Padova 1960, III, 210; P. ALONSO, *Carvajal (Bernardin Lopez de)*, DHGE XI (Paris 1949), cols. 1239-40.

(²) Chrysostomos A. PAPADOPOULOS, Ἱστορία τῆς ἐκκλησίας Ἱεροσολύμων, Alexandria 1910, 460-61; B. GANZAKETS, Yazordowtʿiwn patriarkʿacʿn Erowaslemi..., Istanbul 1872, 51; my gratitude to Joseph Hermans and Robert Taft, S.J., for their help on the modern Greek and Armenian sources respectively; Fr. TOURNEBIZE, *Arménie*, DHGE 4 (Paris 1930), col. 375; J. MÉCÉRIAN, *Histoire et institutions de l'Eglise arménienne: Évolution nationale et doctrinale, spiritualité – monachisme*, Vol. 30 of *Recherches de l'Institut de Lettre Orientales de Beyrouth*, Beyrouth 1965, 328-329; G. GOLUBOVICH, ed., *Croniche ovvero Annali di Terra Santa de P. Pietro Verniero di Montepeloso*, Vol. 5, which is Vol. 10 of *Biblioteca Bio-Bibliografica della Terra Santa e dell'Oriente Francescano: Nuova serie – documenti*, Quaracchi 1936, 7; C. EUBEL, *Hierarchia catholica*, 210, Hierosolymitan, n. 1 errs in reporting that (Dorotheos) the Greek patriarch of Jerusalem rather than (Theophilus or Philotheus) the patriarch of Alexandria writing in Greek sought confirmation from Rome in 1523. Confer: RAYNALDUS 1523 # 107; J. PAQUIER, *L'Humanisme et la Réforme: Jérôme Aléandre de sa naissance a la fin de son séjour a Brindes (1480-1529)*, Paris 1900, 296; M. LE QUIEN, *Oriens Christianus, in quatuor patriarchatus digestus, in quo exhibentur ecclesiae, patriarchae, caeterique praesules totius orientis*, Paris 1740, II, col. 501.

LATIN REPRESENTATIVE IN JERUSALEM

The affairs of Latin Christendom in Jerusalem during this period of the council were handled by the Franciscan Guardian of the Holy Land, the Venetian patrician Francesco Suriano (11.VI. 1512–24.VI.1514). This seasoned expert on the Near East had recently returned from imprisonment by the Moslems in Egypt to restore the plundered mission in the Holy Land, defend the rights of the Latins (this time against the incursions of Georgian monks), and try to dissuade the Portuguese from raiding Egyptian commerce in the Indian Ocean lest in revenge the Moslems carry out their threat to destroy the Holy Sepulchre. Given his earlier endeavor to encourage the Maronite patriarch to seek confirmation of his election by Rome, Suriano may once again as Guardian have collaborated in similar efforts by his fellow Franciscans in Syria (¹). Although the highest ranking Latin churchman resident in the Holy Land, Suriano apparently did not enjoy the right of direct representation at the council. His interests were handled in the Roman Curia by the Franciscan commissar Cristoforo de Numai da Forli and in the Lateran Council by the Minister General Bernardino Prato de Chieri (²). Besides, it would be quite unusual for the Guardian to be listed as a patriarch and among the temporal powers.

PATRIARCH OF THE MARONITES

The patriarch in the Levant most friendly to Rome at this time was Simʿān ibn Dāwūd ibn Ḥassān al-Ḥadaṭī (1492-1524), spiritual head of the Maronite Christian community. In his struggle against monophysite influences coming from Jacobite missionaries at work among his people and from the apostate Maronite mouqaddam who encouraged them, Simʿān was helped

---

(¹) G. GOLUBOVICH, *Series cronologica dei reverendissimi superiori di Terra Santa ossia dei provinciali custodi e presidenti della medesima*, Jerusalem 1898, 35-37, 43; and *Il Trattato di Terra Santa e dell'oriente di frate Francesco Suriano missionario e viaggiatore del secolo XV*, Milan 1900, liv-lix.

(²) L. WADDING, *Annales Minorum seu Trium Ordinum*, rev. J.M. FONSECA DA EVORA, Quaracchi 1933, XV, 539; M 831a, 862c.

by the Franciscans ([1]). As early as 1494 Suriano urged him to give but one more testimony of his fellowship in the faith by seeking confirmation in his office by Rome. The aged patriarch wrote Rome, but for some reason the lines of communication were not then opened ([2]). Twenty years later Sim'ān once again sought confirmation by the pope. To this end he dispatched the Maronite Buṭrus Būlus with letters of recommendation from the Franciscan Guardian of Beyrouth, Marco da Firenze, written in the name of the patriarch. This nuncio arrived in Rome in time for the ninth session ([3]). Like the three Maronite nuncios who came for the council a year later, Buṭrus Būlus may also have resided with the Latin patriarch of Jerusalem, Cardinal Carvajal ([4]). If this nuncio attended the ninth session, confusion arising from his place of residence at Rome may have resulted in the misnomer *orator patriarchae Hierosolymitani.*

In 1514 Rome was reserved in its reception of this Maronite mission. On the advice of the college of cardinals, Leo X (1513-21) refused to confirm Sim'ān's election as patriarch without first being assured of his orthodoxy and furnished with the proper documents. The papal curia seems to have lost track of its own records regarding the Maronite Church and needed to know how the patriarch was elected, what pontifical insignia he wore, and where he resided. Rome was also concerned about his orthodoxy ([5]). While the pope later rejoiced to learn from Suriano of the Maronites' steady fidelity to Rome, Leo, nonetheless, sent two Franciscans, Gianfrancesco Cina da Potenza and Francesco da Rieti, to instruct

([1]) P. DIB, *Histoire de l'Eglise Maronite*, Vol. I of *Mélanges et Documents*, Beyrouth 1962, 99-102.

([2]) B. GHOBAIRA AL-GHAZIRI, *Rome et l'Eglise Syrienne-Maronite d'Antioche (517-1531)*: *Théses, documents, lettres*, Beyrouth 1906, 160-62; P. DIB, *Histoire de l'Eglise*, 100.

([3]) L. WADDING, *Annales Minorum*, XV, 805, 812; Joseph HERGENROETHER, *Regesta Leonis X*, Freiburg im Breisgau 1884-91, #17, 325.

([4]) Teseo Ambrogio degli ALBONESI, *Introductio in Chaldaicam linguam, Syriacam, atque Armenicam, et decem alias linguas. Characterum differentium alphabeta, circiter quadraginta, et eorumdem invicem conformatio. Mystica et cabalistica quamplurima scitu digna. Et descriptio ac simulachrum Phagoti Afranii*, Pavia 1539, 14ʳ.

([5]) T. ANAISSI, *Bullarium Maronitarum complectens bullas, brevia, epistolas, constitutiones aliaque documenta a Romanis pontificibus ad patriarchas Antiochenas Syro-Maronitarum missa*, Roma 1911, 25-28, 44.

the patriarch in the Catholic faith should he have erred (¹). A year later permission was denied to the Maronite legation in Rome for celebrating the divine liturgy until their liturgical texts were first examined and approved (²). Since Buṭrus Būlus in 1514 could produce no documents from the patriarch himself, but only letters of recommendation from the Franciscan Guardian of Beyrouth, the pope sent him back to Lebanon to secure the necessary documents (³). Given this caution on the part of Rome and the nuncio's lack of instruments, the Maronite may well have been denied incorporation into the council's membership had he requested it.

By the time del Monte published the acts of Lateran V, few, if any, would have confused the seat of the Maronite patriarch with Jerusalem. At the eleventh session on 19 December 1516, the three orators of this patriarch (Yūsuf al–Ḥūri, a priest, Ilyās ibn Zarzūr al–Ḥadaṭī, a deacon monk, and Ilyās ibn Ibrāhīm, a subdeacon monk — accompanied by the Franciscan Gianfrancesco Cina) paid obedience to the pope and read to the council in Arabic the mandate of the Maronite patriarch. A Latin translation immediately followed. From this document Maronite orthodoxy and loyalty to Rome were evident. It was also clear that the patriarchal seat was the monastery of Qannūbīn on Mount Lebanon in Syria (⁴). When contemporaries made mistakes about

---

(¹) G. GOLUBOVICH, *Il Trattato*, lix-lxi; T. ANAISSI, *Bullarium Maronitarum*, 32-35, 46.

(²) T. A. degli ALBONESI, *Introductio in Chaldaicam linguam* 14ʳ⁻ᵛ.

(³) T. ANAISSI, *Bullarium Maronitarum*, 28-29, 44.

(⁴) M. 942a-43e, 1003c-16a; I. ḤARFŪŠ, *Al–Kunūz al–Makhfiyyah*, in *Al-Manārat* 4 (1933), 595, n.; C. CAVEDONI, *Notizia letteraria di alcuni codici orientali e greci della Reale Biblioteca Estense che già furono di Alberto Pio principe di Carpi, Memorie di religione, di morale e di letteratura,* Series 3, XVII (Modena 1834), 5; G. LEVI DELLA VIDA, *Ricerche sulla formazione del più antico fondo dei Manoscritti orientali della Biblioteca Vaticana* (Vol. 92 of *Studi e Testi*), Città del Vaticano 1939, 133 n. 2; E. EL-HAYEK, *Maronite Rite, New Catholic Encyclopedia*, New York 1967, IX, 250. The conciliar program sent to the pope in 1513 clearly identified the center of the Maronites as Mount Lebanon - confer: P. GIUSTINIANI and P. QUIRINI, *Libellus ad Leonem X. Pontificem Maximum, Annales Camaldulenses Ordinis Sancti Benedicti,* ed. G. B. MITTERELLI and A. COSTADONI, Venezia 1773, IX, col. 660. I am grateful to Yousef Jamal Alami, Assistant Director General of the Jordanian Department of Antiquities, for his assistance with the Arabic.

the location of the Maronite seat, they confused it with Antioch in Syria and not with Jerusalem ([1]). When correcting the acts of Lateran V before publication ([2]), del Monte could easily have changed Jerusalem to Maronites or Mount Lebanon — had it been necessary. Since it was also known that Simʿān was only spiritual head of the Maronites ([3]), it is puzzling why his orator, if he were present, would be listed among the representatives of temporal powers.

A CLUE?

The Maronite orators in Rome were at times confused with the dark skinned people from Ethiopia ([4]). This error may help to explain an ambiguous statement coming from the pen of an eye-witness to the events in Rome at the time of the council. Teseo Ambrogio degli Albonesi (1459-c. 1540), the famous professor of oriental languages from Pavia, reported in a book published in 1539 an argument he had with Johann Potken from Schwerte in Westphalia (c. 1470-1524) ([5]). While Potken was still working on his *Psalterium Aethiopicum* printed in Rome in 1513 ([6]), Ambrogio tried in vain to dissuade him from accepting as true what the

---

([1]) E.g. While *Il Diario di Leone X di Paride de Grassi*, ed. P. DELICATI and M. ARMELLINI, Roma 1884, 39 does not give the title of the patriarch, the fuller version in the Biblioteca Apostolica Vaticana, Mss. Vat. Lat. 5636, fol. 153ᵛ, describes his legation at Lateran V as "tres oratores nigri ex Ethiopia nomine patriarche Antiocheni".

([2]) M. 652c.

([3]) T. ANAISSI, *Bullarium Maronitarum*, 29-30, 34-37; Elias filius Junes (Ximes) filii Jacob seems to have been temporal ruler of only the Maronites on Cyprus, L. WADDING, *Annales Minorum*, XV, 811, 820; P. DIB, *Histoire de l'Eglise*, 101-02; M. 1010c; RAYNALDUS 1516 n. 6.

([4]) *Il Diario*, 39; N. WISEMAN, *Horae Syriacae seu commentationes et anecdota res vel litteras Syriacas spectantia*, Roma 1828, I, 188, n. 31.

([5]) T. A. degli ALBONESI, *Introductio in Chaldaicam linguam* 13ᵛ-15ʳ; G. LEVI DELLA VIDA, *Albonesi, Teseo Ambrogio degli, Dizionario biografico degli Italiani*, II (Roma 1960), 39-42; A.-D. von den BRINCKEN, *Johann Potken aus Schwerte, Propst von St. Georg in Köln, Der erste Äthiopologe des Abendlandes, Aus kölnischer und rheinischer Geschichte: Festgabe Arnold Güttsches zum 65. Geburtstag gewidmet*, ed. H. Blum, Köln 1969, 81-114.

([6]) J. POTKEN, *Psalterium aethiopicum: psalmi, cantica veteris et novi testamenti, et canticum canticorum, quibus accessit specimen alphabeti et numeri aethiopice studio Ioannis Potken cum ejus praefatione latina*, Romae 1513.

German's native Ethiopian instructors had told him about their liturgical language Ge'ez: that it was a Chaldaic language. Ambrogio continued his account:

> Verum paucos ab hinc annos ab Iulio, eius
> nominis, Secundo, Pontifice maximo, conuocato
> oecumenico, incohatoque Concilio, et sub Leone
> Decimo perseuerante. Venere Romam ad Synodum,
> a Presbytero Iano, seu Ioanne directi Indi.
> Venerunt et Syri Chaldei, Iosephus Sacerdos,
> Moyses monachus, Diaconus, et Elias, subdiaconus (¹).

This statement is open to different interpretations.

From the context it may seem that Ambrogio has identified the Maronites with Ethiopians, and the *et* following *Venerunt* functions as a conjunction of emphatic apposition. This interpretation, however, is full of difficulties. Ambrogio knew the difference between Ge'ez and Syrian script. He had examined Potken's edition closely enough to give him detailed criticisms; and he was commissioned by Carvajal to translate the liturgical works of the Maronites into Latin with the help of the subdeacon monk Ilyās ibn Ibrāhīm and of Joseph Gallus, the son of the famous Jewish doctor Samuel Zarfati. In return for instructions in Latin, Ilyās taught Ambrogio Syrian (²). It is hard to believe that after two years of so close a relationship with this Maronite, he could still err in referring to these Syrian Christians as true Ethiopians sent by Prester John. Cardinal Wiseman went so far as to deny that the Maronite nuncios were Syrians at all, but instead were really Ethiopians (³). Cavedoni, however, holds that there was a separate Ethiopian embassy distinct from the Maronite (⁴).

If an Ethiopian delegation did come for the council, it is still unclear as to when it arrived. Ambrogio indicated that it was a

---

(¹) T. A. degli ALBONESI, *Introductio in Chaldaicam linguam* 14ʳ; Teseo Ambrogio, writing some twenty years after the close of the council, apparently erred in reporting that Mūsā, instead of Ilyās ibn Zarzūr al-Ḥadaṯi, was a member of the legation to Lateran V. He probably confused this legation with that sent six years later to Hadrian VI. Confer: I. ḤARFŪŠ, *al–Kunūz al–Makhfiyyah*, 595, n.

(²) *Ibid.*, 13ᵛ, 14ᵛ-15ʳ; W. ROSCOE, *The Life and Pontificate of Leo the Tenth*, rev. W. HAZLITT, London 1846, I, 355.

(³) N. WISEMAN, I, 188, n. 31.

(⁴) C. CAVEDONI, *Notizia letteraria*, 14.

couple or few years after his argument with Potken (*paucos ab hinc annos*) and during Leo's presidency of the council (*sub Leone Decimo perseuerante*) — thus somewhere between 1513 and 1517. Since the Ethiopians are mentioned before the Maronites, this may imply that they came before the 1515/16 legation from Syria and perhaps in time for the ninth session in 1514. The existence of such a delegation to the Lateran Council would mean that the famous Zaaga Zab embassy of 1529-39 need not be considered the first serious effort to establish relations between Ethiopia and Rome (¹).

PRESTER JOHN AND THE ABUNA OF ABYSSINIA

In the early sixteenth century, the Portuguese explorer in the Indian Ocean, Tristão da Cunha, sent a delegation to the court of Ethiopia where, he heard, the fabled Prester John ruled. When these Portuguese arrived there in 1508, they found a Christian country ruled in the name of the twelve-year old emperor Lebna Dengel (1508-40) by his step-grandmother, the capable and popular dowager empress Eleni (1508-28). Upon learning of a powerful Christian naval force nearby, the Ethiopian monarch conceived that an ancient prophecy of the final defeat of the Moslems was soon to be realized and decided to secure a military alliance with the Portuguese by sending a delegation to their king (²).

To avoid calling attention to itself as the embassy passed through hostile Moslem lands, its composition was small and its gifts inconspicious. The legation was headed by an aged Armenian merchant, the brother of a servant of the Emperor. Of Christian birth, Matthaeus travelled under the pseudonym of Abraham, bringing with him a letter of introduction from the young Emperor approved by the "patriarch" of Abyssinia, the metropolitan or abuna Mārqos (d. 1530), and such gifts as a number of gold medallions, a relic of the true cross from Jerusalem, and a bene-

---

(¹) Asa J. DAVIS, *Background to the Zaaga Zab Embassy: an Ethiopian Diplomatic Mission to Portugal*, Studia 32 (1971), 211-302.

(²) A. DAVIS, *Background to Zab Embassy*, 213-14; Girma BESHAH and Merid Wolde AREGAY, *The Question of the Union of the Churches in Luso-Ethiopian Relations (1500-1632)*, Lisbon 1964, 20-23; I Diarii di Marino Sanuto, ed. F. STEFANI, G. BERCHET, N. BAROZZI, Venezia 1887, XVIII, col. 141.

diction sent by the Ethiopian priests of Jerusalem. The letter of introduction empowered Matthaeus to speak on unspecified topics in the name of the Emperor. Accompanying the ancient merchant was a young distinguished Ethiopian of noble birth. It is unknown if the delegation were any larger in size. After a series of long delays the embassy from Prester John arrived in Europe by way of Goa in India and with the assistance of the Portuguese [1].

Soon after his arrival in Lisbon on 19 February 1514, Matthaeus was warmly received by Manuel, king of Portugal, and by his royal court. In addition to military matters discussed, the merchant ventured to speak on the topic of religion. He claimed that the Church of Ethiopia recognized the pope as head of all Christians and had wished to send representatives to Rome to acknowledge his supremacy, but had been prevented thus far by the distance and intervening lands of hostile Moslems. The Portuguese, however, had now opened up a way by sea. In the event of Mārqos' death, this Church requested the pope to appoint a successor. When questioned further by the prelates of the Portuguese court on the doctrine and religious practices of the Ethiopian Church, the Armenian layman made a number of mistakes which were discovered only years later [2]. Matthaeus apparently remained in Lisbon for over a year, leaving for Ethiopia on 7 April 1515 with the armada of the new Portuguese governor in the East, Lopo Soares de Alvarenza. Not until 1520, however, did he reach his destination due to Moslem hostilities [3].

Tristão da Cunha, who had been earlier involved in this successful effort to contact the court of Prester John, was sent to Rome at the head of an impressive legation representing the extent and variety of the lands under the sway of the Portuguese monarch. Given the reported desire of the Ethiopians to pay obedience to

---

[1] *I Diarii*, col. 141-142; A. DAVIS, *Background to Zab Embassy*, 242, 281-82; RAYNALDUS 1514 #103.

[2] D. de GÓIS, *Cronica do felicissimo rei D. Manuel*, Coimbra 1954, 219-23; *Corpo diplomatico Portuguez contendo os actos e relações politicas e diplomaticas de Portugal com as diversas potencias do mundo deside o seculo XVI até os nossos dias*, Vol. 1: *Relações com a Curia Romana*, ed. L. A. REBELLO DA SILVA, Lisbon 1862, 248-59.

[3] de GÓIS, *Cronica*, 278; A. DAVIS, *Background to Zab Embassy*, 242-43; G. BESHAH and M. W. AREGAY, *Question of Union*, 26, 29.

the pope, it would be surprising if among its seventy members there were not also an Abyssinian — but available documents make no mention of an African member of this delegation. Arriving in Rome on 12 March 1514, this embassy made a very favorable impression on the people of the city who were amazed at the splendor and diversity of the costumes worn and at the wild animals brought as gifts, especially the elephant. In a series of audiences following the presentation of their credentials on 20 March, the Portuguese orators informed Pope Leo of what the Ethiopian ambassador Matthaeus had told their king (¹).

Leo responded to the news with great joy. Within a month a long papal letter was sent to king Manuel in which Leo professed his readiness to grant all the pious desires of the Ethiopian Emperor and his "patriarch". Without the instruments and profession of orthodoxy demanded of the Maronite patriarch, the pope proceeded to confirm (the monophysite!) Mārqos in his office. While tolerating their paschal practices, Leo demanded that the rite of circumscision be abolished. He also promised to send a nuncio (perhaps Antonio Pucci, the homilist at the coming ninth session of the Council) to king Manuel to treat these and other religious matters and to gain further information. The pope also pledged to write the Abyssinian Emperor and his Regent (²). In October of that year Leo sent his own legate to Ethiopia, the Florentine Andrea Corsalo, to bring papal greeting and exhortations in the faith (³). Given the enthusiasm shown by Leo for the news of the submission of the Ethiopian Church to Rome and of the projected alliance of Abyssinia with Portugal against the Moslems, it would not be unreasonable for the pontiff to have an Ethiopian representative present at the Fifth Lateran Council called to secure, among other things, peace among Christian princes, a crusade against the infidels, and unity in the Church (⁴).

(¹) E. RODOCANACHI, *Histoire de Rome: Le Pontificat de Léon X, 1513-1521*, Paris 1931, 69; A. BRĀSIO, *Embaixada do Congo a Roma em 1514? Studia* 32 (1971), 77-87.

(²) *Corpo diplomatico*, 248-50.

(³) RAYNALDUS 1514 #102.

(⁴) M. 667b-d, 788de, 796ab, 843e-45d; N. H. MINNICH, *Concepts of Reform Proposed at the Fifth Lateran Council, Archivum Historiae Pontificiae* 7 (1969), 237-38; Giustiniani who had visited Jerusalem in 1507 and come in contact with the oriental communities there, including the

The Portuguese sent to Rome in 1514 may not have been the first to inform pope Leo of the Ethiopians. Toward the beginning of his reign, a delegation of Ethiopians from Jerusalem arrived in Rome to pay homage to the pontiff (¹). They may have come on instructions of Lebna Dengel, in accordance with the Abyssinian monastic practice of pilgrimages, or at the urging of Franciscans. Ethiopia maintained close ties with Jerusalem with new monks visiting it annually and some going on from there to the shrines of Western Christendom (²). The Franciscans of the Holy Land had earlier sent a delegation of Abyssinian monks to Sixtus IV to seek his blessing on the coronation of their emperor (negus) Eskender (1478-94). The friars remained over the years on good terms with the Abyssinian community of Jerusalem and may have been involved once again in this mission to Leo X, just as they were instrumental at the time of the council in bringing the Maronites into closer relations with Rome (³). This second Ethiopian legation (to Leo X) may be the one which Ambrogio claimed was sent to the council by Prester John.

A member of this delegation came to the attention of pope Leo, the Dominican abbā Tomās (c. 1484-1518) from Scios in the Ethiopian heartland. Son of high nobility whose sisters had married tributary kings, Tomās entered the Dominicans at fifteen years of age, being ordained at twenty. Learned and pious, he was sent by obedience and his own desires to visit the major shrines

---

Ethiopian, urged Leo X to invite bishops and priests from these separated churches to attend the Lateran Council — confer: *Libellus ad Leonem*, 664; S. TRAMOTIN, *Il problema delle chiese separate nel 'Libellus ad Leonem X' dei veneziani Paolo Giustiniani e Pietro Quirini (1513)*, Studia Patavina 11 (1964), 276, 280.

(¹) E. CERULLI, *Etiopi in Palestina: Storia della comunità etiopica di Gerusalemme*, I (Vol. 12 of *Collezione scientifica e documentaria a cura del Ministero dell'Africa Italiana*), Roma 1943, 397-98.

(²) R. LEFEVRE, *Riflessi etiopici nella cultura europea del medioevo e del rinascimento*, Annali Lateranensi 8 (1944), 74; A.-D. von den BRINCKEN, *Johann Potken*, 92, 99-100, 105.

(³) M. CHAÎNE, *Un monastère étiopien à Rome au XV et XVIᵉ siècle: San Stefano dei Mori*, Mélanges de la Faculté Orientale de la Université Saint-Joseph, Beyrouth 5 (1911), 7; G. GOLUBOVICH, *Il Trattato*, xxxviii-xxxix, n. 1, 80.

of Christendom: Jerusalem, Rome, and Compostella. While in the Holy Land he was elected prior of the Dominican convent of the Nativity at Bethlehem. Arriving in Rome he was warmly received by the pope who inquired first of the Portuguese ambassador about this friar's national origins and then spoke to Tomās himself through interpreters about his country. The pope took a special interest in him, having him named prior of the Ethiopian monastery-hospice of San Stefano dei Mori at Rome. Tomās may have been in Rome at the time of the ninth session since it was not until the spring of the following year that he appeared in Valencia on his way to Compostella ([1]).

In addition to the young Ethiopian nobleman who accompanied the aged Matthaeus to Lisbon and who may have gone on from there to Rome, Tomās who was also of noble birth and whose orthodoxy as a Dominican was probably not questioned would have been a logical candidate to represent at Lateran V the Ethiopian negus and his abuna. Since the exact location of the land of Prester John was for years yet beyond the ken of most people, while the Ethiopian community at Jerusalem was known as the source of this legation to Leo, it would not be that surprising if the representative of the negus Lebna Dengel who was considered both a spiritual and temporal ruler (Prester John) and his abuna Mārqos whom Leo had just confirmed in his office would be listed as *orator patriarchae Hierosolymitani* ([2]).

([1]) MAURO DA LEONESSA, *Santo Stefano Maggiore degli Abissini e le relazioni Romano-etiopiche*, Città del Vaticano 1929, 187; R. LEFEVRE, *Reflessi etiopici*, 71; S. RAZZI, *Vite de i santi e beati, così huomini, come donne del sacro ordine de' fratri predicatori*, Firenze 1577, 292-95; E. CERULLI, *Etiopi in Palestina*, 397-98. By the time Tomās reached Pisa in September of 1516, he had already spent altogether eighteen months in Italy. Given the leisurely pace of his pilgrimages and his appointment as prior before departing for Compostella, his arrival in Pisa may have been on his return trip from Spain with the year and a half spent in Italy thus falling during 1513-14.

([2]) R. LEFEVRE, *Riflessi etiopici*, 46-47, 58-89; S. RAZZI, *Vite de i santi*, 293; Giustiniani, Quirini, and Suriano, however, placed the land of Prester John at the upper reaches of the Nile: *Libellus ad Leonem*, col. 660 and *Il Trattato*, 80.

CONCLUSION

While this evidence would seem to point to an Ethiopian representative at Lateran V, it is too inconclusive to rule out definitively the other candidates. The Latin, Greek, and Armenian patriarchs of Jerusalem and the Franciscan Guardian of the Holy Land are, however, not very strong contenders for having an orator at the council. The Maronite nuncio Buṭrus Būlus seems to be the only other likely candidate. Not until new documents are discovered can the identity of the "orator of the patriarch of Jerusalem " at Lateran V be finally resolved.

III

The Function of Sacred Scripture in the Decrees of the Fifth Lateran Council (1512–17)

At the time of the Fifth Lateran Council (1512–1517), Sacred Scripture had come to command the attention of some of Latin Christendom's leading thinkers. In Spain, a group of eminent scholars assembled by cardinal Francisco Jimenez de Cisneros was preparing the famous Complutensian Polyglot Bible which was published at Alcala from 1514 to 1517. In France, Jacques Lefèvre d'Etaples published in 1512 his corrections of the Vulgate version and commentaries on the Pauline epistles, which he revised for publication in 1515. With the encouragement of John Colet who led the way in England with his historical and philosophical exegesis of selected books of the Bible, the Dutchman Desiderius Erasmus of Rotterdam caused a stir in learned circles with his publication on the Froben press in Basel in 1516 of his *Novum Instrumentum*. This work, praised by Leo X and dedicated to him in its 1518 revised second edition, became the first publicly sold printed edition of the Greek text, together with a fresh Latin translation and scholarly annotations. In their 1513 *Libellus ad Leonem X,* written as a program of reform for the Lateran Council, the Venetian Camaldolese hermit-humanists Paolo Giustiniani and Pietro Quirini urged that the Bible become the basis of clerical studies and of sermons preached to the laity, and that it be translated into the vernacular, so that it will be more

---

[1] For a recent overview of Renaissance scriptural studies which devotes special attention to the Complutensian New Testament and to the work of Erasmus, see Jerry H. BENTLEY, *Humanists and Holy Writ: New Testament Scholarship in the Renaissance* (Princeton, N.J., 1983), esp. 70–193. On Lefèvre's scriptural scholarship, see Eugene Rice, ed., *The Prefatory Epistles of Jacques Lefèvre d' Etaples and Related Texts* (New York, 1972) esp. xxi – xxiv and 295–302; Heiko A. OBERMAN, *Forerunners of the Reformation: The Shape of Late Medieval Thought, Illustrated by Key Documents,* trans. Paul L. NYHUS (New York, 1966), 281–307; and Philip Edgcumbe HUGHES, *Lefèvre: Pioneer of Ecclesiastical Renewal in France* (Grand Rapids, Michigan, 1984), 53–73. On Colet, see P. Albert DUHAMEL, "The Oxford Lectures of John Colet," *Journal of the History of Ideas* 14 (1953), 493–510 and Catherine A. L. JARROTT, "Erasmus' Annotations and Colet's Commentaries on Paul: A Comparison of Some Theological Themes", in *Essays on the Works of Erasmus,* ed. Richard L. DE MOLEN (New Haven, 1978), 125–144. On Giustiniani and Quirini's emphasis on Scripture in their reform proposal, see their "Libellus ad Leonem X Pontificem Maximum" in *Annales Camaldulenses Ordinis Sancti Benedicti,* ed. G. B. MITTARELLI and A. COSTADONI, IX (Venice, 1773), 612–719, esp. 676–683. On Reuchlin, see Lewis W. SPITZ, *The Religious Renaissance of the German Humanists* (Cambridge, Mass., 1963), 61–80 and James H. OVERFIELD, *Humanism and Scholasticism in Late Medieval Germany* (Princeton, N.J., 1984), 159–63, 247–97. Among the numerous works on Luther's scriptural scholarship, see Jaroslav PELIKAN, *Luther the Expositor* (St. Louis, 1959); J.S. PREUS, *From Shadow to Promise: Old Testament Interpretation from Augustine to the Young Luther* (Cambridge, Mass., 1969), and Jared WICKS, *Man Yearning for Grace: Luther's Early Spiritual Teaching* (Washington, D.C., 1968), esp. 41–143.

III

readily read. Meanwhile in Germany Johannes Reuchlin was arguing for the preservation and study of ancient Hebrew literature, while Martin Luther was lecturing on the Psalms and on the Epistles to the Romans and Galatians, and coming to a new theological understanding of the Scriptures which would soon lead to a profound splintering of the Church.[1] Of these contemporary approaches to the Scriptures, only the slightest echo can be detected in the decrees of the Council. Instead, Sacred Scripture is treated in these documents as a font of literary adornments, in the form of citations and allusions, or as an armory of theological arguments.

Some of the major scriptural themes, which appeared as ornamentation primarily in the narrative portions of the conciliar decrees, were enunciated from the start. Biblical imagery that focused on the devil and on the metaphors of flock, field, and vineyard can be found already in Julius II's bull *Sacrosanctae Romanae Ecclesiae* of 18 July 1511 which convoked the Lateran Council. Thus, the controversy between the pope and Pisan cardinals is due to the devil who sows the weeds of dissension among the clergy (Mt 13:25). The disobedience of these cardinals is likened to Lucifer's attempt to raise his own throne to the level of God's (Is 14:13). The flock of the Lord has been committed to the pope (Jn 21:15–17) who seeks to heal the division in it (Jn 10:16, 17:21–23). The Church is also viewed as the vineyard of the Lord, and the pope's function is to expel from it the little foxes who come to feast on its fruit (Song 2:15). These scriptural metaphors are also prominent in the brief homily Julius II gave at the first session. In it, the pope claimed that Christ's flock had been entrusted to his care, that the field of the Lord was overrun by weeds, poisonous plants, and vipers, and that Satan was sabotaging good works and plotting against mankind. These themes run through many of the conciliar decrees, even after the death of Julius II.[2]

Because of their pre-conciliar selection and a similarity of themes, the Gospel passages chanted at the beginning of the earlier sessions may be viewed as another possible source for the biblical imagery found in the decrees. This imagery focuses on the pastoral and agricultural metaphors of shepherd and flock, sower and seed, vinedresser and vineyard. The likely explanation for this similarity is not what one would initially think. In his ceremonial prescriptions for a council, Agostino Patrizi ruled that the Gospel text be changed according to the materials treated in each session. This ruling would suggest that the decrees were first written and then the Gospels selected accordingly. The diary of the master of ceremonies for the Lateran Council, Paride de Grassi, however, shows that this was not the procedure followed for the opening and first four sessions. Instead, the preparatory commission of nine cardinals, among whom were Alessandro Farnese and Marco

---

[2] For this biblical imagery in the bull of convocation, see *Sacrorum conciliorum nova et amplissima collectio*, ed. G.D. MANSI *et al.*, vol. 32 (Florence, 1759), cols. 681C, 682A – hereafter this volume is cited as "M".

For the text of Julius' homily, see M667B–D and Appendix 1 of my "Concepts of Reform Proposed at the Fifth Lateran Council," *Archivum Historiae Pontificiae* 7 (1969) 163–251, here 237–38. For examples of these themes in the Lateran decrees, see M 691E–92A, 846B, 870A, 905CD, 913A, and 974C for field of the Lord; M 681C, 685C, 691E, 693D, 944A, and 990C for flock of the Lord; and M 681E, 682A, 687A, 768C, 842AB, and 965D for the devil.

Vigerio, decided what these Gospel texts would be, before the agenda of the sessions had been determined. The commission explicitly chose the Gospel on the sending out of the seventy-two disciples (Lk 10:1 ff.), on the good shepherd (Jn 10:7 ff.), and on the warning against false prophets (Mt 7:15 ff.) It ordered de Grassi to follow the Pontifical for the third and fourth sessions, and thereafter either to repeat these selections or to follow the advice of cardinal Vigerio in choosing a new text, for he was expert in such matters. For the third session, the Gospel of the good shepherd was repeated, and for the fourth the Gospel of the seeds which fell on various soils (Mt 13:3 ff.). Only with the fifth session, where a decree against simony in papal elections was reconfirmed, does an effort seem to have been made to select a Gospel appropriate to the agenda: Christ's warning against the thief who does not enter the sheepfold by the door (Jn 10:1 ff.). The suspicion thus arises that these initial, predetermined Gospel texts on the good shepherd and sower of seeds may have influenced the scriptural imagery found in the decrees, rather than the opposite as prescribed by Patrizi. Cardinal Farnese, who seems to have supervised the composition of some of the decrees under Julius II, had also helped to select the initial Gospel texts.[3] That these selections may have influenced the scriptural imagery in the early decrees is thus not surprising.

Another possible source of the Lateran Council's biblical language was that used in the formal statements of its opponents, those associated with the rival Pisan Council. In their response to Alessandro Guasco, the nuncio of the Roman college of cardinals, the Pisan cardinals on 11 September, 1511 claimed that because the five councils of the previous century (Pisa, Konstanz, Siena, Basel, and Florence) had not brought about church reform, it was necessary to go forward with theirs so that the field of the Lord, which was already thick with weeds and thorns whose daily increase was boundless, might at last be purged by a council. At the fourth session in the cathedral of Milan on 4 January 1512, the abbot-general of the Premonstratensians, Jacques de Bachimont, also insisted that the briars which then surrounded on every side and occupied the vineyard of the Lord (especially the ecclesiastical state) could not be uprooted except by the pruning hook and censure of a general council. Similarly at the tenth and final session of the council at Lyon

---

[3] The Gospel texts used at the Lateran sessions are as follows: The Lord appointing seventy-two disciples and sending them out (Lk 10:1 ff.) – opening session (M 667AB) and session VII (M 809DE); the good shepherd (Jn 10:7 ff.) – sessions I (M 680CD), and III (M 731D); warning against false prophets – session II (M 713E); parable of the sower and the various soils (Mt 13:3 ff.) – session IV (M 747C); enter the sheepfold by the door (Jn 10:1ff.) – session V (M 766D); apparition to the ten and giving of Holy Spirit (Jn 20:19 ff.) – session VI (M 788D); parable of wheat and weeds (Mt 13:24 ff.) – session VIII (M 831E); last discourse on love and promise of Holy Spirit (Jn 14:15 ff.) – session IX (M 863B); parable of the wedding feast (Mt 22:1 ff.) – session X (M 905A); signs of the end times (Mt 24:3 ff.) – session XI (M 942A); Christ walking on water (Mt 14:22 ff.) – session XII (M 983DE). For Patrizi's ruling, see the *Caeremoniale Romanum of Agostino Patrizi, Piccolomini*, ed. Cristoforo MARCELLO (Venice, 1516, reprinted Ridgewood, N.J., 1965), fol. LXII^r; for the membership of the preparatory commission, see Walther von HOFMANN, *Forschungen zur Geschichte der kurialen Behörden vom Schisma bis zur Reformation,* Band I (Rome, 1914), 309 n.4; for the ruling of this commission, see "Le cinquième Concile du Latran d'après le Diaire de Paris de Grassi," ed. Marc DYKMANS, in *Annuarium Historiae Conciliorum* 14 (1982), 271–369, here 283 and 287, nrs. 842:15 and 842:32 super 15; on cardinal Farnese's role in shaping the decrees, see my "Paride de Grassi's Diary of the Fifth Lateran Council," *Ibid.*, 370–460, here 453.

on 6 July 1512, the Church once again was likened to the vineyard of the Lord which has suffered from various mistreatments.[4]

The prominence of these themes sets off the Lateran Council from the two major councils of the previous century, Konstanz and Basel. Given these councils' difficult relations with the pope, the absence of the imagery of the shepherd from their decrees is not surprising. But given their efforts to root out the heresies of Wyclif and Hus, one might have expected to see more prominence given to the metaphor of the weeds and to the figure of the devil. The attention which the officials of the Lateran Council gave to the proceedings of these two councils was apparently limited to their juridical and ritual forms and did not extend to the scriptural imagery of their decrees. The only biblical text notably common to all three councils was one used as a literary ornament: "through the tender mercy (viscera) of our God" (Lk 1:78).[5]

As might be expected of a council tightly controled by popes who were eager to assert the authority of the restored papal monarchy, the Fifth Lateran inserted into its decrees numerous biblical allusions to the papal office. These are found primarily in the narrative sections where an effort was made to assert and spell out a theology of papal power with references to supporting scriptural texts. Thus Christ promised that to the end of time He will not desert His flock. Before ascending to His Father, He instituted on a rock foundation as His vicars, Peter and his successors. To them He committed His flock and set them as watchmen over peoples and nations. To them is owed obedience. They in turn will have to render to God an accounting for the souls entrusted to their care. God chooses these vicars, and no one is to attempt to enter the sheepfold except by the door.[6] The family name of the Medici pope, Leo X, became the occasion for seeing the present pontiff as the fulfilment of biblical figures who acted as medical men: the good Samaritan of the Gospel and the doctor who administers the balm of Gilead.[7] The cardinals who opposed the papacy and supported the Pisan Council are identified with the biblical figures of Dathan and Abiram, the Levites who rebelled against Moses and were punished by God.[8] Bishops are depicted as sharers in the papal office of pastor, men called upon to be shining examples to their flock.[9]

---

[4] *Acta primi concilii Pisani celebrati ad tollendum schisma anno Domini MCCCCIX et concilii Senensis MCCCCXXIII ex codice MS. item constitutiones sanctae in diversis sessionibus sacri generalis concilii Pisani ex bibliotheca regia* (Paris, 1612), 71, 107; *Promotiones et progressus sacrosancti Pisani concilii moderni indicti et incohati anno Domini MDXI* (s.l., s.d.), 43.ᵛ

[5] For a modern edition of these decrees, see *Conciliorum Oecumenicorum Decreta,* ed. G. ALBERIGO *et al.* 3rd ed. (Bologna, 1973), 405–513: for the quotation of Luke 1:78, see *Ibid.,* 439, 458, 467, 471, and in the Lateran decrees, M 974C and 992A. On the attention paid by Lateran officials to Konstanz and Basel, see my "De Grassi's Diary", 423.

[6] For these statements on papal power and their biblical prooftexts, see M 965C, 874D (Mt 28:20, Jn 13:1, 21:15–17, Mt 16:18–19, Deut 17:12), M 947E (Ezek 3:17, Jer 1:10), M 988BC (Jer 1:10), M 944A (Ezek 3:17, 33:7), M 965D (Heb 13:17), M 681C (Jn 10:7–10), M 869CD (Jn 21:15–17).

[7] M 842AB (Lk 10:34, Jer 8:22).

[8] M 684C, 686B (Num 16:1–32)

[9] M 971A (1 Cor 12:18–20), M 974CD (Mt 5:14–15, Ps 83:8), M 970E (Tit 1:5)

When referring to the pastoral office of the pope at the beginning of a decree, the language used was often solemn and exalted. Papal authority was placed in a cosmic context and the current pope seen as part of a providential plan. Such a vision accords well with that of the psalmist. Because the decrees allude instead to the description, found in James' Epistle, of God as the Father of lights from Whom descends every good and perfect gift, one may suspect that the Neo-Platonic thought world of the Medici's Florentine Academy may also be operative here.[10]

Other scriptural imagery was also used to give authority and dignity to the statements in the decrees. God, Whose works are perfect, is looked to for lending His right hand for the achievement of the Council's goals. His Church is the bark of Peter, the tunic of the Lord which should not be torn. The rival Pisan Council is a synagogue, and its supporters have the lying tongues denounced by the psalmist, for they falsely accused Julius of negligence in not calling a council. This pope will delay no longer in moving against these schismatic cardinals, lest continued tolerance of them bring upon him the condemnation of the prophet Ezechiel against those who fail to defend Israel. The conciliar exhortations for peace among Christians are replete with scriptural references. God is seen as fostering peace and concord in the heavens, and in the person of Christ as bequeathing peace to His disciples as their legal inheritance. The Council set as one of its goals the realization of the psalmist's prophecy that peace and justice will embrace in a kiss. To further that goal it sent to Christian princes special legates who are described as angels of peace. And in the Council's reaffirmation of Julius II's 1509 bull, anyone who would attempt to obtain the papal office by simoniacal means is equated with Simon Magus and to be shunned as a publican.[11]

In addition to the Council's use of Scripture as a literary adornment in its decrees, biblical texts were quoted as prooftexts and their sources identified by name. The words of Christ were introduced as being those of the Lord, the Savior, Truth. The term "prophet" by itself usually referred to the psalmist, but certain prophets such as Amos, Jeremiah, and Ezechiel were identified by name. Paul was called the Apostle or teacher of the Gentiles.[12] Citations could also be made without attribution.

The long reform bull of the ninth session, *Supernae dispositionis arbitrio,* incorporated scriptural allusions and citations as justifications for its prescriptions. Concern that clerics set a good example in their public conduct was reinforced with scriptural exhortations to let one's good works shine before men and to seek to be pleasing in the sight of both God

---

[10] For examples of solemn introductory phrases, see M 874D and 944A. The allusions to Jam 1:17 are in M 817C and 844B. Psalm 103 praises God as Creator and ruler of the universe.

[11] God: M 733E (Deut 32:4) and 992B (Ex 15:6 and Ps 117:6–7); Peter's bark: M 768B (Mt 14:29); tunic of Lord: M 769DE, 946D (Jn 19:23–25); synagogue: M 754A (Apoc 2:9, 3:9); lying tongues: M 684B, D (Ps 11:2–3, 108:3); Ezechiel's condemnation: M 686A (Ezech 13:5); peace: M 687B (Ps 84:11), 843E (Job 25:2, Jn 14:27), 844E (Is 33:7); simony: M 769B–D (Acts 8:18–22, Mt 18:15–17).

[12] E.g. M 842C: *Quod manifeste constat ex evangelio, cum Dominus ait . . .* For examples of citations by name, see: M 842C (Lord), 946C, 971D (Savior), 971D (Truth); M 684B, 945D (psalmist); M 946E (Amos), M 842A (Jeremiah), M 686A (Ezechiel), M 988BC (prophet, not psalmist, but Jeremiah), M 842C, 843A, 877D, 946E, 965C (Paul the Apostle), M 792C (Teacher of Gentiles), M 988BC (Apostle, meaning John).

and man. To cardinals were applied Paul's admonitions that bishops live sober, chaste, and pious lives, and take care to rule over their households. The bull's prescription on the religious education of youth was deemed necessary because of a statement in Genesis that the human heart is prone to evil from the time of adolescence onward. Its ruling that the penalties of canon and civil law be imposed on those convicted of sodomy appeals to a scriptural circumlocution which the decree's author mistakenly thought referred to this crime and God's punishment of it.[13]

The decree *Dum intra mentis arcana* of the eleventh session, regulating the relations between bishops and exempt religious, appealed to Scripture for a rationale of harmony. It invoked Christ's command that we love one another as He has loved us. It found a basis for unity in the common Lord and Faith each professed and in the metaphor of being members of the same body.[14]

The decree *Supernae maiestatis praesidio* of the same session, which set down rules to govern preaching, paid particular attention to statements in Scripture on this topic. The narrative preamble of the decree traces the history and theology of preaching from Christ's example and instructions to the practice of His apostles and disciples and their vicars. This section is almost a chain of biblical texts whose purpose is to point to the importance and usefulness of preaching, to exhort clerics to engage in it according to the model of Christ and His first followers, and to condemn certain abuses in contemporary practice. By quoting Paul's warning to Timothy that men would arise who would abandon sound doctrine to preach fables and things to their own liking, the decree claims that this prophecy is realized in contemporary preachers who propagate fables and errors and seek self-glorification rather than what is helpful to their listeners. Preachers should use their talents not to tear the seamless tunic of Christ by scandalous attacks on prelates and by heterodox teachings, but to preach to all creatures the same message, the way of the Lord, and seek to dwell as one in His house. As tempted as the conciliar fathers may have been to impose a blanket proscription against prophecies, their decree noted both that biblical text which denied that anyone can know when the end of the world will arrive, but also those which insisted that God will reveal secrets to His servants and that His Spirit is not to be spurned. To resolve this dilemma, the Council invoked John's warning not to put credence in every prophecy, but to test them to see if they come from God. And the Council set up procedures to be followed in testing these spirits.[15]

---

[13] Public conduct: M 877D (Mt 5:16), 877DE (Prov 3:4), 879B (2 Cor 8:21); exhortations to cardinals: M 877D (Tit 2:12), 879BC (1 Tim 3:5); education: M 881C (Gen 8:21); and sodomy: M 882E (Eph 5:6) – according to Joseph A. GRASSI, in the *Jerome Biblical Commentary* (London, 1968), p. 348, this scripture text does not refer to sodomy but to Gnostic teachings that those who were enlightened were above considerations of good and evil.

[14] Christ's command: M 971D (Jn 15:12), common Lord and Faith: M 971D (Eph 4:5), one body: M 971D (Eph 4:4).

[15] Chain of biblical texts: M 944BC (Acts 1:1, Mk 16:15, Ps 18:2, Ps 106:14, Acts 26:18, Rom 13:12, Ps 18:5, Mk 16:20); purpose of citations: M 944B–E; Paul's warning: M 944E (2 Tim 4:3–4); duties of preacher: M 944D–946B; use talents: M 946E (Mt 25:14–29); not to tear tunic: M 946D (Jn 19:23); preach to all creatures: M 946D (Mk 16:15); same message: M 945D (Ps 67:7, Mt 22:16); end of world: M 946C (Acts 1:7); some prophecies true: M 946E–947A (Amos 3:7, 1 Thes 5:19–20); test spirits: M 947A (1 Jn 4:1).

This decree on preaching also contains the only two statements of the Council which deal directly with Scripture. Preachers are instructed to base their sermons on the Sacred Scriptures which they are to explain. And their explanations of the Bible are to accord with the interpretation of those church fathers and theology teachers whom the Church or long usage have approved and whose specific exegesis the Church has thus far accepted.[16]

The biblical text cited in the decree *Inter multiplices* of the tenth session functioned neither as a literary adornment nor as a prooftext, but as a potential condemnation of what the Council was about to approve. In order to give its approval to the *mons pietatis,* a form of pawn shop/lending institution, the Council had to deal with the prohibition in the Sermon on the Mount against taking interest on a loan, which was considered the sin of usury by the medieval Church. Christ's exhortation to "lend, expecting nothing in return" (Lk 6:35) had been invoked by Urban III in his 1187 condemnation of usurious practices, and this same passage was cited by the opponents of the *mons pietatis.* The Church recognized that other biblical texts also prohibited usury, but no explicit or implicit reference was made to them in the decree of the Fifth Lateran.[17]

Tommaso de Vio (Cajetan), who sat on the conciliar deputation which drafted this decree, opposed the *mons pietatis,* but claimed that the Lucan text did not constitute a clear prohibition. His objections were on the basis of natural reason, derived from an application of the principles of commutative and distributive justice to the current practices of the *montes pietatis.* He felt that those who debated the question of their licitness should not invoke external authorities, but follow the method of moral philosophy. The Lateran decree reported some of Cajetan's objections based on considerations of justice but also the Lucan text cited by others as here applicable.[18]

---

[16] Base sermons on Bible: M 945DE, 946B; interpret Scriptures according to approved teachers: M 944CD, 945A, 946BC.

[17] For the Lucan prohibition in *Inter multiplices,* see M 906A; for its earlier use by Urban III, see *Enchiridion symbolorum definitionum et declarationum de rebus fidei et morum,* ed. H. DENZINGER and A. SCHÖNMETZER, S.J., 34th rev. ed (Freiburg im Breisgau, 1967), p. 243, nr. 764. For the condemnation of usury by the Second Lateran Council (1139) which invoked unspecified prohibitions in the Old and New Testaments, see *Conciliorum oecumenicorum decreta,* ed. G. Alberigo *et al.,* p. 200, canon 13: *per Scripturam in veteri et novo Testamento abdicatam* . . . Among the biblical texts cited as prohibitions against usury were Deut 15: 4,8; 16:11; 23:19; and Mt 5:40, 42. For the appeal to the Lucan text by the opponents of the *mons pietatis,* see Michele MONACO, "La questione dei Monti di Pietà al Quinto Concilio Lateranense," *Rivista di Studi Salernitani* 7 (1971), 85–136, here 98, and Paolo PRODI, "La nascita dei Monti di Pietà: tra solidarismo cristiano e logica del profito," *Annali dell' Istituto storico italo-germanico in Trento,* VIII (1982), 211–224, here 218. For a study which emphasizes the role of the Deuteronomic condemnations, see Benjamin N. NELSON, *The Idea of Usury: From Tribal Brotherhood to Universal Otherhood* (Princeton, 1949), 19–25.

[18] For a modern edition of Cajetan's 1498 *De Monte Pietatis,* see *Scripta philosophica: Opuscula oecumenica-socialia,* ed. P. ZAMMIT (Rome, 1934), 41–89. This edition does not take cognizance of the reprinted edition of Jacopo Mazzochio, published in Rome on 27 February 1515. This Roman edition is prefaced by a letter to Leo X (Sig. Aiᵛ) in which Cajetan acknowledges papal teaching authority, yet states: *Et propter duo rogaverim: alterum ne sinistro spectentur oculo que capite secundo contra locum ab auctoritate in his que certa ratione sciti possunt, dum partes philosophie moralis tuerer non in virorum vere doctorum qui ratione utuntur, sed in eorum qui promiscue omnia ex sola auctoritate autumant sigillationem scripsit: Alterum ne quis brevitate doctrine in .3. aut .4. capite allate ex dictis autoribus terreatur. Fateor in genue congenitum mihi ne scio quem spiritum pudoris, quo*

The conciliar decree dealt with the question of the Lucan prohibition by making a distinction. This biblical text was interpreted as condemning only that interest based on the money loaned and taken as profit. But the *mons pietatis* was a public, not-for-profit institution whose fees were viewed as non-usurious, moderate compensations for the expenses (e.g., space, labor, and personal responsibility) involved in providing custody for the items pawned. Thus, the *mons pietatis* did not fall under the Lucan prohibition.[19]

By its approval of the *montes pietatis* the Lateran Council took sides in a theologico-philosophical debate. Franciscan theologians had been the most avid backers of the *montes,* although a few Dominicans also supported them. But most of the members of the Order of Preachers, under the leadership of their master general, Cajetan, opposed the *montes,* as did a number of Augustinian friars.[20]

The question of the soul's immortality, on which the Lateran Council issued the decree, *Apostolici regiminis solicitudo,* at its eighth session, was another topic hotly debated by philosophers and theologians. Averroists held that the soul was naturally mortal. Nominalists such as Gabriel Biel maintained that the soul's immortality could not be proven by natural reason alone. Scotists contended that by the mere use of natural reason one could arrive only at the probability of the soul's immortality. Thomists argued that the soul was by nature immortal and this can be proven by reason alone. In addition to these Aristotelian schools of thought, the Neo-Platonists also wrote on the topic. They held that the soul was both immortal and knowable as such. Apart from the Averroists and Nominalists, members of each of these schools sat on the deputation which drafted the decree on the soul's immortality. And the three cardinals probably charged with giving final form to the decree came from different scholastic backgrounds and were cardinal-protectors of rival religious orders.[21]

---

non allegatione sed prolixa recitatione aliene doctrine repletos codices edere erubesco: quo fit ut malim lectoribus ostendere unde procedam: que ex libro (ut aiunt) scribere in libello. For studies of Cajetan's thinking on the *mons,* see I. MANCINI, *Cardinalis Caietanus et Montes Pietatis (Disquisitio historico-moralis)* (Jerusalem, 1954) and John T. NOONAN, Jr., *The Scholastic Analysis of Usury* (Cambridge, Mass, 1957), 296–299. For a study which shows that Cajetan's views were often enough at odds with those of his fellow Dominicans, see Reginaldo FEI, "Fra Tomaso Gaetano (1468 + 1534): 'L' Uomo delle singolari opinioni'," *Rivista di filosofia neo-scolastica,* XXVII (Special Supplement), March, 1935, pp. 127–147.

[19] M 906A–907A; PRODI, "La nascita," 220.

[20] For a brief survey of the major thinkers on each side of the *montes pietatis* issue, see *Ibid,* 218 and MONACO, "La questione," 114–121.

[21] For a survey of the schools of thought at the time of the Council, see Siro OFFELLI, "Il pensiero del concilio lateranense V sulla dimonstrabilità razionale dell' immortalità dell' anima umana," *Studia Patavina* 1 (1954), 7–40; for a study of the positions of the members of the faith deputation, see the study of M. Daniel PRICE, "The Origins of Lateran V's *Apostolici Regiminis,*" in *Annuarium Historiae Conciliorum,* 17 (1985), 464–72 and my "Alexios Celadenus: A Disciple of Bessarion in Renaissance Italy" forthcoming in the 1988 Spring issue of *Historical Reflections.* The three cardinals probably charged with giving the decree its final form were: Bernardino ! opez de Carvajal (protector of the Mimins), Niccolo Fieschi (protector of the Dominicans), and Domenico Grimani (protector of the Franciscans). See the letter of Franceso Vettori to the Dieci di Balia, Rome, 24 October 1513, in Archivio di Stato, Firenze, Dieci di Balia, Carteggi – Responsive Nr. 118, fol. 317ʳ: *et pure hieri furono in strecta consulta . . . di rassectare molte cose circa la religione a che sono proposti li Reverendissimi di Santa Croce et Grimani et Flischo . . .* On these cardinals, see especially: G. FRAGNITO, "Carvajal, Bernardino

Instead of siding with one school over another, the decree affirmed that the human soul is truly, by itself, and essentially the form of the human body, separate and distinct in each body in which it is infused, and immortal. In addition to citing a canon of the Council of Vienne, the Lateran decree sought to prove its affirmations by referring to a series of scriptural texts. Christ's statements that "they cannot kill the soul" (Mt 10:28) and that "he who hates his life in this world preserves it unto life eternal" (Jn. 12:25) were quoted as proofs. His promises of eternal rewards and punishments according to each person's merits or demerits (e.g., Mt. 25:46) were also brought forward as arguments. So too was Paul's statement that if there is no resurrection, those who follow Christ are the most miserable of men (1 Cor. 15:19). Those schools of philosophy which taught the mortality and unicity of the human soul were declared erroneous and the need to season human philosophy with elements of revealed wisdom was justified by an appeal to Paul's observation that God has made foolish the wisdom of this world (1 Cor 1:20). By this recourse to Sacred Scripture, the conciliar deputation and cardinalitial commission had come up with the compromise formulation of a decree that had affirmed church doctrine without offending any of the major Christian schools of thought or the religious orders which promoted their teachings.[22]

If Sacred Scripture played such a central role in some of the Lateran decrees, it also played no role or next to none in others. Thus, in three of the four decrees of the tenth session, there are no explicit references to Scripture and only the faintest echoes in one. These decrees treated disciplinary matters: the privileges of exempt clerics, the summoning of those who defend the Pragmatic Sanction to appear before the Council, and censorship restraints on book publication. The one decree which treated a doctrinal issue, that on the *montes pietatis,* did make explicit reference to a scriptural text.[23]

Lopez de," in *DBDI*, 21 (Rome, 1978), 28–34; Pio PASCHINI, *Domenico Grimani Cardinale di S. Marco († 1523),* Vol. 4 of *Storia e letteratura* (Rome, 1943), esp. 5, 77–79; and I. CREVELLI, "Fieschi di Lavagna (Nicolà)," in *DHGE* 16 (Paris, 1967), cols. 1440–41.

[22] M 842C, 842E–43A. For canon 1 of the Council of Vienne (1311–12), see *Conciliorum oecumenicorum decreta,* ed. G. ALBERIGO *et al*, 361. The Averroists and Alexandrinists, who followed non-Christian philosophers, would have been unhappy with this decree. Pietro Pomponazzi had explicity excluded the data of revelation from his reasoned considerations of the soul's nature which concluded that it was mortal – see Dominick A. IORIO, "The Problem of the Soul and the Unity of Man in Pietro Pomponazzi," *The New Scholasticism* 37 (1963) 293–311. According to Offelli "Il pensiero", 39–40, the decree's command – that all philosophers, who publicly teach in universities of general studies or elsewhere, are to make every effort to present arguments defending such truths of the faith as the soul's multiplicity and immortality – should be seen not as a doctrinal statement that the human reason can demonstrate with certitude the human soul's immortality, but as a disciplinary decree in the same spirit as the injunction of Pietro Barozzi in 1489. In this episcopal ordinance aimed at putting a stop to similar debates at the University of Padua, the same text from St. Paul's first letter to the Corinthians (1:20) was cited. Barozzi's intention was not to take sides in a philosophical debate, but to prevent harm being done to those who might come to doubt the soul's immortality. Instead of stopping all debate, Lateran V took a more positive stance in ordering that arguments for the soul's immortality be presented. Thus the Council's intention was also pastoral and not aimed at resolving a philosophical debate. The quotation from Paul was used to justify putting limits on philosophical discourse in public.

[23] E.g., M 905C–915E. In the decree on book censorship, echoes of 1 Cor 9:19–22 and of Is 42:16 can probably be heard in the opening sentence – see M 912C.

In conclusion, Sacred Scripture had various functions in the Lateran decrees. Most often it was used as a literary adornment lending dignity and authority to the conciliar statements and to the office of the pope who issued them with the Council's approval. The Bible also provided both prooftexts to justify various reform decrees and guidance for its prescriptions on preaching. In the case of the decree on the *montes pietatis,* the Council had to show how the prohibition in the Lucan passage did not apply. In the decree on the soul, Scripture provided a way to avoid taking sides in a debate among orthodox theologians. The only time when the Council seemed to be echoing contemporary approaches to Scripture was in its decree on preaching where it urged that this be based on the Gospels which were to be interpreted in accord with the church fathers.

The Council's stance toward other contemporary developments in the area of biblical studies can only be inferred. It issued no decrees praising or condemning the scriptural scholarship of Jimenez's group at Alcala or that of Lefèvre, Colet, and Erasmus. It placed no prohibitions on vernacular versions of the Bible. Given the controversies which swirled around these biblical projects and given the Council's mentality of countering the devil's ploys and removing weeds from the field of the Lord, conciliar silence on these topics can perhaps be seen as tacit approval. The duke of Burgundy and future emperor Charles V had urged the Council to intervene in the Reuchlin affair, but instead, the topic of ancient Hebrew learning was handled in a special commission whose work dragged on for years and the Council approved only a decree on the censorship of books aimed in part at putting an end to the pamphlet war raging around this issue.[24] The Council's insistence that preachers interpret Sacred Scripture according to the mind of the church fathers and of other approved theologians pointed the way to an inevitable conflict with Luther over his innovative understandings of Scripture.

Can any conclusions be drawn from the records of Lateran V regarding the Church's attitude toward Sacred Scripture on the eve of the Reformation? As shown in my earlier study, the diary of the master of ceremonies suggests that those concerned with liturgical matters at Lateran V, while attentive to the precedents of the previous century, exalted the position of the pope to the point of almost disparaging at times the Bible: it was placed at his feet during the oath-taking ceremony and placed under the altar for quick reference, instead of being enthroned on it during the formal sessions. Canonists who drafted most of the conciliar decrees seldom sought to justify their prescriptions by appeals to Scripture. Its role was reduced to a font of literary adornments. The principal concern of these canonists was also apparently that the Council conform to earlier legal precedents. Only the theologians who had to grapple with the doctrinal questions of the soul's immortality, usury, and rules for preaching made serious appeals to the Bible.[25] The other places where

---

[24] On the effort to have the Lateran Council take up the Reuchlin case, see Ludwig von Pastor, *The History of the Popes from the Close of the Middle Ages,* Vol. VII, trans. Ralph Francis Kerr, 2nd ed., (St. Louis 1923), 319–25, esp. 323, Overfield, *Humanism and Scholasticism,* 265, *and the letter of Martin Gröning to Johannes Reuchlin, Rome, 12 September 1516 in Staats- und Stadtbibliothek – Augsburg, 2° Cod. Aug. 389, p. [9]: "Prius causam ad Lateranensem Concilium trahere moliebantur. Nunc proprio sessionario Concilio agitata fuit."*
[25] See my "De Grassi's Diary," 457–58.

Scripture was often cited were those passages referring to the papal office. In its efforts to conform to liturgical and legal precedents and to refute the conciliarist thesis, Lateran V functioned under the shadow of its predecessors Konstanz and Basel, and of its rival, the schismatic Council of Pisa-Milan-Asti-Lyon. The decrees of the Lateran Council show that the Church on the eve of the Reformation viewed Scripture as a treasury of prooftexts and literary ornaments and as the basis, when interpreted traditionally, of sermons preached to the people. These decrees register no awareness or concern that scholars were coming up with a new interpretation of the Scriptures that challenged common beliefs – and this lack of concern continued even after the eleventh session had dealt its almost fatal blows to the conciliarist thesis.[26] This conciliar failure to provide leadership and guidance in the crucial area of scriptural scholarship would have lasting detrimental effects.

---

[26] For the report of a well-placed observer of the mentality of the conciliar leadership regarding the Council's achievements and its unfinished business, see the corrected draft of a letter of the imperial ambassador, Alberto Pio, to emperor Maximilian, Rome, 12 March 1517, in the Henry Charles Lea Library of the Rare Book Collection at the Charles Patterson Van Pelt Library, University of Pennsylvania, Philadelphia, Ms. 414, item 4–32: *Quo ad synodam non dissoluendam, respondit* [Leo] *videri Reuerendissimis Cardinalibus et plurimis alijs prelatis consultius esse illam dissoluere, quam diutius continua*[re] *praesertim, cum ea, ob que ipsa indicta fuit, iam ferè omnia peracta sint, maxime autem potissima scisma sublatum esse, pacem inter Principes esse conciliatam, nonnulla, circa mores, esse reformata, et castigata quod restat aeque commode agi posse absoluta synodo, sicuti ea vigente, ut est de reductione Boemorum et Rhutenorum ad vnitatem, et obedientiam Cath*[olicae] *Ecclesiae, et de expeditione assummenda contra infideles, in quo negocio, quod difficilius erat, peractum est, videlicet principum conciliatio, cum vigente bello inter ipssos, nec de inuadendis infidelibus nec de obsistendo ipsis nihil statui aut decerni potuisset, confecta autem pace, ad utrunque peragendum amplissimam reseratam esse viam, singulos quoque Principes respondisse sibi suadenti, et admonenti de ea re, promptos et paratos esse pro viribus contribuere ad eam expeditionem, non . . . synodos* [ms.: synodus] *perpetuas esse, hanc autem multis annis iam uig*[ere] *solere cum diuturniores sint quam res exquirat, nonnumqum* [ha]*bere occasionem scandalorum in ecclesia dei, cum malitia et iniquitas et temmeritas semper apud aliquos locum habent inquietos et turbulentos spiritus semper, ideo omnem* [occasionem] *ad noua molienda aspirare eis auferendam esse, quam arripire, synodo abuti possint preuertentes finem in quem sinodus ipssa determinatur* [?] *indici ad tollenda scandala, et succidendos uepres, et tribulos e vinea domini, prauos autem et temerarios ad ea serenda . . . Quamobrem rogare et hortari Maiestatem Vestram ut a coepto opere non desistat, Vestra ob tam pium opus receptura a summo omnium Creatore mercedem* [et g]*loriam eximiam, aut excluderemur, caeterorum Regum et principum oratoribus et potissime illo Regis Franciae maxime nobiscum in hac re non conuenientibus, quamobrem certo nihil proficeremus, obesse autem rerum Maiestatum Vestrarum plurima possemus, si acrius hanc causam prosequeremur, quia forte interpretaretur iniquius operam nostram et in misteriorem partem, quapropter potius tacere et in die congregationis* [pa]*tribus quam loquendum existimamus.* I am most grateful to Prof. F.A.C. Mantello for his assistance in checking my transcription and suggesting various revisions. Responsibility for any errors, however, remains solely mine.

IV

Incipiat Iudicium a Domo Domini:
The Fifth Lateran Council and the Reform of Rome*

For five years from 1512 to 1517, under two popes Julius II (1503-13) and Leo X (1513-21), and with the official participation of over four-hundred leading ecclesiastics and laymen representing the nations of Latin Christendom, the Fifth Lateran Council was celebrated amid the splendors of Renaissance Rome.[1] Its agenda included the healing of schism, eradication of heresy, pacification of Christian princes, preparation of a crusade, and reformation of Christendom.[2] Although this council tended to shy away from the traditional formula used by the rival council at Pisa of "a reformation in head and members," the mentality encapsulated in that phrase was prevalent among the conciliar fathers meeting at the Lateran. The tears many shed when the inaugural homelist, Egidio Antonini, predicted the success of their reforming efforts were not unrelated to an awareness that earlier councils had labored mostly in vain and popes had drawn up but never promulgated various bulls to bring about this renewal of the Church's head, that is, of the papal court, the Curia, and in an extended sense, the city of Rome.[3] The importance of initiating such a reform was also recognized by the two popes associated with the council.

The official documents, by which Julius II convoked the Lateran Council and Leo X continued it, spoke only in general terms about

---

*An earlier version of this paper was delivered at a joint session of the American Catholic Historical Association and American Historical Association conventions meeting in San Francisco on 28 December 1978.

[1] The official acts of the council edited by Antonio del Monte are reprinted in *Sacrorum conciliorum nova et amplissima collectio*, ed. Giovanni Domenico Mansi *et alii*, vol 32 (Paris, 1902 reprint), cols. 665A-999C, hereafter cited as Mansi. The most recent general study of this council is that by Olivier de La Brosse in *Latran V et Trente*, vol. 10 of *Histoire des conciles oecuméniques*, ed. Gervais Dumeige (Paris, 1975), 12-114, an up-to-date bibliography is provided on 471-73.

[2] Mansi, 667D, 687BC, 688D, 692B, 695B.

[3] *Acta primi concilii Pisani celebrati ad tollendum schisma anno Domini M.CCCC.IX et concilii Senensis M.CCCC.XXIII. ex codice MS. Item constitutiones sanctae factae in diversis sessionibus sacri generalis concilii Pisani ex bibliotheca*

the need for universal Church renewal. In his allocution to the sixth session, however, Leo X singled out Rome as an appropriate object of the council's reforming efforts. In a bull read at the eighth session, Leo claimed that his predecessor Julius had convoked the council "both for many reasons and because of the frequent complaints about the Roman Curia."[4] In practice both pontiffs used the council as an occasion for curial reform. Before the council opened Julius charged the preparatory commission of cardinals to cleanse the city of Rome--its people, Curia, and papal court--lest the prelates coming to the council be easily scandalized. Based on the cardinals' recommendations the pope issued at the end of March 1512 a decree reforming the curial officials and reducing their fees. At the fourth session Julius had the council give its formal approval to this decree.[5] Leo followed a similar procedure at the eighth session. He had earlier urged the conciliar reform deputation to address itself to a reform of his own office, of his household, and of the lives of members of the Curia.[6]

A dominant theme in many of the reform proposals from the time of the council was the necessity of initiating church renewal at Rome. In their *Libellus* (1513) addressed to Leo X, the two Venetian patricians, Camaldolese hermits, and papal confidants, Paolo Giustiniani and Pietro Quirini, enuniciated a principle implicit in the writings of many others: reform should begin at the top. According to their metaphysical model, what happens at the apex of the ecclesiastical hierarchy will necessarily influence the lower orders. The Hungarian bishop and preacher at the council, Šimum Bejna-Kožičić, insisted that the church of Rome be first restored, because from that head as from a fount flows health or illness into

regia (Paris, 1612), 25, 36, 101, etc.; the phrase rarely if ever appears in the documents of the Lateran Council; Odocio Rainaldi, *Annales Ecclesiastici post Baronium ab anno 1198 ad annum 1565*, rev. and ed. G.D. Mansi and A. Theiner (Paris, 1877) ad annum 1512, nr. 35, 40, hereafter cited as Rainaldi; Léonce Celier, "L'idée de Réforme à la cour pontificale: du concile de Bâle au concile de Lateran," *Revue des questions historiques* 86 (1909), 418-435 and his "Alexandre VI e la Réforme de l'Eglise," *Mélanges d'archéologie et histoire de l'Ecole Française de Rome* 27 (1907), 65-124. For the centrality of Rome in the thinking of this prominent reformer at the council, see John W. O'Malley, "Giles of Viterbo: A Reformer's Thought on Renaissance Rome," *Renaissance Quarterly* 20 (1976), 1-11.

[4]Mansi, 667AB, 687BC, 688D, 692B, 695B, 783AB, 845E; Rainaldi, 1513, nr. 24; Paride de Grassi, *Diarium Leonis*, Bibliotheca Apostolica Vaticana (hereafter cited as B A V) Vat. Lat. 12275, fol. 38r.

[5]Mansi, 753AB, 772E; Rainaldi, 1512, nr. 29-31; Paride de Grassi, *Diarium Julii*, BAV, Vat. Lat. 12412, fol 151v, 206v.

[6]Mansi, 845D-47A; Rainaldi, 1513, nr. 27, 97; Nelson H. Minnich, "Concepts of Reform Proposed at the Fifth Lateran Council," *Archivum Historiae Pontificiae* 7 (1969), 245; Raffaele Lippo Brandolini, *Dialogus Leo Nuncupatus...*, ed. Francesco Fogliazzi (Venezia, 1753), 121.

the other members. Antonio Pucci, the cleric of the Camera and servant of Medicean interests from Florence alluded to the statement of this theme found in 1 Peter 4:17 when he observed in his sermon at the ninth session that judgment most fittingly proceeds from the House of the Lord and spreads to the world: "Urbem primum, ut judicium incipiat a domo Domini, inde orbem . . . restitue.[7]

Appeals were made that the pope begin the reform with himself. The two Camaldolese and the court humanist, Gianfrancesco Poggio Bracciolini, urged the pope to be a model of virtues and sound teachings since others will follow his example. While Poggio stressed his role as inspirer, another court humanist, Raffaele Lippo Brandolini, portrayed Alessandro Farnese (the future Paul III) as hoping that Leo will not neglect severity and justice, should his kindness and clemency fail to inspire a reform. The same message was found in the oration sent to Leo by Gianfrancesco Pico della Mirandola. This humanist prince claimed that only the pope can reform the Church and to be successful Leo should add rigor to his accustomed mildness.[8]

The papal household was singled out to be among the first to experience the pontiff's zeal for reform. Leo's personal friend, Quirini, gave specific recommendations. Let the pope's relatives who are not engaged in necessary tasks be sent back to Florence. His personal staff should be reduced by a third and the attire of its members be simple and befitting clerics. Precious metals and fabrics ought not adorn his retainers, horses, mules, or halls, but be dedicated to liturgical purposes. The papal table should serve a simple fare and the meals be accompanied by spiritual reading or edifying conversation.[9]

Together with Giustiniani, his fellow Camaldolese, Quirini also urged the pope to investigate and correct the conduct of the cardinals and to assign them salaries rather than benefices. The royal instructions for the Spanish ambassadors to the council were also concerned about the cardinals, insisting that financial offerings

---

[7]Paolo Giustiniani and Pietro Quirini, *Libellus ad Leonem X. Pontificem Maximum* in *Annales Camaldulenses Ordinis Sancti Benedicti*, ed. G. -B. Mittarelli and A. Costadoni, IX (Venezia, 1773), col. 698, hereafter this work is cited as *Libellus;* Mansi, 803B, 897D.

[8]*Libellus*, 691-92; Gianfrancesco Poggio Bracciolini, *De veri pastoris munere liber,* B A V, Vat. Lat. 3732, fol. 6ʳ, 10ʳ; Brandolini, *Dialogus Leo, 124;* Gianfrancesco Pico della Mirandola, *Ad Leonem Decimum Pontificem Maximum et Concilium Lateranense . . . de reformandis moribus oratio,* App. 146 in William Roscoe, *The Life and Pontificate of Leo the Tenth,* 2nd ed. rev. (London, 1806), VI, 69.

[9]Pietro Quirini, "Fragment eines Reformgutachtens für Leo X (1513)," in Hubert Jedin, "Vincenzo Quirini und Pietro Bembo (1946)," reprinted in *Kirche des Glaubens, Kirche der Geschichte: Ausgewählte Aufsätze und Vorträge,* (Freiburg, 1966), I, 165-66.

130

have no influence in their appointment or in their election of the pope.[10]

A reform of the Curia was urgently demanded by writers from many countries. The Venetian Camaldolese hermits warned Leo soon after his election that if he failed to correct the Curia, nothing great could be expected from his reign. The Florentine humanist, Brandolini, educated at Naples and Rome, denounced the widespread immorality, greed, and ambition of the Curia.[11] Both Diego de Deza, the Dominican archbishop of Seville, and Jakob Wimpfeling, the Alsatian humanist and ardent defender of the council, lamented that those who were rejected by their local ordinaries as unfit either for ordination or for holding a benefice easily obtained from the Roman Curia authorization to be ordained and appointment to church office. Among the abuses to be remedied by the council, according to Deza, was the appointment by Rome as cathedral canons of those who were uneducated and ignorant of church doctrine, not even tonsured and mere children. The Curia did not honor its agreement with the Spanish Church to reserve at least two canonries in each cathedral for university graduates. The royal instructions for the Spanish ambassadors to the council repeated this accusation. The archbishop also complained of the Curia's appointment of absentee, unsuited, and negligent clerics to benefices in Spain.[12] The French ambassador at the Lateran Council, Claude de Seyssel, observed that curial connections and favoritism advanced the careers of ambitious and unqualified men. The correction of these abuses will come, according to the Venetian hermits, when Leo insists on a strict observance of curial regulations.[13]

Spanish prelates advocated an end of various curial practices. Pascual Rebenga, the ascetical bishop of Burgos appointed as delegate of Castile to the council, denounced Rome's granting for a fee all kinds of dispensations from church law. Deza attacked in particular those dispensation's allowing *conversos* to have their own confessors and the Mass celebrated in their homes. He also wanted exemptions from local jurisdiction to be effective only in Rome or within the confines of a monastery's walls. Religious should not be permitted to transfer to laxer orders nor should Rome grant to prelates the administration of religious houses and their revenues.

---

[10]*Libellus*, 694-96; José M. Doussinague, *Fernando el católico y el cisma de Pisa* (Madrid, 1946), 539-40, hereafter this work is cited as Doussinague.

[11]*Libellus*, 711; Brandolini, *Oratio ad Lateranense Concilium excogitata*, BAV, Ottob. Lat. 813, fol. 24r-v, 25v, 51r.

[12]L. Dacheux, *Un réformateur à la fin du XVe siècle. Jean Geiler de Kaysersberg, prédicateur à la Cathédrale de Strasbourg 1478-1510. Etude sur sa vie et son temps* (Paris, 1876), 153, n.1; Doussinague, 533, 536-38, 541.

[13]Claude de Seyssel, *La grand monarchie de France* (Paris, 1541), 21r; *Libellus*, 712-13.

The archbishop also enumerated a host of curial practices which must be terminated: appointment to almost all the major and minor benefices of Spain in disregard of local rights, reservations, untimely expectatives, coadjutorships, commendations, fraudulent provisions without open hearings, lengthy litigations, dispensations from residency and ordination, pluralism, and confiscation of the spoils and legacies of deceased prelates. Many of Deza's complaints were incorporated into the instructions for the Spanish ambassadors.[14] With the exception of the *conversos* question, complaints similar to these of the Spanish would probably have been registered across Europe had other Christian princes also solicited the opinion of their subjects in preparation for the council.

The curial abuse most harshly criticized was simony. Rebenga wanted its practitioners declared heretics and punished according-ly. The Spanish ambassadors were instructed to denounce its pernicious presence in the election of popes, bishops, canons, and other church officials. The eminent curial canonist and bishop, Domenico Giacobazzi, noted that due to the simoniacal purchase of church office, Rome had become the prize of prostitutes--an elusive but suggestive statement.[15]

The city of Rome both papal bureaucracy and local residents was also the subject of a few reform proposals. The bishop of Burgos who had visited this capital of Christendom on a number of occasions and died there during the council denounced the terrible turpitude and outrageous public sins of both the clergy and laity of Rome. Such conduct, he claimed, blasphemed God and confirmed infidels in their opposition to the Faith. Of particular concern to Rebenga were the tolerance shown toward the idolatrous practices of pagans and the religious rites of Jews, the protection given to apostate *conversos*, and the conferral on them of Roman citizenship with the right to hold public office and rule over the lands of the Church. The Camaldolese hermits made much of the numerous prostitutes, claiming that they swarmed the City's streets in broad daylight, even around the papal palace, that priests and prelates had not one but many concubines on whom they lavished church revenues, and that so prevalent was the problem that the City had become a stinking and sordid brothel. The solutions recommended were the expulsion of these ladies from Rome or at least their restriction to a remote corner of the City. These measures were, however, felt by these hermits to be inadequate, and new, more serious and efficacious remedies needed to be devised.[16]

[14]Doussinague, 531, 533-41.

[15]Doussinague, 530, 539-40; Domenico Giacobazzi, *De Concilio tractatus* (Roma, 1538), 228B: "Hodie, autem, propter hoc, perdita est omnis devotio: quia Roma facta est frons meretricis."

[16]Doussinague, 530-31; Joaquin Luis Ortega, "Un reformador pretridentino: don Pascual de Ampudia, obispo de Burgos (1496-1512)," *Anthologica Annua* 19 (1972), 413-35; *Libellus*, 706-07.

132

Some of the writers were insistent that the pope embrace their reforms. Giustiniani and Quirini were remarkably blunt. If Leo did not see these widespread abuses under his very nose, it was questionable that he would ever fulfil his function as overseer of the Church. If he saw, but ignored them, he shared in the guilt of the sinners he tolerated and should beware lest he also incur the dreadful punishment God inflicted on Eli, the priest of Siloh, for a similar negligence.[17] Bracciolini warned Leo that men in high office are prone to forget their virtuous past and claim a license for sin. Alert to his own frailty, let Leo surround himself with wise councillors. A doctor once grown ill is not likely to cure others.[18] The current civil and ecclesiastical powers of the pope in Rome are such, according to Rebenga, that Julius II has no excuse for failing to correct the evils there.[19] These admonitions were not lost on the popes.

Both Julius II and Leo X used the Lateran Council to issue decrees reforming various aspects of Rome. The papal office was, however, virtually untouched by the council. As he lay on his deathbed, Julius had the conciliar fathers reaffirm his bull of 1505 which prescribed detailed measures for preventing simony in the election of a successor as bishop of Rome. In spite of his instructions to the Lateran's reform deputation that it reform his own office, Leo X failed to promulgate a single conciliar decree affecting specifically his own personal life or performance of duty. That Leo gave some thought, however fleeting and fuzzy, to self reform is suggested by a statement he made soon after his election. On refusing to wear certain vestments of his predecessors, Leo affirmed that he wished to reform himself first both internally and externally in order the better to reform others. There is no evidence, though, that he undertook any significant personal reform.[20] His commissioning of the conciliar deputation to reform his own household resulted in an important sentence inserted into the bull *Supernae dispositionis arbitrio* of the ninth session. It stated that all the provisions of this decree also applied to the members of the papal household, with the exception that they could continue to wear traditionally red garments.[21]

The cardinals were the subject of some of the prescriptions of this same bull. These papal advisors were forbidden to act as special advocates of political interests or to divulge anything said or done

[17]*Libellus*, 707; 1 Samuel 3:13-14, 4:11-18.
[18]Bracciolini, *De Munere*, 10r - 11v.
[19]Doussinague, 530.
[20]Mansi, 768A - 72D; de Grassi, *Diarium Leonis*, Vat. Lat. 12275, fol. 36r.
[21]Minnich, "Concepts of Reform," 245; Mansi, 880A.

in secret consistory. In processing consistorial provision to major benefices, they were to follow set procedures. While obliged to maintain their residence in Rome, they were also to become knowledgeable about conditions throughout Christendom and keep the pontiff properly informed. After appointment as legate, they were bound to betake themselves within five months to the region assigned. Fixed portions of the revenues from their consistorial benefices were designated for specific purposes. Qualified clerical and religious staffing, plus funds for its support and the maintenance of church property, were to be provided in the cardinals' major commendatory benefices. Their titular churches in Rome required an annual visitation either in person or through a vicar, and careful provision for the pastoral needs of the people and for the material maintenance of the buildings. Distinguished persons seeking the cardinals' assistance at the Curia were to be dealt with in a kindly and courteous manner. Special concern was to be shown to the cases brought by the poor, by religious, and by those oppressed and unjustly burdened.[22]

The cardinals were to give attention to the personnel of their households. If they employed a bishop, they were to treat him as a brother and not assign him menial tasks. Clerical members of their staffs were to wear the attire proper to their status, keep their hair trimmed and scalps tonsured, and avoid costly coverings and ornaments on their beasts of burden. When absent from Rome and not engaged in official business or recreation, these staff members lost their exemptions from the jurisdiction of their ordinaries. Cardinals were to concern themselves with the moral integrity of their servants lest the faithful be scandalized by them. Their households were to be havens of hospitality for the learned and upright, especially for impoverished nobility and men of high repute. But care was also to be taken lest the number of their retainers be beyond their means or judged excessive. Moderation and frugality were to be exercised, too, regarding the material aspects of their households: its building, furnishings, table, and stable.[23]

The personal lives of cardinals were the subject of a series of exhortations. These prelates were to conduct themselves with moderation, sobriety, chastity, and piety, abstaining not only from evil but even from its slightest appearance. They were to have their own chapels and be devoted to the recitation of the divine office and celebration of the Eucharist. Their revenues were to be spent on good and pious purposes and not consumed in extravagant, wasteful, and thoughtless expenditures. When providing for their

---

[22] Mansi, 875C - 77A, 877E - 79A, 880B - 81C.
[23] Mansi, 877E-78A, 879A-80A, 909BC.

relatives, especially those who were worthy and in need, cardinals should not so enrich them with church revenues that others sustain losses. And finally, the total expenses for a cardinal's funeral were not to exceed one and a half thousand florins.[24]

A reform of the Roman Curia, first of the functions and then of the lives of its officials, was promulgated in the council. At the fourth session, Julius had the conciliar fathers reaffirm his bull of March 1512 which reduced fees and eliminated some of the more scandalous practices of the Curia.[25] Leo followed the same procedure. The findings of his reform deputation became the basis for various changes in the number and functions of curial officials and in the fees they could charge for their services.[26] A lengthy bull covering a wide range of curial officials was issued by Leo six days before the eighth session. This document known as *Pastoralis officii* mandated a return of curial practices to the time of Paul II, reduced taxes, fixed service fees, listed prices for various absolutions, and prohibited such abuses as writing with white ink and keeping transactions secret. It also required a careful examination of all candidates for holy orders who requested of the Curia letters authorizing their ordination. When Leo sought conciliarly mandated sanctions to secure its enforcement, the council fathers gave a reluctant approval complaining that the bull failed to reform the reformers, that is, the curial officials who had helped in the composition of the bull. Leo promised to tackle that problem in the following session.[27] The other reforms of curial practice which Leo legislated through the council were prohibitions on special reservations and on the division and union of benefices, limitations on pluralism, reaffirmations of the canonical requirements for promotions, transfer, or deprivation of bishops and abbots, and restrictions on exemptions and appeals to Roman tribunals.[28]

The personal lives of curialists were treated both explicitly and implicitly in the bull *Supernae dispositionis arbitrio*. The third and

---

[24]Mansi, 877DE, 878DE, 881A.

[25]Julius II, *Bulla reformationis officialium Romanae Curiae:* "Et si Romanus Pontifex," B A V, Raccolta I. IV. 961, int. 11 and in the Bibliotheca Angelica, Y.10.39/1; Mansi, 753 AB, 772E, 846A.

[26]Mansi, 816E, 846B; Walther von Hofmann, *Forschungen zur Geschichte der kurialen Behörden vom Schisma bis zur Reformation*, vols. 12 and 13 of *Bibliothek des kgl. preuss. historischen Instituts in Rom* (Roma, 1914), II, 54-64, 240-48, e.g., nr. 239, 248-50, 260; Guilelmus van Gulik and Conradus Eubel, *Hierarchia catholica medii et recentioris aevi sive summorum pontificum S.R.E. Cardinalium ecclesiarum antistitum series*, Vol. 3: *Saeculum XVI ab anno 1503 complectens*, rev. Ludovicus Schmitz-Kallenberg (Münster, 1923), 81-84; *Bullarum diplomatum et privilegiorum sanctorum Romanorum pontificum Taurinensis editio*, ed. Francisco Gaude *et alii* (Torino, 1860), V (1431-1521), 566-67, Leo X, nr. IV.

[27]*Bullarum Taurinensis editio*, V, 571-601, Leo X, nr. V.

[28]Mansi, 875A-76A, 877A-C, 907E-10B.

final section of this conciliar decree specifically prohibited the practice of simony in the Roman Curia and ordered a careful investigation of the Curia for the presence of any persons ill-disposed toward the Faith or feigning to be Christian, especially heretics, those tainted with heresy, and those practicing the Jewish religion. If found and convicted, they were to be duly punished. The bull concluded with a statement affirming that even those of its prescriptions regarding life, customs, and ecclesiastical discipline which did not explicitly mention curialists were also binding on them whether dwelling then in the Roman Curia or elsewhere. The measures which most likely affected these officials were those which made mention of clerics. Those failing to recite their breviary or engaging in blasphemy were liable to deprivation of benefices. Those found guilty of fornication, sodomy, or concubinage were to be punished according to canon law. Deposition, imprisonment, and removal from church office awaited any cleric who once reprimanded continued to invoke demons or practice incantations, divinations, or other superstitions.[29]

Attempts to enforce the Lateran's decrees reforming the procedures and fees of the Curia were not successful. In his desire to please all, to keep papal finances solvent, to protect the investment curialists made in their offices, to reward their labors, and to remove reasons for illicit exactions, Leo allowed questionable practices to continue, granted many exemptions from the conciliar decrees, and raised the fees curialists could legally charge for their services.[30] Given the sporadic nature of his threats and imposition of penalties, unqualified candidates continued to be approved for ordination by the Curia.[31] The piecemeal efforts of his successor Hadrian VI to reform curial practices were opposed by the bureaucrats and undone when his brief pontificate was followed by that of Clement VII. The one area in which reform did make some headway and triumphed for a while under Clement was the careful examination and certification in the Curia of candidates for holy orders. This is attributable to the zeal of Giampietro Carafa whom both pontiffs entrusted with this responsibility.[32] Clement, unfortunately, lacked the determination

[29]Mansi, 881D-82A, D-E, 883A-C, 884D-85A.

[30]Leo X, *Bulla super societatibus officiorum Romanae curiae:* "Romanum Pontificem" (12 January 1514), aii^r, in B A V, Raccolta I.IV.961, int. 15; Hofmann, *Forschungen,* I, 275,314; Ludwig von Pastor, *Storia dei papi dalla fine del medio evo,* Italian version by Angelo Mercati, IV-I (Roma, 1960), 545-47—hereafter cited as Pastor-Mercati.

[31]G. Pelliccia, *La preparazione ed ammissione dei chierici ai santi ordini nella Roma del secolo XVI* (Roma, 1946), 53-76, 82-84.

[32]Robert E. McNally, "Pope Adrian VI (1522-23) and Church Reform," *Archivum Historiae Pontificiae* 7 (1969), 283-84; Antonio Caracciolo, *Vite e gesti di Giovanni Pietro Carafa, cioè di Paolo IIII. Pont. Mas.,* B A V, Barb. Lat. 4953, fol. 53v-54r. Pastor-Mercati, IV-II, (Roma, 1956) 29, 77-78; Mandell Creighton, *A History of the Papacy from the Great Schism to the Sack of Rome,* new ed. (New York, 1897), VI, 242; Pelliccia, *Preparazione ed ammissione,* 90-92.

of Carafa. In spite of the complaints of the German diets, the exhortations of the Emperor, and the advice of such loyal Catholics as Eck, Clement like his cousin Leo did not enforce with vigor the Lateran decrees reforming curial taxes and practices. In its response of autumn 1530 to the twenty-nine complaints of the German diet, a commission of eight cardinals, half of whom had attended the Lateran Council, made thirteen explicit references to the Lateran's decrees which if enforced would remedy abuses often current in the Curia.[33] Serious reform had to wait until Paul III. Soon after his election, he ordered the observance of the conciliarly mandated bull *Pastoralis officii* and subsequently issued other measures which echoed at times the decrees of the Lateran Council.[34] The prudence and resolve of this pontiff accomplished much for the reform of the Curia.

By following the attempts at enforcing the conciliar bull *Supernae dispositionis arbitrio*, some indications can be gathered as to the seriousness of papal efforts at reforming the lives of curialists and other residents of Rome. The same month that the bull was issued (May of 1514), Leo entrusted to cardinals Lorenzo Pucci and Bernardo Dovizi da Bibbiena responsibility for enforcing its provisions against Marranos and Jews respectively.[35] In spite of the bull's stern language about imposing rigorously the penalties prescribed by canon law for fornication, sodomy, and concubinage, Leo seems to have tolerated lax sexual mores in Rome. The census taken three years after the decree's promulgation reveals large numbers of courtesans, mostly female but some male, spread throughout the City and no longer confined to their former district along the Tiber between the Aventine and Capitoline hills. Instead of relegating prostitutes to a corner of the City and imposing stiff penalties, Leo made provision for prevention and repentance. On the feast of the Annunciation he distributed alms to poor girls so that they would have the dowry needed for a respectable marriage. The convent of Santa Maria Maddalena for penitent prostitutes was founded with the financial support of the Compagnia della Carità under the direction of the pope's cousin, cardinal Giulio dei Medici. On the advice of the imperial ambassador, Alberto Pio, who had

---

[33]Gerhard Müller, *Die römische Kurie und die Reformation 1523-34: Kirche und Politik während des Pontifikates Clemens' VII.*, Vol. 38 of *Quellen und Forschungen zur Reformationsgeschichte* (Gütersloher, 1969), 53-54, 172; *Concilium Tridentinum diariorum actorum epistularum tractatuum nova collectio*, ed. Societate Goerresiana, Vol. 12: *Tractatuum pars prior (1513-1548)*, ed. Vincent Schweitzer (Freiburg im Breisgau, 1930), 59:18, 52; 60:7, 33; 61:1, 15 bis, 31, 57; 65:12, 41–66:2— hereafter this collection is cited as *C.T.*

[34]Stephan Ehses "Kirchliche Reformarbeiten unter Papst Paul III. vor dem Trienter Konzil," *Römische Quartalschrift* 15 (1901), 153-74, 395-409, esp. 154 and 168; *C.T.*, IV, 451-57, esp. 451 n.3.

[35]Marino Sanuto, *I Diarii*, ed. Federico Stefani, Guglielmo Berchet, and Nicolò Barozzi (Venezia, 1879ff), XVIII, 210.

seen similar institutions in France, Leo gave it an Augustinian rule modeled on the French and imposed a strict, perpetual cloister, closed even to cardinals. The money left by curial prostitutes who died without wills was assigned to this convent; and when making their wills, prostitutes were required, under threat of having their legacies confiscated, to bequeathe at least a fifth of their wealth to this house of refuge.[36]

When the conciliar bull, *Supernae dispositionis arbitrio*, was initially ignored at Rome, Leo X ordered his official, Amadeo Berruti, to secure observance. Berruti was given exceptional powers as governor in the City and vice-camerlengo in the Curia with jurisdiction over both civil and ecclesiastical cases. Lest anyone claim ignorance of Latin as an excuse for non-compliance, Berruti issued in Italian an edict summarizing the measures contained in the bull. He warned that the penalties therein mandated would be imposed according to the degree of disobedience.[37] Another edict was promulgated on 1 October 1516 by Girolamo de Ghinucci, who in virtue of his office as general auditor of cases in the apostolic camera was the ordinary executor in the Roman Curia of apostolic decrees. He demanded observance of the council's bulls and noted that they were available for consultation in the office of the notary Guglielmo de Vergio and included specific reforms of the practices and officials of the Curia. Leo, he claimed, was resolved on getting compliance everywhere, but especially at Rome which must be freed of its unsavory reputation as teacher of sin to the rest of Christendom.[38] Twelve days later the vicar general for spiritual affairs in the diocese of Rome, Domenico Giacobazzi, issued his edict requiring those in his jurisdiction, whether lay, clerical, exempt, or Jews, to comply with the decrees of the council. He affirmed that it was fitting that the renowned city of Rome which divine mercy established as the head of the world, should put these decrees into immediate execution.[39]

---

[36]Mariano Armellini, "Un censimento della città di Roma sotto il pontificato di Leone X tratto da un codice inedito dell'Archivio Vaticano," *Gli Studi in Italia: Periodico didattico scientifico e letterario*, Anno IV, Vol. II (1881), 890-909, esp. 897 and Anno V (1882), Vol. I., 69-84, 161-92, 321-55, 481-518, but esp. 162-84 and 328-29; Emmanuel Rodocanachi, *Courtisanes et bouffons: Etude de moeurs romaines au XVIe siècle* (Paris, 1894), 21-22, 59-64, 69-71; *Histoire de Rome: Le Pontificat de Léon X 1513-1521* (Paris, 1931), 195, n. 3; Leo X, *Bulla Monasterii Sanctae Mariae Magdalenae Ordinis Sancti Augustini Convertitarum de Urbe:* "Salvator Noster" (19.V.1520), in Archivio di Stato di Roma, Bandi e buste, nr. 293, int. 34, fol. Aii[r-v]; Peter Partner, *Renaissance Rome, 1500-1559: A Portrait of a Society* (Berkeley, 1976), 97-111.
[37]Amadeo Berruti, "Monitorio per la observatione de la reformatione del sacro concilio Laterano," in Mansi, *Sacrorum conciliorum collectio*, vol. 35: *In quo continentur reliqui textus ab anno MCDXIV ad annum MDCCXXIV pertinentes* (reprint Paris, 1902), 1586A-88B.
[38]Mansi, XXXV, 1584A-85D.
[39]Mansi, XXXV, 1582B-83D.

138

These edicts of the papal vicars were not without effect. In mid-January of 1517 Alessandro Gabbioneta wrote from Rome to the Marquis of Mantova that a reform of the clergy was evidenced by their wearing of priestly attire. Clerics who came to the City on business bringing with them expensive and colorful wardrobes were surprised to discover that they were required to wear ankle-length robes closed at the collars with large hoods in the style of a canon. Girolamo Aleandro, former rector of the University of Paris and now agent of the prince-bishop of Liège, Evrard de La Marck, conformed externally to these reforms lest he hinder his negotiations; but beneath the approved robes, he wore more stylish ones even in the summer heat of the City. Much to his relief, the rigors of this reform which lasted several months finally abated.[40] That reports from Rome singled out for comment the phenomenon of ecclesiastics wearing the attire prescribed by the council, as if this dress code constituted a central element in church reform, suggests that the principal papal concern was for a visual symbol of the restored clerical order: withdrawn from secular affairs, dedicated to its spiritual mission, and obedient to the mandates of the hierarchy. Had not Leo soon after his election described reform in terms of wearing a set of priestly robes not associated with the attire of his delinquent predecessors and thereby signaling an interior renewal? His efforts to enforce effectively, even if only temporarily, the other provisions of this bull are not easily documented.

That the reforms of the Lateran Council did not become a permanent feature of Leonine Rome is suggested by their absence from a collection of statutes compiled for the governance of the City. The first three books are basically Paul II's 1471 codification of civil, criminal, and administrative legislation. While the preface claims that these laws were revised,[41] there is no evidence that they were brought into line with the council's decrees. The stiffest penalties for blasphemy in the Roman code were a ten pound fine and eight days of detention. The council allowed judges to condemn repeated offenders to life imprisonment or the galleys.[42] Although detailed civil legislation prohibited concubinage, fornication between single consenting adults was not made illegal; indeed, the code provided protection for prostitutes: from rape and kidnapping, and from having their doors set aflame or manure deposited at their windows and doors. Imprisonment, torture, and exile awaited

---

[40]Pastor-Mercati, IV-I, 546, n.7; IV-II, 650; Léon Dorez, "Une lettre de Gilles de Gourmont à Girolamo Aleandro (1531) suivie de documents nouveaux sur Aleandro," *Revue des Bibliothèques* 8 (1898), 214.

[41]*Statuta et novae reformationes urbis Romae eiusdemque varia privilegia a diversis romanis pontificibus emanata in sex libros divisa novissime compilata* (Romae: per Stephanum Guilereti de Lunarivilla Tullensis diocesis, 1523), A$_{ii}$r, A$_{iii}$r; Creighton, *History of the Papacy*, VI, 31.

[42]*Statuta*, Book II, chp. 102; Mansi, XXXII, 882B.

the perpetrators of such crimes. The conciliar fathers directed their legislation not to the protection of these ladies, but to the severe punishment of their clerical clients.[43] The Lateran's decree against false Christians of Jewish descent did not apparently affect provisions in the code condemning heretics or regulating Jewish life in the City.[44] A partial explanation for these discrepancies may be found in the composition of the commission entrusted with revising the code.[45] Of its six members, only one (provided Bishop Farnese is cardinal Alessandro) ever attended the council and by the time the revised code was promulgated Hadrian VI was pontiff.

Reform-minded prelates urged Leo's successor, Hadrian Florenszoon Dedel who had never attended the council, to bring about church renewal. The Swiss cardinal and former member of the conciliar reform deputation, Matthias Schiner, wrote the new pope advising him to begin his reforms with Roman officials, their households, and their venal performance of curial functions. A knowledgeable curialist, cardinal Lorenzo Campeggio, lamented the fact that the Lateran Council's decrees regulating clerical life were approved by all, but thus far observed by few. He exhorted the Dutch pope to obtain enforcement not only of these conciliar measures but also of those prohibiting a plurality of benefices.[46] A former member of both the Pisan and Lateran Councils and now bishop of Guardialfiera, Zaccaria Ferreri, directed the pope's attention to the city of Rome, especially the Curia. Like Christ with whip in hand, His vicar was to drive from the Temple those who bought and sold spiritual favors and also those who scandalized the faithful by their lewdness. If Rome, the head, mother and teacher of the other churches were reformed, the other churches would follow: "Purge Rome, and the world is cleansed; restore and reform Rome and the whole world is restored and reformed."[47]

The new pontiff accepted this criticism of Rome. In his allocution to the cardinals following his coronation, Hadrian solicited their help in correcting the vices, injustices, and immoral conduct of the Curia so that once again it would become a model of righteousness and norm of proper conduct. His instructions to the bishop of Feramo, Francesco Chieregati, sent as papal nuncio to the imperial diet at Nürnberg in September of 1522, promised to begin church reform with the Curia "from which has come perhaps all this evil." Illness has spread from the head to the members and must be cured

---

[43] *Statuta*, II, 60, IV, 22-23; Mansi, 882DE.
[44] *Statuta*, I, 2, III, 159-61; Mansi, 884E-85A.
[45] *Statuta*, A$_{iii}$r-v
[46] *C.T.*, XII, 8-9; Pastor-Mercati, IV-II, 693-94.
[47] *C.T.*, XII, 23,27.

at its source. Christ also began his work of reform by purging the Temple.[48]

Hadrian began his reform with the Curia. Instead of issuing a sweeping set of regulations, he took up each question as it came to his attention and after mature reflection issued the appropriate corrective measure. The curial cardinals resented his curtailment of their privileges. He brought to Rome, housed in the Vatican palace, and appointed as his agents for the reform of Rome two men he had met in Spain: Giampietro Carafa, bishop of Chieti, and Tommaso Gazzella, a jurist from Gaeta. It seems they were charged to move especially against blasphemers, usurers, simoniacs, fictive *conversos*, despisers of the Faith, corrupters of youth, and ordainers of unworthy candidates.[49] They, thus, became in effect the enforcers at Rome of a number of the Lateran's decrees.

Soon after his election as pope Clement VII, Giulio dei Medici, who had figured prominently at the Lateran Council and had applied its decrees to his archdiocese of Florence, took measures to reform the city and Curia of Rome in accordance with these same decrees. On 24 February 1524 he urged the cardinals gathered in consistory to see that members of their households wore clerical tonsure and garb, that prelates were attired with rochet (*rochetto*) and felt cap (*pileo*), and that the cardinals, especially Lorenzo Pucci (the grand penitentiary) and Pompejo Colonna (the vice-chancellor) warned the curial officials subject to them to observe the Lateran decrees.[50] Clement appointed men like Giampietro Carafa, Jacopo Sadoleto, and Matteo Ghiberti to a commission charged with bringing the City into compliance with the council. On learning from their report about the abuses and corruptions practiced by curial officials, the pope registered his official displeasure. In hopes of eliminating continued disregard of the conciliar decree governing promotion to sacred orders, Clement put the officials in charge of examining and certifying candidates under the sole authority of Carafa whom he appointed as his special vicar.[51] At the consistory of September ninth, the cardinals agreed with the pope's proposal to

[48] *C.T.*, XII, 31; Creighton, *History of the Papacy*, VI, 254-60; John C. Olin, *The Catholic Reformation: Savonarola to Ignatius Loyola. Reform in the Church 1495-1540* (New York, 1969), 125.

[49] See above note 32 and Rainaldi, 1523, nr. 117.

[50] Fondo Consistorialia, Acta Miscellanea, Vol. 20, fol. 13V in Archivio Segreto Vaticano; Müller, *Römische Kurie*, 17-19, 26; Richard C. Trexler, *Synodal Law in Florence and Fiesole 1306-1518*, vol. 268 of *Studi e Testi* (Città del Vaticano, 1971), 10-11; Mansi, XXXV, 215-318, esp. 232D-34B, 270E-72B, 274D-75D, 283B-D, 290B-D, 304B.

[51] A. Caracciolo, *Vite e gesti*, fol. 54V-55V, 57r-V; Pelliccia, *Preparazione ed ammissione*, 90-91, 462; Richard M. Douglas, *Jacopo Sadoleto 1477-1547, Humanist and Reformer* (Cambridge, Mass., 1959), 36-37. Douglas's assertion that Carafa was vicar-general is not, however, supported by the partial list found in Konrad Eubel, "Series vicariorum Urbis a. 1200-1558," *Römische Quartalschrift für christliche Alterthumskunde und für Kirchengeschichte*, 8 (1894), 499.

prepare Rome for the Holy Year. All churches were to be visited and corrected, parish clergy to be examined and those found unworthy prohibited from celebrating the Mass at least during the Jubilee, and regular clergy to be prepared as confessors. By the end of October the zealous Carafa had produced notable results: candidates for the priesthood were strictly examined free of charge, ordained priests were carefully checked before being allowed to celebrate the liturgy, religious services were put on a regular basis and churches filled. Carafa was soon hailed as the reformer of the papal court.[52]

In November Clement renewed his efforts at a reform of the City. At a consistory on the seventh he ordered the cardinals to correct their households, especially the attire and morals of their retainers. The decrees of the Lateran Council were to be applied and the Curia reformed. Lorenzo Pucci was charged with preparing the minutes of a bull on this subject. After mature deliberation and with the advice and consent of the college of cardinals, Clement published on the twenty-first of that month, almost a year to the day of his election as pope, the bull *Meditatio cordis nostri.*[53]

In this document, Clement recalled the efforts of his cousin Leo X to reform morals and secure observance of canon law by his bull *Supernae dispositionis arbitrio* of the ninth session of the Lateran Council. Clement affirmed his own chief desire to see that decree observed. He recounted its contents generally by repeating verbatim its provisions with minor stylistic changes in the text and a rearrangement of some of its sections. The only exception from its provisions he explicitly mentioned was an exemption for non-resident curialists from the obligation of wearing the capuche.[54] A comparison of Clement's account with the original Lateran decree, however, reveals a number of more important alterations. Over one-half of the conciliar bull has been dropped. Deleted were those sections dealing with curial procedures in the provision of benefices and any measures directly affecting the cardinals' personal life style, consistorial or curial duties, legations, limitations on benefices, and responsibilities for informing the pope about conditions throughout Christendom. Also dropped were: prohibitions against lay interference in clerical affairs; condemnations of sodomy, sorcery, superstition, and feigned belief, especially in the

[52]Letters of Valerio Lugio to Francesco de Zuane de la Seda, 21·X·1524 and of Di Marin da Pozo to Francesco Spinelli, 21·XII·1524 in Sanuto, *I Diarii*, XXXVII, 88-89, 357; Müller, *Römische Kurie*, 37; Hubert Jedin, *A History of the Council of Trent*, trans. Ernest Graf (New York, 1957) I, 422.

[53]Fondo Consistorialia, Acta Miscellanea, vol. 20, fol. 15^v; Clement VII, *Meditatio cordis nostri assidue*, (Romae, XI Kal. Dec. 1524), B$_i^r$ in BAV, Raccolta I.IV, 1680, int. 14, fol. 58^r-63^r.

[54]Clement VII, *Meditatio cordia*, B$_i^r$.

142

Roman Curia; and requirements that youths be given religious instructions and clerics recite the divine office.[55] The only thing Clement added to the Lateran decree was a prohibition against beneficed and ordained clerics wearing linen shirts with effeminate ruffles and pleats, insisting instead that clerical garb be simple and decent in style and somber in color, and thus witness to a priestly dignity, purity of mind, and fitting service in the heavenly militia of Christ. This bull *Meditatio cordis* was to be published as soon as possible in Rome and elsewhere and observance in the City was to be secured by the vice-camerlengo, the governor, the auditor, and other competent judges.[56]

These actions of Clement in the first year of his pontificate would seem to indicate that the Lateran decrees were considered central to his plan for a reform of Rome. The alterations he made in the bull of the ninth session suggest a desire to deal with higher prelates in private, to reissue only those portions of the Lateran decree which he could realistically hope to enforce, and to eliminate the more obvious sources of scandal by insisting on externals.[57] Observance of this decree seems to have lasted at least until the Sack of 1527 temporarily removed Carafa, its zealous enforcer, from the Roman scene.[58]

This brief survey of the first decade at Rome following the council has shown that the Lateran decrees were not forgotten in the wake of the Wittenberg theses. The papacy in the person of Hadrian and Clement saw them as tools for correcting some of the abuses in the head, in the church at Rome, which had given added force to the Protestant critique. In some sense a culmination of the pre-Lutheran Catholic Reform, the Lateran decrees went on to become an element in the Counter-Reformation program for Rome. In the edict on the reform of the clergy of Rome issued after the Council of Trent, echoes of the Lateran legislation can be detected, there is even a specific reference to the Lateran Council in this edict.[59] The Lateran's reforms, especially those touching clerical garb, tonsure, and livery had become part of the Roman patrimony. They had helped in a limited way to bring about a reform in the head, in the House of the Lord, which would eventually affect the members, and spread to the world, *ab urbe ad orbem*.

---

[55] Sections dropped by Clement include the following: Mansi, 874D-79D, 881CD, 882E-85B.

[56] Clement VII, *Meditatio cordis*, B$_i$v - B$_{ii}$r

[57] In his undated memorial, Tommaso Campeggio acknowledged the possible need to revise this Lateran decree: "In primis videtur innovanda Bulla reformationis edita per felicis recordationis Leonem X in nona sessione novissimi Lateranensis concilii sed prius in consultatione posita an aliqua sint moderanda addenda vel minuenda propter quae forte non fuit usu recepta." - see his *Consilium quoddam de reformanda ecclesia*, BAV, Cod. Reg. Lat., 451, fol. 225^r.

[58] Pelliccia, *Preparazione ed ammissione*, 92.

[59] Jacobus Sabellus, *Edictum super reformatione cleri Urbis* (Romae, 30.X.1566), fol. 1^r-2^r in BAV, Stamp. Chig. II. 1073, int. 15.

V

THE AUTOBIOGRAPHY OF ANTONIO DEGLI AGLI (ca. 1400-77), HUMANIST AND PRELATE *

Until this century publications concerning Antonio degli Agli (ca. 1400-77) have been confined to brief and repetitious outlines of his life and writings. In 1924 Vladimiro Zabughin surprised the scholarly world with two paragraphs on Agli's life and hagiographical interests, which contained exciting new material, but this Russian émigré neglected to indicate in this study published posthumously the source of his information. More recently the printed inventory of the Florentine State Archives (1951-), and those on humanist manuscripts by Mario Cosenza (1962) and Paul Oskar Kristeller (1965-67) have identified a variety of manuscripts which can serve as the basis for new research on Agli's career and literary works. A. D'Addario (1960) and John H. Swogger (1975) have added to our understanding of Agli, but they did not have access to Zabughin's source.[1] Undoubtedly this consisted of the autobiographical dialogue written in 1475 and identified by Bernardino Feliciangeli (1917) in a footnote to a study devoted to another theme.[2] An annotated edition of Agli's dialogue is currently in preparation. Meanwhile, it may be helpful to share with scholars some of the highlights of that dialogue together with occasional references to other sources which help to explain particular points.

But before examining this document, a few words about Antonio's family seem appropriate. The Agli were an old respected Florentine family. His father was Bellincione, son of Bernardo d'Aglio degli Agli ("oggi dell'Scalogni") and of Tommasa di Bellincione di Messer Cece Donati. In 1395 Bellincione and his brother Bartolommeo married sisters, Dianora and Bartolommea, the daughters of Francesco di Ser Neri. Bellincione and Dianora had seven known children, the oldest a daughter, the rest sons, of whom Antonio was the eldest, born ca. 1400. An early death or religious vocation claimed all of his brothers but one, Francesco. In 1438 he married Vaggia, daughter of Giovanni Matteo Corsini. Of their offspring, a daughter Dianora, who in 1456 married Tedice degli Albizzi (d. 1480) and then Marcello di Giovanni di Marcello di Strozza Strozzi, was Antonio's principal heir.[3]

According to his own account, Antonio's youth was plagued by his family's financial difficulties. Owing to poverty he grew up in the countryside. His father, unable to pay the tax levied on him, had to fend off its collectors. When he died leaving behind a wife, daughter of marriageable age, and six sons, the oldest of whom, Antonio, was a mere fourteen years old, creditors and tax collectors descended on the grieving family and threatened imprisonment or the loss of what few goods were still in the house. Household utensils and furnishings were sacrificed for freedom. To earn some income, the widowed Dianora and her daughter worked day and night with wool. The boys went about dirty and ragged, almost naked, begging for the barest necessities of food and drink. Eventually the house and a few pieces of land were sold to provide a dowry for Antonio's sister and pay back taxes. With her daughter married, Dianora and her sons headed for Florence where she rented a small dwelling.[4]

In Florence Antonio became the principal bread-winner of the family. The only one of the sons who knew letters and arithmetic, he found remunerative employment handling the accounts of a wool merchant. When a serious famine hit Florence, however, Antonio's salary proved scarcely enough to support one person, much less his family. His mother, who in the face of repeated adversity trusted in God and maintained a cheerful spirit, found help for her family from a miller she regarded as God's true servant, who provided food for many in need. The burden of providing for his family in such difficult times was for Antonio a source of intolerable worries.[5]

With great difficulty, Antonio tried to meet his family obligations, while not neglecting totally his own personal development. Once his work was ended, he spent his nights in study, but even these precious moments were reduced by the need to earn a little extra income by illuminating the large letters in manuscript books. In the hope of learning new things, he joined a confraternity most of whose members were mechanics and artisans. But instead of helping him advance intellectually, these sodalists generally had only contempt for learning, claiming that letters inflamed one with pride and not charity, and warning him that his avid pursuit of letters could lead to insanity. In later life he acknowledged that secular letters can, indeed, lead to pride and corrupt morals by their teachings contrary to the Christian message. He also admitted to having been enamoured as a youth with the vanities of painting, sculpture, and theatre, and to having struggled earnestly with the temptations of the flesh. From such snares God rescued him. His membership in the confraternity and circle of pious friends helped him eventually to find and follow God's will for him. The time he spent at the confraternity's quarters was given over to singing psalms and hymns to the praise of God and flagellating himself. The miller, who had supported Antonio's family in its need, was a member of the same confraternity and he took a genuine interest in the lad and gave him encouragement. Antonio also found support in a group of friends who met on feast days to share their enthusiasm for learning. But so depressing was the daily spectacle of his family's misery that Antonio thought of fleeing to Bologna where he might pursue an education. The unresolved conflict between his family responsibilities and personal ambitions so exhausted him that he suffered a breakdown. By day he was racked with worries, in the dark terrorized by nightmares.[6]

Antonio slowly recovered with the help of friends who on occasion supplied his material needs and who appear to have been very pious. With them he would discuss the Scriptures, and on feast days he attended services and sermons in various churches. So intent was Antonio on hearing the word of God, that he grew impatient with preachers who neglected the Bible on which he now focused his interest. In this new frame of mind, his former anxieties no longer weighed him down.[7]

New difficulties soon befell him. At the textile company where he worked Antonio discovered that a large sum of money for which he was responsible was missing. He suspected that it had been stolen by someone with access to the storeroom, but feared that he himself would be accused of the crime, be arrested, and questioned under torture. He hardly expected that the supervisor of the storeroom, who was related to the thief, would help expose the real criminal. Antonio appealed for divine assistance and decided to go himself to the police offering to be the first of the workshop members to undergo interrogation. When his co-workers learned of his plan, the thief's relative begged him to delay. Within a few days, a friendly friar secretly brought Antonio a coffer containing the stolen money. After a year Antonio resigned his post and shortly thereafter found employment outside the wool trade.[8]

Antonio's new position not only provided a good income but introduced him to the world of humanism. His employer was a learned Florentine, probably Antonio Corbinelli, who hired him to direct final construction of his spacious home, a task which consumed Antonio's daylight hours. In exchange, this Florentine promised to instruct him in Latin literature. Antonio learned the rudiments with astonishing speed and his employer read to him some books of the poets and smaller works by Cicero. With the vigor of a twenty-year old, Antonio spent entire nights and the summer months lost in study of the classics. From books and charts he also derived the necessary technical information to complete the construction work. Whether riding or walking he was busy with his books. He later claimed that books were his only real teacher. From Cicero, Seneca, and Jerome he derived inspiration to carry on, even though he knew he did not understand all he read and hesitated to try his own hand at writing Latin, despite his teacher's exhortations. This routine of work and study was abruptly ended by a new financial problem.[9]

Family obligations once again pressed upon Antonio when the 250 gold pieces pledged on his uncle's behalf fell due. Realizing that he could pay not even the smallest part of this sum, Antonio took refuge in a Church-sponsored hospital to escape imprisonment for debt. To earn some income for himself and his family, Antonio hired himself out as a scribe and teacher of grammar, thereby increasing his knowledge of Latin. The tedious life in the hospital however made it seem like a prison. His mother and brother, moreover, mourned him as dead. Rather than face the alternative of imprisonment in the Stinche or exile from Florence, Antonio decided to become a cleric. Later he repented his ignoble motives for becoming God's minister, yet felt his decision was part of God's providential plan which draws good from evil.[10]

As a cleric he continued to support his mother and brothers on income derived from his school. In 1428 Giovanni di Bicci dei Medici had the young priest appointed as the first rector of the canonry of SS. Cosimo and Damiano which he had just established in the church of San Lorenzo. Antonio was eventually forced to resign this rectorship in 1436 because his duties as prior of SS. Apostoli in Florence and as provost of S. Maria di Poggibonsi prevented him from fulfilling personally the obligations of residency and of celebrating Mass and singing choir at San Lorenzo. But even before receiving the other benefices, the revenues from this canonry proved sufficient to meet the needs of Antonio and his family, and he soon gave up the school and instead devoted his energies to sacred letters.[11]

Tragedy followed with the death of his saintly mother and three brothers whom he deeply mourned. Of these brothers, the pious Jacopo, whom he personally instructed in Latin, died at the age of twenty; and a few years later, in 1431, soon after ordination as a Dominican priest, Fra Pietro, Jacopo's junior, died at the monastery of S. Maria Novella. Except for Francesco, all of Antonio's other brothers also became religious.[12]

As a canon of San Lorenzo, Antonio devoted himself to his priestly duties, celebrating the liturgy and preaching. His special ministry seems to have been with youth, and among the many young noblemen was probably Piero dei Medici for whom Antonio was "preceptor olim tuus." Foreshadowing what another member of his mother's Neri family would do in Rome a century later, Antonio gathered the lads on feast days and accompanied them to a monastery or to some other quiet place away from the noisy city. Once there they would discuss among themselves some sacred theme. In order the better to understand the biblical passages thus discussed, Antonio took up the study of Greek using as his texts the *Iliad* of Homer, hymns of Pindar, the *Cyropaedia* of Xenophon, and orations of Isocrates. New responsibilities, however, prevented him from mastering Greek as he had Latin.[13]

Antonio would have loved to have continued this simple, tranquil, and pleasant pattern of life, but fell victim to a severe abdominal pain ("pugna enim intra praecordia"), which so strained his nerves that he was unable to write. On learning of the arrival in Florence on 23 June 1434 of the papal refugee Eugenius IV, Antonio summoned a friend and dictated a letter which he sent to the pope once his own illness ended.[14]

No sooner had the pope read the letter than he summoned Antonio and subsequently appointed him teacher of his seventeen-year old nephew, Pietro Barbo. According to Vespasiano da Bisticci Antonio held this post as long as the Roman curia remained in Florence. But these duties forced him to discontinue his study of Greek just when he was almost able on his own to understand the Gospels and Psalter. It is unclear whether some of the benefices he received under Eugenius were in recompense for his services. He was appointed prior of the church of S. Niccolò oltr'Arno and in 1438 succeeded Andrea Vannozzi as a canon of S. Maria del Fiore. In the following year the pope appointed him as presiding priest of S. Maria dell'Impruneta, a baptismal collegiate church some six miles south of Florence. Its miraculous picture of Mary made it a popular pilgrim's shrine and its revenues were second only to those of the local archbishop.[15]

The handsome revenues which he derived from these benefices and from his later episcopal offices were lavished on various causes. While his only reference in the autobiography to Impruneta was an allusion to his rural refuge from public life, this church occupied a central place in his thoughts and affections. For this haven in the hills he drew up a program of renovation and spent huge sums hiring architects and artists of such stature as Michelozzo and the della Robbias to execute his plans. His earlier interest in painting and sculpture which he had formerly considered as mere vanities, together with his experience in the building trade, were now given full scope in a pious endeavor with a sound theological rationale which he propounded in his *De racionibus fidei*. In this work he defended, among other things, miraculous pictures and shrines.[16] When remodeling the shrine at Impruneta, he seems to have skillfully eliminated traditional, superstitious objects and practices. To prevent the church's revenues from being later misused, he endowed nine chaplaincies and agreed with a plan of the church patrons, the Buondelmonti, to convert the collegiate chapter into a Benedictine house of the Santa Giustina congregation—which, however, was never carried out.[17] Apparently Antonio also contributed to the renovations of his others churches as well as helping to support a convent of nuns where for many years he served as chaplain and spiritual father. He also endowed some benefices which he reserved for members of the Buondelmonti and Agli families.[18]

In other ways, too, he came repeatedly to the aid of his relatives, providing a dowry for a cousin and rescuing an uncle and nephew from debt, even to the point of jeopardizing his own finances. Deserving humanists and numerous unnamed poor were also recipients of his benefactions.[19]

In 1464 Antonio's life took a new turn when his former student, Pietro Barbo, was elected pope, taking the name Paul II. According to Vespasiano the pope summoned his old teacher and had him take up residence in the curia where Antonio was honored and loved by the highest ranking prelates. But he found Rome so uncongenial that he resolved to return to the rustic simplicity of Impruneta with his integrity intact. Contrary to his own wishes, however, Antonio was appointed on Christmas eve of 1465 archbishop of Ragusa in Dalmatia. He felt himself unfit and unable to carry out these new responsibilities, which brought him not only envy but also a series of misfortunes. Subsequently, on 4 May 1467, Paul II transferred Antonio from Ragusa (a see he apparently never resided in) to Fiesole, a diocese just outside Florence. But even this post was not to his liking, and on 30 April 1470 Antonio was transferred again, this time to Volterra, a see he actively sought.[20]

Antonio, however, also soon found this position disagreeable, seeing it as fitting punishment for his former ambition. Becoming embroiled in a legal battle over the recently opened alum pit owned by the bishopric, he appealed to Lorenzo dei Medici to work out a settlement that would protect the interests of the Church yet be useful and agreeable to the citizens. He later suggested that a local commission of impartial Florentine clerics or a committee named by the pope work out the differences. Meanwhile the city was in turmoil; urged on by pledges of support from some Italian princes, factions of the Volterran citizenry grew so contentious as to rebel openly against Florentine authority. Antonio tried desperately to mediate matters between the town and the Medici, but contrary to his wishes, the episcopal residence became a secret rebel military center. In vain did he try to regain possession of it. The crisis came to a tragic end when the army sent by Florence to restore peace sacked the town after it had surrendered. Among the victims was the bishop who lost everything including his house which was demolished to build a fortress on the site. Efforts to regain a residence in the town apparently came to nothing and Antonio ruled his diocese through a vicar while living at Impruneta.[21]

Diocesan problems, involving greed, corruption and insubordination, also troubled the bishop. Frustrated at not being able personally to resolve such difficulties, Antonio often turned to Lorenzo dei Medici.[22] In autumn of 1474 an attractive solution to all his problems as bishop of Volterra appeared. When the archbishopric of Pisa was about to become vacant, he begged Lorenzo to support his transfer. But Antonio's hopes were disappointed and three years later he died still bishop of Volterra and was buried in his church at Impruneta.[23]

Despite continuing ill health and various clerical and familial responsibilities, Antonio produced an impressive corpus of writings. As of 31 August 1475 he listed by title 123 works.[24] In addition there are the letter of consolation to Eugenius IV, his sermon on the power of a supreme pontiff and of a universal council, his essay on the immortality of the soul, his oration on behalf of the Volterrans, his book on envy, and the autobiographical dialogue itself, bringing the number to 129.[25] Besides these are numerous letters of an administrative nature which are still extant.

Among the recipients of Antonio's texts were: popes Eugenius IV, Nicholas V, Pius II, Paul II, and Sixtus IV; cardinals Ioannos Bessarion, Jacopo Ammannati, and a certain Niccolo of Pistoia (!); his fellow Florentines Cosimo and Piero dei Medici, Marsilio Ficino, Niccolò Corbizzi, and Filippo Ugolini; the Lucchese Niccolò da Fivizzano ; the citizens of Volterra ; and the nephews of Paul II.[26] Several of these writings were consolatory pieces.[27]

The occasions for some of his writings are suggested by their titles. Thus, for example, from the heading on surviving copies of his poem on friendship, we know that he participated in the 1441 laurel crown competition in Florence. The sacking of Volterra in 1472 inspired an invective against mercenary troops and an attack on their commander Federico II da Montefeltro.[28]

A large group of Antonio's writings were in the epideictic form of a *laudatio* or *panegyricus*. Those praised ranged from God, saints, and heroes of old, to his contemporary Florentines. He tried to complete Traversari's project by compiling ten books on the lives and deeds of the saints of apostolic and patristic times. St. Francis of Assisi merited a separate work. But he also found many figures from classical antiquity deserving of a special *laudatio* such as Bias of Priene and Pittacus of Mitylene, Socrates, Aglaus the poorest man of Arcadia, Mucius Scaevola, and many others. Florentine contemporaries who were singled out for an encomium were archbishop Antonino Pierozzi, abbot Ambrogio Traversari, Cosimo dei Medici, the poet-chancellors Leonardo Bruni and Carlo Marsuppini both of Arezzo, and the humanists Niccolò Niccoli, Filippo Ugolini, and Antonio Corbinelli, his own former teacher.[29]

As targets of invective or disagreement were Judas Iscariot, the Neopythagorean theories of Apollonius of Tyana, Democritus' ideas on physics, the Brachmanes' philosophy of ancient India, and the "mathematicians" of his own day.[30]

Antonio also wrote treatises on moral virtues and vices, such as his four books on the conduct of life and an exhortation to good morals.[31] He claimed that writing was one tactic he used to overcome his own temptations.[32]

He also enjoyed explaining to others abstruse and difficult texts.[33] One of his favorite literary activities was writing biblical commentaries.[34].

A number of Antonio's writings reflect an element of sadness. He penned a book containing various lamentations, another on illness and the doctor, and yet another on old age. Death in general and his own approaching demise were the subjects of three works. A vision of the cries of the damned was described in a book he entitled *Infernus*.[35]

A happier destiny for man because of God's grace was also explored in his writings. In his earliest work, a short dialogue, Antonio sought to explain why God allows a tyrant to inflict intolerable suffering on a martyr. To prevent the persecution of Christians, he also wrote an exhortation to stir princes to fight the infidels.[36]

Public affairs also interested Antonio; he wrote a book on offices and also treated church offices individually. Thus there is a sermon on the power of the supreme pontiff and of a general council; a treatise on the difficulty, labor, and dangers of administering the Roman pontificate; a book on those things to be observed by a bishop; on whether the episcopal office should be resigned; and on the dignity, office, and morals of priests. What he treated in his work on the republic or empire of the god of gods is not clear. For his former student Piero dei Medici he wrote on the defense of the republic.[37]

A variety of other topics also captured his attention. He recorded the dreams he had about his good friend Leonardo Dati, the secretary of Paul II and bishop of Massa. Dante and Cicero were compared in another piece. On women he wrote a defense in four books, on pleasure a single book. For history he seems to have had a particular predilection. He wrote on its utility and attempted to trace the history of the world from creation to his own day, but stopped in the mid-thirteenth century. He wrote a biography of pope Eugenius IV, and of course, his own life was the subject of the dialogue here studied.[38]

Of these 129 literary works only about a seventh has survived.[39] The ideas they contain, especially his Platonic theology and profound piety, deserve to be studied by scholars.

What Antonio degli Agli attempted to convey at some length and with interesting detail in the autobiographical dialogue and in his other writings was succinctly summarized in an epitaph for his tomb written by Sebastiano Salvino but never used:

Here lies Antonio degli Agli, bishop of Volterra and outstanding theologian whom the chorus of Muses and the paupers mourn: the poor because they have lost, alas, the kindest refuge; the Muses because they no longer have both the melodious lyre and song. Who in his time wrote more books? Who was more elegant? Who finally more learned? Did he not preside over the churches of Ragusa, Fiesole, and finally Volterra? The temple of his holy Mary in the Pine Grove preserves his bones and name. While life remained, as you can see, he always served and embellished it. What now? [His] soul is safe in heaven where he has happily attained the rewards of his labors.[40].

V

186

NOTES

* The American Philosophical Society has graciously provided the funding for the research on which this article is based. I am especially grateful to Dottoresse Paola Peruzzi and Caterina Schupfer of the Archivio di Stato, Florence, for their help in tracking down Agli's genealogy and to Don Giacomo Boccanera of the Biblioteca Valentiniana Comunale, Camerino, for assisting me with my work on the manuscript copy of the *Dialogus*. Dr. Arthur Field kindly furnished valuable bibliographical references. Mr. James Todesca of the Catholic University of America helped to provide a working transcription of the text.

[1] For extensive bibliographies on Antonio degli Agli, see M. E. Cosenza, *Biographical and Bibliographical Dictionary of the Italian Humanists and of the World of Classical Scholarship in Italy 1300-1800*, I, Boston, 1962, p. 141; A. D'Addario, "Agli, Antonio," in *Dizionario biografico degli Italiani*, I, Rome, 1960, pp. 400-01; and J. H. Swogger, *Antonio degli Agli's "Explanatio symbolorum Pythagore:" An Edition and a Study of Its Place in the Circle of Marsilio Ficino*, Ph. D. Thesis, University of London, 1975, pp. 314-20. For his manuscripts see especially: *Archivio mediceo avanti il Principato: inventario*, Rome, 1951ff, I, II, IV passim, and P. O. Kristeller, *Iter Italicum*, I-II, London/Leiden, 1965-67, passim.

[2] B. Feliciangeli, "Le proposte per la guerra contro i Turchi presentate da Stefano Taleazzi vescovo di Torcello a papa Alessandro VI," *Archivio della Reale Società Romana di storia patria*, xl (1917), pp. 5-63, here p. 29 n., and V. Zabughin, *Storia del Rinascimento cristiano in Italia*, Milan, 1924, pp. 134-36. This autobiographical dialogue is entitled *Dialogus de vita eiusdem auctoris* and is entry nr. 4 of Cod. 78 (III R 1-15 bis)—*Miscellaneo di argomenti e autori diversi*—ff. 93-138v. The paper measures 14×20.5 cm and bears the watermark of the Paschal lamb bearing in his mouth the staff of the banner of victory, all inscribed within a circle. This mark appears on ff. 98-100, 102. It is reproduced and dated to Florence 1511 and Treviso 1514 in C. M. Briquet, *Les filigranes: Dictionnaire historique des marques du papier dè leur apparition vers 1282 jusqu'en 1600*, ed. A. Stevenson, Amsterdam 1968, I, p. 21, nr. 49, III, nr. 49 Agneau pascal. The dialogue manuscript consists of 4 quires: 1) a-a$_{12}$^{v} (= 93-104v) sewn at a$_v$ ^{v}/a$_6$; 2) b-b$_{11}$^{v} (= 105-16v) sewn at b$_v$ ^{v}/b$_6$; 3) c-c$_{14}$ (= 117-30v) sewn at C$_{vi}$ ^{v}/c$_7$; and 4) d-d$_{10}$ (= 131-38v) sewn at d$_{iiii}$ ^{v}/d$_5$. Only fols. d$_{8-10}$ (= 139-41) are blank. In the 1960s the codex which contains this manuscript was rebound and the original parchment cover with paper lining was replaced with thick cardboard covers. Given the companion pieces which precede it, all of which relate to the Roman scene ca. 1512-13, and one with an explicit dedication to Alberto Pio, the imperial ambassador to the Fifth Lateran Council then in session, this dialogue may have once belonged to Pio. Don Boccanera suggests that the whole codex may have later been in the possession of Lorenzo Cardona, O.P., bishop of Zamora who died in Camerino and whose books and manuscripts went to the monastic library there of San Domenico. With the expulsion of these Dominicans under Napoleon and the confiscation of their library at the time of the unification of Italy, a large part of their collection was incorporated into the Biblioteca Valentiniana of Camerino. See Don Boccanera's forthcoming catalogue of this communal library. For a survey of autobiographical literature in the West from antiquity to the mid-fourteenth century, see G. Misch, *Geschichte der Autobiographie*, 3rd ed., Berne, 1949-69. For a study which examines the influence of St. Augustine's *Confessions* and of medieval penitential practices on such literature in Renaissance Italy, see T. C. Price Zimmermann, "Confession and Autobiography in the Early

Renaissance," in *Renaissance Studies in Honor of Hans Baron*, ed. A. Molho-J. A. Tedeschi, De Kalb, Ill., 1971, pp. 119-40.

3 Genealogists have had difficulty in tracing Antonio's family and its descendents. Their identity became an important legal question in the mid-seventeenth century owing to a benefice in the Order of St. John of Rhodes (later Malta) which he had endowed for a member of his family on 9 September 1473. For the documents on this case, see Archivio di Stato, Firenze (ASF), *Acquisti e doni*, 288, serie II, esp. nrs. 4-8 and 11. The scarcest information on this family is to be found in D. Tiribilli - Giuliani di Pisa, *Sommario storico delle famiglie celebri toscane*, ed. L. Passerini, I, Florence, 1855, entry 4, pp. 3-4. The working papers for this published account are just as weak on Antonio's immediate family—see ASF, *Raccolta Sebregondi*, n. 23 Agli di Firenze, material of Passerini 158 bis, nr. 15. The Agli genealogical chart in ASF, *Carte Pucci*, scatola I, inserto V, c. 1, traces Antonio's lineage from Aglio to Jacopo to Aglio or Agliuzzo (1256) to Caro and Seglia di Segliaio Cavalcanti (1310) to Aglio and Francesca di Lamberto Frescobaldi to Bernardo and Tommasa di Bellincione to Bellincione and Dianora di Francesco di Ser Neri. For their children it gives Giovanni and Francesco, with Francesco marrying Vaggia di Giovanni Matteo Corsini and having as their sons Antonio (the bishop) and Bernardo (the knight of Rhodes) who had as offspring: Giovanni, Antonio and Dianora. D'Addario, 1960, p. 400, following this chart, errs in making Antonio's brother Francesco his father and in making Dianora's brother Bernardo her father. For reliable information on Antonio's family, see ASF, *Carte Dei*, filza IV, nr. 14 Agli, ff. 2v, 3v, 5, 6. On his niece Dianora, see P. Litta, *Famiglie celebri di Italia*, V, Milan, 1839, "Strozzi di Firenze," tavola III, and *ibid*. XIV, Milan, 1876, "Albizzi di Firenze," tavola X. Her extensive property holdings appear in ASF, *Decima repubblicana*, 29 (1498), S. Giovanni Drago, f. 392. The year of Antonio's birth is either 1399 or 1400. The latest date would be 19 February 1400 since his epitaph states that he died in 1477 at the age of 77 years, 10 months, and 10 days—see D. Moreni, *Continuazione delle memorie storiche dell'Ambrosiana imperial Basilica di San Lorenzo di Firenze*, II, Florence, 1817, p. 137. The earliest date would be 1 September 1399 since he gives his age on 31 August 1475 as 75 years old—see *Dialogus*, f. 119. Antonio had a deep devotion to St. Antony the Hermit whose feast day is January 17th.

4 *Dialogus*, ff. 96v-98.

5 *Dialogus*, ff. 98-99. The year of this famine was probably 1417—see R. Bianchini, *L'Impruneta: Paese e Santuario*, Firenze, 1932, p. 90.

6 *Dialogus*, ff. 99-101, 109v, 113, 120v, 125. On confraternities, see the studies of G. Meersseman and G. P. Pacini, *Ordo Fraternitatis: Confraternite e pietà dei laici nel Medioevo*, Rome, 1977, and R. F. E. Weissman, *Ritual Brotherhood in Renaissance Florence*, New York, 1982.

7 *Dialogus*, f. 101.

8 *Dialogus*, ff. 101v-103.

9 *Dialogus*, ff. 103-104. Among his writings Antonio lists, under nr.105, *Laudatio Antonii Corbinelli auctoris preceptoris civis Florentini*—(*ibid*., f. 118v). Antonio Corbinelli (ca. 1377-1425), whose family had investments in textile manufacturing and farm lands, was an avid collector of Latin and Greek manuscripts. He was still in Florence in 1424, but then moved to Rome to escape local taxes and died there in 1425. His library went to the Benedictine abbey of S. Maria in Florence. See Cosenza, II, 1962, pp. 1096-97; G. Holmes, *The Florentine Enlightenment 1400-50*, New York, 1969, p. 37; R. Blum, *La biblioteca della badia fiorentina e i codici di Antonio Corbinelli*, Vatican City, 1951, pp. 39-47; and P. W. G. Gordon (ed.), *Two Renaissance Book Hunters: The Letters of Poggius Bracciolini to Nicolaus de Niccolis*, New York, 1974, esp. pp. 93-99, passim.

¹⁰ *Dialogus*, ff. 104-106v.

¹¹ *Dialogus*, ff. 106v-107; for a copy of the documents of appointment, residential obligation, and resignation of the canonry in San Lorenzo, see ASF, *Mediceo avanti il Principato* (MAP), nr. CLV, fols. 8-10 and 17v-18; for an example of his duties as canon and of the stipends attached to them, see Biblioteca Medicea Laurenziana, Firenze (BMLF), *Archivio San Lorenzo*, nr. 2407, f. 58. The reason for his resignation is given on f. 72—I am grateful to Arthur Field and Jeffrey Ruda for this reference; on his priorship of SS. Apostoli, see G. Richa, *Notizie istoriche delle chiese fiorentine*, IV/2, Firenze, 1751, p. 57; on his position as provost at Poggibonsi, see B. Salvini, *Catalogo cronologico de' canonici della chiesa metropolitana fiorentina*, Firenze, 1782, nr. 346, p. 41.

¹² *Dialogus*, f. 107; Fra Petrus Belliccioni appears as early as 1422 in the records of the monastery; his death notice is "Fr. Petrus de Aleis aspectu decorus et moribus ac omnibus gratus et amabilis noviter effectus sacerdos devotissime obiit florentie 1431"—see S. Orlandi, *"Necrologio" di S. Maria Novella*, Firenze, 1955, I, p. 152, nr. 607, II, pp. 481, 500, 596-97. The genealogical chart in ASF, *Carte Pucci*, scatola I, inserto V, c. 1, seems to suggest that one of Antonio's brothers' names was Giovanni. According to the translation of Ficino's letter to Antonio on 28 April 1474 he was mourning the recent death of his "brothers"—see Marsilio Ficino, *The Letters*, I, London, 1975, pp. 167-68.

¹³ *Dialogus*, ff. 107v-108, 130v; on Piero dei Medici as Antonio's student, see the letter of consolation of Antonio to Piero on the death of his father Cosimo, S. Maria Impruneta in 1464, in BMLF, Pluteo LIV, n. 10, f. 123 and his letter to Lorenzo dei Medici, s.l., 25 September 1474, ASF, MAP, filza XXX, nr. 902: "Petri genitoris tui ac Johannis patrui preceptor utriusque fui;" on the Neri family in Florence and Filippo's apostolate in Rome, see L. Ponnelle-L. Bordet, *St. Philip Neri and the Roman Society of His Times (1515-1595)*, trans. R. F. Kerr, London, 1932, e.g. pp. 48-49, 87-88, 170-72, 217-20; and A. Mengarelli, *La pastorale di Filippo Neri, giovane fiorentino e sacerdote romano 1515-1595*, Perugia, 1974, pp. 7-29.

¹⁴ *Dialogus*, ff. 108, 109v; letter of Antonio to Piero, BMLF, Pluteo LIV, nr. 10, f. 127: "Inde ego calculi acerbissima molestia uexari affligi, et ad obitum usque rapi," letter of Antonio to Lorenzo dei Medici, s.l., 6 March 1473, MAP, XXX, nr. 124: "Impero ch'io o auuto mal di fiancho e di pietra..." On the flight of Eugenius IV, see C. Eubel, *Hierarchia catholica medii aevi*, 2nd ed., Münster, 1914, p. 7, n. 4.

¹⁵ *Dialogus*, ff. 109v-130; the papal court left Florence on 18 April 1436 to spend the next two years in Bologna—see Eubel, II, 1914, p. 7, n. 4. On 1 July 1440 Eugenius raised his nephew to the cardinalate—see *ibid.*, p. 7, n. 4 and p. 8. For Vespasiano da Bisticci's account see his *Le vite*, ed. A. Greco, I, Firenze, 1970, p. 295. On his appointment as prior of San Niccolò, see Moreni, II, 1817, p. 132. On his canonry in the cathedral and appointment in 1462 as its first dean, see Salvini, 1782, pp. 41, 173. For 1439 as the date of his appointment as pastor at Impruneta, see D'Addario, 1960, p. 400. In addition to the older studies on Impruneta, such as that of Bianchini, see the more recent D. Herlihy "Santa Maria Impruneta: A Rural Commune in the Late Middle Ages," in N. Rubinstein (ed.), *Florentine Studies: Politics and Society in Renaissance Florence*, Evanston, Ill., 1968, pp. 242-76, esp. 242-45, and the collection of studies, *Impruneta, una pieve, un paese: Cultura parrocchia e società nella campagna toscana*, Florence, 1983, esp. the study by F. Quinterio, "Riflessi umanistici negli interventi di Antonio degli Agli al Santuario dell'Impruneta," pp. 137-51.

¹⁶ *Dialogus*, f. 130; Quinterio, 1983, pp. 140-51; Biblioteca Nazionale Cen-

V

trale-Firenze (BNCF), *Conventi Soppressi* B. 9. 1268: Agli, *De racionibus fidei quinque libri*, ff. 50-52, esp. 51-52.

17 D'Addario, 1960, p. 400; Vespasiano, I, 1970, pp. 295-96; on the proposal to affiliate Impruneta with the Benedictine Badia fiorentina of S. Maria, see the letters of Antonio to Lorenzo dei Medici, s.l., 22 August and 17 September 1474, in ASF, MAP, filza XXX, nrs. 730 and 871.

18 *Dialogus*, f. 129; D'Addario, 1960, p. 400; Richa, IV, 1756, p. 57; and W. and E. Paatz, *Die Kirchen von Florenz*, I, Frankfurt am Main, 1940, pp. 243, 252, n. 8.

19 *Dialogus*, ff. 108, 112; according to ASF, *Carte Pucci*, scatola I, inserto V, c. 1 Agli, Antonio's paternal uncles were Zacchena (no offspring given) and Bartolommeo whose sons were Piero and Giuliano. For his generosity toward humanists and paupers, see *Dialogus*, f. 108; Vespasiano, I, 1970, p. 296; and the proposed sepulchral inscription, *Epithaphium Antonii Allii editum a Sebastiano Salvino in funere eius*, in Biblioteca Apostolica Vaticana (BAV), Vat. Lat. 5140, ff. 123v-124, translated at the end of this study. Among the recipients of Antonio's benefactions was Marsilio Ficino—see Ficino, II, 1978, pp. 24-25.

20 *Dialogus*, ff. 109v-110, 131; Vespasiano, I, 1970, p. 295; Eubel, II, 1914, pp. 154, 220 and 271.

21 *Dialogus*, ff. 110-111; H. Acton, *The Pazzi Conspiracy: The Plot against the Medici*, Southampton, Hants., 1979, p. 26; and for an account of the sack of Volterra and of Antonio's role as unsuccessful negotiator of a settlement, see L. Landucci, *A Florentine Diary from 1450 to 1516*, ed. I. del Badia, trans. A. Jervis, London, 1927, pp. 10-11; Kristeller, I, 1965, p. 71 reports an oration of Antonio in 1472 on behalf of Volterra; for the letters of Antonio to Lorenzo dei Medici, Volterra and s.l., 10 April and 21 June 1471, 26 February, 9 and 19 March, 5, 25, and 30 April, 1, 2, and 10 June, 17 August, 14 September, 2 November 1472, 6 February 1473, 8 January 1475, see in ASF, MAP, filza XXIV, nrs. 239, 474; filza XXVII, nrs. 130, 158, 183, 223, 338; filza XXVIII, nrs. 187, 194, 220, 331, 520, 638; filza XXIX, nr. 52; filza XXX, nr. 25, filza XXXIV, nr. 75.

22 See the letters of Antonio to Lorenzo dei Medici, Impruneta and s.l., 6 and 26 March, 23 June, 22 and 29 August 1474, 8 January 1475, and 10 March 1476, in ASF, MAP, filza XXX, nrs. 25, 124, 203, 541, 730, 792, filza XXXIII, nr. 20. On 3 March 1471 Antonio as apostolic delegate and commissioner of Paul II had given a set of constitutions to the collegiate church at S. Gimignano. On 20 September 1471 Sixtus IV ordered Antonio to carry out a reform of that church and resolve the conflict between provost and chapter, something Antonio failed to accomplish— see Moreni, II, 1817, p. 136.

23 See the letter of Antonio to Lorenzo dei Medici, s.l., 25 September 1474, in ASF, MAP, filza XXX, nr. 902.

24 *Dialogus*, ff. 95v, 111v-119 v; Antonio's statement that his writings deserved to be burned does not reflect his attitude three years earlier. He wrote to Lorenzo dei Medici on 10 June 1472 expressing concern for the many texts he had taken to Volterra to edit. He did not want any evil to befall them and pointed out that they were of no value to the soldiers—see ASF, MAP, filza XXVIII, nr. 220. Perhaps most of them were destroyed in the sack of the city and demolition of his residence there. A letter of Sebastiano Salvino to Bernardo degli Agli, Antonio's nephew, indicates that Bernardo had a copy of his *Liber hystoriarum* still needing emendation— see BAV, Vat. Lat. 5140, f. 99.

25 The evidence for these unlisted works includes: the letter of consolation mentioned in *Dialogus*, f. 109v; his sermon on the power of pope and council cited in Kristeller, II, 1967, pp. 150 and 572; his treatise on the immortality of the soul in

B. Nogara, *Codices Vaticani latini*, III, Rome, 1912, pp. 24-27 (Vat. Lat. 1464, ff. 91-97v); and his book on envy in the *Laus librorum Allii amicicie et invidie* in the *Porcelli carmina* in BNCF, *Conventi soppressi*, J. IX. 10, ff. 114-115 (old pagination) or 131-132 (new).

[26] For the references to his readers see: for popes Eugenius IV (1431-47), *Dialogus*, f. 109v; for Nicholas V (1447-55), BAV, Vat. Lat. 3742, f. 1v; for Pius II (1458-64), *Dialogus*, f. 119, nr. 119; for Paul II (1464-71), BAV, Vat. Lat. 1064, ff. 1-2v, and BNCF, *Conventi Soppressi*, B. 9, 1268, ff. iv-2v; Sixtus IV (1471-84), *Dialogus*, ff. 116v, nr. 41, 117, nr. 63, 117v, nr. 80, and BAV, Vat. Lat. 3698, ff. 1-2; for Bessarion (ca. 1403-72), Biblioteca Nazionale di Napoli (BNN), *Fondo principale*, VIII. F. 9, f. 33v—this work was originally dedicated to Leonardo Dati; for Ammannati, *Dialogus*, f. 116, nrs. 20 and 24; for Niccolò of Pistoia (*ad Nicolaum Cardinalem Pistoriensem*), *Dialogus*, f. 117, nr. 53 [Niccolò de Pandolfinis was bishop of Pistoia 1474-1518, but never a cardinal; contemporary cardinals named Nicolaus include: Acciapaccio, d. 1447; Albergatis, d. 1443; Cusa, d. 1464; and Fortiguerra, d. 1473—see Eubel, II, 1914, pp. 6, 7, 11, 13, 216]; for Cosimo dei Medici, *Dialogus*, f. 117v, nr. 73, and BNCF, *Conventi Soppressi*, A. 2. 1737, f. 1, BMLF, Pluteo LIV, nr. 10, ff. 97-104, and BNN, *Fondo Principale*, VIII, F. 9, ff. 97-102v; for Piero dei Medici, BMLF, Pluteo LIV. nr. 10, ff. 123v-134, *Dialogus*, f. 117, nrs. 50-51; for Marsilio Ficino, BNN, *Fondo Principale*, VIII. F. 9, f. 19; for Niccolò Corbizzi, *Dialogus*, ff. 115v-16, nrs. 8, 9, 11-13; for Filippo Ugolini, *Dialogus*, f. 116, nr. 15; for Niccolò da Fivizzano, *Dialogus*, f. 117v, nr. 72; for the citizens of Volterra, *Dialogus*, f. 117v, nr. 70; for nephews of Paul II, *Dialogus*, f. 116v, nr. 38. On Niccolò Corbizzi, another canon of Florence's cathedral and the man entrusted with carrying out the testament of Antonio Corbinelli, see the letter of Jacopo Ammannati to Antonio, Rome, 15 February 1462, in BMLF, *Acquisti e doni*, 82, f. 47v, and Cosenza, II, 1962, p. 1098. On Ugolini, see *ibid.*, IX, p. 3507.

[27] *Dialogus*, ff. 109v, 115v-118v, nrs. 8, 28, 38, 48, 50, 66, 70, 115.

[28] *Dialogus*, ff. 115v-117v, nrs. 8, 37, 39, 62, 70, 71; for examples of the heading on his poem on friendship, see BAV, Chig. L. VIII, 301, f. 117v, BNCF, MSS, 1939, f. 83v, and 2732, f. 42v.

[29] *Dialogus*, ff. 116-118v, nrs. 18, 61, 74, 82-85, 87-88, 91, 96-100, 102-110, 113; for St. Francis, see BAV, Vat. Lat. 3698, ff. 1-32v.

[30] *Dialogus*, ff. 117v-118v, nrs. 80, 94-95, 101, 111.

[31] For virtues, *Dialogus*, ff. 115v-17, nrs. 6, 19, 21, 25, 43, 61; for vices, *ibid.*, nrs. 10, 11, 16, 17, 30, 52, 54, 57, 58, for that of envy, see BNCF, *Conventi Soppressi*, J. IX. 10, ff. 131-132 (new pagination).

[32] *Dialogus*, f. 119v.

[33] *Dialogus*, ff. 115-118v, nrs. 7, 14, 16, 22, 44, 45, 116.

[34] *Dialogus*, ff. 116-118v, nrs. 12-13, 27, 33-35, 40, 46, 47, 59, 64, 77, 112, 116, 117.

[35] *Dialogus*, ff. 115v-117v, 119, nrs. 3, 9, 23, 31, 49, 68, 120.

[36] *Dialogus*, ff. 115v-117v, 118v-119, nrs. 1, 5, 42, 56, 65, 69, 73, 118, 122; the treatise on the soul's immortality is BAV, Vat. Lat. 1494, ff. 91-97v.

[37] *Dialogus*, ff. 116-119, nrs. 19, 51, 55, 67, 72, 121, 123; for his treatise on the power of a pope and council, see Kristeller, II, 1967, pp. 150, 572.

[38] *Dialogus*, ff. 115v-118v, nrs. 2, 36, 53, 79, 81, 82, 104.

[39] Among Antonio degli Agli's extant works are: 1) *Sermo de summi pontificis atque universalis concilii potestate* (Kristeller, II, 1967, pp. 150, 572); 2) *Capitolo sopra la amicitia* (*ibid.*, I, 1965, pp. 215, 222, 257; II, pp. 488, 606); 3) *Vite gestaque sanctorum* (*ibid.*, I, p. 172; II, p. 323); 4) *Explanatio symbolorum pythagore* (*ibid.*, I, p. 427); 5) *Liber de mystica statera* (loc. cit.); 6) *Liber iubelei* (loc. cit.); 7) *Explanatio in Eccle-*

siastem (loc. cit.); 8) *Hystoriarum libri* (*ibid.*, I, p. 154); 9) *Epistola consolatoria ad Cosmum Medicem obitu filii* (loc. cit. and A. M. Bandini, *Catalogues codicum latinorum Bibliothecae Mediceae Laurentianae*, II, Florence, 1975, col. 647); 10) *Epistola consolatoria ad Petrum Medicem obiti patris* (Bandini, II, 1775, col. 648, and Kristeller, II, p. 556); 11) *Epistola ad Jacobum cardinalem Papiensim* (*ibid.*, I, p. 14); 12) *Epithalamium* (A. Pelzer, *Bibliothecae Apostolicae Vaticanae Codices manu scripti recensiti: Codices Vaticani Latini*, II/1, Vatican City, 1931, pp. 618-19); 13) *De racionibus fidei quinque libri* (Kristeller, I, p. 156); 14) *Panegyricus in D. Franciscum* (*ibid.*, II, pp. 322, 582); 15) Oration on behalf of the citizens of Volterra (*ibid.*, I, p. 71); 16) *De immortalitate anime* (Nogara, III, pp. 24-27); 17) *Dialogus de vita eiusdem auctoris* (Feliciangeli, 1917, p. 29 n.).

[40] On Sebastiano Salvino, see P. O. Kristeller, "Sebastiano Salvini, a Florentine Humanist and Theologian, and a Member of Marsilio Ficino's Platonic Academy," in *Didascaliae: Studies in Honor of Anselm M. Albareda*, ed. S. Prete, New York, 1961, pp. 205-43; and Ficino, I, 1975, pp. 122-23, who states that he and Antonio brought him up. This epitaph is from BAV, Vat. Lat. 5140, ff. 123v-124: "Hic situs est Antonius Allius episcopus uolaterranus theologus insignis. Quem musarum chori pauperesque deplorant. Pauperes quoniam piissimum sibi (heu) amisere refugium. Muse quia dulcem amisere lyram simul et cantum. Quis plures suo scripsit tempore libros? Quis elegantior? Quis denique doctior? Nonne ragusine fesulane uolaterraneque tandem prefuit ecclesie? Cuius denique seruat ossa nomenque sue dive Marie inpinete templum, quod dum uita manebat, ut uides, seruauit semper et auxit. Quid tandem? Seruatur anima celo ubi tot suorum laborum est feliciter premia consecutus est."

VI

Alexios Celadenus:
A Disciple of Bessarion in Renaissance Italy

Of the Greek exiles who achieved some fame in the West, Alexios Celadenus (1450-1517) has yet to be the subject of a full biographical study. Only in recent time has he attracted the attention of scholars. For the most part, they have examined either his orations or crusade proposals and have depended on seventeenth- and eighteenth-century works for the outlines of his life. A few years ago some new material came to light which corrected some of the chronology of his career and documented his early association with the Greek cardinal, John Bessarion (1402-1472).[1] This study will briefly

---

1. The first attempt to sketch the life and career of Celadenus was probably that in the series of bishops of Molfetta in the 1662 collection of Fernando Ughelli, *Italia Sacra*, rev. ed. Niccolò Coleti, vol. 1 (Venice, 1717), col. 918, and of Gallipoli, vol. 9 (Venice, 1721), cols. 105-106; see also Francesco Lombardi di Bari, *Notitie istoriche della città e vescovi di Molfetta* (Naples, 1703), pp. 111-113, 115-116; Michele Romano, *Saggio sulla storia di Molfetta* (Naples, 1842), p. 122, no. 2; Richard Garnett, "A Contemporary Oration on Pope Alexander VI," *The English Historical Review* 7 (1892):311-314; Emile Legrand, *Bibliographie Hellénique*, 4 vols. (Paris, 1885-1906), 3 (1903):446; M. Jugié, "Alexis Celadoni," *Dictionnaire d'histoire et géographie ecclésiastiques*, vol. 2 (Paris, 1914), col. 395; Nicolae Iorga, *Notes et extraits pour servir à l'histoire des croisades au XVe siècle*, 5 vols. (Paris and Bucharest, 1899-1916), 5 (1915):313-330; Hans Joachim Kissling, "Militärisch-politiken Problematiken zur Turkenfrage im 15. Jahrhundert," *Bohemia: Jahrbuch des Collegium Carolinum* 5 (1964):108-136; Franz Babinger, "Alessio Celidonio (+1517) und seine Türkendenkschrift," *Beiträge zur Südosteuropa-Forschung* (Munich, 1966), pp. 326-330; Nelson H. Minnich, "Concepts of Reform Proposed at the Fifth Lateran Council," *Archivum Historiae Pontificiae* 7 (1969):163-251, here pp. 179-181; John M. McManamon, "The Ideal Renaissance Pope: Funeral Oratory from the Papal Court," *Archivum Historiae Pontificiae* 14 (1976):9-70, here esp. pp. 17, 54-70; H.J. Kissling, "Celidonio, Alessio," *Dizionario biografico degli Italiani*, vol. 23 (Rome, 1979), pp. 421-423; and John Monfasani, "Alexius Celadenus and Ottaviano Ubaldini: An Epilogue to Bessarion's Relationship with the

survey the biographical data and look at him more closely as a disciple of Bessarion.[2]

Alexios was Greek by birth. The epitaph on his tomb in San Agostino's church in Rome describes him as sixty-seven years old at the time of his death in mid-April of 1517 and as *Spartensi ex nobili genere oriundus.* While some authors give Mistra (a fortress city near ancient Sparta) as his birthplace, it is not clear whether he came from that city or its neighbouring territory. In the early fifteenth century, Mistra achieved prominence as the virtual political and cultural capital of Greece. Its ruler, the despot of Morea, appointed by the Byzantine emperor, was usually an important member of the imperial family. The noted Platonist, Georgios Gemistos Plethon (c. 1360-1452), established his Academy in this Peloponnesian city, and from 1431 to 1436 the Basilian monk John Bessarion attended his lectures there. As one of the emperor's three erudite lay advisers, Gemistos attended the Council of Ferrara-Florence (1438-1439). While Gemistos opposed a union of the Greek Church with the Latin, his disciple Bessarion, by then archbishop of Nicaea, promoted this union in his formal speeches and committee activities. Bessarion's return to Greece was brief: by 1440 he was back in the West, where for the next thirty years he encouraged the study of Platonist philosophy, assisted Greek exiles, promoted a crusade to free his homeland from the Turk, and laboured for church reform, especially of monasteries. After the Council of Florence, Gemistos returned to Mistra where he worked against the union with Rome, wrote against Bessarion, and continued to direct his Academy. It survived his death, only to be doomed by the Turkish conquest. Alexios Celadenus was most likely aware of the former cultural and political prominence of Mistra and proud to have this place of origin registered on his tomb stone. That Alexios did, indeed, also come from a prominent family is suggested by his father's later gift of two codices to Pope Paul II (1464-1471) and by his own use of a coat of arms. When Mehmed II Fatih invaded the Peloponnese in 1460, Demetrios II Palaeologus, brother of the last Byzantine emperor and

Court of Urbino," *Bibliothèque d'Humanisme et Renaissance* 46 (1984):95-110.

2. This study does not seek to reopen questions surrounding the life, career, and writings of Bessarion. For the standard study of this Greek cardinal, see Ludwig Mohler, *Kardinal Bessarion als Theologe, Humanist und Staatsmann,* 3 vols. (Paderborn, 1923-1942); for a briefer account, see Joseph Gill, *Personalities of the Council of Florence and Other Essays* (New York, 1964), pp. 45-54, and for contemporary accounts, see Vespasiano da Bisticci, *Renaissance Princes, Popes, and Prelates: The Vespasiano Memoirs: Lives of Illustrious Men of the XVth Century,* trans. William George and Emily Waters (New York, 1963), pp. 137-141 and Mohler, *Kardinal Bessarion* 3:405-414.

himself despot of Morea, surrendered to the Turk. Thomas, the other brother of the despot Demetrios, fled to Corfù and then to Rome, accompanied by many Greek nobles. Among them appears to have been Alexios and his father.[3]

Alexios spent at least part of his youth in Rome. Paul II provided subsidies and pensions for the Greek exiles residing in the Papal States. The Greek cardinal, John Bessarion, offered unselfish assistance to those at Rome and made of his home at Santi Apostoli a meeting place for learned Greeks and Italian Hellenists. He also became tutor of Thomas Palaeologus' sons. Among the cardinal's other disciples was Alexios, whose stay in Rome dates from at least 1464. His formal education in the liberal arts was received in Italy, and, like his master Bessarion, he learned to write Latin with some literary skill. In 1466, at about sixteen years of age, he entered the service of the Roman Church–whether this dates his conversion from Orthodoxy or entrance upon a clerical career in the Latin Church is

---

3. The epitaph on his tomb reads: "Alesius Celadenus episc. Malfit. Ap. Sec. Geminaeque linguae Orator Et interpres. acutiss. Sparten. Ex nobili genere oriundus Religione et sanctis semper operibus admirabilis LXVII. annos foelix obijt. XIII. Cal. Maias MDXVII"; see Monfasani, "Alexius Celadenus," p. 101, nn. 41-43 and Vicenzo Forcella, *Iscrizioni delle chiese e d'altri edifizi di Roma dal secolo XI fino ai giorni nostri*, 14 vols. (Rome, 1869-1885), 5 (1874):35. Among the authors giving Sparta as his birthplace are Lombardi, *Notitie istoriche*, p. 111, and Kissling, "Celidonio," p. 421; on the importance at this time of Mistra and of Gemistos' Platonic Academy there, see François Masai, *Plethon et le Platonisme de Mistra*, Classiques des l'Humanisme: Etudes, vol. 5 (Paris, 1956), pp. 38-54, 319-363. On Bessarion at Plethon's Academy, see Mohler, *Kardinal Bessarion* 1:45-50. Alexios' coat of arms is in the form of a shield with a dark blue background. At the centre of it is a golden sun with a human face, eight protruding flames of fire, and multiple rays of light. Above the sun is a red Latin cross. Whether this Latin cross was inserted later in his career or there from the beginning and whether this coat of arms was the traditional one of his family or devised on Alexios' promotion to the episcopate are not clear. This coat of arms appears at the bottom of the miniature frontispiece which adorns the Greek lectionary he gave to Julius II. In his 1512 dedicatory letter to Julius II, Alexios referred to two ornate codices "quos meus parens Paullo Secundo Pontifici dono dedit..."; see Angelus Maria Bandinius, *Bibliotheca Leopoldina Laurentiana seu Catalogus Manuscriptorum qui nuper in Laurentianam translati sunt*, 3 vols. (Florence, 1791-1793), 3:498. On the fall of Morea and flight of Thomas, see *The Fall of the Byzantine Empire: A Chronicle by George Sphrantzes 1401-1477*, trans. Marios Philippides (Amherst, 1980), pp. 80-85, and Enea Silvio Piccolomini, *Memoirs of a Renaissance Pope: The Commentaries of Pius II, an Abridgment*, trans. Florence A. Gragg, ed. Leona C. Gabel (New York, 1959), pp. 241-243. In his dedicatory letter to Julius II, Alexios relates that he went into exile while yet a boy: "puer patriam et omnia quae in hac vita bona nuncupantur...mihi amisi..."; see Bandinius, *Bibliotheca* 3:497. On the date of Celadenus' death, see Marino Sanuto, *I Diarii*, ed. Federico Stefani et al., vol. 24 (Venice, 1889), col. 182 (the report of Marco Minio from Rome, dated 17 April 1517, stating that yesterday the bishop of Molfetta had died); and Monfasani, "Alexius Celadenus," pp. 104-105, n. 62.

not clear. He claimed his father had given the codices to the pope as a sign of his family's devotion to the Holy See and its pontiffs. As a member of Bessarion's household, Alexios enjoyed the friendship of Theodore of Gaza. Alexios seems to havè remained in the service of Bessarion up until the death of this Greek cardinal in 1472, attending him in his final illness and seeing that his master's promised treatise on Aristotelian politics was in fact sent to its intended recipient, Prince Ottaviano Ubaldini, a relative and adviser of Federico da Montefeltro, lord of Urbino.[4] Bessarion's remains were eventually interred in his church of Santi Apostoli. His influence on the young Alexios was probably enduring, for in many ways the disciple's subsequent career and intellectual interests mirrored those of his master.

For the next quarter century after the death of Bessarion, Alexios pursued his career in the kingdom of Naples. His father apparently resided in Taranto, and Alexios seems to have spent some time in that city. In 1480 he was appointed bishop of Gallipoli, a centre of Greek exiles located about forty miles to the southeast down the coast of the Gulf of Taranto. In this diocese his efforts to bring

---

4. On Paul's use of regular revenues and those from the alum mines to support Greek exiles, see Ludwig von Pastor, *The History of the Popes from the Close of the Middle Ages*, trans. Frederick Ignatius Antrobus et al., 40 vols. (St. Louis, 1923-1953), 4 (1923):193-194; on Bessarion as patron of the Greek exiles, see ibid. pp. 127-128 and Egmont Lee, *Sixtus IV and Men of Letters*, no. 26 of *Temi e Testi*, ed. Eugenio Massa (Rome, 1978), p. 24; the identification of Alexios as "Card. Bessarionis auditor" comes from the endnote on fol. 76 of Alexios' three sermons favouring a crusade, MS 12 of the Cathedral Chapter of Toledo; see José Maria Octavio de Toledo, *Catalogo de la Libreria del Cabildo Toledano:* Ia Parte–Manuscritos, vol. 3 of *Biblioteca de la Revista de Archivos Bibliotecas y Museos* (Madrid, 1903), p. 15. Niccolò Perotti identified fourteen members of Bessarion's "Academy," the last of whom he named as "Alexi." Giovanni Mercati identitied this "Alexi" as a member of the Stati de Thomarotiis family who died about 1489; see his *Per la cronologia della vita e degli scritti di Niccolò Perotti, arcivescovo di Siponto*, vol. 44 of *Studi e Testi* (Rome, 1925), p. 80. In his 1512 oration at the Lateran Council, Alexios indicated that he had been in Rome since at least 1464; see *Sacrorum conciliorum nova et amplissima collectio*, ed. Giovanni Domenico Mansi, vol. 32 (Florence, 1759), col. 737A (hereafter cited as Mansi). For a description of a manuscript copy of this speech, see below note 21. In his letter to Egidio Antonini, from Rome, 30 November 1506, he admits that he was educated in Italy: "verum Regis cuius virtuti et laudi sum vehementer addictus, simulque regionis Italiae, quae mihi tecum in eo comunis est, quod amissa ab annis teneris patria educationem instituta et pauculum quicquid est in me disciplinae ei acceptum debeo"; see Biblioteca Nazionale "Vittorio Emmanuale III," Napoli, MS 5 F. 20, fol. 172[r]. For his forty-six years of service in the Roman Church, see his 1512 statement in Bandinius, *Bibliotheca* 3:495-496. On Alexios' associations with Theodore of Gaza and Ubaldini, see Monfasani, "Alexius Celadenus," pp. 100, 106, 108-109 and Mohler, *Kardinal Bessarion* 3:580-586, esp. n. to Ep. 8.

about a reform of morals and ritual and to recover church property led to slanderous charges being brought against him in Rome. He asked to be transferred to another see, and in 1508 Julius named him bishop of Molfetta on the Adriatic coast where he expended large sums beautifying his cathedral church. As commendatory abbot of SS. Petrus et Andreas de Insula Parva in the diocese of Taranto, Alexios worked to make this monastery viable by increasing its number of monks and its revenues.[5] As a reform-minded Latin churchman, he was in the mold of his master Bessarion.

During his stay in the Neapolitan kingdom, Alexios developed personal ties with members of the royal family. His reputation for learning was such that Ferrante I (1458-1494), king of Naples, called him to court to serve as tutor and adviser to his natural son Alfonso. Having failed in his attempts to marry this possibly half-Cypriot son into the royal house of Cyprus, Ferrante destined him for an ecclesiastical career. This pleasure-loving royal bastard, however, lacked the proper humanistic and religious formation required for his new position as bishop-elect of Chieti. Until 1491, Francesco Pucci tried to educate him; thereafter Alexios was in charge. Alfonso resigned his see of Chieti in 1496 and resisted being appointed archbishop of Reggio-Calabria. What influence Alexios may have exerted on Alfonso is unknown. But, like Bessarion, he had served as tutor to royal offspring; in this case, however, the scion's Greek lineage was only partial and probable. When Alfonso's half-brother succeeded to the throne as Alfonso II (1494-1495), Alexios was present at the coronation ceremony. By the time Alfonso's other half-brother Federigo (1496-1501) had resigned the throne and opened the way for the Aragonese conquest of Naples, Alexios was in Rome. Probably in part because of his ties to the former royal family, Alexios was relieved when Egidio Antonini and not the former tutor was called upon to give an oration in October 1506, welcoming Fernando of Aragon to Naples. Alexios' relations with the former royal family continued in Rome, for he ordained to the subdiaconate

---

5. Monfasani, "Alexius Celadenus," pp. 102-103, nn. 47, 51-52; Monfasani's correction of the date of his appointment as bishop is confirmed by an otherwise elusive 1512 statement of Alexios on having served for the past thirty-two years in the ministry of the Roman Church; see Bandinius, *Bibliotheca* 3.496. On the relocation of Greeks in southern Italy, notably Naples, and the survival of the Greek tongue in Gallipoli, see Apostolos E. Vacalopoulos, *The Greek Nation, 1453-1669: The Cultural and Economic Background of Modern Greek Society*, trans. Ian and Phania Moles (New Brunswick, 1976), pp. 46-49. On his adornment with marble of the Marian chapel in the cathedral of Molfetta, see Lombardi, *Notitie istoriche*, p. 115. On his reform of the monastery, see Monfasani, "Alexius Celadenus," p. 102 n. 51 and p. 103 n. 54.

and diaconate on 23 June 1504 another natural son of Ferrante, cardinal Luigi de Aragonia.[6]

Although he is not usually listed among those associated with the Accademia Pontaniana of Naples, Alexios probably had some ties to these humanists. As tutor of a royal scion, he most likely had contact at court with these men of letters, among whom were royal councillors, secretaries, historians, administrators, soldiers, and fellow tutors. An allusion to Alexios seems to be suggested by a name found in Jacopo Sannazaro's third piscatorial eclogue, probably written between 1501 and 1504. A speaker identified as "Celadon" asks his friend to recount what happened when storms forced him and his fishing party to take refuge on the island of Ischia. The response begins with a lengthy lament on how, from the shores of that isle, King Federigo and his country's youth set sail for exile in France. The rest of the eclogue deals with the theme of the pain of separation. Because Sannazaro accompanied into exile his close friend, King Federigo, the half-brother of Alexios' former student, it may not be unreasonable to see this third eclogue as addressed to his former colleague at the court in Naples, Alexios Celadenus, now in

6. On Alfonso de Aragonia, see Konrad Eubel, *Hierarchia catholica medii aevi sive summorum pontificum, S.R.E. cardinalium, ecclesiarum antistitum* series, vol. 2: *Ab anno 1431 usque ad annum 1503 perducta*, 2nd rev. ed. (Münster, 1914), pp. 222-249; Harry Luke, "The Kingdom of Cyprus, 1369-1489," *A History of the Crusades*, ed. Kenneth M. Setton, vol. 3: *The Fourteenth and Fifteenth Centuries*, ed. Harry W. Hazard (Madison, 1975), pp. 361-395, here pp. 390-392, and F. Forcellini, "Strane peripezie d'un bastardo di casa d'Aragona," *Archivio storico per le provincie napoletane* 37 (1912):553-563; 38 (1913):87-114, 441-482; 39 (1914):172-214, 268-298, 459-494, 767-787; here 39 (1914):470-482.

For Alexios' presence at the coronation of Alfonso and ordination of Luigi, see Johann Burchard, *Liber notarum ab anno MCCCCLXXXIII usque ad annum MDVI*, ed. Enrico Celani, vol. 32 of *Rerum italicarum scriptores* (Città di Castello, 1906-1942), 1:515; 2:455. The edition by Louis Thusane *Diarium sive rerum urbanarum commentarii (1483-1506)* (Paris, 1883-1885), 3:360 reports the ordination to the subdiaconate missing in *Liber notarum*, ed. Celani, 2:455.

On the Neapolitan succession and Fernando's 1506 entrance into the city, see Giovanni Antonio Summonte, *Dell' historia della città e regno di Napoli*, vol. 4 (Naples, 1675), prima faciata and pp. 2-9, and William H. Prescott, *History of the Reign of Ferdinand and Isabella the Catholic*, 3rd rev. ed. (New York, 1838), 2:32, 54, 154, 275; in his letter from Rome of 30 November 1506 to Egidio Antonini, Alexios claimed that he had helped prepare for a sumptuous reception of Fernando, in keeping with Neapolitan tastes, but was freed from the need to prepare a welcoming speech when Egidio was chosen for this task. He discretely suggested that the Augustinian friar use the occasion for exhorting the Spanish monarch to fight the Moslems; see his letter in Biblioteca Nazionale "Vittore Emmanuale III" di Napoli, MS 5 F. 20, fols. 171ᵛ-77ʳ, here 172ʳ, 175ʳ-76ᵛ. Dr. Annamaria Voci is currently preparing a critical edition of this letter for her edition of the correspondence of Egidio Antonini.

Rome. An association with the local circle of humanists would be in keeping with the pattern laid down by Bessarion.[7]

From 1499 until his death in 1517, Alexios pursued a career at the papal court and curia, in the same city where his master Bessarion had spent his mature and final years in the service of the Roman Church and of Greek interests. On several occasions Alexios chanted the epistle or gospel in Greek at the papal liturgies. He seems to have developed some expertise in liturgical matters for he openly criticized the decision of the new master of ceremonies, Paride de Grassi, when he placed the ambassador of Monferrato (probably the Greek, Constantinos Arianiti Comneni) in front of, rather than behind, the representative of Florence. Alexios found employment also in the curia where, from at least October of 1500 until his death, he served as an apostolic secretary. That he actually functioned in this post is attested by his signature on numerous papal documents. His residence in Rome was on the via Tor Sanguigna in the fashionable district near the church of San Agostino. His reputation for frugality was such that "Pasquino" sarcastically called him prodigal, while Aretino claimed he ate his servants' food and died of hunger. Despite a papal brief allowing him to bequeathe his personal goods, Leo apparently gleefully confiscated from his estate the eight thousand ducats in coin and another five thousand in vouchers of deposit.[8]

7. For an overview of the members of the Accademia Pontaniana, see Antonio Altamura, *L'Umanesimo nel mezzogiorno d'Italia: storia, bibliografie e testi inediti, Biblioteca dell' "Archivum Romanicum,"* ed. Giulio Bertoni, ser. 1: *Storia-Letteratura-Paleografia,* vol. 29 (Florence, 1941), pp. 49-160. Alexios' letter to Egidio Antonini (see above n. 4) shows that he was on good terms with this noted humanist who joined the circle of Pontano in Naples shortly after his arrival there in 1498. For background on Sannazaro and his piscatorial eclogues, see especially William J. Kennedy, *Jacopo Sannazaro and the Uses of Pastoral* (Hanover, 1983), pp. 10-27, 149-180; on his reference elsewhere to another contemporary in these eclogues, see ibid., p. 163; on the third eclogue, see esp. pp. 166-168. For the Latin text of this third piscatorial eclogue and an English translation of it, see Jacopo Sannazaro, *Arcadia and Piscatorial Eclogues,* trans. with introduction by Ralph Nash (Detroit, 1966), pp. 170-177; Nash does not identify "Celadon" as Alexios Celadenus, but traces the etymology of the name to the Greek word *kelados,* which he translates as an outpouring of sound; see ibid., p. 204. In his notes to this eclogue, Wilfred P. Mustard also makes no effort to identify "Celadon"; see his *The Piscatory Eclogues of Jacopo Sannazaro* (Baltimore, 1914), pp. 64-67 (text), pp. 82-84 (notes).

8. For Alexios' presence at papal liturgies, see Celani, *Liber notarum* 2:196, 215, 275, 310, 324, 371, 372, 392; for his challenging the decision of de Grassi, see ibid. 2:455-456. For his appointment as apostolic secretary, see Walther von Hofmann, *Forschungen zur Geschichte der kurialen Behörden vom Schism bis zur Reformation,* vol. 2: *Quellen, Listen und Exkurse* (vol. 13 of Bibliothek des königlich-preussischen historischen Instituts in Rom, [Rome, 1914]), p. 118 n. 201. For some examples of Alexios

Alexios had died without achieving one of his treasured ambitions. Like his early patron John Bessarion, Alexios had laboured to convey Greek learning to the West and to encourage a crusade to liberate his homeland; but unlike the archbishop of Nicaea, the bishop of Molfetta never attained the dignity of cardinal. He had cultivated the friendship of such powerful cardinals as Oliviero Carafa, Bernardino López de Carvajal, Francesco Tedeschini Piccolomini, and Jorge de Costa by dedicating to them various literary works. He looked to Giuliano della Rovere as a patron and hoped that his longings would be satisfied once he was elected Julius II. But the only favours Julius showed him were permission to install Latin monks in the Basilian monastery of which he was commendatory abbot, and the transfer from Gallipoli to Molfetta. In the hope of inducing Julius to name him a cardinal, Alexios gave him as a gift for the new St. Peter's Basilica a beautiful Greek lectionary formerly used in the cathedral at Trebizond. When the Turks took that city in 1461, they despoiled the lectionary of its ornate covers, but spared the carefully copied text with its elegant illuminations. This lectionary made its way to Italy where émigré Greeks asked Alexios to offer it to the pope. Julius accepted the gift, praising the beauty of the text but deploring its missing covers. At his own expense, Alexios had the manuscript refitted with very ornate covers of pure gold and silver. He also furnished it with a beautifully illuminated frontispiece depicting in two panels: (1) the voyage of the codex aboard a ship with full sail apparently bound for Italy, with the cities of Constantinople and Trebizond depicted in the background; and

functioning as secretary or collator, see Archivio Segreto Vaticano (hereafter, ASV), Reg. Vat. 987, fols. 8^r, 31^r, 33^r, 46^r, 108^v, 243^r, 271^r, 273^r, 286^r, 299^v, 363^v, 500^r (spanning January 1510 to October 1511). For his residence, see Monfasani, "Alexius Celadenus," pp. 103-104; for satirical comments on his frugality, see Vittorio Rossi, *Pasquinate di Pietro Aretino* (Palermo, 1891), pp. 15, 84-85. Reports on the extent of his estate are found in Sanuto, *I Diarii* 24:182, 197. For the brief of 10 August 1515 granting Alexios permission to bequeathe his personal goods, see ASV Reg. Vat. 1205, fol. 202^v-203^v; for a discussion of such papal licenses to bequeathe personal goods, see Barbara McClung Hallman, *Italian Cardinals, Reform, and the Church as Property* (Berkeley 1985), pp. 80-94; for Leo's reservation of all his benefices and offices, see ASV Archivio Consistoriali, Acta Vicecancellarii cod. 2, fol. 24^v.

Why Alexios was so intent on accumulating wealth is not clear. As a member of the exiled Greek nobility, he may have tried to recuperate in part his family's lost fortune and pass it along through the line of his brother Johannes (on Johannes, see Monfasani, "Alexius Celadenus," p. 104 n. 59). Like his contemporary, Cardinal Ximénes, he could have saved the money in the hope of donating a good portion of it to the cause of a crusade, or he may have seen the money as a key factor in achieving another of his life's goals, promotion to the cardinalate, these savings providing him the means for paying the customary *honorarium* on the occasion of such a promotion.

Fig 1. Frontispiece for a Greek lectionary (Florence, Biblioteca Medicea Laurenziana, Ms. Palat. 244, fol. 1v) depicting (above) the presentation of this codex by Celadenus to Julius II, and (below) the journey of this codex from Trebizond and Constantinople toward Rome and Celadenus' family coat of arms. Photo: Guido Sansoni.

Fig 2. Detail from the frontispiece of Ms. Palat. 244, fol. 1v, of the Bibliotheca Medicea Laurenziana, Florence, depicting Alexios Caledenus presenting this Greek lectionary to Julius II flanked by two cardinal deacon assistants. Photo: Guido Sansoni.

(2) Alexios kneeling before the enthroned pope to whom he hands the Greek lectionary.[9]

In the presentation preface, Alexios praised Julius for having liberated Italy from "barbarian" forces and pleaded with him now to rescue Greece from the cruel Turks. He also begged the pope to appoint him as cardinal, arguing that the decree of Konstanz mandated an international college, and that while the British, Hungarian, Spanish, German, French, and other "barbarian" nations were currently represented in it, the Greek peoples were not. Granted that he was not trained in law as were most cardinals, nonetheless, his age, innocence of life, curial service, talents, virtues, and devotion to the pope recommended him for this position. It was not for his own sake that he sought it, but that he might represent his fellow Greeks and contribute their perspective and wisdom to the highest counsels of church government. The refurbished lectionary would serve as a perpetual witness of his devotion to Julius and the Holy See. Until it could be used in the new St. Peter's, it should be preserved in the pope's personal library kept in the papal chamber

9. For the dedicatory letters of Alexios, see Bibliotheca Apostolica Vaticana (hereafter, BAV), Vat. Lat. 14174, fol. 1^r-2^v (Carvajal), 3^r-6^v (Francesco Tedeschini Piccolomini), 7^r-9^r (Oliviero Carafa); Vat. Lat. 8736, fol. 1^{r-v} (Jorge de Costa), and Bandinius, *Bibliotheca* 2:142-144 describing Codice Gaddiani 130 dedicated to Carafa alone; for the text of his dedicatory preface to Julius, see ibid. 3:495-498. On Julius' favours, see Monfasani, "Alexius Celadenus," pp. 102-103, nn. 52-54. For Alexios' protestation that he was faithfully dedicated to the cause of Julius before his election as pope, see Bandinius, *Bibliotheca* 2:498-499. For a fuller description of this twelfth-century lectionary, see ibid. 3:494-504. The frontispiece is Biblioteca Medicea Laurenziana (Florence), Codice Mediceo Palatino 244, fol. 1^v.

Pope Julius is depicted wearing a full beard. He began to grow one in October of 1510 and it disappeared slowly in March of 1512. While he wore it, the beard became somewhat fashionable in Rome. It is not surprising that the two cardinals depicted also sport a beard. On the Julian beard, see Loren Partridge and Randolph Starn, *A Renaissance Likeness: Art and Culture in Raphael's 'Julius II'* (Berkeley, 1980), pp. 2-3, 43-46. Alexios' beard probably predated Julius', for the beard was often worn by Byzantine emigres such as his former master Bessarion; see Deno John Geanakoplos, *Byzantium and the Renaissance: Greek Scholars in Venice: Studies in the Dissemination of Greek Learning from Byzantium to Western Europe* (Cambridge, Mass., 1962), p. 299.

The representation in this miniature of Julius' throne with golden acorns mounted on the corner posts of the back and arms and a similar depiction of the back of his throne in Raphael's famous portrait of this pope would seem to suggest that such acorns in fact decorated the Julian throne and were not the iconographic inventions of artists. On these acorns, see Partridge and Starn, *Renaissance Likeness*, pp. 56-59.

The depiction of Trebizond is a reference to where this lectionary was originally used and from which place it made its journey by sea to Rome. Trebizond was also the birthplace of John Bessarion, whose disciple Alexios had been and whose successor in the college of cardinals he hoped yet to be—with an assist from the gift of this lectionary.

where he received cardinals and ambassadors, i.e., the room which Raphael had recently frescoed and is now known as the Stanza della Segnatura.[10]

That the college of cardinals should contain a Greek was not a novel proposition. In the days following the union of Greek and Latin Churches at Florence, the Greeks were represented by Bessarion until his death in 1472. While Sixtus IV (1471-1484), the uncle of Julius II, did not name a Greek successor during his pontificate, his confessor, the Hispano-Portuguese Franciscan, Beato Amadeo Menez de Silva prophecized a future angelic pope and a college of cardinals containing ten men from the East. On reading this prophecy in 1502, Cardinal Carvajal became convinced that his own destiny was here foretold. His companion, the Bosnian Franciscan, Juraj Dragišič, had similar delusions that he himself would someday be named a cardinal, if not also pope. Dragišič was appointed bishop of Cagli in 1507. He too was a disciple of Bessarion and promoted himself as that cardinal's true heir.[11] Thus Alexios was not alone in seeking the red hat, based on a Balkan birth and discipleship of the famous Greek cardinal.

Why Julius passed over Alexios can be only surmised. Had this pope intended to name a Greek cardinal, he may have preferred some member of the exiled imperial Palaeologi or Arianti Comneni families. Greek clerics more eminent in learning than Alexios were also likely candidates. In his struggle against the French and the schismatic Pisan cardinals and their council, Julius needed the support of cardinals who would offer unquestioning support for his policies, win for him outside support by their personal prestige and

10. On the location of Julius' library, see Deoclecio Redig de Campos, *Raphael in the Stanze*, trans. John Guthrie (Milan, 1973), p. 7, n. 2.

11. On Beato Amadeo and the 1502 reading of his prophecy of oriental cardinals and of an angelic pope, see Anna Morisi Guerra, *Apocalypsis Nova: Ricerche sull' origine e la formazione del testo dello pseudo-Amadeo*, fasc. 77 of *Studi Storici* of the Istituto storico italiano per il medio evo (Rome, 1970), esp. p. 4 and p. 30, n. 56. On Dragišič, see Cesare Vasoli, "Notizie su Giorgio Benigno Salviati (Juraj Dragišič)," in *Studi storici in onore di Gabriele Pepe*, ed. Giosue Musca (Bari, 1969), pp. 429-498. In the dedicatory letter to Leo X introducing his *In librum VII Quaestionum a Magnifico Laurentio Medicis propositarum olim amissum nuper inventum*, Dragišič claimed Bessarion often told him, "Tu eris haeres meus" (fol. 1ᵛ) and that Antonio Barbarini stated "cogitamus itaque te ad Tusciae ministeriatum deinde ad Generalatus officium, tandem ob scientiam et humanissimos mores tuos ad cardinalatus dignitatem erigere" (fol. 2ʳ). See Biblioteca Medicea-Laurenziana, Pluteo 83, cod. 18. The Cypriot Ludovicus Podocatharus was cardinal from 1500 until his death in 1504; see Eubel, *Hierarchia catholica* 2:24. Marcus Musurus was also reported to have eagerly sought the cardinalate and to have died of grief for not having been named to the sacred college; see Geanakoplos, *Byzantium and the Renaissance*, p. 163.

powerful connections, or add to his coffers a large sum as an honorarium for their promotion. But Alexios was known for being independent in his judgement, did not enjoy a wide reputation for learning, was associated with the powerless, exiled ruling families of Greece and Naples, and seems to have kept others in the dark as to the extent of his personal wealth. Furthermore, on two issues for which Julius was attacked for failing to make progress despite his election oaths, namely, launching a crusade against the Turk and carrying out church reform, Alexios had repeatedly demanded papal action. Julius II's uncle, Sixtus IV, had suffered keen discomfiture in the presence of Cardinal Bessarion who also openly espoused these causes. The papal nephew, Julius II, was not eager to add to his college a new Bessarion.[12]

Alexios' dedication to the cause of a crusade to liberate Greece permeates many of his works. In 1500, he penned three sermons which he addressed to three of the leading cardinals of the day: Carafa, Carvajal, and Piccolomini. He spelled out for the cardinals' consideration a detailed plan for a coordinated attack on the Turks aimed primarily at freeing Greece and the old imperial city of Constantinople. In the first sermon he set out the spiritual and material preconditions for a successful crusade: praying, fasting, doing penance, reforming morals, levying and collecting a crusade tax, establishing peace among Christian princes, and convening a congress where agreement on a unified command could be reached. In the second sermon he suggested a grand strategy which this congress might adopt. Let a land army from Germany, Bohemia, Poland, Hungary, and Dacia attack the Turks in the regions surrounding Constantinople: Thrace in Europe and Mysia in Asia. Another army composed of the French and British should attack the Turks along the Adriatic coast and push into Macedonia. A third contingent with ships and sailors from Spain and Portugal and equipment and soldiers from Italy should ravage the Aegean coast and land a force in Asia Minor or elsewhere on the Anatolian peninsula.

---

12. That Alexios was known to Roman circles as a student of Greek literature is suggested by his name in the register of those borrowing books from the Vatican library. On 9 February 1503 he borrowed a codex containing works by Aristotle, Plutarch, Aelianus, Athenaeus, and Strabo. He returned it on July 28th. See Maria Bertòla, *I due primi registri di prestito della Biblioteca Apostolica Vaticana: Codici Vaticani Latini 3964, 3966* (Città del Vaticano, 1942), p. 52, n. 2. For a brief survey of some prominent learned Greeks in Italy at that time, esp. Marcus Musurus who eventually was promoted to archbishop of Monemvasia, see Geanakoplos, *Byzantium and the Renaissance*, esp. 111-166. On the tension between Sixtus IV and Bessarion, see Vespasiano, *Memoires*, p. 140; Lee, *Sixtus IV*, pp. 29-31.

In the final sermon Alexios analyzed Turkish tactics, trickery, and weaknesses, and suggested how the Christian force could best exploit these. To motivate the Christian troops, he wanted to enlist the support of their wives. To increase the ranks of the Christian forces while simultaneously eliminating a social problem in Europe, he encouraged drafting into the army criminals currently in jails. Legates were also to be sent to the duke of Moscovy, encouraging his cooperation with the offer of Pontus and Thrace as booty, to the shah of Persia offering Trebizond, and to the sultan of Egypt holding out Cyprus as a tributary state.[13]

When nothing came of this appeal to these cardinals, Alexios' hopes turned toward others. In the conclave of September 1503 he urged the assembled cardinals to elect a pope who was able by his reputation for impartiality to mediate a peace between Louis XII of France and Fernando II of Aragon. The deep animosity between these kings has kept Christendom in a state of warfare which favours the Turks.[14] In his letter of 30 November 1506 to Egidio Antonini, Alexios urged him in his oration welcoming Fernando II to Naples to exhort this king to turn his victorious forces against the Turks, retake Constantinople, and become an all-conquering Christian Alexander, truly the *rex catholicus*.[15] In his 1512 letter prefaced to the Greek lectionary and addressed to Julius II, Alexios congratulated him on having driven the French from Italy and asked the pope to liberate Greece. God will not abandon it forever to the Turks, its faults can be expiated over time. This lectionary should remind Julius of the church's children still in captivity.[16] And in his speech before the third session of the Lateran Council on 3 December 1512, Alexios recalled the crusades of old, from that proclaimed by Urban II at the synod of Clermont (1095) to that called by Innocent III at the Fourth Lateran Council (1215). Alexios

13. This collection of three sermons exists in at least three copies: BAV Vat. lat. 14174, fols. 1ʳ-9ʳ (three letters), 9ᵛ-76ᵛ (sermons); Biblioteca Medicea-Laurenziana, Gaddiana 130, fols. 1ʳ-3ʳ (letter to Carafa), 3ᵛff. (sermons)–described in Bandinius, *Bibliotheca* 2:142-144; and codex 12 of the Cathedral Chapter Library at Toledo described by José Maria Octavio de Toledo, *Catalog de la Libreria del Cabildo Toledano*, Ia parte: *Manuscritos* (Madrid, 1903), pp. 14-15. For studies of these sermons, see the above mentioned studies by Iorga, Kissling, and Babinger (n. 1).

14. Alexios' 1503 sermon is reproduced in McManamon, "Ideal Pope," pp. 62-70, esp. pp. 67-68 (crusade plea) and 57 (identification of warring kings as Louis and Fernando).

15. For the relevant section of Alexios' letter, see Biblioteca Nazionale "Vittorio Emmanuale III," Napoli, MS 5 F. 20, fols. 173ᵛ-174ʳ, 175ʳ-176ᵛ, or the copy in the Biblioteca Statale Angelica–Rome, MS 1001, fols. 133ᵛ-134ʳ, 135ʳ-137ʳ.

16. Bandinius, *Bibliotheca* 3:496-497.

urged the fathers of the Fifth Lateran to put an end to the mutual slaughter of Christians so that they could unite in an expedition against their common enemy, the Turks.[17]

Alexios feared that the Western Church could also collapse before Islamic might, if it did not reform itself. God may use the Turks to punish it. The church can ill afford another pope like Alexander VI who used devious means to garner power and attain the papacy. He sought to dominate all, like Alexander of old, would be denied nothing, and thus engaged in sexual misconduct, excessive nepotism, and government by fear rather than love. Alexios urged the cardinals in conclave to vote only for good men who do not lust after that papal office but are dedicated pastors–a criticism which probably did not sit well with the future Julius II. For not only was Julius suspected of simony in his election to the papacy, but his uncle Sixtus IV may well have been guilty of the same and was apparently openly criticized by his former patron Bessarion for such misconduct. The Greek cardinal's disciple Alexios also attacked the papal court. In Rome there is great license for sinning. The clergy live lives of luxury and spare no labours to accumulate wealth. The laity perceive them as parasites and fitting food for vultures. Corruption also permeates the lay order of the church with its crimes, ambition, warfare, fraud, venality, cupidity, licentiousness, and blasphemies. Let representatives from all levels of the church assemble to work out a reform program and may the pope enforce it.[18]

The agenda set for the Fifth Lateran Council (1512-1517) must have appealed to Alexios. Among its principal goals were a restoration of unity to the church, a reform of morals, and the launching of a crusade. If his master Bessarion had come to the attention of Latin churchmen by the active role he had played at the Council of Ferrara-Florence, his disciple Alexios would seek to be no less active at this Roman council three-quarters of a century later.[19]

Although not a member of the inner papal circle which sought to control the activities and direction of the Lateran Council, Alexios

---

17. Mansi 32.739A-C, 741D, 742A.

18. Celadenus, *Fraterni obitus tolerantiam*, BAV Vat. Lat. 8736, fols. 4^r-5^v, and *De ratione belli in Turcos ineundi*, BAV Vat. Lat. 14174, fols. 5^v, 8^v-9^r, 10^v-12^r, 13^v-16^r; Mansi 32.740D, 741D-42A; McMananon, "Ideal Pope," pp. 54-59; and John W. O'Malley, *Praise and Blame in Renaissance Rome: Rhetoric, Doctrine, and Reform in the Sacred Orators of the Papal Court, c. 1450-1521* (Durham, 1979), pp. 213-214, 216, 229-230.

19. On the goals of the Lateran Council, see my "Paride de Grassi's Diary of the Fifth Lateran Council," *Annuarium Historiae Conciliorum* 14 (1982):431-433. On Bessarion's role at the Council of Ferrara-Florence, see Joseph Gill, *The Council of Florence* (Cambridge, 1959), and his *Personalities of the Council*, esp. pp. 46-53.

played one of the more prominent roles allowed to a bishop. He attended all of its formal sessions, except for the fifth and twelfth, and served as procurator for the bishop of Melfi (Raffaele de Cerva) at the fourth and for the bishops of Girgento (Giuliano Cibò) and of Bergamo (Pietro Lippomani) at the eleventh session. He was chosen by the pope to be one of the twelve clerics who delivered sermons at its sessions, Julius choosing Celadenus to speak at the third session. Alexios' name appears several times in the conciliar *acta* as someone who gave a personal opinion when voting. At the second session he alone opposed the wording of the decree condemning the Pisan cardinals whose leader was Carvajal. Alexios had been forewarned of this decree and came to the council with a written statement explaining why the adherents of the Pisan council should not be condemned without a hearing. At this session he voiced his objection and entrusted to the master of ceremonies, Paride de Grassi, his written statement which was to be given to the pope later. Julius' response to Alexios' protest was to laugh it off, saying, "There is nothing surprising about Molfetta, for he is a Greek and Greeks always disagree with Latins." Leo took Alexios more seriously and named him to the twenty-man deputation of faith on 3 June 1513. At the eighth session Alexios joined his voice to that of the chorus of prelates demanding a conciliar reform program that was wider in scope. When the bishops were asked at the general congregation on 29 April 1514 to approve a reform decree drawn up by the reform deputation, Alexios insisted on first seeing a draft of this proposal. On the following day he was elected by his colleagues as one of the eight bishops to represent episcopal interests in the preparatory conciliar deliberations and negotiations. He was the only bishop at the tenth session to protest censorship in the publication of ancient authors. His final intervention was at the eleventh session where he expressed satisfaction with those provisions of the bull which restored to ordinaries control over religious, and he agreed to the other measures in that decree provided they did not prejudice the rights of present and future ordinaries.[20] In addition to occasions when Alexios was mentioned by name in the *acta* were the many times when without further comment he joined his fellow bishops in

20. Minnich, "The Participants at the Fifth Lateran Council," *Archivum Historiae Pontificiae* 12 (1974):157-206, here 184, no. 98; Mansi 32.736E-742E, 797DE, 847A, 849CD, 850D, 913D, 975A; Marc Dykman, "Le cinquième Concile du Latran d'après le diaire de Paris de Grassi," *Annuarium Historiae Conciliorum* 14 (1982):271-369, here 314-315, no. 848:27-28; and my forthcoming "The Proposals for an Episcopal College at Lateran V," in *Ecclesia militans: Studien zur Konzilien-und Reformationgeschichte. Festgabe für Remigius Bäumer*, ed. Herbert Immenkötter (Paderborn, 1988).

approving overwhelmingly the proposed conciliar decree.

Because few of the council's working papers survive, it is difficult to evaluate Alexios' contributions. His sermon at the third session was rhetorical and traced in general terms the nature and history of the church and its councils. His recommendations were mostly pious generalities regarding a crusade and reform. He did assign to the council the task of explaining the truths of the Faith, formulating these in appropriate chapters and articles, and expelling error from the world.[21] What role he may have played in the deputation of faith is open to speculation.

Scholars have argued over the origins of *Apostolici regiminis*, the council's decree on the human soul's multiplicity and immortality. John O'Malley, Felix Gilbert, and Paul Oskar Kristeller have suggested that the proponents of the decree were Platonists, led by such prominent humanists as Egidio Antonini, Gianfrancesco Pico della Mirandola, Francesco da Diacceto, and others. Antonio Poppi and Daniel Price have pointed to the Scotist and Thomistic oppo-

---

21. Mansi 32.738E-739A. This sermon also exists in a manuscript copy bound into a codex formerly owned by Alberto Pio, the imperial ambassador to the Lateran Council. This codex is preserved in the Biblioteca Valentiniana di Camerino as MS 78 fols. 85ʳ-92ᵛ bearing the title "Alexii Episcopi Melfitani oratio quam habuit in tertia sessione sacri Lateranensis Concilii, cui Julius huius nominis ii Pont. Max. auctor factus interfuit et prẹsedit." This sermon is bound together with various writings of Stephanus Teglatius and of others. The codex appears in a catalogue of Alberto Pio's library as "Variae Orationes et tractatus Steffanii Patratensis et alia, scritto à penna con pergam"; see Leon Dorez, "Latino Latini et la bibliothèque capitulaire de Viterbo," *Revue des bibliotheques* 2 (1892):377-391, here 386, section E. Alexios' oration is written on paper measuring 14.7 by 20.5 cm. Folios 87 and 90 constitute one sheet as do also 85 and 92. These sheets contain a circular watermark divided into two equal sections. In the top half is depicted most of a common anchor: a large section of its shank and the protruding end sections of the two arms with their flukes. In the other half appear some marine animals: a fish or dolphin, three starfish, and other items not clearly delineated. This watermark does not appear in the collection of Charles Möise Briquet, *Les filigranes: Dictionnaire historique des marques du papier dès leur apparition vers 1282 jusqu' en 1600*, 4 vols. (Paris, 1907). The differences between the text of his oration here given and that reproduced in Mansi are minor, mostly having to do with peculiarities in orthography, but also offering alternate readings on occasion: e.g., in hoc perangusto Europae angulo discordia et ignavia coarctatae (M741E1-2) *vs* in hoc perangusto Europae angulo per discordias et ignaviam coarctatae (fol. 91ʳ); propterea (M741E7) *vs* ob haec (fol. 91ʳ); idcirco (M742A9) *vs* propterea (fol. 91ᵛ); felicitatis (M742C3) *vs* facilitatis (fol. 92ᵛ); apud te coram sacro senatu et his patribus (M742C14-15) *vs* apud te, hunc sacrum senatum, et hos patres (fol. 92ʳ), etc. While a critical edition of this oration will have to take into consideration such variant readings, they do not seriously alter the sense of the text printed by Mansi. The manuscript version does not contain the material removed from Alexios' original version of this sermon which would have taken about three hours to deliver (M742B).

nents of the Averroists such as the Franciscan Antonio Trombetta, the Dominican Tommaso de Vio, and the Franciscan eclectic Scotist-Platonist Dragišič.[22] I should like to add to the list of significant contributors to this decree the name of Alexios Celadenus.

Alexios' views on the immortality of the soul are spelled out in his 1501 letter of consolation to Cardinal Jorge de Costa on the death of his brother. To console the grieving cardinal, Alexios reviewed some of the ancient arguments for the soul's immortality: it moves itself, its nature is simple with no corruptible element mixed in, it is indivisible, it has innate knowledge and knows the past and future, its speed of operation is remarkable, its arts and inventiveness are astonishing. Noble persons have died with equanimity in the conviction that a good future awaits them. These arguments and others he drew from the writings of the ancients: Plato, Xenophon, and Cicero, authors whom Bessarion had earlier translated or defended. Their arguments based on experience and reasoning he complemented with those drawn from the Christian Faith.[23] Thus, a dozen years before the council's deputation on faith discussed this topic, Alexios had already held that the soul was immortal and that this could be argued from reason.

Rather than seeing the decree *Apostolici regiminis* as the product of either the Platonists or the scholastic anti-Averroists, it may be more useful to see it as a reflection of the views of both groups. There is nothing in the wording of the decree which would have been unacceptable to Thomists, Scotists, or Platonists. The decree was the

22. John O'Malley, *Giles of Viterbo on Church and Reform: A Study in Renaissance Thought* (Leiden, 1968), p. 42; Felix Gilbert, "Cristianesimo, umanesimo, e la bolla '*Apostolici Regiminis*' del 1513," trans. M.V. Malvano, *Rivista storica italiana* 79 (1967):976-999, here p. 978; Paul O. Kristeller, "Francesco da Diacetto and Florentine Platonism in the Sixteenth Century" (1946), in his *Studies in Renaissance Thought and Letters* (Rome, 1956), pp. 287-336, here p. 303; Antonio Poppi, "Lo scotista, Antonio Trombetta," *Il Santo* (1962), pp. 349-367; and M. Daniel Price, "The Origins of Lateran V's 'Apostolici Regiminis,'" *Annuarium Historiae Conciliorum* 17 (1985):464-472, esp. 465-467, 472.

23. Celadenus, *Fraterni obitus tolerantiam*, Monfasani, "Alexius Celadenus," cites another copy in Paris on p. 106 n. 70. Although learned in Greek, Alexios curiously seems to have taken his quotations from Plato and Xenophon not from their original Greek texts, but from their translations in Cicero's *De senectute*, esp. xxii, pp. 78-83 (Loeb edition). Bessarion had earlier translated into Latin Xenophon's *Memorabilia* of Socrates, into Greek Cicero's *De senectute* and *Tusculan Disputations*, and had composed in both Latin and Greek a lengthy *In Calumniatorem Platonis libri IV*. In this latter work, he presented Plato's reasons for the soul's immortality based on its self-movement and also the arguments of Albert the Great, Thomas Aquinas, Duns Scotus, and others. See Mohler, *Kardinal Bessarion*, 1:253, 404-405, 2:141-165, 365-413, and 3:410.

product of a deputation containing known exponents of each school: Vio, Trombetta, Dragišič, and Celadenus. Of the three cardinals proposed as supervisors of the decree's final formulation, two were the cardinal protectors of the Franciscans and Dominicans, Domenico Grimani and Niccolò Fieschi respectively. The third was the reconciled former Pisan cardinal, Bernardino López de Carvajal, patron of Bessarion's two disciples: Dragišič and Celadenus, both of whom sat on the faith deputation and espoused Platonist views. By representing forcefully the arguments of Plato for the soul's multiplicity and immortality, Bessarion's disciples could have discouraged the deputation from adopting an Aristotelian line of reasoning. Indeed, the final decree avoided taking sides with either school and provided instead a series of scriptural prooftexts.[24]

In March of 1517 the Lateran Council closed without Alexios having achieved the fame of his master, and one month later this Greek bishop died without ever having been named a cardinal. In his lifetime, however, he had recapitulated many of the career choices, causes, and ideas of his former teacher and guide: tutoring the probably half-Greek scion of the king of Naples, associating with the local humanists there, labouring as a Latin bishop for church and monastic reform, writing humanistic works in Latin, espousing Platonist ideas, serving in the central bureaucracy in Rome, calling for untainted papal elections, participating actively in a church council, representing Greek interests at the papal court, especially by his advocacy of a crusade to free his homeland, and finding a final resting place appropriately enough in one of the churches of Rome. Alexios Celadenus deserves, then, to be seen as a faithful disciple of John Bessarion.

Alexios' failure to achieve the fame and rank of his master suggests a change in the status of things Greek in Renaissance Italy. Italian humanists had so successfully appropriated much of ancient Greek culture in the half-century since Bessarion that they ceased to stand in awe of a learned Greek.[25] Italians were also no longer

24. Letter of Francesco Vittori to the Dieci di Balià, Rome, 24 November 1513: "et di rassectare molte cose circa la religione a che sono proposti li Reuerendissimi di Santa Croce et Grimani et Flischo..." in Archivio di Stato–Firenze, Dieci di Balià, Carteggi Responsive, no. 118, fol. 317ʳ. For the wording of the decree, see Mansi 32.842A-843C. For a fuller explanation of how this decree used Sacred Scripture to avoid taking sides between the Platonists and Aristotelians, see my forthcoming "The Function of Sacred Scripture in the Decrees of the Fifth Lateran Council (1512-1517)," in *Annuarium Historiae Conciliorum.*

25. Geanakoplos, *Byzantium and the Renaissance,* pp. 299-300 and his "Italian Renaissance Thought and Learning and the Role of the Byzantine Emigrés Scholars in Florence, Rome, and Venice: A Reassessment," *Rivista di Studi Bizantini e Slavi* 3 (1983):129-157, here 153-155.

shocked by the fall of Constantinople to the Turks nor fearful of an imminent invasion of their homeland. Hope for a permanent healing of the schism between the Latin and Greek Churches had faded after the hostile reception in the East to the union negotiated at the Council of Ferrara-Florence. The papacy turned its attention increasingly to the politics of the Italian peninsula as a way of safeguarding the independence of the Papal States. In this environment the cause of serious church reform was put temporarily onto hold. Times had changed since the days of Bessarion and a disciple who mirrored so closely his learning, concerns, and career choices could no longer hope to achieve the same eminence as his master.

VII

VOCATIONAL CHOICES: AN UNKNOWN LETTER OF PIETRO QUERINI TO GASPARO CONTARINI AND NICCOLÒ TIEPOLO (APRIL, 1512)

BY

Nelson H. Minnich and Elisabeth G. Gleason*

Inserted into a codex of manuscripts formerly belonging to the Chigi family and now in the Vatican Library are two inconspicuous sheets which, according to the table of contents, were written by a "fra Pietro." In actuality, they are autographs of a complete letter with postscript by Vincenzo Querini (ca. 1479-1514), who as a monk took on the name of Pietro, to Niccolò Tiepolo (+1551)[1] and Gasparo Contarini (1483-1542).[2] On the verso page of the postscript Querini addressed them as "my dearest friends," and the tone he adopted throughout is one of confidence and affection. What we have before us, however, is more important than a mere letter of friendship. It is a valuable, hitherto missing piece of a particularly famous epistolary exchange. Despite its brevity it throws new light on a central figure among proponents of church reform in early sixteenth-century Italy.

Let us look at the context of this letter and postscript. In 1953 Hubert Jedin published thirty letters, all but two previously unknown, written

*Nelson H. Minnich is an associate professor of history and church history in the Catholic University of America. Elisabeth G. Gleason is a professor of history and holder of the National Endowment for the Humanities Chair of Humanities for 1988-89 in the University of San Francisco. The authors would like to thank Dean Carl J. Naegele and the Faculty Development Fund of the University of San Francisco for their financial support.

[1]For the scant bibliography on him, see James Bruce Ross, "Gasparo Contarini and His Friends," *Studies in the Renaissance*, XVII (1970), 195, n. 9.

[2]For his biography and extensive bibliography, see Gigliola Fragnito, "Contarini, Gasparo," in *Dizionario Biografico degli Italiani*, Vol. 28 (Rome, 1983), pp. 172-192, expanded as "Un patrizio veneziano alla corte pontificia," in her *Gasparo Contarini: un magistrato veneziano al servizio della Cristianità* (Florence, 1988), pp. 1-78.

between 1511 and 1523 by Gasparo Contarini to his friends Tommaso Giustiniani and Vincenzo Querini, Venetian nobles like himself, who had left their city to join the strict Camaldolese order.[3] These letters have attracted such attention from scholars that their exegesis by now forms a short chapter in the historiography of religious thought in sixteenth-century Italy.[4] Many of the letters describe the inner states of the young Contarini, future statesman and cardinal, to two men with whom he was linked by deep friendship. What he poured out to his friends with candor and lack of stylistic conceits creates a rare sense of immediacy for his modern readers. Jedin's view that Contarini, too, seriously considered the monastic life[5] is rejected by most recent scholars. But their opinions diverge concerning the relative importance of themes touched upon in the letters of the three friends.

It is not easy to understand the many levels of meaning in this corres-pondence because only some of the responses by Giustiniani and

[3]The letters were published in *Contarini und Camaldoli* (Rome, 1953), actually a preprint of the article from *Archivio Italiano per la Storia della Pietà*, II, which appeared only in 1959. All references are to page numbers of the preprint "Contarini und Camaldoli."

[4]In addition to "Contarini und Camaldoli," see Jedin, "Ein 'Turmerlebnis' des jungen Conta-rini," *Historisches Jahrbuch der Görresgesellschaft*, LXX (1951), 115-130, and "Gasparo Con-tarini e il contributo veneziano alla riforma cattolica," in *La Civiltà veneziana del Rina-scimento* (Florence, 1958), pp. 105-124. These two articles were reprinted: "Ein 'Turmerleb-nis'," in the collection *Kirche des Glaubens—Kirche der Geschichte: Ausgewählte Aufsätze und Vorträge* (Freiburg im Breisgau, 1966), I, 167-180, and in an Italian translation in *Chiesa della Fede, Chiesa della Storia: Saggi scelti*, ed. Giuseppe Alberigo, trans. A. Destro, A. M. Fidora and G. Poletti (Brescia, 1972), pp. 606-623; and "Contarini e il contributo" in *Chiesa della Fede*, pp. 624-639. See also Heinz Mackensen, "Contarini's Theological Role at Ratisbon in 1541," *Archiv für Reformationsgeschichte*, 51 (1960), 36-57; Roberto Cessi, "Paolinismo preluterano," *Rendiconti dell'Accademia dei Lincei*, Classe di scienze morali, storiche e filologiche, XII (1957), 3-30; Felix Gilbert, "Religion and Politics in the Thought of Gasparo Contarini," in *Action and Conviction in Early Modern Europe: Essays in Memory of E. H. Harbison*, ed. T. K. Rabb and J. E. Seigel (Princeton, N.J., 1969), pp. 90-116; Gigliola Fragnito, "Cultura umanistica e riforma religiosa: il «De officio viri boni ac probi episcopi» di Gasparo Contarini," *Studi veneziani*, XI (1969), especially pp. 97-115, reprinted in her *Gasparo Con-tarini*, pp. 79-211. Innocenzo Cervelli, "Storiografia e problemi intorno alla vita religiosa e spirituale a Venezia nella prima metà del '500," *Studi veneziani*, VIII (1966), especially pp. 466-467; Delio Cantimori, "Le idee religiose del Cinquecento. La storiografia," in *Storia della Letteratura Italiana*, ed. E. Cecchi and N. Sapegno, Vol. V: *Il Seicento* (Milan, 1967), pp. 7-87; James Bruce Ross, "Gasparo Contarini and His Friends," *Studies in the Renaissance*, XVII (1970), 192-232; Giuseppe Alberigo, "Vita attiva e vita contemplativa in un'esperienza del XVI secolo," *Studi veneziani*, XVI (1974), 177-225; the somewhat shorter French version appeared as "Vie active et vie contemplative dans une expérience chrétienne du XVIᵉ siècle," in *Théologie: le service théologique dans l'Église*. Mélanges offertes à Yves Congar pour ses soixante-dix ans (Paris, 1974), pp. 287-321; Giovanni Miccoli, "La storia religiosa," in *Storia d'Italia*, Vol. 2, Pt. I (Turin, 1974), pp. 947-955.

[5]"Contarini und Camaldoli," p. 9.

Querini are available to us.[6] Contarini's thinking is fairly fully represented, Giustiniani's less so. But Querini's, because of the dearth of published letters from the period after his religious profession, remains at times puzzling. The letter before us adds a new dimension to his thought and reveals his approach to the discussion between himself and Giustiniani on the one hand and Tiepolo and Contarini on the other.

Giustiniani, Querini, and Contarini were all students at the University of Padua at the turn of the sixteenth century and established a whole network of friendships during that period.[7] Close bonds existed between the three men. J. B. Ross noted that "at the center of Contarini's affective life before 1514 there lay, one might say, a triangle, the apex representing Giustiniani, his spiritual mentor and elder by seven years, the other angles himself and Quirini, his *alter ego*, about four years older than himself."[8] After all three had returned to Venice from Padua, they formed a tightly-knit circle which included their closest friends Niccolò Tiepolo, Sebastiano Zorzi, Giovanni Battista Egnazio, and Trifone Gabriele.[9]

This group of young men (all aristocrats except for the commoner Egnazio) was part of a generation of Venetian *nobili* who shared common experiences of religious quest and, in some cases, crisis at a time of political turmoil caused by the war of the League of Cambrai.[10] But little that is definite is known about the circle which was formed around Giustiniani and apparently met in his house on the island of Murano. Giustiniani may well have been the central figure of this group not only because he was the oldest, but on account of his intense intellectual and spiritual travails during several years after 1505, when he left Padua.

Giustiniani's odyssey from a Venetian patrician, by his own admission a sensuous and passionate man,[11] to an ascetic reformer of the Camal-

---

[6]They are printed in *Annales Camaldulenses ordinis Sancti Benedicti*, eds. Giovanni Benedetto Mittarelli and Anselmo Costadoni (9 vols.; Venice, 1755-1777), IX (Venice, 1773), cols. 446-611 (Epistolicum Commercium).

[7]For a discussion of these friendships, see especially Ross, *op. cit.*, pp. 195-213.

[8]*Ibid.*, p. 195. Jedin used the spelling Quirini. Querini was the Venetian form of the name which was latinized as Quirinus.

[9]*Ibid.*, p. 195, notes 9-12 for bibliography on these men. See also Ross, "Venetian Schools and Teachers, Fourteenth to Early Sixteenth Century: A Survey and a Study of Giovanni Battista Egnazio," *Renaissance Quarterly*, XXIX (1976), 521-560 for Egnazio.

[10]For the first use of the term "generation" in this sense, see Carlo Dionisotti, "Chierici e laici nella letteratura italiana del primo Cinquecento," in *Problemi di vita religiosa in Italia nel Cinquecento* (Padua, 1960), p. 176. The essay appears in a fuller version as "Chierici e laici" in the author's *Geografia e storia della letteratura italiana* (Turin, 1967), pp. 55-88; the passage on the Venetian group is on p. 78.

[11]See Jean Leclercq, *Un humaniste ermite: le bienheureux Paul Giustiniani* (Rome, 1951), pp. 17-22.

dolese order and an advocate of church reform is yet to be told fully. A modern edition of his works and letters has been planned for a long time.[12] Judging from his available writings, he was a charismatic figure whose opinions strongly influenced his friends. Gradually detaching himself from the social and political activities expected of a young man of his class, he repudiated civic life for monastic withdrawal, and his humanist education for theological learning.[13] Like a new St. Jerome, Giustiniani travelled to the Holy Land in search of a peaceful retreat. Not finding it, he returned and in 1510 decided to enter the Camaldolese hermitage in the mountains near Arezzo, taking the name of Paolo. A year later he was joined there by Querini, who left both Venice and a promising public career.

Because we lack a modern biography of Querini, and his correspondence still remains to be edited, it is not possible to understand his thought and character clearly.[14] He seems a more complex figure than Giustiniani, who was his spiritual guide. After an early start in public life as ambassador to the Court of Burgundy and to Emperor Maximilian,[15] Querini decided to follow in the footsteps of Giustiniani. Despite his profound religious zeal, he revealed a remarkable measure of uncertainty and ambivalence even after making his profession as a Camaldolese hermit on February 22, 1512. His letters provide evidence that he was an emotional, high-strung man for whom deeply-felt bonds to friends and family were an important part of life. Often moved to tears, he was not afraid to weep; perhaps he was encouraged by Giustiniani's view that "not weeping does not show strength of mind."[16] His debate about what choices to make forms the substance of his published correspondence

[12]See Eugenio Massa, *I manoscritti originali del Beato Paolo Giustiniani custoditi nell'Eremo di Frascati* (Rome, 1967), and his article "Paolo Giustiniani" in *Bibliotheca Sanctorum*, VII (Rome, 1966), cols. 2-9, with bibliography. The work of Leclercq, cited in n. 11 above, while based on much original material, remains only a useful beginning.

[13]On Giustiniani's and Querini's attitudes toward humanist learning, see Felix Gilbert, "Cristianesimo, umanesimo e la bolla 'Apostolici Regiminis' del 1513," *Rivista Storica Italiana*, 79 (1967), 976-990.

[14]Still useful: Emmanuele Cicogna, *Delle Inscrizioni Veneziane*, Vol. V (Venice, 1842), pp. 62-73; for bibliography, see Jedin, "Vincenzo Quirini und Pietro Bembo," in *Miscellanea Giovanni Mercati*, Vol. IV (Vatican City, 1946), pp. 407-424, now also in Jedin, *Kirche des Glaubens—Kirche der Geschichte*, I, 153-166, and *Chiesa della Fede, Chiesa della Storia*, pp. 481-498. Querini's correspondence was gathered after his death by Giustiniani in codices belonging now to the Camaldolese monastery near Frascati.

[15]For bibliography concerning Querini's embassies, see Jedin "Contarini und Camaldoli," p. 7, n. 2.

[16]Letter of Giustiniani to Tiepolo and Contarini, March, 1517, in *Annales Camaldulenses*, IX, col. 498, and the same to the same, July 15, 1510, *ibid.*, col. 457.

with his friends. He is intense, almost relentless in his self-examination, which reveals how difficult leaving Venice was for him. As he unfolds his thoughts to Giustiniani, he signs several letters not with his own name but with "Licenope," as if that were someone else participating in the debate.[17] Licenope is his better self who would like to follow Giustiniani and overcome Vincenzo's doubts, weaknesses, and hesitations. But even as a hermit, Querini continued to be attracted to Florentine humanist circles and the court of Leo X, where he was called to help conduct diplomatic negotiations between Venice and the Holy See in the spring of 1514.[18] At the time of his death on September 23, 1514, he was in line to be named cardinal.

Querini's planned and then realized departure from Venice in 1511 produced an exchange of letters between the three friends that was continued until Brother Pietro died.[19] Except for the account of Contarini's religious experience on Holy Saturday, 1511, written to Giustiniani on April 24,[20] the most personal topic they discussed before Querini took final vows was whether or not the novice had a monastic vocation.[21] This soon led to the related issue of the merit of monastic withdrawal. The two poles in the debate were the views of Giustiniani and Contarini, who mustered arguments designed to convince their mutual friend of the validity of their respective positions. Brother Paolo unequivocally espoused the traditional view that among the ways of life a Christian could choose, monastic withdrawal from the world for the purpose of serving God was the highest, while Contarini was equally convinced that the life of contemplation and that of action were not arranged in hierarchical order, with the second occupying a lower position than the

---

[17]For example, throughout the letters to Giustiniani of July 15, 1511, *ibid.*, cols. 452-454, and 454-461, he writes of Lycenope as of a third person; also in letters of August 1 and 13, *ibid.*, cols. 261-267 and 515-517. A long, undated letter of 1511 is signed with "Lycenope": *ibid.*, cols. 496-509, and another September 15 of the same year with "Licenope": *ibid.*, cols. 517-518. Once he has decided to join the Camaldolese, he again signs his letters with his full name.

[18]Jedin in "Vincenzo Quirini und Pietro Bembo" tried to explain Querini's behavior and defend him against the accusation of being hypocritical and self-seeking made by V. Cian, "A proposito d'un ambasceria di Pietro Bembo (dicembre 1514)," *Archivio Veneto*, 30 (1885), 355-381. The documents which Cian cites raise questions concerning Querini's motives which Jedin does not answer entirely.

[19]They include Contarini's letters 5-15, from the end of November, 1511, to July 11, 1514, in Jedin, "Contarini und Camaldoli," his letter to Querini written after February 22, 1512, in *Annales Camaldulenses*, IX, cols. 539-543, and the letters of his friends, *ibid.*

[20]"Contarini und Camaldoli," pp. 12-15. See also Jedin, "Ein 'Turmerlebnis' des jungen Contarini," pp. 115-130.

[21]On this point, see Alberigo, "Vita attiva e vita comtemplativa," esp. pp. 194-195.

first. He firmly maintained that there was no privileged status for one form of Christian life over another, holding fast to his insight that one can serve God by remaining "in the midst of the city" and living "among the multitude of the city."[22] What mattered was not the place where one lived, but one's disposition to unite oneself with Christ, "our head, in faith, hope, and the little love of which we are capable."[23]

The evidence for Querini's views in this debate has so far rested on a long letter he wrote to Giustiniani in January, 1511.[24] Comparing the thought of the two men, Giuseppe Alberigo was struck by Querini's "notably more flexible positions"[25] concerning the salvation of those who remained in the world and lived with their families and friends. Knowing Querini's hesitations, Contarini made an attempt in December of 1511 to dissuade his friend from espousing the eremitical life. He warned Querini that such a life was not natural to man, and that anyone who wanted to embrace it had to possess perfection which was almost beyond human nature, attainable only by the few. Contarini's distrust of what he perceived as an attempt on Querini's part to force his monastic vocation by sheer will-power surfaced in his warning that one cannot do violence to one's nature without running serious risks.[26] In another letter, written probably toward the end of February, 1512, Contarini stressed Querini's obligations to his family and his civic duty, and noted that many Venetians accused his friend of leaving his homeland in the hour of need during the war by behaving like a soldier who deserted or a sailor who abandoned ship.[27]

Apparently Niccolò Tiepolo had written in a similar vein, for Giustiniani replied jointly to him and Contarini. In an immoderate, sharply worded letter he called them instruments of the devil, persecutors of Christ, miserable souls, and even antichrists. In their letters "all is falsity, ignorance, impiety, and manifest heresy."[28] Contarini's reply to this torrent of

---

[22]"Contarini und Camaldoli" pp. 14 and 15.

[23]*Ibid.*, p. 14.

[24]*Annales Camaldulenses*, IX, cols. 496-509.

[25]"Vita attiva e vita contemplativa," p. 210.

[26]"Contarini und Camaldoli," p. 23.

[27]*Annales Camaldulenses*, IX, cols. 539-543. To Jedin's doubt that this letter was actually sent, expressed in "Contarini und Camaldoli," p. 30, n. 29, Gigliola Fragnito offers a convincing reply: "Cultura umanistica e riforma religiosa," p. 94, n. 73.

[28]The letter is dated February, 1512: *Annales Camaldulenses*, IX, cols. 544-550. The heresy mentioned by Giustiniani could refer only to Contarini's denial of the superior value of monastic life, since Giustiniani did not attribute any specific doctrinal errors to him and Tiepolo. See Alberigo's incisive and informative discussion of this issue in "Vita attiva e vita contemplativa," pp. 206-213, and the bibliography, p. 218, n. 82.

accusations was a gentle, meditative letter which reminded Giustiniani not to judge everyone by his own example.[29] After asking to be corrected if he had committed errors, he again underlined his firm belief that everyone had to follow his own way to salvation in accordance with his nature, and that the life of a hermit was only for the few. He thought that Querini "was maybe presumptuous" in wanting to reach such a rare state of perfection immediately, without prior experience, and candidly assessed Brother Pietro's nature as "not much inclined to solitude."[30] Giustiniani answered in a strangely meek tone, excusing himself to Tiepolo and Contarini, and promising to speak in the future in a more circumspect fashion with friends and others.[31] This exchange about Querini's vocation terminated on Contarini's part with the somewhat perfunctory acceptance of his friend's choice, accompanied by routine exclamations like: "Oh, on what kind of service are you embarked!"[32] But his own way was different: although his "most beloved friends" were his examples, he wanted to come for a visit without imitating them.[33]

This, then, is the immediate context for Querini's letter to Tiepolo and Contarini of April 12, 1512.[34] Chronologically, it follows Giustiniani's denunciations at the end of February, 1512, and Contarini's response of March 10. It precedes and foreshadows Giustiniani's conciliatory letter of April 18, 1512. Querini's intent is clear: he wants to reconcile his friends in Venice with Giustiniani, whose strongly worded letter of February he obviously knew. He excuses Brother Paolo by stressing that it was zeal for the honor of Christ which made him reprove his friends so sharply. Actually, the entire final paragraph is a defense of Giustiniani, written in the interest of making peace.

But more significant is the fact that Querini does not share his fellow-monk's views about the hierarchy among Christians. He sounds much more like Contarini than Giustiniani in his discussion of civic and monastic life. His striking affirmation that salvation can be found everywhere and that it depends on man's closeness to God and not on the choice of vocation echoes not only Contarini's letter which related his Easter experience of 1511,[35] but the future cardinal's consistently held views

---

[29] March 10, 1512: "Contarini und Camaldoli," p. 32.

[30] *Ibid.*, p. 31.

[31] April 18, 1512: *Annales Camaldulenses*, IX, col. 561.

[32] To Querini, March 10, 1512, "Contarini und Camaldoli," p. 34.

[33] *Ibid.*, p. 35.

[34] Massa, *I manoscritti originali*, makes reference to two other letters of Querini to Tiepolo and Contarini without, however, giving any indication of their content: p. 131, no. 64, and p. 149, no. 173. The manuscripts remain inaccessible.

[35] "Contarini und Camaldoli," pp. 12-15.

on this subject. For Brother Pietro, the decisive element in the process of salvation is conformity to God's will. One cannot help wondering whether Giustiniani read Querini's poignant question to his friends: "Who knows? Maybe you will reach your goal before many who go to live in solitude," or what he thought of Brother Pietro's praise for "all the different forms of good life," including the civic life, which "Christ never disapproved."

This letter helps us to understand Querini's willingness and perhaps even eagerness two years later to become a cardinal and lead the life of an active decision-maker at the highest level of the Church. He could not accept Giustiniani's categorical views about the primacy of a monastic vocation, although he repeatedly stated that it was the right choice for himself. Even as a monk he remained in essential agreement with Contarini's conviction that every choice of life could advance man on the way to his salvation, provided it rested on a truly Christian disposition. In this respect Querini and Contarini stood on the modern side of the great religious divide of the sixteenth century.

The postscript to this letter of Querini suggests the larger political, military, ecclesiastical, and cultural context in which he wrote. His postscript refers to a battle that has just occurred, to news about the council, to being loyal to Pope Julius II, and to his concern for his friends in Venice.

As Querini was writing this postscript, probably during the night of Easter Monday and into Easter Tuesday morning (April 12-13, 1512),[36] he received word of the terrible slaughter that had occurred on Easter Sunday at the Battle of Ravenna, less than fifty miles from Camaldoli.[37] On the great plain, which was once the ancient port of Classe, the armies met. The forces of the League of Cambrai (primarily French, German, and Ferrarese, under the military command of Gaston de Foix) fought in the name of the Council of Pisa-Milan, and its legate, the deposed cardinal Federigo de Sanseverino in military garb, took an active role in the conflict. The opposing army of the Holy League (principally Spanish and papal, with supporting Venetian troops and ships, all led by the Spanish Viceroy of Naples, Raimondo de Cardona, as captain general of the allies) was accompanied by the papal legate in cardinal's robes,

---

[36] That this postscript was written at night is clearly stated in the text. It is a companion piece to the letter dated April 12. His reference to "the day on which the battle occurred" suggests at least some distance in time from the event, as does also the report that Zorzi was in Faenza.

[37] Giustiniani calculated the distance by winding road from Ravenna to the Eremo as 65 *miglia*: see *Annales Camaldulenses*, IX, cols. 469-471.

Giovanni dei Medici, the future Leo X. When the battle ended at least ten thousand soldiers had died: the Holy League losing two-thirds of its forces, the League of Cambrai one-third, but also its leader, de Foix. While de Cardona managed to escape eventually to Ancona, dei Medici was taken prisoner.[38] With the army of his allies destroyed, the cause of Julius II (1503-1513) was in desperate straits.[39] Word of this defeat brought consternation to Querini on a number of accounts. He wept for the many who had died; he worried about his Venetian countrymen; and he feared for the pope.

Querini followed with great interest the latest developments regarding a church council. In his sworn election capitularies of 1503, Julius had promised to convoke a council within two years and agreed that should he fail to do so the cardinals could convene on their own authority. Seven years later he had yet to convoke the promised council. When he similarly backed out of his obligations as a signatory of the League of Cambrai, the pope's former allies, Louis XII of France (1498-1515) and Maximilian I of the Empire (1493-1519), agreed at Blois in November of 1510 that if Julius refused to abide by the provisions of the League, a council should be called. Negotiations having failed at Mantua in April of 1511 to resolve the differences, the emperor, king of France, and several dissident cardinals proceeded to convoke a council to meet in Pisa later that year. On November 1, 1511, that council held its opening ceremonies in the Church of S. Michele of the Camaldolese monastery in Pisa, where the council's president had taken up residence. Three formal sessions followed within eleven days, but nothing of substance was treated except for a reiteration of *Haec sancta*. Attendance at these sessions hovered at around thirty prelates, almost all Frenchmen. Following the council's transfer to Milan and Julius' refusal to deal with its emissaries on the question of choosing a mutually agreeable site for its meetings, the council set at its fourth session on January 4, 1512, a forty-day deadline for a papal response, threatening him thereafter with a conciliar censure.[40] While recuperating in Florence, Querini had writ-

---

[38]On the Battle of Ravenna, see Francesco Guicciardini, *Storia d'Italia*, ed. Costantino Panigada (5 vols.; Bari, 1929), Book X, chapters 12-13, Vol. III, pp. 179-193; *Storia della lega fatta in Cambrai frà Papa Giulio II. Massimiliano I. Imperatore, Luigi XII. Re' di Francia, Fernando V. Ré d'Aragona, e tutti i Principi d'Italia contra la Repubblica di Vinegia*, trans. from French into Italian (Antwerp, 1718), pp. 237-246.

[39]Nelson H. Minnich, "The Healing of the Pisan Schism (1511-13)," *Annuarium Historiae Conciliorum*, 16 (1984), 59-192, here 85-89.

[40]*Ibid.*, pp. 59-84; *Acta primi concilii Pisani celebrati ad tollendum schisma anno Domini M.CCCC.IX. et concilii Senensis M.CCCC.XXIII. Ex codice manuscripto, item constitutiones sanctae in diversis sessionibus sacri generalis concilii Pisani ex bibliotheca regia* (Paris, 1612), pp. 16-18

10   VOCATIONAL CHOICES

ten to Giustiniani on January 21 to report this latest development and
the fears of the local bishop, presumably Cosimo dei Pazzi, the archbishop of Florence, that this council could lead to schism with the
election of a new pope if the French were not driven from Italy.[41]
Querini's interest in the proceedings at Milan did not diminish with his
return to the Eremo on January 30 and his profession as a monk on
February 22.[42] From this postscript of mid-April, it is not clear whether
Querini had learned of the council's appointment at its fifth session of
February 11 of Federigo de Sanseverino as its legate to Bologna and vicar
general for temporal and spiritual matters in the Papal States, or of its
condemnation at its sixth session on March 24 of Julius II for contumacy
and its nullification of his censures against this council and of his convocation of his own council to meet at the Lateran on April 19.[43]

Querini's response to the contest between the rival councils was to
study the theological and canonical issues involved. For arguments that
would support claims of papal superiority to all councils, Querini went
to the writings of Juan de Turrecremata (1388-1468), who authored the
then standard works of papal ecclesiology. Querini ignored those sections of his *Commentaria super Decreto* (1449-1464) and *Summa de
Ecclesia* (1449-1453) where the theologian allowed the cardinals or the
emperor and the Christian princes or even lesser prelates to convoke a
council to examine the case of a pope who endangered the welfare of
the Church.[44] Instead, Querini excerpted passages which supported his
position that the pope was superior to any council and that a council
could be called only by his authority and could judge his case only if
he so authorized it. Querini used this material for his *Tractatus super
concilium generale.*[45]

(relevant sections of election capitularies), 22-51 (convocations), 79-119 (first four sessions); and
L. Sandret, "Le Concile de Pise (1511)," *Revue des questions historiques*, 34 (1883), 425-456, here
436-438 for attendance.

   [41]*Annales Camaldulenses*, IX, cols. 530-531, 538.

   [42]On Querini's stay in Florence, see Jedin, "Contarini und Camaldoli," p. 27, n. 8.

   [43]For these measures taken by the Council of Pisa-Milan at its fifth and sixth sessions, see *Acta
primi concilii*, pp. 139-147, 152, 170-182; for the twice prorogued opening date of the Lateran
Council, see Marc Dykmans, "Le cinquième concile du Latran d'après le Diaire de Paris de Grassi,"
Annuarium Historiae Conciliorum, 14 (1982), 271-369, here 274-275, No. 840:3.

   [44]Thomas M. Izbicki, *Protector of the Faith: Cardinal Johannes de Turrecremata and the Defense
of the Institutional Church* (Washington, D.C., 1981), pp. 90-93, 167-170.

   [45]For Querini's excerpting from Turrecremata, see Jedin, "Contarini und Camaldoli," p. 35, n. 34,
and Silvio Tramontin, "Un programma di riforma della chiesa per il Concilio Lateranense V: il Libellus
ad Leonem X dei Veneziani Paolo Giustiniani e Pietro Quirini," *Venezia e i Concili*, ed. Antonio Niero
et al. (Venice, 1962), pp. 67-93, here 88, n. 77. The treatise is printed in *Annales Camaldulenses*,

Querini also worked to move others to an ardent defense of Julius II. His fellow Camaldolese hermits had already declared themselves as partisans of the pope. Their prior general, Pietro Delfino, had not participated in the proceedings of the Council of Pisa-Milan but would later be represented at the papal Lateran Council by Pietro Bembo and attend personally its eighth and ninth sessions.[46] Querini sought now to bolster his friends' support for Julius II. The new Camaldolese monk did not put credence in the accusations made against this man whom he regarded as the true pope.[47] He also declared that the Roman pontiff is the true vicar of Christ and urged his friends Contarini and Tiepolo to share his convictions. Years later Contarini would argue the same position before the Venetian Senate, and at the urgings of his friend Tiepolo he reiterated these ideas in the form of an epistolary treatise *De potestate Pontificis quod divinitus sit tradita*, first published in 1533.[48] Querini hoped that his friends might use their influence in Venice to persuade others to support the pope's cause. Although Venice was now an ally of Julius II, its leadership did not share the former Venetian-diplomat-turned-monk's papalist views, as evidenced three years earlier in its having appealed against the Julian bull *Pastoralis officii* to a council which it exhorted Tamas Bakòcz, the cardinal primate of Hungary and Latin patriarch of Constantinople, to convoke.[49] Membership in the Holy League did not seem to improve the fortunes of Venice. Brescia had recently fallen to

---

IX, cols. 599-611; for some of his strongly papalist statements, see Nos. 11, 22-25, 30-35, and 38. Querini seems to have adopted the position of Huguccio of Pisa (fl. ca. 1190) that a council cannot depose a pope but merely declare that he has automatically ceased to be pope because of his crimes.

[46]Delfino did not share Giustiniani and Querini's fear of a schism: see Jedin, "Contarini und Camaldoli," p. 35, n. 34. For Delfino's representation by his procurator Pietro Bembo at a session of the Lateran Council in December, 1512, see *Veterum scriptorum et monumentorum . . . collectio*, eds. Edmond Martène and Ursin Durand (9 vols.; Paris, 1724-1733), III, cols. 1180-1181; for his appointment to the conciliar deputation on reform and his participation at the eighth and ninth sessions of this council, see *Sacrorum conciliorum nova et amplissima collectio*, eds. Giovanni Domenico Mansi et al. (60-vol. reprint, Paris, 1899-1927), Vol. 32 (1438-1549), cols. 797B, 830E, 862C.

[47]For a satirical summary of the various accusations made against Julius II, see Erasmus' *Dialogus, Julius exclusus e coelis*, reprinted in *Erasmi opuscula: A Supplement to the Opera Omnia*, ed. Wallace K. Ferguson (The Hague, 1933), pp. 65-124.

[48]A critical edition of Contarini's treatise was published by Friedrich Hünermann in his collection Gasparo Contarini, *Gegenreformatorische Schriften (1530 c.-1542)*, Vol. 7 of *Corpus Catholicorum* (Münster, 1923), pp. xiii-xv (Introduction), 35-43 (text); on the dating on this treatise, see Franco Gaeta, *Un nuncio pontifico a Venezia nel cinquecento (Girolamo Aleandro)* ("Civiltà Veneziana," Saggi, Vol. 9 [Venice, 1960]), pp. 115-116, n. 2; for the publication date of 1533 and variants between a manuscript copy and that printed, see Franco Gaeta, "Sul 'De potestate pontificis' di Gasparo Contarini," *Rivista di Storia della Chiesa in Italia*, 13 (1959), 391-396.

[49]Federico Seneca, *Venezia e papa Giulio II* (Padua, 1962), pp. 121-122.

the French, and the pope was pressuring the Republic to make numerous concessions to the emperor. With the demoralization that would surely follow the League's defeat at Ravenna, Venetian support for the papal cause needed bolstering.[50]

Another section of Querini's postscript shows that his entrance into the Camaldolese hermitage did not mean his severing all connections with former friends. He asked Contarini and Tiepolo, his regular correspondents, to recommend him to four specified persons and to others unnamed. Marco Gradenigo, whom he describes as *mio carissimo*, was a fellow patrician, doctor of arts in 1503 from the University of Padua, candidate both for an ambassadorship and for a lectureship in philosophy, and mutual friend of Querini, Giustiniani, and Tiepolo.[51] Girolamo Savorgnan, the *generoso*, was also a patrician, listed apparently among the *medici illustres* together with the *philosophi* Querini, Tiepolo, and Zorzi who attended in 1508 a learned lecture of the Scuola di Rialto. When Giustiniani discussed with him his plan to enter the Camaldolese in 1510, Savorgnan advised against it, pointing out that one did not need to become a hermit in order to be saved but that one could serve God well while living at home, with the support of family and friends. Girolamo himself remained an active and loyal citizen of Venice. He even served with the army of Venice near Cremona in November of 1511.[52] Marcus Musurus (ca. 1470-1517), a cleric from Crete, was a prominent member of the Aldine Academy in Venice, professor of Greek in the University of Padua (1503), and since January of 1512 a public lecturer in the same language at Venice.[53] He was among those who had openly wondered if Querini would indeed embrace the solitary life, and it was he who furnished his former student Contarini with the reference to St. Basil's letter to Gregory of Nazianzus (ca. 358) wherein Basil

[50]Venice had reason to be unsure of its alliance with the papacy and in March of 1513 formed a new alliance with France: see *ibid.*, pp. 161-169.

[51]On Gradenigo's career, see Bruno Nardi, *Saggi sulla cultura veneta del Quattro e Cinquecento*, ed. Paolo Mazzantini ("Medioevo e Umanesimo," 12 [Padua, 1971]), pp. 40, n. 3, p. 73, n. 3, and p. 88, n. 1, and *I Diarii di Marino Sanuto*, ed. Federico Stefani et al. (58 vols.; Venice, 1879-1903), XIV, cols. 47, 55, and 57 (for Gradenigo's serving in March of 1512 together with Tiepolo as part of the honor guard of gentlemen who greeted and accompanied the Swiss embassy and Cardinal Schiner in Venice).

[52]Nardi, *op. cit.*, p. 172, n. 1; Sanuto, *I Diarii*, XIII, col. 232, and XIV, col. 283; *Annales Camaldulenses*, IX, col. 479.

[53]On Musurus, see Deno John Geanakoplos, *Byzantium and the Renaissance, Greek Scholars in Venice: Studies in the Dissemination of Greek Learning from Byzantium to Western Europe* (Cambridge, Massachusetts, 1962), pp. 111-166, and Thomas B. Deutscher, "Marcus Musurus of Iraklion, c. 1470-17 October 1517," in *Contemporaries of Erasmus: A Biographical Register of the Renaissance and Reformation*, ed. Peter G. Bietenholz (3 vols.; Toronto, 1985-1987), II, 472-473.

confessed that his soul's disquiet had followed even after fleeing city life for one of solitude.[54] The last of the four singled out for greeting was Andrea Navagero (1483-1527), a fellow student at Padua and pupil of Musurus, a member of the Aldine circle and noted Latinist, who had fought in the battle of Agnadello (1509) and in despair over the defeat had considered becoming a priest. When Giustiniani informed him of his own intention to become a monk, Navagero feared that he had gone mad and pointed to the many useless and evil monks of the day.[55] Their mutual friend Tiepolo warned against tempting God by embracing the austerities of the Camaldolese and suggested instead that Giustiniani consider joining the model Benedictines of Santa Giustina.[56] By asking Tiepolo and Contarini to recommend him to Savorgnan, Musurus, and Navagero, Querini here seems to be reaching out to all his old friends in an effort to maintain their bonds of friendship, even though they are now separated by distance, disparate views of the eremitical life, and differing vocational choices.

The concluding section of this postscript clearly demonstrates his concern for a friend. Marino Zorzi (ca. 1466-1532) was a distinguished patrician, public servant, and promoter of learning. He obtained his doctorate in arts from the University of Padua ca. 1490, was listed among the philosophers of the Scuola di Rialto, and eventually reformed the academic program at his *alma mater* after the end of the War of the League of Cambrai. His views were highly esteemed in the Venetian Senate, and at the time of this letter he was serving as ambassador to the Spanish Viceroy of Naples, Raimondo de Cardona. Querini's claim that on the day of the battle of Ravenna Zorzi was in Faenza is not confirmed by the ambassador's dispatches. He retreated with the Spanish troops to Forlì and eventually made his way to Ancona, where he took a ship to Pesaro, hoping to return to Venice. He was never a prisoner of the French, but his wife would still need comforting, for the Venetian government did not allow him to return home but promptly reassigned him as ambassador to the duke of Urbino, Francesco Maria della Rovere, the nephew of Julius II.[57] Querini's concern for Marino is probably also related to the fact that a fellow Venetian monk at the Eremo was Sebastiano Zorzi.

---

[54]Jedin, "Contarini und Camaldoli," pp. 32-33.

[55]Martin J. C. Lowry, "Andrea Navagero of Venice, 1483-July 1527," in *Contemporaries of Erasmus*, III, 8-9; *Annales Camaldulenses*, IX, cols. 479, 482-485.

[56]*Annales Camaldulenses*, IX, cols. 478-479.

[57]Nardi, *op. cit.*, pp. 72, n. 1, and 84, n. 1; Sanuto, *I Diarii*, XIV, cols. 11, 108, 111, 119, 193-194, 196-197. Querini may have assumed that Zorzi was among those Spanish who had fled toward Faenza: see *ibid.*, XIV, 122.

Querini was eager to see his friend Contarini. Warfare had prevented him from visiting the Eremo in the summer of 1511. In his letter of December 26, 1511, Gasparo signaled his intention to visit Querini, Giustiniani, and Zorzi at Easter. On February 26, 1512, he hoped to meet them in Ravenna at the time of their general chapter. Because of the warfare in progress, Contarini wrote on March 10, 1512, that he now hoped to spend a month that summer in the woods with Querini.[58] In his letter, the monk encouraged his lay friend to come, suggesting that for a variety of reasons, including the beauty of the place, he would be glad he came. If Querini no longer thought that he could convince Contarini to join him in the eremitical life, he probably hoped that the visit would at least repair the bonds of friendship strained by the recent epistolary exchanges with Giustiniani and would demonstrate that there need not be a tension between the monastic and civic life, but that both can be ways of serving Christ.

APPENDICES

I. LETTER OF PIETRO QUERINI TO NICCOLÒ TIEPOLO
AND GASPARO CONTARINI
EREMO DI CAMALDOLI, APRIL 12, 1512

Biblioteca Apostolica Vaticana, Chigi L. III. 60: Raccolta di Diverse Scritture Minute, Entry No. 43, fols. 79r-80r. Autograph. On fol. 80v: "Alli mei carissimi amici Theupolo et Contareno. In Venetia." In another hand: "Tre Latinae."

Iesu.

Iesu Christo sola vera et perfecta via, per la quale possamo dirizzare alla salute sia quello, che vi racconsoli, che vi guidi Theupolo et Contareno miei per questo triste, et cieco mondo: et prestavi gratia insieme con Paulo, et Pietro vostri di potere sempiternamente fruire quella immensa dolcezza, ch'egli promete a qualunque lo amera di cuore.

Non voglio, amici miei sopra gli altri tutti, che sono per habitare tra gli huomeni carissimi, che noi separiamo tanto le institutione delle vite

[58]Jedin, "Contarini und Camaldoli," p. 15, n. 25, pp. 24, 29, 35.

col lodare una, et biasimare l'altra, che quella inconsutile tunica di Iesu Christo s'habbia in alcun modo a dividere. Non siano piu tra voi, et il buon Paulo nostro differentie qual stato sia da seguire, qual da fuggire. Tutti siamo Christiani: non si vergognamo pure col nome insieme havere la lingua, il cuore, et l'opere nostre. Amiamo solo Iesu benedetto, et ameremlo, servando e sue commandamenti. A lui dirizzamo l'intelletto. la mente nostra ad haverlo per vero iddio, a cognoscere per discorso la potenza, la maesta, la bellezza sua, l'amore immenso, ch'egli semper ci ha portato, et ci porta anchora. Et andiamo drieto questo amore, cosi belando, come il pecorino suole drieto il suo pastore: infiamandoci, raccendosi il cuore d'un dolce et amoroso foco, che levi, scacci, consumi ogni affeto terreno, ogni mondano desio, che ci potesse dal nostro vero bene allontare. Cerchiamo d'immitare le dotti, ch'en lui si possono immitare, amando il proximo nostro di cuore, non seguendo i proprii voleri, cognoscendoci drento et di fuori essere in tutto niente, pieni d'errori, pieni di colpe, deboli, tristi, et sciagurati. Et da lui ricognoscamo quanto di buon ci puo essere in noi. Seguiamo l'opere sante di pieta, et caminiamo per questo mondo come peregrini. Et questo sia il sentiero, che ci conduca alla via principale, a Iesu Christo salvatore, che ci habbia poi per bonta sua infinita a racconciliar col patre eterno: il che in so-litudine, nelle citta, tra le genti, nelle publice administrationi, con mog-lie, con figliuoli si puo coll'ajuto di sopra et non altrimenti benissimo fare.

Et se io non son tale, che mi dia il cuore di seguire il mio Signore nella patria mia [79ʳ/79ᵛ] imputasi questo alla dapocagine mia, alla superba mia natura; che non puo schifarsi, anzi non sa ne vuole dagli errori altrimenti che fuggendo, et non alla vita seculare, o piu tosto civile, non mai da Iesu Christo biassimata. Et se nel mio cuore io ho gia buon tempo sentito questo stimulo, che mi sprona et caccia alla re-ligione, siane di questo lodato Iesu Christo, ch'usa in diversi modi l'opere di coloro, ch'a lui si danno.

Siano adunque tra noi poste da canto le contentioni; et quello solo si existimi essere nella vera via di salute, che si sente di cuore amare Iesu Christo, et per lui operare, secondo il voler suo. Et se voi sarete nella patria, tra vostri, et chi sa? Forse che precorrerete a molti, che nelle solitudini vengono ad habitare. Tutte le sorte di buone vite i lodo; et in ciascuna quello meglio camina, che piu ardentemente ama il suo Signore. Ne altra misura so io ritruovare della perfectione della vita, che l'amore di Iesu benedeto. Et se quello amarenno tutti intrerenno tutti per uno istesso sentiero. Et egli lodato ne sia, se di piu accendere il cuore dell'uno si vora degnare, che dell'altro il che non ponera pero tra noi una differentia tale, che separi la vera et unica via, per la quale tutti i christiani debbon caminare.

Tutto questo ch'io vi dico dicevi frate Paulo, con questo insieme; che le tante ripressioni fectevi fu per zelo dell'honore di Iesu Christo; potendosi interpretare gli animi vostri essere inclinati a piu tosto biassimare la vita de religiosi che la civile. Et se ben questo non sonavano expresse, et absolutamente le parole, ma di me solo favellavano, volsse nondimeno il buon Paulo prevenire, et a chi volesse cosi intendere e deti vostri, et a raffrennare anchora gli animi vostri, che non si lassassino, quando verra talhora il tentatore, sedure a blandirsi a loro medessimi, et credere, che quel stato in che essi voluntariamente si ritruovano sia il piu perfetto. State sani, scrivete, et amate Iesu Christo.

Die 12 aprile 1512 piu per la stretezza del tempo et la presta partita del messo non scrivo

Fr. Pietro vostro piu [illegible] et piu contento che mai

[Postscript, undated]

Se verrete a vederci n'havete qualche contento, per il loco, et per moltaltri rispeti. Se da guerre, et rumori sarete impediti, passerano, non durerano sempre. Noi di loro tanto ci 'ncresce, quanto le nuocono a proximi nostri, alla chiesa di Dio [parenthetical clause cancelled]. Questo solo rispeto talhora ci fa udire le nove del concilio, che per altro non l'udiressimo forse tanto: siamo tutti uniti a mai non abandonare il vero papa, ad esso ubedire et per lui exponere, piu tosto, che negarlo, la propria vita, sperando nell'ajuto di sopra. Cosi vi conforto tutti: un dio, Iesu benedeto; una chiesa, la Santa Sede romana; un pontifice vero vicario di Christo, Julio.ii.: a chi donni iddio tuto quello di bene, che si puo ad un pontefice donare in questa vita, et nell'altra anchora. Desidero la salute sua, ne son iudice de mancamenti, ch'en lui overo nel grege suo fusseron quantunque publici, ch'io credere non debbo. Et voi similmente feitte: et se vi conforto a simil opere, incolpatene l'amore che mi da ardire di passare talhora il segno, che mi si conviene.

Raccomandatime al mio carissimo Gradenico, al generoso Savorgnano, al Musuro, Navaiero, et gli altri. Non scrivo a molti per non haver tempo. La nota di che io vi scrissi si va tanto crescendo, ch'io mi dubito poi, che prima ritorni il giorno ch'ella sia al meggio, non ch'al fine aggiunta. Sforzeromi compirla questa estate a dio piacendo.

Doppo scritto odo rumori, rotture de campi, fughe, presure, morte de genti; cose da movere e saxi a lachrimare, non che noi, che sempre a questo tenuti siamo. Iddio ajuti la chiesa sua. Noi qui sopra siamo tutti unitamente disposti a patir ogni tormento, et la morte istessa prima che per nostra bocca altro pontifice si confessi, che Julio.ii.: siamo in questa nostra solitudine, et con questa dispositione si rimaremo fino che a Iesu Christo piacera. Il qual sempre pregamo, et pregeremo di cuore che vogli prestarci gratia, vigore, fortezza de finire e giorni nostri nella confessione del nome suo, della sua santa chiesa, et del vicario suo vero in terra. Voi tutti amici miei disponeteve allo istesso, ne dubitate, che l'ajuto di sopra non è per mancarvi giamai.

A voi Theupo[lo] raccommando la famiglia del nostro messer Marino, de chi temo assai. Un tratto so certo ch'el giorno del fatto d'arme l'era in Faenza; è sicuro di vita, non so di priggione. Consolate la moglie, et siate in scambio mio; tenuto sete et a Iesu Christo nostro farete cosa grata.

II. TRANSLATION

May Jesus Christ, who is the only true and perfect way by which we can turn toward our salvation, console you, my Tiepolo and Contarini, and may He guide you through this sad and blind world. May He grant His grace to you together with your [friends] Paolo and Pietro, so that we can forever enjoy the boundless sweetness which He promises to those who love Him from their hearts.

My friends, you who are dearer to me than all the others who live among men, I do not wish to make such a sharp distinction between modes of life by praising one and condemning the other as to tear in any way the seamless robe of Christ. Let there not be any more quarrels between you and our good Paolo about which state of life should be embraced and which avoided. We are Christians all; let us not be ashamed to add to that name also our words, our hearts, and deeds. Let us love only our blessed Jesus; we shall love Him by keeping His commandments. Let us direct our understanding and mind to Him so as to accept Him as the true God and to recognize through reason His power, majesty, beauty, and immense love which He always had for us and which He still bears us. Let us follow that love, bleating like the lamb which follows its shepherd: let us become inflamed and let our hearts be ignited with a sweet and loving fire, which takes away, banishes, and consumes every earthly affection, all terrestrial desire which could separate us from our true good. Let us seek to imitate those of His qualities which can be imitated, loving our neighbor from our heart, not following our own will, knowing that inside and out we are nothing, full of errors and of faults, weak, sad, and wretched. But from Him let us realize what good there can be in us. Let us perform holy works of piety, and walk in this world like pilgrims. This should be the path leading us to the main road, to Jesus Christ our savior, who through His infinite goodness will reconcile us with our eternal father. Only with help from above and not otherwise, this can be done equally well in solitude, in the city, among people, while engaged in public administration, or with wife and children.

If I am such that I lack the courage to follow my Lord in my fatherland, this should be attributed to my own worthlessness and to my proud nature. I am not able to feel repugnance at my errors: on the contrary, my nature does not know or want to know how to free itself from them other than by fleeing. [It should not be attributed] to secular, or rather, civic life, of which Christ never disapproved. If I in my [innermost] heart have already for a long time felt the urge which spurs me on and drives me toward life in a religious order, let Jesus be praised because of it; He uses in different ways the works of those who give themselves to Him.

Therefore, let contentions among us cease. We should consider only that man to be on the true path of salvation who feels himself loving Jesus Christ from his heart, and who acts in accordance with His will and through Him. If you remain in your fatherland, among your family, who knows? Maybe you will reach your goal before many who go to live in solitude. I praise all the different sorts of good life. In each of them he who loves his Lord most ardently proceeds best. I do not know how to find another measure of perfection in one's life than the love of our blessed Jesus. If all love Him, all will proceed along the same path. Let Him be praised for deigning to set aflame the heart of one more than that of another. This should not create such differences among us as to cut us off from the true and only way by which all Christians must walk.

All that I am telling you, Brother Paolo does as well, including this: that his many reprimands were because of his zeal for the honor of Jesus Christ, since it is possible to get the impression that your minds are inclined to censure monastic life more readily than civil life. Even though your words did not state this expressly and absolutely, but dealt only with me, our good Paolo wanted to guard against those who would understand your words in this way, and even more to curb your minds from allowing themselves to be seduced, when the tempter sometimes comes, and to flatter themselves into believing that the state which you have voluntarily embraced is the most perfect. Stay healthy, write, and love Jesus Christ.

April 12, 1512. I am not writing more because of the pressure of time and the impending departure of the courier.

Your Brother Pietro more [illegible] and more content than ever

[POSTSCRIPT]

If you come to visit us you will be pleased because of the place and for many other reasons. If wars and rumors prevent you, they will pass, and not last forever. We regret them as much as they harm our neighbors and God's church. Only because of these things do we sometimes hear news of the council, which we would otherwise maybe not hear so often. We are all of one mind that we will never abandon the true pope, that we will obey only him, risking our lives rather than denying him, and we hope in help from above. I exhort you thus: there is one God, our blessed Jesus; one church, the holy Roman See; one pope and true vicar of Christ, Julius II. May God grant him all the good which He can give a pope in this life, and also in the next! I wish for his health, and am not a judge of his failings, or rather, those of his flock however public they might be, and which I do not have to believe. Do likewise; if I encourage you to such action, attribute it to the love which is responsible for my daring to overshoot the proper mark at times.

Recommend me to my dearest Gradenigo, to the generous Savorgnan, to Musuro, Navagero, and the others. I do not write to many because I do not have the time. The note about which I wrote you is growing so long that I doubt it will reach the half-way mark, let alone its end, before daylight returns. But I shall make myself finish it this summer,[59] God willing.

After I wrote this, I am hearing reports about military defeats, flight, capture, people's deaths: these are things to make the stones weep, and much more us, who are always inclined to it. May God help His church!

[59] It is unclear what topic was to be treated in this *nota* and when Querini had earlier written to his friends about it. Few of his letters seem to have survived. Perhaps Querini is here referring to his treatise defending papal authority over councils written about this time. A letter from Giustiniani dated April 1512 provided Querini with his views on two questions regarding the Lateran Council, perhaps to help him compose this *nota* - see Leclercq, *Un humanist ermite*, 151.

We up here [in the hermitage of Camaldoli atop a mountain] are unanimous in our resolution to suffer every torment and death itself rather than to declare that there is any other pope than Julius II. We are here in our solitude and will remain firm in our resolution as long as it pleases Jesus Christ. We beseech Him, and we shall continue to pray to Him from our hearts to grant us grace, power, and strength to live out our days confessing His name, His holy church, and His true vicar on earth. And you, all my friends, resolve to do likewise, and do not fear that help from above will ever fail you.

To you, [my] Tiepolo, I commend the family of our Messer Marino, about whom I am quite worried. Of one thing I am certain: that on the day of the battle he was in Faenza. He certainly is alive, but he may be in prison. Comfort his wife, and be in my place. Fulfill your obligation and you will please our Lord Jesus Christ.

ON THE ORIGINS OF ECK'S „ENCHIRIDION"

Few works of sixteenth-century Catholic controversalist theologians were as popular and influential as the *Enchiridion locorum communium adversus Lutherum et alios hostes ecclesiae* of Johann Maier von Egg (Eck), first published in 1525, revised nine times before its author's death in 1543, translated into German, Flemish, and French, and reprinted about ninety times before the close of that century.[1] Thanks especially to the Herculean labors of Pierre Fraenkel, much is now known about the sources Eck drew upon and the various printings of his manual. But despite the assertions and conjectures of scholars, the origins of this book have remained obscure.

[*] Dr. Minnich is associate professor of church history and history at The Catholic University of America. This year of 1986 marks not only the 500th anniversary of the birth of Johann Eck, but also the academic year in which Professor Samuel J. Miller has retired from teaching at Boston College. Almost a quartercentury ago Professor Miller introduced an undergraduate from his native state of Ohio to the fascinating study of the Renaissance and Reformation. This article is dedicated to him as a token of lasting appreciation and esteem. The author would also like to thank Profs. W. Jared Wicks, S. J. and Walter L. Moore for their helpful suggestions on how to improve this paper.

[1] On the publication history of the *Enchiridion,* see Theodor WIEDEMANN, *Dr. Johann Eck, Professor der Theologie an der Universität Ingolstadt: Eine Monographie* (Regensburg, 1865), 528–553; Johannes METZLER, S. J., ed., *Tres orationes funebres in exequiis Ioannis Eckii habitae. Acceserunt aliquot epitaphia in Eckii obitum scripta et catalogus lucubrationum eiusdem (1543); nach den Originaldrucken mit bio-bibliographischer Einleitung, einer Untersuchung der Berichte über Ecks Tod und einem Verzeichnis seiner Schriften,* Band 16 of *Corpus Catholicorum: Werke katholischer Schriftsteller im Zeitalter der Glaubensspaltung* (Münster in Westfalen, 1930), XCI–CII; Pierre FRAENKEL, „Erste Studien zur Druckgeschichte von Johannes Ecks Enchiridion locorum communium", *Bibliotheque d'humanisme et Renaissance: travaux et documents* 29 (1967), 649–678, his „John Eck's *Enchiridion* of 1525 and Luther's Earliest Arguments against Papal Primacy", *Studia Theologica: Scandinavian Journal of Theology* 21 (1967), 110–163, „Neue Studien zur Druck- und Textgeschichte von Johannes Ecks Enchiridion locorum communium", *Bibliotheque d'humanisme et Renaissance* 30 (1968), 583–600, his „Johann Eck und Sir Thomas More 1525–1526: Zugleich ein Beitrag zur Geschichte des ‚Enchiridion locorum communium' und der vortridentinischen Kontroverstheologie", in *Von Konstanz nach Trient: Beiträge zur Kirchengeschichte von den Reformkonzilien bis zum Tridentinum, Festgabe für August Franzen,* ed. Remigius BÄUMER (Paderborn, 1972), 481–495, and his edited volume Johannes Eck, *Enchiridion locorum communium adversus Lutherum et alios hostes ecclesiae (1525–1543),* Band 34 of *Corpus Catholicorum* (Münster, 1979), 27*–101* – hereafter references to the text of Fraenkel's edition of the *Enchiridion* are cited as E–F, references to his introductory material as Fraenkel, ed., *Enchiridion;* and John Eck, *Enchiridion of Commonplaces Against Luther and Other Enemies of the Church,* trans. Ford Lewis Battles (Grand Rapids, Michigan, 1979), 4*–7*.

The Standard Explanation

The standard explanation of the origins of Eck's famous manual, based on Ulrich Zwingli's 1526 opinion that Eck had imitated Philip Melanchthon, asserts that his *Enchiridion* was the Catholic equivalent and a direct response to the 1521 *Loci Communes* of Luther's younger colleague.[2] Not content with this explanation, Fraenkel has reviewed the evidence in great detail and proposed a number of hypotheses. During his 1523 stay in Rome Eck had repeatedly urged the pope and Curia to issue a new bull condemning Luther, to list his old errors and new ones, and to provide each condemnation with a commentary consisting of arguments drawn from the Bible, especially the Gospels and Pauline epistles, and from the church fathers and councils. Eck hoped that such a bull could play a significant role at the upcoming Third Nürnberg Reichstag.[3] Eck's ideas may have been incorporated into the memorial prepared by Girolamo Aleandro for the papal legate to that German assembly. According to this document, the legate is to try to win back Lutherans with arguments drawn from the Scriptures, Fathers, councils, and doctors, and to avoid the sophistry of the scholastics. He should excerpt from the works written against Luther those commonplaces which defend Catholic teachings on the Church and its authority, on the primacy of Peter, on the sacraments and church rites, and on purgatory and indulgences. He can find in the writings of the church fathers arguments on confession, monasticism, celibacy, and the cult of the saints and their images. Among other topics to be prepared were fasting, nuptial impediments, annates and tithes.[4] However, the legate

---

[2] *Huldreich Zwinglis Sämtliche Werke,* Band VIII: *Briefwechsel 2: 1523–1526,* ed. Emil EGLI, Georg FINSLER, and Walther KÖHLER (= *Corpus Reformatorum,* XCV) (Leipzig 1914, reprint Zürich 1982), 574–575, letter of Zwingli to Joachim Vadian, Zürich, 22 April 1526, Ep. 472: 28–31: „Eccius quosdam locos explicuit, communes ut arbitror, Melanchthonem imitatus, misere tamen, in quibus admonet Lutherum ac Luteranorum genus non disputatione, sed igni, ferro laqueisque superandum esse." FRAENKEL, ed., *Enchiridion,* 7* and 15* citing Wilhelm MAURER, *Der junge Melanchthon.* 2 vols. (Göttingen, 1967–69), I, 246; BATTLES, *Enchiridion,* 4*; and Erwin ISERLOH, *Johannes Eck (1486–1543): Scholastiker, Humanist, Kontroverstheologe,* Heft 41 of *Katholischen Leben und Kirchenreform im Zeitalter der Glaubensspaltung* (Münster, 1981), 54.

[3] FRAENKEL, ed., *Enchiridion,* 8*–10*; Eck's thirteen memorials of 1523 are printed in „Dr. Johann Ecks Denkschriften zur deutschen Kirchenreformation, 1523", ed. Walter FRIEDENSBURG, *Beiträge zur bayerischen Kirchengeschichte* II (Erlangen, 1896), 235–243 an in *Acta Reformationis Catholicae ecclesiam Germaniae concernentia saeculi XVI: Die Reformverhandlungen des deutschen Episkopats von 1520 bis 1570,* Band I, ed. Georg PFEILSCHIFTER (Regensburg, 1959), 109–150, nrs. 28–40 – see esp. pp. 116–117, 143–144.

[4] FRAENKEL, ed. *Enchiridion,* 11*; Aleandro's memorial for the legate is printed in *Beiträge zur politischen, kirchlichen und cultur-Geschichte der sechs letzten Jahrhunderte,* ed.

sent by Clement VII, cardinal Lorenzo Campeggio, brought with him neither a new bull nor a compendium of controversalist theology. Fraenkel hypothesizes that at the time of the Nürnberger Reichstag (March and April of 1524), Campeggio may have turned to Eck to write such a manual. In a dedicatory letter of 1529, Eck states that the cardinal had urged him to publish the Enchiridion.[5] Fraenkel also finds a stimulus for writing the Enchiridion in Campeggio's admonition to Eck that he cease engaging in disputations with obstinate heretics. Campeggio could have urged him to return to his earlier ideas of listing Lutheran errors and the reasons for their rejection and to pay special attention to the themes proposed in Aleandro's memorial, or Eck could have come to these ideas on his own, or they could have been suggested to him directly by Aleandro or someone else. When Fraenkel attempts to explain how the Enchiridion was actually composed, he emphasizes the importance of Aleandro only for the first few loci of the work. Prior to the addition of the Auctarium chapters in 1526, the Enchiridion consisted of three sections. Part I (loci 1–4) dealt with church authority, and here Aleandro's ideas held sway. Part II (loci 5–11) treated the doctrine of salvation and the Church's sacraments. This section was influenced by the Köln and Louvain condemnations of Luther's teachings, by the bull Exsurge Domine, and by the writings of Schatzgeyer, Henry VIII, and Fisher. Part III (loci 12–27) defended church practices and drew on the writings of Schatzgeyer and Clichtove. On the supposition that Campeggio's admonition to stop disputing with heretics gave birth to this work, Fraenkel moves away from the Spring date and suggests that it was written between November of 1524 and January of 1525.[6]

Johann Josef Ignaz VON DÖLLINGER, III (Vienna, 1882), 243–267 – see esp. 247–248. Eck also had urged that the legate come prepared: „legatus qui pie mansuete ac cum scripturae rationibus consultet, quibus modis et ipsi iuvare et assistere possint ac condemnationem proxime factam confirment" – see PFEILSCHIFTER, Acta, I, 144.

[5] „Enchiridion and Luther", 114, his „Erste Studien", 652, and Enchiridion 7*, 13*; in the dedicatory letter to Konrad von Thüngen prefaced to the 1529 Ingolstadt sixth edition of his Enchiridion, Eck states on signature A₅ʳ⁻ᵛ: „Eminus uero editis aliquot in Germania et Italia libellis, cum haereticis manum conserui. E quorum numero Enchiridion fuit locorum communium annis ab hinc quattuor praelo commissum (r/v) quod ea quidem ratione, hortatu reuerendissimi D. Cardinalis D. Laurentii de Champegiis sedis apostolicae legati edideram, quo occupatiores, quibus non uacat grandia heroum uolumina reuoluere, in promptu et breui, ut aiunt, manu haberent, quo haereticis occurrerent. Et simpliciores, quibus cortice natare opus est, summagium [sic] haberent credendorum, ne a pseudoapostolis subuerterentur." Fraenkel does not note this Ingolstadt edition in his study – see 61*, 71*–72* – the copy I use is in the BAV, Stamp. Chig. VI. 963.

[6] FRAENKEL, „Erste Studien", 652–653, „Enchiridion and Luther", 110–114; and Enchiridion, 13*–17*; in his letter to Jacopo Sadoleto from Vienna on November 17, 1524, Campeggio wrote: „La disputa de lo Echio ho sempre improbata et scrittolo a lui

40

Fraenkel also illuminates the context in which the *Enchiridion* was published. Eck's deepening despair over conditions in a Germany infected with Lutheran heresy and plunged in the chaos of the Peasants' Revolt led him on February 1, 1525, to dedicate the work to Henry VIII, hoping that this fellow opponent of Luther might provide him with a refuge and teaching position in England. In April of 1525 the *Enchiridion* was finally published by Johann Weyssenburger in Landshut, Bavaria.[7]

New Evidence

With the help of three documents that have previously escaped the attention of scholars the origins of the *Enchiridion* become much clearer. First, Eck's letter to Gian Matteo Giberti from Ingolstadt on February 27, 1524 provides a graphic description of the immediate context in which he had begun work on the *Enchiridion*.[8] Second, a manuscript presentation copy of the *Enchiridion* with a dedicatory letter to Campeggio is full of clues as to why, when, and how Eck composed his manual.[9] And third, the fragment of another manuscript copy shows another stage of revision prior to the first printing.[10]

perche con questi obstinati non si po guadagnare alcuna cosa et, iuxta doctrina apostoli, haeretici post unam et alteram monitionem evitandi sunt, quia suo proprio iudicio iudicati sunt." See Petrus BALAN, *Monumenta Reformationis Lutheranae ex Tabulariis secretioribus S. Sedis* (Regensburg, 1884), 398. Fraenkel speculates that Campeggio probably wrote to Eck in September or October and that this letter may have functioned as the exhortation referred to in Eck's 1529 dedicatory letter – see his *Enchiridion*, 13*.

[7] FRAENKEL, „Erste Studien", 655–656 and his „Eck und More", 484–485; for Eck's despair over Germany and plans for his trip to England, see his letter to Giovanni Matteo Giberti of June 29, 1525 from Ingolstadt in „Beiträge zum Briefwechsel der katholischen Gelehrten Deutschlands im Reformationszeitalter: V. Dr. Johann Eck", *Zeitschrift für Kirchengeschichte* 19 (1899), 211–264, 473–485, here 213–215.

[8] Eck's autograph letter to Giberti, preserved in the Bibliotheca Apostolica Vaticana, under Mss. Chigiani, L. III. 59, fol. 267^{r-v}, is written on a single folio measuring 21.5 x 32.5 cm and bearing a watermark of the same design (a caster for ink-drying sand) and same dimensions (2.5 x 2.7 cm) as those described below in notes 30 and 57. This letter is transcribed in Appendix I of this article. I am grateful to Professor A. Lynn Martin of the University of Adelaide for having called my attention to this letter in 1974.

[9] For a description of this manuscript, see Henricus NARDUCCI, *Catalogus codicum manuscriptorum praeter graecos et orientales in Bibliotheca Angelica olim coenobii Sancti Augustini de Urbe: Tomus Prior* (Rome, 1983) 286, Nr. 665 – (Q 3.15). Hereafter this manuscript is cited as E–A (= *Enchiridion* – Angelica). For a fuller description of this manuscript, see below note 30.

[10] *Phareta Locorum Communium pro catholicis contra Ludderanorum haeresim, Johanne Eckio Autore*, in Bibliotheca Apostolica Vaticana, codex Vaticanus Latinus 6211, fols. 203^{r}–210^{v} – hereafter cited as E–V (= *Enchiridion* – Vatican).

Letter to Giberti

From Eck's letter to Giberti it is clear that he began work on the *Enchiridion* in early 1524, very soon after returning to Ingolstadt. Although his work in Rome as a special agent of the Bavarian dukes was coming to an end in November of 1523, Eck stayed on to preach there on December 13th and to give advice on the appointment of a legate to Germany. On January 8, 1524, cardinal Lorenzo Campeggio, with whom Eck had been on good terms for over a dozen years, was named legate with a commission expanded along the lines of Eck's recommendation. Campeggio did not leave Rome until February 1, 1524 and he stopped in Bologna for the ceremonies of installation as its bishop. Eck preceded him into Germany and collected information along the way that might be of use to the legate in his negotiations at the Third Nürnberg Reichstag where Campeggio hoped to rally support for a crusade against the Turks and for the suppression of Lutheran heresy.[11]

Eck gave what later proved an overly optimistic assessment of the political situation. His likely return route would have allowed him to gather information at the courts of the prince-bishops of Trent and Brixen, of the Austrian archduke at Innsbruck, and of the Bavarian dukes at Munich, where he probably gave a report on his mission in Rome. Eck concluded that almost all the secular princes were on the side of the papacy, the only exception being probably Friedrich III (the Wise), elector of Saxony. Lutheranism had, however, taken over the imperial free cities of Franconia. In Augsburg the inhabitants showed disrespect for church rites, no longer went to confession, and publicly sold and ate fresh meat as if the Lenten fast were not in effect but Easter had already arrived. But such manifestations of

---

[11] For Eck's third sojourn in Rome beginning in March of 1523 and the Bavarian business he negotiated with Hadrian VI and Clement VII, see WIEDEMANN, *Eck*, 185–193, 440, 660–673, 684–692 and Gerald STRAUSS, „The Religious Policies of Dukes Wilhelm and Ludwig of Bavaria in the First Decade of the Protestant Era", *Church History* 28 (1959), 350–373, here 360–361; for his advice on the legatine mission, see PFEILSCHIFTER, *Acta*, I, 147–150. Campeggio's title of legate to Germany, Denmark, Poland, Prussia, and Livonia closely parallels Eck's recommendation – *Ibid.*, 150. On the date of Campeggio's appointment, *Ibid.*, 106. For Campeggio's itinerary, see Edward V. CARDINAL, *Cardinal Lorenzo Campeggio: Legate to the Courts of Henry VIII and Charles V* (Boston, 1935), 82–85 and Ludwig PASTOR, *The History of the Popes from the Close of the Middle Ages*, X, translated Ralph Francis KERR, 3rd. ed. (St. Louis, 1923), 110–111. On the long-standing good relationship between Eck and Campeggio, see Eck's letter to Girolamo Ghinucci, 18 February 1537, from Ingolstadt: „Scribo Rmo. cardinali Campegio, a 26 annis michi familiariter noto . . ." – see FRIEDENSBURG, „Beiträge", 227. For Campeggio's mission to Nürnberg and for his need of scouting reports, such as those which Girolamo Rorario was to collect, see BALAN, *Monumenta Reformationis Lutheranae*, 312–316, 321–324.

heresy were confined to the cities, and Eck felt that there was reason for hope, provided emperor Charles V and his brother, Ferdinand of Austria, resisted the Lutherans. The proceedings at Nürnberg two months later showed that Eck's confidence was poorly founded and his fear misplaced. The emperor's representative pressed vigorously for the implementation of the Edict of Worms, but the final decision of the Reichstag was much diluted, due to Luther's numerous supporters among the secular rulers.[12]

Eck had also collected advice from Catholic leaders and laity. Some bishops recommended a number of remedies they considered useful and effective which Eck could forward to Campeggio on his arrival. In open discussions and in letters many laymen not only asked, but indeed urged him to collect all the topics contested by the heretics and to append to each topic a brief compendium of prooftexts drawn from the Bible and sayings of the church fathers to bolster the Catholic position. Where the Lutherans had twisted the texts to give them a meaning contrary to church teachings and practice, Eck should expose their errors. From this report it becomes clear that the broad outlines and method of the *Enchiridion* were formulated on Eck's return trip in response to the urgings of many unnamed Catholics. Eck adds in his letter to Giberti in late February of 1524 that although he had not yet recovered from his journey, he had already set to work on the project. When the compendium was completed, he promised to send to Giberti at his recently built palace near the Vatican gates this modest work, blushing perhaps over its humble origins in comparison to its new home.[13]

The environment at Ingolstadt in which he composed what later became the *Enchiridion* is also suggested in this letter to Giberti. During the previous year when Eck was away in Rome, his colleagues in the theology faculty had scored a propaganda victory in the

---

[12] For Eck's opinion that Friederich the Wise was the single most important obstacle to the implementation of the Edict of Worms, see his earlier letter to Girolamo Aleandro from Ingolstadt, February 1522: „Timeo autem Ducem Fridericum Saxoniae, ne ille obstrepet." – in BAV, Vat. Lat. 3918, fol. 180ʳ. Eck's misreading of the German scene whereby he limited Luther's princely support to the Saxon elector was shared by Rome, until proven erroneous by the Third Diet of Nürnberg. Philip of Hesse supported Luther since the end of 1523 – see PASTOR, *History of the Popes,* X, 115, 119. A very similar assessment of conditions in Franconia was made in the letter of Paolo Ziani on March 29, 1524 – see Beresford J. KIDD, ed., *Documents Illustrative of the Continental Reformation* (Oxford, 1911), 134–135.

[13] Giberti had his residence constructed according to a design of Giulio Romano. It was located near the gate to the Vatican palace and was connected with it. He was one of Clement VII's closest advisors – see M. A. TUCKER, „Gian Matteo Giberti: Papal Politican and Catholic Reformer", *The English Historical Review* 18 (1903), 24–51, 266–286, 439–469, here at 34, 454, 465.

struggle against Lutheranism. A young instructor at the university, Arsacius Seehofer, who had recently taken his master's degree there but had studied earlier at Wittenberg under Melanchthon, was discovered inserting Lutheran doctrines into his lectures. He was haled before the faculty of the university on charges that seventeen propositions taken from his teachings were heretical. On September 8, 1523 he formally abjured these errors. In a series of publications the faculty proudly proclaimed its victory. Upset that no prominent Lutheran had stepped forward to defend Seehofer's teachings, Argula von Grumbach, the daughter and wife of impoverished Bavarian nobility, published an open letter in which she attacked the actions of the faculty and offered to come in person to defend the disputed doctrines. As a response, Eck reportedly sent her a distaff. The other members of the faculty totally ignored her challenge, and she had to content herself with an exchance of doggerel rhymes with Johann of Landshut, a student at Ingolstadt. In his letter to Giberti, Eck reported on the victory of his colleagues and sent along what was probably one of the published accounts of Seehofer's retraction. He also mentioned how unhappy neighboring Lutherans were on learning of the abjuration and how he pushed his colleagues into provoking debates with these heretics. Two other professors joined Eck in his petition to the university's procurator that he secure the expulsion from the school and town of anyone holding Lutheran positions. In keeping with this counter-offensive, the university celebrated on April 11, 1524, a public disputation at which seventy-five propositions on faith, hope, love, and a comparison of the old Law and Gospel were debated by his colleague Nicolaus Apel, and another hundred on true Christian liberty were defended by fellow professor of theology, Leonhard Marstaller. This continued offensive turned up another student, Andreas Helmschrott, who was charged with holding heretical views on the authority of the pope, on justification by faith alone, on the celebration of saints' feast days, and on fasting. He fled but later returned on orders of the Bavarian chancellor to answer charges of heresy before the faculty of Ingolstadt. On June 8 the assembled professors demanded that he retract under oath the Lutheran articles found in his writings. Like Seehofer before him, Helmschrott also submitted. At the request of nearby church authorities, Eck and his fellow professors also travelled about the region to refute those who espoused heresy. The professors of theology from Ingolstadt were out to console Catholics and confound their adversaries. In this environment the *Enchiridion* took shape.[14]

---

[14] On Seehofer and his seventeen propositions which treat faith, justification, the uselessness of works, the preaching of God's Word, divorce, swearing, the Mosaic

Eck complained in his letter to Giberti that Rome seemed most unappreciative of his labors in defense of the Catholic faith and Apostolic See. He noted that he had not remained in the Curia looking for personal financial gain but had returned to troubled Germany where he could be of greater help to the papacy. But whether in Rome or in Ingolstadt, Eck was ignored when benefices were bestowed. Perhaps he should have spoken up when the prepositura of Spalt in his own diocese of Eichstätt fell vacant. He would have been content with its small revenues, but instead it was given to a mere boy, the son of someone known for his lack of restraint in taverns. Now that vacancies have occured in Speyer, Eck hoped Giberti would see that his needs were met, for he had incurred expenses in his defense of the faith. He put his trust in Giberti, let the Datarius not deal with him as had Hadrian VI. He too wanted to experience what Paul and Cyprian had so loudly praised, namely, that trust in Romans was well placed.[15] This effort to convince Roman officials that he was deserving of a reward for his many labors on behalf of the Catholic faith may have been one of the factors in determining to whom he would dedicate his *Enchiridion*.

Eck ends his letter to Giberti with the prayerful hope that Campeggio will be able to achieve some good for the Church of God and notes that the legate's failure to arrive on time displeases many people.

Law, and the Gospel, see Johann Heinrich ZEDLER, *Grosses vollständiges Universallexikon*, XXXVI (Leipzig and Halle, 1743), cols. 1325–1327. For listings of some of the editions of Seehofer's abjuration on September 8, 1523 and of the articles debated on April 11, 1524 by Nicolaus Apel and Leonhard Marstaller, see: *The British Museum General Catalogue of Printed Books: Photo-lithographic Edition to 1955*, Vol. 218 (London, 1964), col. 332; *Gesamtkatalog der Preussischen Bibliotheken*, Band V (Berlin, 1934), col. 737; and *Katholische Kontroverstheologen und Reformer des 16. Jahrhunderts: ein Werkverzeichnis*, ed. Wilbirgis KLAIBER, Heft 116 of *Reformationsgeschichtliche Studien und Texte* (Münster, 1978), 14 nr. 153, 119 nr. 2064. On Argula von Grumbach, see Roland BAINTON, *Women of the Reformation in Germany and Italy* (Boston, 1971), 97–109; WIEDEMANN, *Eck*, 195–196; STRAUSS, „Religious Policies", 359, and James MACKINNON, *Luther and the Reformation*, III: *Progress of the Movement (1521–29)* (New York, 1962), 148 n. 36 – Luther later wrote in defense of Seehofer. On the Ingolstadt counteroffensive, see WIEDEMANN, *Eck*, 194–198.

[15] Giberti seems to have made an honest effort to meet Eck's needs. He worked in the Roman Curia on his behalf (see Campeggio to Giberti, Vienna, September 23, 1524, in Archivio Segreto Vaticano [= ASV], Principi I, fol. 36ʳ). He tried to assist him in his efforts to be freed from the vexations caused by the vicar of Eichstätt (see Giberti to Eck, Rome, February 25, 1525, in ASV, Particolari 154, fol. 105ʳ). When Eck wrote begging help to have his *Enchiridion* and other works printed, Giberti promised to write to neighboring bishops on his behalf and to do whatever he could (see FRAENKEL, „Erste Studien", 664).
But when Eck inquired about financial assistance, Giberti responded with no particulars and only with assurances that he was mindful of his merits, that Eck

already enjoyed fame among all good men, and that God had surely a reward prepared for him in the next life (see Giberti to Eck, Rome, February 25, and December 26, 1525, in ASV, Particolari 154, fols. 104ᵛ and 124ʳ⁻ᵛ). Perhaps aware that Giberti's patronage was not to be relied upon, Eck turned to duke Wilhelm of Bavaria for assistance when he found himself locked in a Roman legal suit over his pension from the parochial church of Gunzburg. The duke wrote to Clément VII on September 24, 1525 pleading Eck's many years of devoted, even heroic service of the Catholic Faith and asking that the case be remitted to the bishop of Augsburg for a decision (see BALAN, *Monumenta Reformationis Lutheranae,* 540–541).

If Giberti was not always effective in providing material assistance to Eck, he was generous in his words of fulsome praise and in his protestations of affection: e. g., „Nunc responsionibus omnibus ad tuas literas absolutis, restaret, mi Eckio, uti meis te verbis succenderem ad pergendum in tuo proposito sancto, nisi tua pietas numquam stimulo aut hortatione quiesset. Per se enim illa tot iam annos diu militas semper ardens ac velox, cuius si multos similes haberemus, non tam sera malis remedia coemeremus. Ego vero [non]modo ut fidei et apostolicae dignitatis, sed tuaeque laudis et utilitatis avidus, pergere te cupio . . ." – see Giberti to Eck, Rome, February 25, 1525, in ASV, Particolari 154, fol. 105ᵛ; and „Quod enim te semper et bonum et doctum hominem pientissimumque iudicam quibus ex rebus amam te atque amo plurimum . . . Interim te ipsum sequere et ceptis insta, nam et Summum Dominum Nostrum tibi benevolum tuaque pietate conciliatum semper habiturus es, nec deerunt fautores apud illum, inter quos non committam ut postremus, [si] amore et benevolentia erga te iudicer." – see Giberti to Eck, Rome, December 26, 1525, *Ibid.,* 124ᵛ.

In a letter to Aleandro from Innsbruck on June 5, 1522, Eck begged that he urge Hadrian to reward him for his labors with a benefice in a southern German diocese, or with an apostolic indult, or by some other means – see BAV, Vat. Lat. 6199, fol. 59ʳ. In an almost contemporary letter written probably at the beginning of July, 1522, from Spain to his brother Giambattista, Girolamo Aleandro described Hadrian VI's habitual way of dealing with requests for favors: „A cardinali, a Principi et altri qualunque grandi che dimandono gratia responde *videbimus,* et fa poi quello li pare." – see Jules PAQUIER, *Lettres familières de Jerome Aleandre (1510–1540)* (Paris, 1909), 101. Eck's colleague, Leonhard Marstaller, also wrote to Aleandro in November of 1525 from Ingolstadt sending along two works he had written against the heretics and asking that the pope reward him with a canonry in Bavaria – BAV, Vat. Lat. 6199, fols. 6ʳ–7ʳ. It should be pointed out that while Eck was a harsh critic of benefice hunters, he himself came to hold two parishes, one in Ingolstadt and the other in Günzburg where a vicar served in his stead. Eck was notable for the conscientious way in which he fulfilled his pastoral duties. He was the only theologian among the canons of the cathedral church of Eichstett. When one considers the many poorly qualified clerics on whom Rome lavished its benefices, Eck indeed had reason to complain – see Joseph LORTZ, *The Reformation in Germany,* trans. Ronald WALLS (London, 1968), II, 100–101, 108–109, ISERLOH, *Eck,* 71–74, and Johann ECK, *De primatu Petri adversus Ludderum . . . libri tres* (Paris: P. Vidoue, 1521), Lib. 1, cap. 41, fol. LXVʳ.

It is interesting to note Eck's reference to Cyprian of Carthage in the same letter which tells of his beginning work on the *Enchiridion.* In his *Testimonia,* this third-century saint collected biblical proof texts into three books and arranged them under subject headings.

Campeggio's Legation and Eck

Campeggio had a memorable journey to the German Diet of 1524. The principal cause of his delay seems to have been the nine days he spent in his native Bologna where the city celebrated with a procession, fireworks, and banquet his installation as its new bishop. The receptions he received in Germany were markedly different. When he entered Augsburg and unwittingly attempted to give his legatine blessing to assembled crowds of Luther's sympathizers, he was greeted with jeers and vulgar insults. To avoid a similar public humiliation at the Diet, the legate discreetly set aside his ecclesiastical robes and entered Protestant-leaning Nürnberg on March 16th in lay dress escorted by prominent Catholics nobles. The displeasure of the populace at Nürnberg over the legate's arrival was not primarily due to his tardiness.[16]

Campeggio had come to seek the enforcement of the imperial edict against Luther and his followers. But so effective were Luther's supporters at the Diet that the most Campeggio and his allies could achieve was an agreement by the members of the Reichstag to enforce the Edict of Worms „as well as they were able, and as far as possible." Complaints against the Roman Church were to be aired again at the next meeting of the Diet scheduled for Speyer on November 11th. At that meeting the religious questions facing Germany were to be settled, pending a general council. This first phase of Campeggio's mission to Germany came to a troublesome end on April 19th with the legate unsuccessfully protesting these evasive and dangerous decisions of the Diet.[17]

Despite the demands of his teaching post and parish in Ingolstadt and of his offensive against local heretics, Eck managed to find time to visit the legate at Nürnberg. In addition to lobbying him on behalf

---

[16] For Campeggio's visit to Bologna, see Carlo Sigonio, *De vita Laurentii Campegii Cardinalis liber* (Bologna, 1581), 52–53; on his entrance into Augsburg, see Creighton, *History of Papacy*, VI, 282, and Kidd, *Documents*, 135: „idem facienti Augustae asinum ostendisse dicebantur"; and for his Nürnberg entrance, *Ibid.*, 134–135. On the religious situation in Nürnberg at this time, see Gerald Strauss, *Nuremberg in the Sixteenth Century: City Politics and Life Between Middle Ages and Modern Times*, rev. ed. (Bloomington, Ind., 1976) 154–186, esp. 174.

[17] On the third Nürnberger Reichstag, see Odorico Rainaldo, *Annales ecclesiastici ab anno MCXCVIII. ubi desinit cardinalis Baronius*, rev. G. D. Mansi, XII (Lucca, 1755), 457–462, ad annum 1524, nrs. 1–14; and Pastor, *History of Popes*, X, 111–114, Creighton. *History of Papacy*, VI, 282–284 and Cardinal, *Campeggio*, 85–89. For Campeggio's instructions from Rome, see Pietro Balan, *Monumenta saeculi XVI. historiam illustrantia*, I (Innsbruck, 1885), 14–17, and Enrico Carusi, „Una lettera al Card. Lorenzo Campeggio legato pontificio nella dieta di Norimberga (An. 1524)", in *Scritti storici in memoria di Giovanni Monticolo*, ed. C. Cipolla *et al.* (Venice, 1914), 141–145.

of the South German bishops for a revocation of the one-third crusade tax, Eck probably used the opportunity to report on his own activities in opposing the Lutherans, perhaps even informing the cardinal of his work on what became the *Enchiridion*. In the dedicatory letter to Campeggio which eventually prefaced it, Eck claims to have been ordered to instruct the legate on how to answer the Protestants – perhaps Nürnberg was the occasion of that command. As a strong and outspoken advocate for a reform of the German clergy, Eck may also have helped the legate formulate the plans for such a Catholic reformation. From Rome Campeggio received authorization to call a conference of loyal Catholic princes and bishops to enact this reform.[18]

The Regensburg Conference lasted about nine days. On June 28, 1524, Campeggio opened the meeting and set as its agenda a resolution of the complaints of the clergy and laity against each other and of the controversy over the one-third crusade tax. Once work began, he was almost overwhelmed by the quantity and diversity of the issues which were brought to him as legate to decide. Eck, together with Johann Dobeneck (Cochlaeus), Johann Heigerlin (Faber) and Friedrich Nausea, was on hand to advise him and the other participants. On the final day of the Conference, Eck preached the sermon and Campeggio issued thirty-eight decrees which mandated a reform of the lower clergy in such areas as preaching, dress, entertainment, fees, celibacy, qualifications for ordination, blasphemy, simony, and superstitious practices, and regulated the bishops' relations with their clergy. The legate also promulgated a resolution to the crusade tax controversy. The eleven South German prince-bishops together with the poorer clergy were declared exempt from the tax. The other clerics were to pay it in two installments and Archduke Ferdinand promised that the revenues would be used solely for the crusade against the Turks.[19]

---

[18] On Eck's presence at the Nürnberg Diet, see Pfeilschifter, *Acta,* I, 262, Joseph Hergenroether, *Histoire des conciles,* trans. Henri Leclercq, VIII–II (Paris, 1921), 907–908, and Iserloh, *Eck,* 53; on Rome's permission to call the Regensberg Conference, see Balan, *Monumenta saeculi XVI,* 14–17; on the command to offer instruction, see E–A, fol. 1ᵛ, transcribed here in Appendix II.

[19] For Campeggio's inaugural speech and the final reform measures, see Pfeilschifter, *Acta,* I, 323–324, 334–344, and the summaries in Rainaldo, *Annales,* 1524, nrs. 25–38, and in Hefele-Leclercq, VIII–II, 909–913; it could be noted that at about the same time that Campeggio was enforcing church law against concubinage, he himself was siring an illegitimate daughter, Ludovica – see Cardinal, *Campeggio,* 17 n. 19; on the numerous issues to be treated, see Campeggio's letter to Nicolaus Schönberg, Vienna, August 12, 1524, in Balan, *Monumenta Reformationis Lutheranae,* 361–362; on Eck's sermon, see Wiedemann, *Eck,* 440. On the crusade tax compromise, see Pfeilschifter, *Acta,* I, 345–346.

For the history of the *Enchiridion*, this Regensburg Conference was important in three respects. Once again Eck was called upon to advise Campeggio. Among the issues treated were some which later appeared in the *Enchiridion:* clerical celibacy and immunity, feast days and fasts, and the Turkish crusade. Also advising the legate were two of the four contemporary Catholic writers whom Eck later named as sources in his first version of the *Enchiridion,* Cochlaeus and Faber.[20] From the latter, the vicar general of Konstanz who in January of the previous year had debated Zwingli in Zurich, Eck probably learned first-hand of the growing threat of heresy in the Swiss cantons.

Following the Regensburg Conference, Eck turned his attention to the reformation in Zurich. On August 13th he addressed an open letter to the leaders of the oldest cantons of the Swiss Confederation which were Catholic. He claimed to have found many doctrinal errors in Zwingli's writings and proclaimed his own willingness to debate him at a time and place of the Catholic leaders' choosing. He wanted the preacher from Zurich to be bound by the decisions of those appointed to judge the disputation.[21] The writings of Zwingli which Eck had examined and found heretical apparently included the same sixty-seven articles used at the First Zurich Disputation.[22] That Eck's

---

[20] For issues which reappeared later in the *Enchiridion,* see PFEILSCHIFTER, *Acta,* I, 337–344, nrs. 16, 21, 23–24, 26. On Campeggio's theological advisers: Cochlaeus, Eck, Faber, and Nausea, see PASTOR, *History of the Popes,* X, 114. On Faber's debate with Zwingli, see Keith LEWIS, *Johann Faber and the First Zurich Disputation: 1523. A Pre-Tridentine Catholic Response to Ulrich Zwingli and His Sixty-Seven Articles* – Ph. D. dissertation, C.U.A. (Ann Arbor, 1985). The Catholic controversalists Eck cited were Cochlaeus – E–A, fol. 12ʳ, Faber – E–A, fols. 23ᵛ, 30ʳ, 108ʳ, Henry VIII – E–A, fol. 99ᵛ, and Schatzgeyer, E–A, fol. 105ʳ. While Kaspar Schatzgeyer, O.F.M., was apparently not at the Regensburg Conference, Eck and he were personal friends for many years now and soon after the Regensburg Conference they were both appointed as members of the Bavarian ducal commission for the Faith where they functioned as inquisitors – see Kaspar SCHATZGEYER, O.F.M., *Schriften zur Verteidigung der Messe,* ed. Erwin ISERLOH and Peter FABISCH (*Corpus Catholicorum,* 37) (Münster, 1984), 1–2, 121–122 n. 36.

[21] For a summary of this letter citing August 17, 1524 as its date, see WIEDEMANN, *Eck,* 207–208; for the full text of Eck's letter from Ingolstadt dated August 13, 1524, see *Johannis Ecken Missiue und embieten, Den Frommen, Vesten, Ersamen, Wysen, etc. gmeyne Eydgnossen botten, zu Baden imm Ougsten versamlet überschickt. Über solchs embieten Huldrichen Zwinglis, so vyl er darinn angerürt, Christenlich unnd zimlich verantwurt* (Zurich, 1524), fols. 1ᵛ–2ʳ.

[22] On the 67 Articles as the material Eck had read, see George R. POTTER, *Zwingli* (Cambridge, 1976), 154. For the standard modern editions of these Articles, see *Huldreich Zwinglis Sämtliche Werke,* Band I, ed. Emil EGLI and Georg FINSLER (*Corpus Reformatorum,* LXXXVIII) (Berlin, 1905; reprint Zurich 1982), 451–465, and Carl S. MEYER, ed., *Luther's and Zwingli's Propositions for Debate: The Ninety-Five Theses of 31 October 1517 and the Sixty-Seven Articles of 19 January 1523* (*Textus Minores,* XXX) (Leiden, 1963), 35–57.

preparations for such a debate are reflected in the *Enchiridion* is suggested both by a similarity of topics treated and by explicit references to Zurich reformers. Of the twenty-seven *loci* in the copy of the *Enchiridion* presented to Campeggio, eighteen treated themes similar to those in Zwingli's articles. And of the nine remaining chapters, two (on the veneration of saints and images) made explicit reference to the heretical views of the Zurich reformers Zwingli, Leo Jud, and Balthasar Hübmaier. Due to an inability to agree on the location and judges for such a disputation, Eck did not debate the Swiss reformers until the Spring of 1526. Because the disputation was held at Baden, instead of Zurich, Zwingli refused to attend. Campeggio seems to have been initially uncomfortable with Eck's offer to debate Zwingli and advised against this disputation.[23]

---

[23] For the similarity of themes between the *Enchiridion* and Zwingli's Articles, compare the following chapters and article numbers: 1 (Church) – 7, 8; 3 (Primacy) – 17 (implicit?); 4 (Scripture) – 1, 13–14; 5 (Faith and Works) – 22; 6 (Confirmation) – 67; 7 (Holy Orders) – 20, 61–62; 8 (Confession) – 50–55; 10 (Matrimony) – 28 (implicit?); 12 (Human Ordinances) – 10–11, 16, 25; 13 (Feasts, Fasts, Abstinence, Consanguinity) – 24–25; 16 (Mass) – 18; 17 (Vows) – 26–27; 18 (Celibacy) – 29, 49; 20 (Excommunication) – 31–32; 22 (Clerical Immunity and Church Wealth) – 11, 23, 33–34, 36–38; 23 (Indulgences) – 66 (implicit?); 24 (Purgatory) – 57–60; 27 (Disputing) – 67. In chapter 14 (Veneration of Saints), Eck cites Zwingli twice – see E–A, 89^r and 90^r; in chapter 15 (Images) Eck cites Balthasar Hübmaier of Freiburg and Leo Jud – see E–A, 92^v and 93^r.
For the negotiations and actual debate, see WIEDEMANN, *Eck*, 208–248, 440–441 and POTTER, *Zwingli*, 155, 209, 228–238. In his letter to Sadoleto from Buda of December 29, 1524, Campeggio reported the alarming news from Konstanz that the Swiss nation was completely infected with heresy – see ASV, Secretariato di Stato (= SS.), Germania 53, fol. 50^v (the relevant passage is missing from BALAN, *Monumenta Reformationis Lutheranae*, 405–406). Writing to Eck in the name of Clement VII, Giberti on February 25, 1525 promised to contact the papal nuncio in Germany, Girolamo Rorario, urging him to consult with Eck and devote much effort to combatting heresy among the Swiss. Giberti also reported the pope's praise for Eck's efforts to debate the heretics first at Nürnberg and then at Zurich and the pope's assertion that God's honor has been advanced by the usefulness of Eck's services and his piety – see ASV, Particolari 154, fols. 104^r–105^r. On Campeggio's stance, see his statement above in Note 6. Given the context, the legate's admonition seems aimed at the proposed Swiss disputation and is not a prohibition against all debates. Campeggio was apparently fearful that the negative outcome of a debate might provide the occasion or pretext for an assembly of laymen and clerics to make laws altering the faith and religious ceremonies. To prevent this he wanted to ban all public debates about the faith. He also thought it advisable to have present at the meetings of the Diet some learned men who appeared to come on their own out of concern for the „common cause" and not as persons sent by the pope. When the need arose, they were to defend the truth and refute heresies. Given the Germans' hostility to a papal legate, he did not think it „fitting, honorable or necessary" that a legate be also present. (See Campeggio to Sadoleto, Buda, February 8, 1525, in BALAN, *Monumenta Reformationis Lutheranae*, 426–427. Campeggio thus came to esteem in some respects what Eck was already doing. Eck had a more optimistic view of the

50

Following the Regensburg Conference, the paths of Eck and the cardinal legate no longer crossed. Campeggio was in Vienna by mid-August of 1524. But they remained in correspondence. At the end of August, the legate conferred on the Ingolstadt professor full apostolic power to hear and decide the case of Wolfgang Wurfinger, a choir-priest of the church of St. Andreas in Freising, who was charged with neglect of his duties and heresy. After some complicated legal manoeuvring by Wurfinger, Eck finally on December 19th formally excommunicated him for heresy, deposed him from his benefice, and conferred it on his own nephew, Michael Knab. Eck was, however, much less successful in his effort to secure for himself and his colleague at Ingolstadt, Leonhard Marstaller, any benefices from Campeggio. Probably just before the legate left for the Hungarian capital of Buda toward the end of December, Eck sent him a manuscript copy of his *Enchiridion* on which he had been working ever since his return from Rome. Eck prefaced the text with a frontispiece depicting Campeggio's coat of arms and with a dedicatory letter addressed to the cardinal. The legate's response was not to reward Eck's efforts with a benefice, but to encourage him to publish it.[24]

utility of a legate being present at a Diet and recommended to Rome that Campeggio attend the meeting at Augsburg – see Giberti to Campeggio, Rome, October 10, 1525, in ASV, Particolari 154, fol. 119[r].

[24] On the Wurfinger case, see WIEDEMANN, *Eck,* 198–200, and Eck's letter to Giberti, Ingolstadt, June 29, 1525, ed. FRIEDENSBURG, „Beiträge", 213–214; to Clement VII on July 25, 1525 and to Giberti on September 30, 1525 in BALAN, *Monumenta Reformationis Lutheranae,* 497, 544. On Eck's nephew, see WIEDEMANN, *Eck,* 429, where Michael Knab is described as his cousin, the son of his mother's sister. On Eck's efforts on behalf of his colleague, see Leonhard Marstaller to Girolamo Aleandro, Ingolstadt, November, 1525, BAV, Vat. Lat. 6199, fol. 6[r-v]: „Solicitavit superiori anno (ut rem teneas) pro me collega meus Dominus Eckius Apostolicum Legatum ut susceptos meos ob fidei causam adversus Lutheranam perfidiam labores atque perpessas inde calumnias illatumque mihi damnum sacerdocio aliquo rependeret atque relevaret. Et obtinuissem procul dubio nisi inopinatus in Italiam reditus gratificandi occasionem illi abstulisset." Regarding Campeggio's itinerary: on December 7th he was still in Vienna, but by December 29th he was in Buda reporting „l'altro giorno mentre eramo in Vienna" – see BALAN, *Monumenta Reformationis Lutheranae,* 403, 405–406.

The frontispiece is on E–A, 1[r]. Four colors are used in the design. The outline of the shield and the T-shaped cross atop it are in brown. The background of the shield is a yellowish brown. The cardinal's hat, its cords and tassels are in red. And black is used as a shading device and to depict the full figure of a rampant hound in the right half of this divided shield and the left half of a two-headed imperial eagle in the other half of the shield.

For the dedicatory letter, see E–A, 1[v] and Appendix II below. Campeggio's exhortation, reported above in note 5, would seem to point to publishing *(praelo commissum . . . edideram),* rather than to composing the work.

The Dedicatory Letter of the Manuscript Copy

The dedicatory letter reveals some shifts in Eck's thinking from that time in February when he first reported on the project to Giberti. While pastoral concerns remain paramount, Eck is no longer responding to the behests of the Catholic laity for a refutation of Lutheran heresies, but has written out of obedience. The most likely superior to have commanded this work is the man to whom it is dedicated, Lorenzo Campeggio. Giberti, who closely followed Eck's work and encouraged him, was not as Datarius in a position to put the Ingolstadt professor under such an obligation. Also, instead of writing a work that would be of immediate use to the German faithful, Eck has written in Latin a book which the cardinal can use to defend these simple Catholics. Echoing the words Leo X had used when conferring on Campeggio the cardinal's hat, Eck exhorted him to defend even to death the faith preserved by the Holy See.[25]

Eck reluctantly assumed the role of the cardinal's teacher. Campeggio was very learned in canon and civil laws, but lacked a specifically theological education. In his own memorial on the legation, Eck had urged that the papal emissary be accompanied by secretaries skilled in Sacred Scripture. In the instructions drawn up for the legate by Aleandro, the papal representative himself is to be able to defend Catholic positions with arguments drawn from Scripture and the church fathers. While still at the Nürnberg Diet, the legate received a letter from his fellow cardinals in Rome urging him to be the agent of the Holy Spirit through whom the heretics would be freed from their blindness. Eck had been on hand in Nürnberg and Regensburg to advise him when he seemed almost overwhelmed by the topics discussed. But now the legate was about to leave the Empire for Hungary and the professor from Ingolstadt would not follow. By a tactful use of classical proverbs to imply that the cardinal did not need his assistance, Eck excused himself on the grounds of obedience and pastoral concern for presuming to instruct Campeggio in controversialist theology. Perhaps in response to the legate's admonition not to debate Zwingli, Eck claimed that his book was not written to help himself debate heretics, but to aid Campeggio in the defense of Catholic teachings. Eck described the work as the sketch of a collection of commonplaces for quick reference in formulating answers to heretics. As a cardinal Campeggio was called upon to defend not the Roman See, but the faith it espoused. The twenty-seven *loci* which followed this letter would have provided Campeggio with numerous arguments on a wide range of controverted teachings. Eck

---

[25] E–A, 1ᵛ; Prosperi, *Tra Evangelismo*, 126.

52

ended his letter by wishing the legate success and divine assistance: „Vale, prosperare, et vince."[26]

The First Printed Edition of the Enchiridion

Campeggio was probably surprised when he eventually saw a printed copy of the *Enchiridion*. In response to the legate's exhortation that he publish the work, Eck looked about for a printer, even writing to Rome for assistance. In the name of pope Clement VII, Giberti responded on February 25, 1525. He promised to write to the papal nuncio in Germany, Girolamo Rorario, to have him approach neighboring bishops and urge them to assist Eck in the publication of his recent work against the heretics. Eck eventually found a printer in Landshut, some forty miles southwest from Ingolstadt. By the time the work came off the press of Johan Weyssenburger in April of 1525, Eck had revised the text and appended a new dedicatory letter. Campeggio would have found it difficult to complain about the altered dedication. Eck's years of devoted service in the cause of orthodoxy and repeated pleas for assistance, some directed to the legate, had produced only rhetorical words of appreciation but no new benefices. Even the two modest ones he had were now threatened by the outbreak of the Peasants' Revolt and the advances of Lutheranism. Eck looked for a new patron and refuge in England.[27]

---

[26] On Campeggio's educational background, see CARDINAL, *Campeggio,* 15–16; for Eck's memorial, see PFEILSCHIFTER, *Acta,* I, 150; for Aleandro's instructions, see above note 4; the cardinals urged: „istique heresiarche aut Sancti Spiritus illustratione a tanto luto tantaque autore te, cecitate liberabuntur aut tuae potentie dextra conterentur." – see CARUSI, „Una lettera", 145; for the text of the dedicatory letter, see E–A, 1ᵛ and Appendix II.

[27] For Eck's inquiries about a possible Roman printer, see FRAENKEL, „Erste Studien", 663–665 and the draft of the letter which Fraenkel cites – ASV, Particolari 154, fols. 104ʳ–105ᵛ. From the context of this letter and from others (esp. Giberti to Eck, December 26, 1525, *Ibid.,* 124ᵛ), it becomes clearer that Eck's request was for financial assistance to have this book printed in Germany. On his general difficulties in finding a publisher, see FRIEDENSBURG, „Beiträge zum Briefwechsel: Eck", 214, letter to Giberti, Ingolstadt, June 29, 1525: „Aliqua chartacea opuscula nondum impressa mecum fero si forte contingat me Christianum praelum invenire, ut illic excudantur." On the Landshut edition, see FRAENKEL, ed., *Enchiridion* 27*–28*, 63*. In the above cited letter to Giberti, *Ibid.,* 214, Eck complained: „nec Reverendissimus dominus legatus nec sedes apostolica est memor pauperis Eckii; non scio profecto quomodo tranquillitati studiorum meorum consulam . . ."
Eck's complaints were justified. Campeggio did not provide him with significant support. Except for a promise to tell Eck about the efforts of Giberti on his behalf in the Roman Curia (Campeggio to Giberti, Vienna, September 9, 1524, in ASV,

Eck made a shrewd decision to dedicate the *Enchiridion* to king Henry VIII of England. The king shared a similar concern to defend the Catholic faith and had distinguished himself by composing the *Assertion of the Seven Sacraments*. On Leo X's orders, Eck had been given a copy of it while in Rome in 1521. In May of 1523 Eck published there a defense of Henry's book against the attacks of Luther. During his time in Rome he had also made the friendship of the English ambassadors to the papal court, Richard Pace and John Clerk, the bishop of Bath and Wells. Eck hoped, too, to count on the support of

Principi I, fol. 36^r), Campeggio's reports to Rome are remarkably either silent about or critical of Eck (see above, note 6), yet full of praise for Cochlaeus and others. Campeggio had funds at his disposal with which he could have helped to underwrite the costs of publishing the *Enchiridion*, initially dedicated to himself. For the 200 florins Campeggio had for such purposes, see his letter to Sadoleto from Buda, January 5, 1525, in ASV, SS. Germania 53, fol. 56^v (the relevant passage is missing from BALAN, *Monumenta Reformationis Lutheranae*, 409). Instead of assisting Eck, the legate wanted to help Cochlaeus with this money and have two canonries and prebends already conferred on Johann Bruen assigned to Cochlaeus, once the pope has pressured Bruen into resigning them in Cochlaeus' favor – all this in response to Cochlaeus' explicit request. *(Ibid.)*. Ever since the Regensburg Conference where Cochlaeus had been one of the legate's principal advisers, Campeggio was impressed by his abilities. He asked him afterwards to send him reports on ecclesiastical affairs in Franconia which Cochlaeus faithfully did. The „goodness and honesty of his life" also commended him to the legate, and to help him publish his works against the heretics, Campeggio had already given him an initial grant of 250 florins. He prized his writings over those of Emser and Dietenberger and repeatedly praised him to Roman officials. Given this aggressive furthering of Cochlaeus' career, Campeggio's neglect of Eck's needs is noteworthy. See: BALAN, *Monumenta Reformationis Lutheranae*, 476, and Campeggio to Giberti, Vienna, October 9, 1524, in ASV, Principi I, fol. 40^r (the relevant passage is missing from BALAN, *Ibid.*, 380); Giberti to Campeggio, Rome, October ?, 1524, in ASV, Particolari 154, fol. 32^v; Campeggio to Sadoleto, from Buda, January 5, May 26, and June 5, and from Bologna, August 29, 1525, in ASV, SS. Germania 53, fols. 56^v (the relevant passage is missing from BALAN, *Ibid.*, 409), 95^v (the relevant passage is missing from BALAN, *Ibid.*, 466–467), 124^r. For an overview of the Campeggio – Cochlaeus relationship at this time, see Martin SPAHN, *Johannes Cochläus: ein Lebensbild aus der Zeit der Kirchenspaltung* (Berlin, 1898), 115–119.
In Campeggio's defense, it should be noted that the legate had great difficulty conferring even a few benefices in Germany due to the rights and privileges of patrons and princes and to the interference of heretics. Even when he did make a provision, it often had little effect. (See his letter to Sadoleto, Buda, January 22, 1525, in ASV, SS. Germania 53, fol. 64^v – the relevant passage is missing from BALAN, *Ibid.*, 410–417). He also proposed that Rome establish a fund to pay each of from six to eight very learned persons in different parts of Germany (among whom would probably have been Eck) an annual fee of two hundred ducats for their labors and expenses in writing and publishing prompt responses to the books of the heretics – see Campeggio to Sadoleto, Buda, February 8, 1525, in BALAN, Ibid., 426–427.
On the background of Eck's decision to seek English support, see FRAENKEL, „Erste Studien", 654–656.

John Fisher, bishop of Rochester and noted Catholic controversalist whose writings he had read and praised. The dedicatory letter dated February 1, 1525, extolled the king's literary defense of the Church and called upon Clerk and Pace to testify to Eck's own book defending Henry's. Elsewhere in the *Enchiridion* he cited the king's and Fisher's writings against Luther. With such a book as a gift to Henry VIII, Eck expected and eventually received in August of 1525 a warm reception in England – but not the hoped-for rewards of a benefice or teaching position. As the recent nominee of Henry VIII to the lucrative posts of cardinal protector of England and bishop of Salisbury, Campeggio could hardly complain of Eck's dedication of the printed edition of the *Enchiridion* to the English king.[28]

By recourse to an epistolary epilogue, Eck paid his dues to Giberti. The Datarius could have expected a dedication since Eck had promised to send him a copy of the *Enchiridion* when it was completed. This papal adviser had encouraged Eck in his work and had offered him his protection in the Curia, but Giberti like Campeggio had failed to provide him with a benefice. The Datarius was also in no position to complain, especially of a dedication to Henry VIII, with whom he was on good terms ever since his visit to the English court in 1522. He was probably content that what may have been intended as the original dedication letter now became a mere epilogue.[29]

---

[28] On the nearly thirty printed copies of the *Assertion* sent by Henry to Rome which arrived there in September of 1521, on its reception there, and Leo's order that Eck receive a copy, see J. J. SCARISBRICK, *Henry VIII* (Berkeley, 1968), 111, 116; Erwin DOERNBERG, *Henry VIII and Luther: An Account of Their Personal Relations* (Stanford, 1961), 16–20; E–F, 3, and FRAENKEL, „Erste Studien", 653 n. 5. For Eck's 48-page defense of Henry's book, *Asseritur hic invictissimi Angliae regis liber de sacramentis a calumniis et impietatibus Ludderi,* see METZLER, ed., *Tres orationes,* p. LXXXVIII, nr. 44; on Pace and Clerk in Rome, see Jervis WEGG, *Richard Pace: A Tudor Diplomatist* (New York, 1932), 184–193 and William E. WILKE, *The Cardinal Protectors of England: Rome and the Tudors before the Reformation* (Cambridge, 1974), 120–129, 133–139. For the dedicatory letter and citations of Henry VIII and Fisher, see E–F, 1–4, 34, 208, 415–416. On Eck's trip to England, see Hubertus SCHULTE HERBRÜGGEN, „A Letter of Johann Eck to Thomas More", *Moreana* 8 (1965), 51–58, esp. 52–53, and FRAENKEL, „Eck und More", 485. On Campeggio's appointment as cardinal-protector and bishop while on his legation in Germany, see WILKE, *Cardinal Protectors,* 143–147. On Campeggio's close friendship with Pace who was personally opposed to Luther's teachings, see WEGG, *Pace,* 169, 188. For Eck's letters to Rome on the trip to England, see that to Giberti on June 29, 1525 in FRIEDENSBURG, „Beiträge zum Briefwechsel: Eck", 214, and that to Clement VII, Ingolstadt, September 17, 1525 in BALAN, *Monumenta Reformationis Lutheranae,* 538.

[29] For the text of this letter, see E–F, 415; on Giberti's encouragement and offer of protection, see PROSPERI, *Tra Evangelismo,* 126 n. 87; on Giberti's 1522 visit to England, see TUCKER, „Giberti", 50.

An Analysis of the Text of the Ms. Copy Dedicated to Campeggio

An examination of the manuscript copy of the *Enchiridion* dedicated to Campeggio reveals a number of pecularities. Three different scripts are evident: Eck's own hand which wrote the dedication letter, table of contents, and marginal comments; a Teutonic hand which copied *loci* 1 to 3 and returned midway through *locus* 18 to continue through *locus* 25; and a humanistic hand which penned the *loci* from 4 to the first half of 18, and the final two *loci*, 26–27. The Germanic script appears on paper with an elaborate crown watermark; the humanistic script on paper bearing the watermark of a covered, fluted caster for ink-drying sand. Blank pages appear at the beginning and end of both sections of humanistic script. And finally the numeration of the *loci* in the text is not continuous nor does it agree with the table of contents.[30] The challenge is to find a coherent theory

---

[30] The scripts are found as follows: Eck's, E–A, 1^r–2^v and marginalia *passim;* Teutonic, 3^r–42^r, 112^r–132^r; and humanistic, 48^r–110^r, 134^r–142^v; for the crown with two curved bows (a raised arch) surmounted by a star over a cross but without an accessory sign which appears in part in fols. 5, 8, 10, 12, 16, 17, 27, 28, 30, and 32, see example 18 on pages 39 and 99 in Gerhard PICCARD, *Die Kronen-Wasserzeichen. Findbuch I: der Wasserzeichenkartei Piccard im Hauptstaatsarchiv Stuttgart* (Stuttgart, 1961), Abteilung VIII – example 18 is found in numerous German cities and dates from 1513–44. The closest example of this crown in Charles Moise BRIQUET, *Les filigranes: Dictionnaire historique des marques du papier des leur apparition vers 1282 jusqu'en 1600: A Facsimile of the 1907 Edition with Supplementary Material Contributed by a Number of Scholars,* ed. Allan STEVENSON (Amsterdam, 1968) is on I, 298, III, no. 4966 (dated 1525); of the „sablier" design in the *Enchiridion* which appears fully or in part on fols. 52, 64, 72, 73, 78, 85, 88, 89, 90, 91, 92, 93, 134, 139, and 143, no example is identical in Briquet, but the closest (lid divided into two instead of seven sections, and the lines on the stand are horizontal instead of a series of curved droplets) is no. 2172 in *Ibid.,* I, p. 160 (dated 1520) and later in Munich, Augsburg, Memmingen, Nürnberg, etc.; the blank pages are in E–A, 43^r–47^v, 110^v–111^v, 132^v–133^v, 143^r–144^r. Because the codex has recently been rebound in such a way as to hide its present quire divisions and because no report was made of its original organization, the following reconstruction of its earlier quires seems best to conform to the evidence at hand in the form of visible threads and catchwords in Eck's autograph and to reasonable hypotheses based on this evidence. The quires are:

1, fols. 1–2, no thread visible, Eck's handwriting;

2, fols. 3–13, sewn at 6^v–7^r, catchword *quam* on 13^v. German script;

3, fols. 14–25, sewn at 19^v–20^r, catchwords *quod solus* on 25^v. German script;

4, fols. 26–37, sewn at 31^v–32^r, catchword *pont.* on 37^v. German script;

5, fols. 38–47, sewn at 42^v–43^r, catchwords *ex scripturis* on 47^v. German script but fols. 43–47 are blank;

6, fols. 48–55, sewn at 51^v–52^r, catchwords *locus VII* on 55^v, humanistic script;

7, fols. 56–65, sewn at 60^v–61^r, catchwords *qui trusus* on 65^v, humanistic script;

8, fols. 66–73, sewn at 69^v–70^r, catchword *laudo* on 73^v, humanistic script;

9, fols. 74–81, sewn at 77^v–78^r, catchword *gradus* on 81^v, humanistic script;

10, fols. 82–89, sewn at 85^v–86^r, catchword *unus* on 89^v, humanistic script;

which explains these anomalies and sheds light on how the *Enchiridion* was originally put together.

One might claim that most of these peculiarities are merely the result of two different scribes working simultaneously on copying different sections of a finished manuscript. But this theory has difficulty explaining the strange division of materials, namely, that *locus* 18 is in two hands and seven *loci* in Teutonic script separate almost fourteen continuous *loci* in humanistic script from the final two in the same hand.

A theory of stages of composition seems to conform to the internal evidence of this manuscript. Thus *loci* 1–3 dealing with the Church, councils, and primacy form an intelligible unit (they even end with the phrase „Laus deo") and are probably the chapters on which Eck first worked when he returned from Rome to Ingolstadt in early 1524. While he had already written on the question of papal primacy, he did not merely summarize his earlier work but cited Luther's writings. These three chapters are in Germanic script.[31]

The next section, from *locus* 4 which begins „praeter superius dicta" to the first part of *locus* 18 on clerical celibacy, and including the final two *loci,* 26 on burning heretics and 27 on not disputing with them, is written in a humanistic hand and deals with issues actually debated by the faculty at Ingolstadt or topics which Eck may have prepared in

---

11, fols. 90–97, sewn at 93ᵛ–94ʳ, catchwords *et omnibus* on 97ᵛ, humanistic script;

12, fols. 98–103, sewn at 100ᵛ–101ʳ, catchword *consilia* on 103ᵛ, humanistic script;

13, fols. 104–111, sewn at 107ᵛ–108ʳ, no catchword, humanistic script but fols. 110ᵛ–111ᵛ are blank;

14, fols. 112–123, sewn at 117ᵛ–118ʳ, no catchword, German script;

15, fols. 124–133, sewn at 128ᵛ–129ʳ, no catchword, German script but fols. 132ᵛ–133ᵛ are blank;

16, fols. 133–142, sewn at 137ᵛ–138ʳ, no catchword, humanistic script, ends with Eck's signature;

17, fols. 143–144, sewn at 143ᵛ–144ʳ, no catchword, both folios are blank.

It is unclear to which quires belong the unnumbered cut-off folios which appear between fols. 25ᵛ–26ʳ and 133ᵛ–134ʳ.

The *loci* are numerated in the table of contents from 1 to 25, but the *locus: De ordine* is added at the bottom of 2ʳ with a marginal indicator that it should be inserted between nos. 6 and 7, *locus: Non disputandum cum haereticis* is not listed in the table. In the Landshut edition, *De ordine* became *locus* 7, the subsequent *loci* were raised in numeration by one and *Non disputandum* was assigned no. 27. Within the text, Eck's hand has assigned Roman numeral XX to *De haereticis comburendis* – the other *loci* (from 19 to 25, 27) have no nunbers.

[31] On the composition of *locus* 3 on papal primacy, see FRAENKEL, „*Enchiridion* and Luther", esp. 114. For the phrase *Laus deo,* see E–A, 42ᵛ and E–F, 74, n. k7. That this section was revised to reflect later *loci* is evidenced by cross-references in *locus* 1: „Plura inferius de scriptura vide" and „Unde infra de constitutionibus humanis" – see E–A, 7ᵛ and 8ᵛ.

anticipation of a debate with Zwingli. Campeggio's admonition against this Swiss disputation may have led to the composition of chapters on shunning and executing heretics. That this material once formed a unit is suggested by the uncorrected numeration of *locus* 26 as *locus* 20 in the text.[32]

The third section, the second half of *locus* 18 to *locus* 25, written in a German hand, appears to have been inserted at the last minute. Except for its initial page, it lacks Eck's typical marginal annotations and was not carefully proofread for scribal errors. Many of the topics here treated were probably ones of special interest to the legate Campeggio.[33] Three of them (clerical celibacy, excommunication, and purgatory) were topics Zwingli was prepared to debate. The original

---

[32] For the numeral XX assigned to chapter 26, see E–A, 134ʳ.

Locus 13 on feasts, fasts, abstinence from meat, and degrees of consanguinity can be related to Zwingli's articles on feasts, fasts, and abstinence, but also to Campeggio's legation. In preparation for the Jubilee fo 1525, Clement VII published a bull ordering three days of fasting. At the end of September 1524, Campeggio received many copies of a new papal bull against those who violate the prohibited degrees of consanguinity which he distributed among the archbishops of the Empire. See BALAN, *Monumenta Reformationis Lutheranae*, 379, 415.

Locus 16 on the sacrifice of the Mass was probably composed before the German Peasants' Revolt seemed to be getting out of control. In the version dedicated to Campeggio, Eck ends this *locus* on the note of praise of Christ forever. By the time the *Enchiridion* was published in April of 1525, Eck altered the ending and spoke now of the coming of antichrist and the end of time. In the manuscript version he also made no reference to his book on the sacrifice of the Mass. In the Landshut edition he explicitly refers to it, even though it would not be printed until 1526. For the endings, compare E–A, 100ʳ and E–F, 209. On the causes and course of the Peasants' Revolt in Eck's region, see Rudolf ENDRES, „The Peasant War in Franconia", in *The German Peasant War of 1525 – New Viewpoints*, ed. Bob SCRIBNER and Gerhard BENECKE (London, 1979), 62–83, esp. 70–73. For the missing reference to his book on the Mass, see E–A, 96ᵛ; for its inclusion, see E–F, 202–203; on 202, n. 37 Fraenkel notes that the book was ready but not yet published. On Campeggio's admonition as the source of chapter 27, see FRAENKEL, „Erste Studien", 652, n. 2. The statement in E–A, 139ʳ („At latius hic agamus cum haeretico non disputandum"), which is missing from the printed editions (see E–F, 278) and here concludes *locus* 26 on burning heretics, suggests, however, that the following *locus* grew logically out of a theme treated in this previous *locus* and was not a direct response to Campeggio's admonition.

[33] *Locus* 19 on cardinals and legates of the apostolic see is unlike earlier chapters in that it does not explicitly answer the attacks of heretics but traces the history of papal legates, ending with the story of two who were sent to the council of Frankfurt in 794 to condemn the Adoptianist heresy of Felix of Urgel in Spain. In addition to this earlier German legation, other allusions to Campeggio are suggested by Eck's references to the titular churches of San Lorenzo and of S. Anastasia. See E–A, 114ʳ, 115ᵛ.

Locus 21 on the war against the Turks treated a topic that was a major concern of Campeggio's legation, especially the question of the tax to finance it. At Regensburg this issue was resolved, as was also that regarding the taxation and punishment of clerics, topics treated in *locus* 22.

58

locus 19 of the second section, which was removed when the third section was inserted, may have treated one of the topics already studied in that third section. A likely candidate would be purgatory, on which Eck had recently published a work in four books.[34] The third section was probably written prior to the second one and may have originally included the whole of *locus* 18 on clerical celibacy and *locus* 17 on vows, since there is both a thematic and literary link between these two *loci*. All of 17 and half of 18 may have been eliminated from the section copied by a German hand in order to be revised and hence had to be recopied by the humanistic hand.

The fourth and chronologically last section to be added to the *Enchiridion* contained those elements in Eck's own hand: the dedicatory letter, table of contents, marginalia, insertions, and corrections.[35]

In addition to its specific introductory material, the 1524 version dedicated to Campeggio differs in over one hunded and fifty places from the first printed edition. In some of these cases, the manuscript reading would seem to be preferred. Spontaneous prayers which reveal Eck's piety have been eliminated.[36] Had the printer copied correctly certain words, later editors would not have had to speculate on the proper reading or readjust the punctuation to make sense.[37] Arguments which Eck made that advanced his position were inexplicably eliminated.[38] Words were dropped which were never replaced

---

[34] For Eck's 1523 *De purgatorio,* see METZLER, ed., *Tres Orationes,* LXXXVIII, nr. 45.

[35] Eck's marginal notations served different purposes, e. g., highlighting sections with series of dots (30[r], 87[v], 93[v], etc.), numbering objections and their responses (31[r]–41[v], 52[v]–54[r], 75[v]–77[v], etc.), providing guides to themes treated (25[r], 33[v], 38[r], 67[r], etc.) or to authors cited (21[v], 48[v], 90[r], 99[v], etc.), inserting omissions (34[r], 48[r], 50[r], 77[v], 94[v], 141[r], etc.), canceling an incorrect word (87[r], 134[v], etc.), and correcting misreadings by the scribe (22[r], 32[r], 37[r], 75[v], etc.). Eck often supplies in the margins references to the scriptural and patristic sources he has used. The German and humanistic hands also corrected themselves and there is even an example of the humanistic hand inserting a clause into the text copied by the German hand (34[v]), but the German hand does not correct the humanistic.

[36] For examples of Eck's prayers: „Domine, prosperare et adiuua nos" (2[v]), „In nomine tuo datas (?), Iesu" (3[r]), „Christus . . . in saecula benedictus" (100[r]), „Soli deo gloria" (142[v]). This phrase, *„Soli deo gloria"* with which he concluded his manual, was also the motto Eck placed on a silver medallion bearing his portrait and dated 1529. It is reproduced as the frontispiece to Fraenkel's edition of the *Enchiridion.*

[37] E. g., „in terris" (20[r]) became „interius" in the 1525–34 editions, and „exterius" thereafter – see E–F, 48 n. e; „ita" (119[v]) became „vi" of „via" – see E–F, 243 n. k1; „Petrum fuisse Romae" (26[v]) stating Eck's counter-thesis to Urban Rieger became „Petrus numquam fuisse Romae" with a change in punctuation to make it appear as Rieger's position – see E–F, 57.

[38] E. g., that Mary's virginity is commonly accepted yet not in Scripture (E–A, 94[v], but not in E–F, 198); if one is to live by the Scriptures only, then circumcision and vows should be observed (E–A, 8[v]–9[r], but not in E–F, 30); quotations from Matt 18 on the

in subsequent editions or at times editors supplied alternatives.[39] Eck's copious marginal references to his sources were occasionally dropped or miscopied.[40] Also subtitles and coordinated numeration which helped the reader follow the arguments were ignored in places by printers. But by and large, the numerous revisions, deletions, and additions found in the printed version were improvements.

The Landshut edition corrected many of the mistakes in the manuscript version. Misspellings were rectified,[41] missing words and lines supplied,[42] scribal errors eliminated,[43] inaccurate citations and quotations emended,[44] and mistaken identifications corrected.[45]

In other ways, too, the first printed edition was an improvement over the copy dedicated to Campeggio. Eck had used the time which separated the two versions to strengthen his presentation. New

authority of the Church (E–A, 13ᵛ, but not in E–F, 37); and Eck's answer to objection 8 of the heretics: „Paulus loquitur de operibus legis" (E–A, 54ʳ) is dropped and the new text gives a different response (E–F, 100).

[39] Words never replaced: e. g., „[mysteriorum] dei" (E–A, 62ᵛ, but not in E–F, 120), „[ex S. Dionysio . . .] liquet" (E–A, 94ᵛ, but not in E–F, 199 n. e); words dropped but others substituted: e. g., „[licet] iniungat" (E–A, 35ʳ) with substitutes of „coniungere" and „coniunget", although the Dresden 1526 edition had it correctly (E–F, 67 n. h5), and „[et] nega[vi]t [episcopos]" (E–A, 39ʳ), with „nega" (E–F, 71).

[40] The citations of 1 Cor xii and Rom xii are in the text of E–A, 3ʳ, but dropped in the printed versions (E–F, 17 n. i). Eck's autograph citation of his own work on not removing images (bottom of E–A, 93ᵛ) is missing in the printed versions (E–F, 197). For examples of marginal citations later miscopied, see: Deut 17 (E–A, 49ᵛ), but later editors cited incorrectly Deut. 14 (E–F, 81, n. n1). Eck's autograph reference inserted into the text to Augustine's „xviii li. de ciui. dei" (E–A, 90ʳ) was miscopied to become in the marginalia libro 8 (E–F, 187, n. 122). Eck's effort to coordinate the heretics' objections with his own responses by using numbers was occasionally ignored by editors – e. g., E–A, 52ʳ–54ʳ where used, but E–F, 97–100 numeration dropped.

[41] E. g., „renunerunt" (E–A, 32ᵛ) corrected to „renuerunt" (E–F, 65), „temperales/ temporales" (53ʳ/98), „bresbiterum/presbyterum" (58ʳ/112), and „apperuit/apparuit" (97ʳ/203). Also corrected were numerous incidents where the scribe failed to double the appropriate consonant: e. g., „pecatum" and its variants (60ᵛ/119, 61ʳ/120), „imolatus" (64ʳ/134), „eclesia" (68ʳ/139), „imo" (79ᵛ/162).

[42] E. g., „occupavit" (9ʳ/54), „si" (37ᵛ/69), „ad" (56ᵛ/108), „sumptio" (65ᵛ/136), „ab" (66ᵛ and 67ʳ/137). Whole missing lines were supplied: e. g., „tributum . . . tribuat ei" (40ᵛ/72), „historiae volunt sub Pontiano" [dropping repetition of „aliquae sub Marcello"] (113ᵛ/232), „manifestum . . ." (130ʳ/267).

[43] E. g., „annexant/annexam" (51ᵛ/95), „in/sine" (104ᵛ/218), „promisit/promiserunt" (105ʳ/218), „ducis/dicis" (112ᵛ/229), „huic/hinc" (113ᵛ/232), „si/sub" (118ᵛ/241), „caesare/ caesares" (121ᵛ/250), „quadam/quasdam" (127ᵛ/261), „et/est" (128ᵛ/262), etc. Inappropriate words/errors were also deleted: e. g., „est" (25ʳ/55, 27ᵛ/58), „ibi" and „domian" which should have been cancelled (30ᵛ/61 and 31ʳ/62).

[44] E. g., 1 Cor 3 corrected to 1 Cor 10 (24ᵛ/55), in the quotation of 2 Cor 4:3 „multis" was corrected to „in hiis" (49ʳ/80), and in 1 Tim 1:20 the missing „non" was supplied (116ʳ/236).

[45] E. g., John of Constantinople was corrected to John of Jerusalem (32ʳ/64), and Helvidius to Vigilantius (87ᵛ/182).

VIII

60

arguments were devised,[46] more prooftexts from Sacred Scripture found,[47] and examples from patristic sources, from later church history, and from contemporary tracts and events were added.[48] Eck provided more information on the identity and opinions of current heretics.[49] The tone of his criticisms became more polemical and insulting, but toward the end he prayed that God in His mercy would convert Luther and his followers.[50] Eck also supplied fuller explanations of historical events.[51] He made minor stylistic changes,[52] reorganized his materials,[53] and clarified and expanded elements in his arguments.[54] He also modified one of his positions. Since the printed work was no longer dedicated to Campeggio, who admonished him against disputing with heretics, but was prefaced by a letter praising

---

[46] E. g., Christ's descent into hell and Sunday observance [earlier at 7ᵛ] are not found in Sacred Scripture (48ʳ⁻ᵛ/76–77 and 94ᵛ/198), and the important thing is not reading but understanding Scripture (49ᵛ/83).

[47] E. g., Song 4 (3ʳ/18), Exodus 19 (15ʳ/40), Ezech. 44 (49ᵛ/81), John 6, 8, 9 and Gen. 15 (51ᵛ/94–95), Acts 20:28 (75ʳ/150), 1 Peter 2:16 (77ᵛ/156), and 1 Cor 9:27 (84ᵛ/172).

[48] Patristic sources: e. g., Gregory the Great (24ʳ/54), Jerome (61ᵛ/182; 80ʳ/163 ul; 107ʳ/224), Ignatius of Antioch (80ᵛ/163 and 95ᵛ/201), Eusebius (84ᵛ/171), Dionysius the Areopagite (87ᵛ–88ʳ/183 and 129ᵛ/263–264); Church history: e. g., Porchetus de Selvaticis (76ᵛ/155), legend of St. Savinianus (88ʳ/183), story of Charlemagne writing four books on images (91ᵛ/194), decree of the Council of Carthage (106ᵛ/223), Platina's account of the early pontificates (113ᵛ/231–232), history of indulgences (126ᵛ/257–258); contemporary authors and events: e. g., John Fisher (12ʳ/34), Luther's Protestant opponents Carlstadt, Zwingli, Haetzer, and Hubmaier (17ʳ/44 and 91ᵛ/194), and Eck's own book on papal primacy (115ᵛ/234).

[49] E. g., Luther resisted Carlstadt and had him expelled from Saxony for destroying images (91ᵛ/194); Baltasar Hubmaier presently calls himself Fridberger (92ᵛ/196); and Leo Jud is at Zurich (93ʳ/196); and disputations judged by cold and hostile laity are dangerous (141ᵛ/282).

[50] E. g., Lutherans are insane and insolent (14ᵛ/39), Luther's followers constitute an „imperium vulgus" of heresy (49ᵛ/83), Lutheran theologians are superficial and twist texts (50ʳ/83), may Luther's argument boomerang on him and his followers (50ʳ/83), the Lutherans remit all penalities for sin yet complain when the pope remits only a part (126ʳ/257). But Eck came to hope that God in His mercy may convert Luther and his followers (139ᵛ/276, n. o2).

[51] E. g., once the simple Western bishops realized that they had been seduced at Rimini, they abrogated their decisions (16ᵛ/43); Magdeburg is the primatial see (37ᵛ/69); only the apostles were present at the Last Supper (67ʳ/137); communion under both species was not the universal practice of the primitive Church (67ᵛ/137); and the Council of Frankfurt condemned the Felician heresy (91ʳ/193).

[52] E. g., „datur/tradetur" (56ʳ/107), „rex/reges" (59ᵛ/115), „prodesse/prodere" (62ʳ/122), „omittentes/obmittentes" (66ᵛ/137), „ratio legis/legis ratio" (134ᵛ/272).

[53] E. g., Scriptural citations (3ʳ⁻ᵛ/17–18, 4ᵛ/21 and 73ʳ/147), patristic references (21ᵛ/49), adding a cross reference (74ʳ/148).

[54] E. g., to live only by the soul, not according to bodies (48ᵛ/77), the Mass as a testament requires the death of the testator (100ʳ/208), by the apostles and elders (74ᵛ/150), animator of the brothers and people of Israel (86ʳ/175), other items Solomon had carved (93ʳ/196).

Henry VIII for writing against Luther, Eck added that when suitable judges could be found, one should by all means engage in disputations so that truth would be preserved and heretics confounded. Eck's outright defense of these debates may also reflect a renewed enthusiasm for this tactic, after learning from Giberti in early 1525 that Clement VII had praised the professor's efforts to refute such heretics as Zwingli.[55]

The Revised Ms. Copy Without a Dedication

Evidence exists that the *Enchiridion* went through an intermediate stage of revision before it was revised again for publication. This evidence is in the form of eight folios preserved in the Vatican collection. These sheets contain a title page with a listing of the contemporary Catholic authors Eck used and the text of the first two *loci* plus the beginnings of the third. The catch words at the end of the last folio suggest that the manuscript at one time continued on. None of the *loci* are numbered.[56] The paper bears the watermark of a caster for ink-drying sand, a design similar to that found in the Campeggio dedication copy.[57] The handwriting is in a clear humanistic script.[58] The recipient or owner of this manuscript is nowhere indicated.

A close examination of this Vatican manuscript reveals a stage of revision that is inbetween the version presented to Campeggio and that printed at Landshut. For the most part the Vatican text follows

---

[55] E–A, 142ᵛ, E–F, 284. See above note 23.
[56] BAV, Codex Vaticanus Latinus 6211, fols. 203ʳ–210ᵛ. See note 10 above. For a listing of other items contained in this volume of miscellany, see BAV, Inventarii Bibliothecae Vaticanae, Tomus VII, pp. 180–184 and Paul Oskar KRISTELLER, *Iter Italicum*, II *Italy: Orvieto to Volterra, Vatican City* (Leiden, 1977), 338. The listing of contemporary Catholic authors on the title page is identical to that which appears in the Landshut 1525 edition, even to the identification of Faber as *Constancien* – see Landshut edition, fol. Aiᵛ (where spelt *Constantien*). The version dedicated to Campeggio makes no explicit mention of Fisher, Marcello, Emser, Politi, Usingen, and Alveldt. Although Fisher is mentioned on E–V, 203ʳ, he does not appear in the text (E–V, 208ʳ) at the place where he is cited in the Landshut edition (E–F, 34). The *loci* titles are on E–V, 204ʳ, 208ʳ, 210ᵛ; the catchwords *sed pater* appear at the bottom of 210ᵛ. This fragment of the *Pharetra* is written on paper measuring 21.3 x 31.7 cm.
[57] See above n. 30. The Vatican watermark differs from that in the Campeggio copy in that is has nine instead of seven fluted sections showing and the design is perpendicular and does not lean toward the right.
[58] This scribe has introduced a few peculiarities into the script: spelling „penitus" as „poenitus" (E–V, 209ʳ and 210ʳ), substituting a „z" for an „s" in „Baptisma" (206ᵛ) and „evangelisaverit" (209ʳ), and abbreviating the syllable „ser" as in „conseruandam" and „reseruamus" (210ʳ).

62

closely the version dedicated to Campeggio: it retains sections
eliminated in the Landshut printing[59] and is missing many of the
sections added to that version.[60] It improves the earlier text by
correcting errors, reversing word orders, and inserting or dropping
words.[61] But it also makes a number of its own mistakes by
miscopying, misspelling, and skipping words.[62] The expository part of
locus one, however, shows significant revision: a tightening up of the
argumentation, rearrangement of materials, addition of new subsec-
tions, and more references to heretics. These revisions bring this part
of *locus* one much closer to the Landshut version.[63] In order to arrive
at the text printed in the 1525 Landshut edition, Eck continued his
process of revision: adding to the Vatican version more scriptural
citations, providing historical explanations, expanding the lists of
heretics, and making minor stylistic changes.[64]

Why was the version preserved in fragmentary form in the Vatican
collection produced and who was its intended recipient? Given the
German watermark and the revisions which could have been made
only by Eck, it seems reasonable to assume that this manuscript was
produced under Eck's direction. Having sent the earlier version to
Campeggio, did Eck now turn his attention to his patron in Rome to

---

[59] E. g., „Act. xvi, Hunc . . . in Cenchiis" (E–A, 8ᵛ–9ʳ/E–V, 206ᵛ – but not in E–F, 30) and
„Si peccaverit . . . et in caelo" (E–A, 13ᵛ/E–V, 208ʳ – but not in E–F, 37).

[60] See below note 64.

[61] Corrected errors: e. g., „qua" (E–A, 13ᵛ) becomes „quam" (E–V, 208ᵛ and E–F, 37) and
„dixerunt" (E–A, 20ʳ) becomes „dixerint" (E–V, 210ᵛ and E–F, 47); reversed word
order: e. g., „ecclesiam dilexit" (E–A, 3ʳ), becomes „dilexit ecclesiam" (E–V, 204ʳ and
E–F, 18), „ipse exhiberet" (E–A, 3ᵛ) becomes „exhiberet ipse" (E–V, 204ʳ and E–F, 18),
„se non" (E–A, 12ᵛ) becomes „non se" (E–V, 208ʳ and E–F, 36), but in other incidents
subsequent printed versions retained the earlier word order: e. g., „non concilium
fuit" (E–V, 209ᵛ) ignored for „fuit non concilium" (E–A, 16ᵛ and E–F, 42) and
„Augustinus contra donatistas libro vii" (E–V, 208ᵛ) ignored for „Augustinus libro vii
contra donatistas" (E–A, 15ʳ and E–F, 39); inserted words: e. g., „est" inserted
between the words „consectarium multo" (E–A, 7ʳ, E–V, 206ʳ, and E–F, 27) and „et"
between „est sacerdotum" (E–A, 18ʳ, E–V, 210ʳ, and E–F, 46); and dropped words:
e. g., „et" from „et suffocato" (E–A, 9ᵛ, E–V, 206ᵛ, and E–F, 31. n. h6 for later
edition).

[62] Miscopying: e. g., „videtur" (E–V, 207ʳ) for „iudicium" (E–A, 10ᵛ and E–F, 32) and
„sibi" (E–V, 207ʳ) for „tibi" (E–A, 10ʳ and F, 32); misspelling: e. g., „poenitus" (E–V,
209ʳ, 210ʳ) for „penitus" (E–A, 17ᵛ, 19ʳ and E–F, 45, 46); skipping: e. g., „in mundum
universum" (E–V, 205ᵛ but retained in E–A, 6ᵛ and E–F, 26), „ad legem Moyse" (E–V,
206ᵛ but retained in E–A, 8ᵛ and E–F, 30), „Paulus" (E–V, 209ʳ but retained in E–A,
16ʳ and E–F, 42), „varie" (E–V, 209ᵛ but retained in E–A, 17ʳ and E–F, 45).

[63] E–V, 204ʳ–205ᵛ compared to E–A, 3ʳ–5ᵛ and E–F, 17–24.

[64] More scriptural citations: e. g., „Praelatus . . . Salomonem etc." (E–V, 205ᵛ, E–F, 24)
and „Ideo lex . . . Hiere. xxxi" (E–V, 205ᵛ, E–F, 26); historical explanation: e. g., „et
simplices episcopi . . . conclusa Arimini" (E–V, 209ᵛ, E–F, 43); lists of heretics: e. g.,
„ut iam . . . Zvinglius" (E–V, 205ᵛ, E–F, 22), „sic Zvinglius . . . Pacimontanus" etc. (E–V,
205ᵛ, E–F, 25), „unde et Carolostadius . . . damnati sunt" (E–V, 209ᵛ, E–F, 44).

whom he had promised a year earlier a copy of his work once it was completed? In that letter to Giberti, Eck stated that this work was in response to the urgent requests of „tot fideles et catholici". On the title page of the Vatican manuscript this work is described as „pro catholicis contra Ludderanorum haeresim".[65]

The Evolution of the Manual's Title

Before concluding this study on the origins of the *Enchiridion*, the question of the book's title should be addressed. The copy presented to Campeggio has no title page. At the top of the table of contents the words *Loci communes* have been inserted by Eck.[66] On the spine of the original vellum binding are inscribed the words DE ECCLESIA ET EIVS AUTORITATE. A later hand has also written on this spine the words *Loci communes Joanne Echÿo*. On the page bearing Campeggio's coat of arms a later hand has inserted too the words *Echii Joannis de Auctoritate Ecclesiae*.[67] Given these descriptions of the work, it is easier to understand how this manuscript could go unnoticed for so long.

The Vatican manuscript bears the title *Phareta Locorum Communium pro catholicis contra Ludderanorum haeresim Johanne Eckio Autore*.[68] Once again the word *Enchiridion* appears nowhere in the title; instead, Eck uses another Greek word referring to a quiver for holding arrows. This imagery of armament in defense of the faith accords well with the quotation from Paul's epistle to the Ephesians which appears immediately after the table of contents in the Campeggio dedication copy and on the title page of the Landshut printing: „Above all, taking up the shield of faith with which you can quench all the flaming darts of the most evil one."[69]

By switching from *Phareta* to *Enchiridion*, Eck has both retained the weapon imagery (hand dagger) and placed his work in the tradition of manuals (a handbook) popular among clerics.[70] But Eck also aimed at a lay audience. Just as Erasmus some twenty-three years earlier

---

[65] E–V, 203[r].

[66] E–A, 2[r].

[67] Although this codex has been rebound in recent times, the original spine has been preserved inside the new cover. The cardinal's coat of arms is on 1[r]. By assigning to the whole work the title of the first chapter, *de ecclesia et eius autoritate*, the two later scribes seem to show that they did not realize that they were dealing with the original version of the famous *Enchiridion*.

[68] E–V, 203[r]. The scribe seems to have been unaware that the correct spelling of this Greek word is *pharetra*.

[69] E–A, 2[v] and for a reproduction of the title page of the Landshut edition, see FRAENKEL, „Erste Studien", 667. The reference to this quotation is Eph. 6:16.

[70] FRAENKEL, ed., *Enchiridion*, 13*–16*.

assigned the double-meaning word *Enchiridion* as the title of his famed summa on Christian living written for the lay knight and manufacturer of armament, Johann Poppenruyter, so now Eck used the same word in his title when dedicating his summary of controversalist theology to the most eminent layman of his day who was openly engaged in fighting heresy, king Henry VIII of England. Eck thus hoped that his small handbook of arguments would serve as a dagger in the hands of the royal warrior who had recently assumed the papally acclaimed title of „Defender of the Faith".[71]

Conclusion

This study of Eck's letter to Giberti, of related documents, and of the two manuscript copies of what was eventually entitled the *Enchiridion* has shed some new light on the origins of this manual of controversalist theology. On the urgings of numerous clerics and lay persons with whom he conversed or corresponded on his return trip from Rome in early 1524, Eck began work on the manual as soon as he arrived in Ingolstadt. Many of the twenty-seven topics he treated can be related to his activities during the remainder of that year: his debates with Lutherans in Bavaria, his advisement of the cardinal-legate Campeggio at the Diet of Nürnberg and the Regensburg Conference, and his efforts to engage Zwingli in a public debate and his likely preparations for such. When Campeggio proved unsupportive of his efforts by discouraging a public disputation and failing to provide him with funds, Eck turned to Giberti who assured him of Clement VII's approval of his efforts and who worked to find him a printer in Germany for his new manual. The manuscript copy dedicated to Campeggio contains a prefatory epistle which helps to clarify the cardinal's role in its composition. And the three different hands used in copying this text suggest stages in the composition of the *Enchiridion*. The fragment of another manuscript shows that the *Enchiridion* went through a revision before being revised once again and printed in Landshut in April of 1525. These two manuscript copies also show that the title of the manual evolved from *Loci communes* to *Phareta locorum communium pro catholicis contra Ludderanorum haeresim,* to finally *Enchiridion locorum communium adversus Lutherum et alios hostes ecclesiae.* Thanks to the documents here studied, the origins of the *Enchiridion* are no longer so obscure that they can be elucidated only by scholarly conjectures.

[71] Roland BAINTON, *Erasmus of Christendom* (New York, 1969), 66; E–F, 2–4; WILKE, *Cardinal Protectors,* 122–125, 140.

Widmungsbrief Ecks an Kardinal Campeggio: Rom, Biblioteca Angelica,
Ms 665, fol. 1ᵛ.

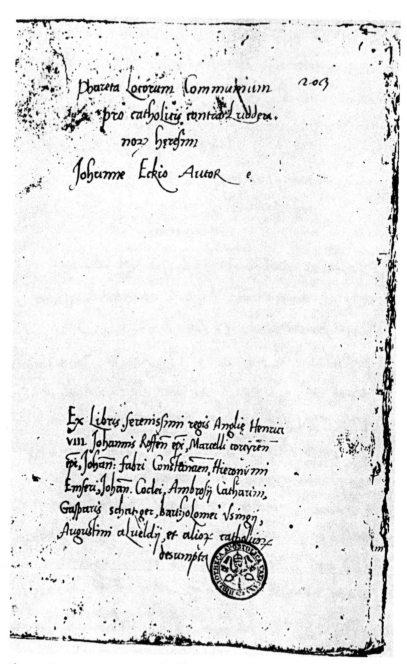

Phareta Locorum Communium pro catholicis contra Ludderanorum haeresim, Johanne Eckio Autore: Rom, BAV, cod. Vat. Lat. 6211, fol. 203ʳ (Titelblatt).

De ecclesia et eius autoritate. 204

Ecclesia est corpus christi, sponsa christi, regnum celorum: paulus ad
ephesios 1. Omnia subiecit sub pedibus eius, et ipsum dedit caput
super omnem ecclesiam, que e corpus ipsius et plenitudo eius, qui
omnia in omnibus adimpletur.

Ephes. 4 digne ambuletis vocatione qua vocati estis cum
omni humilitate et mansuetudine cum pacientia suppor-
tantes inuicem in charitate, solliciti seruare vnitatem spiritus
in vinculo pacis, Vnum corpus et vnus spiritus, sicut vocati
estis in vna spe vocationis vestre, Vnus dominus, vna fides
vnum baptizma: vnus deus et pater omnium qui est super omnes
Can. vi. Vna est columba mea, perfecta mea, vna est matri
sue, electa genitrici sue. Can. iiii. Ortus conclusus soror mea
sponsa, ortus conclusus fons signatus.

Ad Ephes. v. mulieres viris suis subditae sint, sicut domino: quoniam vir
caput est mulieris, sicut christus caput ecclesie, ipse saluator
corporis eius: sed sicut ecclesia subiecta est christo ita et mulieres
viris suis in omnibus. Viri diligite vxores vestras, sicut et christus
dilexit ecclesiam: et seipsum tradidit pro ea ut illam sanctificaret:
mundans eam lauacro aque in verbo vite, ut exhiberet ipse
sibi gloriosam ecclesiam, non habentem maculam aut rugam aut aliquid
huiusmodi, sed ut sit sancta et immaculata.

1. Cor. xii. Vos autem estis corpus christi, et membra de membris.
Sic ergo vna est ecclesia, non est foris et intus, sicut vna fuit
archa Noe 1. pe. 3. que fuit figura huius ecclesie: extra illam vnum

[signatum]

Johannes Eck, Phareta Locorum Communium: erste Textseite (fol. 204ʳ).

68

Appendices*

I. *Letter of Johann Eck to Gian Matteo Giberti, Ingolstadt, February 27, 1524*

Bibliotheca Apostolica Vaticana, Mss. Chigiani, L. III. 59, fol. 267ʳ⁻ᵛ

iiii Kalendas Martias 1524, Eckii
Reverendo patri et domino, domino Johanni Matthaeo Giberti Summi Domini Nostri Datario,[1] Mecaenati suo,[2] Romae.

Salutem plurimam cum sui commendatione.
Attigi Germaniam,[3] reverende pater, propiciis numinibus, reperi quoque principes saeculares recte animatos in negotio fidei et sedis apostolicae uno dempto, qui ab initio in veritate non stetit.[4] Civitates vero Francae (quas imperiales solemus appellare)[5] ultra modum infectae sunt illa haeresi. Augustae iam publice comedunt, vendunt passim carnes, non secus, ac si iam pascha ageremus; non confitentur; divina omnia et fidei nostrae mysteria contemnunt.[6]
Adii quosdam episcopos et eos consului, quid remedii utile et efficax ipsi existiment, ut reverendissimum dominum legatum adventantem[7] certius informare possim.

---

* In my transcription of these two letters, I have standardized spellings, avoided contractions and abbreviations, and modernized to some extent the use of capital letters and punctuation.

[1] Immediately after his election, Clement VII appointed as Datarius his secretary Giberti – see PROSPERI, *Tra Evangelismo*, 35; Giberti continued for a while as Datarius even after his appointment as bishop of Verona on August 8, 1524 – see Walther VON HOFMANN, *Forschungen zur Geschichte der kurialen Behörden vom Schisma bis zur Reformation*, II (Rome, 1914), 103, nr. 26.

[2] Giberti took Eck under his protection in the Roman curia – see PROSPERI, *Tra Evangelismo*, 126 n. 87. Francesco Minizio Calvo, the Roman publisher in 1525 of Eck's *Enchiridion*, also referred to Giberti as his Maecenas – *Ibid.*, 97 n. 7; FRAENKEL, „Erste Studien", 656–657; and his *Enchiridion*, 64*.

[3] On his return from his third trip to Rome, see WIEDEMANN, *Eck*, 194.

[4] Probably a reference to Frederick III (the Wise), elector of Saxony. See above n. 12.

[5] Among these imperial cities of Franconia were Nordlingen, Weissenburg, Nürnberg, and Regensburg. On the spread of Reformation teachings in Franconia, see ENDRES, „Peasant War", 70–73.

[6] For similar reports on conditions in Augsburg and Nürnberg, see CARDINAL, *Campeggio*, 83–85 and BALAN, *Monumenta Reformationis Lutheranae*, 329. In 1524 Lent began on February 9th.

[7] Campeggio reached Augsburg on March 9th and Nürnberg on March 14th – see PASTOR, *History of the Popes*, X, 111 and above n. 16.

In summa, res in manu Caesaris est et Ferdinandi,[8] qui si non colludant cum Ludderanis, res acta est, et foeliciter. Nam hos solos curant civitates.

Tot fideles et catholici, coram aliqui, alii per literas, non modo me rogant, sed urgent potius ut locos omnes controversos ab haereticis colligam et breviter subnectam sacrae scripturae autoritates ac patrum dicta. Adiiciam quoque autoritates a Lutteranis perperam torsas contra ecclesiam et ecclesiae usum, brevissime excutiendo sinistras inductiones. Itaque hunc laborem subii, nondum etiam respirans ex itinere. Cum absolutus fuerit, verecunde aedes tuae paternitatis adibit.[9]

Porro, reverende pater, sicut fidei paternitatis tuae abiens me commisi, ita et nunc ad memoriam revoco; nam plus est ex re sedis apostolicae, ut hoc turbulento tempore sim in Germania quo consoler catholicos et terream adversarios,[10] quam quod pro privato lucro starem in curia Romana. Tamen non minores favores et gratias debet michi impendere, sede apostolica absenti, immo ampliores, quo magis utiliter laboro absens quam praesens facerem. Ideo super commissione facta per Sanctissimum Dominum Nostrum nuper in vacationibus Spirensis[11] paternitas tua curet ut Eckius aliquid habeat. Nam sic in causa fidei expensas utiliter facere potero et sufferre. Quod si nulla ex praeposituris illis libera est, potes semper curare alia via occurrente quottidie. Miror quod, proximo decembri vacante praepositura Spaltensis Eistetensis diocesis,[12] michi praesenti Romae

---

[8] Emperor Charles V and his younger brother Ferdinand, archduke of Austria.

[9] Eck included in the first printed edition of his *Enchiridion* (Landshut, 1525 on fol. Rii^v, reprinted in E–F, 415) a letter addressed to Giberti in which he described what he had hoped to achieve in writing this work „Cuius te quoque volui participem esse . . ." For the possibility of a manuscript copy sent to Rome before the printed edition, see above n. 65 of the text. On Giberti's residence in Rome, see above n. 13.

[10] Immediately upon returning to Ingolstadt in early 1524, Eck moved against Lutheran influences in the university, city, and surrounding territories – see WIEDEMANN, *Eck*, 194–200.

[11] In his letter to Clement VII from Nürnberg dated April 11, 1524, Campeggio reported on the recently vacated position in the church of Our Lady and SS. Peter and Paul in the town of Bruchsal. Invoking its papally confirmed privileges, this aristocratic collegiate chapter elected Philip von Anglach to fill the post. This election was, however, contested by Peregrinus de Taxis. Campeggio urged the pope to dismiss de Taxis' suit and to silence him lest complaints be raised about Roman violation of local rights. See ASV, SS. Germania 53, fol. 7^r–v. On the town of Bruchsal (located 12 miles northeast of the later-founded Karlsruhe) and on its collegiate church during this period, see Lawrence G. DUGGAN, *Bishop and Chapter: The Governance of the Bishopric of Speyer to 1552* (New Brunswick, New Jersey, 1978), 151, 176–179.

[12] By his brief of May 6, 1527, Clement VII conferred on Ambrosius von Gumppenberg the church, canonry, and prebend of S. Emeran in lower Spalt. These benefices

de ea non provisum fuerit, cum ego in ea resideam diocesi. Et cum illa ego fuissem contenus, licet parvula sit; et magis delegeritis eam dare puero unius immodice diversariis faventi; at forte negligentiae meae imputabis, qui eam non petierim. At adhuc omnis spes in te pendet; noli itaque, observande pater, mecum Hadrianisare;[13] et fidem, tantopere a Sanctis Paulo et Cypriano[14] laudatam in Romanis, fac ut experiar, et quanto citius, tanto gratius.

Doctores studii nostri, quod quendam Ludderanum ad revocationem adigerunt,[15] male audiunt a Ludderanis civitatum vicinarum,[16] induxi eos et quasi coegi, ut ad disputandum provocent adversarios quod, incluso libello[17] eos fecisse intelliget paternitas vestra reverenda, cui me quam maxime possum commendo.

Spero in Deum, reverendissimum et dominum legatum aliquid boni pro ecclesia Dei expediturum, licet tardior adventus suus, pluribus displiceat.

Valeat musice in Deo, paternitas tua reverenda.

Ex Ingolostat, iiii Kalendas Martias, Anno salutis M.D. XXIIII.

Reverendae paternitatis tuae deditissimus cliens, Eckius.

---

became vacant through the death in the Roman Curia of Georg Stuner. Ambrosius also worked in the papal service, was of noble birth by both parents, and was already the praepositus of the church in the town of Onugen (?) in the diocese of Würzburg and canon of the church in upper Spalt. See ASV, Reg. Vat. 1437, fols. 12^r–13^r. On von Gumppenberg, see Ilse GUENTHER, in *Contemporaries of Erasmus: A Biographical Register of the Renaissance and Reformation*, ed. Peter G. BIETENHOLZ and Thomas B. DEUTSCHER, II (F–M), (Toronto, 1986), 154.

[13] Hadrian VI was accused of responding to those who asked for benefices with the vague promise „We shall see" and then doing what he thought best – see above n. 15 and Barbara McCLUNG HALLMAN, *Italian Cardinals, Reform, and the Church as Property, 1492–1563* (UCLA Center for Medieval and Renaissance Studies, 22), (Los Angeles, 1985), 17.

[14] For examples of Paul's trust in the Romans, see his appeal to the Roman emperor (Acts 25:11–12) and his complimentary statements on the faith and benevolence of the Christian community in the capital city (Rom 1:8, 15:14, 30–33). On Cyprian of Carthage's praise of the Romans' faith, see his Epp. 59.14.1 and 60.2.1 in *S. Thasci Caecili Cypriani opera omnia*, ed. Wilhelm HARTEL, *Corpus Scriptorum Ecclesiasticorum Latinorum*, III–II (Vienna, 1871), 683, 692. I am grateful to Rev. Thomas Halton for his assistance in locating this reference. There is a certain irony in Eck's statement, in that Paul's trust in the emperor was rewarded with beheading and Cyprian's appeal to Rome resulted in his condemnation and excommunication. While Eck did not experience the same favors accorded these saints, he was also to find that his trust in Roman largess was misplaced.

[15] Arsacius Seehofer – see above n. 14 and WIEDEMANN, *Eck*, 195.

[16] Among the critics of Seehofer's treatment was Argula von Grumbach – see above n. 14 and WIEDEMANN, *Eck*, 195–196.

[17] See above n. 14.

II. *Dedication letter of Johann Eck to cardinal Lorenzo Campeggio, s. l., s. d.*

Biblioteca Angelica, Rome, Ms. 665, fol. 1ᵛ

Reverendissimo in christo patri et domino, Domino Laurentio, Sanctae Romanae Ecclesiae tituli Sanctae Anastasiae Cardinali[18] ac per Germaniam, Daciam, Poloniam, Prussiam, Livoniam et cetera legato,[19] Johannes Eckius optat Spiritus Sancti unctionem et indefectibilis fidei sedis apostolicae defensionem.

Noctuas Athenis mittit[20] Eckius, et sus Minervam docet;[21] at obedientia haec imperat, et salus animarum expostulat. Locos communes, tua reverendissima paternitas, depinxi; non ut ex proposito hic cum haereticis pugnem, sed ut per te habeant simplices Catholici in promptu quo haereticis respondeant.[22]

Tu, vero, memor galeri cardinei rubei ut nichil addubites roseum sanguinem, non dico pro sede, sed pro fide sedis apostolicae fundere,[23] nam reddet tibi Deus coronam iusticiae.[24]

Vale, prosperare, et vince. Fiat bone Deus. Amen.

---

[18] Campeggio held this title of cardinal priest of S. Anastasia from 1519 to 1528, see EUBEL, *Hierarchia Catholica*, III, 16, 59.

[19] Campeggio's legation dated from January 8, 1524 when he was named legate in a consistory. He left Rome on February 1st and returned on October 13, 1525. See EUBEL, III, 16a, n. 8. Eck had urged that Campeggio's legation be expanded beyond Germany to include „sed etiam Datiam, Suecam, Norbegiam, Bohemiam, Prussiam et Livoniam" – see PFEILSCHIFTER, *Acta Reformationis Catholicae*, I, 150: 31–32.

[20] A common proverb, the equivalent of the English phrase „sending coals to Newcastle" – see *Roget's International Thesaurus of English Words and Phrases*, rev. C. O. Sylvester MAWSON (New York, 1932) No. 641: Redundance, p. 262 – „send owls to Athens".

[21] For variants of this proverb about a pig instructing Minerva and their meanings, see Adagiorum Chilias I, Centuria I, Proverbium XL: „Sus Minervam", in *Desiderii Erasmi Roterodami opera omnia*, ed. Jean LECLERC, II (Leiden, 1703), col. 43 A–F.

[22] This wording is echoed in Eck's 1529 dedicatory letter to Konrad von Thüngen – see above n. 5 of text. W. Jared WICKS, S. J., has made the interesting suggestion that the „simple Catholics" here mentioned were those ordinary faithful without time or inclination to read Eck's tomes on papal primacy, confession, purgatory, and so forth. They would be helped by Campeggio if he were to underwrite the costs of printing Eck's manual which summarized many of the arguments contained in these longer works.

[23] During the ceremony creating a cardinal, the pope places on the appointee's head the tasselled red cardinal's hat and prays: „accipe galerum rubrum insigne singulare dignitatis Cardinalatus, per quod designatur quod usque ad mortem et sanguinis effusionem inclusive pro exaltatione sanctae fidei, pace, et quiete populi Christiani augmento, et statu Sacrosanctae Romanae Ecclesiae te intrepidum exhibere debeas. In nomine Patris et Filii, etc." See *Caeremoniale Romanum of Agostino Patrizi Piccolomini*, ed. Cristoforo MARCELLO (Venice, 1516, reprint Ridgewood, N. J., 1965), fol. XXXXIʳ. Eck had the presentation copy adorned with a frontispiece depicting Campeggio's coat of arms in black surmounted by a cardinal's hat in red – see E-A, 1ʳ.

[24] 2 Tim 4:8.

Zusammenfassung

ZUR ENTSTEHUNG VON ECKS ENCHIRIDION

Nur wenig ist über die Entstehung von Johannes Ecks *Enchiridion locorum communium adversus Lutherum et alios hostes ecclesiae* (Landshut, April 1525) bekannt, der wohl populärsten unter den katholischen Entgegnungen auf protestantische Lehren. Pierre Fraenkel stellte in einer Reihe von Aufsätzen, sowie in der Einleitung seiner kritischen Ausgabe des *Enchiridion* (Münster 1979) die Hypothese auf, daß es auf Verlangen des päpstlichen Legaten in Deutschland, Lorenzo Campeggio, gegen Ende 1524 geschrieben worden sei, und zwar mit der Absicht, Ecks Bemühungen von öffentlichen Disputationen mit den Protestanten weg und auf andere Bahnen zu lenken. Eck habe es Heinrich VIII. in der Hoffnung gewidmet, den Unruhen des Bauernkriegs entgehen und eine sichere Bleibe in England finden zu können.

Durch drei wichtige, bisher aber unveröffentlichte und unbenützte Dokumente wird es möglich, die Entstehungsgeschichte des *Enchiridion* aufzuhellen. Ein Brief Ecks an Gian Matteo Giberti vom 27. Februar 1524 beschreibt, wie Eck aufgrund drängender Bitten zahlreicher Kleriker und Laien, mit denen er auf seiner Rückreise von Rom entweder in Unterhaltung oder Korrespondenz in Kontakt gekommen war, sofort nach seiner Rückkehr nach Ingolstadt die Arbeit begann, die allmählich zum *Enchiridion* ausgestaltet wurde. Der Vortrag analysiert Ecks Tätigkeit von diesem Zeitpunkt an bis zum Ende des Jahres auf Basis veröffentlichter Quellen sowie der noch unveröffentlichen Korrespondenz im Archivio Segreto Vaticano und zeigt, wie Ecks Beschäftigung im Jahre 1524 den Inhalt des *Enchiridion* beeinflußt haben könnte. Dazu gehören zum Beispiel seine Disputationen mit Lutheranern in Bayern, seine Teilnahme am Nürnberger Reichstag und an der Regensburger Konferenz, seine Herausforderung Zwinglis zu öffentlicher Debatte, seine wahrscheinlichen Vorbereitungen für diese Debatten, das Lob Clemens VII. für seine Bemühungen, die Häretiker zu widerlegen, und seine Beziehungen zu Campeggio.

Durch die sorgfältige Analyse einer Handschrift des *Enchiridion* mit einer Widmung an Campeggio, die bis jetzt unbekannt geblieben ist und von der bisher noch niemals bewiesen worden ist, daß sie den Urtext des berühmten Traktats enthält, können Aussagen über den ursprünglichen Zweck der Arbeit, die einzelnen Kompositionsphasen sowie nicht zuletzt über den genauen Inhalt von bisher kontroversen Passagen gemacht werden. Die Untersuchung eines Fragments einer weiteren Handschrift, die bisher von Gelehrten ebenso wenig beachtet worden ist, ergibt, daß es sich hier um eine Überarbeitung handelt, die ein Zwischenstadium zwischen der Campeggio gewidmeten Handschrift und der Heinrich VIII. dedizierten, im Druck vorliegenden Ausgabe darstellt. Gründe für diesen Wechsel der Widmung und der dem Werk gegebenen Titel (von *Loci communes* über *Pharetra locorum communium* zu *Enchiridion locorum communium*) können wahrscheinlich gemacht werden.

The Character of Erasmus

THE CHARACTER OF DESIDERIUS ERASMUS OF ROTTERDAM (ca. 1467–1536) has over the years been the object of widely divergent opinion. He is often presented as the gentle, but insistent, voice of moderation and toleration amid Reformation polemics, a view popularized by recent generations of "liberals" and skeptics, but modified by current scholarship. Yet, in his own lifetime and for centuries thereafter, conservative Catholics vilified him as the sower of bitter discord and the followers of Luther denounced him as a cowardly traitor to the Gospel.[1] These varying views are due not only to differing theological and philosophical perspectives, but also to the apparently contradictory evidence to be found in Erasmus' writings and actions. With the help of psychology a few explicit attempts have been made to understand the complexities of Erasmus' character.[2] Unfortunately, their findings are limited

We are grateful to William J. Bouwsma, Myron P. Gilmore, John W. O'Malley, Thomas and Catherine West, and others for having suggested a number of helpful revisions. Whatever deficiencies remain should be attributed solely to the authors.

[1] For a bibliographical survey of some of the vast literature on Erasmus, see Andreas Flitner, *Erasmus im Urteil seiner Nachwelt: Das literarische Erasmusbild von Beatus Rhenanus bis zur Jean Leclerc* (Tübingen, 1952); Bruce E. Mansfield, "Erasmus in the Nineteenth Century: The Liberal Tradition," *Studies in the Renaissance*, 15 (1968): 193–219; Preserved Smith, *Erasmus: A Study of His Life, Ideals, and Place in History* (New York, 1923), 421–41; Jean-Claude Margolin, *Douze années de la bibliographie érasmienne (1950–1961)* (Paris, 1963); and Rudolf Padberg, *Personaler Humanismus—Das Bildungsverständnis der Erasmus von Rotterdam und seine Bedeutung für die Gegenwart: Ein Beitrag zur Revision des Humboldtschen Bildungsideals* (Paderborn, 1964), 21–38. For some of Erasmus' principal modern biographers, see Augustin Renaudet, "Érasme, sa vie et son oeuvre jusqu'en 1517," *Revue historique*, 111 (1912): 225–62 and 112 (1913): 241–74, *Érasme, sa pensée religieuse et son action d'après sa correspondance, 1518–1521* (Paris, 1926), *Études érasmiennes, 1521–1529* (Paris, 1939), and *Érasme et L'Italie* (Geneva, 1954); Smith, *Erasmus*; Johan Huizinga, *Erasmus*, Eng. trans. F. Hopmen (New York, 1924); Albert Hyma, *The Youth of Erasmus* (Ann Arbor, 1930; rev. ed., 1968), and *The Life of Desiderius Erasmus* (Assen, 1972); Margaret Mann Phillips, *Erasmus and the Northern Renaissance* (London, 1949); Louis Bouyer, *Autour d'Érasme: Études sur le Christianisme des humanistes catholiques* (Paris, 1955); Ronald H. Bainton, *Erasmus of Christendom* (New York, 1969); and James Tracy, *Erasmus: The Growth of a Mind* (Geneva, 1972).

[2] The most important remains the three chapters of Huizinga's *Erasmus* which presents a psychologically perceptive, if overly negative, picture of an unhappy, self-centered, spiteful, ambivalent, and lonely man. The physician John Joseph Mangan portrays a sickly man of great literary talent whose personality was unimpressive: supremely egotistic, neurasthenic, morbidly sensitive, volatile, variable, and vacillating, injudicious, irritable, and querulous, yet "always . . . a baffling but interesting character"; *Life, Character and Influence of Desiderius Erasmus of Rotterdam: Derived from a Study of His Works and Correspondence*, 1 (New York, 1927): xi. Victor W. D. Schenk claims that Erasmus was a volatile neurotic, latent homosexual, hypochondriac, and psychasthenic; "Erasmus' Character and Diseases," *Nederlandsch tijdschrift voor gen-*

to description rather than analysis, formulated in an outmoded terminology, presented only in passing, or marred by inaccuracies when authors venture outside their areas of competence. Furthermore, these studies do not integrate their valuable insights into a coherent psychological pattern, nor do they help to explain the course of Erasmus' career. The following collaborative study of a psychiatrist and a historian seeks to resolve the seeming contradictions of Erasmus' character and arrive at a psychoanalytically intelligible configuration consistent with the historical data.

MOST OF OUR SCANTY INFORMATION ABOUT the earliest years of Erasmus' life comes from the *Compendium Vitae*, a purportedly autobiographical piece whose covering letter is dated 1524. Although its authorship has been contested, a number of the events it records find confirmation in other documents of the period, and the pattern of Erasmus' adult attitudes and behavior is psychologically consistent with the circumstances of childhood described in this *Compendium*.[3] Erasmus was born on October 27/28, probably in 1467,[4] of an unlawful and, "as he feared, a sacrilegious union." His mother was a widow, and the father was unmarried and probably already a cleric. According to the *Compendium* the father was named Gerard. There is some confusion about his identity because a papal brief referred to Erasmus as the son of Rogerius.

eeskunde, 91 (March 22, 1947): 702–08. The recent publication by Harry S. May, *The Tragedy of Erasmus: A Psychohistoric Approach* (St. Charles, Mo., 1975) attempts to find the psychological roots of Erasmus' anti-Semitism. And for a blistering review of this work, see Wallace K. Ferguson, in the *American Historical Review*, 82 (1977): 376–77. The secondary literature on Erasmus and his times is already enormous. We do not attempt to list the many works that have influenced our thinking on Erasmus, but cite in the appropriate places a few that were important for our understanding of a particular issue or event. Whenever possible and desirable we have cited primary rather than secondary sources. Preference has been given here to Erasmus' letters since they reveal in a special way his thoughts, feelings, and ways of dealing with friends, acquaintances, religious superiors, patrons, and opponents. References to his other writings cite the standard edition of Jean Leclerc: Desiderius Erasmus Roterodami, *Opera omnia emendatiora et auctiora ad optimas editiones, praecique quas ipse Erasmus postremo curavit, summa fide exacta doctorumque virorum notis illustrata* (Lugduni Batavorum: Cura et impensis Petri Vander Aa, 1703–06); hereafter this edition is cited as LB. The more recent but as yet unfinished critical edition *Opera omnia Desiderii Erasmi Roterodami recognita et adnotatione critica instructa notisque illustrata* (Amsterdam, 1969-) is hereafter cited by its standard abbreviation ASD.

[3] For a critical edition of this work, see Percy Stafford Allen, ed., *Opus Epistolarum Desiderii Erasmi Roterodami*, 12 vols. (Oxford, 1906–48), 1: 47–52; hereafter this edition of correspondence, notes, and indexes published with the assistance of Helen Mary Allen *et al.* will be cited as *EE*, an abbreviation of its shorter title *Erasmi Epistolae*. References to the individual letters of Erasmus cite the arabic number of the appropriate letter (no.) and relevant lines (ll.); all other references to material in Allen's collection are by volume and page number (e.g., 1:47–52). For a treatment of the arguments surrounding the authorship of the *Compendium Vitae*, see Francis Morgan Nichols, *The Epistles of Erasmus*, 1 (New York, 1901): xlvii–li, 2–3; *EE*, 1: 575–78, app. 1; Roland Crahay, "Recherches sur le Compendium Vitae attribué à Érasme," *Bibliothèque d'Humanisme et Renaissance*, 6 (1939): 7–19, 135–53; Tracy, *Erasmus*, 21, n. 2; Huizinga, *Erasmus*, 5; and Hyma, *The Youth of Erasmus*, 52. Our discussion of the character of Erasmus does not rest on or derive from the circumstances recounted in the more than likely romanticized *Compendium Vitae*; rather our reconstruction rests on more specific evidence derived from Erasmus' life, patterns of behavior, frequently expressed attitudes and sentiments, letters, and writings of various sorts. The *Compendium Vitae*, with its apparent coloration of the story of Erasmus' origins, merely blends into this overall picture. It is not essential to the argument of our analysis.

[4] For a detailed discussion of the problems involved in dating Erasmus' birth, see A. C. F. Koch, *The Year of Erasmus' Birth and Other Contributions to the Chronology of His Life*, trans. E. Franco (Utrecht, 1969), 1–7, 39–44; and the annotated references in Bainton, *Erasmus of Christendom*, 27, n. 2.

Erasmus called his brother Peter Gerard. Some historians suggest that his father's name may have been Roger Gerard.[5] The *Compendium* recounts that the father had, with the expectation of marriage, an affair with Margaret, the daughter of a physician. They may even have been secretly betrothed, but Gerard's family staunchly opposed the union. Nine brothers, all married, insisted that one of the family be consecrated to God. In the face of this opposition, Gerard fled, leaving his intended wife with child. Learning that Gerard was in Rome, his parents wrote him that the girl he had planned to marry was dead. He believed this, and in his grief became a priest and applied himself to religion. Only after returning home did he discover the deception.[6]

Erasmus probably knew that this story was an apparent if convenient idealization, inaccurate in detail. More likely, his father was already a cleric at the time of the affair, and the conception was not the result of impatient passion, but of an irregular union of several years standing—Erasmus' brother had been born three years earlier.[7] If Erasmus was the author of the *Compendium*, he would naturally have wished to obliterate the sordidness of his origins by creating such a romanticized myth. The "family romance," in which the child fantasizes that he is the offspring not of his present parents but of some more important or powerful persons, is a familiar phenomenon. The fantasied parents possess the idealized characteristics with which the child had endowed his parents during the period of infantile narcissism. The child must somehow rationalize the discrepancy between this romanticized infantile image and his parents as they actually are.[8] The author of the *Compendium* seems to have idealized not only the circumstances of Erasmus' conception but also the father's subsequent absence. Gerard was depicted as the helpless victim of the imposed wishes of his family. In desperation he secretly fled to Rome, where he "lived like a young man," applied himself to the liberal arts, thereby gaining an excellent knowledge of Latin and Greek, and was forced by grief and cruel circumstances to become a priest. After discovering the deception, the father honorably refrained from touching Erasmus' mother again and provided for the education and support of their child.[9] The *Compendium* thus seems to absolve the father of blame for both Erasmus' illegitimacy and the father's continued absence.

The early experiences apparently had a significant influence on Erasmus'

[5] *EE*, no. 517, ll. 7–8; no. 187a, ll. 4–5; *EE*, 1: 578, app. 1; and Huizinga, *Erasmus*, 6. For arguments suggesting Gerard as his father's baptismal name and Rogerius as his mother's surname, see Hyma, *The Youth of Erasmus*, 55–56; and Nichols, *Epistles of Erasmus*, 37–39.
[6] *EE*, 1: 47–48, *Compendium*, ll. 1–28.
[7] Bainton, *Erasmus of Christendom*, 8; Huizinga, *Erasmus*, 5; and Hyma, *The Youth of Erasmus*, 52–54. In another work Hyma cites a local tradition recorded by Loos later in the sixteenth century whereby Erasmus' mother was the housekeeper at Gouda of his priest-father and was sent away to her mother's house in Rotterdam after becoming pregnant; see *Life of Desiderius Erasmus*, 10–12. If Erasmus' mother were a widow as claimed in the papal brief, Peter could also have been his half brother; see *EE*, no. 187a, l. 5. The question of the immediate sources of the account in the *Compendium* is open to speculation.
[8] Sigmund Freud, *Family Romances* (1909), in *The Standard Edition of the Complete Psychological Works of Sigmund Freud*, trans. James Strachey et al., 24 vols. (London, 1953–74), 9 (1959): 235–41.
[9] *EE*, 1: 47, 48, *Compendium*, ll. 21, 28–31.

development.[10] From the account of the father's absence, we can hypothesize a deep yearning in Erasmus for closeness with his father. Erasmus' inclination toward learning and his dedication to classical literature and to religion suggest a considerable identification with the father.[11] The son's tendency to present himself as the helpless victim of malicious forces is strikingly similar to the portrayal of the father in the *Compendium*. But it also seems reasonable to postulate that this father's remoteness and abandonment of him frustrated Erasmus' longing for closeness and produced a deeper resentment which was repressed only to manifest itself in later life. The *Compendium* reports that he was raised at his grandmother's house, presumably by his own mother. When at the age of nine he went off to school at Deventer where, he stayed until 1483, his mother followed along to watch over and care for him.[12] She was probably a devoted and doting mother, upon whom Erasmus became all the more dependent owing to his father's absence. Children who are forced into excessive dependence on parental figures tend to develop ambivalence toward them.[13] If Erasmus conformed to the model, he both identified with the mother and resented her. The patterns of masculine and feminine identification and the influences which give rise to them are important for the analysis of character development. A very likely consequence of the child's unsatisfied desire to be loved by his father is an identification with the mother who is the

[10] In order to keep in focus the delicate interplay between historical judgment and clinical interpretation, it is useful to quote Erik H. Erikson's comments on the available data concerning Luther's childhood. He observes, "Except for bits of often questionable amplification here or there, and some diligent background study by the biographers . . . these are all the facts we have. If any determining insight had to be drawn from this material alone, it would be better not to begin. But a clinician's training permits, and in fact forces, him to recognize major trends even where the facts are not all available; at any point in a treatment he can and must be able to make meaningful predictions as to what will prove to have happened; and he must be able to sift even questionable sources in such a way that a coherent predictive hypothesis emerges. The proof of the validity of this approach lies in everyday psychoanalytic work, in the way that a whole episode, a whole life period, or even a whole life trend is gradually clarified in therapeutic crises leading to decisive advances or setbacks sufficiently circumscribed to suggest future strategies. In biography, the validity of any relevant theme can only lie in its crucial recurrence in a man's development, and in its relevance to the balance sheet of his victories and defeats." See Erikson, *Young Man Luther: A Study in Psychoanalysis and History* (New York, 1958; reprint ed., 1962), 50. For scholarly critiques of this work, see Roger A. Johnson, ed., *Psychohistory and Religion: The Case of "Young Man Luther"* (Philadelphia, 1977); a bibliography of other reviews is given on pages 197–98.

[11] This description of his father's interest in classics comes from the *Compendium*. Corroborating evidence is meager. His father, apparently a skilled copyist, is known to have possessed a number of books, the sale of which Erasmus urged after his father's death; see *EE*, no. 1, ll. 7–15. The elements of paternal identification which appear in the *Compendium* are reflected in Erasmus' experience. The link between Erasmus and the *Compendium* remains open to question, but the psychological force of the argument points in the direction of such a paternal identification.

[12] *EE*, 1: 47–48, *Compendium*, ll. 18–19, 32–34. Explicit references to his mother are rare in Erasmus' writings. This characterization is consistent with the slender references to her and is congruent with Erasmus' character. The nature of a child's relationship to his parents can often be clinically inferred from the patterns of his adult behavior. See Sigmund Freud, "Some Character-Types Met Within Psychoanalytic Work" (1916), in *Standard Edition*, 14 (1957): 309–33; Sigmund Freud, "The Ego and the Id" (1923), in *Standard Edition*, 19 (1961): 1–66; and H. H. Tartakoff, "The Normal Personality in Our Culture and the Nobel Prize Complex," in R. M. Loewenstein et al., eds., *Psychoanalysis: A General Psychology* (New York, 1966), 252–72.

[13] M. S. Mahler, "On Human Symbiosis and the Vicissitudes of Individuation," *Journal of the American Psychoanalytic Association*, 15 (1967): 740–63; and Gregory Rochlin, *Griefs and Discontents: The Forces of Change* (Boston, 1965).

602

object of the father's romanticized love. This can serve as the basis for homosexual yearnings for closeness with the father.[14]

Erasmus was sensitive on the issue of illegitimacy. Occasional remarks made in later years show that his tainted origins affected him. He noted that children known for their virtue do not usually spring from evil parents. Repeating the commonplace wisdom of humanists, he also insisted that only personal sin makes one base, while the practice of virtue produces nobility. Since God does not impute the sins of parents to their offspring, children should not be treated as though they share in the parents' sins.[15] Erasmus' illegitimacy did, however, color the rest of his experience. According to the psychology of "exceptions," originally discussed by Freud, persons born with some physical defect feel that because of the wrong done to them at birth they are special individuals free of the constraints placed on ordinary men.[16] Illegitimacy was Erasmus' congenital defect. We can infer that it made him feel special and privileged. The efforts of a doting mother would have contributed to these feelings. The continued absence of his father must have extended the initial sense of deprivation, for which Erasmus' narcissism may have demanded compensation in the form of maternal attention. A suggestion that Erasmus may have succeeded in gaining this attention and later reflected on its harmful effects is found in a letter to Severin Boner, written when Boner sent his young son away to be educated. Erasmus declared that the child would be better off without the excessive kisses of his mother and the hugs of nurses and would spend his time in more useful pursuits.[17]

Erasmus described in dismal terms his fate after the premature death of both parents at the time of the plague.[18] The three guardians placed over him by his father's will consulted a "haughty" Franciscan, whose "sense of

---

[14] Freud, "The Ego and the Id," 1–66. We do not wish to overstate the argument for homosexual elements in Erasmus' personality. But it is consistent with the data. Remoteness from the father and close dependence on the mother is common among male homosexuals.

[15] Erasmus, *Moriae Encomium* (1509/11) (LB), 4: 429c and *Liber de sarcienda ecclesiae concordia* [equals LB's *De amabili ecclesiae concordia liber: Enarratio psalmi LXXXIII*, 1533] (LB), 5: 474a.

[16] Freud, "Some Character-Types Met within Psychoanalytic Work," 309–33. The "exceptions" were Freud's first attempt to describe a form of character pathology based on narcissistic elements. The concept of narcissism was advanced in his 1914 paper, "On Narcissism: An Introduction," in *Standard Edition*, 14 (1957): 67–102. The pathological aspects of Erasmus' character can best be understood as a form of narcissistic character disorder or narcissistic personality. Not all narcissism is pathological. Healthy and well-integrated narcissism can serve as the basis of positive character traits such as ambition, ideals, values, self-esteem. Narcissism, in a simplified sense, can become pathological either by excess or by defect. The pathological excess of narcissism expresses itself in traits of pride, hypersensitivity, demandingness, a sense of entitlement and specialness, the expectation of privilege, special consideration, and the desire for recognition beyond what has been merited. The pathological defect of narcissism appears in traits of depression, feelings of inadequacy and lack of worth, shame, envy, jealousy, and a sense of vulnerability and impotence. The "exceptions" would then be a typical form of narcissistic character pathology by excess. In Erasmus, as in most narcissistic personalities, the elements were mixed.

[17] *EE*, no. 2533, ll. 66–70; Erasmus urged, however, a close physical and affectionate relationship between a mother and her baby during the child's earliest years. See *Colloquia*, "Puerpera" (1526), ed. Léon-E. Halkin *et al.* (ASD), 1, pt. 3 (1972): ll. 161–91, 514–51, pp. 457–58, 467–68.

[18] The age of Erasmus at the death of his father varies between fifteen and eighteen years depending on the date of his birth. He left Deventer after his mother died, probably in the plague of 1483. His father died soon afterwards. See *EE*, 1: 582, app. 2; Koch, *Year of Erasmus' Birth*, 27–28; and Regnerus R. Post, *The Modern Devotion: Confrontation with Reformation and Humanism*, trans. Mary Foran, vol. 3 of *Studies in Medieval and Renaissance Thought*, ed. Heiko A. Oberman *et al.* (Leiden, 1968), 351, 658.

judgment was no better than that of common folk" and who thought "that he was sacrificing to God a most pleasing victim whenever he dedicated one of his pupils to the monastic life." On his advice, the guardians sent Erasmus to 's-Hertogenbosch rather than to a university. As he noted bitterly, "They feared the university, for they had decided to rear the boy for the religious life." At 's-Hertogenbosch Erasmus lived in a house of the Brethren of the Common Life, where, he later claimed, his teacher was bent on ruining good natural talents and instilling monasticism. His guardians also put pressure on him to enter the religious life. Others were enlisted in an effort "to entice, intimidate, and sway his unsteady mind." For a time Erasmus resisted these pressures by pleading his lack of knowledge about himself and the world he would renounce. In frustration, one of his guardians threatened to resign his charge. Erasmus' older brother Peter, upon whom he probably became dependent, was subjected to the same pressure. When his brother yielded, Erasmus felt betrayed. Deserted by Peter and weakened in health, Erasmus finally gave in to the wishes of his guardians and entered the monastery of the Augustinian Canons at Steyn, where he took vows in 1488. He later stated that he had reached this decision only after having visited the monastery and having found there an old school chum from Deventer who pointed out to him some of the advantages of monasticism—particularly "the holiest way of life, the abundance of books, leisure, peace, and angelic companionship."[19]

In later life Erasmus remembered the transfer to Steyn as something forced on him. Yet his letters from there do not indicate a deep-seated aversion to monastic life. However much he may have chafed against its restrictions, he probably still found much in the monastic setting that was congenial, especially the leisure and relative freedom to pursue his intellectual interests. During this period he penned an encomium on monastic life which he later excused as a favor for a friend who wished to persuade a nephew to enter the monastery—a naive rationalization at best.[20] In later years he claimed that the members of his monastic community were intellectually dull—"naturally slow in comprehension, partial fools, untouched by the Muses, and greater lovers of their bellies than of learning"—and that anyone who showed unusual talent or capacity for learning was squelched and his talent prevented from blooming. Erasmus buried himself in his studies, for "by means of literary pursuits he escaped the tedium of his captivity." Indeed, if the Bishop of Cambrai had not rescued him from the monastery in 1493, there was danger that he would have succumbed to temptation and that "his remarkable talents would have rotted away through idleness, allurements, and drinking parties."[21]

Erasmus tended to look back with scorn on his early education at Deventer, 's-Hertogenbosch, and Steyn. His gloomy accounts, however, need qualification. While he gives the impression of having been in large part a struggling,

---

[19] *EE*, 1: 49–50, ll. 50–86; and no. 447, ll. 81, 86, 92–94, 282–84.
[20] Hyma, *The Youth of Erasmus*, 167–81.
[21] *EE*, no. 447, ll. 373–77, 451–57.

self-made scholar, he probably owed to his teachers and peers at Deventer more than he was ready to admit. The noted grammarian John Xinthen, one of the Brethren of the Common Life, who supervised the studies of and gave supplementary lessons to those staying in the student hostel there, affectionately praised the young Erasmus and encouraged him in his Latin studies, predicting that some day he would reach the summit of learning. Alexander Hegius—friend of Rudolf Agricola, eventual collaborator with Xinthen on a grammar commentary, and headmaster of the school at Deventer—provided Erasmus with a model of the Northern humanist. Hegius exhorted his students in the new learning during Erasmus' final period at the school. While esteeming this schoolmaster, Erasmus claimed in later life that he owed him little. The youthful Erasmus was not the only pupil at Deventer interested in classics. We know of two other students, the cousins Cornelius Gerards and William Hermans, who shared with him their enthusiasm for the classics and later joined him at Steyn in common literary pursuits.[22]

Erasmus' attacks on his former teachers and their methods were not without some basis. His allegation that the Brethren of Common Life, who supervised his studies at Deventer and 's-Hertogenbosch, systematically "tamed" the lively spirits of talented youths in order to mold them for monastic life is partially confirmed by evidence found in other sources.[23] His claims that schooling was made a painful experience, that what was learned had later to be unlearned, and that his teachers were less skilled in Latin than their student probably also contained elements of truth. The training received by the youthful Erasmus had centered on medieval Latin grammars with rules based on logic rather than usage. His propensity for seeing himself as oppressed, however, probably colored his accusations against his teachers. That he exaggerated his plight is suggested by the leadership exerted by some of the Brethren in popularizing a scholarly study of Latin.[24]

What drew the brilliant student Erasmus to classical studies, rather than to rival disciplines such as scholastic theology and canon law, is open to speculation. The initial attraction may have been related to an effort to identify with his absent, classically trained father and to win the attention and affection of his Latin teachers, the father figures most available to him. He was no doubt encouraged in his studies by the exceptional success which greeted his efforts, as he was said to have surpassed all his classmates in his knowledge of Latin.[25] Classical studies also lifted him from his sordid origins and dull surroundings to the great minds of the past and eventually to the learned circles of his own day with their aristocratic patrons. As his comprehension of the humanist culture matured, he probably found a remarkable symmetry between many of the major themes it espoused and his own deeper needs: a flight from this

[22] *Ibid.*, 1: 48, *Compendium*, ll. 39–40 and n.; 1: 57, no. IV, ll. 11–16, 20–27; and Post, *The Modern Devotion*, 576–79, 659, 674–75.
[23] *EE*, 1: 49, *Compendium*, ll. 53–56; no. 447, ll. 103–07; and Post, *The Modern Devotion*, 254–55, 396–97, 660.
[24] *EE*, 1: 48, *Compendium*, ll. 34–36; no. 447, ll. 118–20; no. 2584, ll. 25–29; Post, *The Modern Devotion*, 577, 658–59; and Hyma, *Life of Desiderius Erasmus*, 18–21.
[25] *EE*, 1: 57, no. IV, ll. 16–18.

decadent world to an idyllic past unlike his own; a refined language that allowed him to cloak his own emotions; a quest for peace and concord that provided a defense against his own sense of vulnerability; rhetorical ambiguities that abhorred the clear distinctions, stark assertions, and univocal truths characteristic of scholastic theology (and to a lesser degree of canon law) and that matched the ambiguities of his own personality; a belief that the path of wisdom lay in rhetorical eloquence rather than in the rational analysis of the scholastics, which he found too difficult; and membership in an elite international community of scholars, which allowed him to escape his origins, avoid entangling loyalties, and sink few roots.[26] Erasmus came to appropriate this culture so passionately that he was hailed as its embodiment, the prince of humanists.

One of the more interesting incidents of his years at Steyn was Erasmus' friendship with Servatius Roger. The letters to Servatius reveal an aspect of Erasmus' character that rarely appeared elsewhere: a certain feminine sensitivity and a sentimental need for friendship. Erasmus begged for a return of affection, protesting that Servatius was always in his heart, his only hope, his other self, the solace of his life. "I shall never stop loving you," he finally affirmed.[27] This outburst of sentimental affection seems to reveal a latent homosexuality, which may in part reflect the persistent yearning for his lost father. Servatius, we can note, had the same name Roger as did Erasmus' father. But this sharing of names is not at all necessary. Attempts have been made to excuse this excessive affection by references to models of intimate friendship found in Erasmus' readings of classical literature, to the sentimental friendships then in vogue within and without the monastery walls, to the likely response of one debarred from love and placed in a crude and cold environment, and to a monastic tradition of rhetorical letters. Although such literary expressions of affection were commonplace among Renaissance humanists, Erasmus seldom used them. Apparently Servatius did not reciprocate his effusive and exclusive affection. Erasmus learned to be more restrained; only rarely did he again give expression to his tender feelings. Instead, he became the guarded, yet witty and urbane, humanist who engaged others on a primarily intellectual level. Emotions were measured before being expressed, and it was increasingly the litany of his sorrows that he chose to share.[28]

---

[26] John W. O'Malley, "Erasmus and Luther: Continuity and Discontinuity as Key to Their Conflict," *Sixteenth Century Journal*, 5 (1974): 47–65.

[27] Of his letters to Servatius, see especially *EE*, no. 7, all, and no. 8, ll. 61–68.

[28] Huizinga, *Erasmus*, 11–12; and D. F. S. Thomson, "Erasmus as Poet in the Context of Northern Humanism," *De Gulden Passer*, 47 (1969): 192–97. Hyma sees these letters as expressions of neurotic affection; *The Youth of Erasmus*, 160–62. While the expression of tender affection was common enough in literary, humanistic circles of the period for it to be regarded more or less as a stylistic convention, this does not contradict the interpretation of such utterances as expressing basically homosexual impulses. One of the points at issue between the historical perspective and the psychoanalytic perspective is the extent to which patterns of behavior and expression may be taken to reflect stylistic conventions or cultural variants as opposed to unconscious psychodynamic motivations. There is no inherent reason, however, why such conventions and cultural expressions should not concurrently express psychodynamically significant and multiply (including unconsciously) determined influences. The historical approach prefers to disregard or,

606

A year after ordination to the priesthood, Erasmus left the monastery at Steyn to become secretary to Henry of Bergen, bishop of Cambrai and important member of the Burgundian court. Pleased at first with his new job, Erasmus grew despondent when his duties became routine. The bishop lost interest in him, and a projected journey to Rome never materialized. Brought by his secretarial position into the harsh, bustling world of politics, Erasmus—not unlike other court humanists of his day—longed at times for the leisure to study that Steyn had afforded.[29] We can surmise that Erasmus' apparent depression arose in part from his loss of the safe and protecting—we might almost say "maternal"—environment of the monastery and its quiet seclusion. More significant, however, was the loss of the close and meaningful relationships that he had developed, not only with Servatius, but apparently also with William and Cornelius, his companions at Steyn. Erasmus' dejection is understandable in terms of his need to mourn such an important loss. Yet, on another level, an element of mild dissatisfaction, restiveness, disillusionment, dejection, and even bitterness and resentment pervaded much of his career, suggesting that he felt in some basic sense deprived of what he had a right to expect.

With help from his friend James Batt, Erasmus persuaded his employer to send him to Paris to study theology. The parsimony of his patrons and the difficulty of his scholastic studies at Paris gave Erasmus much room for complaint. He objected to scholastic theology's barren and thorny subtleties, to its indifference to stylistic elegance, and to the arrogance and counterfeit lives of its proponents, especially those "pseudotheologians" who were his Scotist teachers at the Sorbonne.[30] We can grant a significant "kernel of truth" in Erasmus' complaints and still suggest that his hostility and contempt, which persisted over the years, reflected an aspect of Erasmus' narcissism, which found it difficult to acknowledge worth in that which he could not understand or master and hence perceived such an affronting object as hostile.

Erasmus' life at Paris was one of uncertainty and unrest. His health was never very good, and the austerity of his living conditions there weakened it further. He seemed to be continually depressed. He saw himself as an undeserving victim, without the support of friends and so crushed by misfortune that he no longer wished to live. While studying at the Sorbonne he had tried to cultivate friendships with the leading local humanists. But these men were not very responsive to his writings. Unfavorable reports about him reached his

---

at least, to de-emphasize a more remote or esoteric explanation when more tangible, obvious, common sense and historically verifiable explanations are at hand. The psychoanalytic approach, for its part, prefers to emphasize the psychodynamically relevant aspects of the evidence in addition to other available explanations. Thus, the ascribed historical reasons, however valid, do not abrogate the inherent homosexuality of Erasmus' romanticized effusions. One reason, perhaps, for this frequently encountered tension in viewpoints is the congeniality of overdetermination to the psychological mind in contrast to the historian's preference for linear causality.

[29] *EE*, 1: 57–58, no. IV, ll. 39–63; and Huizinga, *Erasmus*, 16–17.
[30] *EE*, no. 64, ll. 6–92, esp. 45–46, 88–92; and no. 108, ll. 20–31.

episcopal patron in Cambrai, endangering his pension. In the hope of supporting himself, Erasmus increasingly turned to tutoring. One of his pupils in Paris was the young Lord Mountjoy, William Blount, who urged Erasmus to visit England. In early 1499, Erasmus made the trip in Mountjoy's retinue.[31]

The year in England opened up new horizons for Erasmus. Traveling in aristocratic circles, he met men of culture and gladly shared in the diversions of court life. At Oxford he came under the influence of the humanist-theologian John Colet, whose exegesis of Scripture departed from the traditional scholastic method, adopted a neoplatonic framework, and employed philology to uncover theological truths in the texts. This approach appealed to the inclinations and linguistic skill of Erasmus. Colet even urged him to lecture on Scripture. In turning down this offer, Erasmus explained that, while secular studies were beneath his ambitions, he lacked as yet the tools necessary for this new theology.[32] First, he must master Greek, the language of the New Testament and of many of the leading Church Fathers. The linguistic skills he perfected in the following years resulted in critical editions of these early Christian writings. His scholarly interests turned more and more to the field of theology—not the speculative theology he had struggled with at Paris, but the philological exegesis of sacred Christian texts learned from Colet.

The strong impression which Colet made on the Dutch humanist may have been related to Erasmus' probably frustrated, but perduring, desires for closeness to a father whose image matched the reality of Colet. Like Colet, his father was reportedly a priest, a man of classical learning, a student of Greek, and a visitor to Italy—the home of humanism. Erasmus openly sought Colet's affection and years later frankly rejoiced in winning it: "He loves me deeply, as everyone knows, and prefers my company to that of anyone else."[33] While there were antecedents in Erasmus' intellectual development for his eventual interest in both Greek literature and a theology utilizing his linguistic skills, the personal example and encouragement of Colet may have led him to dedicate his talents to this "new theology."

On his return to the Continent in 1500, Erasmus devoted himself to the study of Greek, published a collection of Latin and Greek proverbs known as the *Adagia*, and penned his popular handbook on piety, the *Enchiridion Militis Christiani* (1503). Two years after its publication, Erasmus was once again in England, this time in close association with Thomas More. He stayed in More's home, and together they worked on translations of the Greek satirist Lucian. From 1506-09 Erasmus wandered about Italy, gaining a doctorate in theology at Turin, tutoring at first the sons of the English royal physician, Gian Battista Beorio, and then Alexander Stuart, the youthful archbishop of St. Andrews, publishing an enlarged edition of the *Adagia*, visiting with Italian humanists and their patrons, and securing at Rome the friendship of high

---

[31] *Ibid.*, 1: 58, no. IV, ll. 63-80; no. 83, ll. 85-100.
[32] *Ibid.*, no. 108, ll. 95-101.
[33] *Ibid.*, no. 107, ll. 37-69; no. 296, ll. 141-42. For a letter implying that Erasmus was one of Colet's closest friends, see *EE*, no. 1211, ll. 371-78.

churchmen and a dispensation to hold benefices. Hopes of preferment with the accession of the young humanist Henry VIII to the throne of England brought Erasmus back across the Alps. On his journey northward he looked forward to visiting again with his good friend Thomas More, the wisest and wittiest of men, whose surname in Greek ironically means "fool." This piece of philology inspired Erasmus to reflect on the role folly plays in human affairs and to compose mentally a declamation on folly in the style of Lucian as a gift for his friend More.[34]

On arriving in England, Erasmus lived in More's household in Bucklersbury, near London. Here he found warmth, quiet kindliness, and acceptance in a normal family life such as he had never known in his youth. Without his precious books to comfort him (they were still in shipment) Erasmus wrote, within a short time, what must stand as the most uncharacteristic of his works—the *Moriae Encomium* (*Praise of Folly*). It is as if, after years of restraint and repression, all that was capricious, playful, and witty in Erasmus was suddenly given license, and we are allowed to see a part of Erasmus' soul that elsewhere is little visible.

The *Praise of Folly* was more than a satiric commentary on human foibles and delusive self-love; it was a revelation of Erasmus himself, an exquisite and elaborate self-parody. Erasmus—the man of learning, of even pre-eminent learning—made Folly declare "that man is truly the happier who acts the fool in many ways." Or again, "as therefore those professions are the happier which have the greater affinity with Folly, so those people are the happiest by far who have been allowed to abstain absolutely from commerce with all learning and follow nature alone as their guide." It is not learned men, but Folly's followers who are candid and speak the truth, a function not to be despised. "What, moreover, is more praiseworthy than truth?"[35]

The relationship between the mind of Erasmus and the words of Folly has troubled commentators on the *Moriae Encomium*. Literary analyses reveal deliberate ambiguities that at times effectively disguise the author's true views.[36] From another perspective, however, these ambiguities form a consistent pattern explained by Erasmus' personality. In portions of the *Praise of Folly* the more characteristic voice of Erasmus is easily recognizable in its biting cynicism and especially in its excoriating attack upon his favorite targets—the theologians and monks. When the mask of Folly slips, the face of Erasmus is revealed. But even when the mask stays in place, the disguise can still be penetrated. Folly is indeed Erasmus—not the Erasmus usually in evidence, but the Erasmus who, though usually concealed behind a facade of

[34] *Ibid.*, no. 222, ll. 1–24.

[35] Erasmus, *Moriae Encomium* (LB), 4: 440d, 435c, 437e.

[36] A. H. T. Levi, Introduction to Erasmus of Rotterdam, *Praise of Folly and Letter to Martin Dorp, 1515*, trans. Betty Radice (Baltimore, 1971), 15–16. For a careful delineation of the various roles played by Folly, see Bainton, *Erasmus of Christendom*, 91–95. Also see Lynda Gregorian Christian, "The Metamorphoses of Erasmus' Folly," *Journal of the History of Ideas*, 32 (1971): 289–94; Geraldine Thompson, *Under Pretext of Praise: Satiric Mode in Erasmus' Fiction* (Toronto, 1973), 51–85; and Walter Kaiser, *Praisers of Folly: Erasmus, Rabelais, Shakespeare* (Cambridge, Mass., 1963), 91–93.

intellectual urbanity, is much closer to his actual character. The key may be in Folly's claim that shame and fear keep men from learning by experience. Shame clouds the mind, while fear advises against apparent dangers. Folly frees men from both. Few mortals realize the heights they could attain if only they could overcome these two obstacles.[37]

Erasmus, we suggest, was seldom free from the constraints of fear and shame. Perhaps more truly than he knew, the folly of his little *jeu d'esprit* freed him, if but briefly, from their burden. By satirizing self-importance and self-deception, Erasmus in a sense attacked his own weakness and fallibility. Paradoxically, his own folly released him from the tyranny of his shame and self-doubt, but this very release he felt compelled to parody and satirize. If these are the trappings of injured narcissism, we can infer that this burden of self-doubt not only lay at the root of his inner torment, but also served as the prod of his genius.

Once in print, the *Praise of Folly* did not go unnoticed. Erasmus believed that as a man of learning he was entitled to satirize with impunity the foibles of humanity, especially since he had provoked in the process serious reflection. Besides, the ideas and goals of the *Praise of Folly* were much the same as those of his widely acclaimed but more straightforward *Enchiridion*—advice on the true Christian life. While friends such as More appreciated his *Moriae Encomium*, others could neither forgive nor forget those large sections of the work in which they found themselves scoffed at and satirized. But it was perhaps his playful use of the text of the Holy Scripture that caused the most trouble. Many found it too adventuresome. Erasmus' attempts to convince his critics that the purpose of the work was no more than to encourage people to lead virtuous lives were not convincing. Repeatedly, he felt the need to defend it and even commented that, if he had known the book would offend so many, he might not have published it. In later years Erasmus always spoke somewhat disparagingly of this work, regarding it as a trifle, quite out of keeping with his character.[38]

This unique performance, the *Praise of Folly*, must be placed in the context of Erasmus' recollection of the intellectual stimulation and emotional release he had found in the company of English courtiers and humanists, especially of Thomas More. After years of demanding study in the cold confines of a Dutch monastery and amid conditions of hardship and poverty at Paris, Erasmus had encountered in England some of life's pleasures—the aristocratic diversions of banquets and hunts, the polite company of women, and what pleased him most, "men well acquainted with good learning." Recalling these pleasures brought him joy when he was away from England. The friendly encouragement of Colet had inspired his study of Greek and the Christian classics,

---

[37] Erasmus, *Moriae Encomium* (LB), 4: 427c–28a.
[38] *EE*, no. 222, ll. 40–57; no. 337, ll. 26–28, 91–94, 141–45, 569–72, 585–93; no. 597, ll. 7–16; no. 622, ll. 21–30; no. 739, ll. 3–16; no. 749, ll. 3–31, esp. 7–8; no. 967, ll. 180–88; no. 1706, l. 6; no. 2465, ll. 288–309; and no. 2566, ll. 83–84.

and in the companionship of More, Erasmus confessed finding "the most delicious experience life has granted."[39]

More seems to have been for Erasmus the bright sun that broke through the dark clouds. In reply to Ulrich von Hutten's inquiry, Erasmus wrote in 1519 a glowing encomium of More. The portrait of More was enthusiastically idealized, possessing a quality of almost adolescent adulation. More was "the sweetest friend of all." To portray him was like trying to portray Alexander or Achilles, and even those heroes were no more deserving of immorality than More. His kindness and charm were most winning, while his wit gladdened even the most melancholic. He inspired the *Praise of Folly* and was thus responsible "for making the camel dance."[40] We can speculate at this point that More's charm and personal gifts stirred Erasmus' deep yearning for affection. Even though More was twenty years Erasmus' junior, he nonetheless embodied the ideals of learning and loving devotion with which Erasmus probably endowed the memory of his father. The relationship with More perhaps concealed a homosexual longing that had for long been denied—now sublimated and ennobled by an attachment to the character of the saintly Thomas More. It allowed the release and channeling of long repressed energies in Erasmus, which found expression in an outburst of playful inspiration that gave birth to the *Praise of Folly*.[41]

After the passage of a quarter century, Erasmus could no longer express with spontaneity his affection for More. Under Henry VIII More rose to the office of chancellor of England, only to fall from favor because his conscience would not let him take the Oath of Supremacy. Like another of Erasmus' friends, John Fisher, bishop of Rochester, More mounted the scaffold in the summer of 1535. Less than a year away from his own death, Erasmus showed the effects of years of bitter controversy. His shell had thickened, and he could no longer openly express his deep emotions. The fate of Fisher drew dry comments about England's loss and about some details of the execution; More merited both a sigh—a wish that he had left the king's business to theologians—and a philosophic confession: "In More I seem myself to have died since there was but one soul between us both, as Pythagoras says. Yet such is the turbulent course of human affairs."[42]

Erasmus' relation to his other major father figure, Servatius, posed a serious problem for a while. Servatius was now prior of Steyn, to which Erasmus was

---

[39] *Ibid.*, no. 103, ll. 6–25; no. 107, ll. 50–53; and no. 222, ll. 4–8.

[40] *Ibid.*, no. 999, ll. 19–24, 111–20. Louis Bouyer suggests that the *Moriae Encomium* should be attributed to a wholesale appropriation of and intoxication with More's style of humor; *Autour d'Érasme*, 89–90.

[41] One aspect of the dynamics of homosexuality involves the seeking of a narcissistic love object, someone like the idealized self. Usually this pattern is related to a deeper longing for an idealized father, for his love and approval. This may even take the form of identification with the mother, who was loved by the father. The evidence in support of this latter aspect in Erasmus is meager, but the other elements seem clear. It should be noted that More's position, gifts, and personality amply fitted him to fulfill the functions of such a narcissistic object choice by Erasmus. And Erasmus' affiliation with More provided him with a warm family context within which he was received and accepted—something his style of life had otherwise denied him. And of course, More was a loving and genial father. Consequently, the difference in age was incidental since the unconscious is little troubled by dimensions of time.

[42] *EE*, no. 3037, ll. 98–105; no. 3048, ll. 59–60; and no. 3049, ll. 163–64.

ultimately expected to return. Erasmus dreaded this possibility, which became more pressing when the deaths of his patron, Henry of Bergen, and his influential friend, James Batt, left him in precarious financial circumstances. A dispensation allowed him to accept benefices, however, and in a letter to Servatius dated April 1, 1506, Erasmus reported receiving the promise of a curacy from eminent and erudite Englishmen who held him in great esteem. The letter, however, was a study of repentance and renunciation, in which Erasmus demeaned himself as though he despised such worldly honors.[43] But Servatius knew him better than most. Yet for eight years he refrained from exercising his authority as prior to order Erasmus back to Steyn. On July 7, 1514, soon after leaving England and while a guest of Mountjoy at the castle of Hammes near Calais, Erasmus finally received the dreaded order. This terrible blow came at a time when Erasmus had the prospect of fulfilling some of his highest ambitions.

In his reply, written on the following day, Erasmus refused to return and gave a justification—an *apologia pro vita sua*. Erasmus traced the history of his unhappy vocation: how he had been pressured and shamed into entering the religious life; how he had realized that he was unsuited in mind and body for the monastic routine, but for fear of scandal had continued as a canon of St. Augustine with proper dispensation from the rules on dress; how he was revolted at the thought of returning to the boorish and ritualistic routine at Steyn; and how his health, already impaired, would give out completely there. Steyn spelled death—both mental and physical. In counterpoise to this catalogue of complaints about his unhappy vocation, Erasmus enumerated the many scholarly works he had published and influential friends he had made since leaving the monastery. On account of his literary accomplishment he was welcomed everywhere with affection and respect. He claimed as his admirers the most eminent civil and ecclesiastical leaders of England and Rome. He mentioned some of these by name, as if to list the forces he could muster to resist his return to Steyn.[44] The letter was a polite, if firm, rejection of Servatius' summons. It also seems to have served notice on the termination of a type of relationship.

Ironically, Erasmus addressed Servatius as his "kindest Father," and at the end of the letter said, "Farewell, once the sweetest companion of my intimacy, now a Father to be respected."[45] Although some of Erasmus' resentment toward the monastery at Steyn arose from the circumstances of his coming there, another factor was his relationship with Servatius, the "companion of my intimacy," who had apparently rejected his adolescent adulation and affection. And beyond Servatius there likely stood on an unconscious level the figure of his idealized, yet rejecting and abandoning, father. This rejection of his religious superior, his "Father to be respected," can be seen as a manifes-

---

[43] *Ibid.*, no. 189, ll. 1–18.
[44] *Ibid.*, no. 296, ll. 1–5, 8–17, 23–33, 45–69, 98–170.
[45] *Ibid.*, ll. 1, 236–37.

tation of the hidden and repressed anger at the abandoning father of his childhood.

Erasmus made no secret of his feelings about monastic life as practiced at Steyn and elsewhere. He described his fellow monks as lacking a spirit of Christ and priding themselves on their pharisaical ceremonial observances. He decried "the huge mass of monasteries where the practice of piety has so declined that, by comparison, brothels are more temperate and modest." The monastic obligation—"I almost said servitude—is not to be found in the Old or New Testament." And he eased his conscience by declaring that his monastic vows had been taken under duress and were, therefore, not binding.[46] In two letters written by his secretary, Jacopo Sadoleto, on January 26, 1517, Pope Leo X granted Erasmus dispensations that permitted him to dress as a secular priest, to hold ecclesiastical benefices despite his illegitimacy, and to live outside the monasteries of his religious order.[47]

Erasmus' long refusal to maintain a permanent residence reveals a deep inner restlessness. Fear of the plague, demands of health, hope of patronage, collaboration with his publishers, and reasons of scholarship and public service—all were offered as justifications for his endless pilgrimage across Europe. Even toward the end of his life, when he settled at Basel, he was still planning to move on. When contemporaries commented on his seeming instability, he replied that his home was wherever his library and furniture were located. This restlessness may have been an unconscious searching for a family life denied him in youth but enjoyed for a while in the warm and accepting households of men like Thomas More and the printer Hieronymus Froben. His anxieties lest the plague overtake him were probably rooted in the memory that it had killed both his parents. His seeming inability to become attached to a permanent residence may also have been related to a need to see himself as an abandoned victim, without home or loved ones, driven from place to place by the vagaries of cruel fate.[48]

ERASMUS CONTINUED TO PUBLISH WORKS which others found controversial. In the decade after leaving his teaching post at Cambridge, some of the most famous of these writings appeared in print: his edition of the Greek New

---

[46] *Ibid.*, no. 447, ll. 464–65, 554–55, 563–70. For a contrary attitude toward his vows, see *Colloquia*, "Ichtuophagia" (1526), ed. Léon-E. Halkin *et al.* (ASD), 1, pt. 3 (1972): ll. 778–80, p. 516. His unflattering comparison of monasteries to brothels shows a certain sensitivity to and defensiveness against the denunciations of clerical concubinage preached by these friars. Given the circumstances of his own birth, Erasmus on occasion was at pains to play down the wickedness of priestly concubinage and to disparage those who called attention to this evil. He favored the option of marriage for priests and monks since this would help to end concubinage, legitimize their children, and allow noncelibate priests to live in peace. See *Antibarbarorum Liber*, ed. Kazimierz Kumaniecki (ASD), 1, pt. 1 (1969): ll. 1–7, p. 75; *EE*, no. 858, ll. 417–39; no. 1188, ll. 8–14; *Epistola apologetica de interdicto esu carnium* (1522) (LB), 9: 1201a–02a; and *De conscribendis epistolis* (1521), ed. Jean-Claude Margolin (ASD), 1, pt. 2 (1971): l. 7, p. 417; l. 10, p. 418.

[47] *EE*, no. 517, esp. ll. 36–60; and no. 518.

[48] *Ibid.*, no. 296, ll. 94–101; no. 809, ll. 117–26; no. 1236, ll. 177–84; no. 1319, ll. 15–17; no. 1479, l. 181; and no. 3032, ll. 197–232. The dimensions of abandonment, deprivation, vulnerability, and victimization are the negative correspondents of the investments of the narcissistic sense of entitlement and omnipotence. See Heinz Kohut, *The Analysis of the Self* (New York, 1971).

The Character of Erasmus 613

Testament, the *Novum Instrumentum* and subsequent *Paraphrases*, his *Querela Pacis*, the *Colloquia*, and his editions of Church Fathers. These publications won him patrons and praise and a host of critics with whom he often engaged in extended public controversy. Of all his opponents, the most important was probably Martin Luther, and the issues over which they fought were neither moot points in an obscure text nor the potential for scandal in Erasmus' works. The argument was for both men essentially theological, but it also reached the core of their respective personalities and intellectual traditions.[49]

At the beginning of the Reformation controversy, Erasmus found himself in sympathy with Luther's call for a more interior religious experience, with his criticisms of certain Church practices and of current scholasticism, and with his return to the Scriptures. He was unhappy, however, with the harsh tone of the friar's writings, with the suspicions they stirred of Erasmus' co-authorship, and with the danger they posed of arousing further opposition to a theology based on early Christian writings.[50] In his initial letters to Luther and other leaders, he professed a friendly but noncommittal attitude toward the Reformer, claiming that he had not as yet read Luther's works, while advising him to avoid anger, arrogance, and ambition. He also counseled both sides to moderation and tried to arrange arbitration of the controversy.[51] Eventually, Erasmus realized that the disparity between himself and Luther was not merely one of tone but of teaching. Erasmus stood firmly with the humanistic reform tradition, some of whose elements he had delineated as early as 1503 in his *Enchiridion*, a tradition which called for a reform of morals and not of doctrine. By the time Luther arrived on the scene, however, the moralism of Erasmus' earlier works was already giving way to a concern for doctrine that centered on the "mystery of Christ." Luther's increasingly vehement demand for a change in Church teachings reinforced Erasmus' orientation toward traditional dogma. Even though Erasmus found himself in disagreement with aspects of the German's theology, he still shied away from drawing that ultimate conclusion that would have served as the postulate for decisive action. Only when pressured at last into confronting Luther in print did Erasmus submit to calm and careful scrutiny the Wittenberg theologian's position on free will.[52] Because Luther responded with open invective to the Dutchman's gentle, but semi-Pelagian, treatise, Erasmus felt himself

---

[49] For a clear presentation of the differences between their respective intellectual traditions, see O'Malley, "Erasmus and Luther," 47–64. For a psychoanalytic study of the roots in Luther's personality for his embittered attacks on the Church, see Erikson, *Young Man Luther*.

[50] For a brief summary of the principal features of Erasmus' reform program, see Cornelis Augustijn, *Erasmus en de Reformatie: Een onderzoek naar de houding die Erasmus ten opzichte van de Reformatie heeft aangenomen* (Amsterdam, 1962), 305. *EE*, no. 939, ll. 44–113; no. 980, ll. 4–10; no. 1033, ll. 59–175, 195–200, 204–28, 238–40; no. 1119, ll. 36–37; no. 1141, ll. 24–30; no. 1153, ll. 30–38; no. 1156, ll. 35–48; no. 1202, ll. 31–50, 207–12, 257–60; and no. 1688, ll. 28–35.

[51] *EE*, no. 980, ll. 17–18, 37–51; no. 1033, ll. 38–40, 50–58; no. 1141, ll. 8–13; and no. 1202, ll. 34–65, 178–84, 262–66.

[52] Erasmus, *De libero arbitrio diatribe sive collatio* (LB), 9: 1215–48, and his later reflections in *De amabili ecclesiae concordia* (LB), 5: 500b–e; and Georges Chantraine, *"Mystère" et "Philosophie du Christ" selon Érasme: Étude de la lettre à P. Volz et de la "Ratio verae theologiae" (1518)*, Bibliothèque de la Faculté de Philosophie et Lettres de Namur, part 49 (Gembloux, Belgium, 1971), 227–35, 368–93.

wronged. His initial attempts at arbitration and subsequent dissociation from the controversy had proved unsuccessful. Pressured into taking a public stand, he sided with the traditional Church. While he affirmed his own orthodoxy, his sympathies on many nondogmatic points lay with the reformers, although for reasons different from theirs.[53]

Erasmus' stance in the Lutheran controversy can be variously explained. He was part of—indeed, an unwilling spokesman for—that group known as the Moderates, which included among its adherents important men from the liberal wings of both the traditional Church and the camp of the reformers. The dynamics of polarization which exaggerated the distance between Wittenberg and Rome made this moderate position increasingly difficult for Erasmus to maintain. He was under both external and internal pressures to side with one of the groups against the other. Catholic conservatives like Pio and Aleander questioned his orthodoxy when he refused to join their party. Followers of Luther accused him of betraying the Gospel out of cowardice and in hopes of personal profit. Forces within his psyche also urged him to abandon the religious position he had evolved over many years. To side with the more destructive elements within the Lutheran faction would have allowed him to vent his resentments against the parental Church, but would also have meant giving up the security and authority it represented. To join the conservative camp within the Church would have implied a rejection of the rebellious spirit Luther embodied and an endorsement of the Church with all its faults. Erasmus could disown neither his resentments nor his longings for acceptance. By maintaining this moderate religious stance, he could not only remain consistent with his long-standing religious beliefs, but also leave unresolved this transferred ambivalence toward the parental Church. He was both drawn to controversy and repelled by it.[54]

Erasmus was probably sincere in professing a dislike for confrontation, but polemics provided him with an outlet for his pent-up resentment. Once engaged in verbal combat, he could not resist inflicting wounds with his derisive and rapierlike pen. The venom of his attacks and the apparent relish

[53] *EE*, no. 1688, ll. 2-9; no. 1033, ll. 256-60; and Erasmus, *De amabili ecclesiae concordia* (LB), 5: 497c-98b. Augustijn has traced the humanist's stance with regard to the reformers in much greater detail; *Erasmus en de Reformatie*, esp. pp. 305-09. The publication of Luther's *De captivitate Babylonica* in 1520 apparently hindered Erasmus' first attempts at securing an arbitration, but he tried again under Adrian VI and Clement VII only to find both sides intransigent. For several years Erasmus thought the controversy was over nonessentials, but he became aware of significant differences when the debate focused on the Eucharist. Then Erasmus came to a recognition of the doctrinal issues at stake and to a deeper appreciation for the role of tradition in interpreting the Sacred Scriptures. He felt that the failure of the Diet of Augsburg effectively ended all hopes of compromise. During the last fourteen years of his life Erasmus more and more came to accept the traditional Church and urge that reform remain within its fold.

[54] Smith, *Erasmus*, 440; and Phillips, *Erasmus and the Northern Renaissance*, 219-21. Erasmus' posture in contrast with Luther's more declarative stance was echoed in a well-known sixteenth-century epigram: "Where Erasmus merely nodded, Luther rushed in; where Erasmus laid the eggs, Luther hatched the chicks; where Erasmus merely doubted, Luther laid down the law"; as quoted in Crane Brinton *et al.*, *A History of Civilization*, 1 (Englewood Cliffs, N.J., 1957): 455. For a detailed study of his relations with each of his conservative Catholic opponents, see Myron Piper Gilmore, "Erasmus and Alberto Pio, Prince of Carpi," in Theodore K. Rabb and Jerrold E. Seigel, eds., *Action and Conflict in Early Modern Europe: Essays in Memory of E. H. Harbison* (Princeton, N.J., 1969), 299-318.

with which he launched them are perhaps most clearly seen in his comments on monks and theologians. While Erasmus sincerely wished to live in peace and quiet and to dedicate himself to "good learning," he also needed to justify himself in the eyes of the world, as well as in his own eyes. Toward the end, the constant struggle took its toll. He confessed to being so exhausted that he was seriously thinking of withdrawing from controversies.[55] In the closing decade of his life, Erasmus retired from the Reformation battles at Basel for the quiet of Freiburg im Breisgau, continued his critical editions of the Fathers, and penned works of piety and pleas for peace: on preaching—*Ecclesiastes sive De Ratione Concionandi* (1535), on mending the peace of the Church—*De Sarcienda Ecclesiae Concordia* (1533), and on preparing for death—*De Preparatione ad Mortem* (1534). He returned to Basel in 1535, dying there on July 12, 1536.

A REMARKABLE DISPARITY EXISTED BETWEEN the public persona and intellectual achievement of Erasmus and his personal attitudes and behavior. Although hailed as the leading humanist of his day and esteemed as a gentle man of peace and moderation, he was often haunted by unhappiness, dissatisfaction, and despondency. In his dealings with others he usually maintained his distance, was guarded and suspicious, and at times even spitefully small and resentful. Self-doubt and insecurity pervaded his life. Although philosophic considerations and social conditions not unlike those common among Italian humanists may have reinforced tendencies already within his character, they do not of themselves adequately explain his pessimism.[56] Poor health, faithless friends, inveterate poverty, and Herculean labors without reward pursued him relentlessly—or at least so it seemed.[57] He presented himself as utterly wretched and worthy of mankind's scorn, riddled with self-contempt and self-doubt. Revenge on his enemies—his weapon was the pen—could on occasion give him reason to go on living.[58] Even marriage promised no happiness—"Any man who marries must prepare his mind for the

---

[55] *EE*, no. 237, ll. 6–7; no. 476, ll. 67–71; no. 980, ll. 46–51; no. 2136, ll. 150–84; and no. 2522, ll. 53–65.
[56] Charles Edward Trinkaus, *Adversity's Noblemen: The Italian Humanists on Happiness* (New York, 1940), 141–50.
[57] *EE*, 1: 51, *Compendium Vitae*, ll. 141–44; no. 31, ll. 5–11; no. 83, ll. 85–102; no. 145, ll. 51–62; no. 296, ll. 23–33; no. 325, ll. 58–63; no. 551, ll. 3–4, 15–16; no. 552, ll. 10–11; no. 893, ll. 1–28; no. 1102, ll. 2–9; no. 1136, ll. 19–20; and no. 1352, ll. 115–17. For the plottings of Eppendorff against him, see no. 1437, ll. 8–209. For a recent treatment of Erasmus' physical ailments which raises the question of psychological origins, see Hyacinthe Brabant, *Érasme: Humaniste dolent* (Quebec, 1971), 103–04.
[58] Erasmus on occasion could be so depressed that he almost longed for death as an end to his woes. See, for example, *EE*, no. 83, ll. 90–109; and no. 2798, ll. 26–37. On one occasion, when he thought his death was imminent, he was determined to strain every nerve in order to get a fitting revenge on his critics before the end; see *EE*, no. 138, ll. 44–57. The desire for revenge remained with him even when fame and fortune came his way. Granted that bitter polemics are readily found in the words of some of the humanists, the biting passages in Erasmus' writings, while generally much muted in comparison, are not mere imitations of his peers' invectives nor only a response in kind but replies that served his own inner needs.

eventualities that are common to mankind: sterility in his wife, childlessness, loneliness."[59]

Erasmus was disillusioned. The religio-humanistic ideals of peace and concord, which, together with moderation, he so fervently espoused, were seldom realized.[60] A smoldering rage seemed to color his experience and to diffuse itself more generally against all mankind. It was a rage he recognized and tried to rationalize: "Besides, one whose criticism leaves no class of men untouched is, it would seem, angry at no single man but at all forms of vice. Therefore, if there is anyone who will cry that he has been insulted, he will betray either a guilty or certainly a worried conscience." Buried in this passage is one of those clues for which the psychologist looks. Erasmus may well have been angry at *one single man*—the father who had rejected and abandoned him. This anger was, however, displaced as generalized hostility.[61] Erasmus saw himself abandoned in a world where there were few wise men (one of whom was himself) and many who were willing to settle for those illusions that sustained their shallow happiness. Not only did the world ignore his wisdom, but his literary works and the taxing and time-consuming task of editing old manuscripts seemed to win him little recognition or appreciation and brought upon him only a storm of ill will. He was dissatisfied with himself and his work. Almost as soon as his publications came off the press he found it necessary to revise and supplement them. The burdens of scholarship weighed upon him, and he longed to escape. In his brief autobiography he appears discontented with his literary accomplishments. While he held wealth and honor in contempt, he treasured leisure and freedom for scholarly pursuits.[62]

From the mouth of Folly came a description of the "wise man," which must pass at least in part as a self-portrait:

Imagine some model of wisdom to set up against this fool, a man who has frittered away all his boyhood and youth in acquiring learning, has squandered the most pleasant part of his life in endless vigils, cares, and labors. Lest indeed in the whole remainder of his life he taste even a drop of pleasure, he is always thrifty, impoverished, sad, gloomy, harsh and unjust to himself, severe and unpopular with others, worn out with a pallor, thinness, ill-health, sore eyes, and with an old age and hoary

---

[59] *Ibid.*, no. 541, ll. 1–6; no. 2684, ll. 35–39; he could also express conditional optimism on the chances for a happy and fruitful marriage, e.g., *Colloquia*, "Proci et Puellae" (1523) (ASD), 1, pt. 3: ll. 227–357, pp. 283–87.

[60] We do not want to give the impression that Erasmus was always disillusioned with life or disappointed in his friends. He experienced bursts of optimism, and he also maintained a number of close friends even in his periods of deepest despondency. These positive experiences, however, did not significantly alter his more typical and habitual patterns of thinking, feeling, and relating to others.

[61] *EE*, no. 222, ll. 62–68. The psychological interpretation of this passage requires some explanation. On a conscious level, Erasmus was protesting equivalently: "If my criticism touches all classes of men, then I am not angry with any one man but with all vices." An unconscious translation would take the following form: "If I criticize all men, it is because I am really angry at one." The one primary figure who stood forth as the leading object of this denied, repressed, and unconscious resentment was Erasmus' abandoning father. In the clinical setting the analyst might wait for additional evidence to confirm this hypothesis. The psycho-historian can only appeal to its congruence with other known elements of the subject's life. For the role of negation as the conscious substitution for repression, see Sigmund Freud, "Negation" (1925), in *Standard Edition*, 19 (1961): 233–39.

[62] Erasmus, *Moriae Encomium* (LB), 4: 451d–452a; *EE*, 1: 51, *Compendium*, ll. 141–45; 2: 183–84; no. 325, ll. 58–63; no. 402, ll. 1–3; no. 966, ll. 30–33; and no. 2299, ll. 103–08.

crop of hair acquired long before their time, someone fleeing from life before his final day. And yet what difference does it make when a man like that, who has never lived, does die? There you have that admirable image of a wise man.[63]

None of this, of course, rings entirely true; the image which Erasmus presents of a humble, self-effacing, and deprived scholar is only half of the picture. Even his attempts at resignation, honest and sincere though they may have been, are not really convincing. Erasmus pictured himself as resignedly playing the part assigned to him in life, yet he continued to grumble, for he saw his role as a lowly and miserable one.[64] On a deeper level existed another Erasmus who was arrogant and vengeful, intent on his own convenience, and resentful of his lot in life. He found this Erasmus difficult to acknowledge either to himself or to others.

Although he continued to long for intimacy, he kept his friends at a distance, as though he feared they might recognize his vulnerability, which may have been related to, but not entirely derived from, the circumstances of his birth. The threat posed by intimacy made him suspicious of friends and fearful of ever being his idealized self—the open, sincere, and loyal friend with only his heart to offer. His difficulties in establishing close friendships had a deeper origin in his narcissism. He was fundamentally a solitary person, whose loneliness was in large measure self-centered. Friends, he found, could be fickle and inconstant—and he turned from them to learning, the only thing that seemed to survive the flux of fortune. His ideas, his accomplishments, his position, his name increasingly became the criteria for viewing everything else. The fame which scholarship won only served to reinforce that side of him which saw the world in terms of his own needs and ambitions. As the years passed, his enormous correspondence became little more than a protracted self-justification and self-defense.[65]

Particularly galling to the independent spirit of Erasmus was his need for financial support, particularly in the early years of his career. The necessity for begging and wringing money from his friends, however willing they were to contribute it, was a source of inner discontent.[66] Early on, Erasmus sought to make himself less dependent on unreliable patrons by taking back to the Continent the money he accumulated while in England during 1499–1500. Having been misinformed by More and Mountjoy that a recent law prohibiting the export of species did not apply to foreign currencies, he watched helplessly while English customs officials confiscated his savings as he was about to sail. The English tyrant had robbed him of the rewards of his learning, yet Erasmus feared to lose the affection of Englishmen like Mountjoy should he take revenge with his pen. Instead, he published a collection of classical proverbs known as the *Adagia*, dedicating it to Mountjoy. But his

---

[63] Erasmus, *Moriae Encomium* (LB), 4: 438e–39a.

[64] *EE*, no. 2443, ll. 417–19.

[65] *Ibid.*, no. 107, ll. 44–46; no. 272, ll. 1–5; no. 1206, ll. 113–14; and no. 145, l. 70; and Huizinga, *Erasmus*, 122.

[66] *EE*, no. 138, ll. 36–44; no. 139, ll. 25–31, 50–52; no. 145, ll. 51–99.

bitterness lingered. Nine years later, Mountjoy hoped that the accession of Henry VIII would finally end his resentment.[67] The episode is revealing. Fate had snatched a comfortable sum of money from his pocket; to be without money was to become like a slave.[68] The misfortune at Dover demonstrates Erasmus' readiness to see himself as oppressed, to cast blame even on a helpful friend, and to remain for years resentful of an injury.

The marked ambiguity of Erasmus' mind can be interpreted as a matter of philosophic conviction. But it also reflects his basic indecision, ambivalence, and reluctance to commit himself to a decisive course of thought or action. He asserted, while behind the mask of Folly, that "man's happiness . . . depends on opinions. For human affairs are so varied and obscure that nothing can be clearly known of them, as has been rightly stated by my Academicians, the least arrogant of the philosophers. . . . Finally, man's mind is so formed that it is far more susceptible to pretence than to truth."[69] In his debate with Luther, Erasmus expressed this same sympathy with the academicians or skeptics, but was careful to circumscribe it: "And, in fact, so far am I from delighting in 'assertions' that I would readily take refuge in the position of the Skeptics, wherever this is allowed by the inviolable authority of the Holy Scriptures and by the decrees of the Church, to which I everywhere willingly yield my assent, whether I grasp what it prescribes or not."[70] When revealing his inner convictions, Erasmus often took pains to qualify or disavow them. This is perhaps most evident at the end of the *Moriae Encomium* where he disclaimed his many critical statements on the artful ground that they came from the mouth of Folly. Confrontation was not to his taste. There was frequently a reserve, an uncertainty, a partial displacement of the center of intention, so that his readers were never sure whose sentiments and opinions they were reading. He tended to avoid direct action, not merely out of suspicion or caution, but because he immersed himself in the eternal uncertainties of human existence.[71]

This desire to persevere in ambiguities is evident in his relationship with Martin Luther. When Luther first openly sought his support, Erasmus retreated to a policy of studied ambiguity. This action was consistent with his fear of controversy, his inner sense of weakness and vulnerability, and also his characteristic dislike of taking sides with any person or any cause save those

---

[67] *Ibid.*, 1: 16–17, no. 1, ll. 1–10, 19–37; no. 145, ll. 53–58, 92–94; and no. 215, ll. 23–27.

[68] *Ibid.*, no. 119, ll. 7–8; no. 139, ll. 51–52; and no. 227, ll. 20–22.

[69] Erasmus, *Moriae Encomium* (LB), 4: 450c; and *EE*, no. 713, l. 18.

[70] Erasmus, *De libero arbitrio diatribe* (LB), 9: 1215d.

[71] *EE*, 5: 76, no. 1292. Allen's introduction quotes B. Hubmaier on Erasmus' reluctance to write down his opinions on controversial matters; while commenting on controversial topics in his *Colloquia*, Erasmus claimed a different purpose. See *EE*, no. 1262, ll. 11–15; and no. 1476, ll. 8–11; and Preserved Smith, *A Key to the Colloquies of Erasmus*, Harvard Theological Studies, no. 13 (Cambridge, Mass., 1927), 2. In his *De utilitate colloquiorum* (1526/29) (ASD), 1, pt. 3 (1927): ll. 29–368, pp. 742–51, Erasmus admitted that his purpose went beyond teaching a refinement of language; *EE*, no. 337, ll. 89–120, 432–48, 542–47; *The Polemics of Erasmus of Rotterdam and Ulrich von Hutten*, trans. and annotated by Randolph J. Klawiter (Notre Dame, 1977), p. 209, section 243; and Erasmus, *Moriae Encomium* (LB), 4: 504c; and *Responsio ad Annotationes Eduardi Lei in Erasmum Novas* (1520) (LB), 9: 273b. Erikson refers to him as "Erasmus the All-Adjustable"; *Young Man Luther*, 147.

most general causes of religious reform and "good learning." In addition, it conformed to his deep and abiding conviction that neither of the conflicting opinions could express or encompass the whole truth and that human passions of hatred and excessive enthusiasm tend to distort men's minds. While committing the final outcome of the conflict to Christ, he eventually embraced an active policy of mediation. "I urge everyone I can to keep from taking sides and exhort both factions to come together on fair terms, if possible, so that little by little harmony might return."[72] This position was also characteristically Erasmian. He opted for the safe middle course, preserving all aspects of ambiguity, committing himself to no faction, and holding what proved to be a vain hope that, by not giving offense, peaceful accord would be achieved.

Erasmus' style was neither to seek out followers nor to form a faction. He avoided leadership, even of the so-called Moderates. He claimed no disciples for himself, but urged all to follow the teachings of Christ and persevere in the traditions of the Church.[73] If his loyalties remained with the Church, he refused to commit his prestige and energies to an ardent defense. The *De Libero Arbitrio Diatribe* was written reluctantly, and the leadership it offered was transient and ephemeral. His craving for affection and acceptance led him to try to give the least displeasure to the most people and, if possible, to placate all. Ironically, this effort aroused the wrath of both parties. His real enemies, he claimed, were only those who opposed good learning and evangelical truth.[74]

IN APPARENT CONTRADICTION TO HIS LONGING for acceptance was Erasmus' desire to play the part of a silent victim, one who avoided controversy wherever possible and did not respond to personal attacks.[75] Beneath this "Erasmian" spirit of moderation lay the wish to be a patiently suffering, disadvantaged, and unfortunate victim. Although Erasmus' personality contained many vagaries that can be regarded as more or less normal, he also displayed paranoid tendencies. He was plagued by persecutors: boorish teachers who sought to break his spirit, guardians who wasted his inheritance and pressured him into the monastery, a brother who left him in the lurch, false companions who seduced him into the religious life, fellow monks who opposed his literary interests, professors at the Sorbonne who squandered his time with their "supersubtleties," patrons who let him live in poverty, customs officials who robbed him of his earnings, ignorant critics of his *Moriae Encomium* and *Novum Instrumentum* who ridiculed him before the illiterate rabble, Luther and his followers who accused him of skepticism and Epicureanism, conservative Catholics who blamed him for having laid the egg

---

[72] *EE*, no. 337, ll. 414–29; no. 933, Introduction and ll. 1–37; no. 939, ll. 87–102; no. 980, esp. ll. 17–18, 47–49; no. 1033, ll. 57–68; and no. 1526, ll. 140–44.

[73] *Ibid.*, no. 2690, ll. 37–40; and no. 2845, ll. 3–6, 33–38.

[74] *Ibid.*, no. 1156, ll. 35–45; no. 1167, ll. 436–41; no. 1352, ll. 42–78, 115–17; no. 1411, ll. 13–28; no. 1419, ll. 2–3; no. 1488, ll. 24–35; no. 1496, ll. 167–92; no. 1526, ll. 48–85; and no. 1670, ll. 20–24.

[75] *Ibid.*, no. 2443, ll. 115–19.

which Luther hatched, Heinrich von Eppendorff whose spies constantly surveyed his activities and even intercepted his correspondence, Aleander who set others in opposition to his ideas and wishes and stood guard lest Erasmus withdraw from the Catholic camp, and Italians who slandered him for mocking their national pride. The list seems endless.[76]

Erasmus saw himself as an innocent victim struggling for survival. After spending himself in the service of others by his dedication to belles-lettres and to the advancement of true religion, he seemed to have gained little but hostility. The right of self-defense was the least he could claim. Even his favorite saint, the irascible Jerome, had retaliated on less provocation.[77] Erasmus dealt with attackers in a number of ways. While avoiding the coarse invectives typical of his time, he did resort to occasional name-calling and dismissed some critics as ignorant slanderers, playing to riffraff. He accused others of envy and fear of his learning. He tried to ignore the injuries inflicted on him but was not always successful.[78] Although Erasmus longed at times for vengeance, he was ambivalent about it. The need to refute false charges of impiety, he insisted, was all that led him to counterattack. The desire for revenge he discounted as a pinprick that touched the surface and went no deeper. His advice as a Christian was to ignore provocation, provided one's silence did not lead to scandal.[79] In spite of such denials and restraints on venting anger, Erasmus repeatedly succumbed to his desire for revenge. His attack on the Scottish guardian of his former pupil Thomas Grey was spiteful and scurrilous. In his quarrel with the youthful critic Edward Lee, Erasmus impugned his opponent's motives and belittled his abilities. Ulrich von Hutten did not live long enough to read Erasmus' vindictive *Spongia Adversus Aspergines Hutteni* (1523). Hutten's defender, Heinrich von Eppendorff, was in turn mercilessly defamed.[80] As in other incidents, a false charge of impiety was not Erasmus' sole reason for retaliation.[81]

To rationalize and justify his paranoid disposition was also consistent with Erasmus' personality. He spiritualized it so as to see himself as a second Suffering Servant, a humble sinner, the innocent victim of evil and malicious

---

[76] *Ibid.*, no. 1268, ll. 61–75; no. 1342, ll. 134–47; no. 1352, ll. 91–104; no. 1479, ll. 184–85; no. 1528, ll. 11–17; no. 1690, ll. 18–47; no. 1934, ll. 255–356; no. 2395, ll. 2–4; no. 2400, ll. 27–36; no. 2565, ll. 7–13; no. 2892, ll. 37–44; no. 2906, ll. 67–70; no. 2936, ll. 46–77; no. 3032, ll. 115–601, esp. 233–70; no. 3130, ll. 17–18; and 11: 226, n. to no. 3052, together with 11: 322, Introduction to no. 3120. These last two references suggest that Erasmus' paranoid disposition had reached the frankly delusional state of a "diseased imagination."

[77] *Ibid.*, no. 222, ll. 68–72; no. 778, ll. 222–50; no. 1139, ll. 67–75; no. 1144, ll. 15–19; and no. 1352, ll. 115–17.

[78] *Ibid.*, no. 64, ll. 89–92; no. 108, ll. 20–37; no. 138, ll. 53–58; no. 337, ll. 327–29; no. 476, ll. 67–69; no. 541, ll. 81–82; no. 809, ll. 18–21, 64–67, 83–84; no. 2443, ll. 115–19; and no. 2651, ll. 38–42.

[79] *Ibid.*, no. 778, ll. 237–38; no. 980, ll. 46–49; no. 2136, ll. 150–84; and no. 2443, ll. 83–84.

[80] *Ibid.*, no. 58, ll. 13–126; no. 998, ll. 26–55; no. 1053, ll. 197–207, 299–317; no. 1437, ll. 8–9; no. 1934, ll. 251–435; no. 2088, ll. 125–30; and *The Polemics of Erasmus and von Hutten*, 177, 186, 196, 208, 221, 223, 233, 240–41, 243, secs. 127, 163, 197, 236, 294, 304–05, 354, 390, 393, 399, 402.

[81] *EE*, no. 138, ll. 49–51; no. 2203, ll. 8–12; and no. 2443, ll. 46–196. The motif of revenge is closely interwoven with the fabric of narcissistic vulnerability, sensitivity, and injury. See Heinz Kohut, "Thoughts on Narcissism and Narcissistic Rage," *Psychoanalytic Study of the Child*, 27 (1972): 360–400. Kohut's description of aspects of narcissistic rage is a general one and not directly applicable in every way to Erasmus. Its purpose is to support the links between the revenge motif and other aspects of a narcissistically vulnerable character structure.

men, who abused him and even sought to drive him to the cross. Behind their actions Erasmus saw the hand of God scourging him to correct him. He was willing to submit to God's judgments with patience and peace.[82] How better to be a suffering victim than to be scourged by the hand of God?

The whole corpus of Erasmian writings was, in a sense, an elaborate self-justification. When Erasmus described himself to Colet, he combined, while protesting the contrary, false modesty and boasting: he was poor in material goods since he shunned ambition; he lacked learning but admired it ardently; he acknowledged his own deficiencies, while esteeming the good in others; he was unassuming, for he decried pretense; in sum, he was diffident but honest. As if to balance off these few negative qualities, he concluded by claiming to be "simple, open, free, with . . . only his heart to offer"[83]—a rather idealized self-conception! Now and again appeared a touch of self-glorification, even grandiosity. With rhetorical flourish he wrote to his friend Batt, comparing himself to other theologians: "Their sermons are full of trite sayings; I am writing words destined to live forever. Their ignorant nonsense is heard in one church or other; my books will be read by students of Latin and Greek in every nation of the world. A superabundance of ignorant theologians exists everywhere, while one like me is rarely found in many centuries." But then he felt compelled to disqualify what he had written as "a few little white lies."[84]

Side by side with these dark elements in Erasmus' character were ennobling qualities. He embraced honorable ideals and longed for a Christian society raised on an ethical basis and permeated with a fervent faith. He passionately desired simplicity, gentleness, kindliness, moderation, tolerance, and peace. For him the road to true happiness lay along the path of "good learning" and particularly the study of Sacred Scripture and of ancient commentaries upon it. He affirmed that a truly religious impulse lies in the direction of charity and love of neighbor, which should manifest itself in doing good for others no matter how meager the rewards.[85] Yet, to a significant degree, the ideals and virtues that he espoused were not altogether divorced from the more pathological aspects of his character. Thus, for example, his ardent advocacy of gentleness, moderation, tolerance, and peace arose in part from his need for a defense against his sense of vulnerability. And yet he himself was repeatedly guilty of the very anger, arrogance, and pettiness he urged others to avoid.

The contradictory and enigmatic element in the character of Erasmus is revealed by the dispute over his motto, *Concedo nulli* ("I yield to no one"). His critics charged that it showed an arrogance that Erasmus vehemently denied. His spirit, he protested, was closer to the Socratic adage, "This alone I know, that I know nothing."[86] But his denial and labored rationalization ring

[82] *Ibid.*, no. 2892, ll. 132–43; and no. 2205, ll. 23–58.
[83] *Ibid.*, no. 107, ll. 38–46.
[84] *Ibid.*, no. 138, ll. 63–66, 82–85; no. 139, ll. 36–42, 60–62; see also no. 421, ll. 100–02; and no. 2299, ll. 103–13. With due regard to the rhetorical tradition evident in letters such as no. 139, we maintain that psychological factors are also operative.
[85] *Ibid.*, no. 186, ll. 10–12; no. 237, ll. 83–85; and no. 364, ll. 26–32, 38–42.
[86] *Ibid.*, no. 2018, ll. 1–72.

hollow. Curiously, he argued that the motto did not apply to himself, a position similar to one already noted in his *Praise of Folly.* Erasmus' defense suggests that the charge contains the seed of truth. Erasmus was, indeed, an arrogant man. His urbane and gentle bearing and the polished style of his writings were an elaborate attempt to veil this inner arrogance—itself the mask of his deeper sense of vulnerability and victimization.

ENOUGH FRAGMENTS HAVE BEEN GATHERED to assemble a final portrait. In so doing it is important to note that the perspective and language change. Until now emphasis has been on documenting aspects of Erasmus' character and situating them in the context of his life and times. Attention to the limitations of more commonly accepted historical evidence has resulted in those numerous qualifications on statements about his character that probably appear overly cautious to the experienced psychoanalyst. He is also not satisfied with the aggregate data, no matter how valid, until it begins to take shape in some consistent and clinically recognizable form. In conclusion, then, emphasis on a cautious historical investigation and validation will be replaced by concern for a clear and coherent psychoanalytic interpretation of Erasmus' character.

The thread that joins many aspects of his character is injured narcissism. From the very beginning his self-esteem was under attack. His early life, as described in his letters and in the *Compendium Vitae*, was for him a continual saga of deprivation, disappointment, frustration, resentment, and caustic criticism of many with whom he came in contact—a bitter tale of entitlements denied and expectations disappointed. The absent and longed-for father cannot be taken as the single cause for the injury. Nor can it conclusively be asserted that the circumstances of Erasmus' birth, his illegitimacy, and the early abandonment by his father did, in fact, shape his adult character. But it can be said that the overall *Gestalt* of Erasmus' personality and behavior is congruent with such a model derived from clinical experience. Undoubtedly, other hypotheses could be generated to explain the data, but such hypotheses, too, would have to meet the same criteria of validity and are likely to be less convincing than the more obvious one on which this article is based.

Erasmus lived under what Gregory Rochlin calls "the tyranny of narcissism."[87] His life appears to have been an incessant seeking for recognition, acceptance, and adulation from his fellow man. Questioning or criticism of his

---

[87] Rochlin, *Man's Aggression: The Defense of the Self* (Boston, 1973), esp. 217–48. Since narcissism is central to an understanding of the character of Erasmus, some definition of the term may be useful. Rochlin's description will serve this purpose: "The compelling imperative for self-preservation is self-love. It expresses itself in an endless lust for a rewarding image of oneself, whether that image is seen in a glass or in another's eye. The further passion for praise, honor and glory makes for an endless marathon. We enter it remarkably early in our existence and leave it only when we expire. Self-love is a process subject to development, responsive to the vagaries of our fantasies as well as to the circumstances of our lives; it is a governing tyrannical principle of human experience, to which aggression responds as a bonded servant. Neither metaphor nor a mere label, narcissism, this love of self, is the human psychological process through which preserving the self is assured. In infancy, childhood, maturity and old age, the necessity of protecting the self may require all our capabilities. And, when narcissism is threatened, we are humiliated, *our self-esteem is injured, and aggression appears*"; Rochlin, *Man's Aggression*, 1.

motives or performance could prompt in him an anxious and threatened response which mobilized his resources and rushed them to the defense of his embattled narcissism. Erasmus' sense of self-worth and self-esteem was continually in jeopardy and required constant reinforcement. His feelings of inadequacy were reflected in his depression, disillusionment, skepticism, and isolation. Much of his Herculean literary labor can be seen as a gigantic effort to redeem some sense of inner value, as though he sought to build an outer facade of accomplishment and sophistication to conceal a self-perception of worthlessness and vileness.

Erasmus' despondency, the result of denied or frustrated narcissism, can be related to the paranoid dimensions of his character. His inevitable inability to achieve his narcissistically invested high standards—whether of piety, peace, friendliness, moral reform, scholarly industry and expertise, or of some other ideal—was experienced by him as a shameful and intolerable failure, bringing in its wake an increased sense of inadequacy, worthlessness, and shame. To protect himself against these painful depressive effects, he resorted to the narcissistic defense of paranoid projection and denial. He read into the faces of others the self-contempt he more than likely felt due to his own failures. To compensate for this injured self-esteem, he also wanted to devalue and scorn others, while secretly envying their apparent well-being. He looked on them as opponents, projected onto them his own desires to demean an adversary, and expected that these hostile feelings would be returned. Although any scholar in his position could not avoid a certain amount of criticism and opposition, Erasmus was led on occasion, because of these paranoid projections, to verify his expectation of enemies by eliciting hostile responses and by depicting himself as their helpless victim. He also resorted to the paranoid defense of denial, absolving himself of responsibility for his failings, and casting blame on others whom he placed in the role of his persecutors, whether they were his Scotist teachers, religious superiors, or fellow scholars. His guardedness, suspiciousness, inability at times to trust or become firmly attached to his friends, repeated persecutory preoccupations, and even frankly delusional states of paranoia toward the end of his life also reflect this aspect of his personality. The paranoid attitudes and behavior of Erasmus can thus be placed within a clinical framework which sees connections between this neurosis, a defense against despondency, shame at failing to achieve lofty ideals, compensations for feelings of inadequacy, and the painful experience of being illegitimate and abandoned.[88]

On the basis of clinical experience, a number of hypotheses can also be made that relate certain aspects of Erasmus' career development to what was reported about his earliest years. Through his dedication to classical letters and to religion, he unconsciously attempted to identify with his learned priest-father and to win the approval of his pious Latin teachers, the father figures

---

[88] For a fuller treatment of the inner logic of narcissism and paranoid distortions, see J. M. Murray, "Narcissism and the Ego Ideal," *Journal of the American Psychoanalytic Association*, 12 (1964): 477–511.

624

most available to him. His numerous literary and scholarly writings represented an endless endeavor to win from a host of paternal substitutes the acceptance and approval denied him by his abandoning father. Erasmus' sweeping satirical attacks, especially on such father figures as prelates and teachers, allowed him to vent the repressed anger he felt for his unavailable father. The ambivalent relations Erasmus maintained with the Church were the product in part of an unconscious transference of his conflicting feelings about his father. To reject the Church would have implied surrendering his need to both attack and cling to it, or in psychological terms, both to rage against and to seek his abandoning father. To defend it would have meant depriving himself of the object of his wrath and admitting that the good element in the Church far outweighed those deficiencies the criticism of which was so important to him. By siding with neither conservative Catholics nor Protestant reformers, Erasmus found himself attacked by both and could thus preserve his sense of victimization. The course of Erasmus' career can, therefore, be seen as conforming in many ways to the psychological needs which clinical experience suggests could have arisen from the peculiar circumstances of his birth and early childhood. If injured narcissism drove Erasmus to extraordinary efforts to fulfill the demands of paternal identification and gain acceptance and approval through learning, that same narcissism would have set the limits and inhibitions that significantly contributed to the course of action he followed in his historical context.

ERASMUS AND THE FIFTH LATERAN COUNCIL (1512 – 17)

On 30 March 1522, Erasmus let slip in a letter to Willibald Pirckheimer, the patrician humanist of Nürnberg, the following comment: "As for councils, the only statement I would dare to make is that perhaps the recent Lateran Council was not really a council."[1] Four years later in his colloquy "The Fishmonger," Erasmus, speaking through the butcher, would no longer dare to pass open judgment on this council, but he did observe that the Lateran Council was not presently considered to be among the "orthodox" councils. The criteria for true councils he had the fish salesman enunciate: they must be in the Holy Spirit properly (*rite*) gathered (*congregatis*), carried out (*peractis*), promulgated (*aeditis*), and accepted (*receptis*).[2] In his other writings Erasmus provided evidence for why the Fifth Lateran Council did not meet all of these criteria for validity.

For a variety of reasons Erasmus held that the Lateran Council had not been properly gathered in the Holy Spirit. Most of these arguments focused on the authority of the papal office and its occupant Julius II (1503 – 13).

Erasmus questioned the power of popes over councils. Given his decade of intermittent theological study at the Sorbonne, that center of Gallican conciliarist thinking, it is not surprising that Erasmus initially sympathized with those who espoused the superiority of councils.[3] In the *Julius Exclusus* he defended the validity of the Council of Pisa-Milan-Asti-Lyon (1511 – 12) which was based on conciliarist ideas.[4] When the Dominican master general, Tommaso de Vio (known as Cajetan), published two treatises and an oration attacking the Pisan Council as schismatic and arguing that only its rival Lateran Council was valid for it had been called by the pope, Erasmus criticized the friar for writing immoderately about papal power.[5] Erasmus insisted that papal powers were joined to obligations and he feared that a pope's unlimited power could lead to tyranny and become a plague on Christendom. He looked to Christian princes to correct abuses of papal power and praised emperor Maximilian I and king Louis XII of France for carrying out their responsibilities by calling the Pisan Council, when the behavior of Julius II showed that Erasmus' concerns were not groundless.[6]

Another factor calling into question the validity of the Lateran Council was the dubious authority of its convoker. The way Julius II attained the papal office and his conduct in it led to open discussions as to whether he

X

was to be considered a true pope.[7] That he attained the tiara by a simoniacal election was widely suspected. To show that he occupied the chair of Peter unworthily, Erasmus produced a litany of charges against Julius II: sexual misconduct (fathering an illegitimate daughter, sodomy, pederasty, being covered with syphilitic sores), habitual inebriation, simoniac selling of bishoprics, indulgences and dispensations, ignorance of things spiritual, consulting a fortune-teller, resorting to excommunication for frivolous reasons, violating an oath, inciting others to warfare, and engaging himself in such fighting.[8]

Julius II's war-making activities were for Erasmus perhaps the most serious of the pope's moral failings. While visiting the papal court when the question of fighting Venice was being debated by the pope and cardinals, Erasmus composed an oration in which he argued that to wage war was all the more so forbidden to the pope since it was already prohibited for secular princes, Christians, priests, and bishops. In the *Julius Exclusus* he accused the pope of having caused the death of countless men, but of having gained not one soul for Christ.[9] Did such a man still enjoy the authority of the papal office?

Erasmus felt that the Lateran Council was not properly assembled because another council, that of Pisa, was already in session and producing worthy reform decrees. The Pisan Council had been called to prevent the utter ruin of Christendom. As a condition of his election as pope, Julius had sworn to call such a reform council and had agreed that others could convoke it if he failed to do so within two years. When he neglected his promise, reform-minded cardinals, the emperor Maximilian, and king Louis XII of France joined in calling for such a council and invited Julius II to preside. Despite the pope's refusal to attend and repeated threats against its adherents, the council assembled at Pisa under the presidency of the upright and learned Spanish cardinal, Bernardino López de Carvajal. It enacted reform measures limiting the wealth and pompous display of prelates, ending the pluralism of cardinals, prohibiting simony in the election of pope and bishops, and allowing for the deposition of manifestly criminal clerics. If the Council of Pisa came to be considered schismatic, it was not because of something it did, but because its supporters suffered military and diplomatic reversals.[10]

The motive Erasmus attributed to Julius II in calling the Lateran Council could only diminish its claim to being a true council. In *Julius Exclusus* the pope proclaimed his intention to use the Council to reform himself, Christian princes, and the people as a whole. But in stating this, he was totally cynical, for his only purpose in calling the Lateran Council was to destroy the Pisan, to drive out a nail with a nail. He could have approved the Pisan Council and no schism would have occurred. But Julius claimed that he was exempt from all criticism, even by a general council, and he feared that the Pisan Council, which he could not control, might remove him from the papal office he had purchased simoniacally.[11]

The way in which Julius II gathered and manipulated the Lateran Council's members weakened its claim to be a true council representing the Church. By means he was unwilling to divulge, the Julius of the Erasmian dialogue supposedly seduced former supporters of the Pisan Council, such as emperor Maximilian and some of the cardinals, to switch their adherence to his Council. To pack his Council with men friendly to himself, Julius had it meet in Rome and created a number of new cardinals who would cooperate with his plans. To restrict its membership as much as possible, he advised the local church in each region to spare expenses by spending only one or other representative. Lest too many delegates arrive, among whom would inevitably be some upright men, Julius wrote to them saying he had postponed the opening of the Council. Having thus headed off their arrival, he anticipated the date set for the initial session and convened the Lateran Council with only his friends in attendance. While it is true that Julius was careful to control the Lateran Council, Erasmus' account of his ploys to limit its membership was not based on contemporary events and documents, but on a conspiratorial interpretation of what led to the recall and recomposition of the English delegation which initially had included bishop John Fisher of Rochester who had invited Erasmus to accompany him.[12]

Erasmus' description of the proceedings of the Lateran Council under Julius II suggests that he felt the Council had not been properly carried out and hence was invalid. He summarized the achievements of the first session as the mere faithful following of traditional ceremonies and the delivery of an oration praising the pope. The second session condemned the Pisan cardinals and their proceedings; the third placed most of France under an interdict and transferred the market-fair from Lyon to Geneva. He characterized these measures as nothing more than curses, threats, and cruelty mixed with cunning and declared that the Lateran assembly under Julius was not "a true council."[13]

The death of Julius II on 21 February 1513, five days after the fifth session of the Fifth Lateran Council, not only occasioned the *Julius Exclusus* with its satirical vilification of the deceased pope, but led to the selection on 11 March 1513 of a new pope, Leo X, whom Erasmus initially idealized, claiming he possesses the virtues opposed to his predecessor's vices. Thus noble lineage, an excellent education, and a love of letters replace a menial origin, a youth wasted on oars, and an ignorance of things academic, especially theology. Whereas Leo pursues spiritual and cultural goals and has ushered in an age of gold, Julius was preoccupied with

material wealth and questions of jurisdiction and had plunged the world
into an age inferior even to that of iron. He sowed discord, and with
severity and violence incited men to war, the great disrupter of learning.
With military might he harassed his former ally, Louis XII, and thereby
rent Christendom by a schism. But by his mildness, Leo has restrained
the threats of princes and restored concord and peace, the nurse of letters.
His piety and prayers have won over the French king. So thoroughly has
he healed the Pisan schism that not even its scars remain. He was elevated to his high office not by the simoniac methods of his predecessor, but
by a divine decree, for he had not even desired or expected this honor.
His untainted election and Christ-like conduct in office attest that he is
unquestionably the supreme pontiff and Christ's vice-regent.[14]

With Leo as pope, Erasmus could no longer denounce the Lateran
Council as improperly assembled and carried out. Leo, who inherited the
presidency of this Council, was indisputably the supreme pontiff and enjoyed high moral authority. After the demise of the Pisan Council and
formal adherence of all major Latin lands to the papal Council, the issues
of conciliarist theology and of a rival council embodying its claims all but
disappeared. Leo openly encouraged all prelates to attend and Erasmus
himself repeatedly stated his own intention to go to Rome.[15]

Such eagerness is not difficult to understand. Among the Council's
goals were three dear to the heart of Erasmus: a reform of morals, a resto-
ration of Church unity, and the establishment of peace among Christians.
The Council had already or soon would list among its members many prelates whom Erasmus considered his patrons and friends: pope Leo X, cardinals Grimani, Giubé, Pucci, and Riario, and bishops Luigi de Canossa,
Giampietro Carafa, Silvestro Gigli, Pietro Griffi, and Thomas Halsey.
The ordinary of his native diocese, Friedrich III von Baden, bishop of
Utrecht, and the local Bursfelder abbot of St. Adalbert's in Egmond,
Meynard Man, would both be represented by procurators. As a place to
promote his highest goals for Christendom and to obtain the personal dispensations he so eargerly sought, Rome at the time of the Lateran Council had no equal. Nonetheless, Erasmus never came and his knowledge of
the Council's proceedings and decrees remained fragmentary.[16]

What influence if any he had from afar on the Council is difficult to determine. Three of the orators denounced, but not by name, those who attacked the pious customs of the Church. But given their humanistic backgrounds and open esteem for Erasmus, Egidio Antonini and Antonio
Pucci probably aimed their comments at others. Giambattista de Gargha, the knight of Rhodes, excoriated those who boldly spurn ecclesiastical custom, but he gave no indication that he had the author of the *Moriae
Encomium* in mind.[17]

Among the reforms proposed to the Council were many similar to those favored by Erasmus. Thus, Simun Kožičić de Begna, bishop of Modrus, urged at the sixth session in 1513 that Christ be taken as the exemplar and archetype of a reform which was to begin with bishops—a proposal close to that detailed in Erasmus' *Paraclesis*. Two memorials submitted for the consideration of the Council focused on Sacred Scripture. The Camaldolese hermits Paolo Giustiniani and Pietro Quirini wanted the Epistles and Gospels read at Mass to be translated into the vernacular and the Bible in Latin to become the core, together with the church fathers and canonical decrees, of a cleric's education. Gianfrancesco Pico, count of Mirandola, in 1517 urged that the scriptural text of both Testaments (*utriusque instrumenti*) be purged of their errors by comparing them to copies of the earliest texts—something Erasmus had just attempted for the New Testament. Pico also made the typically Erasmian suggestion that good example may prove more effective than weapons in the struggle with Islam. The call for peace among Christian princes was common to almost all the sermons and memorials.[18]

Erasmus' judgment on what the Lateran Council achieved under Leo X can be found both in his general statements and in his comments on particular decrees. In 1515 he praised the pope for his synodal constitutions which are repairing and restoring the Christian religion and which manifest an apostolic spirit and fatherly concern, rather than a quest for despotic power and financial gain. Which of the Lateran decrees he was thus praising is not clear.[19] The only decrees on which he commented in some detail were those on the soul's immortality and on book censorship.

Whether Erasmus knew all the provisions in the decree *Apostolici regiminis solicitudo* of the eighth session (19 December 1513) is not clear. While he seems not to have cited explicitly its statements on the soul's immortality, he agreed on the importance of this tenet of belief, ridiculed those who tried to find in Aristotle a proof for it, yet freely provided his own arguments based on Platonic philosophy, even though the decree bound only teachers of philosophy to advance such reasons. Erasmus cited approvingly and in detail the final provision of this decree which held that those in sacred orders could not continue the formal study of poetry and philosophy for more than five years after completing their training in grammar and dialectics, unless they pursued at the same time some study of theology or canon law. He used this decree in his battles with theologians who berated as unreligious someone who studied the classics. Given his fear that too avid a study of ancient literature might resurrect paganism, he also approved of this decree's curtailments of such study.[20]

Erasmus initially observed the conciliar decree *Inter solicitudines* of the tenth session (4 May 1515). He admitted to knowing its provision requir-

X

ing the censorship of books prior to their publication and cautioned his critics to note that the Council had entrusted such censorship to the local ordinary and to those whom he designated as examiners. Erasmus insisted that in the publication of his *Novum Instrumentum* in February of 1516 he was in strict compliance with this ruling, for he had secured the prior approval of the local bishop of Basel, Christopher von Utenheim. He also prided himself in having obtained a letter afterwards from pope Leo who approved this first edition after it was examined by the learned cardinals Grimani and Riario. And the pope went on to give implicit approval even for a revised edition two years later. The demand of Erasmus' English critic, Edward Lee, that he should have secured this papal permit prior to publication, and the suggestion of others that a council should have examined and licenced the *Novum Instrumentum* were both answerable by pointing to the more reasonable provisions of the Lateran Council which allowed for merely episcopal approval, which Erasmus had obtained, and by citing the later Leonine letter.[21]

Erasmus had mixed feelings about censorship. He favored it to silence the combatants in the Reuchlin affair, his own critic Diego Lopéz de Zuñiga, and anyone who published anonymous or calumnious works or urged in print resistance to lawful governmental authority. The effective censorship of all books he saw as unenforceable, given the great numbers produced each year and the numerous opportunities to evade such controls. The law of nations which already banned the printing of seditious and defamatory works, and not some "new constitution," was sufficient to police book publication.[22]

Most of the Lateran Council's decrees elicited no explicit response from Erasmus. He may have had early on only the vaguest knowledge of their contents or have been completely ignorant of their existence. The decrees approving the *montes pietatis* and prohibiting the plunder of cardinals' homes during a conclave seem to have drawn no comment. His statement in May of 1515 that Leo was issuing synodal constitutions which reflect the spirit of Christ and His apostles probably referred to the conciliar decrees reforming curial officials and their fees and to the "great reform bull" of 1514 which regulated cardinals and their households, limited the number of benefices one person could hold, condemned simony, blasphemy, superstition, heresy, and the fictive conversion of Jews, required priests to pray the divine office and lead a chaste life, and prescribed measures to assure the religious education of youths in schools. Given his own situation as the illegitimate son of a priest and as someone in search of more benefices, Erasmus probably had mixed feelings about the Council's condemnation of clerical concubinage and its restraints on pluralism. None of the provisions of the decree restraining the privileges of some of those enjoying papal exemptions touched him personally. Given his often troubled relations with ''monks,'' he may have privately welcomed the decree reining in the friars' privileges.[23]

Although he seems never to have cited the conciliar decree on preaching, many of its provisions were in line with his own thinking: exhortations to preach the Gospel, restrictions on predicting future events, prohibitions on foretelling the end times, abstention from personal attacks on the character of ecclesiastical officials, and the screening by bishops of those permitted to preach to the people. While Erasmus agreed with the general principle that Scripture be interpreted according to the traditional teachings of the doctors of the Church and of professors of sacred theology, he did not want to rule out, as the Council did, any interpretations which were at variance.[24]

In line with Erasmus' efforts to promote Church unity, but apparently never explicitly mentioned by him, were three conciliar items. The healing of the Pisan schism was registered in the acceptance of the French mandate of adherence and any legal basis for its renewal was removed by the abrogation of the Pragmatic Sanction of Bourges and approval of the Concordat of Bologna. Erasmus praised Leo X for ending the Pisan schism. The Council's effort to heal the Hussite schism by sending cardinal Tamas Bakócz to negotiate with the Bohemians a resolution of the conflict, which would allow them to receive the Eucharist under both species, was seemingly unknown to Erasmus. His own proposals were similar to the Council's. The conciliar reaffirmation of the Maronites' adherence to the Roman Church seems also to have elicited no response from Erasmus.[25]

The role of the Lateran Council in promoting peace among Christian princes was not recognized in Erasmus' writings. Instead, he repeatedly gave credit for these efforts to Leo X. On the other hand, Leo was also blamed for urging an armed crusade against the Turks and no responsibility for this undertaking was laid against the Lateran Council, even though Julius II had made this one of its principal aims and Leo's labors can be seen as an attempt to carry out the Council's purpose.[26]

The one decree to which Erasmus may have refused full assent was *Pastor aeternus* of the eleventh session. In the process of abrogating the Pragmatic Sanction of Bourges, this decree made two doctrinal statements. It reaffirmed an earlier teaching based on Sacred Scripture, the church Fathers, and the constitution *Unam Sanctam* of Boniface VIII that it is necessary for salvation that all Christians submit to the Roman pontiff. It also declared that the Roman pontiff, just as he has authority over all councils, so too does he alone have the power and full right of convoking, transferring, and dissolving them. While Erasmus eventually came to accept the first statement, he probably never would have agreed to the validity of the second if it were interpreted as an outright rejection of the *Haec sancta* charter of conciliarism, for he consistently refused to take a stand on whether a pope or a general council is superior.[27]

This brief review of the Lateran Council's proceedings under Leo X and of Erasmus' expressed or probable responses to its decrees does not support a conclusion that he rejected the validity of the Council because of something carried out (*peractis*) under Leo's presidency—the one possible exception being the Lateran's statement on papal superiority to all councils.

Could the Council have been nullified by the way in which its decrees were promulgated or published (*aeditis*)? Most unlikely, for the procedures followed were in strict conformity with existing legal and liturgical practices. Drafts or *cedulae* of the decrees were read aloud and voted upon in the formal sessions of the Council. No decree was voted down and, where opposition was registered by some prelates to particular provisions, Leo X often intervened to assure the opponents that their views would be taken into consideration when putting the decree into final form (*Scribatur in forma*). Once its text was finalized, the decree was recorded in the *acta* of the Council and written up in the form of a papal bull—e.g. *Leo episcopus servus servorum Dei, ad futuram rei memoriam, sacro approbante concilio*. As a bull it was copied into the papal registers. Usually within several days of the session, papal cursors would publish the bull in Rome by reading aloud and posting a copy of it on the doors of the basilicas of St. John Lateran and of St. Peter, on those of the apostolic Chancery, and *in acie* of the Campo dei Fiori. Also within days of the session one of the local Roman printers would usually publish an edition of the bull which the ambassadors would quickly send to the government they represented. At the last session on 13 March 1517, Leo and the Council reaffirmed all that had been carried out in the earlier sessions. Toward the end of July, 1517, Etienne Guillery was apparently commissioned by the Curia to print a collection of the Council's decrees. A year later on 15 September 1518 another collection was published in Milan by Alessandro Minuziano. And on 31 July 1521 the press of Jacopo Mazzocchi in Rome issued the official *acta* of the Council edited by cardinal Antonio del Monte on order of Leo X.[28]

It is doubtful that Erasmus was either aware of this complicated process of promulgation and publication or found any fault with it. In the *Julius Exclusus* he noted that the pope had taken the decrees of the Council and published them as bulls to give them more authority. Julius II then sent these to all princes. While the Lateran decrees were not issued in the name only of the Council as was done at Basel and Pisa, neither were they published merely in the pope's name as happened at Florence. The Lateran formula, combining both papal and conciliar authorities, was that laid down in the ceremonial book of Agostino Patrizi a quarter century earlier.[29]

That the decrees of the Lateran Council were not properly received and enforced (*receptis*) was probably the strongest reason Erasmus had for considering that Council invalid. In the final decree of the Council, *Constituti juxta verbum*, the execution and enforcement of the decrees were entrusted to the local ordinaries, but in the jurisdiction of the Roman Curia to the governor of the city of Rome and to the general auditor of the apostolic Camera. Both officials, Amadeo Berruti the governor and Girolamo de Ghinucci the auditor, issued edicts mandating observance, especially of the "great reform bull." The vicar general for spiritual affairs, Domenico Giacobazzi, issued a similar edict. For a while the clergy reluctantly conformed to the dress code. If Leo showed little enthusiasm for the conciliar decrees reforming curial practices and readily granted dispensations, his successors Adrian VI concentrated his efforts on curial reform while Clement VII actively worked to enforce at Rome many of the provisions of the "great reform bull."[30]

Outside of Rome little effort seems to have been made to implement the Lateran decrees. In Italy the ecclesiastical province of Florence promulgated many of the decrees as statutes of the provincial council held in 1517 on order of cardinal Giulio dei Medici. Cardinal Alessandro Farnese implemented the decrees in Parma, Federigo de Sanseverino in Novara, and Antonio del Monte in Pavia. The Venetian government chose to apply the decree on book censorship in its peculiar way. In Spain cardinal Francisco Ximenes de Cisneros worked to put the Lateran decrees into effect. Leo entrusted to cardinal Philippe de Chaumont (or de Luxembourg) the task of seeing that the decrees were given effect in France. But the only decree to be registered as the law of the land, despite much opposition, was the conciliarly approved Concordat of Bologna. The French ambassador to Rome, Guillaume Briçonnet, bishop of Meaux, was specially empowered to apply the Lateran decrees in his own diocese. His brother Denys, fellow ambassador and bishop of San-Malo, was charged to enforce the Lateran decree on clerical garb at the church of St. Martha in the diocese of Avignon. The attempts in 1515 to defend in England the Lateran provision on ecclesiastical immunity were blocked when Henry VIII intervened to protect its critic Henry Standish, O.F.M., and Thomas Wolsey was forced to make a submission for the clergy. In Germany the decrees remained for the most part unknown. By 1520 Luther was criticizing those on the immortality of souls, on the Bohemians, and on the authority of the pope over councils. In his 1523 memorial to Adrian VI, Johann Eck suggested that, if ever implemented, the Lateran decrees on clerical reform, book censorship, and the holding of provincial councils would do much to stem the Reformation in Germany. Even Cajetan, the great defender of the Lateran Council, eventually admitted that many of its censures were probably not binding because their non-observance, by itself, had the legal force of abrogation.[31]

Erasmus followed current practice in regard to observing the Lateran decrees. When he learned of a decree, he tried initially to observe it, as happened when he published the *Novum Instrumentum* with episcopal approval. But most of his contemporaries were either ignorant of or ignored the Lateran's decrees. Since these measures were not put into common practice, he felt no longer bound by them. In the *Ecclesiastes* he stated what can be seen as his justification: "Those things, which the public authority of the Church prescribes, especially in ecumenical councils, and which are approved by public practice over a long period of time, should be reverently observed, nor should those things be spurned which pontiffs have ordered on just grounds for the public weal." Given the great difficulties he could have encountered had the decree on book censorship been put into strict practice, Erasmus must have been relieved that this Council's legislation was not approved by public usage and hence did not bind.[32]

It seems reasonable to conclude that Erasmus' rejection of the Lateran Council as a true council was not based primarily on the way in which it had been assembled, carried out, or promulgated, but rather on the way it had been given only a limited reception at first and then came to be ignored.

Erasmus' keen awareness that both the Pisan and Lateran councils had failed to reform the Church may help to explain his initial reluctance to urge a conciliar solution to the Reformation. Instead, he recommended a court of arbitration whose members would be appointed by emperor Charles V and by kings Henry VIII of England and Louis II of Hungary. But later Erasmus returned to the idea of a church council to reform morals and define central doctrines. Unfortunately, he did not live to see such a council assemble at Trent, and he may have been surprised to learn that this papal council did effect a reform of the Church, in part by reaffirming a number of the Lateran decrees—but this time they were enforced.[33]

NOTES

1 *Allen* 1268, 35–36: "De conciliis non ausim aliquid dicere, nisi forte proximum Concilium Lateranense concilium non fuit."

2 *Ichthyophagia* (February, 1526), in *Colloquia*, I – 3, 508, lines 466 – 67: "Bona verba, ne de conciliis quidem rite in Spiritu Sancto congregatis, peractis, aeditis et receptis." And lines 470 – 71: ". . . loquor de his qui nunc habentur orthodoxi, ne quid dicam de proximo Concilio Lateranensi."

3 Erasmus did not at first think that papal primacy was instituted by Christ, even though it was necessary for the unity of the Church. He opposed exaggerations of papal power and held that the authority of councils should confirm important papal teachings. Like his friend Thomas More, Erasmus too probably initially looked for such a decree to define whether a pope or a council was superior. He praised the ability of councils to correct errant pontiffs. Those who defended papal superiority were scoundrels like the Julius II depicted in *Julius Exclusus* or like mendicant friars whose exemptions and powers depended on the good will and authority of the popes. See *LB*, V, 90F – 91A, IX, 1087DE, X 1305B; *ASD* I – 3, 508, lines 455 – 64; *Erasmi Opuscula: A Supplement to the Opera Omnia*, ed. Wallace K. Ferguson (The Hague 1933), page 92: lines 465 – 70, 94: 517 – 36, 98: 601 – 14; Harry J. McSorley, "Erasmus and the Primacy of the Roman Pontiff: Between Conciliarism and Papalism," *Archiv für Reformationsgeschichte* 65 (1974), 37 – 54—McSorley, while admitting conciliarist influences (38 n. 10), attempts to play them down (49 – 52), fails to distinguish between Erasmus' early and later thinking on conciliarism (49 – 54), and tries to focus the discussion on whether a council can depose a pope which he calls "the conciliarist question" (49) and "the most notable characteristic of conciliar theory" (51), when Erasmus himself framed the question in terms of whether the pope or council is superior (e.g. *LB*, X, 1305B); and Willi Hentze, *Kirche und kirchliche Einheit bei Desiderius Erasmus von Rotterdam* (= *Konfessionskundliche und kontroverstheologische Studien* XXXIV), (Paderborn, 1974), 121 – 26.

In agreement with the current state of scholarship, this paper accepts the Erasmian authorship of the *Julius Exclusus*. See the excellent historiographical surveys by J. Kelley Sowards in his edition of *The "Julius exclusus" of Erasmus*, trans. Paul Pascal (Bloomington, Indiana, 1968), 97 – 98 n. 32 and that of James K. McConica, "Erasmus and the 'Julius': A Humanist Reflects on the Church," in *The Pursuit of Holiness in Late Medieval and Renaissance Religion*, eds. Charles Trinkaus with Heiko A. Oberman (Leiden, 1974), 444 – 71, esp. 467 – 71.

4 On the conciliarist thinking behind the Pisan Council, see especially Olivier de la Brosse, *Le pape et le concile: La comparaison de leurs pouvoirs à la veille de la Réforme* (= *Unam Sanctam*, 58), (Paris, 1965), and Remigius Bäumer, *Nachwirkungen des konziliaren Gedankens in der Theologie und Kanonistik des frühen 16. Jahrhunderts* (= *Reformationsgeschichtliche Studien und Texte*, 100), (Münster, 1971). On Erasmus' defense of the Pisan Council, see his *Julius Exclusus* in *Erasmi Opuscula*, 38 – 124, esp. 89 – 102.

5 *Allen* 1033, 144 – 46; 1275, 77 – 78; 1412, 49 – 52. In *Allen* 1225, 198 – 203 he praised Cajetan's 1521 defense of papal primacy for its objectivity, temperance, unadorned arguments, and sources cited. On Erasmus and Cajetan, see Christian Dolfin, *Die Stellung des Erasmus von Rotterdam zur scholastischen Methode: Inaugural-Dissertation* (Osnabrück, 1936), 92 – 93 and the entry of Danilo Aguzzi-Barbagli in *Contemporaries of Erasmus* I (Toronto, 1985), 239 – 42.

6 *LB* V, 90F – 91A, 128C, E; *Allen* 872, 16 – 21; *Erasmi Opuscula*, 90: 426 – 32, 98: 612 – 14.

7 *Erasmi Opuscula*, 90: 415, 106: 813 – 17.

8 *Erasmi Opuscula*, 66: 37 – 39, 73: 175 – 79, 88: 392, 90: 413, 114: 953 – 61 (bought papal office); 89: 402 – 03 (illegitimate daughter); 77: 249 – 50, 88: 392, 108: 858 (sodomy, pederasty); 68: 80 – 81, 72: 160 – 61 (syphilitic); 36: 20, 65: 12 – 13, 67: 57, 68: 83, 85, 90: 413 (drunkenness); 73 – 74: 185 – 93, 105: 770 – 71 (simony); 65: 6, 70: 131 – 32 (ignorance); 72 – 73: 165 – 70 (fortune-teller); 69 – 70: 106 – 09, 79: 274 (frivolous excommunications); 90: 417 – 23 (violating oath); 36: 8 – 9, 75: 211 – 14, 108 – 14: 860 – 939, 115: 977 – 80 (inciting others to warfare); 80: 286 – 87 (engaging as a priest in fighting).

9 *Allen* I, 37, lines 7 – 16 and *LB* II, 968C – E; the outlines of this oration seem to have been preserved in *LB* V, 898B – 99A; for other comments on the Venetian war, see *LB* IV, 608AB, IX, 360EF, and *Erasmi Opuscula*, 86: 370 – 79, 118: 1060 – 64.

10 *Erasmi Opuscula*, 90 – 91: 415 – 32, 97 – 99: 595 – 626, 99 – 100: 639 – 57, 102: 708 – 12.

Of the reform measures Erasmus attributes to the Pisan Council, only that limiting the prelates' pompous displays, and that only for the time of the Council, is to be found in its published acts—see the decree of the sixth session at Milan on 24 March 1512, in *Acta primi concilii Pisani . . . item constitutiones sanctae in diversis sessionibus sacri generalis concilii Pisani ex bibliotheca regia* (Paris, 1612), 152–56. Erasmus' knowledge of the Pisan Council came in part from the reports of friends—see, for example, the letters of Andrea Ammonio in *Allen* 236, 42–43; 239, 48–50; 247, 16–18, and the letter of Girolamo Aleandro, *Allen* 256, 44–60. Augustin Renaudet in his *Préréforme et humanisme à Paris pendant les premières guerres d'Italie (1494–1517)* 2nd ed., rev. (Paris, 1953), speculates that Erasmus' knowledge of the Pisan Council came from his contacts with Ammonio, Budé, and Lefèvre and from conversations he may have had in Paris during his June, 1511 visit when he had his *Moriae Encomium* published there. Whether Erasmus ever read the *acta* of the Pisan Council, published in Paris by Jean Petit on 23 August 1512, is not clear. Apparently he may well have read Jacques Almain's *Libellus de auctoritate ecclesiae . . .* (Paris, 1512) in response to Cajetan—see McSorley, "Erasmus and Primacy," 52–53. For the arguments of a modern scholar on the initial legitimacy of the Pisan Council, see Walter Ullmann, "Julius II and the Schismatic Cardinals," in *Schism, Heresy, and Religious Protest*, ed. Derek Baker (= *Studies in Church History*, 9) (Cambridge, 1972), 177–93, esp. 189. For a study of Julius' dealings with the Pisan Council, see my "The Healing of the Pisan Schism (1511–13)," *Annuarium Historiae Conciliorum* 16 (1984), 59–192, esp. 62–96.

11 *Erasmi Opuscula*, 74: 199–201, 91: 440–49, 95–96: 558–68, 99: 628–30, 101: 660–61, 114: 950–55. For a study of the goals set for the Lateran Council, see my "Paride de Grassi's Diary of the Fifth Lateran Council," *Annuarium Historiae Conciliorum* 14 (1982), 370–460, esp. 431–32.

12 *Erasmi Opuscula*, 95–97: 547–83. For Julius' efforts to control the Council and for a detailed study of those who attended, see my "De Grassi's Diary," 436–50 and "The Participants at the Fifth Lateran Council," *Archivum Historiae Pontificiae* 12 (1974), 157–206, esp. 159–60. For Erasmus' failed efforts to attend the Lateran Council in 1512, see *Allen* 252, 2–8; 255, 2–4; 334: 90–94. For the document proroguing the opening of the Council, see *Sacrorum conciliorum nova et amplissima collectio*, ed. J.D. Mansi *et al.*, vol. 32 (Florence, 1759), cols. 692DE, 694C—hereafter this volume is cited as "M".

13 *Erasmi Opuscula*, 101: 661–86, 102: 699. Erasmus' account of what occurred at the Council was deficient. He confused the opening ceremonies with the first session, passed over completely the first session at which the conciliar officials were appointed, and made no mention of the fourth and fifth sessions at which actions were taken against the defenders of the Pragmatic Sanction of Bourges, a reform of curial officials and their fees was confirmed, and an earlier constitution against simony in papal elections was approved. Whether these omissions were from ignorance or deliberately made to strengthen his case against the Council is not clear.

14 *Allen* 288, 83–85; 333, 10–14, 94–95; 335: 37–38, 43–46, 65–66, 77, 80–83, 93–97, 109–113, 122–25, 132–35, 192–99, 202–03, 331–35; 446, 11–13, 38–41, 84–86; and *LB*, IV, 636 D.

15 On the complicated process by which the schism was ended, especially Leo's dealings with the French, see my "Healing of the Pisan Schism," 11–54; on the temporal rulers adhering to the Lateran Council, see my "The Participants," 205–06; on Leo's exhortations to attend and grants of safe conduct, see, e.g., M 783B–D, 793B–D, 815D–816C; for Erasmus' announced intention to go to Rome in the winter of 1514, see *Allen* 296, 225–26, in March of 1515, see *Allen* 324, 26–27, and in the winter of 1515 and 1516, see *Allen* 334, 94–95, 207–09, and 360, 12–14.

16 For some of Leo's early restatements of the goals set for the Lateran Council, see M 783B, 788E, 792E–93A, 816D–17D, 818DE, etc. For Erasmus' patrons and friends as conciliar participants, see my "The Participants," 181–92 nrs. 5, 56, 71, 80, 173, 182, 184, 218, 310, 320, and M 975E and 976AB. The sources of Erasmus' knowledge of what happened at Lateran V are difficult to determine. He may have received in-

formation from his German correspondents such as Konrad Peutinger, Willibald Pirckheimer, and Beatus Bild, but this is not evidenced in their surviving letters. On Peutinger's knowledge of Lateran V, see John Headley, "Luther and the Fifth Lateran Council," *Archiv für Reformationsgeschichte* 64 (1974), 55–78, here 58. How Erasmus obtained copies of the decrees on clerical education and book censorship is unknown. The papal nuncio to England, Giampietro Carafa, may have furnished him with a first-hand report on the Council; see *Allen* 335, 186, 250–65.

17 For Antonini, see M 675BC and the entry of David S. Chambers in *COE*, I (1985), 64–65; for Pucci, see M 893E–94A, *Allen* 855, 6–14, and the entry of Rosemary D. Jones in *COE*, III (1987), 122–23; for de Gargha, see M 853E.

18 For Begna's statements, see M 799D, 805B; for Giustiniani and Quirini, see their *Libellus ad Leonem X. Pontificem Maximum* in *Annales Camaldulenses Ordinis Sancti Benedicti*, ed. J.B. Mittarelli and A. Costadoni, IX (Venice, 1773), cols. 676–79, 681–82. For Pico's statement on the Bible, see William Roscoe, *The Life and Pontificate of Leo the Tenth*, 2nd ed., rev. (London, 1806), VI, Appendix 146, p. 76: "Non in vestibus modo et sumptibus, sed in studiis sacrae literae utriusque instrumenti recognoscendae, et cum antiquis et castigatis primae originis exemplaribus conferendae . . . ."; for the crusade strategy, p. 75.

19 *Allen* 335, 184–91. That Erasmus used the term "synodal" synonymously for "conciliar" is evident from *Allen* 456, 61–63.

20 The decree is printed in M 842A–43C. For some of Erasmus' statements on the soul's immortality, see *Allen* 916, 275–84; 1039, 46–50, 55–56, and *LB*, IV, 621C–E. For his statements on the clerical education provision, see his scholion on Jerome's letter to Eustochius in *Omnium operum Divi Eusebii Hieronymi Stridonensis Tomus Primus . . . una cum argumentis et scholiis Des. Erasmi Roterodami . . . .* (Basel, 1516), fol. 61v, and *Allen* 1164, 15–22. For Erasmus' fear of a revival of paganism, see *Allen* 541, 133–37. For some classical poets who were considered dangerous, see the statutes of the Council of Florence (1517), in Mansi, XXXV, cols. 269C–70A.

21 The conciliar decree on book censorship is printed in M 912B–13D. For Erasmus' statements that he observed this decree, see *Allen* 446, 57–59; 456, 144–57, 215–16. For Leo's approval through Grimani and Riario, see *Allen* 456, 195–213; 843, 331–35; 864, 1–17. For Lee's demand of prior papal approval, see *Allen* 843, 441–46; for his later charges that Erasmus had no letter from Leo or only a counterfeited one and that even an authentic letter was of no weight unless the pope had first examined the work exactly, word for word, see *Erasmi Opuscula*, p. 271, lines 819–33. For Dorp's concern for conciliarly approved texts, see *Allen* 304, 98–108; 337, 768–89; 843, 317–19; for other critics suggesting prior conciliar approval, see *Allen* 456, 27–32.

22 For censorship of the Reuchlin-case pamphlets, see *Allen* 701, 30–31; for censorship of Zuñiga, see *Allen* 1418, 25–28; 2443, 350–55; *LB*, IX, 384E–85B; for reining in the German press, see *Allen* 785, 41–42; for his advice on book censorship to the Basel town council, see *Allen* 1539, 51–74; for his response to Zuñiga and observation that censorship was odious, see *LB*, IX, 383E; on the condemnation of Luther's writings, see *LB*, IX, 353A; on friars as censors, see *LB*, II, 967C; for the disparity between judgments based on expertise and authority, see *Allen* 843, 319–21; for his own licence to teach, see *Ibid*, 491–92. On the impracticality of the Lateran decree, see *Allen* 1539, 64–68.

23 The texts of the following decrees are reprinted in Mansi: *Montes pietatis* M 905C–07B, plundering cardinals' households M 987A–88B, curial reform M 845D–46E, "great reform bull" M 874C–85D, papal exemptions M 907D–12A, mendicants' privileges M 970D–74E. For Erasmus' general statement approving Leo's synodal constitutions, see *Allen* 335, 182–91.

24 For the decree on preaching, see M 944A–47D, esp. 944CD and 946B (criteria for interpreting Scripture). For Erasmus' views on preaching and interpreting Scripture, see *Allen* 446, 61–65; 916, 359–62, and *LB*, V, 798EF, 825D–26C, 1026C–28D, 1068C–69C.

25 For the conciliar texts related to the healing of the Pisan schism, see M 832A–36B, 947E–70D; to the Hussite schism, see M 845AB and the bull granting Bakócz the power to reconcile the Bohemians according to the terms approved at Basel, reprinted in Augustinus Theiner, ed., *Vetera monumenta historica Hungariam sacram illustrantia*, vol. II: *1352–1526* (Rome, 1860), Nr. 807 (20 September 1513), pp. 610–12; and to the Maronite adhesion, see M 942B–43E. For Erasmus' praise of the healing of the Pisan schism, see *Allen* 335, 81–83; for his suggestions on how to resolve the Hussite schism, see *Allen* 950, 45–56; 1039: 81–267, and Konrad Bittner, "Erasmus, Luther, und die Böhmischen Brüder," in *Rastloses Schaffen: Festschrift für Dr. Friedrich Lammert*, ed. Heinz Seehase (Stuttgart, 1954), 107–29, esp. 111, 113–14.

26 For conciliar efforts to promote peace, see M 817A–D, 843D–44E, and 870B–72B. For some of Erasmus' statements extoling peace, urging prelates to work for it, and praising Leo for his efforts, see *Allen* 288: 76–82; 335, 196–204; 541, 6–12, 29–35; 542: 12–15; 694, 41–43; 1202, 9–10, and *LB*, II, 966CD, IV, 636CD. See also Robert P. Adams, *The Better Part of Valor: More, Erasmus, Colet, and Vives on Humanism, War, and Peace, 1496–1535* (Seattle, 1962), esp. 43–121, 158–85. For the conciliar decree calling for a crusade, see M 988CD, 990D–92B. For Leo's efforts, see Kenneth M. Setton, *Papacy and the Levant (1204–1571)*, vol. III: *The Sixteenth Century to the Reign of Julius III* (Philadelphia, 1984), 142–97. For some of Erasmus' statements favoring conversion efforts rather than warfare, see *Allen* 335, 166–84; 775, 5–6; 781, 25–31; 785, 21–23; 786, 24–29; 858, 103–54, 378–87; 891, 24–33.

27 For the doctrinal statements in *Pastor aeternus*, see M 967D, 968E; for Erasmus' acceptance of the necessity to submit to papal authority, see *ASD* I–3 (*Ichthyophagia*, 1526), p. 505, lines 357–61; for Erasmus' refusal to take a stand, see *Allen* 1596, 35–42, and *LB*, IX, 1087D, X, 1305B. For an interesting study which argues that *Pastor aeternus* should not be interpreted as a repudiation of *Haec sancta*, see Francis A. Oakley, "Conciliarism at the Fifth Lateran Council?" *Church History* 41 (1972), 452–63, here 459–63.

28 For the procedures followed in making conciliar law, see Stephan Kuttner, "Conciliar Law in the Making: The Lyonese Constitutions (1274) of Gregory X in the Manuscript of Washington," in *Miscellanea Pio Paschini* (= *Lateranum*, N.S. 15), II (Rome, 1949), 39–81, here 39–44 and 49–50; and Minnich, "De Grassi's Diary," 441–45, 453–57. For copies of decrees which included rubrics testifying to the legal procedures followed, see the *Bulla intimationis Generalis Concilii apud Lateranum per summum dominum nostrum Julium Papam ii edita* (Nürnberg: Johannes Weyssenburger, 1512), Aiᵛ (Girolamo Ghinucci's verification of lead seal, of the red and saffron colored threads, and of the bull's publication and posting by three papal cursors in the customary places), Bivʳ (verification that the text here printed is correct and authorization to print), see M 689DE, 691A–E for how this bull was read and posted (for from one to two hours) in various places around Rome. For the publication of the bull *Cum inchoatam*, see *Bulla Secunda sessionis sacrosancti Concilii Lateranensis approbans et renovans damnationem et reprobationem Pisani conciliabuli et annullans omnes et singula in illo gesta et gerenda, celebrate die xvii Mai M.d. xii* (s.l., s.d.), 4ᵛ. For the formula "*Scribatur in forma*" following a positive vote, see *Bulla Concilii in Decima Sessione super materia Montis pietatis: Lecta per Reverendum patrem dominum Bertrandum Episcopum Adriensis Oratorem Ducis [Ferrariae]* (s.l., s.d.), ivʳ. For revision of a *cedula*, see M 886D, 987A; for registration in the *acta* of the Council, see M 930CD; for extant copies in bull form of *Constituti juxta verbum*, see Archivio Segreto Vaticano (= ASV), AA. Arm. I–XVIII, nos. 1905 and 1906. For the printing of the decrees within days and ambassadors' concern to obtain copies, see Baltassaro Turini to Lorenzo dei Medici, Rome, 6 May 1514, Archivio di Stato—Florence (= ASF), Mediceo avanti il Principato, Filza 107, no. 18, fol. 18ᵛ, and Francesco Vettori to the Dieci di Balia, Rome, 25 May 1514, ASF, Dieci di Balia, Carteggio-Responsive, no. 118, fol. 706ᵛ. For a listing of bulls which were printed separately, see Fernanda Ascarelli, *Le Cinquecentine romane: "Censimento delle edizioni romane del XVI secolo possedute delle biblioteche di Roma"* (Milan, 1972), 145–47, 153–56. For the reaffirmation of the twelfth session, see M 991BC; for the July 1517 printing of the con-

ciliar decrees, see Hubert Elie, "Un Lunevillois imprimeur à Rome au début du XVIème siècle: Etienne Guillery," *Guttenberg-Jahrbuch* (1939), 185–96, (1944–49), 128–37, here 129–30, 137. The Milan collection, which does not contain such important bulls as those abrogating the Pragmatic Sanction and approving the Concordat, is entitled *Bullae sacri concilii Lateranensis*; the *acta* were published at Rome as *Sacrosanctum Lateranense Concilium Novissimum sub Julio II at Leone X Celebratum*.

29 *Erasmi Opuscula* p. 101, lines 674–76; Agostino Patrizi, *Rituum ecclesiasticorum sive sacrarum cerimoniarum SS. Romanae Ecclesiae libri tres non ante impressi*, ed. Cristoforo Marcello (Venice, 1516), fol. 62ʳ.

30 For the delegation of execution, see M 991BC; for the enforcement at Rome, see my "'*Incipiat iudicium a domo Domini*': The Fifth Lateran Council and the Reform of Rome," in *Reform and Authority in the Medieval and Reformation Church*, ed. Guy Fitch Lytle (Washington, 1981), 127–142, esp. 135–42 and ASV, Arm. XLIV, vol. 5, fol. 251ᵛ and Reg. Vat. 1200, fols. 391ʳ–95ᵛ, esp. 391ᵛ.

31 For the Florentine statutes, see Mansi, XXXV, 215A–318C, esp. 229D, 230AB, 232D–34B, 269D, 270D–73A, 274C–75C, 283C, 290C, 304B, etc. For Farnese's efforts to implement the conciliar decrees at Parma, see Ludwig Pastor, *History of the Popes*, 2nd ed., vol. XI, trans. Ralph Francis Kerr (St. Louis, 1923), 20–21; for Sanseverino's efforts at Novara and del Monte's at Pavia, see Angelo L. Stoppa, "Quattro decreti generali novaresi simultanei al Concilio Lateranense V finora sconosciuti e inediti," *Novara* 2 (1968), 48–104, esp. 48, 64–65, 84, 89, and 92; for the Venetian measure, see Marino Sanudo, *I Diarii*, XXI, col. 485; for Ximenes' efforts in Spain, see Joseph Hergenroether, *Histoire des conciles*, VIII–I, trans. Henri Leclercq (Paris, 1917), 564–65. For the registration of the Concordat, see *Recueil général des anciennes lois Françaises depuis l'an 420, jusqu'a la Révolution de 1789*, ed. F. Isambert *et al.*, XII (Paris, 1828), 75–97, 114–18; for the charge to Philippe de Luxembourg and Guillaume Briçonnet, see ASV, Reg. Vat. 1204, fols. 198ᵛ–99ᵛ, for that to Denys Briçonnet, Reg. Vat. 1200, fols. 277ʳ–78ʳ.

For this English effort, see J. Duncan M. Derrett, "The Affair of Richard Hunne and Friar Standish," in *The Complete Works of St. Thomas More*, vol. 9: *The Apology*, ed. J.B. Trapp (New Haven, 1979), 215–46, esp. 226, 229, 231–32.

For Germany, see Headley, "Luther and Lateran," 65–73, and *Acta Reformationis Catholicae ecclesiam Germaniae concernentia saeculi XVI: Die Reformverhandlungen des deutschen Episcopats von 1520 bis 1570*, Band I, ed. Georg Pfeilschifter (Regensburg, 1959), 121–24, for a memorial urging the implementation of the Lateran decrees in the province of Salzburg, see pp. 21, 32.

On the principle of abrogation through non-observance, see Geoffrey King, "The Acceptance of Law by the Community: A Study in the Writings of Canonists and Theologians, 1500–1750," *The Jurist* 37 (1977), 233–65, here 237–38 (for the opinion of Felinus Sandaeus, d. 1503, an auditor of the sacred Rota). For Cajetan's application of this principle to Lateran V in 1523 and his doubts about the binding force of certain decrees, see his *Peccatorum Summula novissime recognita . . . per Gaugericum Hispanum* (Douai, 1613), "Excommunicatio," cap. LXXXII, pp. 295–97. Carranza, in his conciliar collection which first appeared in Venice, 1546, reiterated approvingly Cajetan's doubts, see Bartolomé Carranza de Miranda, *Summa conciliorum et pontificum a Petro usque ad Pium iiii collecta . . . .* (Lyon, 1570), fol. 403ᵛ

32 *LB*, V, 1076E.

33 *Erasmi Opuscula*, pp. 352–61, esp. lines 134–54; *ASD*, IX–2, 481, lines 51–54; *Allen* 2988, 70–72; and for some examples of Lateran decrees reiterated at Trent, see *Conciliorum Oecumenicorum Decreta*, ed. G. Alberigo *et al.*, 664–65 (book censorship), 670 and 763 (preaching), 730 (union of benefices), 761 (provincial councils), etc.

The Debate between Desiderius Erasmus of Rotterdam and Alberto Pio of Carpi on the Use of Sacred Images

From 1526 to 1532 Alberto Pio of Carpi (1475-1531) and Desiderius Erasmus of Rotterdam (c. 1467-1536) debated the appropriateness of venerating sacred images. In response to Erasmus' attack on certain practices as superstitious and erroneous, Pio mounted a fulsome defense on the grounds of scripture, church teachings and practice, confirmatory miracles, and an appeal to reason and experience. So thorough and insightful was his defense that Erasmus insisted that this lay prince could not possibly have been its author and the historian Hubert Jedin has stated that "[u]p to the Council [of Trent] no one had better confronted the problem in its philosophical-religious aspect with the profundity and care of the count of Carpi."[1]

---

[1] Alberto Pio's response, entitled . . . ad Erasmi Roterodami expostulationem responsio accurata et paraenetica, Martini Lutheri et asseclarum eius haeresim vesanam magnis argumentis, et iustis rationibus confutans, circulated in a manuscript, the draft of which contains Pio's autograph insertions and corrections and is preserved today in the Biblioteca Ambrosiana of Milano, Archivio Falcò Pio di Savoia, Prima Sezione, Ms. 282, entry 6. On the basis of this manuscript, which survived the Sack of Rome in 1527, a revised version was printed in Paris by Joost Bade of Assche on 7 January 1529 and reprinted on 15 May 1529 in Paris by Pierre Vidoue. It was also incorporated into the collection of Pio's writings edited after his death by Francesco Florido of Sabina and published in Paris by Bade on 9 March 1531, reprinted later that year in Venice by Luigi Antonio Giunta, and issued in a Castilian version in Alcalá de Henares by Miguel de Eguya in 1536. Sometime after Pio's death on 7 January 1531, a French translation of this work was made, decorated with beautiful miniature illuminations, and presented to King Francis I. It is preserved in the Bibliothèque Nationale de Paris as Ms. 462.

Pio's second response to Erasmus, entitled Tres et viginti libri in locos lucubrationum variarum D. Erasmi Roterodami, quos censet ab eo recognoscendos et retractandos, was published postumously in Paris by Bade and in Venice by Giunta in 1531 and in Alcalá by Eguya in 1536. Unless otherwise indicated, all references to Pio's writings against Erasmus will be based on the 1531 Bade edition and cited as Pio, Responsio or XXIII Libri.

Erasmus' writings have been edited by Jean LECLERC as Opera omnia emendatiora et auctiora . . . 10 vols., Leiden: Peter vander Aa 1703-06 - hereafter this work is cited as LB. In modern times Erasmus' letters have been critically edited by Percy S. ALLEN et alii and

To what extent Pio was an independent critic of Erasmus or the mere spokesman for conservative Catholic circles first at Rome and then at Paris is difficult to say.

Pio was clearly capable by training, natural talent, and inclination to critique Erasmus' writings. On the advice of his pious and learned uncle, Giovanni Pico della Mirandola (1463-94), Pio's widowed mother entrusted his earliest education (1480-90) to the humanist Aldo Manuzio who trained him in the classical Latin and Greek languages, letters, and philosophy. Pio continued his studies in Latin letters throughout his life, devoting many hours daily to the reading of authors who wrote in the Ciceronian style. His own skill in Latin was such that even as a youth he enjoyed a reputation for clas-

---

published as Opus epistolarum Des. Ersami Roterodami, 12 vols., Oxford 1906-58 - hereafter this collection is cited as ALLEN. A new critical edition of Erasmus' other writings, which will eventually replace the work of Leclerc, is in the process of publication under the title Opera Omnia Desiderii Erasmi Roterdami recognita et adnotatione critica instructa notisque illustrata, Amsterdam and Oxford 1969 ff. - hereafter cited as ASD.

Erasmus' writings against Pio were four in number: Responsio ad epistolam paraeneticam Alb. Pii Carporum principis, Basel: Froben 1529, reprinted with Pio's Responsio by Vidoue in Paris on 15 May 1529 and in LB, IX cols. 1095A-1122E; Apologia adversus rhapsodias calumniosarum querimoniarum Alberti Pii quondam Carporum principis, Basel: Hier. Froben and Nich. Episcopius 1531, Antwerp: Michael Hillen 1531, and in LB, IX 1123A-1196D; the satirical colloquy on Pio's funeral, entitled "Exequiae Seraphicae" Basel: Hier. Froben and Nich. Episcopius, September 1531, reprinted in ASD, I-3, 686-99; and In elenchum Alberti Pii brevissima scholia per eundem Erasmum Roterodamum, published at the end of his Dilutio eorum quae Iodocus Clithoueus scripsit aduersus Declamationem suasoriam matrimonii, Basel: Froben 1532, sigs. m_2^r-n_8^r - hereafter cited as 'Scholia'.

The debate between Pio and Erasmus has been surveyed by Myron P. GILMORE in four studies: Erasmus and Alberto Pio, Prince of Carpi, in: Action and Conviction in Early Modern Europe: Essays in Memory of E.H. Harbison, edd. Theodore K. RABB and Jerrold E. SEIGEL, Princeton, New Jersey 1969, 299-318; 'De modis disputandi': The Apologetic Works of Erasmus, in: Florilegium Historiale: Essays Presented to Wallace K. Ferguson, edd. J.G. ROWE and W.H. STOCKDALE, Toronto 1971, 62-88 (this is revised version of the next item); Les limites de la tolerance dans l'oeuvre polémique d'Érasme, in: Colloquia Erasmiana Turonensia, 2 vols., Toronto 1972, II, 713-36; and Italian Reactions to Erasmian Humanism, in: Itinerarium Italicum: The Profile of the Italian Renaissance in the Mirror of its European Transformations. Dedicated to Paul Oskar Kristeller on the Occasion of His 70th Birthday, edd. Heiko A. OBERMAN and Thomas A. BRADY, Jr., Leiden 1975, 61-115.

I am grateful to Dr. Sergius Michalski for calling to my attention a more recent study, Giuseppe Scavizzi, Arte et architectura sacra: Cronache e documenti sulla controversia tra riforamti e cattolici (1500-1550), Reggio Calabria 1981, that contains a section (pp. 154-79 and 206-12) dedicated to the Erasmus-Pio debate. Unfortunately, because of a passed deadline is was not possible to take cognizance of his views in the following study.

sical eloquence, and Erasmus later listed him among the leading Ciceronian stylists of Italy. With daily lessons from the Cretan scholar Marcus Musurus, Pio continued his study of Greek at his court in Carpi from 1500-03. Another companion of his Greek studies was the Dalmatian Tryphon Bizantius, who became in 1514 bishop of his native Cattaro (Kotor). So skillfull was Pio in Greek letters that he was admitted to the Aldine "New Academy" in Venice whose members were required to speak Greek among themselves. His reputation for classical learning was such that while serving as the Imperial and French ambassador to the papal court he was also welcomed into the refined literary circles of the Roman Academy and was honored by three poems of the *Coryciana*.[2] Pio's ability to write an elegant Latin response to Erasmus which cited classical authors is not in doubt.

Hubert JEDIN's statement is found in his Genesi e portata del decreto tridentino sulla venerazione delle immagini, first published in: TTHQ 116 (1935) 143-88, 404-29, with additions in: ZKG 74 (1963) 321-39, and republished in the Italian version of his collected works Chiesa della Fede, Chiesa della Storia: Saggi scelti, introduction by Giuseppe AL-BERIGO, trans. A. DESTRO, A.M. FIDORA, and G. POLETTI, Brescia 1972, 340-90, here 346.

For examples of Erasmus' claim that Pio reiterated others' views, see LB IX 1124B, 1125DE, etc. and below notes 11-16. Pio was not alone in being accused by Erasmus of being the spokesman of others. He made a similar charge that Jakob Latomus was the mouthpiece of the Louvain theologians - see Gilbert TOURNOY, Jacobus Latomus, in: Contemporaries of Erasmus, edd. Peter G. BIETENHOLZ and Thomas B. DEUTSCHER, II, Toronto 1986, 304-06, here 305.

A later critic of Erasmus' views on sacred images was Ambrosius CATHARINUS (Lancellotto de' Politi) who attacked Erasmus and defended Pio in his De certa gloria, invocatione ac veneratione sanctorum disputationes atque assertiones catholicae adversus impios, Lyon: apud Mathiam Bonhomme 1542, 59-88, esp. 60 (Pio), 61-62, 66-69, 73, 76, etc. (Erasmus).

2   Cesare VASOLI, Alberto III Pio da Carpi, Carpi 1978, 13-15; Francesco FLORIDO, In M. Actii Plauti aliorumque Latinae linguae scriptorum calumniatores Apologiae, nunc primum ab autore aucta atque recognita . . . Basel 1540, page 116, lines 15-17, 30; Juan Ginés de SEPULVEDA, Antapologia pro Alberto Pio comite Carpensi in Erasmum Roterodamum, Rome: Antonio Blado 1532, $C_{ii}{}^v$; Martin LOWRY, The World of Aldus Manutius: Business and Scholarship in Renaissance Venice, Ithaca, N.Y. 1979, 52; LB, I 1011 AB; Deno John GEANAKOPLOS, Byzantium and the Renaissance: Greek Scholars in Venice; Studies in the Dissemination of Greek Learning from Byzantium to Western Europe, Cambridge, Mass. 1962, 125-35; Konrad EUBEL, Hierarchia Catholica, III, 160, Catharen. n. 3; L. Jadin, Bizanti (Triphonio), DHGE 9 (Paris 1937) col. 42; and Blosio PALLADIO (ed.), Coryciana, Rome: L. de Henricis and L. Perusinus, 1524, sigs. $DD_{iii}{}^r$-$EE_{iii}{}^r$. Pio claimed that in his youth, unless he was mistaken, he saw Erasmus in Venice. In 1508 the Dutchman was an honorary resident member of the Aldine Academy. See Pio, Responsio, fol. II ^{v}B; Chris L. HEESAKKERS, Argumentatio a persona in Erasmus' Second Apology against Alberto Pio, in: Erasmus of Rotterdam: The Man and the Scholar, edd. J. SPERNA WEILAND and W.T.M. FRIJHOFF, Leiden 1988, 79-87, here 79; and GEANAKOPLOS, 260.

Pio was also skilled in Aristotelian philosophy and in scholastic, patristic, and biblical theology. He had as his teachers of Aristotle the noted Pietro Pomponazzi, Juan de Montes de Oca, O.E.S.A., and Andrea Barro. Although learned in Thomism, he favored Scotism, studying the writings of John Duns with the help of Graziano da Brescia, O.F.M. In his youth he enjoyed debating some of the thornier problems posed by the Scotists. But as he grew older his theological tastes changed and he took up, in addition to the scholastics, the writings of the church fathers, especially Sts. Augustine and Jerome. The hermit Valerio had trained him as a youth in the study of Sacred Scriptures and he read them so frequently that no one in his household could match his understanding of the Old and New Testaments. When theological issues came up for discussion among leading churchmen at Rome, Pio's views were welcomed and carried weight.[3] Although only a layman and employed in one of the most demanding diplomatic posts in Europe, he also enjoyed a reputation for theological learning.

That Pio was pressured by others into writing against Erasmus does not seem likely. As ambassador of France to Clement VII at the time of the League of Cognac, as someone known to suffer debilitating bouts of gout, and as someone who had never before published a theological work, Pio would have been an improbable target of such pressure. In response to Erasmus' letter to him dated 10 October 1525, Pio eventually composed a lengthy reply, completed in Rome on 15 May 1526. Pio had not been persuaded by Erasmus' denials of having given birth by his books to the tragedy of the Protestant Reformation or of his claims of having been willing but unable to stop it by his pen once it had begun. Pio was convinced that Erasmus must shoulder blame because of the less than grave, inconsistent, and unorthodox way in which he had treated religious questions. Having detailed his objections to the positions espoused by Erasmus and Luther and his followers, Pio sent a copy of his lengthy letter to Erasmus with no intention of ever publishing it.[4]

---

[3] SEPULVEDA, $C_{iii}{}^{r}$-, $_{iv}{}^{r}$; the inventory of Pio's library lists works by his teachers, e.g., Gratiani Brixensis in 4^m Sententiarum, Annotationes Jo. Montis Dova(?) in parva Naturalia, and Pomponatii quaedam - see Léon DOREZ, Latino Latini et la bibliothèque capitulaire de Viterbe, in: Revue des bibliothèques 2 (1892) 377-91, here 389-90; FLORIDO, Apologia, 116:24-25; letter of Erasmus to Pio, Basel, 10 October 1525, ALLEN VI 201-02 Ep. 1634: 10-15, 39-42; letter of Erasmus to Thomas More, Basel, 30 March 1527, ALLEN VII 12, Ep. 1804: 248-56; letter of Erasmus to Johann Choler, <Freiburg> 22 December 1530, ALLEN IX 97, Ep. 2414:12.

[4] SEPULVEDA $B_{iii}{}^{r}$-$C_i{}^{v}$, $D_i{}^{r}$, $L_{iv}{}^{r-v}$; FLORIDO Lectionum succisivarum Libri III iam quoque primum et nati et in lucem editi, Basel 1540, page 264, lines 20-21; letter of Erasmus to Pio, Basel, 10 October 1525, ALLEN VI 201-03, Ep. 1634:1-111; letter of Erasmus to Si-

If pressure from others did not lead to the composition of Pio's response, it did result in its eventual publication in Paris three years later. Besides the working draft of his response which contained numerous marginal and inter-lineal insertions, corrections, and deletions, Pio had one good copy which he lent to others in such a way as to prevent its publication. During the Sack of Rome in 1527 this good copy was lost. By accident the rough draft survived because it had been mixed in with his diplomatic papers and account books which were rescued at the last minute by a member of his household. When Pio took up residence in Paris, he brought with him this rough draft. In March of 1528 Erasmus published his dialogue *Ciceronianus* in which he men-tioned Pio's response as having been written in a style close to Cicero's. Be-cause they could not obtain a copy of his work from book dealers, Pio was bombarded with requests from scholars to lend them his personal copy. The more Pio refused their petition, the more persistent became their pleadings. Erasmus' announcement of the existence of this letter seemed to Pio to take it out of the realm of the private. He even wondered if it were already in print in Germany. Finally yielding to the pressure of friends, Pio put into publish-able form the rough draft. He also made a few insertions of new materials. On 7 January 1529 it came off the press in Paris of Joost Bade van Assche, bearing the title *Ad Erasmum Roterodami expostulationem responsio accurata et paraenetica, Martini Lutheri et asseclarum eius haeresim vesanam magnis ar-gumentis et iustis rationibus confutans.* After his death, two years later, most of this work was translated into French and presented to King Francis I in the format of a beautifully illuminated manuscript.[5]

---

mon Pistorius, Basel < ca. 2 September > 1526, ALLEN VI, 403, Ep. 1744: 130; Pio XXIII Libri, fol. LXIX^v-LXX^r.

[5] *Ibid,* XLVIII^r, LXIX^v-LXX^v; Pio's description of the rough condition of this draft is confirmed by an examination of what remains of it today in the Ambrosiana - see note 1 above. Erasmus admitted that even he had thought of publishing Pio's Responsio - see LB, IX 1134 E; in 1522 he had Froben print both Sancho Carranza of Miranda's Opusculum in quasdam Erasmi Annotationes, plus his own Apologia - see ALLEN V, 52-53, n. on line 22; the French translation of the Responsio, entitled . . . la response de magnifique et noble homme albert pius Conte de Carpe sur lepistre a luy envoiee par maistre didier herasme . . . [fol. 5^v], is preserved in the Bibliothèque Nationale de Paris as Ms. Français 462, 221 fols. The names of neither the translator nor of the person who commissioned the work are given. From a prefatory letter to King Francis I it is clear that Pio has died: "le noble Conte de Carpe duquel dieu veuille par sa grace lame auoir en son paradise . . ." (fol. 2^v). The author of this letter elsewhere also states why this translation was made: "Affin que ceulx qui nentendent pas latin puissent veoir iuger et congnoistre combien grandement a erre failly et devie ce malemoeux luther enemy de la foy catholique et des sainctz decretz de leglise" (fol. 5^v). He admits that the whole of Pio's epistle has not been translated; thus, in the section treating sacred images [division A(AA) of the Latin original and chapter 41 of the French translation] the deletion of clauses becomes apparent by comparing fols.

384

Pio needed no one to urge him to write his final refutation. Soon after receiving from Pio a copy of his letter in 1526, Erasmus began work on a reply. By October of 1528 he had completed a draft of it, but he claimed he did not send it to Pio because he was not sure of his whereabouts following the Sack of Rome. Upon being informed by a friend that Pio was in Paris, that his letter to Erasmus was being circulated about, and that Pio was thinking of publishing this *Responsio*,[6] Erasmus sent him a letter dated 23 December 1528. In it Erasmus urged him to desist or at least to soften or delete those passages in which Erasmus was censured. He offered to send him privately his earlier written reply or even to meet with him in person in an effort at reconciliation.[7] Unfortunately, unbeknownst to Erasmus, this letter was intentionally not delivered to Pio until a year later.[8] Angered that Pio had published his *Responsio,* Erasmus brushed off and revised in several days time his earlier reply, completing the task on 13 February 1529.[9] This at times sarcastic rejoinder he had printed on the Froben press in March of 1529 under the title of *Responsio ad epistolam paraeneticam Alberti Pii Carporum principis.* In this work he tried to answer Pio's charges and made countercharges of his own,

---

LXXVIII^v and LXXIX^v-LXXX^r of the Bade 1529 edition with fols. 179^r-181^v of the French translation. What is not acknowledged by the editor is the addition of materials evident from a comparison of fol. LXXIX^v with fol. 180^r where a clause is inserted on the weakness of the human memory and the permanence of scripture, or of fol. LXXX^r with fol. 181^r where a whole section on the brazen serpent of Moses has been added. Pio admitted that he himself had made a few insertions of new material into the Latin Roman draft prior to publication in Paris - see his XXIII Libri, fol. LX^{r}y and Erasmus' rejoinder, LB, IX 1131D. The editor of the French translation states that in order to make it easier to read this lengthy epistle, he has divided it up into chapters (fol. 5^v). These chapters are numbered from one to fifty three ("ce dernier chapitre" - fol. 219^r), but the numbering system falls into problems when chapter 30 is listed as 31 (fol. 127^r) and the limits of chapter 36 (somewhere between fols. 147^v and 162^r) are not indicated (probably the chapter heading should have been inserted on fol. 151^r). Often the chapter divisions coincide with the marginal letter divisions in the 1529 Bade edition.

   [6]   LB, IX 1134 E-F; letter of Louis Berquin to Erasmus, <Paris, ca. 13 October 1528>, ALLEN VII 525, Ep. 2066: 60-65, letter of Erasmus to Antonio Salamanca, Basel, 10 March 1529, ALLEN VIII 79-80, Ep. 2118: 16-22.

   [7]   Letter of Erasmus to Pio, Basel, 23 December 1528, ALLEN VII 544-45, Ep. 2080:1-31.

   [8]   LB, IX 1134D, and Pio, XXIII Libri, fol. LV^{v}K.

   [9]   Erasmus states that he gave five or scarcely six days to the task of revising and polishing his earlier response - see LB, IX 1122E and his letter to Haio Herman, Basel, 25 February 1529, ALLEN VIII 67, Ep. 2108:15 (six days) or to Antonio Salamanca, Basel, 10 March 1529, ALLEN VIII 80, Ep. 2118:24-25 (five days); for the date of completion, see LB, IX 1122 E. Pio doubted that Erasmus had composed his response in so few days - see his XXIII Libri, fol. LXXI^{r-v}M.

impugning Pio's motives, sole authorship, and the accuracy of his criticisms. Until his death on 7 January 1531, Pio labored on a lengthy reply. He finished a rough draft of it on Holy Saturday, 16 April 1530, and was able to revise it only as far as book nine. The full work was published posthumously by Bade on 9 March 1531 under the title *Tres et viginti libri in locos lucubrationum variarum D. Erasmi Roterodami, quos censet ab eo recognoscendos et retractandos.*[10] In his own extensive *Apologia adversus rhapsodias calumniosarum querimonarum Alberti Pii quondam Carporum principis,* issued by August of 1531 in Basel, Erasmus once again gave answer and elaborated on his earlier charges that Pio was not the sole author of either the *Responsio* or the *XXIII Libri.*

Erasmus accused various persons of having furnished Pio with materials, of having composed diverse sections of his responses, and of having polished up his writings for publication. He claimed that he based these charges on confessions he had received in letters and in face-to-face depositions made by those who had rendered Pio this assistance.[11] Erasmus found it difficult to believe that a layman could write a work of theological erudition. He insisted that Pio had drawn his material for the *Responsio* from the discussions of theologians at Rome and in particular from Diego López de Zúñiga's catalogue of censures. Erasmus also claimed that Pio had revised this work with the help of scriptural proof texts supplied to him by the theologians of Paris. He cited in particular a reference taken from a work of Pierre Cousturier and a passage from the Book of Deuteronomy [4:2].[12] He made more sweeping charges as to how the *XXIII Libri* was composed. Not up to reading Erasmus' works himself, Pio hired a team of young scholars to comb the Erasmian corpus for any passages which could be twisted into seeming to agree with Lu-

---

[10] PIO, XXIII Libri, fols. CLXXI^r and CCXLII^r.

[11] These charges were leveled primarily at how the XXIII Libri was composed and seem to date from the time of Morrhy's letter. See especially the letter of Erasmus to Vigilius Zuichemus, <Freiburg>, 14 May 1533, ALLEN X 227, Ep. 2810: 104-06. Gerard Morrhy, a Paris printer, reported to Erasmus on Pio's hired hands who combed Erasmus' writings for anything damaging. Morrhy claimed that he got this information in a letter from Gerard, a certain Frisian who was then in Tournai and who had been earlier engaged for some months by Pio to investigate Erasmus' New Testament writings - see Morrhy's letter from Frankfurt, 16 April 1530, ALLEN VIII 423-24, Ep. 2311: 19-35. Erasmus repeated this charge in his 1534 *Purgatio,* LB, IX 1545 CD or ASD, IX-1, 418:437-39, and elsewhere in his letters, e.g. Epp. 2329:99, 2371:32-34, 2375:74-76, 2414:10, 2441:67, 2443:341-44; 2466:98, etc. In his letter to Jacopo Sadoleto, Freiburg, 7 March 1531, ALLEN IX, 165, Ep. 2443:331, Erasmus claims that the Responsio was also written with the help of hired hands.

[12] Letter of Erasmus to Thomas More, Basel, 30 March 1527, ALLEN VII 12, Ep. 1804: 253-56; letter of Erasmus to Antonio Salamanca, Basel, 10 March 1529, ALLEN VIII 80, Ep. 2118:26-28, and LB, IX 1114 C-D, 1115A, and 1118E.

ther's positions. Assistance was also rendered at Paris by theologians such as Noël Bédier, the syndic of their faculty at the Sorbonne, and by the Franciscans led by the sharp-cutting guardian of their convent there, Pierre de Cornes.[13] From Venice came material collected from Erasmus' writings by the papal nuncio, Girolamo Aleandro.[14] To give stylistic polish and consistency to this disparate material, the talents of the Spanish humanist and theologian, Juan Ginés de Sepúlveda, were employed.[15] And it was the Franciscans who saw the final product through the press of Joost Bade.[16]

Two former members of Pio's household gave answer to these charges. In his *Antapologia pro Alberto Pio Comite Carpensi in Erasmum Roterodamum,* published at Rome in January of 1532 and reprinted in Paris on 22 March 1532, Juan Ginés de Sepúlveda (ca. 1490-1573) argued from direct observation that Pio was the sole author of the *Responsio.* Even before finishing his doctoral studies in 1523 at the Spanish College of San Clemente in Bologna, Sepúlveda had joined the household of the count of Carpi. They shared to-

---

[13] Letters of Erasmus to Eleutherius, Freiburg, 6 March 1531, ALLEN IX 155, Ep. 2441:69-70; to Jacopo Sadoleto, Freiburg, 7 March 1531, ALLEN IX 165, Ep. 2443:336-38; to Nicolas Maillard, Freiburg, 28 March 1531, ALLEN IX 226, Ep. 2466:99-101; to Nikolas Winmann, Freiburg, 16 April 1531, ALLEN IX 260, Ep. 2486:38-40.

[14] The basis for Erasmus' charge that Aleandro was collecting material against Erasmus was apparently a report to Erasmus from Etienne Dolet who in 1531 served as secretary to Jean de Langeac, bishop of Limoges and French ambassador to Venice - see the letter of Jerome Aleandro to Erasmus, Regensburg, 1 April 1532, ALLEN X 8, Ep. 2639:7-14 and Judith Rich HENDERSON, Etienne Dolet, in: Contemporaries of Erasmus, ed. Peter G. BIETENHOLZ and Thomas B. DEUTSCHER I (Toronto 1985), 394-96, here 394.

For examples of this charge by Erasmus, see Erasmus' letters to Andrea Aliciati, Freiburg, <ca. 24 June> 1530, ALLEN VIII 454, Ep. 2329:105-06, to Willibald Pirckheimer, Freiburg, 29 August 1530, ALLEN IX 21, Ep. 2371:34-36, to Andrzej Krzycki, Freiburg, 1 September 1530, ALLEN IX 25, Ep. 2375:78-79, to Germain de Brie, Freiburg, 5 September 1530, ALLEN IX 33, Ep. 2379:111-13, to Lorenzo Campeggio, Freiburg, <ca. end of November> 1530, ALLEN IX 92, Ep. 2411:49-50, to Nicolas Maillard, Freiburg, 28 March 1531, ALLEN IX 226, Ep. 2466:98-99.

For Aleandro's responses, see his letters to Erasmus, Regensburg, 1 April 1532, ALLEN X 8-9, Ep. 2639:7-48 and 4 July 1532, ALLEN X 51, Ep. 2679:21-33, and Aleandro's letter to Giambattista Sanga, Köln, 28 January 1532, in: Monumenta Vaticana historiam ecclesiasticam saeculi XVI illustrantia, ed. Hugo LAEMMER, Freiburg 1861, p. 99, Ep. LXXIV. On Aleandro's activities in Venice, see Franco GAETA, Un nunzio pontificio a Venezia nel Cinquecento (Girolamo Aleandro) (= Civiltà Veneziana, Saggi 9), (Venice 1960.).

[15] Letters of Erasmus to Andrea Aliciati, Freiburg [ca. 24 June] 1530, ALLEN VIII 454, Ep. 2324: 99-102; to Andrzej Krzycki, Freiburg. 1 September 1530, ALLEN IX 25, Ep. 2375:76-77, and LB, IX 1125D.

[16] Letter of Erasmus to Eleutherius, Freiburg, 6 March 1531, ALLEN IX, 155, Ep. 2441:69-70.

gether a great interest in Aristotle whose writings Sepúlveda was retranslating into Latin. When both decided to write against the northern Reformers, the lay theologian and clerical doctor of theology agreed to critique each others works. Pio's *Responsio* against Erasmus and Luther and his followers was completed on 15 May 1526. Sepúlveda's *De fato et libero arbitrio libri tres*, written against Luther's necessitarian position, was published in Rome the following month with a prefatory letter dated June 6th. Sepúlveda claimed that they pointed out to each other whatever was displeasing or found wanting. He also swore that beside himself the only other person to see Pio's *Responsio* before its completion was the count's scribe, a teenager trained in the classical languages. Following the Sack of Rome and Pio's departure for exile in France, Sepúlveda never again saw the count. That the Spanish theologian had remained in Italy was known to Erasmus, for he was informed by Alfonso Valdes in the Fall of 1529 that Sepúlveda had accompanied Cardinal Francisco de Quiñones from Rome to Piacenza. Sepúlveda had given Pio no help in composing the *XXIII Libri*.[17]

The person who gave help of the most practical sort to Pio was Francesco Florido (ca. 1511-1548) who functioned from 1525 to 1531 as his secretary, scribe, librarian, reader, research assistant, and editor. At fifteen years of age he discontinued his humanistic studies in Rome under the direction of Decio Sillano di Spoleto to work as an amanuensis in the household of the count of Carpi. In addition to the typical tasks of taking dictation and making copies, Florido became in effect the eyes and hands of his ailing employer. Pio was so debilitated by chronic gout that he was confined to bed for months on end. Racked by pain and unable to open a book or hold a pen, he sought relief by having Florido read to him or by discussing with others issues of concern. If Pio heard something he wished later to recall, he would have Florido copy it out. Should a topic arise which the count could not personally investigate, he would call upon the services of others. He needed no assistance, however, in recognizing a controversial passage in Erasmus' writings. Even when his health improved Pio maintained a routine of giving at least eight hours a day to study. No time was lost: while he ate lunch and dinner Florido would read to him. In refutation of Erasmus' claims that Pio hired numerous research assistants and had the theologians of Paris supply him with materials, Florido insisted that while Pio was writing the *XXIII Libri* the only person in his domestic employ in Paris was himself, a youth, and that Erasmus' accusation of assistance from the Sorbonne was "far from the truth." Florido admitted that Pio had died before being able to put the finishing touches on the work and

---

17 Angel Losada, Juan Ginés de Sepúlveda a traves de su *"Epistolario"* y nuevos documentos, Madrid 1949, 37, 46-61, 306-09, 357-59, 361-63; Sepulveda, Antapologia, sigs. D_i^v-E_i^r, Allen VIII 241, introduction to Ep. 2198.

388

that part of it had been revised by "us" for publication.[18] In his letter to the reader, the printer Joost Bade stated that he and Florido had with the greatest accuracy and fidelity possible seen to the transcription and revision of Pio's rough draft for publication. At about sixty percent of the way into the *XXIII Libri,* toward the end of Book IX, Bade even identified the exact point at which Pio's own revisions ended. Toward the end of Book IX Bade interjected that the premature death of Alberto Pio had prevented him from personally revising what followed, all of which however, Pio had written.[19]

The one section which Pio most likely never authored but probably came from the pen of Florido or Bade, was the twenty-six column index to the volume arranged alphabetically according to the initial key word in summary statements. Erasmus found so offensive one hundred and twenty-two of these items that he wrote brief responses to each and published them in 1532 as *In elenchum Alberti Pii brevissima scholia.*[20]

Not addressed by either Sepúlveda or Florido was the extent to which Pio derived his materials from the writings of other contemporary Catholic controversialists. The style he adopted for the *Responsio* was similar to that adopted by Johann Eck and Josse Clichtove: Pio tried to refute his opponent with his own weapons by citing scriptural, patristic, and canonical texts and ancient church historians. But in his marginalia on Erasmus' rejoinder and in his *XXIII Libri,* Pio made reference to contemporary authors whose writings he cited in such a way as to indicate that he had read them. Although insisting that he had not seen the writings of Diego López de Zúñiga prior to their publication and had not borrowed anything from them, he admitted to having read while in Rome some of Zúñiga's criticisms and Erasmus' responses. Pio pointed out that Jacques Masson had not questioned the divine institution of the sacrament of penance, but merely wondered when and how it was so insti-

---

[18] Remigio SABBADINI, Vita e opere di Francesco Florido Sabino, in: Giornale storico della letteratura italiana 8 (1886), 333-63, here 333-34 (relevant biographical data), 337-38 (his veracity), 360 (Pio as patron); SEPULVEDA, Antapologia, sigs. D_i^{r-v}, D_{iii}^v, E_i^r-E_{iii}^r; FLORIDO, Apologia, 116:10-48 and his Lectionum libri III, 264:20-39.

[19] PIO, XXIII Libri, fols. a_i^v and $CLXXI^r$I; LB, IX 1167A. Book VIII of the XXIII Libri, on the use of sacred images, thus received its final form from Pio himself. Internal evidence would also point to his authorship, for Book VIII repeats the earlier arguments of the Responsio and makes references to civil rituals, classical Latin poetry, the advice of Vitruvius, the cultic practices of pagan antiquity, and popular miraculous images in Italy - topics on which the Sorbonne theologians and Franciscan friars were probably not well informed - see XIII Libri, fols. $CXXXIV^v$, $CXXXVI^{r-v}$, $CXLIII^r$, and $CXLVII^r$.

[20] PIO, XXIII Libri, fols. a_{ii}^r-[a_{viii}^r] contains this index; Erasmus' answers to 122 of these statements, together with his preface, were appended to his Dilutio eorum quae Iodocus Clithoveus scripsit adversus Declamationem suasoriam matrimonii . . . Basel: Froben 1532 on sigs. m_2^r-[n_8^r].

tuted. Henry VIII of England was lavishly praised for his learned and pious refutation of Luther and in particular for his proof that the sacrament of penance has a divine power. Noël Bédier was hailed as an outstanding theologian and the best of men who knowingly and truthfully affirmed that Luther's writings on Law and Gospel were obnoxious to read. Pio cited approvingly Sancho Carranza de Miranda's interpretation of the Pauline prohi-   ✱ bition against being greedy for gain as an inhibition on clerics engaging in secular business. He also applauded the Franciscan Frans Tittelmans for having proved conclusively that Erasmus' paraphrases were an innovation. About two of Erasmus' critics Pio claimed to have been ignorant until Erasmus himself called his attention to them. In both cases Pio then read their writings approvingly: the Carthusian Pierre Cousturier's critique of Erasmus' version of the New Testament was, according to Pio, learned, serious, and pious, while Maarten van Dorp's letter was lauded for its having faulted with good reason Erasmus' *Moriae Encomium*.[21]

Pio also cited three authors in such general terms that it is not clear whether he read their works. Johann Faber was praised as an early and most learned opponent of Luther. John Fisher confounded with such erudition and piety the various assertions of Luther that he too deserved mention. Pio's hero was Johannes Eck, that exceptional man who early on and with great strength attacked Luther with his own weapons.[22] As will be seen later, the similarity between the arguments in defense of sacred images advanced in Eck's *Enchiridion* (1525) and those propounded in Pio's *XXIII Libri* (1531)

---

[21] William B. JONES and Thomas B. DEUTSCHER, Luis de Carvajal, in: COE, I (Toronto 1985) 275-76, here 275; PIO, XXIII Libri, fols. LII^{v}a (Eck's style), XLVIII^{v}p, LI^{v}i, LIV^{r}n, LXIX^r (Zúñiga), LVIII^{r-v} s,b (Masson), LVIII^{v}b, LXIII^{v}f (Henry VIII), LXIX^{v}H, CCXXX^{r}A, CCXXXVII^{v}I (Bédier), CXCIV^{r}T (St.Cher's),LX^{v}i (Tittelmans), LIX^{r-v}o, f (Cousturier), LVI^{r}1 (Dorp).

[22] PIO, XXIII Libri, fols. L^v n (Faber), LXIII^v f (Fisher), L^{v}n, LII^{v}a (Eck). Pio could have met Eck and Faber in Rome where both published works against Luther. Just as Eck represented the interests in Rome of the Bavarian dukes Wilhelm IV and Ludwig, so too did Pio help their brother Ernst Wittelsbach, the administrator of the diocese of Passau - see Georg PFEILSCHIFTER (ed), Acta Reformationis Catholicae, I, Regensburg 1959, 152, 156 n.4, 159-61, 245 n.13, 275, and 287. In 1569 duke Albert ordered that among the works contained in the monastic libraries of Bavaria should be the writings of Alberto Pio - see the list in Franz Heinrich REUSCH (ed.), Die indices librorum prohibitorum des sechzehnten Jahrhunderts, Tübingen 1886, 329-37, here 332. On the pretext that Pio's XXIII Libri had been poorly translated, this book was placed on the Spanish Indices of Forbidden Books of 1551 and 1559 and the Portuguese ones of 1547 and 1551 - see J.M. de BUJANDA, Index de l'inquisition espagnole 1551, 1554, 1559 (= Index des livres interdits 5), Sherbrooke (Québec) 1984, 248-49, 451.

✱ For 'Sancho Carranza de Mirands's' read 'Hugh of St. Cher's (d.1263)'.

leads one to suspect that Pio had more than a mere general knowledge of his hero's writings.

Although not cited by Pio, three other authors are probable sources for his ideas. Juan Ginés de Sepúlveda stated that while in Rome Pio had read and critiqued his *De fato et libero arbitrio* written against Luther and published there in June of 1526.[23] Given Josse Clichtove's published works against Luther and Erasmus, his admiration for Pio's uncle Giovanni Pico, his numerous visits to Paris while Pio was there, his attack on Oecolampadius' Eucharistic views which Pio also denounced, and his theological writings which combined humanistic and scholastic learning, it is not unlikely that Pio was familiar with his writings.[24] Another source for Pio could have been the massive *Doctrinale* of the English Carmelite of the previous century, Thomas Netter of Walden (d. 1450). His theological summa, published in Paris from 1521 to 1532 by Pio's friend Bade, was written against the followers of Wycliffe and Hus, two heretics who are often denounced in Pio's writings. Among the items in the catalogue of Pio's library is a work entitled *Doctrinale*.[25]

If Pio received advice and encouragement from French theologians who had not published against Erasmus or the Protestants, his helpers' identities can only be surmised. The most likely candidate would be Pierre de Cornes, a conservative Paris theologian, guardian of the Franciscan convent there, and preacher at Pio's funeral. Another conservative theologian on the Paris Faculty of Theology who opposed Erasmus was the Cluniac Benedictine Christophe Boucher. The influential theologian and friend of Bédier, Nicolas Le Clerc (d. 1558), also found reprehensible Erasmus' writings.[26]

---

[23] Sepulveda, Antapologia, sigs. $D_{iv}{}^r, E_i{}^r$.

[24] Jean-Pierre Massaut, Josse Clichtove, l'humanisme et la réforme du clergé, 2 vols., Paris 1968, I, 43, 150-55, 184, II, 26, 44, 387, 405; for an attack on Erasmus' departures from Church practice, see Clichtove's Propugnaculum ecclesiae, Köln 1526, 141-17; for Pio's reference to Oecolampadius, see his XXIII Libri, fol. LIV^{r}l.

[25] For examples of Pio's attacks on Wycliffe and Hus, see his XXIII Libri, fols. LII^{v}d, LIII^{r}e, LXII^{r}g, LXIV^{v}f, etc.; for the first Paris printing of Netter's Doctrinale by Pio's friend Joost Bade, see Philippe Renouard, Bibliographie des impressions et des oeuvres de Josse Badius Ascensius, imprimeur et humaniste, 1462-1535, 3 vols, Paris 1908, III, 387-90; for a work entitled Doctrinale in Pio's library, see Dorez, Bibliothèque de Viterbe, 388; and the edition of Netter cited below is that by Bonaventura Bianciotti, Thomas Waldensis Carmelitae Anglici Doctrinale antiquitatum fidei catholicae ecclesiae, 3 vols. Venice 1757-59. It is interesting to note that the only works in the inventory of Pio's library written by contemporary Catholic controversalists and possibly relating to his controversies with Luther and Erasmus are: Christofori Longolii orationes (382), Epistolae Benedicti Jovii (385), and Jacobi Sadoleti de duobus Gladiis Evangelii (386).

[26] James K. Farge, Biographical Register of Paris Doctors of Theology 1500-1536 (= Subsidia Mediaevalia 10), Toronto 1980, 52, 110-12, 248-52; Georg Schurhammer,

XI

Pio's ideas on the veneration of sacred images could have come from various sources. Although Hieronymus Emser and Hugo von Hohenlandenberg had published works in defense of sacred images in 1522 and 1524 respectively, their writings were in German, a language which Pio apparently did not know. A more likely candidate would be Eck's *Enchiridion* which contained even in its first edition of 1525, reprinted that year in Rome, a chapter on images which repeated the arguments of his earlier *De non tollendis Christi et sanctorum imaginibus* (1522). Clichtove's *Propugnaculum ecclesiae* published in 1526 also contained a section defending the use of these images. But one of the richest collections of scriptural and patristic texts supporting the veneration of sacred images was that compiled by Netter and included in the third volume of his *Doctrinale* published in Paris by Bade in 1523. Many of the arguments which appear in these three writings are also found in Pio's treatment.[27]

Alberto Pio's attitudes toward religious art are discernible long before his debate with Erasmus. After the death of his father in 1477, Alberto spent much of his youth in exile at the court of Ferrara while his uncle and cousin ruled in Carpi. The then duke of Ferrara, Ercole d'Este, made large expenditures on the construction and decoration of religious buildings, on the production and illumination of pious books, and on the celebration of religious festivals and dramas. Upon assuming control of Carpi, Alberto also engaged in ambitious building projects involving the cathedral, ancient parish church of S. Maria (known as the Sagrada), and the churches of S. Nicolò fuori le mura, of the Madonna della Rosa, and of S. Maria delle Grazie. On architectural questions he consulted with Baldassarre Peruzzi and perhaps also Raffaello, and hired as decorators the painters Bernardino Loschi and Marco Meloni. He commissioned for these churches and for his own personal use a number of religious paintings in which he had himself represented as one of the on-lookers or participants: thus Giovanbattista Cima da Congeliano painted 'Christ Teaching in the Temple' with Alberto as one of the stupified teachers of the Law, the 'Pieta' with a bald and bearded Pio kneeling next to Mary whom he consoles, and the 'Deposition' with a turbaned and sad Al-

---

Francis Xavier: His Life, His Times, trans. Joseph COSTELLOE, 4 vols., Rome 1973-82, I, 250-51; Philip Edgcumbe HUGHES, Lefèvre: Pioneer of Ecclesiastical Renewal in France, Grand Rapids, Mich. 1984, 129-30.

[27] Wilbirgis KLAIBER (ed.), Katholische Kontroverstheologen und Reformer des 16. Jahrhunderts (= RST 116), Münster 1978, Nos. 981, 983, 1573; Johannes ECK, Enchiridion locorum communium adversus Lutherum et alios hostes ecclesiae (1525-1543), mit den Zusätzen von Tilmann Smeling O.P. (1529, 1532), ed. Pierre FRAENKEL(= CC 34), Münster 1979, 64*, 191-98; CLICHTOVE, Propugnaculum ecclesiae, 62-68; and NETTER, Doctrinale, III, tituli XIX (De religiosis domibus), XX (De adoratione sanctae crucis), and XXI (De peregrinando ad imagines), capita 150-161, cols. 902-972.

berto depicted as Joseph of Arimathea who holds the body of Christ for all to see. In Bartolomeo Veneto's 'Circumscision', Alberto once again is depicted in beard and turban, perhaps as Joseph, at the center of the painting between the infant Jesus and the Jewish priest. Pio also commissioned for the cathedral of Carpi a cedar statue of the Assumption carved at Paris in 1516 by Gasparo Simechi (or perhaps Francesco Sibecchi, alias Cibelli, of Carpi). Cima's 'Deposition' Pio is known to have kept in his possession while serving as ambassador in Rome.[28] Apparently only in his youth did Alberto have a secular portrait of himself painted. A work, known as 'The Portrait of Alberto Pio' and dated 1512, depicts a young man in princely robes, holding a book in his left hand, with classical figures in the background between the temples of Apollo and the Muses. The artist is variously identified as Bernardino Loschi, Bartolomeo Veneto, Baldassarre Peruzzi, or some other member of the "Italian School".[29] Given his prominence in the elite literary and social circles of papal Rome, Alberto probably knew personally such artists at Raffaello, Michelangelo, and Giulio Romano, but he seems to have given them no commissions.[30]

Erasmus had a generally favorable attitude toward painting. The claim that as a canon at Steyn he had painted a crucifixion panel is no longer given much credence by scholars.[31] But there is evidence that he once illuminated books with floral designs and later dabbled in doodles and caricatures of him-

---

[28] Werner L. GUNDERSHEIMER, Ferrara: The Style of a Renaissance Despotism, Princeton, New Jersey 1973, 195-99, 209; Marco BERNUZZI and Thomas B. DEUTSCHER, Alberto Pio, in: Contemporaries of Erasmus: A Biographical Register of the Renaissance and Reformation, ed. Peter G. BIETENHOLZ and Thomas B. DEUTSCHER, 3 vols (Toronto, 1985-87) III, 86-88, here 87; Achille SAMMARINI, L'Antica Pieve di Carpi - Memorie Storico-Artistiche, in: Memorie storiche e documenti sulla città e sull'antico principato di Carpi, IV (Carpi 1888), 83-252, here 118-25, 234-38, 246-49; and Carlo CONTINI, Alberto III Pio e il suo tempo: Iconografia con note storiche nel quinto centenario della nascita, Carpi 1475-1975, s.l. 1975, [12-13, 27-28, 30-35, 47].

[29] CONTINI, Iconografia, [24-26].

[30] On Pio's relations with the Roman Academy and leading artists, see Cesare VASOLI, Alberto III Pio da Carpi, Carpi 1978, 41-44.

[31] The case for Erasmus as the painter of a tableaux of Christ on the cross between Mary and John has been advanced in a series of studies by Maurice W. BROCKWELL, A Painting by Erasmus, in: Art in America 6 (1917), 61-66; Erasmus, Humanist and Painter: A Study of a Triptych in a Private Collection, New York (?) 1918; and Erasmus as Painter: Christ on the Cross, in: The Times (London), letters to the editor (2nd column), 17 July 1936.

For the contrary arguments, see especially Rachel GIESE, Erasmus and the Fine Arts, in: The Journal of Modern History 7 (1935) 257-79, here 263-65, and Erwin PANOFSKY, Erasmus and the Visual Arts, in: Journal of the Warburg and Courtauld Institutes 32 (1969) 200-27, here 202-04.

self and others.[32] He was on good personal terms with Quentin Massys and Albrecht Dürer, and also with Hans Holbein the younger until the latter took advantage of his kindnesses. Erasmus had discriminating taste in art and sat to have his portrait sketched by each of the above-mentioned leading northern artists of his day. While he hired these artists to make representations of himself and of others, there is no evidence that he ever gave a commission to them or to anyone else to paint a pious subject, even though these artists were also known for their fine religious paintings.[33] The only sacred images listed among his possessions in his two surviving wills are a silver laddle bearing the image of St. Jerome and a silver spoon with a carved figure of Sebastian[34] - they probably entered his possession more as gifts than as purchases and had a utilitarian rather than cultic function.

The context in which Erasmus formulated his views on the veneration of sacred images was one in which people took violently opposed positions on the issue. In his writings Erasmus frequently observed that the efforts to eliminate cultic abuses or to remove offensive images can easily meet stiff opposition from the people resulting even in civil disturbances. The historical record, however, shows that Erasmus' fears were misplaced, for violence was much more often perpetrated by iconoclastic reformers. In Basel where Erasmus resided a series of attacks on sacred images, beginning in 1525, culminated in the riots of 8-10 February 1529 when rampaging mobs broke into churches and destroyed whatever sacred art work remained. On February 10th, the new city council decreed the abolition of all images from lands under the jurisdiction of Basel, and on February 13th granted amnesty to rioters. On that same day Erasmus finished revising his answer to Pio who had accused him of many things, including that of having been a source of the Germans' hostility toward sacred images. While Erasmus gave detailed answers to other charges in his *Responsio* of 1529, he avoided the issue of images and merely admitted that on occasion he had censured church practices which are extravagant, superstitious, and silly, but did not make sport of divine things. In later letters to friends, in May to Willibald Pirckheimer and in July to Andrzej Krzycki, while reporting on the iconoclastic riots in Basel, he quipped that considering the insults inflicted on the images of the saints

---

[32] Letter of Erasmus to Sasbout, <Steyn>, <c. 1488>, ALLEN I 90-91, Ep. 16:10-12; Emil MAJOR, Handzeichnungen des Erasmus von Rotterdam, in: Historisches Museum Basel: Jahresberichte und Rechnungen (1932), 35-44 (cited by GIESE, 263 n.22 and 265 n. 30 and by PANOFSKY, 203-04 n. 11), see also GIESE, 264-66 and PANOFSKY, 203-04.

[33] GIESE, 266-71; PANOFSKY 214-27.

[34] ALLEN VI, 503-06, here 503-04, Appendix XIX, lines 22-23, 32; IX 363-65, Appendix XXV; letter to Battista Egnazio, <Freiburg>, <c. January 1530>. ALLEN VIII 318, Ep. 2249:16-18.

during this tumult he was amazed that no miracle occurred, for in times past saints, such as St. Francis, were accustomed to punish severely less serious offenses. While personally not sympathetic to sacred images, Erasmus was opposed to their violent ejection from churches.[35]

In his writings Erasmus presented a fairly consistent stance on the questions of images. This position which criticized abuses but tolerated the practice itself was worked out prior to and independently of his debate with Pio. The prince's ardent defense of this traditional devotion did, however, force Erasmus to think more deeply about the issue. To avoid a theology of images that would allow for the adoration of an inanimate object, Erasmus proposed that the picture was the mere occasion for the cultic act. He also borrowed from Pio a number of examples to show that the Old Testament prohibition on images was not absolute and that pictures can have a powerful influence on the emotions of the onlooker. The positive expositon of a theology of images found in his two works of 1533, *Explanatio symboli apostolorum sive catechismus* and *De sarcienda ecclesiae concordia,* seem at times to echo Pio, but Erasmus was ultimately not comfortable with such an affirmative stance and he soon retreated to his more typical positions of grudging tolerance or even advocacy of their total abolition.[36]

---

[35] For examples of Erasmus' concern about people resisting the removal of sacred images, see his comments in Modus orandi Deum (1524), ASD, V - 1, 156:206, Explanatio symboli (1533), Ibid. 304:958, letter to? <Freiburg>, <August 1533>, ALLEN X 282, Ep. 2853:3-5, and De concordia (1533), ASD V - 3, 305:672-73.

For a recent study of early sixteenth century iconoclasm, see Carlos M.N. EIRE, War Against the Idols: The Reformation of Worship from Erasmus to Calvin, New York 1986, esp. 50-51 (Erasmus' ideas on sacred images) and 114-19 (iconoclasm in Basel). Also on the events in Basel, see Carl C. CHRISTENSEN, Art and the Reformation in Germany, Athens, Ohio 1979, 93-102.

For Erasmus' account of the events in Basel, see his letter to Willibald Pirckheimer, Freiburg, 9 May 1529, ALLEN VIII 162, Ep. 2158:13-33, to Jan Antonin, Freiburg, 9 June 1529, Ibid. 192, Ep. 2176:65-69, to Andrzej Krzycki, Freiburg, 23 July 1529, Ibid. 245, Ep. 2201:37-49, to Jean de Lorraine, <Freiburg> <September 1529>, Ibid, 281, Ep. 2217:28-35, and to Pietro Bembo, Freiburg, 25 March 1530, Ibid. 390, Ep. 2290:57-65.

For his indirect answers in the Responsio, see LB, IX 1102 E, 1110 E, 1111 A. For his criticism of violence in removing images, see for example, his letter to Caspar Heido, Basel <c. July 1524> ALLEN V, 482, Ep. 1459: 82-85, to Philip Melanchthon, Basel, 6 September 1524, Ibid. 547, Ep. 1496:80, to Juan Vergara, Basel, 24 March 1529, ALLEN VIII, 107, Ep. 2133: 64-71, to Justus Decius, Freiburg, 8 June 1529, Ibid. 190, Ep. 2175:11-13, and his Epistola ad fratres (1530), ASD, IX-1, 374-76:33-67.

[36] For his extended expositions of a theology of images, see his Explanatio symboli (1533), ASD V-1, 302-05:885-972 (for tolerance and abolition, see 956-61), and De concordia (1533) ASD, V-3, 305-06:672-713 (for tolerance and partial abolition, see 691-93, 705-06).

Erasmus recognized the great potential for inspiration and instruction inherent in sacred images. He called art a silent poetry which is more eloquent and better able to convey an idea or emotion than can the words of the orator. A picture speaks to the eyes instead of the ears and shows us more than we can perceive from words. It can also penetrate more deeply and quickly to the seat of the emotions. Who is not moved by seeing a picture of Christ on the cross? The usefulness and power of pictures cannot be denied. He who takes away religious art also eliminates from life one of its special pleasures.[37]

He counseled others to decorate their houses with religious paintings and praised Johann von Botzheim for having such frescos in his. Events from the life of Christ and the saints, when decently depicted, should adorn every wall of every house. Such images help our memories and provide us with material for pious reflection. They are the books of the uneducated and can also further the piety of the learned. The murals in the home of the learned canon of Konstanz which Erasmus viewed in the autumn of 1522 became the objects of fulsome praise. In a published letter of 1523, Erasmus described approvingly the frescos in the open-air courtyard. On the wall by the dining table stood St. Paul instructing the people and on another wall was a seated Christ delivering His sermon on the mount. Also depicted were the Apostles going through the mountains to preach the Gospel. In a heated room were painted the priests, scribes, and Pharisees conspiring with the elders against the Gospel which is already beginning to spread. Erasmus found these scenes edifying and delightful.[38]

Reverence shown toward sacred images can be pleasing to God. There is no superstition necessarily implied if someone holds dear an image of Christ, occasionally kissing it and putting it in a place of honor. By analogy, no fault would be found should a newlywed kiss the ring or chapelt left with or sent to her by her absent spouse. Thus, the demonstration of affection for a sacred image, when it proceeds from an abundance of love and not superstition, is surely pleasing to God. In accord with the opinion of St. Paul on such matters (Rm 14:5), let each person do what seems to him proper.[39]

Erasmus rejected the notion that the image itself is adored. He found offensive to his sense of piety, even if it were philosophically true, an opinion he

---

37 ERASMUS, Institutio christiani matrimonii (1526) LB, V 696 D, 719 B; Epistola ad fratres (1530), ASD, IX-1, 374:39-42; Explanatio symboli (1533), ASD, V-1, 305-06:930-34; De concordia (1533), ASD, V-3, 305-06:676-78.

38 Letter of Erasmus to Marcus Laurijn, Basel, 1 February 1523 (printed April 1523), ALLEN V, 212, Ep. 1342:342-47; ERASMUS, Epistola ad fratres (1530) ASD, IX-1, 374:47-48, Explanatio symboli (1533) ASD, V-1, 304:927-37, De concordia (1533) ASD, V-3, 306:685-86, 689-91.

39 ERASMUS, Explanatio symboli (1533), ASD, V-1, 304:952-55, De concordia (1533), ASD, V-3, 306:700-06.

attributed to John Duns Scotus, namely, that a wooden representation of the Trinity is reverenced with the same adoration (*latria*) used in worshipping the Godhead Itself, for there is but one and the same act of adoration which moves toward its end through a means.[40] In opposition to this teaching, Erasmus insisted that nothing devoid of reason is suitable either for adoration (the external veneration through gestures) or for cult (the internal veneration or worship). He insisted that the stupid are so confused as to honor a statue instead of the thing represented. The informed worshipper does not honor the wood when he bows his head to a Cross, nor does he reverence a decorated leather binding when he kisses a Gospel lectionary, but rather the crucified Christ there depicted or Christ's doctrine therein contained. A sacred image provides an occasion for adoring God or venerating the saint thus represented.[41]

Erasmus' attempt to define idolatry tended to focus on its moralistic implications. He saw it as a horrible crime which equated an image with God. Dismissing the common notion of it as the burning of incense before an idol, he asserted that idolatry is any denial of God or disdaining of Christ which occurs whenever we seek to please ourselves or others by doing something offensive to God, such as yielding to base sexual desire, seeking vengeance, tyrannizing over others, or giving in to greed. The idols of his day, he claimed, were carnal affections. The worship of stone or wooden idols had been so eliminated by the message of Christ that the danger of idolatry had ceased. He feared, however, that through demons' deceit the cult of idols could return.[42]

---

[40] ERASMUS, Annotationes in Novum Testamentum LB, VI 1015 DE (on Heb. 11:21), letter to Jacopo Sadoleto, Freiburg, 7 March 1531, ALLEN IX 163, Ep. 2443:230-32, Apologia adversus rhapsodias Alberti Pii (1531), LB IX, 1160 DE. Whether Scotus actually made such a statement is unclear. I have been as unsuccessful in locating this reference as have previous scholars - e.g. ALLEN IX 163 (no note on lines 230-32) and Clarence MILLER in ASD, IV-3, 123 and 135 (not mentioned in the extensive notes on lines 964-66 and 176-78 respectively). Erasmus may have confused Scotus' views with those of Thomas Aquinas and Durand di San Porciano - for a critique of these positions by Tommaso DE VIO in 1520 (published in 1523), see his commentary on Quaestio XXV, articulus III of Thomae Aquinatis tertia pars Summae Theologiae (Leonine edition) (= Opera omnia 11) Rome 1903, 279-81.

[41] ERASMUS, Moria (1511), ASD, IV-3, 134:175-79, Apologia adversus rhapsodias Alberti Pii (1531), LB, IX 1160 F, Explanatio symboli (1533), ASD, V-1, 304:949-52, 955-56.

[42] ERASMUS, De vera theologia (1519), LB, V 120 A, letter to Johann von Botzheim, Freiburg, 13 August 1529, ALLEN VIII 254, Ep. 2205:90-91, Epistola ad fratres (1530), ASD, IX-1, 374-75:53-61, Explanatio symboli (1533), ASD, V-1, 304:946-52, De concordia (1533), V-3, 305:674-76.

Erasmus offered his interpretation of the biblical teachings on religious images. He noted that the first commandment of the Decalogue applied to the Jewish people and does not prohibit the use of all images, for Moses placed two cherubim on the Ark and Solomon decorated the basins in the Temple with figures of oxen and lions and had cherubim carved on the wall panels, while the high priest wore on his mitre the symbol of the moon and on his garment were depicted pomegranates. These figures, however, were not in the style of pagan idols, probably did not represent Yahweh or the gods of the Gentiles, and were not for adoration but for ornamentation and to serve as reminders of wholesome things. But if one were to look at the message of the Bible as a whole, one would have to conclude that the use of images was discouraged and nowhere recommended. To argue that because Jews were forbidden to make and venerate sacred images Christians should similarly refrain is not to propound an absurd consideration.[43]

Only slowly did the ancient Church adopt the practice of venerating sacred images. Prior to the time of St. Jerome, some of the approved men of the Christian religion allowed in places of worship no image, not even of Christ, whether it was painted, sculptured, or woven. They devoted much, even violent efforts to this prohibition for fear of idolatry and of encouraging an anthropomorphic understanding of the Godhead. But then some church Fathers thought they could gradually lead people toward the Christian religion if they allowed them to venerate images of Christ and His saints instead of those of the pagan gods. Because of the popularity of these sacred images, churches quickly became full of them.[44]

Over the centuries the cult of images fell victim to abuses which were denounced by Erasmus who prescribed fitting remedies. He expressed serious concern that sacred art depict appropriate subject matter. He held that images placed in churches should have as their themes events found in the Bible. The decree of an African synod restricting what is read in churches to what is found in the Bible should be extended to the subject matter of art works displayed in these places of worship. But not all biblical scenes are fitting topics, as for example, David's seduction of Bathsheba [2 Rg 11:4] or his sleeping with Abishag [3 Rg 1:1-4] or Salome's dance before Herod Anti-

---

[43] ERASMUS, Epistola ad fratres (1530), ASD, IX-1, 374:42-46, letter to Jacopo Sadoleto, Basel, 7 March 1531, ALLEN IX 163, Ep. 2443:228-30, Scholia (1532), Nr. 74, sig. n₃ᵛ, Explanatio symboli (1533), ASD, V-1, 304:940-46.

[44] ERASMUS, Modus orandi Deum (1524), ASD V-1, 156:200-04, letter to Jacopo Sadoleto, Basel, 7 March 1531, ALLEN IX 163, Ep. 2443:232-34, Explanatio symboli (1533), ASD V-1, 232:795-99, 304:922-25, Erasmus' claim that the use of sacred images was opposed prior to the time of St. Jerome may be based on the letter of Epiphanius (bishop of Salamis) to John (bishop of Jerusalem) in which the bishop tells of tearing down a curtain bearing the image of Christ - see Ep. 51, 9 (PL 22:526-27).

pas [Mr 6:22]. And even when pious scenes are represented, care must be taken lest the artists have introduced into their paintings impious and blasphemous details of their own invention, such as depicting in the background an already inebriated Peter draining another goblet or Martha seducing John while Christ speaks to Mary. Those artists who mix into sacred scenes their own scandalous or ridiculous jokes should be severely punished. Some pious scenes, even those enjoying a partial scriptural basis, have been so over-elaborated as to appear as childish stories and fables. Among these scenes unworthy of the Christian religion are the seven falls of Christ, the seven swords of Mary, and her three vows. All scandalous, obscene, subversive, and stupid panels should also be removed from churches and not be allowed in the homes of Christians or elsewhere. While Erasmus seems to have preferred that only biblically based pictures be allowed in churches, he conceded that images of saints have a rightful place considering the displays within churches of military trophies, heraldic shields, and the figures of animals and birds, real and imagined. Outside the church proper, in its portico, ambulatories, and cloister, scenes from the life of Christ and of His apostles and from secular history, provided they promote good morals, can also be depicted. Paintings of Christ, of the saints, and of edifying topics are the equally fitting ornaments of a Christian home.[45]

The manner in which Christian themes were presented drew comment from Erasmus. He disapproved of the classicizing tendency in Italian art which tried to model Christ and the saints after the pagan gods of Greece and Rome. He was also upset when figures of Christ and St. Paul had been patterned on a drunken rascal and those of the Virgin Mary and St. Agatha on a lascivious young whore. Such paintings lead not to piety but to license and are unworthy of Christ. It would be good if they were eliminated quietly.[46]

The number of sacred images on display in churches seemed excessive at times to Erasmus. In the sanctuary and at side altars where God is worshipped Erasmus wanted placed only a figure of the crucifix. To help eliminate the cluttered appearance of churches, he suggested that only those pictures remain which were pure, modest, becoming, and conducive to religion.[47]

---

[45] ERASMUS, Modus orandi Deum (1524), ASD V-1, 156:207-10, 216-21, Institutio christiani matrimonii (1526), LB, V 697 A, 719 C-F, Explanatio symboli (1533), ASD V-1, 304:934-36, De concordia (1533), ASD V-3, 306:686-96. The decree of the African synod has been identified as Canon 36 of the Council of Hippo (393) by R. STUPPERICH in ASD, V-3, 307 n. 687.

[46] ERASMUS, Modus orandi Deum (1524), ASD, V-1, 156:211-14, Ciceronianus (1528), ASD, I-2, 635.

[47] ERASMUS, Modus orandi Deum (1524), ASD, V-1, 156:204; Interpretatio in Psalmum LXXXV (1528), ASD, V-3, 381:417-20, letter to Johann von Botzheim, Freiburg, 13 August 1529, ALLEN VIII 254, Ep. 2205:89-90, Explanatio symboli (1533), ASD, V-1, 303-

Too much money, in the opinion of Erasmus, was being spent on religious art. The enormous sums paid to build and decorate the white-marble Certosa of Pavia were scandalous. Paintings are also signs of wealth and those who donated them to churches often seek not the cause of piety but the perpetuation of their names to posterity. More pleasing to Christ would be the use of this money as alms for the poor. Rather than spending ill-gotten wealth on church decorations which are emblazoned with the donor's heraldic device, let the would-be benefactor restore the money to his victim.[48]

Erasmus viewed miraculous paintings with some scepticism. Belief in the special powers of certain images he traced to pagan times. He wondered how some Christians did not have a similar devotion to all images of Christ and the saints, but hoped from one what they did not dare to ask of another. But he found credible the ancient accounts of various miracles worked at the tombs of certain martyrs.[49] The cultic function of images, nonetheless, remained for him an area of acute concern.

The rituals and gestures used in venerating sacred images reminded Erasmus of pagan practices. Just as the heathens used similar gestures in worshipping their various idols, so too do Christians honor God and His saints in the same way, as if there were no distinction between Creator and creature. They bow down and prostrate themselves on the ground before wooden effigies. They crawl on their knees toward them, kiss them fondly with their hands, rub their chaplets, gaze upon them intently, speak to them, and pray only in their presence. These statues are carried about in triumphal carts, attended by guilds, and honored by huge standards which are carried by many sweating devotees who need to be revived by drink. Tableaux vivants representing the appearance and deeds of saints often end up doing and saying ridiculous things. It is not surprising if these practices mimic so closely pagan rites. In an effort to attract people to Christianity, the ancient leaders of the Church borrowed from heathen rituals and games honoring the pagan gods. The standard of the Cross or statues of saints replaced the idols carried about in public procession. Church Fathers tolerated these practices not because

---

04:916, 925-27. A similar recommendation that only the cross be placed above the altar was made at the Colloquy of Poissy in 1562 by the Erasmian Claude d'Espence - see Donald NUGENT, Ecumenism in the Age of the Reformation: The Colloquy of Poissy (Harvard Historial Studies 89), Cambridge, Mass. 1974, 196-97.

[48] ERASMUS, Convivium religiosum (1522), ASD, I-3, 257-58:795-822, Vidua christiana (1529), LB, V 729 C, 754 B-D, Enarratio psalmi XIV (1536), ASD, V-2, 313:881-87.

[49] ERASMUS, Modus orandi Deum (1524) ASD, V-1, 153: 115-21, letter to Jacopo Sadoleto, Basel, 7 March 1531, ALLEN IX, 163, Ep. 2443: 238-41, Ecclesiastes (1535), LB, V 778 A.

they contained the Christian religion, but because they seemed to lead to a higher level of piety.[50]

Erasmus proposed various remedies for superstitions. He felt that exposing these practices would effectively confute them. The simple people who engage in them should be admonished, have explained to them the Church's teaching, and be instructed in the proper use of images and in how to pray. Adoration has its own gestures: folded hands should be raised toward heaven, the knees bent, the mouth closed, and the deportment of the whole body directed toward a religious act with great purity and reverence. The eyes can be focused on an image, but the mind must concentrate on things spiritual. Or better, let the eyes be closed, for God can be seen with an upright heart. Try even to worship God apart from the phantasms of the senses, to adore Him in spirit. For images are but stepping-stones that should lead one to something better.[51]

Where education fails to eliminate the evils, Erasmus counselled tolerance, suppression, and substitution. If the removal of all immodest and unbecoming images cannot be gradually effected without civil disturbances, let their continued presence be tolerated.[52] But where it can be peacefully done, Erasmus advised that *all* images should be removed from churches in order to eliminate more easily and safely every form of superstition associated with them.[53] Instead of venerating pictures of Christ and His saints, let the people show true devotion by following the example of Christ in the Gospel and imitating the virtues of the saints. And let a living icon be presented to the people in the person of the preacher who in his words, countenance, and life shines forth the true power of the divine Spirit.[54] Erasmus was amazed at how much solicitude was given to the veneration of images when one can scarcely explain how veneration befits an inanimate thing.[55]

---

[50] ERASMUS, Modus orandi Deum (1524), ASD, V-1, 154-55:130-99, letter to Jacopo Sadoleto, Basel, 7 March 1531, ALLEN IX 163, Ep. 2443:235-41, Explanatio symboli (1533) ASD, V-1, 305:963-64.

[51] ERASMUS, Enchiridion (1503), LB, V 32 EF, Modus orandi Deum (1524) ASD, V-1, 156:205, Interpretatio in Psalmum LXXXV (1528), ASD, V-3, 381:417-20, Apologia adversus rhapsodias Alberti Pii (1531), LB, IX 1102 F, Explanatio symboli (1533), ASD, V-1, 304:921-22, De concordia (1533), ASD, V-3, 305:665-69, Enarratio psalmi XIV (1536), ASD, V-2, 313:881-87.

[52] ERASMUS, Modus orandi Deum (1524), ASD, V-1, 154:162-65, 156:213-15, 221, De concordia (1533), ASD, V-3, 305:669-70, letter to ?, <Freiburg>, <August, 1533>, ALLEN X 282, Ep. 2853:3-5.

[53] ERASMUS, Explanatio symboli (1533), ASD, V-1, 304-05:956-61.

[54] ERASMUS, Enchiridion (1503), LB, V, 31 F, De concordia (1533), ASD, V-3, 712-13.

[55] ERASMUS, Scholia (1532), Nr. 73, sig. n_3^{r-v}.

Erasmus' principal defense against the attacks of Pio was to claim that they were originally aimed at the Zwinglian image-smashers and only later and without justification redirected against him.[56] The section on images in Pio's *Responsio* of 1529 did indeed excoriate the German iconoclasts and made no explicit mention of Erasmus. In Book VIII of his *XXIII Libri* (1531), Pio admitted that what he had published two years earlier was a general refutation of the heretics of his day, but he insisted that the arguments he presented could also be directed against Erasmus. He cited two statements taken from the Erasmian corpus to show how the Dutchman unjustly characterized the veneration of images as something vain, superstitious, erroneous, and sacriligious. The first, taken from the *Enchiridion militis christiani* (1503), lamented the gullibility of most people in thinking that they merit heaven by observing punctiliously mere ceremonies invented by men - this passage makes no mention of images. The second statement came from Erasmus' annotation on the Epistle to the Hebrews [11:2] where Erasmus stated that in Old Testament times the worship of anything created was abhorrent because such honors were reserved only for God, but that nowadays supernatural philosophy has discoverd that a wooden representation of the Trinity is to be worshipped with the same adoration used for the Trinity Itself - a statement Erasmus found offensive to pious ears and which Pio also rejected as most false and calumnious. Pio held that his treatise on images was a refutation of the premises which underlaid Erasmus' two statements. But for most of Book VIII, it was once again the German iconoclasts, and not Erasmus, who were explicitly attacked.[57]

Erasmus' claim that Book VIII was written for Pio by some monk or theologian as is evidenced by the subtlety of the distinctions and arguments used does not seem credible. As shown above, Pio was skilled in biblical, patristic, and scholastic theology. Besides, Book VIII is for the most part but an elabo-

---

[56] Erasmus, Apologia adversus rhapsodias Alberti Pii, LB, IX 1160 F.

[57] For explicit references to the German iconoclasts, see Pio, Responsio, fols. XXXVII^{r}Z-XXXVIII^{r}A, for his implicit references to Erasmus in Book VIII, see, e.g., XXIII Libri, fols. CXXXIII^{v}A-CXXXIV^r, CXXXVII^{r}G, CXLIII^r, CXLVI^{v}Y. The two citations from Erasmus' writings are found in the Enchiridion (1503), LB, V 33 A and in his Annotationes, LB, VI 1015 DE. For Pio's rejection of the "Scotus" statement, see his XXIII Libri, fol. CXXXV^{r-v}D. Pio was aware that Luther had tempered the iconoclasm of some Protestants, see his Responsio (1529), fol. LXVII^{v}R, reprinted in XXIII Libri, fol. XXXII^{r}R: *Hic nihilo secius sacras imagines contempsit, quamvis postea (ut audio) hanc legem sed stultissime temperavit.*

ration of arguments already presented in Pio's *Responsio* of 1529, the authorship of which Erasmus does not seriously challenge.[58]

The first part of Book VIII tries to answer a charge, never explicitated but at times hinted at by Erasmus, that those who venerate scared images are guilty of idolatry because they offer worship owed to God alone to something vile and lifeless. In response to this accusation Pio tried to define idolatry and to analyze the relationships between image and the person represented.[59]

Pio based his definition of idolatry on a section from St. Paul's Epistle to the Romans [1:18-25]. Paul states that although the pagans knew God from natural reason, they refused to offer Him glory and gratitude, but instead shaped their own notions and images which they held to be true gods, animated and living *numina*, or held that these effigies truly represented the proper nature of God and were not mere signs. These they worshipped instead of God. Having surveyed also the church Fathers on this topic of idolatry, Pio concluded that idolatry consists in offering to a creature, preceived as such, the cult owed only to God. It does not consist in making and venerating images. Pagans were not wrong in setting up effigies referring to the *numina*.[60]

Pio sought to clarify the nature of cult. External cult, as practiced by humans in this world, requires, in addition to a time and place, the use of gestures and a sensible object. The gestures used are not prescribed by God. That of kneeling, which can symbolize subjection or penance, does not necessarily imply adoration, for the bended knee is employed indiscriminately in honoring magistrates, kings, saints, and God. The intention or internal disposition of the kneeler, however, differs according to the situation. Worship (*latria*) is rendered only to God, but it can be paid to something intimately joined to the divinity such as the body of Christ. But an image, insofar as it is something created, is not to be adored, no matter how beautiful it is. Because of the divinity or saint represented, the image may be venerated. But as all Christians, even the feeble-minded, know, it is God, the archetype, Whom they worship, when they reverence a wooden or bronze or stone "likeness" of Him. The same adoration is not paid to both the image and the Godhead represented.[61]

Having disposed of the accusation that Christians are idolators, Pio addressed the next charge that the fashioning of images of God is neither al-

---

[58] For ERASMUS' charge, see his Apologia, LB, IX, 1160 F; for an example of Pio's syllogistic argumentation, see his XXIII Libri, fol. CXXXVIII[r]; and for arguments pointing to Pio's authorship, see above note 19.

[59] PIO, XXIII Libri, fols. CXXXIV[r]-CXXXVII[r].

[60] Ibid. CXXXV[v]-CXXXVII[r].

[61] Ibid. CXXXIV[r]-CXXXV[v], CXLVI[v].

lowed, fitting, nor useful. His response contained arguments drawn from a wide variety of sources.[62]

By an appeal to natural reason, Pio tried to answer his opponent's claims that it is impossible to represent by material means the proper nature of a purely spiritual God and that the effort to do so is impious and can result only in a confused, indeterminate, misleading, and unsuitable image. In response to these assertions, Pio examined the various ways in which God can be represented. Not only is an image of the same divine nature possible, but such an image in fact exists in the person of the incarnate Word, Jesus Christ, Who is the image of the Father and shares the same nature and substance with Him. Granted that apart from Christ there is no image that is wholly or partially of the same divine substance, but then an image need not be of the same nature and no representation will be exactly like the thing represented. Any attempt to represent the proper nature of God will indeed result in only a confused form. But some forms are better than others. Because God the Creator contains all the perfections found in His creatures, He can be represented by any creature that mirrors His perfections. Those creatures that possess these qualities more so than others can more fittingly refer to Him, because the more perfect the creature, the closer it comes to Him. The image can even be of a completely different nature and resemble what it represents only in certain qualities. Thus, a piece of marble can represent a living person because it has been carved with his features. An image should not be so similar that it cannot be distinguished from what it represents, for it is of the very nature of an effigy that it refers to someone else. By human convention and custom something dissimilar both in nature and qualities can also be taken to represent something else. The ancient Egyptians worshipped their gods in the form of various animals. If letters of the alphabet, by nature so dissimilar from God, can by human convention be held to signify God, why cannot an image shaped by a paint brush or chisel also come to represent Him?[63] Leaving aside considerations of how God can be properly represented, Pio also argued from the spiritual needs of the physically impaired. Because God wants people to know Him, material images must be allowed, for how else can a deaf person be instructed about God without the help of pictures?[64] Thus, by a variety of arguments based on natural reason, Pio demonstrated that is possible and pious to make images of God.

Pio examined the teachings of the Old Testament to determine if Christians were forbidden to make images of God. Prior to the time of Moses, God taught us that He is representable and revealed Himself on numerous

---

[62] Ibid. CXXXVII^(r-v).

[63] Ibid. CXXXVII^r-CXXXIX^v.

[64] Ibid. CXXXIX^v-CXL^r.

occasions under sensible signs. He told us in Genesis [1:26-27] that He made man in His own image and likeness and thus indicated that He could be appropriately represented in human form. In the valley of Mamre Abraham saw three men and worshipped one as God [Gn 18:1-22]. Daniel saw in a vision God the Father as an aged, white-haired man seated on a throne [Dn 7:9] and the Son as the son of man coming on the clouds of heaven [Dn 7:13]. Ezekiel saw the Lord in a human form that spoke to him [Ez 1:26-2:2]. In addition to the human form, God also appeared in mist [3 Rg 8:12], in a column of fire or of cloud [eg. Ex 13:23-24, 16:10, 19:9, 40:34-38; Lv 16:2], or in other sensible ways [e.g. Ex 3:2-6]. He ordered Moses to make a bronze serpent through which His healing power was exercised [Nm 21:8-9, 4 Rg 18:4]. The natural law is in harmony with this scriptural evidence, for it does not condemn as inherently evil the making of images or sensible representations of God.[65]

The first commandment of the Decalogue which forbade the introduction of foreign gods and the carving and adoration of divine images applied primarily to the Israelites. This prohibition was then necessary because the human race had become corrupted, few men worshipped the true God, while most had gods of their own making. During their sojourn in Egypt, the Hebrews learned of the pagan gods and their rituals. Over the centuries their proclivity for idolatry was such that they continued to worship false gods. Even the wisest among them, Solomon, worshipped Astarte, [the Canaanite fertility] goddess of Sidon, and Molech, [the child-sacrifice] god of the Ammonites [4 Rg 23:13]. Idols and obscene rites were established even in the Temple at Jerusalem. The destruction of this Temple and the punishment of the Babylonian captivity did not cure them of their idolatrous proclivities. The commandment against making graven images was to remove from the Israelites any occasion for idolatry. But even this prohibition was not absolute. The two cherubim on the Ark of the Covenant, the angels on the Temple walls, and the twelve bronze oxen were seen by Pio as images of the divine allowed to the Israelites by God, but not to be worshipped. This prohibition against adoring images is the only part of the first commandment which applies to all men.[66]

Christians are not forbidden to make and venerate images. The laws of Judaism do not apply to them. Unlike the pagans, they give glory and thanks to the true God and do not hold idols to be gods, although they may have somewhat confused ideas about the relationship between the representation

[65] Pio, Responsio, fol. XXXVII^v; La Response, fol. 181^r (this reference to the bronze serpent appears only in the French translation and indirectly in his XXIII Libri, fol. CXLIV^r); XXIII Libri, fols. CXXXV^v and CXXXIX^{r-v}.

[66] Pio, Responsio, fol. XXXVII^{r-v}; XXIII Libri, fols. CXXXIX^r-CXLI^r.

and the person represented. Granted that some Christians cannot describe in great detail the Church's teaching on the use of sacred images; they know, however, that they do not adore the material image but rather God there represented. Because they hold whatever the Church teaches, they avoid any errors and retain implicitly the integrity of the faith.[67]

In the latter part of Book VIII, Pio argued for the usefulness of sacred images by appeals to the teachings of Scripture and the church Fathers. He found further evidence in the practice of the Church from ancient times onward which has been confirmed by miracles and canonical decrees. Common sense based on experience also points clearly to the utility of sacred images.

The Bible and the earliest apostolic tradition show that God Himself is the author of the use of images. He ordered Moses to adorn the Ark with cherubim [Ex 25:18] and Solomon to use other symbols in the Temple [3 Rg 6:23-35]. God would not have commanded Moses to make statues of the invisible angels if it were not useful. He made Himself visible to us by making man in His own image [Gn 1:26] and by sending us His true image, the consubstantial, only begotten Son in the form of man [Jo 1:14]. Pio conceded that the New Testament contains no explicit teaching on the use of sacred images. But he pointed out that all of Christ's words were not written down [Jo 21:25]. And by accepting as true the story narrated by John of Damascus in Book IV of his *De fide orthodoxa*, Pio claimed that Christ had implicitly approved their use when He sent to King Abgar of Edessa, who was anxious to have a picture of Christ, a piece of cloth on which He had imprinted His features when He used it to wipe His face. In his version of these events, Eusebius of Caesarea stated that King Abgar had written to Jesus Who sent him a letter in reply and it was this letter (no mention of an image) which was preserved in Edessa. Not only did Christ leave behind material witnesses to His presence on earth, but He instituted sacraments and thereby taught that spiritual realities can be represented and at times be even adored under sensible signs.[68]

---

[67] PIO, Responsio, fol. XXXVII[r-v]; XXIII Libri, fol. CXLI[r-v].

[68] PIO, Responsio, fol. XXXVII[r-v]; XXIII Libri, fols. CXLI[v]-CXLII[r]; JOHN OF DAMASCUS, Expositio fidei orthodoxae, IV, 16 (PG 94:1174); EUSEBIUS OF CAESAREA, Historiae ecclesiasticae libri decem, I, 13 (PG 20:122) - references to John and Eusebius can also be found in ECK'S Enchiridion (ed. FRAENKEL), 192 n. 12, in CLICHTOVE'S Propugnaculum, 63, and in NETTER, Doctrinale, III, 907 E. The reference to JOHN CHRYSOSTOM seems to be to his Liber quod Christus sit Deus contra Judaeos atque Gentiles (PG 48:826). Pio was probably referring to the Eucharist when he stated that a sensible thing, a sacrament, can be adored. It is interesting to note that Pio made no appeal to the image on the Holy Shroud which in his time was preserved at Chambéry in Savoy and was the object of popular devotion approved in 1506 by the bull *Romanus Pontifex* of Julius II. Pio's concern for scriptural and patristic proofs probably led him to omit this reference.

406

Pio appealed to the testimony of the church Fathers and historians of the early Church to show that the use of sacred images dated from the time of the apostles, was received by the faithful, and continually practiced in subsequent times. He attributed to St. Augustine the story that St. Luke painted Christ and His mother, and he found in Augustine's *De doctrina christiana* the statement that the Christian worshipper, who understands what the image represents, does not venerate what he sees but Him to Whom the image refers. St. John Chrysostom in his commentary on St. Matthew's Gospel [14:13] stated that no one was ashamed of the sign of the Cross but rather embraced it as the consummation of all that led to our salvation, and thus Christians placed the Cross everywhere so as always to venerate it as the trophy of Christ and their own standard. St. Ambrose had in his basilica in Milan not only the crucifix and other sacred images, but he also placed near to the Cross a type of it, namely, a copy of the bronze serpent which Moses had placed on a pole in the desert. When Serenus, the bishop of Marseille, destroyed the images in his churches lest they become occasions for error, St. Gregory the Great wrote to restrain him, explaining that the pictures on the walls were for the benefit of those who could not read. This same pope also sent to Secondinus upon request certain images, comparing them to writings (*pictura quasi scriptura*), describing them as aids to our memories, and teaching him that we do not prostrate ourselves before them, as before a divinity, but we adore through an image Christ Who is now seated upon His throne. Saints Basil the Great, Augustine, Jerome, and John of Damascus all affirmed that the honor rendered to images passes on to the person represented, to the prototype or exemplar. The existence of a famous, miracle-working statue of Christ in the Phoenician city of Caesarea was reported in the *Ecclesiastical History* of Eusebius and, Pio mistakenly claimed, in the *Tripartate History* of Socrates. The reason for setting up statues and sacred images, according to John of Damascus, is to inspire us to imitate the virtues of those represented. Thus, sacred images were used in the early church with the approval of leading church Fathers.[69]

---

[69] Pio, Responsio, fol. XXXVII^v and XXIII Libri, fols. CXLII^r-v, CXLIII^v-CXLIV^r. Unlike Pio, CLICHTOVE does not attribute the story of St. Luke painting Mary and Christ explicity to St. Augustine - see his Propugnaculum, 63; neither does ECK - see his Enchiridion, 192 n. 17; nor does NETTER, Doctrinale, III, 948 C (but his discussion of Luke as a painter follows immediately after a section on Augustine). AUGUSTINE, De doctrina christiana, III, 7 (11) (PL 34:70); JOHN CHRYSOSTOM, Commentaria in Matthaeum, Homilia LIV, 4 (PG 58:536-38); for references in St. AMBROSE to the brazen serpent as a type of Christ on the cross, see e.g., Expositio in Psalmum 118, sermo VI, 15 (PL 15:1340) and De Spiritu Sancto libri tres, III, viii, 50-51 (Pl 16:787); GREGORY THE GREAT, Epistolae IX, Ep. 105 and XI, Ep. 13 (both to Serenus) (PL 77:1027-28, 1128-29), XI, Ep. 52 (to Secundinus) (PL 77:990-91); St. BASIL THE GREAT, Liber de Spiritu Sancto, XVIII, 45 (PG 32:149 C);

These men were inspired by the Holy Spirit to institute the use of sacred images. Christ nowhere in the Bible ordered that His Gospel was to be written down, rather He told His apostles to preach it [Mt 28:19-20]. Later, under the guidance of the Holy Spirit, His message was written down for the common good. A similar thing can be said for images: the Holy Spirit suggested this practice to our fathers in the Faith. Recall, however, this difference: God had earlier set up the use of these images. Only someone with a mental block would assert that it is permissible to represent divine things in a written form which is accessible only to the few who are literate, but forbidden to depict them in images which by natural intuition can be understood by all. The charge that images can lead to idolatry can also be lodged against lectionaries, for Christians kiss and venerate the sacred books of the Bible in the same way they honor images. If using images is considered a paganization of Christianity, then removing them can be equally denounced as a form of Judaization.[70]

The utility of sacred signs, such as that of the Cross, has been proven over the centuries. Persons possessed by unclean spirits are often healed when brought before a Cross or sacred image. Constantine the Great attributed his victory over Maxentius at the Milvian bridge near Rome to the sign of the Cross which he used in battle. His mother Helena, inspired by the Holy Spirit, made a pilgrimage to find the wooden cross on which Christ died and when she had recovered it she adored it, without thereby falling into idolatry. A short time afterwards she sent to her son a crown encrusted with gems and made all the more precious by being adorned with one of the nails from the true Cross. This indicates how useful she felt this relic was. Emperor Heraclius fought a great battle to recover the Cross from the Persian shah Khusrau and scored an impressive victory. The fittingness of this most holy sign of the Cross can also be discerned from the fact that it is always used in the sacred rituals of the Church, and St. John Chrysostom held that it should be introduced and inserted everywhere.[71]

JEROME, Epistolae, Ep. 109.1 to Riparius (PL 22:906-07) and his Liber unus contra Vigilantium, 5-7 (PL 23:343-46); JOHN OF DAMASCUS, Expositio fidei orthodoxae, IV, 16 (PG 94:1170); EUSEBIUS OF CAESAREA, Historia ecclesiasticae libri decem, VII, 18 (PG 20:679) and instead of Socrates, see HERMIAS SOZOMEN, Ecclesiastica Historia, V, 21 (PG 67: 1279-80). Pio seems to have followed Netter in attributing this work to Socrates, see NETTER, Doctrinale, III, 907 A and 954 C. Once again many of these references also appear in Eck and Clichtove, but especially in Netter, and that to Gregory's letter to Serenus in the Corpus juris canonici, c. 27, D. III, de cons. (edd. E.L. RICHTER and E. FRIEDBERG, I, col. 1360).

[70] PIO, Responsio, fol. XXXVII^{r-v} and XXIII Libri, fol. CXLV^v.

[71] PIO, XXIII Libri, fols. CXLV^v-CXLVI^r; AMBROSE, De obitu Theodosii oratio, esp. 46-47 (PL 16:1401-02); for Constantine's victory over Maxentius and use of the Cross, see

The use of sacred images has been formally approved by Church authorities. The decrees of popes and of general councils have defined their use to be in accord with the Faith and have ordered their veneration. In this context Pio does not explicitly mention the decrees of Nicaea II in support of sacred images. There is no Christian people in the whole world, whether Latins, Greeks, or barbarians, whether orthodox or schismatics (such as the Nestorians, Jacobites, Armenians, Copts, Georgians, or others dispersed throughout the East), who do not venerate sacred images. Only the Moslems, who follow in part the Jews, Arians, and pagans, forbid in their Koran the use of images. There are also some heretics, but few in number, who reject sacred pictures due to their lack of common sense, excited minds, and pride. Erasmus is not the first to scoff at sacred images as the history of the iconoclastic heresy well demonstrates. Nonetheless, the authority of the universal Church clearly supports the practice of venerating images.[72]

The usefulness of sacred images has been proven over the centuries by the miracles and marvels that have occurred as a result of intercession before them. Eusebius told of a strange herb that grew at the base of a bronze statue of Christ in Phoenician Caesarea. Juice from this plant could cure a disease only if harvested from those leaves which had grown to such a height that they had touched the bronze hem of the figure of Christ. Implicitly admitting that he had not read the acts of the Second Council of Nicaea at which the event occurred, as evidenced by his repeating an error in the preface to a treatise of Pseudo-Athanasius, Pio mistakenly claimed at the Council of Caesarea in Cappadocia [ca. 376], blessed bishop Peter of Nicomedia read from a book of St. Athanasius of Alexandria which recounted the miraculous flow of blood that came forth from an icon of Christ-crucified when it was abused by the Jews of Beirut in Syria during the time of Constantine I. The blood from this icon, when sprinkled on the ill, was said to cure them of numerous serious maladies. Other church Fathers also report so many prodigies having been performed in diverse places before sacred images that it is impractical to rehearse them all. These wonders have continued over the centuries and in his own time Pio pointed to a number of miraculous images throughout Europe, especially those of Mary at Loreto, in the Annunziata church of Florence, in various churches in Rome, in the church of Santa Maria degli Angeli in Assisi, in Naples and other Italian cities, in Spanish cities such as Seville and at the shrine of Our Lady of Monserrat in the Pyrenees Mountains, and in various places among the French, British, Germans, Poles,

---

Eusebius of Caesarea, Historiae ecclesiasticae libri decem, IX, 9 (PG 20:819-23). Pio may have derived these patristic references from Netter, Doctrinale, III, esp. 954 C - 56 A and 965 C-E.

[72] Pio, XXIII Libri, fols. CXLIII^v and CXLVI^{r-v}Y.

Greeks, Syrians, Ethiopians, and other peoples. Many are the reliable witnesses to the remarkable cures beyond the power of nature that have been worked over the centuries in divers places before these sacred images. If the prodigies were not true, the images would have been removed long ago.[73]

Those who have opposed the use of sacred images over the centuries have incurred divine wrath. Among those who fell into error because they tried to abolish icons were the Byzantine Emperors Philippicus Bardanes [711-13], Leo III, the Isaurian [716-41], and Constantine V, Copronymus [720/41-75]. These emperors forced the patriarchs of Constantinople to publish their edicts against icons or else suffer imprisonment and torture. When Emperor Constantine VI, Porphyrogenitus [born 771, crowned 776, assumed power 789, died 797] came to the throne as a child, his mother Irene ruled initially as regent [780-89]. In order to restore peace to the Church and veneration to sacred images she had celebrated the seventh ecumenical council, that of Nicaea II, at which iconoclasm was condemned. Her son Constantine eventually had her imprisoned, and according to Pio began a fierce persecution of those who honored sacred images. God punished the emperor for these crimes against His martyrs by seeing that Constantine was removed from power and exiled to the island of Lesbos where he died a miserable death. Other emperors who espoused iconoclasm also suffered personal calamities. The Empire itself was punished, for barbarian tribes invaded from all sides and occupied many provinces and the imperial title was transferred to the Franks when pope Leo III on the petition of the clergy and peoples of Rome, Italy, and the western provinces raised Charlemagne to the imperial office.[74] God's

---

[73] Pio, XXIII Libri, fols. CXLII^v-CXLIII^r; Eusebius of Caesarea, Historiae ecclesiasticae libri decem, VII, 18 (PG 20:679); Pseudo-Athanasius, De passione imaginis Domini nostri Jesu Christi, (PG 28:813-24). On Peter of Nicomedia's attendance at the Second Council of Nicaea, see Mansi, XII, 993 B, 1089 AB, 1148 E, and XIII, 366 B, 382 AB, 573 AB, etc. At the fourth session (*actio*) on 26 October 787, Peter asked that a treatise of St. Athanasius be read aloud; the Synod agreed and Stephanus (deacon and notary) read it to the assembly - see Mansi, XIII, 580 B-585 D. Pio's error on the site of the synod probably derived from the preface to this treatise where it is stated that Peter read this work of "Athanasius" at the council "Apud Caesaream Cappadociae urbem" - see PG 28:811 D.

[74] Pio, XXIII Libri, fol. CXLIII^v. On Irene's deposition of her son and blinding of him, from which wound he later died, see Theophanes, Chronographia, A.C. 789 (PG 108:950-51); Karl Joseph Hefele, A History of the Councils of the Church, Vol. 5 (626-787), trans. and ed. William R. Clark, Edinburgh 1896, 339-42, 391-93 and G. Garitte, Constantine VI, DHGE 13 (Paris 1956), cols. 613-15. The notion, not based in fact, that the imperial title was transferred from the iconoclastic Greeks to the orthodox Franks as a punishment for their persecution of venerators of sacred images is also found in Eck, Enchiridion, 193 and Clichtove, Propugnaculum, 64-65, n. 4.

severe punishment of iconoclasts demonstrates that He approves the use of sacred images.

One cannot help wondering why Pio reduced the significance of the Second Council of Nicaea to the story of God's punishment of an iconoclast. He seems to have lacked any precise knowledge of its decrees and was ignorant of its *acta,* as evidenced by his placing Peter of Nicomedia's intervention erroneously at the Council of Caesarea instead of at that of Nicaea. But then, prior to the publication of the Nicene *acta* in 1540, very few scholars knew of their contents. Johann Eck and Johann Faber had been fortunate enough to find a copy of the *acta* in the Vatican Library and later made reference to them. The central provisions of Nicaea's decree on images were, however, readily available, even being incorporated into the *Corpus juris canonici.* Had Pio referred to them, perhaps he could have effectively quieted some of Erasmus' fear of a recurrence of idolatry based on the extreme statement of "Scotus".[75]

Pio argued for the utility of sacred images by appeals to human experience. He pointed to the power of pictures to stir quickly the inner emotions when these images are viewed with pious eyes. He observed that a picture of Christ suffering for our salvation should lead us to prayers of thanks, tears over our own ingratitude, pleas for mercy, and outpourings of love. The victory of His resurrection and ascension should cause us to rejoice, the crowning of His saints inspire in us holy desires to imitate them and hope for a similar reward. And the sight of Christ judging and punishing the sinful should fill us with horror. If we do not experience these emotions, Pio suggests that something is wrong with us: we are contemptuous of religion or else we have hearts of stone and are persons who are cold, bitter, inhuman, and devoid of every emotion. Here Pio seems to be engaging in an *ad hominem* attack on Erasmus' character.[76]

Pio also argued for the superiority of the picture over the written word. Beauty seen is much more attractive than beauty described by mere words.

---

[75] For examples of knowledge of the Nicene decree, see cc. 28-29, D. III, de cons. (edd. E.L. RICHTER and E. FRIEDBERG, I, col. 1360), NETTER, Doctrinale, III, 906 A-C and 945 A, Gabriel BIEL, Canonis missae expositio (edd. H.A. OBERMAN and W.J. COURTENAY), Wiesbaden 1965, II 264-65, lectio XLIX, Q; ECK, Enchiridion, 192-93; CLICHTOVE, Propugnaculum, 66-67, nr. 6. For ECK's reference to the *acta,* see his Enchiridion, ed. FRAENKEL, 192-93 n. 18; on Faber's consultation of the Vatican Library, see Keith D. LEWIS, Johann Faber and the First Zurich Disputation: 1523. A Pre-Tridentine Catholic Response to Ulrich Zwingli and His Sixty-seven Articles, Ann Arbor, Mich. 1985, 50 and 59; on the citations by Eck and Faber of the acta and their publication in 1540, see the forthcoming study of Remigius BÄUMER, Das 2. Konzil von Nizäa in der theologischen Auseinandersetzung des 16. Jahrhunderts.

[76] PIO, Responsio, fol. XXXVII^{r-v} and XXIII Libri, fol. CXLIV^{r-v}.

Visual images penetrate more deeply and make a more lasting and powerful impression on the soul than do written or spoken words. One glance at a picture brings greater comprehension than can be derived from the labor of reading. The power of art to recall to mind and inspire our hearts has long been recognized by secular societies that have bronze and gilded marble statues of standing or equestrian figures erected in prominent places to honor the virtues and achievements of outstanding persons. So too, pictures of distinguished ancestors are displayed in private homes to inspire us to imitate their virtues. Surely saints are also deserving of these honors and their virtuous deeds once represented can also inspire us. Without such statues the memory of these men could die out among the illiterate. Without pictures, how else can those deaf from birth or infancy be taught about the life, death, and resurrection of Jesus Christ? Among the illiterate those would be at a great disadvantage who cannot follow a sermon because of their dense or slow minds or because they cannnot concentrate but are easily distracted. Written accounts can be understood only by those who know how to read that particular language. To remove all sacred images is an elitist act that would seriously harm the ordinary Christian.[77]

Pio recognized that abuses may have crept into the content and display of images. Nothing, he claimed, is so upright and fitting that someone cannot misuse it. But abuses in practice do not justify the abolition of images themselves. Rather, efforts should be made to correct whatever may have gone astray. A great multitude of images was to be avoided for this could lead to confusion, contempt, and derision. Only a few were to be set up in fitting places within a church, their precise locations being a matter of decorum, a proper rationale, and true judgment. Nor should every deed of the saints be depicted. So too in a theatrical comedy, not everything is performed in front of the audience. Actors pass over whatever is turpid and unworthy, claiming it was done off stage or leaving it to the imagination of the spectators. On stage actors portray only what is useful and fitting for the audience, what will edify them. Nor should everything that can be properly depicted be stuffed into a scene. Rather, let the composition be such that harmonious things are rationally arranged with intervals of space. A confused composition distracts rather than instructs the viewer. One should follow in these matters Vitruvius who teaches that pictures and signs should be put in fitting places on the walls. So too, women of culture do not wear excessive jewelry. Nor should rings be on every finger. If such rules of decorum apply to secular affairs, how much greater care should not be given to decorating churches and to representing

---

[77] Pio, *Responsio*, fol. XXXVII^v and *XIII Libri*, fols. CXLIV^r-CXLV^v.

divine things? In these matters consider what benefit will be given to the viewer and what honor and glory to God and His saints.[78]

Pio ended his defense of sacred images with a counter-attack on Erasmus. Having demonstrated that the use of images was supported by the Bible, practiced in the early Church and ever since throughout Christendom, and approved by the testimony of church Fathers and by the decrees of popes and general councils, Pio expressed amazement that Erasmus ever regarded the use of images as a superstitious, erroneous, and insignificant ceremony instituted by little men. Against these fathers in the Faith, Erasmus' "little men," stands the mighty Atlas, Erasmus! Surely he has lost his good sense in opposing such authority. Given his stance, he should be regarded by pious Christians as someone outside the community of faith, as the tax collector and Gentile ostracized in the Gospel [Mt 18:17].[79]

Putting aside Pio's rhetorical flourish, there was much on which the disputants agreed. Both men were favorably impressed by the power of art to teach Christian truths and to inspire men to imitate Christ and His saints. They agreed that indecent and unbecoming material should not be depicted in sacred art. Nor should churches be cluttered with excessive images.

But if the disputants were in accord on the didactic function of religious art, they diverged on its cultic use. Erasmus was scandalized by any theory which would pay to a material image the same adoration owed only to God. He feared that in practice some Christians treat images in the same way as pagans did their idols and that this is because they have erroneous and superstitious notions about them. If care is not taken, outright idolatry could return. Christians should be encouraged to move beyond images to a higher and more spiritual religion. Pio was more confident that beneath the practices of the simple faithful lay an orthodox belief and deep piety. He detected in Erasmus' statements a lack of appreciation for the incarnational and sacramental nature of Catholic beliefs and practices. He too agreed that adoration should not be given to images, but he found their veneration a proper and pious act because the honor passes on to the persons there represented. Pio also exposed the elitism of Erasmus in devaluating images accessible to all and vaunting the written and learnedly preached word popular with the few educated members of society.

---

[78] Pio, Responsio, fol. XXXVII[v] and XXIII Libri, fols. CXLVI[v]-CXLVII[r]Z; Lucius Vitruvius Pollio, De architectura libri decem, trans. from the Latin into Italian with commentary and illustrations by Cesare di Lorenzo Cesariando, Como: Gotardus de Ponte 1521 (reprinted Bronx 1968 by Benjamin Blom), Liber VII, cap. 5, fols. CXVI[v]-CXIX[r].

[79] Pio, XXIII Libri, fol. CXLVI[v]Y.

This debate over the purely didactic or also cultic use of sacred images and the concern to eliminate abuses continued until the time of the Council of Trent. Discussion was particularly sharp in France where Catholic theologians debated how far the Church should go in meeting the concerns of the Calvinists. Because of the insistence of the French delegation, the Council of Trent addressed the issue in a decree of the twenty-fifth and last session of the Council.[80]

This decree spoke to the concerns of both Pio and Erasmus. The didactic purpose of sacred images was clearly laid out and the depiction of any erroneous, profane, or immoral scenes in sacred art was proscribed. It rejected the notion that a special divine presence or force resided in icons. The decree did not, however, support Erasmus' questioning of the cultic function of images, but affirmed that proper veneration was owed them, for by means of them the honor was referred to the prototypes they represent - the position of Basil the Great cited by Pio and formally adopted by the Second Council of Nicaea.[81] Had Erasmus known of the Nicene decree he may not have been so troubled by the extreme statements of "Scotus" which he feared had gained wide acceptance in the Church. He could then have assigned to images a cultic function free of the dangers of idolatry. And Pio perhaps could have been spared writing Book VIII of his already hefty tome.

---

[80] JEDIN, Genesi e portata del decreto, 340-90, esp. 354-78; and his Storia del Concilio di Trento, IV-2, trans. G. CECCHI and G. BEARI, rev. G. ALBERIGO, Brescia 1981, 249-62.

[81] For the text of this decree of the 25th session on 3-4 December 1563, see Conciliorum oecumenicorum decreta, edd. G. ALBERIGO et al., 3rd ed., Bologna 1973, 774-76.

INDEX

INDEX OF MANUSCRIPTS

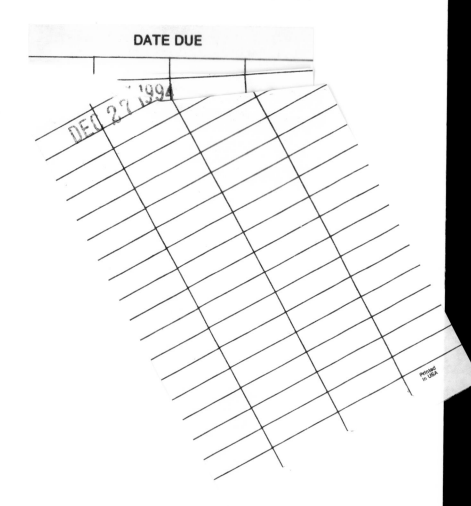

DATE DUE

DEC 27 1994

Printed
in USA